QUANTITATIVE RESEARCH METHODS
FOR COMMUNICATION

Jason S. Wrench
State University of New York at New Paltz

Candice Thomas-Maddox
Ohio University Lancaster

Virginia Peck Richmond
University of Alabama at Birmingham

James C. McCroskey
University of Alabama at Birmingham

QUANTITATIVE RESEARCH METHODS
FOR COMMUNICATION

A Hands-On Approach

THIRD EDITION

New York   Oxford
OXFORD UNIVERSITY PRESS

Oxford University Press is a department of the University of Oxford.
It furthers the University's objective of excellence in research,
scholarship, and education by publishing worldwide.

Oxford   New York
Auckland   Cape Town   Dar es Salaam   Hong Kong   Karachi
Kuala Lumpur   Madrid   Melbourne   Mexico City   Nairobi
New Delhi   Shanghai   Taipei   Toronto

With offices in
Argentina   Austria   Brazil   Chile   Czech Republic   France   Greece
Guatemala   Hungary   Italy   Japan   Poland   Portugal   Singapore
South Korea   Switzerland   Thailand   Turkey   Ukraine   Vietnam

Published by Oxford University Press
198 Madison Avenue, New York, New York 10016
http://www.oup.com

Library of Congress Cataloging-in-Publication Data
Quantitative research methods for communication: a hands-on approach / Jason S. Wrench,
State University of New York at New Paltz; Candice Thomas-Maddox, Ohio University,
Lancaster; Virginia Peck Richmond, University of Alabama at Birmingham; James C. McCroskey,
University of Alabama at Birmingham. --Third edition.
     pages cm
  Includes bibliographical references and index.
  ISBN 978-0-19-045640-5
 1. Communication--Research--Methodology. I. Wrench, Jason S. II. Thomas-Maddox, Candice.
III. Richmond, Virginia P., 1949– IV. McCroskey, James C. V. Title.
  P91.3.Q36   2016
  302.207′2--dc23
                                                                          2015028061

Printing number: 9 8 7 6 5 4 3 2

Printed in Canada on acid-free paper

BRIEF CONTENTS

Preface xxi

CHAPTER 1 An Introduction to Communication Research 1

CHAPTER 2 Empirical Research 12

CHAPTER 3 Research Ethics 29

CHAPTER 4 Searching for Previous Research and American Psychological Association Style 56

CHAPTER 5 Research Structure and Literature Reviews 97

CHAPTER 6 Variables 127

CHAPTER 7 Measurement 165

CHAPTER 8 Reliability and Validity 188

CHAPTER 9 Survey Research 216

CHAPTER 10 Content Analysis 247

CHAPTER 11 Experimental Design 261

CHAPTER 12 Big Data 287

CHAPTER 13 Sampling Methods 309

CHAPTER 14 Hypothesis Testing 326

CHAPTER 15 Descriptive Statistics 347

CHAPTER 16 Chi-Square (χ^2) Test of Independence 377

CHAPTER 17 Independent Samples *t* Tests 406

CHAPTER 18 One-Way Analysis of Variance 426

CHAPTER 19 Correlation 451

CHAPTER 20 Regression 472

CHAPTER 21 Advanced Statistical Procedures 494

CHAPTER 22 Presenting Research 514

Appendix A Qualitative Research (Available online: http://www.oup.com/us/wrench/)

Appendix B Textbook Questionnaire (Available online: http://www.oup.com/us/wrench/)

Appendix C Open-Source Statistical Software Alternatives (Available online: http://www.oup.com/us/wrench/)

Glossary 539

Index 553

CONTENTS

Preface *xxi*

CHAPTER 1   An Introduction to Communication Research 1
The History of the Social Sciences 2
The Nature of Communication 5
Understanding the Book's Format 7
Research Outside the Walls of Academia 10
Conclusion 10

CHAPTER 2   Empirical Research 12
Ways of Knowing 13
  Epistemology 13
  Ordinary Versus Scientific Ways of Knowing 14
The Scientific Approach to Communication Research 16
  Scientific Method 16
    Theories 18
    Describe the National Phenomenon 18
    Predict the Future 19
    Falsification 19
  Predictions/Hypotheses 19
  Observations 21
  Empirical Generalizations 23
Conclusion 25
Research Outside the Walls of Academia 26

CHAPTER 3   Research Ethics 29
Defining Ethics 33
  Good Means–Good End: Ethical Behavior 33
  Bad Means–Bad End: Unethical Behavior 34
  Bad Means–Good End: Machiavellian Ethic 34
  Good Means–Bad End: Subjective Ethic 34
The Belmont Report's Effect on Research Ethics 35
  Informed Consent 35
  Principle of Beneficence 35
  Justice 36
Institutional Review Boards 37
  Institutional Review Board Basics 37
  Informed Consent 39

Institutional Review Board Processes 45
   Basic Institutional Review Board Functions 45
Full-Board Review 48
Specific Ethical Issues for Research 48
  Data Accuracy 48
  Data Sharing 48
  Duplicate Data Publication 49
  Post Hoc Hypothesis Revision 49
  Participant Identity Disclosures 49
  Authorship Credit 50
  Conflicts of Interest 50
  Plagiarism 51
    Source-Not-Cited Types of Plagiarism 51
    Source-Cited Types of Plagiarism 52
Ethical Research Outside Academia 53
Conclusion 53

CHAPTER 4   **Searching for Previous Research and American Psychological Association Style 56**
Step 1: Identifying the Topic 57
Step 2: Clarifying the Research Question and Generating Key Terms 60
  Stating The Topic In The Form of a Research Question 60
  Identifying Key Terms and Synonymous Terms 61
Step 3: Locating Sources of Information 64
  Types of Information Sources 65
  Locating Information Sources 67
    Handbooks and Subject Encyclopedias 67
    Electronic Databases 70
    The World Wide Web 75
  Evaluating Web Sources 78
Step 4: Organizing and Evaluating Information 80
Step 5: Citing Sources of Information Using the APA Format 81
  What Information Must Be Referenced? 84
  Citing Sources of Information 85
    Parenthetical Citations 85
    Quotations and Paraphrases 88
APA Paper Formatting 89
  Creating a Title Page 89
  Creating an Abstract 91
  Creating the First Page 91
  Creating the Reference Page 94
Conclusion 95

CHAPTER 5   **Research Structure and Literature Reviews 97**
The Abstract 98
The Introduction 99
  Attention-Getter 99

Using Statistics or Claims 100
Posing a Rhetorical Question 100
Using an Acknowledged Fact 100
Using a Story or Illustration 101
Quoting or Acknowledging a Source 101
Link To Topic 101
Significance of Topic 102
Espousal of Credibility 102
Thesis and Preview 102
Literature Review 104
Five Reasons for Literature Reviews 104
Previous Research 106
Chronological 106
Cause and Effect 107
Compare and Contrast 107
Problem–Cause–Solution 108
Psychological 108
Categorical/Topical 108
General to Specific 108
Specific to General 109
Known to Unknown 109
Study Rationale 109
Method Section 111
Participants 112
Apparatus 112
Procedure 112
Instrumentation 114
Results Section 115
Discussion Section 116
The Conclusion 119
Research Outside the Walls of Academia 119
Reading and Critiquing Academic Literature 120
Preparing a First Draft 121
Step 1: Identify Your General Topic 121
Step 2: Determine The Type of Study You Are Conducting 122
Step 3: Determine What Variables You Will Examine 122
Step 4: Search for Primary Sources 122
Step 5: Obtain Full Text References 122
Step 6: Look for Other References in Obtained Materials 122
Step 7: Narrow Your List of References 122
Step 8: Organize References by Major and Subtopics 123
Step 9: Look for Gaps in Your References 123
Step 10: Find References to Fill Gaps 123
Step 11: Create a Literature Review Outline 123
Step 12: Write 124
Conclusion 124

CHAPTER 6   **Variables** 127
How Are Research Projects Developed? 128
Variables: Units of Analysis 128
Units of Analysis 129
Aspects of Variables 130
  Variable Attributes 130
  Variable Values 130
  Understanding Relationships and Differences 130
    Relationships 130
    Differences 131
Types of Variables 134
Variable Levels 135
  Nominal Variables 135
  Ordinal Variables 136
  Interval Variables 137
    Likert 137
    Semantic Differential 137
    Staple's 138
    Scalogram 138
  Ratio Variables 141
Communication Variables 142
  Nominal Variables 142
  Ordinal Variables 143
  Interval Variables 143
    Common Interval Variable Measures 143
    Communication Apprehension 146
    Ethnocentrism 148
    Humor Assessment 150
    Nonverbal Immediacy 151
    Sociocommunicative Orientation 153
    Willingness to Communicate 155
    Beliefs and Attitudes 157
  Ratio Variables 159
Writing Up Scales Using APA Style 159
  Participants 159
  Procedures 160
  Instrumentation 160
Conclusion 162

CHAPTER 7   **Measurement** 165
Numbers and Things 166
Review of Measurement Levels 167
  Nominal 167
  Ordinal 167
  Interval 168
  Ratio 169

A History of Measurement 169
  Likert Scales 171
  Semantic Differential 171
Measuring Communication 173
  Personality Traits/States 174
  Beliefs and Attitudes 175
  Knowledge 175
Developing Your Operationalization 177
  Conceptualization 177
  Operationalization 178
Constructing Questions 179
One Measure, Multiple Factors 181
Measurement and Statistical Analysis 184
Research Outside the Walls of Academia 185
Conclusion 185

CHAPTER 8   Reliability and Validity 188
Reliability 188
  Scalar Reliability 189
    Test–Retest Reliability 191
    Alternate Forms Reliability 192
    Split-Half Reliability 192
  Cronbach's Alpha Reliability 192
  Computer Printouts of Cronbach's Alpha 193
    SPSS and Cronbach's Alpha 193
    Excel and Cronbach's Alpha 199
  APA Discussion 200
  Alpha Reliabilities From This Book 201
  Reliabilities In The Real World 201
Improving Reliability of Measurement 202
Validity 206
  Face or Content Validity 208
  Criterion Validity 208
    Predictive 208
    Concurrent 209
    Retrospective 209
  Construct or Factorial Validity 209
Validity Threats 210
Problems with Measurement 212
Research Outside the Walls of Academia 214
Conclusion 214

CHAPTER 9   Survey Research 216
When to Use a Survey 217
  Do You Know What You Want To Ask? 217
  Do You Really Need To Collect New Data? 217

Do Your Participants Know Anything or Will They Even Tell You? 218

Is Your Goal Generalizability? 219

How to Conduct Survey Research 219

   Step 1: Picking Your Questions 220

      Nominal Level Questions 220

      Ordinal Level Questions 221

      Interval Level Questions 221

      Ratio Level Questions 222

      Open-Ended Questions 222

   Step 2: Creating Clear Instructions 223

   Step 3: Study Design 223

   Step 4: Data Processing and Analysis 225

   Step 5: Pilot Testing 225

      Use Actual Survey Population Members 226

      Anticipate Survey Context 226

      Test Parts of the Survey 226

      Determining a Pilot Sample Size 226

      Ask Questions after Someone Completes the Survey 226

Disseminating Your Surveys 227

   Interviewing 227

      Face-to-Face Interviewing 227

      Telephone Interviewing 228

      Self-Administration 229

      Mass Administration 229

      Mailed Administration 229

      Internet Administration 229

   Advantages and Disadvantages of Self-Administered Surveying 230

Problem Areas Associated with Survey Research 231

   Response Rate 231

      Unit Nonresponse 231

      Item Nonresponse 232

      Effects of Nonresponse 234

      Improving Response Rates 234

Translating Surveys into Other Languages 235

   Semantic Equivalence 235

   Conceptual Equivalence 235

   Normative Equivalence 236

   Simple Direct Translation 237

   Modified Direct Translation 237

   Translation/Backtranslation 237

   Parallel Blind Technique 238

   Random Probe 238

Using the Research Project Worksheet 238

   Question 238

Design 240
Setting 240
Participants 241
    Specific Characteristics 241
    Recruitment 241
    Consent 241
Variables 241
    Independent Variables 241
    Dependent Variables 241
Hypotheses/Research Questions 242
Statistical Testing 242
Tentative Study Title 242
Principal Researcher(s) 242
Measurement Outside of Academia 242
Conclusion 245

CHAPTER 10 Content Analysis 247
Conducting a Content Analysis 249
Theory and Rationale 249
Conceptualization 249
Operationalization 250
Coding Schemes 251
Sampling 253
Training and Pilot Reliability 253
    Introduction to Coding Book 253
    Sample Coding 253
    Coding of Initial Data 254
    Initial Reliability 254
APA Write-Up 256
    Retraining 257
    Final Coding 257
    Final Reliability 258
Tabulation And Reporting 258
Conclusion 258

CHAPTER 11 Experimental Design 261
What Are Experiments and Why Do We Do Them? 262
Rationale For Experimental Research 262
Aspects Of Experimental Design 263
    Random Assignment 264
    Manipulation of the Independent Variable 266
    Measurement of the Dependent Variable 269
    Controlling an Experiment 270
Conducting an Experiment 272
    Introducing the Experiment and Obtaining Consent 272
    Random Assignment 272

Manipulate the Independent Variable 272
Measure the Dependent Variable 273
Debriefing 273

Threats to Experimental Validity 274
Historical Flaw 274
Maturation 274
Testing Flaw 274
Regression To The Mean 275
Selection Threat 275
Attrition 276

Common Experimental Designs 277
Preexperimental Designs 277
One-Shot Case Study 277
One-Group Pretest Posttest Design 278
Static Group Comparisons 278
Quasi-Experimental Designs 278
Pretest–Posttest Design 279
Time Series 279
Multiple Time Series 280
Switching Replications Design 280
True Experimental Designs 281
Pretest–Posttest Design 281
Two-Group Posttest-Only Design 281
Randomized Switching Replications Design 282
Solomon Four-Group Design 282

Final Thoughts on Experiments 284
Conclusion 285

CHAPTER 12   **Big Data 287**
What is the Data in Big Data? 288
Human-Generated Data 289
Machine-Generated Data 289

Big Data? 290
Big Data Explained 290
Laney's 3V's 292
Volume 292
Velocity 294
Variety 294
Four More V's 295
Veracity 295
Variability 296
Visualization 296
Value 297

Big Data and the Cloud 297
Understanding The Cloud 298
The Cloud And Data 298
Big Data In The Cloud 299

Big Data Analysis 300
   Data Mining 301
   Monitoring And Anomalies 301
Communication and Big Data 302
Big Data Ethics *303*
   Privacy 303
   Identity 304
   Ownership 305
   Reputation 305

CHAPTER 13 **Sampling Methods 309**
Why Use a Sample? 310
   Population 310
   Sample 310
   The Sampling Process 310
   Selecting a Sample Design 311
   Probability Sampling 312
   Simple Random Samples 312
   Stratified Random Samples 314
   Cluster Samples 315
   Systematic Samples 315
Sampling Error 316
Nonprobability Samples 316
   Convenience Samples 317
   Volunteer Samples 317
   Purposive Samples 317
   Quota Samples 318
   Network Sample 319
Determining Sample Size 319
Common Sense Sample Recruiting 320
   Ethical Recruitment 323
Conclusion 324

CHAPTER 14 **Hypothesis Testing 326**
   Hypotheses 326
      One-Tailed Hypotheses 328
      Two-Tailed Hypotheses 328
   Research Questions 328
      Directional Research Questions 329
      Nondirectional Research Questions 329
   Alternative and Null Hypotheses 329
Hypothesis Testing Case Study 331
   Hypothesis Testing in the Case Study 332
From Random Samples to a Whole Population 332
Testing for Significance 334
   Step 1: Set the Probability Level 335
   Step 2: Conduct a Statistical Test 335
   Step 3: Comparing Calculated and Critical Values 336

Testing for Power 338
Effect Sizes 339
Understanding Error 341
   The Confidence Interval 342
   Power 343
   Type I Error 344
   Type II Error 344
Conclusion 345

CHAPTER 15 Descriptive Statistics 347
   The Benefits of Statistics 348
Descriptive Versus Inferential Statistics 349
Measures of Central Tendency 350
   Mean 350
   Median 351
   Mode 353
   Frequency Distributions 354
      SPSS and Frequency Distributions 354
      Excel and Frequency Distributions 359
      Frequency Distributions and Charts 360
   Skewness and Kurtosis 363
Measures of Variability 365
   Range 365
   Sum of Squares 366
   Variance 367
   Standard Deviation 367
Dataset Variability 371
Conclusion 375

CHAPTER 16 Chi-Square (χ^2) Test of Independence 377
Case Study Introduction 378
Chi-Square Background Information 379
Step-by-Step Approach to the Chi-Square Test of Independence 380
Computer Printouts of the Chi-Square Test of Independence 383
   SPSS and Chi-Squares 384
   Excel and Chi-Squares 389
   APA Write-Up 395
   Discussion of Findings 395
   Post Hoc APA Write-Up 401
Biological Sex and Book Edition 401
   APA Write-Up 401
Discussion of Brummans and Miller's Article 403
   Article Purpose 403
   Methodology 403
   Results 403
Chi-Squares Outside Academia 404
Conclusion 404

CHAPTER 17 Independent Samples *t* Tests 406
Case Study Introduction 407
Independent Samples *t* Test Background Information 407
Step-by-Step Approach to the Independent *t* Test 408
Computer Printouts of the Independent *t* Test 413
SPSS and t Tests 413
Excel and t Tests 417
APA Write-Up (SPSS) 418
APA Write-Up (Excel) 418
Discussion of Findings 419
Biological Sex and Communication Apprehension 419
APA Write-Up (SPSS) 419
Discussion 420
Calculating Effect Sizes 420
Discussion of the Weber, Fornash, Corrigan, and Neupauer Article 422
Article Purpose 422
Methodology 422
Results 423
Paired *t* Tests 423
t Tests Outside Academia 424
Conclusion 424

CHAPTER 18 One-Way Analysis of Variance 426
Case Study Introduction 427
One-Way ANOVA Background Information 427
Step-by-Step Approach to the One-Way ANOVA 429
Computer Printouts of the One-Way ANOVA 434
SPSS and One-Way ANOVAs 434
Multiple Comparison Tests 440
Excel and One-Way ANOVAs 443
APA Write-Up (Without Chart) 443
APA Write-Up (With Chart) 443
Discussion of Findings 445
Political Affiliation and Humor Assessment 445
APA Write-Up 446
Discussion 446
Discussion of the Boiarsky et al. Article 446
Article Purpose 447
Methodology 447
Results 448
One-way ANOVAs Outside Academia 448
Conclusion 448

CHAPTER 19 Correlation 451
Correlation Background Information 452
Types of Relationships 452

Correlation Not Causation 453
Correlation Assumptions 454
Case Study Introduction 455
Step-by-Step Approach to the Pearson Product-Moment
    Correlation 455
Computer Printouts of the Pearson Product-Moment Correlation 458
SPSS and Pearson Product-Moment Correlations 459
Excel and Pearson Product-Moment Correlations 462
APA Write-Up 463
Discussion 463
Relationships among CA, WTC, and Beliefs about Public Speaking 464
APA Write-Up 464
A Note About R 465
Reading Large Correlation Tables 466
Discussion of the Chesebro Article 467
Article Purpose 467
Methodology 467
Results 469
Discussion of the Punyanunt Article 469
Article Purpose 469
Methodology 469
Results 470
Correlations Outside Academia 470
Conclusion 470

CHAPTER 20   **Regression 472**
Case Study Introduction 473
Regression Background Information 474
Step-by-Step Approach to a Linear Regression 475
Computer Printouts of the Linear Regression 477
SPSS and Simple Linear Regressions 477
Excel and the Simple Linear Regression 481
APA Write-Up 481
Discussion 482
Relationships between CA and Beliefs about Public Speaking 483
APA Write-Up 484
Understanding Multiple Linear Regressions 485
APA Write-Up 487
Discussion 487
Discussion of the Wrench and Booth-Butterfield Article 488
Article Purpose 489
Methodology 489
Results 489
Discussion of the Rocca and Vogl-Bauer Article 489
Article Purpose 490
Methodology 490
Results 490

Regressions Outside Academia 491
Conclusion 491

CHAPTER 21 Advanced Statistical Procedures 494
Difference Tests 495
   Factorial ANOVA 495
     Example 495
     Explanation 496
     APA Write-Up 496
     Discussion 496
   Analysis of Covariance 497
     Example 497
     Explanation 497
     APA Write-Up 498
     Discussion 498
   Multivariate Analysis of Variance 499
     Example 499
     Explanation 499
     APA Write-Up 499
     Discussion 499
   Repeated-Measures ANOVA 500
     Example 500
     Explanation 500
     APA Write-Up 500
     Discussion 501
Relationship Tests 501
   Path Analysis 501
     Example 501
     Explanation 501
     APA Write-Up 502
     Discussion 502
   Structural Equation Modeling 503
     Example 503
     Explanation 503
     APA Write-Up 504
     Discussion 505
   Factor Analysis 507
     Example 507
     Explanation 507
     APA Write-Up 508
     Discussion 509
   Canonical Correlations 511
     Example 511
     Explanation 511
     APA Write-Up 511
     Discussion 512
Conclusion 513

CHAPTER 22　Presenting Research　514

Writing a Discussion Section　515

Providing a Summary of Major Findings　516

Providing an Interpretation of Findings　516

Discussing the Relationship Between Findings and Previous Studies　517

Acknowledging Limitations　517

Discussing Implications and Future Directions　518

Writing the Abstract　518

Presenting at Conferences　519

Divisions and Interest Groups　519

Submitting Research For Conference Review　520

Types of Conference Presentations　523

Paper Presentations　523

Poster Presentations　526

Scholar-to-Scholar Posters　528

Panel Discussions　528

Publication　529

Journal Review Process　529

Submission Process　529

Review Process　532

Research Outside the Walls of Academia　533

Writing For Business　533

Research and The General Public　534

Writing Statistical Stories　535

Infographics　536

Conclusion　538

Appendix A Qualitative Research (Available online: http://www.oup.com/us/wrench/)

Appendix B Textbook Questionnaire (Available online: http://www.oup.com/us/wrench/)

Appendix C Open-Source Statistical Software Alternatives (Available online: http://www.oup.com/us/wrench/)

Glossary 539

Index 553

PREFACE

Real Data. Real Studies. Real Life.

Noted science fiction writer H. G. Wells (1866–1946) once wrote, "Statistical thinking will one day be as necessary a qualification for efficient citizenship as the ability to read and write." H. G. Wells realized that understanding how statistics function within our world was no longer a luxury of scientists and mathematicians but a necessary endeavor for all citizens. Sadly, in the twenty-first century increasing numbers of people are functionally numerically illiterate. John Allen Paulos (1988) first tackled the notion of numerical illiteracy or innumeracy by defining innumeracy as "an inability to deal comfortably with the fundamental notions of number and chance" (p. 3). Unfortunately, most people simply do not understand enough about the world of statistics and scientific research to make much sense of the statistics in their daily lives. People are constantly bombarded with statistics, and most are unable to accurately process the information to any usable degree. Milroy (2001) argued that with the proliferation of science and pseudo-science today, people must be able to engage in strategic junk science judo. Most people are completely unaware of the extent to which their lives are controlled by quantitative research. Although the goal of this book is not to discuss nifty marketing tricks or medical research, the basics of quantitative research methods and reasoning are the same across all fields that use social scientific research methods.

Although this book does not attempt to correct all of the problems associated with innumeracy, it is intended to engage communication students on two levels. On the first level, this textbook hopes to teach readers the basics of the scientific process necessary in quantitative communication research. Although college students typically learned the scientific method in elementary school, most cannot accurately translate this understanding outside the physical sciences. In this text we promote a strategic use of the scientific method when conducting quantitative research examining communication topics. Along the way, we hope that students begin to understand the steps necessary for conducting research in a manner that is transferable to other parts of their lives. Scientific and statistical processes are the same whether they are utilized by communication researchers or by medical researchers. Therefore, one of our goals for this text is simply to educate readers about the scientific method and the most commonly used statistical tools. Although the examples used throughout this textbook are focused on communication-related phenomena, we believe that students can learn to transfer this knowledge into other areas of science and statistics when faced with them.

On a second level, we hope to help students engage in real quantitative research projects of real importance. The four authors of this textbook have a history of working with both undergraduate and graduate students to develop, write, present, and publish quantitative research projects. We all believe that the only way for students to truly learn and grasp quantitative research methods is through real examples and hands-on work. In our vast experience teaching quantitative research methods, we have learned that students cannot transfer theoretical knowledge of research methods and statistics to actual projects and datasets unless they have actively engaged the research process when learning. In other words, it is one thing to read about what a correlation is and how correlations work and quite a different thing to find significant relationships in real datasets.

IMPROVEMENTS TO THE THIRD EDITION

As with any new edition of the text, there are always a number of important improvements that are made to ensure that the quality of the textbook meets new demands and reflects the input from the instructors who have used this book in the past. The authors of this text have taught numerous short courses at various national and regional conventions and had the opportunity to get direct feedback from both students and instructors alike. The changes that we made to this book reflect this feedback along with our own insights after having regularly used the first two editions ourselves. Here are the important changes and additions we have made to this edition:

- Starting in the second edition of the textbook, we started making a real effort to demonstrate how the techniques discussed in the book could be used in the real world. We have expanded on these in the third edition.
- We decided to more thoroughly discuss the major epistemological traditions within the field of communication in addition to a more philosophical discussion of epistemology as a whole.
- We looked to see where information in various chapters was valuable but pulled the reader out of the narrative; we kept the information but placed it in sidebars. We also incorporated a number of new interesting tidbits in these sidebars to make them come alive for readers.
- We wrote a whole new section on ordinary versus scientific ways of knowing.
- We added conflicts of interest to the chapter on research ethics. This was a clear oversight within that chapter.
- We added a section in Chapter 22 on presenting research to external audiences. We wanted our readers to see how writing about research for academic and general public audiences differs. Furthermore, we wanted to discuss the modern use of infographics to display complicated statistical information.
- Because Big Data has become a huge talking point within our society, we decided that addressing this topic and explaining what it is and how it is important was necessary. Although this chapter focuses less on how to conduct Big Data, the chapter introduces readers to what big data is and how it is being used by communication and noncommunication researchers to impact people's daily lives.

KEY FEATURES OF THE BOOK

We wanted this book to be extremely practical for both students of quantitative research methods and their instructors. This book is built on decades of pedagogical theorizing and practice engaged in by the authors of this text. We strongly believe that this text is a great first step in understanding quantitative research methods utilized by modern communication researchers. For this reason, we have incorporated five unique factors within this text:

1. **Actual Data Sample**

   One unique component to this text is an actual dataset that was collected by the authors of the project with its express purpose for use in this textbook. A series of research scales written by the authors of this book were used in the creation of a survey instrument:

   Nominal variables (biological sex and political affiliation)
   Ordinal variable (time spent each week online and year in school)
   Interval variables (communication apprehension, willingness to communicate, ethnocentrism, humor assessment, nonverbal immediacy, sociocommunicative orientation—assertiveness and responsiveness, attitude about college, and belief that everyone should be required to take public speaking in college)
   Ratio variable (age)

   This dataset will be made available to book users in three different formats: SPSS, Excel, or text. By having three options available, a teacher can easily choose the format he or she prefers. Furthermore, because data were collected from 654 actual people, students can actually experience what it is like to manipulate data to receive real answers to research questions and hypotheses. Furthermore, the textbook's website also contains the example statistics discussed in the textbook in all three formats.

   In essence, students will be able to conduct statistical tests on actual data and double-check that the findings we report in the textbook match the findings they are able to obtain using a statistical software package.

2. **Actual Studies**

   The authors of this text made an agreement to republish a series of 10 articles published in either *Communication Research Reports* or *Communication Quarterly*, two journals published by the Eastern Communication Association, for inclusion on the textbook's website. The articles were chosen because they tend to be exemplars on how to conduct specific aspects of the research methods process. When selecting the articles for inclusion on the textbook's website, we included articles from a wide array of communication contexts (communication traits, instructional, listening, mediated, organizational, public relations, etc.). The articles chosen for this book are as follows:

SCALE DEVELOPMENT

McCroskey, J. C., Richmond, V. P., Johnson, A. D., & Smith, H. T. (2004). Organizational orientations theory and measurement: Development of measures and preliminary investigations. *Communication Quarterly, 52*, 1–14.

Thomas, C. E, Richmond, V. P., & McCroskey, J. C. (1994). The association between immediacy and socio-communicative style. *Communication Research Reports, 11*, 107–115.

Wrench, J. S., & Richmond, V. P. (2004). Understanding the psychometric properties of the Humor Assessment instrument through an analysis of the relationships between teacher humor assessment and instructional communication variables in the college classroom. *Communication Research Reports, 21*, 92–103.

CHI-SQUARE

Brummans, B. H. J. M., & Miller, K. (2004). The effect of ambiguity on the implementation of a social change initiative. *Communication Research Reports, 21*, 1–10.

t TESTS

Weber, K., Fornash, B., Corrigan, M, & Neupauer, N. C. (2003). The effect of interest on recall: An experiment. *Communication Research Reports, 20*, 116–123.

ONE-WAY ANALYSIS OF VARIANCE **(ANOVA)**

Boiarsky, G., Long, M., & Thayer, G. (1999). Formal features in children's science television: Sound effects, visual pace, and topic shifts. *Communication Research Reports, 16*, 185–192.

CORRELATION

Cheseboro, J. (1999). The relationship between listening styles and conversational sensitivity. *Communication Research Reports, 16*, 233–238.

Punyanunt, N. M. (2000). The effects of humor on perceptions of compliance-gaining in the college classroom. *Communication Research Reports, 176*, 30–38.

REGRESSION

Rocca, K. A., & Vogl-Bauer, S. (1999). Trait verbal aggression, sports fan identification, and perceptions of appropriate sports fan communication. *Communication Research Reports, 16*, 239–248.

Wrench, J. S., & Booth-Butterfield, M. (2003). Increasing patient satisfaction and compliance: An examination of physician humor orientation, compliance-gaining strategies, and perceived credibility. *Communication Quarterly, 51*, 482–503.

3. **Hand Calculations and Statistical Package Summaries**

This book takes students step by step through the statistical computation process. Although many books attempt to teach students the mathematical process for computing statistical tests, this book clearly spells out each step in the necessary sequence to come to an end result. In fact, in the classroom, this process has consistently been used, and students find the mathematical computations to be one of the easiest parts of learning quantitative research methods. We believe that students must learn how to calculate the problems by hand because the physical process of calculating helps to solidify the understanding of how the mathematical process works.

In addition to providing the hand computations, we also provide information on how to conduct statistical tests using the two most commonly used statistical packages: Statistical Package for the Social Sciences (SPSS) and Microsoft Office's Excel. We understand that most researchers do not calculate lengthy tests by hand, so demonstrating how the various statistical processes can be calculated using both programs helps the students conduct their own statistical analyses using the software packages. In addition to the instruction for both SPSS and Excel, we also provide printouts of statistical results utilizing both software packages. We understand that knowing how to correctly use the software packages is one thing and being able to accurately read and interpret the statistical output is completely different.

4. Glossary

The book contains an extensive glossary with commonly confused terms. We always tell our students that learning quantitative research methods is akin to learning a foreign language. For this reason, we have provided the students with a "language guide" to help them remember definitions.

5. Qualitative Research Chapter

Finally, we asked two prominent scholars in the field of qualitative and critical research, James W. Chesebro and Deborah J. Borisoff, to write a chapter for this book on qualitative research. Although the purpose of this text is to focus on quantitative research methods in communication, we strongly believe that students should at least be exposed to qualitative research methods so that they can more clearly differentiate between the two epistemological approaches. We believe that this chapter (now located on the textbook's website) is a balanced and helpful introduction to the differences in epistemology and the tools utilized to draw research conclusions.

Students are often intimidated on the first day of a research methods class. This textbook is based on years of in-classroom teaching experience and was written expressly to help alleviate the fear students may have by structuring a learning environment that clearly helps students succeed. Students who have learned quantitative research methods using the methods discussed in this textbook have gone on to have careers that utilize quantitative research both in the private sector and in academia.

Acknowledgments

Although the bulk of this text is based on our own experiences as both students and teachers of quantitative research methods, we thank the editorial teams at Roxbury Publishers and Oxford University Press for shepherding this project through its various phases. We also thank the reviewers who gave us such great insight along the way as we have written this text:

Cleo Joffrion Allen, Dillard University
Suzanne Atkin, Arizona State University
Daniel Bergan, Michigan State University
Jonathan Bowman, University of San Diego
Amanda Cote, University of Michigan
John Courtright, University of Delaware
Kristin Dybvig-Pawelko, Arizona State University
Douglas A. Ferguson, College of Charleston
Ann Bainbridge Frymier, Miami University
Mark Generous, Arizona State University
Michelle Givertz, California State University, Chico
Rosanne Hartman, Canisius College
Marian L. Houser, Texas State University San Marcos
Kumi Ishii, Western Kentucky University
Seung-A Annie Jin, Boston University

Antwan Jones, George Washington University
Canchu Lin, L., Tiffin University
Yang Lin, University of Akron
Meina Liu, George Washington University
Yung-I Liu, California State University, East Bay
Joseph P. Mazer, Clemson University
Bree McEwan, Western Illinois University
Chris R. Morse, Bryant University
Kekeli Nuviadenu, Bethune–Cookman University
Youngrak Park, Columbus State University
Larry Powell, University of Alabama–Birmingham
David Schuelke, University of Minnesota
Lijiang Shen, University of Georgia
Joanna Showell, Bethune–Cookman University
Ross Singer, Southern Illinois University–Carbondale
Darren Stevenson, University of Michigan
Claire Sullivan, University of Maine
Tara Suwinyattichaiporn, Arizona State University
Celeste Walls
Qi Wang, Villanova University
Katie Warber, Wittenberg University
Kirsten Weber, University of Georgia
Terry L. West, California State University, East Bay
Margaret A. Wills, Fairfield University
Xiaohe Xu, The University of Texas at San Antonio
Kenneth Yang, The University of Texas at El Paso
Shuo Yao, Radford University

DEDICATION

Since the publication of the second edition of this book, we lost the single most published scholar in the field of communication and our coauthor, Dr. James C. McCroskey. This book has been a labor of love for all of us, but Jim's influence is clearly seen in every page of this text. In fact, trying to separate our memories of conducting communication research from our relationships with Jim is impossible. Each chapter brings forward different memories of conversations and research projects we conducted with Jim. Without him, this book never would have been what it is today. Without him, the field of communication would not be what it is today. For these reasons, we dedicate this edition to our teacher, mentor, and friend.

Jason S. Wrench
Candice Thomas-Maddox
Virginia Peck Richmond

INSTRUCTOR ANCILLARIES

If you have not received a copy of the instructor's manual from your Oxford University Press representative, please ensure you get one. The instructor's manual has been completely overhauled for the 3rd edition. Here are some of the important ancillary materials we have included to make your life easier as you prepare to teach this course:

1. **Sample Syllabi**

   In the Instructor's Manual, you will find a variety of different types of courses contexts where this textbook has been previously used (e.g., undergraduate face-to-face class, undergraduate online class, graduate face-to-face class). Furthermore, we offer you multiple approaches a teacher could take with the course. Whether you take a strictly content-based approach to the class or you want to take a project-based approach to teaching research methods, the sample syllabi will definitely help you structure your course.

2. **Chapter Outlines**

   On the textbook's website, every student has access to a skeletal outline of the different chapters' content. In the Instructor's Manual, we have not only the skeletal outlines, but also completely annotated versions of these outlines to help you prepare your course notes. Many instructors tell us that all they need to do is grab the Instructor's Manual and take it with them to class for fully realized class lectures.

3. **PowerPoint-based Slide Deck**

   Many instructors asked for a PowerPoint-based slide deck after the first version of the textbook was released, so we added a comprehensive slide deck to this edition of the book. The comprehensive slide deck reflects the annotated chapter outlines within the Instructor's Manual directly.

4. **In-Class Activities for Each Chapter**

   For each chapter we provide a range of different activity ideas to make your class more engaging. Numerous worksheets and assignments that we have used in the past can be found in the Instructor's Manual. None of the activities or assignments discussed within the Instructor's Manual was created specifically for the Instructor's Manual. All of the activities and assignments have been utilized within our own classrooms.

5. **Test Bank**

   The test bank has been completely updated and revised for the third edition of the Instructor's Manual. We provide a range of multiple-choice, true–false, and short-answer/essay questions for your course's examinations.

Companion Website

Please visit our companion website at http://www.oup.com/us/wrench/ for a range of supplementary materials for both you and your students. The website has links to podcasts related to some of the chapters, sample APA style papers, further discussion of statistical software (with video tutorials), and many other features.

Last Word

To students:

Thank you for taking up the challenge of learning quantitative research methods for communication. For most of you, this is a daunting course and unlike any you have taken within a communication studies department before. Please realize that you can get through the course and succeed. We need a new generation of communication researchers coming through the pipeline for our field to grow and thrive. Furthermore, the methods and practice of conducting research you learn in this book can be applied to any field of research that examines humans or phenomena statistically. Although different fields have their own avenues of interest and advanced statistical preferences, the basics you learn in this course could easily be applied to any social or physical science research undertaking.

To instructors:

Thank you for choosing to use *Quantitative Research Methods for Communication: A Hands-On Approach.* If you would like help or clarification teaching communication research methods, please do not hesitate to reach out to any of the authors of this text. If one us does not know the answer to a question, we will forward it to the others so we can assist you best. Also, please feel free to give us your feedback. As we look toward revising the book in the future, instructor feedback is unbelievably helpful.

REFERENCES

Milroy, S. J. (2001). *Junk science judo: Self-defense against health scares and scams.* Washington, DC: Cato Institute.

Paulos, J. A. (1988). *Innumeracy: Mathematical illiteracy and its consequences.* New York, NY: Hill & Wang.

QUANTITATIVE RESEARCH METHODS
FOR COMMUNICATION

CHAPTER 1

An Introduction to Communication Research

CHAPTER OBJECTIVES

1   Explain the difference between physical and social sciences.
2   Describe the history of social sciences.
3   Understand what led to the rise of quantitative research in the sciences.
4   Explain the debate between James Winans and Everett Lee Hunt.
5   Summarize how both World War I and World War II influenced social scientific research.
6   Define the word *communication*.
7   Explain Claude Shannon and Warren Weaver's (1949) model of communication.
8   Understand the basic layout of this textbook.

Every day, people around the globe participate in an activity that helps shape our understanding of the world. This activity is research. Ever since you were a child in elementary school you have been taught all kinds of facts. What most students do not stop to think about is where these "facts" come from in the first place. Whether it was learning that Newton created his theory of gravity after having an apple fall on his head or memorizing all of the elements in the periodic table, most of your academic endeavors have been built around knowledge that has not always existed. At some point in history, a scientist has actually had to conduct a research study to determine what we today often take for granted as common knowledge.

Although most people are familiar with many basic facts about the **physical sciences**, or the study of the objective aspects of nature (biology, chemistry, physics, astronomy, etc.), as a result of K–12 schooling, people do not tend to be as aware of the research in the area called the social sciences. The **social sciences** consist of a group of fields that set out to study how humans live and interact. These include many different disciplines: anthropology, communication, cultural studies, economics, education, geography, history, linguistics, political sciences, psychology, sociology, social work, and so on. All of these fields have at their core a desire to understand how humans live and interact. Although each social scientific field may approach the study of human life and interaction differently, they all have the same basic origin in history. This chapter will first present a brief history of the development of social science and then talk specifically about how the field of communication has become what it is today.

The History of the Social Sciences

The earliest recorded scientists would be shocked to see the division that exists today between the physical sciences and the social sciences. In ancient Greece, the physical sciences and philosophy were perceived as handmaidens because one informed the other. Most of the ancient Greek philosophers wrote not only about science but also about rhetoric, poetry, drama, and other intrinsically human-oriented topics. For example, Hippocrates of Cos (c. 460 BCE) is most noted for the oath that all physicians take that states that physicians should first do no harm. Hippocrates was also the first researcher in history to start classifying his patients by various temperaments, which is now seen as the general origin of personality theory that modern social scientists study today. To Hippocrates, science was an extremely important part of understanding the world in both the physical sense and the humanistic sense; he wrote, "There are in fact, two things: science, and opinion; the former begets knowledge, the latter ignorance." Even later Greek thinkers such as Plato and Aristotle often wrote on both physical and social scientific topics and sometimes combined the two. Plato used geometric proofs (a physical science tool) to demonstrate his perspective on the intrinsic state of knowledge (a social scientific concept). Aristotle studied planetary motion with the same rigor and scientific processes with which he studied poetry and rhetoric. To the ancient Greeks, both physical nature and human social processes were avenues of research to be done scientifically.

This lack of division between physical and social sciences stayed fairly intact until the publication of the three volumes of Sir Isaac Newton's *Philosophiae Naturalis Principia Mathematica* (*Mathematical Principles of Natural Philosophy*) in 1687. In essence, Newton sets forth in the three volumes the foundation of classical mechanics and his law of gravity. Newton's publication revolutionized scientific thought because he argued that the underlying rule of all physical nature was mathematics. Whereas physical scientists quickly latched onto and successfully applied Newton's writings, eventually many scientists studying the social aspects of humans tried to make their research more mathematically oriented as well. This trend of physical sciences creating revolutions that remake how we understand science continued with the publication of Charles Darwin's **theory of natural selection**. Although mathematics clearly impacted physics and chemistry, natural selection revolutionized how biologists understood biology. Yet again, the physical sciences were light years ahead of social scientists in their understanding of nature, but eventually the social scientists came to understand how Darwin's theory actually applied to the social sciences. In fact, Sigmund Freud (in Austria) and William James (in the United States) were the first social scientists to examine how natural selection could be applied in the social sciences.

During the late 1800s and early 1900s, the rise of quantitative or mathematical measurement in the physical sciences quickly became the norm. Ernest Rutherford, the father of nuclear physics, once wrote that any knowledge that cannot be measured numerically is a poor sort of knowledge. Ultimately, during the early 1900s a rift emerged between humanists, who believed in universal human qualities (rationality, common history, experience, and belief), and social scientists, who saw the need to objectively quantify human experience. In the field of communication, we also saw this debate occurring within our own ranks.

At the turn of the twentieth century, James A. Winans (1915) and Everett Lee Hunt (1915) led an interdisciplinary debate regarding the need for research in public speaking. Winans wanted scientific research conducted on three levels: speech pathology, speech psychology, and rhetorical history. Hunt, by contrast, believed that the scientific approach was antithetical to the enthusiasm and inspiration that was needed for good public speakers. This divergence of ideology created what is commonly referred to as the social science versus humanist debate in the field of communication studies, which has continued for the greater part of the twentieth and into the twenty-first century.

Social scientific research really started finding its own way after World War I as research in a variety of new avenues began to flourish. In 1918, William Isaac Thomas and Florian Znaniecki defined social psychology as "the study of attitudes." Along with the development of attitudinal research, Jowett and O'Donnell (1992) note,

> Other social sciences such as sociology and psychology were also stimulated by the need to pursue questions about human survival in an age in which social strain grew heavy with concerns about warfare, genocide, economic depression, and human relationships. These questions were about influence, leadership, decision making, and changes in people, institutions, and nations. Such questions were also related to the phenomena of propaganda, public opinion, attitude change, and communication. (p. 123)

Overall, the period after World War I saw a quick rate of research in the social sciences. By the 1920s, marketing agencies were surveying consumer behavior and politicians and media outlets realized that the new techniques being created by social scientists to research humans could be used to examine political preferences. With the burgeoning need for social scientific research, Likert (1932), Guttman (1944), and Osgood (1952) developed three measures of attitudes that are still used by researchers today (these will be discussed in greater detail in Chapters 6 and 7).

When World War II broke out in Europe, the U.S. government turned to social scientists to understand propaganda, attitudes, and persuasion (Albarracín, Johnson, & Zanna, 2006). The U.S. government quickly realized that to maintain morale during wartime, the media was going to be extremely important. The creation of the U.S. Office of War Information was one step in this effort (Lazarsfeld & Stanton, 1944). By 1941, Lazarsfeld published the first review of the discipline of communication based on his and others' research at the Bureau of Applied Social Research. Ultimately, Lazarsfeld determined that communication could be broken into four categories: (1) who, (2) said what, (3) to whom, and (4) with what effect. The U.S. government was most interested in the last category as a way to fuel the war effort at home.

At the conclusion of World War II, the shift in social scientific communication research took its next major step as a result of a group of 30 researchers at Yale University led by Carl Hovland. The primary purpose of the research conducted by the Yale group was to analyze how attitude change occurred. Overall, the Yale group examined a wide range of differing variables all shown to influence persuasion: source credibility, personality traits, argument ordering, explicit versus implicit conclusions, and fear appeals (Hovland, Janis, & Kelly, 1953). The legacy of the research conducted by Hovland and his colleagues ultimately led future researchers to examine other communication contexts.

Wilbur Schramm and David Berlo

Wilbur Schramm is largely credited with creating the modern conceptualization of the field of communication studies with the creation of the Institute for Communications Research at the University of Illinois. One of his students, David Berlo, is largely credited with the shift in focus to quantitative research methodologies within the field of communication while at Michigan State University.

Communication concept explored	No. of articles	% of total
General Communication	229	9.8
Relationships	116	4.9
Perception	90	3.8
Apprehension	68	2.9
Students	53	2.3
Self	45	1.9
Television	44	1.9
Behavior	37	1.6
Satisfaction	35	1.5
Culture	35	1.5
Social	34	1.5
Interpersonal	33	1.4
Organizations	32	1.4
Style	31	1.3
Teacher	31	1.3
Public	31	1.3
Gender	28	1.2
Development	28	1.2
Verbal	27	1.2
Anxiety	27	1.2
Roles	27	1.2
Aggression	26	1.1
Competence	26	1.1
Classroom	26	1.1
Motivation	26	1.1
Interaction	25	1.1
Influence	23	1.0
American	23	1.0
Immediacy	22	0.9
Sex	21	0.9
Messages	21	0.9
Group	20	0.9
Japan	20	0.9
Nonverbal	20	0.9

Figure 1.1 Articles Published in *Communication Research Reports*

Today, the contexts for research in the field of communication are numerous. In fact, in 2004 Wickersham, Sherblom, and Richmond published a 20-year retrospective (1984–2004) of the types of empirical articles published in *Communication Research Reports* (*CRR*). Since its first publication, *CRR* has been solely devoted to short, concise, quantitative research articles. As a result of the nature of *CRR*, analyzing the concepts published in the journal allows researchers to see the overarching scope of the field of empirical communication research.

Figure 1.1 contains the results of the Wickersham et al. (2004) study. Overall, the top four concepts explored in *CRR* are general communication, relationships, perception, and apprehension, which have been directly influenced by research in both attitudes and persuasion initiated during the early and mid-1900s. Along with an expansion in the type of research that qualifies as "communication research," our understanding of communication has also changed. For this reason, the next part of this chapter is devoted to an explanation of the approach of communication according to the authors of this text.

Figure 1.2 2005–2014 *Communication Research Reports* Titles Word Cloud

To see what had changed since 2004, we examined the titles of all of the published research articles in *CRR* from 2005 through 2014. Using those 364 titles, we generated a word cloud demonstrating the words that were commonly seen across titles (Figure 1.2). The size of the word directly corresponds to the number of titles in which the word was found.

The Nature of Communication

The word "communication" has many different definitions, but the one we will use in this textbook states that **communication** is "the process by which one person stimulates meaning in the mind(s) of another person (or persons) through verbal and nonverbal messages" (McCroskey, 2006, pp. 20–21). Although other definitions may view communication from a different perspective, we see communication as primarily meaning focused. To comprehend this definition fully, a few of its parts need some clarification. The word "process" suggests that human communication is dynamic and changing, the notion that communication does not start, stop, or break. Berlo (1960) suggested that communication is like the river described by the Greek philosopher Heraclitus, who believed that it was impossible to step in the same river twice because the moment you take your foot out of the water, the river changes so much that it really is not the same river. In life, humans are constantly changing as we go through various events, and our communication with other people also naturally evolves over time. Therefore, humans never communicate in the same way twice. Even professional actors who recite the same lines over and over again never recite them in the same way twice.

The second part of the definition of "communication" involves the phrase "stimulating meaning in the mind(s) of another person (or persons)." The basic goal of communication is to take a thought that you have inside your head and determine the appropriate method for getting that thought into another person's head or into the heads of a group of people. Through the processes of stimulating meaning, we develop, cultivate, share, expand, and reshape ideas. Rare is the occasion when we develop an idea completely on our own. The very thoughts that lead to an idea occur as a result of our experiences of talking with others, reading various literatures, and simply observing and interacting with the world around us. Such ideas or combinations of ideas are the meaning stimulated through the verbal and nonverbal messages that are exchanged. But before we can discuss verbal and nonverbal messages, we must explain the basic model of communication.

Claude Shannon and Warren Weaver (1949) developed a model for describing the process of communication for the Bell Telephone Company. The Shannon and Weaver Model was simple because it was designed to explain how people use telephones. The telephone is designed with two basic parts: a source you talk into and a receiver in which you hear people on the other end. The full Shannon Weaver Model is often referred to as the source–message–channel–receiver (SMCR) model. The **source** is the person(s) who originates a message. This person(s) goes through a process called encoding to create a message. McCroskey and Wheeless (1976) defined **encoding** as "the process of creating messages that we believe represent the meaning to be communicated and are likely to stimulate similar meaning in the mind of a receiver" (p. 24). In other words, encoding involves translating ideas and information inside your head into messages that can be sent to a receiver(s). Encoding requires some degree of accuracy and precision for effective communication to take place because if your receiver cannot understand what you are saying, then communication will be ineffective. Inaccurate and imprecise encoding often leads to confusion. Therefore, it is important to select messages that have similar meanings for us and our receiver(s).

Of course, whereas the source sends messages, a **receiver** receives messages. As receivers of messages, we must receive messages and assign meaning to them. The process we go through as receivers to assign meaning to messages is called **decoding**. The meaning we assign a given message depends to a great degree on previous messages we have received from either the source and/or our previous experiences. Often, the meaning(s) we assign specific messages may not be close to the meaning intended by the source. Remember when you first started analyzing poetry in school and your teacher would tell you about the hidden meanings within a poem that you simply did not see at all? Verbal and nonverbal communication and meaning can function the same way; people often completely miss the meaning of a message or assign a meaning to the message that was not intended. For communication to be effective, it is necessary for us, as receivers, to consider our background and experience compared with the background and experience of the source, which may require that we put ourselves in the other person's shoes. The converse of this is also true. As sources of messages, we must know who our receivers are. If we were going to talk about media to a group of college freshmen, using references to Lawrence Welk and Ed Sullivan might not be useful (if you do not know who either of those men is, you just proved our point).

The next part of the SMCR model is the message. A message is any verbal or nonverbal stimulus that stimulates meaning in a receiver. As our definition of "communication" in this textbook is meaning focused, so is the basic model of communication. The **message** is simply what you want your receiver(s) to know, feel, and/or do when you are done communicating.

The last part of the SMCR model of communication is the channel. A **channel** is the means by which a message is carried from one person to another. In communication, we typically talk about two primary channels: verbal and nonverbal. By **verbal messages** we mean language. **Language** is a system of symbols or codes that represent certain ideas or meanings. The use of symbols and codes is regulated by a set of formal rules, which we call grammar and syntax. We transmit these messages either in spoken or in written form. Today, approximately 5,000 oral languages exist, but no single language is spoken or understood by a majority of humans (although Mandarin is spoken by more people in the world than any other language). Thus, even today, when people travel to various parts of the world, they often resort to communicating messages through nonverbal channels. **Nonverbal messages** refer to any messages other than verbal. These messages include such things as tone of voice, eye movements, hand gestures, and facial expressions. All in all, nonverbal messages are extremely important. Nonverbal researchers have estimated that between 65 and 93 percent of our understanding of a source's message is a result of how we decode the source's nonverbal communication. Humans tend to look more to how a source communicates than to the language choices he or she uses to communicate; this does not mean that language is unimportant, only that meaning is a combination of both verbal and nonverbal messages.

Both verbal and nonverbal channels can be utilized when communicating messages. However, verbal and nonverbal channels are not the only channels available to communicators. A **mediated channel** is any channel that uses some kind of mediating device to help transmit information. Telephones, e-mail, newspapers, television, radio, and text messaging are all examples of technologies that help mediate communication between people. Whether two people are on opposite sides of the world using mediated channels to communicate or sitting side by side text messaging each other to avoid eavesdroppers, people in today's world are constantly communicating via mediated messages. The first medium used to communicate messages was cave drawings, but cave drawings were neither efficient nor particularly effective channels for communicating anything but the most primitive of thoughts. In fact, some people try to make a case for prehistoric extraterrestrial contact based on the drawings found in caves. People can see pretty much anything they want in a cave drawing, so as a historical tool cave drawings are not reliable. Such drawings slowly evolved into more complex picture systems as they took on more substantial forms, where specific pictures were intended to mean things, which ultimately evolved into written language. If the history of human communication were represented by a typical 12-inch ruler, the history of writing would be included in less than the last quarter of an inch.

The most rapid improvement in mediated channels has occurred in the past 150 years. Ever since the first message was sent by Morse code in 1844, mediated technology has constantly been improving. From Morse Code to radios, to televisions, to cable televisions, to the Internet, to whatever comes next, mediated technology is constantly evolving. For this reason, many people in the field of communication devote themselves to the study of mediated **communications**. In the field of communication, the letter "s" at the end of the word "communication" is used to signify mediated technologies. The field of mass communications studies how mediated technologies communicate messages to large numbers of people. However, most of the research within the field of communication does not examine mediated technologies, so the letter "s" must not be added to the word "communication" unless one is specifically talking about communication occurring through mediated technologies.

Now that we have discussed both the history of social science research and the nature of communication, the rest of the chapter will briefly explain the organization of this volume.

Understanding the Book's Format

The authors of this book have more than 100 years combined experience conducting empirical research in the field of communication. Historically, West Virginia University's (WVU) Department of Communication studies has mentored many of the top quantitative researchers in the field, although the department did not technically have its own doctorate program until the fall of 2006. Individuals who graduated from WVU with a doctorate actually received their doctorate in education (either curriculum and instruction or educational psychology), so all WVU graduates have extensive training in both communication and educational theory and practice. Overall, the approach that WVU takes to teach research methods has been successful; in 2003, WVU was listed as one of the top doctorate programs for graduates publishing research in the field (Hickson, Turner, & Bodon, 2003). Furthermore, WVU was the number one program for faculty research publications. For this reason, this book is going to take the approach used at WVU to train many of the most prolific quantitative researchers in the field. All four of the authors of this text have WVU roots: two as faculty (James C. McCroskey and Virginia P. Richmond) and two as program graduates (Candice Thomas-Maddox and Jason S. Wrench). In various analyses of the field, WVU graduates and faculty have consistently made important contributions to the field of communication. Over a 30-year period, the instruction in quantitative research methods at WVU has been fine-tuned to enable both undergraduate and graduate researchers to quickly understand the research process. This book is the culmination of years of teaching instruction in research methods by all of the authors.

Chapters 2 and 3 are designed to introduce you to the basic aspects of communication research. In Chapter 2 we explore the meaning of empirical research and the scientific method, which is what this book is designed to teach you. If you are interested in nonquantitative research methods, in Appendix A (see textbook's website) we have included a chapter written by James Chesebro and Deborah Borisoff that discusses qualitative and critical research methods. In Chapter 3 we discuss the ethical standards that modern researchers are required to follow both philosophically and legally.

Chapters 4 and 5 take you through the basic process necessary for conducting research. In Chapter 4 we examine how to use libraries and other sources for finding research previously conducted on a given topic. In addition to basic library skill discussions, Chapter 4 will clearly lay out how to format papers and cite sources using the fifth edition of the American Psychological Association's style manual. Chapter 5 will then break down each section of a research study and give tips and examples for writing these sections for your own research projects.

Chapters 6, 7, and 8 examine the some of the most fundamental parts of a research project. In Chapter 6 we explain what variables are, the different types of variables that exist in empirical sciences, and various communication variables. The communication variables discussed in Chapter 6 will help you understand the majority of the examples discussed in this text. Furthermore, an actual research dataset was collected on the variables discussed in this chapter; you can find this dataset on the textbook's website. Chapters 7 and 8 explain how social scientists measure human behavior and perceptions and how to ensure these measurements are reliable and valid. In Chapter 7 we discuss how researchers measure communicative behaviors and perceptions. In Chapter 8 we discuss two extremely important characteristics involved in the measurement process that must be clearly followed for research to be meaningful (reliability and validity).

In Chapters 9, 10, 11, and 12 we explore three common techniques for conducting communication research: survey, content analysis, and experiment. In Chapter 9 we examine survey research. The methods discussed in this chapter date back to the techniques created during the 1930s and 1940s by the social scientists studying human attitudes. In Chapter 10 we explore the research method called content analysis. Chapter 11 will present the nature of experiments and various methods researchers can employ to ensure that experiments are successful. Then, Chapter 12 will introduce you to the new world of Big Data and the impact it is having both in the field of communication and in the world around you.

Chapters 13 and 14 explore some basic concepts related to research methods: sampling and hypothesis testing. Chapter 13 explains how to go about finding the appropriate research participants to ensure your research projects are successful and meaningful. Chapter 14 provides the basic explanation for how the statistical process is actually conducted. Although this chapter is the densest chapter to read, the information contained in it is extremely important to understanding the next six chapters.

Chapter 15 will start our discussion of statistics by introducing you to the first category of statistics, called descriptive statistics. Most people are somewhat familiar with the ideas of descriptive statistics, but we will show you how these descriptive statistics are the basic building blocks for more advanced statistics.

Chapters 16 through 20 will each examine a different statistical tool that can help you in answering actual questions about communication phenomena. The first segment in these chapters will walk you through the step-by-step process necessary to compute statistical formulas by hand. This is the part of quantitative research methods that many students are nervous about when first learning. Trust us, if you follow our step-by-step instructions, you will have no problems whatsoever learning how to calculate these mathematical formulas. In the first part of every chapter you will be presented with a scenario for the type of statistical test each chapter represents. These scenarios are designed to help you compute the statistical tests by hand. For this reason, the data used in these examples are fabricated to make the math as easy as possible. Although the first examples in each chapter may be interesting, they are not based on actual empirical data. In addition to calculating the problems by hand, you will also be provided with statistical output using the Windows version of the IBM Statistical Package for the Social Sciences (SPSS), version 20.0, and statistical output using the Windows version of Excel (from Microsoft Office 2010), which are useful tools used by quantitative communication researchers. Additionally, information will be provided on the utility of two open-source statistical software packages called PSPP and R. PSPP is a pared-down version of SPSS that is freely available. R, in contrast, is a statistical programming language and is best suited for those in graduate school. However, there is a graphic user interface called R-Commander that enables R to function in a manner that is similar to SPSS. To learn more about these free statistical software packages, please see Appendix C (see textbook's website).

The second segment in Chapters 16 through 20 will consist of real data–driven research questions from the dataset that was collected for this textbook. In these examples you will be presented first with a research scenario and then with the SPSS and Excel results, similar to the examples in the first part. The biggest difference between these examples and the examples in the first part of the chapters is that these examples are based on actual collected data, so these are real research findings. We could have used the examples in the second half of each chapter to compute the statistics by hand, but that process would have been much more complicated and not beneficial to your understanding of the mathematical processes needed to compute these statistics.

The third and final segment in Chapters 16 through 20 will examine the articles on the textbook's website. To see how each of these statistical tests can actually be used by researchers to answer actual hypotheses and research questions, we recommend that you read the first two sections of every chapter first, then read the corresponding article on the textbook's website, and finally examine the analysis of the article we have provided for you in the chapter. By completing the readings in the way we recommend, you will be able to determine whether you truly understand the statistical concept and how it can be employed in research.

In Chapter 21 we further your understanding of statistical devices by introducing you to eight advanced statistical tools that are commonly seen in communication literature. Although we will not show you how the computations are performed by hand or how to perform the analyses on the computer software packages, we will provide you with the theory behind the statistical tool, a real example, and an American Psychological Association write-up for each device. The goal of this chapter is not to enable you to conduct these statistical procedures, but to provide you with enough information to understand what these procedures are when you run into them in journal articles.

The final chapter in this book, Chapter 22, is designed to discuss the processes that researchers go through to present their findings to other people. This chapter will examine how to design effective research posters for presentation at conferences and conventions, how to deliver papers at conferences and conventions, and how to submit your original research for possible publication.

Research Outside the Walls of Academia

One area that really surprises numerous communication students is the cross-transferability of the skills you learn in a quantitative research methods course to life outside of academia. The reality is that a great deal of your life is governed by information derived through quantitative research. Everything from the medication you take, to the clothes you wear, to how you connect with friends exists because of quantitative research. Although this is not a book about medical research or market research, we do want you to be aware that there are numerous individuals engaged in applied quantitative communication research. Periodically in this text we will end a chapter with a discussion of some key factors to consider when engaging in research outside the confines of higher education. Furthermore, we will discuss how people in the world outside of academia are using the same processes, tools, techniques, and statistics to answer a whole host of different problems outside of academia.

Conclusion

The authors of this textbook have a passion for conducting unique and interesting communication research. We sincerely hope that you will learn to share our passion for research as you take this journey with us through this text. In the next chapter, we will explain the process researchers go through when conducting scientific research in communication.

KEY TERMS

Channel	Language	Receiver
Communication	Mediated channel	Social science
Communications	Message	Source
Decoding	Nonverbal messages	Theory of natural selection
Encoding	Physical science	Verbal messages

REFERENCES

Albarracín, D., Johnson, B. T., & Zanna, M. P. (Eds.). (2006). *The handbook of attitudes*. Mahwah, NJ: Erlbaum.

Berlo, D. K. (1960). *The process of communication*. New York, NY: Holt, Rinehart & Winston.

Guttman, L. (1944). A basis for scaling qualitative data. *American Sociological Review, 9,* 139–150.

Hickson, M. III, Turner, J., & Bodon, J. (2003). Research productivity in communication: An analysis, 1996–2001. *Communication Research Reports, 20,* 308–319.

Hovland, C. I., Janis, I. L., & Kelly, H. H. (1953). *Communication and persuasion: Psychological studies of opinion change*. New Haven, CT: Yale University Press.

Hunt, E. L. (1915). The scientific spirit in public speaking. *The Quarterly Journal of Public Speaking, 1*, 185–193.

Jowett, G. S., & O'Donnell, V. (1992). *Propaganda and persuasion* (2nd ed.). Newbury Park, CA: Sage.

Lazarsfeld, P. (1941). Remarks on administrative and critical communications research. *Studies in Philosophy and Social Science, 9*, 2–16.

Lazarsfeld, P., & Stanton, F. N. (1944). *Radio research, 1942–43*. New York, NY: Duell, Sloan, & Pearce.

Likert, R. (1932). A technique for the measurement of attitudes. *Archives of Psychology, 140*, 1–55.

McCroskey, J. C. (2006). *An introduction to rhetorical communication: A western rhetorical perspective* (9th ed.). Boston, MA: Allyn & Bacon.

McCroskey, J. C., & Wheeless, L. R. (1976). *An introduction to human communication*. Boston, MA: Allyn & Bacon.

Osgood, C. E. (1952). The nature and measurement of meaning. *Psychological Bulletin, 49*, 197–262.

Shannon, C. E., & Weaver, W. (1949). *The mathematical theory of communication*. Urbana, IL: University of Illinois Press.

Thomas, W. I., & Znaniecki, F. (1918). *The Polish peasant in Europe and America: Primary-group organization*. Chicago, IL: University of Chicago Press.

Wickersham, J. A., Sherblom, J. C., & Richmond, V. P. (2004). A twenty year retrospective on a research community: An analysis of scholarship published in *Communication Research Reports* (1984 to 2004). *Communication Research Reports, 21*, 437–444.

Winans, J. A. (1915). The need for research. *The Quarterly Journal of Public Speaking, 1*, 17–23.

FURTHER READING

Chesebro, J. W. (Ed.). (2010). *A century of transformation: Studies in honor of the 100th anniversary of the Eastern Communication Association*. New York, NY: Oxford University Press.

Salkind, N. J. (2012). *100 questions (and answers) about research methods*. Los Angeles, CA: Sage.

Wrench, J. S., McCroskey, J. C., & Richmond, V. P. (2008). *Human communication in everyday life: Explanations and applications*. Boston, MA: Allyn & Bacon.

Empirical Research

Have you ever read a textbook in a communication course and wondered where all the information came from? Have you ever wondered how your university professors became so smart? The simple and complicated answer to both these questions is research. Now for many readers, when we say "research" you may be thinking of the type of research you did in an English class where you looked at various books, articles, and Internet websites and tried to write a paper incorporating the information from those sources into your paper. Although this type of research is extremely important, it is not what we are referring to when we say "research." This textbook's definition of the word **research** can best be understood by looking at one of the definitions provided by Merriam-Webster's *Dictionary* (n.d.): "studious inquiry or examination; especially: investigation or experimentation aimed at the discovery and interpretation of facts, revision of accepted theories or laws in the light of new facts, or practical application of such new or revised theories or laws." This definition implies that "research" is the use of the scientific method to answer questions. We will further explain the idea of the "scientific method" later in this chapter, but before we explain the scientific approach to conducting research, a quick discussion of the major epistemological approaches to research will be presented.

Ways of Knowing

EPISTEMOLOGY

According to Moser (2002), epistemology is "the study of the nature of knowledge and justification: in particular, the study of (a) the defining components, (b) the substantive conditions or sources, and (c) the limits of knowledge and justification" (p. 3). Simply put, **epistemology** is a way of knowing. Of course, along with the idea of "knowing," we must admit that there are various perspectives on the very notion of knowledge. For example, Klein (2002) argued that these foundations of "knowing" are highly controversial because of a range of different standpoints. Klein argues that there are three important considerations to consider when discussing knowledge.

First, how does one analyze knowledge and justification? Or, how does someone use theory, data, and other forms of evidence to ascertain "knowledge?" Diverse epistemological perspectives will have different theoretical traditions to draw on. Furthermore, they often have varied approaches and ways of analysis to interrogate and find meaning within human communication.

Second, what sources of knowledge does one use? Within the field of communication, there are three general branches discussed: social-scientific (also called positivism/postpositivism), qualitative (also called interpretive), and rhetorical (also called critical, postmodern, poststructuralist, etc.). We should mention we divide the three branches through our vantage point as social scientists. If you asked a poststructuralist scholar, their categorizing scheme would look different. Social-scientific researchers rely predominantly on quantitative methodologies and believe that human communication can be examined through the use of both simple and complex statistical models. Interpretive researchers, in contrast, believe that to understand human communication, one must thoroughly explore and appreciate how the individual(s) at the center of specific interactions or communicative acts understands his or her own communication. Last, critical scholars believe that the central role of research is to examine the interplay between ideology and science.

Ideology refers to the common or partial knowledge that people have. Common or partial knowledge is problematic for two reasons. First, common knowledge tends to serve the needs of specific people (generally those with the power and control within a given group or culture). Second, common knowledge is incomplete because people generally do not understand where this common or partial knowledge originated from, so they assume it must be factual, true, doctrine, etc. Research, from the critical perspective, is the process a researcher uses to examine how power and domination create these forms of common knowledge and eventually shed light on how these forms of knowledge are used to subjugate the people who have them. Each of these three epistemological traditions is important within the field of communication. However, they are not always suited for the same types of research questions. For instance, if you wanted to determine whether one group who views an advertisement responds differently toward a product than a second group, then the social-scientific method is the best. If you want to know how people understand what it means to be members of a church from the perspective of the individual members of the church through the interactions that they have, then examining these perceptions interpretively would make the most sense. If you want to examine how crisis messages are steeped in traditions of privilege, power, and hegemony, then a rhetorical/critical tradition is probably the most appropriate. It is important to understand that epistemology is always the driving force behind the research questions someone asks and the methodological traditions someone uses.

Last, Klein (2002) discusses the importance of skepticism and its importance to both knowledge and justification. Klein says there are three approaches to epistemological skepticism that are aligned with the three theoretical traditions: (1) epistemist (acknowledging that knowledge of something is possible), (2) academic (arguing that knowledge of something impossible), and (3) Pyrrhonian (withholding agreement to either the epistemist or the academic perspective). In essence, the term "knowledge" is often utilized without any kind of acknowledgment to what is meant by the word itself. Philosophically, uncertainty helps rein in the notions of what knowledge is and whether something can be known. If you ask people conducting research in the different epistemological traditions (social-scientific, qualitative/interpretive, and rhetorical/critical), the answers you get about what is known or even knowable will vary greatly. The purpose of this book is not to shine a light on all three of these epistemological perspectives.

This book focuses on quantitative/scientific epistemology for research. However, it is important that beginners, which this book presumes you are, be exposed to both epistemological approaches to communication scholarship. After you have completed your initial study of quantitative research you may want to stay with this approach (as all of us have done), or you may decide that you would rather explore one of the other epistemological traditions for research. If you decide that the qualitative/interpretive or critical approach may fit you better, it is certainly not too late to opt to take a course in that approach to scholarship. Many communication programs require you to take courses in quantitative/scientific, qualitative/interpretive, and rhetorical/critical research methods to ensure that you have a broad exposure to how knowledge is arrived at within the field. Many scholars, including the authors of this book, believe that all scholars (undergraduate students, graduate students, and academic professionals) should be exposed to the three main approaches to communication scholarship because the only way to engage in academic discourse is to have a strong foundation in all three methodological approaches to research. Appendix A (see textbook's website) broadly introduces you to the two epistemological traditions not focused on within this text.

ORDINARY VERSUS SCIENTIFIC WAYS OF KNOWING

From the moment we are born, we start attempting to know the world that is around us. Admittedly, our attempts in infancy are minimal and do not get us far, but these attempts get larger and more complex throughout our lifetimes. Part of this understanding involves our ability to understand our current situations and predict what will happen in the future. Over time, we start to realize that "future circumstances are somehow caused or conditioned by present ones" (Babbie, 2010, p. 4). Some of these realizations are easy. If you stick your finger in a light socket, it is going to hurt. Others are more complex: if you get a degree from a prestigious university, you will make more money compared to those individuals who do not go to prestigious universities. However, we also start realizing that these predictions are probabilistic, meaning that they are not accurate 100 percent of the time. For every Ivy League graduate out there making huge amounts of money, there are others who are starving artists, authors, actors, musicians, etc. Over time, we start to realize that our predictions should be narrowed and fine-tuned. For example, maybe getting an Ivy League education is only part of the picture. If you get a degree in business or economics from an Ivy League school, then maybe your long-term financial prospects are better than that of individuals with a degree in creative writing. According to Babbie (2010), "If you can understand why things are related to each other, why certain regular patterns occur, you can predict better than if you simply observe and remember those patterns. Thus, human inquiry aims at answering both 'what' and 'why' questions, and we pursue these goals by observing and figuring out" (p. 5).

Chances are you have never actually read a research report looking at the statistics of Ivy League graduates and incomes, so we often rely on ordinary sources of information. Ultimately, Babbie (2010) argues that two tools people often rely on to gain ordinary or common-sense knowledge are traditions and authorities. First, traditions! Each of us is constrained by the culture we have grown up in. Depending on the culture, you may learn things like when it is best to plant fruits and vegetables to ensure the best harvest. You also learn issues related to gender, sexuality, race/ethnicity, nationalism, etc. Traditions are often dominant and dictate how people think, behave, and communicate with one another. However, traditions can also have a dark side and limit people inherently. For example, in many parts of the world, tradition dictates that unmarried women should never interact with or communicate with men who are not their immediate family members.

Second, we often ascertain knowledge from some kind of authority figure. In any cultural group, there are authority figures whose ideas on knowledge are judged as more valuable than others. Often these values may have a factual basis in reality. If you are told by an astrophysicist that the earth rotates around the sun (as it does), that information would hopefully bear more weight than if a religious leader told you that the sun rotates around the earth (as was Catholic Church doctrine for many years).

Therein lies one of the biggest problems people face with issues of ordinary knowledge: which authority figure one should believe. Should one rely on ordinary knowledge provided by a religious authority or a scientific authority with regard to scientific information? Many authority figures will speak outside of their actual realm of real authority. Inquiry is fundamentally hindered when someone listens to and believes the "common knowledge" of someone who is not an actual authority on a topic. For example, a huge national debate currently exists on the efficacy and outcomes of vaccines. On one side of the debate are the Surgeon General, the medical establishment, and academic researchers from around the world. On the other side of the debate are a handful of celebrities and some rich and vocal parents on the West Coast fueling the "anti-vaccer" debate. In a case like this, who do you listen to? One group of authority figures has studied the issues extensively using science and the other group has anecdotal evidence and opinions. Although for us the choice to align oneself with scientific authority figures makes sense, others have been taught to historically distrust science and even believe in larger scientific conspiracy theories; hence, they believe the celebrity authority figures.

Overall, tradition and authority figures both have positive and negative associations. On the positive side, both tradition and authority give us a grounding to understand our world. Admittedly, these understandings may not be true and must be adjusted as one grows older. For example, you may have been taught that women were second-class citizens without the full rights of men, only to realize that the subjugation of women in the name of religion is abhorrent. As such, it is important to always question common knowledge and why that common knowledge exists. Unfortunately, many traditions and authority figures teach that questioning "their knowledge" is a heresy one should avoid.

What, then, is the difference between common knowledge and science? The knowledge that is arrived at through science is distinctly different from common knowledge because of the rigorous process used to acquire that knowledge. Harris (2014) describes six specific differences between common and scientific knowledge:

1. Conceptualizing the topic: scientists carefully conceptualize their research studies while delineating clear boundaries for what is being studied and what is not.

2. Reading the literature: scientists read a range of research studies on a single topic prior to engaging in a new study or scientific discourse to ensure their positions are backed by evidence and not opinion.

3. Careful measurements: scientists attempt to create and then use precise measures of various phenomena while admitting any specific limitations that may exist in these measurement techniques.

4. Collecting samples: scientists rely not on the opinions and anecdotes of the few, but instead on larger, more carefully assembled samples that represent a specific phenomenon.

5. Analyzing data and presenting results: scientists spend their entire careers learning how to analyze data and new methods for analyzing data in an effort to disseminate their results to both their academic peers and the general public.

6. Ethics and politics: researchers must think through how to ethically collect and report data while minimizing any political and personal biases that may distort the research process.

When you compare these six processes to those that rely on tradition and authority, clear distinctions between what is knowledge and how one gains knowledge emerge. One of the biggest frustrations scientists run into is when they have mounds of evidence on a topic and someone feels that her or his opinion is equally valid to all of the data that have been painstakingly collected and analyzed. Opinions are not science. Unfortunately, we live in an age where opinions are taken as facts if they are repeated often enough. For our purposes, we are interested in science rather than opinions related to how people behave, interact, and communicate.

The Scientific Approach to Communication Research

The idea of a method for determining things scientifically is as old as the notion of **science** itself. The ancient Egyptians and Greeks both created systems for determining knowledge through a process that is loosely related to what we now know as the scientific method. Furthermore, advances were made in the scientific method as a result of Muslim philosophers who believed that experiments should be used to test opposing theories. Our current understanding of the scientific method was first theorized by Sir Francis Bacon and René Descartes and later crystallized by Charles Sanders Peirce in 1878 in his article, "How to Make Our Ideas Clear." Overall, the notion of a specific method for discovering scientific laws has been around for millennia. Whether you are a physical scientist (biologist, chemist, physicist, etc.) or a social scientist (psychologist, sociologist, communication researcher, etc.), the basic processes for conducting research stem from the scientific method. When you were in elementary school, you were probably introduced to the scientific method in much the same way we were. So, before we can go further in discussing the scientific approach to communication research, we must revisit the scientific method.

SCIENTIFIC METHOD

The **scientific method** actually relates to the definition provided earlier from Webster's *Dictionary* for the word "research." In essence, as Figure 2.1 illustrates, there are four primary steps to the scientific process as it is commonly discussed by all scientists. Where one starts in the process is somewhat arbitrary, but it is usually most helpful if we start with the "theories" step and explain from that point forward in the process.

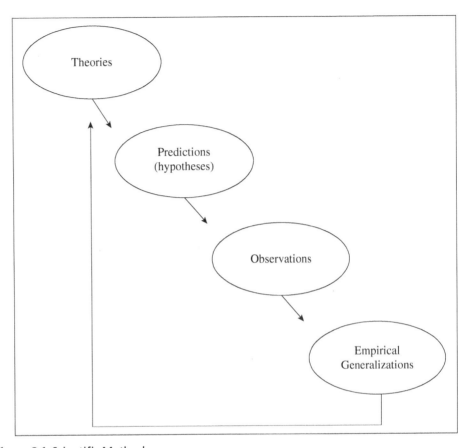

Figure 2.1 Scientific Method

Although most people have a general understanding of what the scientific method is, most do not know the history of this method. The scientific method was first used by a Muslim scientist, Ibn al-Haytham (965–1039 CE), who lived in what is now modern-day Iraq. Ibn al-Haytham can be best described as a polymath, or an individual who studied a wide range of scholarly topics. Ibn al-Haytham wrote about anatomy, astronomy, mathematics, medicine, philosophy, physics, psychology, and religion. However, it was his interest in the area of optics, the branch of science that studies visible and invisible light, and vision that led to the creation of the scientific method. In the *Book of Optics*, Ibn al-Haytham describes a method for conducting experiments, which ultimately became the basis of modern science. Ibn al-Haytham's scientific method consisted of seven basic steps: (1) observation, (2) stating of the scientific problem, (3) formulating a hypothesis, (4) testing the hypothesis through experimentation, (5) analyzing the experimental results, (6) interpreting data and forming conclusions, and (7) publishing research. Although this method of conducting research may seem standard today, this practice was unheard of in his time.

Over the next thousand years, many of our most famous scientists revisited and debated Ibn al-Haytham's method for conducting science. Some of these scientists include Galileo Galilee, Francis Bacon, René Descartes, Isaac Newton, Charles Sanders Peirce, David Hume, and Karl Popper. The version of the scientific method that is most commonly used today stems from the work of Karl Popper (1934, 1968).

Theories

A **theory** is a proposed explanation for how a set of natural phenomena will occur, capable of making predictions about the phenomena for the future, and capable of being falsified through empirical observation (West & Turner, 2006). We will break this definition down and examine its major components.

Describe the National Phenomenon

First, a theory should be able to either explain or describe a natural phenomenon (observable event). According to the sociologist Gwynn Nettler (1970), an explanation is an attempt to satisfy one's curiosity about an observable event. In one of our favorite movies, *The Gods Must Be Crazy*, a Bushman named Xi who lives in Botswana is presented a gift from "the gods." The so-called gift is actually a Coke bottle accidentally dropped by a pilot flying a plane above the tribe. Ultimately, the Bushmen become jealous of each other because there is only one Coke bottle; this causes the tribe to rename the bottle "the evil thing." The majority of the movie tells the story of Xi attempting to take the bottle to the end of the world and return "the evil thing" to the gods. In essence, the Bushmen were faced with a new and unexplainable event, the appearance of the bottle, and were forced to create an explanation for how the bottle appeared in their tribe after falling from the sky. The Bushmen's explanation for the observable event was that the gods had given them the bottle. This example is actually only one type of explanation that people give to observable events and is called **appealing to authority** because the explanation centers around the gods being wise in their decision to give the Bushmen the bottle.

The second way of explaining phenomena is to **label the phenomenon**. Humans use labeling constantly with children to help explain why parents do things. A child might ask, "Why do we wash our hands?," in response to which the parent explains the concept of bacteria and disease in a basic way the child can understand. This is also seen with the Bushmen when the "gift from the gods" causes jealousy among the tribe members and is labeled an evil thing."

The third way to explain phenomena is to **evoke empathy**, or show how a phenomenon had good, just, or moral reasons. For example, when explaining his reasoning to the American public for invading Iraq, President George W. Bush appealed to the American people, explaining that Iraq had weapons of mass destruction and it was the just and moral thing to invade Iraq to prevent Saddam Hussein from being able to use those weapons.

The fourth way to explain a phenomenon is to **define terms or give examples**. For example, university professors often forget how large their vocabularies are and occasionally make the mistake of using a word on an examination that many students do not know. To give an **explanation** of what the word means, we will try to think of other words (synonyms) a student may be more familiar with to help her or him understand what the question is actually asking.

The last way people can go about explaining phenomena is to **appeal to general empirical rules**. For example, when people experience stage fright, they often have sweaty palms. Sweaty palms occur during anxious periods because our body goes into a fight-or-flight mode, so blood is actually being pumped to our extremities (arms and legs) at a fast rate, which causes the internal temperature to rise in our extremities in case we have to fight what is causing the anxiety or run fast. Although this physiological response to fear is useful when you come face to face with a man-eating bear in the wilderness, it is not useful when you have to give a public speech. In this example, we explained why sweaty palms occur by relating the physiological response to what we empirically know about how the body reacts to fear. Ultimately, appealing to general empirical rules as a method for explaining phenomena is extremely important because it is the only way to explain the past and present and help us predict what could happen in the future, which is the second part of the definition of theory provided earlier.

Predict the Future

Our explanation of the behavior (fight or flight leads to sweaty palms) helps us to formulate predictions (when fearful, people's hands are more likely to sweat). When we talk about theories, our ultimate goal is to be able to predict, explain, and control a phenomenon. If a theory is of any use, then the theory for why a behavior occurs should help direct us to ways to control the phenomenon. For example, recent research has shown that certain psychiatric medications can actually decrease an individual's level of anxiety, even in situations where he or she must give public speeches (Stein, Stein, Goodwin, Kumar, & Hunter, 2001; Van Ameringen et al., 2001; Van Ameringen, Mancini, Oakman, & Farvolden, 1999). Overall, we can predict that people who experience high levels of anxiety while giving a speech will have sweaty palms. We can explain why this occurs through the research that has been conducted by scientists in the area of physiological responses to fear that result in a fight-or-flight state. Finally, based on new research conducted in the area of psychopharmacology, we can now better control the physiological tendency to experience anxiety, thus preventing sweaty palms while giving a speech (Richmond, Wrench, & McCroskey, 2013).

Falsification

The last part of the definition of "theory" is often the hardest for nonscientists to completely understand. Karl Popper first argued in the 1930s that a theory must be falsifiable through empirical research (Popper, 1968). In essence, for a theory to truly be a theory, there must be a way to test it empirically. The word **empiricism** was originally coined by the Roman skeptic Sextus Empiricus in reference to Greek physicians, who rejected beliefs in the divine nature of illness (i.e., you are sick because you made Zeus mad); instead, the physicians relied on the observation of phenomena as perceived in experience through the five senses (touch, smell, hear, see, taste). In other words, empiricism is the belief that science is only acceptable insofar as the phenomenon in question can be "sensed" by average people. For example, people may not be able to see atoms with their naked eyes, but they can observe them using powerful microscopes. However, there are no microscopes or telescopes powerful enough to observe little green men living on Mars or any other known planet beyond earth. For this reason, we can create scientific theories about atoms, but we cannot create scientific theories about extraterrestrial life forms.

PREDICTIONS/HYPOTHESES

The second step in the scientific method is the development of predictions about the relationship between phenomena that come in the form of hypotheses. A **hypothesis** is the conclusion that occurs at the end of a series of propositions. A **proposition** is a statement that either confirms or denies something. Although there are many types of propositions, the most important to researchers are conditional or hypothetical propositions, which consist of two primary parts: antecedent and consequent. An **antecedent** is an "if" statement, and a **consequent** is a "then" statement. For example, "If I was born in the United States (antecedent), then I am an American (consequent)." Or "If this month is June (antecedent), then the next month is July (consequent)." In the world of propositions, the antecedent causes the consequent to be true if the antecedent is true. In both examples used here, the consequent is true if the antecedent is true. If someone is born in the United States, then he or she is an American. If the current month is June, the next month on the calendar must be July because we do not randomly shuffle the months just for the fun of it every year.

From hypothetical propositions, we can take the next step to forming arguments. An **argument** is a set of propositions in which one follows logically as a conclusion from the others. In the world of logic, logicians illustrate arguments through the **syllogism**. A basic syllogism has three propositions (two premises and one conclusion). The most famous syllogism was given by the philosopher Aristotle more than 2,000 years ago:

Major Premise:	All men are mortal.
Minor Premise:	Socrates is a man.
Conclusion:	Therefore, Socrates is mortal.

However, one of the problems with syllogisms is that that for the syllogism to be accurate, we must trust that the premises are true. If our syllogism starts with false premises, then the conclusion can never be true. For example:

Major Premise:	All extraterrestrials are rich.
Minor Premise:	I am an extraterrestrial.
Conclusion:	Therefore, I am rich.

This syllogism, although correct in form, clearly is not true, and the conclusion cannot be trusted to tell us anything meaningful about the world around us. There is also a flip side to this problem—a completely invalid syllogism that is based on true statements. For example:

Major Premise:	All mammals are living.
Minor Premise:	All lizards are reptiles.
Conclusion:	Therefore, all lizards are living.

Although all three statements are true, the **major premise** and the **minor premise** do not go together at all. In essence, you are dealing with apples and oranges in the major and minor premises. Therefore, the conclusion that one would draw based on the major and minor premises may be true, but the syllogism is considered invalid because of the breakdown in the logical process. Ultimately, then, a hypothesis is a valid conclusion that is arrived at by a series of hypothetical propositions.

The following is an example from a student research paper attempting to determine the major premise, the minor premise, and the conclusion. See whether you think this argument is logical.

Major Premise:	Lack of conflict discussion leads to insecurity in the workplace.
Minor Premise:	Cooperation among employees minimizes conflict.
Conclusion:	Cooperation aids individuals in the management of conflict, and conflict discussion leads to solution-oriented conflict-management strategies.

Let's examine this argument to see where the problem actually lies. The major premise clearly says that the less people talk about conflict, the more insecure they are. The minor premise goes on to state that employees who cooperate have less conflict. The conclusion then says two different things: (1) if employees cooperate with each other, then somehow the cooperation will aid in the management of conflict, and (2) talking about conflicts helps people find a solution. The first conclusion simply does not make sense because it is not specific and we have no idea what "aids individuals in the management of conflict" actually means. This could indicate that people will have more conflict or less conflict—we simply cannot tell based on the information provided in the syllogism. The second conclusion introduces a new term that was not seen in either the major or the minor premise (solution-oriented conflict management strategies). If the term is not mentioned in any of the earlier propositions, it cannot magically appear in the conclusion of a logical argument. Finally, the major and minor premises have nothing to do with one another. The major premise discusses the lack of conflict, whereas the minor premise talks about minimizing conflict. Although the two ideas may sound similar, they are not the same, so you cannot put them together to form a logical argument.

Let's now examine an example from a student paper that was ultimately published right after the first edition of this book came out (Wrench, Millhouse, & Sharp, 2007). The following argument has true major and minor premises and a true conclusion:

Major Premise:	Passengers on airplanes like flight attendants who use humor.
Minor Premise:	There is a positive relationship between liking someone and trusting them.
Conclusion:	Therefore, flight attendants who use humor will be more trusted by passengers.

In this example, we have a major premise (funny flight attendants are liked) that clearly relates to the minor premise (liking and trust are related), which leads to the conclusion that funny flight attendants will be trusted. In essence, we can now hypothesize that flight attendants who are perceived as humorous will be more trusted than flight attendants who are not perceived as humorous. Note that both propositions are true because previous research in the area of flight attendant communication has generated empirical evidence to make those statements possible. When examining the major and minor premises that are used to create arguments in research, the propositions are based on actual empirical findings from previously conducted research. In other words, the premises are not simply made up because they help someone form an argument. If you do not have previous empirical research to help support your argument's propositions, then the propositions cannot be used to form any kind of conclusion.

OBSERVATIONS

The next step in the scientific method is referred to as observations. The **observations** part of the scientific method is where a researcher attempts to test the hypotheses created in the previous step. The most rigorous way to test a theory is to employ an experiment of some kind that directly allows a researcher to control a variable and then see the ramifications of this variable. For physical scientists, controlling a variable is easy—when one adds baking soda to vinegar we will always get the "volcanic" reaction we saw as a child in our earth sciences class. You could perform this experiment hundreds of times with varying brands of baking soda and vinegar and you will always get the same reaction. Unfortunately, the social sciences are not as neat and easy because people do not always react the same. You cannot always take one funny flight attendant and expect everyone to react to that flight attendant in the same way, because many other characteristics of that flight attendant could influence passengers' perceptions of her or him (e.g., biological sex, hair color, uniform, ethnicity, sexual attractiveness). For this reason, a certain amount of error is inherent in social scientific research simply because humans provide social scientists with too many possibilities. However, there are certain processes that social scientists can use to make sure they weed out as much uncertainty as possible when they are testing theories. These issues will be discussed in greater detail in Chapters 13 and 14; for now, we will test the hypothesis discussed above: "Flight attendants who use humor will be more trusted by passengers."

This hypothesis was actually created by a couple of undergraduate students who wanted to conduct research on the airline industry. There are a number of ways a researcher could go about observing this hypothesis. First, a researcher could fly hundreds of airlines seeking out funny and not-so-funny flight attendants. Clear criteria would have to be used to determine whether a flight attendant was funny. The researcher could then ask passengers whether they trust the flight attendants and keep a record of responses. Unfortunately, flying many different airlines and getting people's responses could be costly, so a researcher may opt to conduct an experiment instead. The researcher could have a video or audio tape of a flight attendant being funny or not so funny and then get participants' reactions to the flight attendant. In this case, the researcher manipulates whether the participants see the funny flight attendant or the not-so-funny flight attendant videos. After viewing one video or the other, the researcher could have the participants fill out a scale that measures the participants' perceptions of the video flight attendant's trustworthiness. Although watching video tapes is not the most accurate way of observing this phenomenon, it is the most cost-efficient.

However, when observing a phenomenon, researchers must take great care that their observations are empirical, objective, and controlled. We discussed the nature of empiricism earlier in this chapter, so we will not go into great detail here other than to say that empiricism with regard to observations basically means that scientists must make sure that what they are observing can be observed. If scientists cannot determine a way to make observations of some kind about a specific phenomenon, then they cannot study the phenomenon, so the phenomenon is beyond the domain of science. Along with this notion is the idea that research must be able to empirically test a phenomenon. You may be wondering how social scientists observe what is going on inside people's heads, and you would be right to question this because social scientists cannot read brain waves and translate them to actual thoughts. For this reason, social scientists have created specific ways to indirectly observe phenomena that cannot be easily observed through one of the five senses. I am sure that at some point in your undergraduate career you have been asked to fill out a research scale or questionnaire of some kind. These scales and questionnaires are examples of indirect methods social scientists have created to observe what is going on inside someone's head.

As previously stated, scientists must be both empirical and objective when they are observing phenomena during research. By "objective," we mean that a scientist must make sure that her or his personal emotions, predictions, and biases do not get in the way of the observation. For example, imagine a scientist interviewing students about their tendency to drink alcohol right before giving a speech in class. The more the student talks about her or his drinking behavior, the more the interviewer starts to scowl and give the student dirty looks. Do you think the student will be forthright and honest about her or his drinking behavior? Probably not. For this reason, scientists must ensure that they are as objective as possible when conducting research. Another aspect of objectivity is reporting exactly what one finds in research, not just what one wants to find. Often when researchers pose hypotheses and test them, the hypotheses will not be supported. Although there can be hundreds of reasons for why a hypothesis does not turn out the way a researcher expects it to, the researcher has an obligation to the scientific community to report those results and make them available for critique.

Finally, when observing a phenomenon, a researcher must ensure that he or she takes every step possible to control the research process. By **control**, researchers refer to the process where an individual both prevents personal biases from interfering with the research study and ensures there are no other explanations for what is seen in the study. We have already discussed the importance of preventing personal biases and will go into greater detail about how to do this in Chapters 13 and 14, so we will focus on how to prevent other explanations for observations.

Story of Clever Hans

A story that is often repeated as a warning when discussing explanations of observations is the story of Clever Hans. Clever Hans was an Arabian stallion (Figure 2.2) purchased in 1888 by Wilhelm Von Osten. Von Osten theorized that animals were intelligent beings and believed that with the proper education he could teach a horse to do

Figure 2.2 Story of Clever Hans (Karl Krall, Denkende Tiere, S. 425)

simple arithmetic. By the end of Hans's education, he could answer many arithmetic questions, from simple square roots to telling the time. The answers given by Hans came in the form of him pounding the number with his hoof the correct number of times on the ground. The horse could even answer mathematical questions when Von Osten was not present. Many researchers observed Hans and believed that Von Osten had educated the horse. Even the esteemed director of the Berlin Psychological Institute, Carl Stumpf, declared that Von Osten had educated Hans in 1904.

One researcher, Oskar Pfungst, decided to empirically test Hans through a simple, controlled experiment. First, Pfungst would have Von Osten look at a flash card to see the answer and then test Hans. When Von Osten knew the answer to the question, Hans's answers were always correct. Then Pfungst had Von Osten show Hans the card without Von Osten knowing the answer, and Hans's answers became very random. Pfungst concluded that somehow Von Osten was giving Hans the answers without even knowing it. At this point, Pfungst turned his attention to Von Osten as the teacher and observed his behavior. Pfungst started noticing that the teacher, whether Von Osten or another person, actually started changing her or his posture by standing up straighter as the horse neared the correct answer. When the teacher would stand fully erect, Hans knew he could stop pounding his hoof. Pfungst published his findings in 1907 in a book entitled *Clever Hans: The Horse of Mr. Von Osten*. In the Clever Hans example, we see both what happens when a scientist is not objective in observing a phenomenon (how Von Osten actually nonverbally cued the horse's responses) and how another scientist, Pfungst, came into the situation and determined how to control for other possible explanations and got to the bottom of what was really going on with Clever Hans.

EMPIRICAL GENERALIZATIONS

The final stage in the process of the scientific method is the creation of empirical generalizations. An **empirical generalization** is an attempt to describe a phenomenon based on what we know about the phenomenon at this time. Of course, our empirical generalizations are based on what we observed in the previous step of the scientific method. For example, in an initial study looking at flight attendant humor, the students conducting the research had participants read flight attendant preflight briefings (this is where the flight attendants show you all the doors, explain what to do with the yellow mask when it falls from the ceiling, and what to do in case you crash). One preflight safety briefing was standard and covered all of the basics required by the Federal Aviation Administration; in the second briefing the students added humor. Overall, the results of the study indicated that people did not trust the flight attendant in the humorous script (Wrench et al., 2007). In fact, participants trusted the bland flight attendant more than the funny flight attendant. In essence, the hypothesis was not supported. Unethical researchers may just pretend this finding did not happen and not present the results because this finding is contrary to previous research in humor. However, even results that go against common opinions on the subject are important for a number of reasons. First, this result could indicate that in situations where people feel their safety is involved, humor is not appreciated. In essence, the airline industry could be a context in which previous research in humor is not applicable. Second, the finding could be a result of the method used in the experiment. The student researchers relied on written scripts where they manipulated humor (one plain script vs. one funny script). The written humor may be interpreted differently if the participants in the study had viewed an actor or actress performing the script instead of the participants reading the script themselves. Overall, there are limitations to this study, and any good study will be up front about those limitations. If we do not know the limitations to a study, people may attempt to overgeneralize the study and start campaigns to pass laws banning flight attendant humor.

Overall, when we attempt to generalize what we have learned in a study to the real world, we must be honest about how we are applying our research findings. There are three common problems that researchers face when generalizing results: hasty generalizations, ecological fallacies, and exception fallacies. First, researchers should avoid **hasty generalizations**, or generalizing to something when not enough evidence is available to make the generalization. Scientists must avoid this problem in their own writing and in how others use their research. In the world of communication, media scholars often investigate how the effects of violence in the media relate to violence in the real world. Although the media scholars will correctly attribute limits to their results, often politicians will inaccurately try to use media research in their attempts to get various media banned. However, scientists should not investigate a phenomenon thinking of the political ramifications of their findings. One area in which there are ramifications to communication research is biological sex differences and communication. Empirical research generally shows that about 1 percent of a person's communicative behavior can be attributed to her or his biological sex (Canary & Hause, 1993); however, this finding contradicts what many people believe, which has largely been supported by pop psychologists such as John Gray, who wrote the book *Men Are from Mars, Women Are from Venus* (1992). Sadly, scientists who conflict with conventional wisdom often have problems in society, and those who buy into conventional wisdom see those scientists who try to thwart convention as "having an axe to grind." Remember, Pope John Paul II fully conceded in 1992 that the Catholic Church's teaching that the sun was stationary was wrong and Galileo's assertion during the 1600s was correct—the earth traveled around the sun. Overall, scientists typically do not think about how their research will be used by nonscientists or how people who disagree with research will react. Unfortunately, research is often used in ways that was never intended, and people who disagree with research can be vocal.

Second, researchers must be careful to avoid the ecological fallacy, or making generalizations about an individual because he or she belongs to a specific group. For example, research has shown us that men are typically more aggressive than women. Does this mean that all men are aggressive? No. Does this mean that no women are aggressive? Obviously not. The ecological fallacy becomes problematic when we meet a male and immediately assume he will be aggressive because research has demonstrated that men are more aggressive than women. As we will discuss in numerous places within this book, quantitative sciences are often looking at and comparing averages of groups. In this case, men are more aggressive on average when compared to the average levels of aggression among women. However, there will always be a great deal of variety that happens within a single group. There are many highly aggressive women and many men who are not aggressive at all.

Last, researchers want to avoid the exception fallacy. The exception fallacy is almost a reverse ecological fallacy. Under this fallacy, people make generalizations about an entire group of people based on one person or a small handful of people. Imagine you hear that a purple person was recently involved in a home burglary and you immediately think to yourself, *Those purple people are a bunch of thieves.* You may be realizing that this fallacy has nothing to do with purple people, but it is often the basis of inaccurate stereotypes. Just because one purple person steals does not mean that all purple people are thieves. However, these types of stereotypes and the resulting discrimination often become deeply ingrained in our society.

Ultimately, the empirical generalizations made should lead to refinements in one's theory. As we learn more about theory, we must change our theory to take into account what we have learned about our theory through the empirical process. For example, whereas a general theory of humor shows that humor is positive in most communicative contexts, we may need to limit the scope of a general theory of humor as a result of the initial findings in the use of flight attendant humor. Maybe our theory needs a new clause that says humor is positive in communicative interactions, except in situations where people feel their safety is involved. However, once you make adjustments to the theory, you must empirically test those adjustments, and thus the cycle of research continues.

Conclusion

Scientists typically begin a program of research with little more than a few questions and speculations. Scientists may also speculate that something causes something else or something is just related to something else. As the research program generates more data and results, these speculations may move toward becoming real theory. If one does not have solid quantitative research results to support one's theory, all that is left is speculation.

Nevertheless, the line dividing speculation and theory is less than perfect. Generally, when researchers are just guessing about what is going on in the real world, they are using speculation and more frequently use research questions to guide their efforts. When a body of data and results allows a scientist to begin building a formal description of what is going on, he or she is developing theory. Depending on the results obtained, the theory may be strongly supported, but it may not be. The theory may get partial support and need to be modified to be consistent with the results obtained, or the theory may fail to receive meaningful support from the research outcomes.

Many scientists work on both describing what goes on and explaining why these things occur. Some scientists focus primarily on the descriptive phase of scholarship. They often are described as employing inductive methods. Other scientists focus primarily on the explanation phase of scholarship. They are described as employing deductive methods. Although some people may want to argue which is more important, inductive or deductive research, this is a pretty much a "Which comes first, the chicken or the egg?" situation. Both are critical to the advance of science.

The term "theory" is used for many purposes and in many ways. There are theories that are meaningless (chicken or egg?) and there are theories that are important (the theory that a certain medication will kill cancer). You can check yourself as to how valuable your theory is in your own mind. Would you bet real money that, if properly tested, your theory would be proven correct? How much? Five cents? Fifty dollars? Fifty thousand dollars? Five hundred thousand dollars? Five million dollars? Although this may seem like a silly game, it is not. Many scientists must get grant support to conduct their research. They must convince granting agencies to provide the resources to do their research. Not only does the scientist have to believe her or his theory is worth the financial risk, he or she must also be able to get others to believe it. People typically are not highly committed to their speculations or guesses. However, people are likely to be committed to theories that they and others believe to be strong, solid theories supported by empirical research (anyone want to jump off a skyscraper and test the theory of gravity?).

Everybody is entitled to an opinion, and as noted by the number of bloggers on the Internet, in most circumstances most people have an opinion. However, not everyone's opinion is equal in value to everyone else's opinion. The value of a scientist's opinion depends on the scientific support he or she has available. What are the data? What are the research results? How many replications are available? How much variance can the theory predict in realistic studies? Are there solid research results reported by credible scholars that suggest the theory is not right? Quantitative researchers depend on the results of data analyses for determining the validity of a theory, not on someone's opinion. Science makes a maximum effort to keep the emotions and beliefs of a researcher separate from the evaluation of a theory. In contrast, the emotions and values of the researcher are a critical part of the decision making in much of the qualitative research (Appendix A; see textbook's website). The researcher's thoughts contribute directly to the results of the research. Although it often is not possible to keep the scientific researcher's thinking and/or believing 100 percent out of decisions about results in quantitative research, at least there is an extreme effort to do so.

Research Outside the Walls of Academia

You may be surprised to find out that a great deal of your life happens because of people's pursuit of the scientific method. One area where quantitative researchers have made an impact in recent years is in how we purchase materials online. In his book *The Man Who Lied to His Laptop*, Clifford Nass and Corina Yen (2010) discuss how his research team helped Dell Computers create an online persona that would "upsell" customers buying from the Dell website. Upselling happens when a customer service agent asks a customer whether he or she wants more of something or makes recommendations for other purchases. The classic upsell is McDonald's "Do you want fries with that?"

In their consulting for Dell, the research team started by selecting 250 male and female models and weeded them out by circulating photographs to hundreds of people and through qualitative focus groups. Ultimately, the team settled on what Nass called the "perfect guy: he was attractive and seemed both friendly and intelligent" (Nass & Yen, 2010, p. 111). The web team videoed hours of the model in an attempt to "help" customers make smarter (i.e., more profitable) purchases.

Unfortunately, after the research team started testing their new-model-enhanced upselling on the website, upselling did not actually happen. According to Nass and Yen, "Everything was there: the agent [model] praised the customer, he had all the markers of honesty and sincerity, and his facial expressions perfectly matched the words he was saying" (p. 45), so what was the problem? Eventually, someone on Nass's team had a spark of recognition that the polo shirt the model was wearing had the Dell logo on it. Once they reshot the video without the logo, people interacting with the website saw the model as credible and were more likely to go along with the model's upselling attempts.

Everything about how this project was conducted happened in line with the scientific method. The project started with social scientific theories for how people communicate credibility including making sure nonverbal behaviors match verbal utterances. The researchers made predictions that upselling would happen when the website went live. The research team then observed customers not finding the model credible or likeable. Once their original hypothesis did not pan out, the researchers looked for a generalizable explanation and then started again with a new theory—the Dell logo is causing problems. Once this was corrected, the team went back through the scientific method; this time, customers found the model likeable and credible and were persuaded to buy more.

Now that we have introduced you to the basic concepts involved in the scientific process of research, we can focus on the necessity of conducting research in an ethical and responsible manner in the next chapter.

KEY TERMS

Antecedent
Appeal to authority
Appeal to general empirical rules
Argument
Consequent
Control
Define terms or give examples

Empirical generalization
Empirical rules
Empiricism
Epistemology
Evoke empathy
Explanation
Hasty generalization
Hypothesis
Label the phenomena

Major premise
Minor premise
Observation
Proposition
Research
Science
Scientific method
Syllogism
Theory

REFERENCES

Babbie, E. (2010). *The practice of social research* (12th ed.). Belmont, CA: Wadsworth, Cengage.

Canary, D. J., & Hause, K. S. (1993). Is there any reason to research sex differences in communication? *Communication Quarterly, 41*, 129–144.

Harris, S. R. (2014). *How to critique journal articles in the social sciences.* Thousand Oaks, CA: Sage.

Gray, J. (1992). *Men are from Mars, women are from Venus: A practical guide for improving communication and getting what you want in your relationships.* New York, NY: HarperCollins.

Klein, P. (2002). Skepticism. In Paul K. Moser (Ed.), *The Oxford handbook of epistemology* (pp. 336–361). New York, NY: Oxford University Press.

Merriam-Webster (n.d.). *Research.* Retrieved from http://www.m-w.com/dictionary/research/

Moser, P. K. (2002). Introduction. In *The Oxford handbook of epistemology* (pp. 3–24). New York, NY: Oxford University Press.

Nass, C., & Yen, C. (2010). *The man who lied to his laptop: What machines teach us about human relationships.* New York, NY: Current.

Nettler, G. (1970). *Explanations.* New York, NY: McGraw-Hill.

Peirce, C. S. (1878). How to make our ideas clear. *Popular Science Monthly, 12*, 286–302.

Pfungst, O. (1911). *Clever Hans (the horse of Mr. Von Osten): A contribution to experimental animal and human psychology* (Trans. C. L. Rahn). New York, NY: Holt. (Originally published in German, 1907).

Popper, K. (1934). *Logik der Forschung* (Amplified English ed., 1959). Vienna: Springer.

Popper, K. R. (1968). *The logic of scientific discovery.* New York, NY: Harper & Row.

Richmond, V. P., Wrench, J. S., & McCroskey, J. C. (2013). *Communication apprehension, avoidance, and effectiveness* (7th ed.). Boston, MA: Allyn & Bacon.

Stein, D. J., Stein, M. B., Goodwin, W., Kumar, R., & Hunter, B. (2001). The selective serotonin reuptake inhibitor paroxetine is effective in more generalized and in less generalized social anxiety disorder. *Psychopharmacology, 158*, 267–272.

Van Ameringen, M., Mancini, C., Oakman, J. M., & Farvolden, P. (1999). Selective serotonin reuptake inhibitors in the treatment of social phobia: The emerging gold standard. *CNS Drugs, 11*, 307–315.

Van Ameringen, M. A., Lane, R. M., Walker, J. R., Bowen, R. C., Chokka, P. R., Goldner, E. M., et al. (2001). Sertraline treatment of generalized social phobia: A 20-week, double-blind, placebo-controlled study. *American Journal of Psychiatry, 158*, 275–281.

West, R., & Turner, L. H. (2006). *Introducing communication theory: Analysis and application* (3rd ed.). Boston, MA: McGraw-Hill.

Wrench, J. S., Millhouse, B., & Sharp, D. (2007). Laughing before takeoff: Humor, sex, and the pre-flight safety briefing. *Human Communication, 10*, 381–399.

CHAPTER 3

Research Ethics

CHAPTER OBJECTIVES

1   Summarize eight actual research studies that have questionable ethical practices.
2   Understand the history of research that led to the creation of the Belmont Report.
3   Define *ethics* and list the four types of ethical stances.
4   Explain the three principles for ethical research spelled out in the Belmont Report.
5   Review the history of research that led to the creation of institutional review boards (IRBs).
6   Explain the basic purposes for IRBs.
7   Distinguish among anonymity, confidentiality, and privacy.
8   Explain the importance of the informed consent process.
9   Explain how researchers balance deception and informed consent.
10 Describe the four additional functions fulfilled by IRBs.
11 Distinguish among exempt, expedited, and full-board reviews.
12 Explain the seven specific issues related to research ethics.

The word "ethics" evokes many images in different people. Typically, determining what is "ethical" falls along two tracks of thinking: theological or philosophical. Theologians will determine the rightness or wrongness of a behavior by searching specific religious texts, oral teachings, or traditions. Philosophers, by contrast, concern themselves primarily with the question, "What should a person do?" Whether a person uses a theological or philosophical stance for determining the ethicality of behavior, understanding ethics is important to almost any endeavor. For example, what do you think of the ethicality of the following eight research scenarios?

1. Researchers use rural African American men to study the course of an untreated disease. During the course of the study, the men receive free examinations and medical care.

However, the men did not receive information about the disease, were not informed that they were participating in research, and were not told that the research would not benefit them directly. Even after a known treatment for the disease was discovered, the participants were not informed of the new treatment and the research continued for decades, which led to the death of many study participants.

2. Researchers studying whether people would intervene when someone was about to experience harm decide to stage a crime. The researchers, with the consent of a shop owner, staged a burglary at a liquor store and then watched how bystanders reacted to the experiment.

3. A researcher wanting to understand the psychological processes involved in men who have sex with other men in public toilets poses as a voyeur or "watchqueen," an individual whose job it is to warn individuals who are engaging in public sex acts if someone is coming. After performing the job of "watchqueen," the researcher would then write down the license plate numbers of the men. The researcher would then trace the men's identities through the Department of Motor Vehicles under the guise of a market researcher. Once the researcher knew who the men were, he would approach them at their residences and interview them a year later to learn more about them.

4. Researchers are interested in understanding how juries decide verdicts. To examine jury deliberations, the researchers get permission from a judge to record the deliberations (using audio means only) of six actual juries.

5. Researchers interested in watching how the roles of "guard" and "prisoner" influence subject reactions create a mock prison in the basement of a university building. Participants were assigned to the category of either "guard" or "prisoner," and they would then live in that role for a 2-week period in the mock prison.

6. A researcher interested in understanding how obedience to authority figures works devises an experiment under the guise of a teacher–learner scenario. In the experiment, participants are told that they are going to deliver electrical shocks at increasing levels to a learner in another room when the learner does not correctly answer a question. The learner is actually a member of the research project and no shocking occurs during the course of the research project. The goal of the project is to determine how long a participant will keep shocking the learner, even after the learner starts protesting, if the participant is encouraged by the researcher to continue with the shocks.

7. A researcher wants to determine whether media campaigns can discourage adolescents from drinking alcohol. To provide baseline measures of actual consumption of alcohol, area adolescents were surveyed with the promise of confidentiality. Unknown to the adolescents, one of the strategies the researchers planned on using was the publication of the data in the local newspaper. The strategy proved effective, with many parents clamping down on their adolescents' drinking behavior.

8. A researcher interested in understanding what it is like to be an undergraduate at a university in the twenty-first century decides to enroll. The researcher enrolls in her university as an entering first-year student and lives in the dorm after getting permission from her IRB. During the researcher's year as an undergraduate, she takes classes, makes friends, participates in intercollegiate sports, and joins various student organizations. The researcher also interviews undergraduate students living in her dorm or taking classes with her. She has her interview participants fill out a consent form, explaining that the researcher is conducting a study on perceptions of undergraduates that may be published. For the most part, the participants do not know that the researcher is actually a university professor and researcher.

9. Researchers interested in the effects that online reading has on moods purposefully manipulate what people see online. The team of researchers manipulates the reading material of 700,000 participants of a large social networking site without any of the participants knowing the research was being conducted.

10. When a researcher does not get the kind of results he wants, he starts to fabricate data. Over a 10-year period, he publishes a number of highly controversial studies in a variety of prominent journals around the world.

You may be thinking to yourself that these research projects are completely ridiculous and no one would ever actually think of completing any projects like these. However, you would be wrong. All of these examples are actual research projects that were conducted during the 1900s and early 2000s.

The first research scenario is commonly referred to as the Tuskegee Syphilis Study and lasted from 1932 to 1972. In 1972, when it became apparent that the U.S. Public Health Services was involved in violating the basic human rights of the research participants, the U.S. public was outraged, especially since penicillin, a good treatment option for syphilis, had been around and available since World War II. In essence, the researchers kept their research project going although adequate treatment options were available for the study participants. Ultimately, the U.S. Senate held hearings on this study and other alleged health-care abuses and passed the National Research Act of 1974, which created a policy for protecting human subjects with federal regulations, and created the National Commission for the Protection of Human Subjects of Biomedical and Behavioral Research. This commission would then go on to produce the Belmont Report, or the *Ethical Principles and Guidelines for the Protection of Human Subjects of Research.*

The second example, staging of a liquor store burglary, was conducted by Bibb Latané and John Darley (1970). In this study, the two researchers conducted a staged burglary to watch bystanders' reactions. One bystander responded by calling the police. The police showed up to the scene of the "crime," guns drawn and ready to arrest the researchers. Needless to say, this research experiment could have ended badly for both the researchers and the bystanders.

The third research example was conducted by Laud Humphreys (1975) to examine what types of men engage in anonymous sex with other men in public restrooms. Humphreys's study was seen as both positive and negative by most researchers. Scholars believed that Humphreys's ability to carefully guard the actual identities of his research participants was to be applauded; however, his failure to obtain consent from his participants, his lying to the Department of Motor Vehicles to obtain his participants' home addresses, and his approaching the participants a year later in their home environments is indefensible. In Humphreys's defense, at the time he was conducting his research, homosexuality was still illegal in most states with the penalty of jail time. Scholars look at Humphreys's research today and believe that it could have caused his participants undue psychological, financial, and legal harm.

The fourth study mentioned is commonly referred to as the Wichita Jury Study of 1954. The researchers were allowed to tape record six jury deliberations in Wichita, Kansas, without the jurors' knowledge of their participation in the research study. When this project came to light, the research was widely criticized by reporters and politicians around the country. This research project was seen as undermining the judicial system because, as Vaughan (1967) said, surveillance "threatens impartiality to the extent that it introduces any question of possible embarrassment, coercion, or other such considerations into the minds of actual jurors" (p. 72). Ultimately, the U.S. Senate passed a law prohibiting the recording of jury deliberations.

The fifth study, the prison simulation study, was conducted by Zimbardo, Haney, Banks, and Jaffe (1973) in a basement at Stanford University (http://www.prisonexp.org/). On the surface, this study may not seem to be controversial. However, the problems with this study lay not in what was being studied as much as in the problems that arose out of the methods used to study the phenomenon. When people were labeled "prisoners" or "guards," a cognitive shift occurred and they started to confuse who they were in real life with their new personas. Guards started to physically and psychologically abuse the prisoners. Prisoners either became rebellious and fought back against the guards or broke down and did the guard's wishes even if those wishes were inhumane. Ultimately, the 2-week experiment was closed after six days. Critics of this study believe that the researchers did not do enough upfront to guarantee the safety (both psychological and physical) of all the participants—guards and prisoners. This study is actually so widely known, a movie based on this study was released in July 2015 called *The Stanford Prison Experiment* starring Billy Crudup as Dr. Philip Zimbardo.

The sixth study is commonly referred to as the Milgram Study. The project leader was Stanley Milgram (1974), who wanted to understand how authority figures impacted people's decisions to comply with requests or mandates. After World War II, many researchers started studying how Hitler had gotten many regular people to blindly follow orders and commit atrocities associated with the Holocaust. Although Milgram's study did not involve killing people, it did involve inflicting pain on another person. Participation in Milgram's study caused many people severe psychological discomfort because the participants actually believed they were inflicting pain on the learner in the other room. Of the 40 members of the general public paid to take part in the study, all complied with the order to administer shocks up to 300 volts (marked intense shock). As many as 26 responded obediently to the experimenter's urging to apply the maximum 450 volts. Videotapes of the Milgram study actually show adult males crying while continuing to shock the learner in the other room. One participant was so overcome by stress that he had a convulsive seizure. Furthermore, Milgram and his colleagues had not thought about the long-term effects of the study on their participants' psyche.

The seventh study, the adolescent alcohol consumption project, was a study conducted by Charles Atkin and reported by Garramone and Kennamer (1989). In this case, the question of ethics came in the form of the adolescents who felt deceived by the researcher. The adolescents had been open with the researcher about their alcohol consumption. When the researcher then published the results in the newspaper, many parents quickly clamped down on their children's behavior, and the adolescents felt their confidentiality had been violated. Atkins argued that the individual participant's confidentiality had not been violated but the confidentiality of the group as a whole had been. However, the adolescents were participating in illegal underage drinking, so the question could also be posed, as Atkin did, "Does one have a *right* to do something illegal?" In essence, the publication of the research findings in the local paper enabled parents to prevent illegal adolescent behavior.

The eighth study was written under the pseudonym Rebekah Nathan and was published in 2005. The book was published under a pseudonym to protect the student participants who volunteered to be interviewed or who lived in the dorm or attended classes with the researcher. However, the researcher's real name, Cathy Small, was discovered long before her book hit the shelves. Although many researchers applauded Dr. Small's use of her anthropological background to study modern college students in their natural environment in a way reminiscent of how Jane Goodall studied chimpanzees in their natural habitat, Small's methods have caused quite a stir in the academic community. Is it ethical to enter a college dorm under false pretenses and watch the students in their natural environment? Is it ethical to have students sign informed consent forms for participating in a research project when the participants do not know who the researcher really is? The participants would naturally assume that Small was a fellow undergraduate and the chances of her research ever reaching print were unlikely, so were Small's participants really informed?

The ninth story really hit home for many people in the summer of 2014 when it was found that that Facebook had been purposefully manipulating users' newsfeeds to see whether it would affect their moods. Facebook purposefully manipulated the emotional level of newsfeeds to see whether users would match the emotional level of the news feeds they were reading. Basically, if someone read a happy newsfeed, would that person write more positive, upbeat posts her- or himself? Of course, the controversy was not that this study was conducted. The problem with this study was that none of the 700,000 people who were part of this study knew they were being manipulated in a study. Of course, Facebook's response is that they were well within their rights under the user agreements that all Facebook members agree to when joining. As such, they argue that they did nothing unethical. Of course, many people disagree with Facebook's stance on ethical research practices.

Facebook has not been the only social networking site to conduct research on its unknowing users. OK Cupid, a dating website, admitted shortly after the Facebook study was revealed that it too had conducted research on their members. In the OK Cupid study, the researchers wanted to see whether purposefully mismatching people had an effect on love. Basically, OK Cupid requires all users to complete a questionnaire and various questions in an effort to demonstrate the compatibility between members (represented as a percentile score). OK Cupid purposefully told people who received a low match (low percentage of compatibility) that they scored higher and vice versa. As you can imagine, people who use dating sites rely on these tools to meet dating partners and potential spouses, so they were disgruntled at having been lied to.

In the tenth ethical scenario, we have the interesting case of Dr. Diederik Stapel, a professor of psychology at Tilburg University. Three younger researchers who had been working with Dr. Stapel brought up ethical charges against the professor when they started noticing inconsistencies within datasets, which led the researchers to think the data had been altered. Over the course of the investigation, researchers found cases of clear fraud in more than 50 published research articles and 10 doctoral dissertations he had shepherded. This case of academic fraud is the largest known incident to be caught.

All 10 of these studies are important to the history of ethics in research because each one has forced researchers to reevaluate how research ought to be done. This chapter will explain the current state of ethics in research and how it applies to the field of communication. To examine ethics in communication research, we will first explore the meaning of the term "ethics" in more detail, examine the three-prong test for ethics established by the 1979 Belmont Report (persons, beneficence, and justice), explain the purpose and place of IRBs in research, and pose some basic ethical questions for communication researchers.

Defining Ethics

Although the study of ethical considerations dates back thousands of years, the modern analysis of **ethics** resides primarily in the understanding of two basic concepts: means and ends (McCroskey, Wrench, & Richmond, 2003; Wrench, McCroskey, & Richmond, 2008). **Means** are the tools or behaviors that one employs to achieve a desired outcome. Means can be either good or bad. **Ends** are those outcomes that one desires to achieve. Like means, ends can be either good or bad. Figure 3.1 demonstrates the four combinations of good and bad means and ends.

GOOD MEANS–GOOD END: ETHICAL BEHAVIOR

The first quadrant of the ethical diagram depicts what happens when someone has good means and a good end (**ethical behavior**). For example, a researcher wants to conduct a research study to examine the influence that health campaign television advertisements have on positively changing health behaviors. The researcher brings in a group of participants and informs them of the project, obtains their consent, does not lie to them, and conducts the study in an ethical manner. The result of the study helps public health officials design appropriate mediated campaigns. Ultimately, in this example the means and the ends are both positive. This would be considered ethical behavior or communication.

BAD MEANS–BAD END: UNETHICAL BEHAVIOR

The second quadrant of the ethical diagram depicts the exact opposite of the first quadrant, or what happens when someone has bad means and a bad end (**unethical behavior**). Some of the results seen in the Milgram study fall into this category. Researchers deceived their participants and then one of the participants had a seizure because of the stress he was under during the experiment. Who knows how many of the participants had severe psychological trauma after the fact?

BAD MEANS–GOOD END: MACHIAVELLIAN ETHIC

The first two quadrants are fairly straightforward in their ethical understanding, but the other two quadrants in the ethical diagram are not as clear-cut. The third quadrant is an example of what happens when a person employs bad means to achieve a good end. This concept is referred to as the **Machiavellian ethic** because Niccolò Machiavelli believed that the ends justify the means. Machiavelli's greatest work, *The Prince*, written in 1513, created much controversy because he wrote that princes should retain absolute control of their lands and should use any means necessary to accomplish this end, including deceit. This notion was so outlandish that Pope Clement VIII described it as heretical.

This ethical perspective is still seen as outlandish and unethical by many today. The following is an example of how the Machiavelli ethic can be seen in a research situation. If a researcher overstates her or his findings (bad means) about the harmful nature of a drug to get people to stop doing it (good ends), is this researcher ethical? Some would consider it ethical behavior if it causes people to stop using a harmful substance, but others would say it is not ethical because the researcher had to lie to get the behavioral change.

GOOD MEANS–BAD END: SUBJECTIVE ETHIC

The fourth quadrant of the ethical diagram (Figure 3.1) examines what happens when a person employs good means that result in a bad end (**subjective ethic**). For example, a media researcher conducts research on how to appropriately deliver communicated messages during a political campaign. A political candidate gets hold of the research and sees how he can use the study's findings to create manipulative messages that will get him elected. In essence,

		ENDS	
		Good	*Bad*
MEANS	*Good*	1. Ethical behavior	4. Subjective ethic
	Bad	3. Machiavellian ethic	2. Unethical behavior

Figure 3.1 Ethical Matrix

the researcher conducted the research in an ethical manner (the mean), which led to the manipulation of the populace by a political candidate (the end). Is research ethical if it can later be used for harm? Many researchers who worked on the Manhattan Project, which resulted in the creation of the atomic bomb, did not think about the loss of life and devastation their research would ultimately bring on the world.

Hopefully by this point you are starting to see that the world of research ethics is not completely clear-cut. For the most part, research is not innately ethical or unethical. Research can be methodologically sound or methodologically problematic, but determining whether a researcher is being ethical is complicated, and there are a number of opinions as to what constitutes ethical versus unethical research behavior. The U.S. federal government has stepped in and provided a number of guidelines that researchers must follow by law.

The Belmont Report's Effect on Research Ethics

In 1979, The National Commission for the Protection of Human Subjects of Biomedical and Behavioral Research completed the report entitled *Ethical Principles and Guidelines for the Protection of Human Subjects of Research*, which is commonly referred to as the **Belmont Report**. The Belmont Report devised three basic principles that all researchers using human subjects, regardless of research area, should be accountable for in their research. First, *researchers should respect all possible research participants as autonomous individuals who have the capability of making decisions about their participation in a research project*. In essence, a researcher must ensure that her or his research participants are informed about their participation in the research process without coercion. Furthermore, researchers should also make sure that possible participants are adequately informed about the purpose of the research, the voluntary nature of research, and the risks that may be associated with participation.

INFORMED CONSENT

This first part of the Belmont Report is commonly referred to as the ethical standard of "**informed consent**." This ethical standard also has a second component that researchers must be aware of because not all possible participants have the ability to intellectually discern for themselves whether participation in a research endeavor is ok, so possible participants with "**diminished autonomy**" may need additional protections. You may be wondering what types of people fall into the category of "diminished autonomy." In essence, the Belmont Report realized that children and adults, who mentally cannot make informed decisions, should not be allowed to volunteer for the research process. Under current standards, prisoners, fetuses, pregnant women, terminally ill individuals, students, employees, comatose patients, and persons under the age of 18 or who are legally given to the care of an adult because of severe developmental disorders or dementias fall into the diminished autonomy category as well. These populations are highly studied groups, so it is not that they cannot be studied, only that you must get informed consent from a legal guardian.

PRINCIPLE OF BENEFICENCE

The second ethical principle spelled out in the Belmont Report is the need for researchers to *guarantee beneficence*. The **principle of beneficence** obligates researchers to ensure that during the research process they maximize possible benefits and minimize possible harms to the research participants themselves. For this reason, one question that is often asked of researchers when designing a research study is, "How will this study benefit the participants?" As a general response, the authors of this book think this question is extremely important, not only because ethically we should be attempting to enhance our participants' lives while minimizing possible harms, but also because good research should make people's lives better. Too often researchers study small aspects of human communication that have no direct impact or bearing on real people's lives. For example, if research in the area of interpersonal relationships does not ultimately help people understand the interpersonal communication process better and lead to more successful interpersonal communication relationships, then what is the point of the research itself? You can peruse any discipline's journals and see many studies that make you wonder, "Why did they do that?!" In fact, there is an association dedicated to ridiculous research that gives out the yearly Ig Nobels and publishes the interdisciplinary journal the *Annals of Improbable Research*. Some of the past Ig Nobel winners have fed Prozac to clams, watched brain activity of locusts while watching *Star Wars*, noted the effect of country music on suicide, noted that when people concentrate they may miss the woman in the gorilla suit, and studied and classified belly button lint. To view the entire list of Ig Nobel winners dating back to 1991, you can visit the *Annals of Improbable Research* website at http://www.improb.com/. In other words, please do not end up on the Ig Nobel list as a researcher. For all the humor this list actually provides, these research projects started as legitimate projects. To avoid creating a research project that is absurd, always ask yourself how your research could actually better the lives of your research participants.

JUSTICE

The third and final Belmont Report ethical standard is that of **justice**. By justice, the authors of the report believed that those who take the risks of research should also receive the benefits from that research. As was seen in the Tuskegee case, lower-income African American men were basically used as guinea pigs and received none of the benefits of the findings. For this reason, researchers today must make sure that risks and benefits are fairly distributed within society without bias. This is not to say that you cannot single out specific groups that you want to research, only that there must be a clear justification for this singling out and that the benefits would ultimately help that group. For example, maybe you want to examine differences in communication phenomena between patients and physicians when the patients and physicians are of different races. You may decide to examine Hispanic patients' perceptions of Anglo/Caucasian (White) physicians. Although the risk of harm as a result of this study would probably be minimal, every study contains some element of risk (either physical or psychological). The basic reasoning behind the notion of justice is that historically a lot of medical research was conducted on ethnically diverse groups or people on the lower rungs of the social hierarchy, but the benefits of the research only impacted those people at the top of the social hierarchy (primarily White males). Ultimately, researchers must ask themselves whether some classes of people are overrepresented in their samples because of their availability, their compromised position, or their vulnerability. If the answer to these questions is "yes," is there a clear justification for their inclusion, or were they selected inappropriately and will thus bear the brunt of the possible risks of the study? For the most part, this is not generally a problem communication researchers have faced. Communication researchers have generally not conducted studies that have serious risks beyond psychological discomfort. And although psychological discomfort can be serious, few studies in communication would violate the justice principle of ethicality.

Institutional Review Boards

By 1981, the Department of Health and Human Services and the Food and Drug Administration approved a series of federal guidelines, Title 45, *Code of Federal Regulations*, Part 46 (45 CFR 46), which established the **Common Rule**. The Common Rule established a set of guidelines for the rights, welfare, and protection of research participants. One of the most important aspects of the Common Rule was the requirement that any institution that received federal funding and federal agencies themselves must establish an **Institutional Review Board** to review all research proposals for possible risks to research participants and to make sure that all research participants are informed of their rights as research participants. To further understand the nature of IRBs, this section will examine IRB basics, informed consent, and the IRB process.

INSTITUTIONAL REVIEW BOARD BASICS

The IRB was established by 45 CFR 46 to ensure that past research atrocities like the Tuskegee experiment did not happen again on U.S. soil. Ultimately, IRBs are charged with the task of ensuring that researchers take appropriate steps in protecting and informing research participants. According to the National Institutes of Health (NIH) (2002), a **research participant** is "a living individual about whom a researcher obtains either: (1) data through intervention or interaction with the individual; or (2) identifiable private information" (p. 16). Data through intervention are data that would occur in biomedical research situations. For example, one common type of medical publication is the case study. A medical case study is when a physician sees an interesting medical case and then writes an article for a medical journal detailing the case. In this research instance, the information was obtained about the patient during a routine medical intervention, so for a physician to publish this information, he or she would need to obtain consent from either the patient or her or his legal guardian. Even if the physician does not use the person's name or photograph in the article, he or she is still obligated to obtain consent. The second type of data can be acquired through interaction with the participant. If a communication researcher runs focus groups, investigates a culture, or hands out surveys, he or she is obtaining information about an individual through interaction, so the individual with whom the researcher is acting is a research participant. Finally, a research participant is someone who could be identified through identifiable private information. For example, maybe you want to determine whether females and males differ in their likelihood of taking communication courses in high school, so you request to see high school transcripts for all incoming first-year students at your university. Although you may not think this is a big deal, when high school students apply for college and forward their transcripts to colleges, they are sending them to the college under the notion that the transcripts would be used to determine applicants' eligibility for entrance to the university, not for a communication research project. For this reason, high school transcripts would be considered private information and a researcher would have to obtain every first-year student's permission to use the transcripts for research purposes.

Another basic ethical dilemma that IRBs tackle is whether a participant should be paid for her or his participation. Researchers often offer some form of payment for an individual's participation in a research study. Whether the payment comes in the form of money or extra credit, payment is payment. Unfortunately, there are no standard rules for how payments should work other than the notion that coercion of participants is wrong. For this reason, undergraduate students who are asked to participate in a research project are often offered extra credit for their participation. Since the extra credit points are above and beyond the points within the course itself, the "payment" is not coercion. Some IRBs will take "payment" a step further and require alternative extra credit opportunities for individuals who do not want to participate in the study itself. One common form of alternative activity is to have students read and abstract an article related to the study. However, if your IRB asks for an alternative exercise for individuals who do not want to participate, make sure the alternatives are equitable. For example, if it takes 10 minutes to fill out a survey, it should take 10 minutes to complete the alternative extra credit opportunity as well. Furthermore, some ethicists take it a step further and actually argue that extra credit sways students to participate in a study, which theoretically will alter the results within a study because without the extra credit, the students would not participate.

The last basic aspect of IRBs is the determination and understanding of anonymity, privacy, and confidentiality. Many researchers when they are first starting research often mistake the terms "anonymity," "privacy," and "confidentiality." However, as far as an IRB is concerned, there are important distinctions among the three concepts. First, **anonymity** occurs when a researcher does not know who participated in a study or which results belong to which participants in a study. For example, one of the authors of this text has done considerable work with online surveying. He sends out e-mails to various target groups requesting participation. Although this method of data gathering is problematic, it does allow him to target groups that would otherwise be out of his reach. Individuals who then decide to participate fill out a survey on a website. Ultimately, the researcher has no way of knowing who filled out his survey, so the process is completely anonymous. The second term, **privacy**, according to the NIH (2002), is "defined in terms of having control over the extent, timing, and circumstances of sharing oneself (physically, behaviorally, or intellectually) with others" (p. 23). Research participants willingly give information about themselves to researchers under the understanding that the researcher will only share this information when it is necessary. For this process to work, all researchers must make sure they keep the information learned from a research participant private. Under the 1996 Health Insurance Portability and Accountability Act (HIPPA), privacy has entered a new stage of understanding. Under HIPPA, there are new classifications for what is deemed **protected health information** (PHI). PHI is any individually identifiable health information (e.g., demographic data and biological specimens) that is transmitted or maintained by a covered entity (Bankert & Amdur, 2006). Although most communication researchers are not going to be investigating any PHI, it is possible that people involved in health communication research may research PHI, so they should make sure they investigate HIPPA's effect on researchers in biomedical research to ensure they are in compliance with HIPPA statutes regarding research. For more on HIPPA responsibilities, talk to your campus's IRB. We should also mention at this point that there are also rules specifically for research conducted in K–12 educational settings. Both the Family Educational Rights and Privacy Act and No Child Left Behind have other guidelines to which researchers conducting research using K–12 participants also must adhere. We note these specific instances to further demonstrate the importance that the federal government has in overseeing social, behavioral, and educational research.

Along with privacy we must explore the third term, **confidentiality**, because the two terms are interrelated. Confidentiality "pertains to the treatment of information an individual has disclosed in a relationship of trust and with the expectation that it will not, without permission, be divulged to others in ways that are inconsistent with the understanding of the original disclosure" (NIH, 2002, p. 24). Confidentiality is making sure that you do not divulge any information about a participant that could lead to her or his identification. Some common ways of keeping confidentiality include removing signed consent forms from surveys, substituting codes for identifiers (instead of male, it becomes "1" on a code sheet), properly disposing of computer data and other paper (generally with a shredder), limiting access to identifiable data (typically only to immediate investigators), and storing files in a secure space. Furthermore, it is also important to educate any research assistants on the necessity of confidentiality. Although most communication projects warrant little risk and confidentiality is not a huge problem, there are studies in communication that have examined more sensitive areas such as illegal, drug, and sexual behaviors that warrant a closer scrutiny of the IRB on a researcher's protection of her or his participants' confidentiality.

Communication Researchers and IRBs

The August 2005 issue of the *Journal of Applied Communication* focused on the process of communication researchers interacting with IRBs. Although there were many horror stories in the issue, most criticisms were met with positive experiences as well. One interesting narrative (pp. 228–230) tells an experience of being subpoenaed by a district attorney. The researcher was investigating what types of evidence jurors used to render decisions. The researcher had conducted interviews with various jurors after the conclusion of a number of trials. After the interviews were conducted, the researcher received a subpoena in which the defense attorney wanted to ask the researcher whether "the jurors had said anything to me about their verdict in the case that did not pertain to the facts presented at the trial" (p. 229). The researcher immediately called the university IRB because the researcher did not know what to do because the participants had filled out a consent form guaranteeing confidentiality. Ultimately, one of the arguments the university attorney made on behalf of the researcher was that the researcher "had a moral and contractual duty to not answer questions about what the jurors told me. The jurors would be put in jeopardy if I was forced to disclose the confidential information they provided" (p. 229). Although the judge in this case agreed with the defendant (the researcher), this is not always the case. Unfortunately, researchers are not granted a privileged status such as patient–physician, lawyer–client, or spouses when it comes to information. In essence, researchers can be compelled to disclose what was learned or be incarcerated for contempt of court. However, federal provisions under the Public Health Act can allow you to petition the Secretary of Health and Human Services for a Certificate of Confidentiality. A **Certificate of Confidentiality** enables a researcher engaged in "biomedical, behavioral, clinical, or other research (including research on mental health and on the use of and effect of alcohol and other psychoactive drugs) to protect the privacy of individuals who are the subjects of such research" (NIH, 2002, p. 25). If you are ever researching a highly sensitive topic that involves illegal activity, you will want to work closely with your IRB to see whether it is possible for you to receive a Certificate of Confidentiality.

INFORMED CONSENT

Throughout this chapter, we have mentioned the need to inform participants about the nature of research and any possible risks associated with research. This section will go into further detail about the nature of informed consent and how to prepare a consent document for distribution during a research study. Informed consent is a "person's voluntary agreement, based upon adequate knowledge and understanding of relevant information, to participate in research" (NIH, 2002, p. 64). In essence, a researcher must provide any potential participants with adequate information about the purpose of the study, how long the study will last, experimental procedures, alternatives, the known risks, and any known benefits. The researcher must also explain to participants how they can ask questions about the research project and about their rights as research participants. Figure 3.2 is an example of an informed consent document used by one of the authors of this text in a project examining how personalized coaching impacted weight loss.

The consent document in Figure 3.2 contains a great deal of information in a brief format. Let's examine the various parts of the document itself. The consent form is clearly broken down into different sections to make it easier for participants to follow the general idea of what is being presented. For example, note that the reasoning for the study is provided only in the section titled "Why Is This Study Being Done?," whereas the explanation for confidentiality is explained in the section titled "What about Confidentiality?" By keeping these sections short and titled, readers are more likely to understand what they are getting into when they agree to participate.

Let's look at the various sections in order. First, the researcher provides her or his contact information, followed by a short statement that indicates that the researcher is asking the individual to participate in a *research* project. We added the emphasis in the previous sentence to the word "research" because most colleges and universities require that the topic sentence clearly state that an individual is being approached about a research project. After this introductory material, there is a brief section where the researcher explains the general purpose of the study. The goal of this section is to help a participant determine whether he or she wants to participate and explain to the participant what the purpose of the study is. Another aspect that helps someone decide whether he or she wants to participate involves the predicted number of participants. If a researcher plans on engaging only 2 or 3 participants, then guaranteeing confidentiality is almost impossible. In a large sample size—for example, 200 participants—guaranteeing confidentiality is much easier for a researcher.

The next section explains what is involved in the study itself. In this paragraph, the researcher explains that there are three steps involved in participation. First, the wellness coach will complete some basic demographic behavior. Second, the participant completes the survey. Finally, the participant places the completed survey in the locked box in the wellness organization's lobby. For the purposes of a survey, a consent form is generally direct with regard to the procedure. However, if a research study is an experiment, a researcher would need to discuss all aspects related to the experimentation including issues involving how participants are randomized into the different groups and any procedures to be conducted (more on this in Chapter 13).

In addition to the basic information about what is expected of a participant, a researcher also must explain to the participant how long he or she will be involved in the study. Some studies involve completing a 15-minute survey, but others could involve years of participation (as is often seen in large clinical trials). The participant is also informed that her or his participation is voluntary and that he or she may quit at any time during the study. This sentence is important because many participants believe that once they start they cannot stop, which simply is not the case. Legally, a person has the right to opt out of research at any point during a research project. Admittedly, researchers prefer for research participants to stay through the entire project, but researchers must respect an individual participant's wishes to stop participating in the study.

Next, the consent form discusses any aspects related to the "risks" of the study itself. Whereas a large sample anonymous survey poses what is called "below minimal risk," or when the participant is exposed to no more risk than he or she confronts in her or his daily life, other studies can involve massive amounts of risk. One of the basic goals of an IRB member is to weigh the risks with the benefits, which is why the benefits to both the individual

Study Title: Communicative Interactions between Clients and Wellness Coaches

Name of Principal Investigator: Name of Researcher
Department: Communication Studies
Position: Associate Professor

Contact Name And Phone Number For Questions/Problems: Researcher's Name, (XXX) XXX-XXXX

This is a communication research study. This research study includes only participants who choose to take part. Please takeyour time to make your decision. If necessary, feel free to discuss your participation with any necessary friends and family. You are being asked totake part in this study because you are currently undergoing weight loss coaching.

WHY IS THIS STUDY BEING DONE?

I am conducting research to examine the impact that your Wellness Coach has had on weight loss and weight loss motivation. As a health communication researcher, I am interested in what you have to say about your wellness coach. I am specifically interested in the interpersonal relationship you have developed and continue to develop with your coach.

HOW MANY PEOPLE WILL TAKE PART IN THE STUDY?

About 200 people will take part in this study.

WHAT IS INVOLVED IN THE STUDY?

If you agree to participate in this survey, your wellness coach will complete the top half of the survey, which includes demographic information related to how long you've been in the program and your current weight loss. Your participation in this project will involve completing the rest of the attached survey.

Please do not write your name anywhere on the survey in an effort to maintain your anonymity as a participant and as a client of the wellness organization.

After you have completed the survey, please return it to the locked box labeled "Research Surveys" in the waiting room. No one other than the principal investigator of this project has access to this locked box.

HOW LONG WILL I BE IN THE STUDY?

Completing the survey will take approximately 15 to 25 minutes.

This study is 100 percent voluntary, so you can stop participating at any time.

WHAT ARE THE RISKS OF THE STUDY?

The risks involved in this study are no more than those you would encounter in your everyday life.

For more information about risks, please feel free to contact the principal investor whose contact information is provided on this document.

ARE THERE BENEFITS TO TAKING PART IN THE STUDY?

If you agree to take part in this research, there may or may not be direct benefit to you.

We hope the information learned from this research will benefitothers who are attempting to lose weight by demonstrating the strategies and tactics that weight loss coaches can utilize to successfully encourage weight loss.

WHAT ABOUT CONFIDENTIALITY?

Efforts will be made to keep your personal information confidential.The survey attached contains no place for your name or other specific identifying information beyond those basic demographics at the top of the survey.

Figure 3.2 Informed Consent Document—Signature Required

Continued

Continued

Furthermore, the researcher will not provide the wellness organization with a copy of your completed survey. The wellness organization will only have access to aggregated data analyses at the completion of the study.

However, we cannot guarantee absolute confidentiality. Your personal information may be disclosed if required by law.

WHAT ARE THE COSTS?

Taking part in this study may lead to added costs to you.

You will receive no payment for taking part in this study.

WHAT ARE MY RIGHTS AS A PARTICIPANT?

Taking part in this study is voluntary. Refusal to participate will involve no penalty or loss of benefits to which you are otherwise entitled. You may choose not to take part, may leave the study at any time, or not answer research questions, which you consider inappropriate. Leaving the study will not result in any penalty or loss of benefits to which you are entitled. And participation will in no way affect the care and coaching you receive from the wellness organization.

We will tell you about new information that may affect your welfare or willingness to stay in this study.

WHOM DO I CALL IF I HAVE QUESTIONS OR PROBLEMS?

For questions about the study or a research-related injury, contact the researcher(s), at (XXX) XXX-XXXX or via e-mail at name@genericaccount.edu.

For questions about your rights as a research participant, contact the *University's Name* Institutional Review Board (which is a group of people who review the research to protect your rights) at (XXX) XXX-XXXX or via e-mail at irb@genericaccount.edu.

OTHER INFORMATION:

The Institutional Review Board at *University's Name* has determined that this research meets the criteria for human subjects according to Federal guidelines. - You will get a copy of this form.

CONSENT:

I have read or have had read to me the preceding information describing the study. All my questions have been answered to my satisfaction and this form is being signed voluntarily by me indicating my desire to participate in this study. I am not waiving any of my legal rights by signing this form. I understand I will receive a copy of this consent form.

Printed Name of Participant	Signature	Date

Printed Name of Person Obtaining Consent	Signature	Date

*Based on the IRB Consent form created by the State University of New York at New Paltz

participant and society are presented. If a study poses below minimal risk, then there really does not need to be a direct benefit to the individual participants. However, if a study does pose a risk then the researcher must explain how being exposed to the risk is beneficial to both the participant and society.

Next, participants are exposed to information about the confidentiality of the study. In this example, the researchers explain that the survey is anonymous and that the wellness organization will only see the concluded data and not the individual surveys. If you ever find yourself working for an organization conducting research, we strongly recommend that you make this process part of your understanding from the beginning. By not giving the organization the participants' completed surveys, you can ensure, as a researcher, that the organization cannot retaliate against a participant if the organization does not like her or his responses on the survey. The consent form also explains that participation or lack of participation will not affect an individual's standing with the organization the researcher was using to conduct the research. This line is also common in research involving students, but would read something like, "Your participation in this study is completely voluntary, and will in no way affect your grade or athletic standing." This clause basically informs a participant that whether he or she decides to participate in a research project, the participation will not negatively affect her or his grade or prevent her or him from participating in athletics.

Next, the consent form clearly articulates that there are no costs to the individual participating and that the individual is not getting paid for her or his participation in the study. If there is a cost or if a participant is getting remunerated in some fashion, then the researcher must spell out how this process would work. For example, a study recently reviewed by one of your coauthors for IRB approval was broken into five phases. At each phase of participation, the participants were given an Amazon.com gift card in increasing values (time one, $5; time two, $10; . . . time five, $25). However, the consent form clearly stated that if a participant dropped out of the study, he or she would be paid for their actual participation and not future participation.

Finally, the consent form reiterates the importance of the participants' rights. Next is a paragraph explaining how to get in touch with the researcher if the participant has any questions. Last is a sentence explaining to a participant how he or she can contact the IRB at the researcher's university if the participant has questions about her or his rights as a participant in a research project.

The final section of the consent form is dedicated to the actual giving of consent by the participant. If the participant decides to participate, then he or she signs the consent statement at the bottom of the page, fills out the questionnaire, and returns the whole packet to the collection box. The actual consent box a participant signs is loaded with legal terminology, basically ensuring the participant understands the nature of the research, is volunteering to be a participant, understands that the university is not liable for injury, is older than 18 (or not a child), has the right to stop participating, and has been given the option of taking a consent form. In addition to getting a signature from the participant, the person who is obtaining consent (usually the researcher, but in this case the wellness coach) also signs the consent form.

This discussion on consent forms is based on the notion that a participant actively reads a consent form and understands the material provided within the consent form. First, in a study conducted by McNutt et al. (2008), the researchers were interested in examining the extent to which participants read consent forms. The researchers timed the participants in a variety of different research studies. Furthermore, McNutt et al. asked the individual obtaining consent to predict how accurately the participant read the consent form and interpreted its meaning. McNutt et al. found that the average participant spends about 30 seconds reading a consent form. However, the individual obtaining consent predicted that the participants read the consent form completely 38–74 percent of the time (depending on the sample). Most educated people cannot adequately read and consider a consent form in 30 seconds, so there are definitely ethical questions about how researchers obtain consent. Second, we must always question the readability of consent forms. Depending on the participant population, highly technical consent forms may meet the requirements of an IRB, but may impede an individual's ability to decide whether he or she wants to participate in a research study. In essence, ethical researchers must think through how they obtain consent in an effort to maximize the understandability of the study for their participants.

Although Figure 3.2 is the most standard kind of consent form one will see in research, there is another form that is often used that does not require an individual to sign something for consent. Researchers can generally request an IRB for permission to not have a signed consent for one of two possible reasons:

1. A signed consent form would be the only record linking the participant and the research, which could result in potential harm resulting from breach of confidentiality. In this case, each participant will be asked whether he or she wants documentation linking her- or himself with research, and the participant's wishes will govern.
2. The research presents no more than minimal risk of harm to the participants and involves no procedures for which written consent is normally required outside of the research context.

In these cases, the following text is added as a paragraph to the consent form seen in Figure 3.2 instead of a signed statement:

> Returning this questionnaire certifies that you have read and understand this consent form and voluntarily agree to be a participant in the research described. Additionally, you agree that known risks for your participation have been explained to your satisfaction and you understand that no compensation is available from [your university's name] and its employees for any injury resulting from your participation in this research. Participation in this study also certifies that you are 18 years of age or older. Please understand that you may discontinue participation at any time without penalty or loss of any benefits to which you may otherwise be entitled.

Note that the same basic information that was in the signed consent form is available in this statement. In this version, however, the participant is not required to sign off on her or his understanding of the consent. Instead, active participation in the research endeavor is a sign of informed consent.

There is one tricky ethical dilemma that must come under scrutiny in the informed consent process—deception. What if telling the participants about the nature of the research will skew their responses? For example, in the study conducted by Stanley Milgram discussed at the beginning of this chapter, he clearly did not inform his research participants that he was studying the effects of how authority figures impact people's decisions to comply with requests or mandates. Instead, he told his participants that they were taking part in a study designed to examine negative feedback (electrical shocks) on the learning process. Should deception be allowed? Lying about the purpose of the study to receive a good study result is a clear example of the Machiavellian ethic discussed earlier in this chapter. IRBs unfortunately do not handle deception in a uniform manner at every university. For this reason, if you are planning on using deception within your study, you will want to make sure you talk to your IRB before developing your IRB proposal (more on this in the next section) to learn what they will and will not allow. One thing can be guaranteed, however, if you are planning on deceiving during your informed consent: you will need to debrief your participants at the conclusion of their participation. In the debrief, you will need to explain to your participants that they were deceived, what the purpose of your deception was, and what the nature of the project really is. You may be thinking to yourself, *well, I won't actually lie to my participants; I just may not be as complete as I should be in explaining the nature of the project itself.* Under typical IRB guidelines, if your disclosure is incomplete, as a researcher you will need to debrief your participants as well.

INSTITUTIONAL REVIEW BOARD PROCESSES

This section will briefly explain the IRB process to which all researchers who use human subjects must adhere. As mentioned earlier, the development of the IRB was set forth in 45 CFR 46 in 1981 as a ramification of the Belmont Report. Every university will have an Office of Research Compliance, Office of Funded Projects, Office of Institutional Research, or some other name where the university's IRB will be housed (we will be using the word university in this section, but it also applies to IRBs in other locations like foundations, research firms, or governmental agencies). Federal regulations mandate that the IRB must have at least five members from various backgrounds. Membership on the IRB should be diverse and often will include both university personnel and members of the community (at least one nonuniversity member). If IRBs are going to be overseeing research involving protected groups (children, pregnant women, prisoners, or physically/mentally disabled persons), then at least one member of the IRB must have a specialization in working with these populations.

Basic Institutional Review Board Functions

Each IRB is also given the job of overseeing all of the research that is conducted at that university. At the most basic level, IRBs ensure that human rights are protected and that informed consent occurs in all research. To do this, IRBs have several jobs they must complete.

First, IRBs must review the full protocols for every planned research study and then determine whether the research protocol exposes participants to unreasonable risks. Generally speaking, an IRB assigns a research protocol to a trained member of the IRB, who then evaluates the IRB protocol and determines whether the benefits of the study outweigh the potential risks. This process can take weeks to complete, depending on the complexity of the case and the guidelines for IRB members established by a college or university.

Second, the IRB must periodically review all research projects currently underway to ensure that human protections are still in place. Research protocols that warrant either expedited or full-board review (more on this in a moment) must undergo, at a bare minimum, an annual review. Research projects that have higher levels of risk (commonly seen in biomedical studies) may undergo reviews even more often.

Third, IRBs should examine adverse events (unexpected harms that result from a study), interim findings, and any recent literature in the project area that could force a change in the IRB protocol. Unfortunately, many types of research are dangerous and could cause unforeseen harm to an individual. If and when this happens during a study, a researcher is obligated to report the adverse event to the IRB, which will then investigate the research protocol to see whether changes must be made or if the project must be shut down completely. Some IRBs will also want to see your findings along the way. In short-term studies (lasting less than five years), IRBs may just want to see the demographic makeup of your participants on a yearly basis. For longer studies (longer than five years), IRBs may want more detailed updates along the way. IRBs should also be up to date on current trends in research that could force a change in an IRB protocol. Again, although not common in communication research, changes made as a result of new research are more common in biomedical research.

The fourth responsibility of the IRB is to investigate suspected or alleged protocol violations, complaints expressed by research participants, or violations of institutional policies. In essence, an IRB must make sure that the researcher is doing what he or she said he or she was going to do.

The last responsibility of the IRB is to ensure that federal guidelines that dictate that all individuals conducting research undergo training are followed. Most colleges and universities today will require what is called CITI training before you can start conducting a study. CITI stands for the Collaborative Institutional Training Initiative (https://www.citiprogram.org/). CITI training is broken into a number of modules that introduce researchers to the nature of ethics and much of the same content discussed in this chapter.

Advanced IRB Functions

Beyond the basic responsibilities of the IRB, IRBs have the authority to engage in four different behaviors. First, university IRBs have the ability to approve, disapprove, or terminate all research activities at the university. Second, IRBs have the ability to require modifications to research protocols (both new and previously approved protocols). Third, IRBs have the ability to require researchers to divulge more information than the information mandated in 45 CFR 46 if the IRB believes additional information will add to the protections of participants' rights and safety. Finally, IRBs have the ability to require or waive informed consent.

Before you get to the IRB stage of a research project, you will be required by your university to fill out an IRB protocol. Every university has the ability to create its own unique IRB protocol, which is adjusted to its specific needs. Some IRB protocols are one page in length, and others could be up to 30–50 pages in length, depending on the nature of your project and the specific documentation your IRB wants to see. Once your IRB protocol is completed, you will generally be asked what kind of review your project should receive. There are three levels of review that IRBs have at their disposal: exempt, expedited, and full board.

EXEMPT REVIEW

Exempt review technically means that you are exempted from undergoing an IRB review that adheres to the guidelines specified in 45 CFR 46. Having an exempt review does not mean that you do not have to submit your IRB protocol; only a trained IRB member or the IRB's designee can make determinations of exemption. However, some institutions will have different sets of IRB protocol documents for this level of review. Other institutions will only have one set of IRB protocol documents for all three levels of review. Again, be sure to check with your individual institution about the IRB process. This chapter is designed to introduce you to the generalities of ethics in research and the IRB process, not to be a definitive answer on how your university's IRB ought to run.

The exempt review can be granted to a research protocol if the project contains below minimal-risk research and is exempted from federal regulations concerning IRB review and approval. In 45 CFR 46, six categories for research exemptions were created, as seen in Figure 3.3.

Much of the research that is conducted by communication researchers will be exempt under 45 CFR 46 101b2. Specifically, much communication research will fall under Category 2 exemption because communication research relies heavily on survey procedures, interview procedures, and/or observation of public behavior. However, just because you think your research will fall under Category 2 for exempt research does not mean that your IRB will

1. Research conducted in established or commonly accepted educational settings, involving normal educational practices (e.g., research on regular and special education instructional strategies or research on the effectiveness of or the comparison among instructional techniques, curricula, or classroom management methods).

2. Research involving the use of educational tests (cognitive, diagnostic, aptitude, achievement), survey procedures, interview procedures, or observation of public behavior, unless:
   (a) Information obtained is recorded in such a manner that human participants can be identified, directly or through identifiers linked to the participants.
   (b) Any disclosure of the human participants' responses outside the research could reasonably place the participants at risk of criminal or civil liability or be damaging to the participants' financial standing, employability, or reputation.

3. Research involving the use of educational tests (cognitive, diagnostic, aptitude, achievement), survey procedures, interview procedures, or observation of public behavior that is not exempt under the previous paragraph, if:
   (a) The human participants are elected or appointed public officials or candidates for public office.
   (b) Federal statute(s) require(s) without exception that the confidentiality of the personally identifiable information will be maintained throughout the research and thereafter.

4. Research involving the collection or study of existing data, documents, records, pathological specimens, or diagnostic specimens, if these sources are publicly available or if the information is recorded by the investigator in such a manner that participants cannot be identified, directly or through identifiers linked to the participants.

5. Research and demonstration projects which are conducted by or subject to the approval of federal department or agency heads, and designed to study, evaluate, or otherwise examine:
   (a) Public benefit or service programs.
   (b) Procedures for obtaining benefits or services under those programs.
   (c) Possible changes in or alternatives to those programs or procedures.
   (d) Possible changes in methods or levels of payment for benefits or services under those programs.

6. Taste and food quality evaluation and consumer acceptance studies.

Figure 3.3 Exempt Categories

agree with you. Many researchers will think their research is exempt, only to have their research bumped up to the next level of review, the expedited review.

EXPEDITED REVIEW

The **expedited review** is designed for research projects that involve no more than minimal risk, do not include intentional deception, do not utilize vulnerable populations, and include appropriate consent procedures. Do not think that just because you are collecting surveys, your project is automatically exempt. Surveys that ask people highly sensitive information (illegal behavior, substance use, or sexual behavior) may be reviewed at this level depending on the specific guidelines of the college or university. The Office of Human Research Protections creates the guidelines for the Department of Health and Human Services within the federal government as a baseline. Different academic institutions have the right to interpret these guidelines differently, so do not think that just because a study was approved as exempt at one institution that a similar study will be approved as exempt at a different institution.

If the research is highly controversial, beyond a minimal risk, or involves confidentiality problems, the IRB chair will require that a research protocol be examined by the full IRB.

FULL-BOARD REVIEW

A **full-board review** occurs when the chair of the IRB believes that a research protocol is beyond a minimal risk and that the complete IRB should make a decision as to whether a research protocol should be allowed. Nearly anything that falls outside the exemptions seen in Figure 3.3 can be cause for a full-board review, depending on the university. Typically, IRBs meet once a month at large universities and quarterly at small ones. Some IRBs only meet as needed, so they do not have a specific time frame for reviewing research protocols. If you suspect that your research study will not be exempt, it is often best to plan on a full-board review. If you get lucky and the IRB chair does not think you need a full-board review but rather an expedited review, you will have already completed the work for that level of review.

Specific Ethical Issues for Research

To this point, this chapter has primarily examined research ethics from an institutional perspective. However, a number of major ethical issues affect the research situation: data accuracy, data sharing, duplicate data publication, post hoc hypothesis revision, participant identity protection, authorship credit, and plagiarism.

DATA ACCURACY

The first ethical issue relates to the accuracy of your data. Historically, a number of researchers have been found falsifying data in the sciences. **Data falsification** occurs any time one manipulates or alters the data to achieve the results wanted by the researcher. For example, perhaps a researcher predicted that men who view magazine advertisements of scantily clad women will have more negative views of women. To examine this research question, the researcher conducts a study and finds out that the hypothesis is not true. If the researcher then decides to change some participants' scores to slant the study in the direction he or she wants, then the researcher would be falsifying data, which is highly unethical. One of the hardest things for researchers is when a hypothesis does not pan out. However, as scientists we cannot have an agenda for our research. For example, maybe the researcher in our example wanted the data to help further a feminist agenda against advertising. Even if the data do not support the hypothesis, the data should still be reported as such. Unfortunately, people both inside and outside of academia will often attach political agendas to scientific research. Although it is tempting to slant our research results in a specific political direction, as researchers we must be honest and forthcoming with all of our results, not just the ones we like.

DATA SHARING

Another reason to avoid falsifying data is because researchers are expected to engage in **data sharing** when other researchers ask to see the data. Because social scientists are expected to further our understanding of the human process, the only way future scientists can build on our work is to have access to both the published analysis of our work and the actual data used for publication. There are several reasons why other researchers might be interested in seeing your actual data. First, other researchers may want to reexamine your results if a finding does not make sense. We all make mistakes, and often researchers will make mistakes when reporting results. Although the review process a research study goes through before publication should catch any glaring errors, this is not always the case. Second, there is an advanced statistical process called meta-analysis, which attempts to pool the results from numerous studies that examine a specific phenomenon to achieve a greater understanding. Although people conducting a meta-analysis can use published results much of the time, meta-analytic research is often much more useful when the original data are used. We must also mention that there is one giant exception to sharing data: If releasing data will violate the participants' rights to anonymity and confidentiality because there is no way to **deidentify the data** (i.e., unlinkable to the participants), then the researcher has an ethical obligation to protect her or his participants.

DUPLICATE DATA PUBLICATION

The next ethical issue that researchers must be aware of is the concept of **duplicate data** publication, or publishing the same set of data in two different research publications. In academia, publication is considered one of the three pillars of an academic's job (along with teaching and service). Although different colleges and universities will have varying degrees of publication requirements for untenured professors, most colleges and universities today expect faculty to publish. For this reason, meeting a college or university's publication requirements is extremely important and extremely competitive. However, some unethical researchers have published the same manuscript or the same data in more than one publication. In essence, these unethical researchers have double-dipped their chip in the salsa, and we all know that is just plain wrong. Along the same lines, other unethical researchers have presented the same paper at numerous conferences. Colleges and universities typically give researchers money to present research at academic conferences, so presenting the same paper at numerous conferences is seen as a way to cheat the college or university. Furthermore, if you are presenting the same paper at multiple conferences or publishing identical research in more than one journal, you are also preventing other researchers from presenting and publishing. Conferences and journals have finite space available, so if you double-dip, you prevent someone else from either presenting or publishing.

POST HOC HYPOTHESIS REVISION

The second major ethical area for communication researchers is related to the first because this ethical dilemma involves the treatment of data in relation to proposed hypotheses. This ethical issue involves the revising of hypotheses once an individual receives her or his results, or **post hoc** (after the fact) **hypothesis revision**. Imagine a researcher predicts, based on previous research, that there will be a relationship between an organization's culture and the organization's web page content. If the researcher then finds that the organization's web page has nothing to do with the organization's culture, her or his proposed hypothesis would be wrong. Most people do not like being wrong, so it is tempting to just alter the hypothesis (or say that an organization's culture and content on the organization's web page would not be related to each other). When a researcher alters her or his hypotheses to fit the data, the scientific method is weakened, which leads to inaccurate research that cannot help foster future intellectual thought.

PARTICIPANT IDENTITY DISCLOSURES

The third ethical consideration for communication researchers relates to information previously discussed in this chapter—protecting our participants' identities. Often, communication researchers will examine sensitive information from participants that could embarrass or harm them (either personally or professionally) if the information were made public. For this reason, communication researchers ensure that the information obtained from participants is protected. In large-scale quantitative projects, individual participant identity is easier to protect because it is impossible to ascertain one person's responses in a dataset that contains 200 participants. However, qualitative researchers often examine data from only a handful of people, so altering demographic information and changing participant names is often necessary to maintain confidentiality.

AUTHORSHIP CREDIT

Authorship credit is basically the notion that ethical researchers give credit where credit is due. According to an article written by the ethics committee of the American Psychological Association (APA) (Ethics Committee, 1992), there are three basic aspects to the ethical standard for authorship credit. First, authors should only take credit for research they have actually conducted or to which they have contributed. Historically, there have been cases where researchers have stolen another person's data and published those data as their own. At the same time, one should also note that there is an ethical obligation to ensure that all parties who have actually contributed to the research get credit for their participation, which also relates to the second standard. The second standard for authorship credit is to accurately give credit to all parties involved in the research process. Although this may seem to be common sense, there have been a few unethical researchers who would not give students credit for their contribution to research. Whether a contributor is an undergraduate, Master's, or doctoral student does not matter—all authors should get credit for their participation in research. Also involved in this ethical standard is the order in which researchers are listed. When listing all of the researchers for an article, authors should be listed in the order of their contribution, not alphabetically or by some other contrived listing format. You may be wondering why the order of authors matters. Academia (especially tenure and promotion committees) views the listing of authors seriously. Often researchers will only get credit from their college or university if they are the principal author or the first author on an article. Ultimately, the order in which authors are listed is somewhat arbitrary, but researchers should be as objective as possible when listing authors to indicate the level of contribution of each one. The final standard for determining authorship credit has to do with a specific type of article, one that stems from a student's Master's thesis or doctoral dissertation. According to the ethics committee, if an article contains multiple authors and is based on a thesis or dissertation, then the student should be listed as the first author.

CONFLICTS OF INTEREST

A **conflict of interest** occurs when financial or other personal considerations prevent a researcher from abiding by or can give the appearance of compromising scientific and ethical principles. For example, maybe you have been asked by a pharmaceutical company to speak about patient health communication. If you then become involved with a research study that involves that same pharmaceutical company, you would have competing conflicts: your financial incentives for the pharmaceutical company and your ability to complete ethical research. Although some people could still conduct ethical research when they have a conflict of interest, the appearance of being in a compromising situation can be enough to discredit the researcher and her or his research.

PLAGIARISM

The last ethical area for communication researchers relates to the commonly discussed academic problem of **plagiarism**. Any time that a writer does not properly cite or give credit to any source of information, he or she is plagiarizing. Communication scholars "do not claim the words and ideas of another as their own; they give credit where credit is due" (American Psychological Association, 2010, p. 15). Although the cited sentence in the previous sentence was taken from the APA's *Publication Manual*, the sentence is equally applicable for communication scholars. Note that although the sentence could equally apply to both psychologists and communication researchers, the authors of this text still have cited the APA for the information because we did not write it originally ourselves. When people plagiarize, they steal other people's intellectual property and quite possibly infringe on copyright laws. In an article by Mahmood, Mahmood, Khan, and Malik (2010), the authors expanded on information from plagiarism.org, examining the two types of plagiarism: source not cited and source cited.

Source-Not-Cited Types of Plagiarism

Source-not-cited plagiarism involves using someone else's work and not attributing the information to a specific author or group of authors. There are five distinct types of source-not-cited plagiarism.

The Ghostwriter

The first type of plagiarism some writers engage in is referred to as the ghostwriter because the writer has another person literally write the entire paper for her or him. There are many highly unethical websites, from which writers can download prewritten papers for a fee. Other websites offer to put a student in contact with a ghostwriter who will write the student's entire paper for a fee. For obvious reasons, this practice is highly frowned on in higher education and can lead to a student being kicked out of school permanently if he or she is caught doing this.

The Photocopier

The photocopier is a form of plagiarism in which the writer takes a chunk of material from a source and copies it word for word into her or his paper. Remember, if you are citing more than four words in a row, you must place those words in quotation marks and inform your readers where the original information is located.

The Potluck Writer

According to plagiarism.org ("Types of plagiarism," 2011), the potluck writer "tries to disguise the plagiarism by copying from several different sources, tweaking the sentences retaining most of the original phrasing" (para. 4). In this form of plagiarism, the writer mashes a bunch of sources together with a sentence from here and a sentence from there all designed to look like the author's own original work.

The Disguiser

The disguiser form of plagiarism occurs when a writer steals a sentence and then tries to rearrange or replace a few words within the sentence to disguise the fact that the sentence is not his or her own. Imagine that we have the following sentence: "A number of factors are responsible for the quality of research" (Mahmood et al., 2010, p. 193). Here is one way a disguiser would try to rearrange this sentence to "make it their own": "A number of *ideas* are *paramount* for *excellence* in research." Has switching out a few words really changed the basic idea in the first sentence? No! As such, this is a common form of plagiarism.

The Self Stealer

The last plagiarizer is one who often does not even realize that he or she is plagiarizing because he or she is just reusing her or his own writing. When a writer takes portions of previously used work (even if it is her or his own work), that work should be cited as such. Although you may have papers that have overlap conceptually or even in the sources utilized, the writing should be unique for each individual paper.

Source-Cited Types of Plagiarism

Source-cited plagiarism involves partial attribution of information to a source but the attribution is incomplete. There are five distinct types of source-cited plagiarism.

The Forgotten Footnoter/Referencer

The forgotten footnote or forgotten referencer is a plagiarizer who may cite a source within her or his paper but forgets to include that source within her or his footnotes, works cited page, or reference page. Again, citing a source is a two-step process. We must (1) attribute information to a source within the paper and (2) provide information on how to locate that source in our footnotes, works cited, or references.

The Misinformer

The misinformer may either cite information within the text or even on a footnotes, works cited, or reference page, but the information is so vague that one cannot locate that source. For example, if you are writing a paper and you cite the information internally as "According to the *New York Times*" and this is all the information you provide, you are misinforming your reader because the *New York Times* has been published since 1851. How is a reader supposed to know who wrote the information, when the information was written, or the context of the information? This is one of the main reasons we rely so heavily on style manuals to help us correctly cite information both within a paper and in our footnotes, works cited, or references. We will talk more about this in the next chapter.

The Too-Perfect Paraphraser

The too-perfect paraphraser happens when an individual lifts a sentence and then attributes that sentence to the author but does not put the sentence within quotation marks. For example, as shown earlier, the correct way to cite a direct quotation in APA style is like this: "A number of factors are responsible for the quality of research" (Mahmood et al., 2010, p. 193). If you just cited the sentence like this: A number of factors are responsible for the quality of research (Mahmood et al., 2010), then we would not be correctly attributing the sentence to Mahmood et al. because it would look as if we had written that sentence ourselves.

The Resourceful Citer

According to plagiarism.org, a resourceful citer is someone who "cites all sources, paraphrasing and using quotations appropriately. The catch? The paper contains almost no original work! It is sometimes difficult to spot this form of plagiarism because it looks like any other well-researched document" (para. 11). In this case, the writer sticks to the "letter of the law" on how to appropriately cite material within the paper and on her or his footnotes, works cited, or references; however, the writer does not have an original thought within the piece of writing.

The Perfect Crime

The perfect crime is a devious type of plagiarism. Generally, the perfect crime occurs because the writer knows that the source of the information is problematic, so the writer purposefully alters information in her or his citation to disguise where the writing came from. For example, maybe you know that you are not allowed to cite material from Wikipedia. Instead of admitting that the information came from Wikipedia, you decide to cite one of the references at the bottom of the Wikipedia page.

In the next two chapters we will discuss how to conduct research and how to write research articles. We will emphasize how to correctly cite information using the style format created by the APA. For more on how to avoid plagiarism, we recommend Stern (2007) or Menager-Beeley and Paulos (2009). If you are not sure about your own plagiarism, you may want to consider using TurnItIn.com's new website specifically geared toward students: Write Check (https://www.writecheck.com/).

Ethical Research Outside Academia

Ethical research in the world outside of academia is just as important as research conducted inside academia, but there are not the same federal protections for research participants. Regardless, we believe that thinking through research using the same basic model proposed originally by the Belmont Report is a good place to start. All of the ethical aspects discussed previously can be applied to conducting any kind of research in the world:

1. You want to ensure that participants know that participation is voluntary.
2. Do not recruit participants under the age of 18 without parental permission.
3. Do not plagiarize.
4. Do not falsify your results just to make your boss (or your boss's boss) happy.
5. Make sure you maintain the anonymity or confidentiality of participants.

And so on . . .

Conclusion

In this chapter, we have examined the ethics of conducting research in today's academic environment. We began by exploring some of the more controversial research that has been conducted. Then we discussed the nature of ethics and what this meant for communication researchers. Next, we examined the legacy of the Tuskegee experiment and how it ushered in a new era of responsibility and oversight in research involving human subjects. Finally, we discussed four ethical dilemmas that communication researchers often face. Although the IRB process is not perfect, it is designed to prevent atrocities that have been seen in previous research. One of the biggest problems that critics have of the IRB process is that it is highly controlled by a biomedical model of research that does not apply well to social scientists (Dougherty & Kramer, 2005; Hamilton, 2005; Koerner, 2005). Maybe one day there will be separate evaluation processes for social scientific and biomedical research endeavors; however, until that happens, we must learn how to present our research protocols in as clear a way as possible for a variety of different audiences.

KEY TERMS

Anonymity	Belmont Report	Common Rule
Authorship credit	Certificate of Confidentiality	Confidentiality

Conflict of interest	Exempt review	Plagiarism
Data falsification	Expedited review	Post hoc hypothesis revision
Data sharing	Full-board review	Principle of beneficence
Diminished autonomy	Informed consent	Privacy
Duplicate data	Institutional Review Board	Protected health information
Ends	Justice	Research participant
Ethical behavior	Machiavellian ethic	Subjective ethic
Ethics	Means	Unethical behavior

REFERENCES

American Psychological Association. (2010). *Publication manual of the American Psychological Association* (6th ed.). Washington, DC: American Psychological Association.

Bankert, E. A., & Amdur, R. J. (2006). *Institutional review board: Management and function* (2nd ed.). Subury, MA: Jones & Bartlett.

Dougherty, D. S., & Kramer, M. W. (2005). A rationale for scholarly examination of institutional review boards: A case study. *Journal of Applied Communication Research, 33*, 183–188. doi:10.1080/0090 9880500149270

Ethics Committee. (1992). Ethical principles of psychologists and code of conduct. *American Psychologist, 47*, 1612–1628.

Garramone, G. M., & Kennamer, J. D. (1989). Ethical considerations in mass communications research. *Journal of Mass Media Ethics, 4*, 174–185.

Hamilton, A. (2005). The development and operation of IRBs: Medical regulations and social science. *Journal of Applied Communication Research, 33*, 189–203. doi:10.1080/00909880500149353

Humphreys, L. (1975). *Tearoom trade: Impersonal sex in public places.* Chicago, IL: Aldine.

Koerner, A. F. (2005). Communication scholars' communication and relationship with their IRBs. *Journal of Applied Communication Research, 33*, 231–241. doi:10.1080/00909880500149395

Latané, B., & Darley, J. M. (1970). *The unresponsive bystander: Why doesn't he help?* Englewood Cliffs, NJ: Prentice Hall.

Mahmood, S. T., Mahmood, A., Kahn, M. N., & Malik, A. B. (2010). Intellectual property rights: Conceptual awareness of research students about plagiarism. *International Journal of Academic Research, 2*, 193–198.

McCroskey, J. C., Wrench, J. S., & Richmond, V. P. (2003). *Principles of public speaking.* Indianapolis, IN: College Network.

McNutt, L. A., Waltermaurer, E., Bednarczyk, R. A., Carlson, B. E., Kotval, J., McCauley, J., . . . Ford, D. E. (2008). Are we misjudging how well informed consent forms are read? *Journal of Empirical Research on Human Research Ethics, 3*(1), 89–97.

Menager-Beeley, R., & Paulos, L. (2009). *Understanding plagiarism: A student guide to writing your own work.* Boson, MA: Houghton Mifflin Harcourt.

Milgram, S. (1974). *Obedience to authority: An experimental view.* New York, NY: Harper & Row.

Nathan, R. (2005). *My freshman year: What a professor learned by becoming a student.* Ithaca, NY: Cornell University Press.

National Institutes of Health. (2002). *Human participant protections education for research teams.* Washington, DC: U.S. Department of Health and Human Services National Institutes of Health.

Stern, L. (2007). *What every student should know about . . . avoiding plagiarism.* Boston, MA: Allyn & Bacon.

Types of plagiarism. (2011). Retrieved from http://www.plagiarism.org

Wrench, J. S., McCroskey, J. C., & Richmond, V. P. (2008). *Human communication in everyday life: Explanations and applications*. Boston, MA: Allyn & Bacon.

Vaughan, T. R. (1967). Governmental intervention in social research: Political and ethical dimensions in the Wichita jury recordings. In G. Sjoberg (Ed.), *Ethics, politics, and social research* (pp. 50–77). Cambridge, MA: Schenkman.

Zimbardo, P. G., Haney, C., Banks, W. C., & Jaffe, D. (1973, April 8). The mind is a formidable jailer: A pirandellian prison. *New York Times Magazine, 122*, 38–60.

CHAPTER 4

Searching for Previous Research and American Psychological Association Style

Formulating an idea for a research project can be intriguing or it can be frustrating. If the researcher already has a question or idea in mind, the process can be relatively easy; in fact, it could almost be considered a "mystery" to be solved. However, there are aspects of the process that can be frustrating if the researcher lacks the knowledge or tools for finding answers.

Chapter 1 focused on the role of theory in social scientific research and provided a model of communication. Although the topics we discuss in this chapter can be applied to any social scientific field, as communication researchers we must always keep communication in our minds when thinking about research. This chapter provides an overview of the research process and will assist in creating a road map for conducting a communication research project. After all, before starting out on a journey it is a good idea to have a game plan for getting there! At the conclusion of this chapter, you will be able to identify a communication topic to research, understand the options available for examining and summarizing the communication research that already exists on your topic, and organize and cite sources of information to report your research.

Research takes time and should be approached in much the same way that a mystery would be analyzed on your favorite television crime drama. Before beginning the investigation, the "detective" (researcher) must establish a game plan. The investigator should have a good idea of the question to be answered, or he or she will spend many hours working to solve nothing at all. To understand the background of the question or mystery, evidence in the form of information and facts must be gathered. All of the evidence must be synthesized or organized to help you, the researcher/detective, establish a logical answer to the research/mystery.

In research, there are five preliminary steps to beginning a research project that will be discussed in this chapter: (1) identifying the question or topic to investigate; (2) clarifying the research question and generating a list of key terms and concepts; (3) locating potential sources of background information on the topic; (4) organizing and evaluating information; and (5) citing sources of information using a standard format.

Step 1: Identifying the Topic

The first step in beginning the communication research project involves choosing a topic or question about communication to investigate. For some people, picking a communication topic can be one of the most daunting tasks. After all, the research project will consume a considerable amount of time, so researchers often put pressure on themselves to find the "perfect" communication topic. Some researchers have indicated that choosing a topic has been the easiest part of their research process because they draw on events that have happened in their own lives and seek answers. For example, maybe you will be reading a research article and a question will pop into your head, or maybe you will just be taking a shower one morning and think, *Hmmm, I wonder if anyone has researched that before!?* Every researcher has a different process he or she goes through when creating a research project. However, there are some tips that can assist you in finding a research topic to start your research journey.

First, be sure that you understand why you are doing the research. Are you doing the research to get published or because you have to take a research methods class and are given an assignment to complete? Even before you begin thinking about a topic, you must clarify why you are conducting the research in the first place. Some questions to consider if conducting research for a college class may include the following:

- Is the focus on a specific communication context or phenomenon? For example, is the goal of the project to select a topic that focuses on communication in the health-care setting? Or is the goal of the project to examine a personality variable as it relates to communication?
- What types of sources are required? Should the search for sources focus exclusively on scholarly journals, or can sources from popular magazines and newspapers be included? Can websites be included as sources?

- Is there a particular number of resources that should be cited?
- What style format should be used? Is American Psychological Association (APA) format acceptable, or should the project adhere to Modern Language Association (MLA) guidelines or another format (*The Chicago Manual of Style*, international medical journal style, etc.)?

If you are not conducting research for a specific class, there are other questions you must consider as well:

- Are you conducting the research for an organization or for your own personal use?
- What do you plan to do with the research after it has been conducted (publish it, present it somewhere, etc.)?
- Will other people be interested in the research you are conducting?

The second step to ensuring a successful research experience involves selecting a topic that interests you personally. You will experience greater motivation to spend time exploring sources and collecting data if the topic is one that you have an interest in studying. Since this book assumes that you plan on focusing your research to examine a communication phenomenon, keep reminding yourself to concentrate on messages and meaning when identifying the research topic.

Research ideas can come from a variety of sources or experiences. Ideas can result from a conversation, other research articles, media examples, current events, or even a professor. If you experience difficulty in identifying a research topic, consider brainstorming. Get together with a group of friends or family members and generate a list of ideas. Browse through current magazines and newspapers to see whether there is a "hot" topic that has been the subject of attention. Examine a textbook or browse a subject-specific online database on a library website (for example, Communication and Mass Media Complete—CMCC in EBSCOhost) for ideas. Conduct a word or subject search using key terms that describe your interests.

As stated previously, an idea for research can result from a casual conversation. For example, the idea for a study conducted by Thomas, Booth-Butterfield, and Booth-Butterfield (1995) resulted from a lunch conversation between friends. During the conversation, the friends discussed what had happened during the previous weekend. One of the women (Stacey) mentioned that she had visited her sister and her niece. During dinner Stacey had casually asked her sister, "So when is Joe [your husband] moving out?" The shocked expression on her niece's face followed by the question, "Why is Daddy moving out?" led her to realize that she had just disclosed to her niece that her parents were divorcing before they had an opportunity to discuss it with her. Her niece became upset and angry and accused her mother of lying to her. Stacey felt horrible! Would Stacey's niece continue to blame her sister for the divorce? As a result of hearing this story, Thomas et al. (1995) decided to investigate the impact of disclosure of the decision to divorce on a child's level of communication satisfaction with her or his parents. More specifically, the researchers wanted to see whether children reported more communication satisfaction with the parent who told them about the decision to divorce. Would the child of a divorce perceive the parent who revealed the decision to divorce as being more honest and the other parent as being more deceptive?

To exhaust all options for identifying the topic for a project, consider a variety of sources for potential topics. Three possible sources include reflecting on personal experiences, reviewing literature, and developing questions from existing theories. Let's build on the earlier example regarding the use of personal experiences. We discussed how the idea for a research study on divorce disclosures evolved from a personal conversation. In research methods classes we have taught, students often use their own experiences to come up with ideas for research projects. One student decided to research the verbal aggressiveness of hockey parents as a result of watching parents yelling at the teams, players, and officials during his son's hockey games. Another student decided to research the use of interpersonal deception after watching several episodes of a reality television show *Big Brother*. Both of these topics were the result of personal experiences. Yet another student focused on communication strategies used to inform employees of impending downsizing in a local organization after reading an article in her local newspaper. Potential research topics are everywhere!

Another major way that researchers often find topics is by reading the literature within a specific communication context. For example, maybe you are reading an article on computer-mediated communication. While reading the article you realize that a lot of research has examined the use of chat rooms and instant messaging, but no one has really looked at how cell phone text messaging affects communication. Most research studies conducted probably stem from this type of initial noting of "gaps" in research. These gaps come in a variety of different forms:

1. Some researchers realize that there is information missing in a specific context, like our example comparing computer instant messaging to cell phone text messaging. Although research on computer instant messaging has been around for a decade, cell phone text messaging is still a recent phenomenon, so it is clearly a new context to revisit older research findings.

2. A second type of gap deals with samples. For example, maybe when looking at research on the use of e-mail, you note that little research has been conducted on retired individuals. Retired people and college students may have different uses for e-mail, so examining a communication phenomenon in different samples is extremely important.

3. A third type of research occurs when you note that information simply needs to be updated. Research in the area of computer-mediated communication dates back to the late 1980s and early 1990s. Although the research results of the late 1980s were interesting, do those results still hold true in the twenty-first century? As computer and Internet technology have rapidly advanced, do people still respond to computer-mediated communication in the same way as they did in the late 1990s? Since people change with time, revisiting older studies in an updated fashion can be extremely important.

4. The fourth type of research gap comes in the form of conceptual gaps, that is, no one has studied a specific concept. While talking with other researchers or reading research literature, we often have "aha" moments where we realize that some aspect of human communication has not been studied at all. Of course, it is always important to double-check the literature to make sure that your "new" concept is actually something someone has not studied under a different term.

5. The last gap that researchers attempt to fill is theoretically driven. If you remember our discussion of theories in Chapter 2, we discussed the notion that theories must be able to be proven false. For this reason, scientists will often examine a theory to make sure the theory stays true across a wide range of communication circumstances. Because theoretically driven research is extremely common in communication, we will look at this area in more detail.

Berger and Calabrese (1975) created one of the most important theories of interpersonal communication, called uncertainty reduction theory (URT). At its basic level, URT posits that people will attempt to reduce uncertainty through our interactions with others in initial interactions. The goal of these initial interactions is to increase our ability to make *predictions* about another person to *explain* the outcomes of the interaction. One of the reasons why URT has longevity in communication is because it is built on eight **axioms** (generally accepted principles or rules). Although we cannot go into detail here about the eight axioms of URT, we do recommend that you read either Berger and Calabrese (1975) or the summary of URT research by West and Turner (2006). For our example, we will examine the eighth axiom from Berger and Calabrese: shared communication networks reduce uncertainty, whereas lack of shared networks increases uncertainty. In essence, this axiom posits the idea that the more people have shared communication networks (they find out they have friends in common, coworkers in common, etc.), the less uncertainty they will experience while interacting. However, the more different their communication networks are (they know none of the same people), the more uncertainty they will have while interacting. When completing theoretically driven research, researchers will look at a part of a theory and think, "How can I test the theory?" Maybe you want to examine parental uncertainty while interacting with their children's teachers. So you set out to determine whether parents who have more communication network ties with teachers (e.g., they go to the same church, have friends in common, belong to the same social group) experience less uncertainty while interacting with their children's teachers than parents who share no common communication networks with their children's teachers. In essence, we have chosen to examine part of a theory, determined how to use the theory in a specific communication context, and can now set out to either provide more support for the theory or possibly provide information that contradicts the theory.

Overall, this section has introduced you to a variety of different methods researchers can use to go about creating research studies. Whether a researcher simply has an "aha" moment at 3:00 AM or sets out to purposely test a theory, the next step in the research process is to further clarify the research question and generate a list of key terms to help you find previously conducted research.

Step 2: Clarifying the Research Question and Generating Key Terms

Once a general topic has been identified, the next step is to develop and refine the topic to begin the search for existing information. There are three primary steps involved in this process: (1) state your topic in the form of a question (realize that this may result in more than one question depending on your topic); (2) identify key terms and concepts from the question(s); and (3) generate a list of key term synonyms that can be used to search for background information.

STATING THE TOPIC IN THE FORM OF A RESEARCH QUESTION

The first step in refining your topic involves stating your research topic in the form of a question. We have included a worksheet (Figure 4.1) that can assist you in working through the process of clarifying the research question and identifying potential sources. Note that the first step asks for the *initial* research question. We use the term "initial" because the research question may undergo multiple revisions as you examine existing sources of information. You may discover that the initial question is too broad or too narrow. Or, once you begin the search for information, you might find out that your initial question has already been answered through previous research.

Suppose that you have recently experienced the end of a romantic relationship. Based on your own experience, you decide that the topic of your research project will be terminating relationships. Because this topic is extremely broad, we must narrow the focus to help formulate a specific research question. Some things that you might want to consider in refining your topic and writing the initial research questions include the following:

• What type of relationship should be examined? Friendships, romantic relationships, or family relationships?

- Is there a particular relational role that should be the focus of the study? The person who initiates the termination? Or the recipient?
- How is communication related to the topic? Should the focus be on strategies used to terminate relationships?

As you can see, there are several "mini-questions" that must be addressed before creating the initial research question. Suppose you decided that the focus of your study will be on the messages used by partners to communicate the end of a romantic relationship. The initial research question could be phrased as, "What communication strategies are used to terminate romantic relationships?" That is simple enough! But keep in mind that this research question may need to be revised as we continue through the remaining steps indicated on the Research Planning Worksheet (Figure 4.1).

Step 2 on the worksheet asks the researcher to identify what information is already known about the topic. Think about your own experiences and what you have studied in communication, psychology, family studies, history, biology, or any other class that you have taken. People in a wide variety of fields help communication scholars more fully understand communication phenomenon. What do you already know about communication strategies that are used to end romantic relationships? Probably the most obvious thing that you already know is that relational partners might avoid engaging in communication behaviors. You might even recall studying relationship dissolution in an interpersonal communication class. Maybe your own experience involved the use of deception. Brainstorm and think of anything that you already know about the topic. This information will be useful as you begin generating key concepts to describe your research topic.

IDENTIFYING KEY TERMS AND SYNONYMOUS TERMS

Once the initial research question has been developed, the next step involves identifying key words and concepts that can be used to describe the ideas included in your question.

Let's take a closer look at how Wrench and Booth-Butterfield (2003) generated the topic and research questions for their study examining physicians' use of humor and patient compliance and satisfaction. This project evolved as a result of their interest in humor, health communication, and compliance. Following are some initial questions that created the foundation for the study:

- Are patients more likely to listen to the advice of doctors who are humorous?
- Are patients more satisfied if their doctor uses humor?
- Do patients perceive doctors who use humor as being more credible?

By examining the questions more closely, key concepts and terms emerge to guide the search for information that has already been published on the topic. Create a list of the key terms included in your questions, but realize that these terms alone might not be sufficient to conduct your review of existing literature. Additional terms that are synonymous with the key terms should be included in the list of words that will be used to conduct the library search. Do not be afraid to list any and all words that could be used to describe your topic. Be sure to include both broad and narrow terms to describe each concept. Figure 4.2 includes sample questions and key terms that could be used to find sources for Wrench and Booth-Butterfield's study. The column on the far right lists synonyms for the key terms that were taken directly from potential research questions.

As you generate lists of key terms to represent the research question, it may be useful to visually represent and organize your ideas by creating a concept map (also known as a web diagram). Doing so will create a picture of concepts that fit together and can assist in organizing

1. What is your initial research question(s)?
2. **What do you already know about this topic?** List any information you currently have about your topic

3. What keywords can you use to assist you in conducting a library search? Be sure to include synonyms for all terms identified!

4. What resources should you examine to begin your review of literature?

Electronic databases	Websites	Encyclopedias/ Handbooks

5. Begin your search for information. Be sure to complete a summary sheet for each source you think will be useful for your study!

6. Review and evaluate the information. What did you discover from your research?

What questions have been answered?
What questions remain unanswered?
Should any studies be replicated?

7. Evaluate your sources. Now that the initial research process is complete, revise your initial research question.

Figure 4.1 Research Planning Worksheet

Questions	Key Terms from Questions	Related Terms
Are patients more likely to listen to the directions of doctors who are humorous?	patient listen doctor	obey compliance requests message physician health
Are patients more satisfied if their doctor uses humor?	patient satisfaction doctor humor	physician message health
Do patients perceive doctors who use humor as being more credible?	patient doctor humor credibility	physician expertise

Figure 4.2 Key and Related Search Terms

ideas as you begin writing your review of literature (see Chapter 5). Think of the concept map as a "tree" for organizing ideas. The central concept of the research project serves as the tree trunk or the foundation for the project. The branches of the tree represent the concepts or ideas that the researcher wants to examine in relation to the central concept. Finally, the twigs are used to represent the terms that are synonymous with those represented by the branches. A brainstorming map of Wrench and Booth-Butterfield's (2003) study might look like Figure 4.3. Because the concept of physician humor is central to the study, it is placed at the center of the diagram. Next, patient compliance, patient satisfaction, and expertise are included in the surrounding circles since the goal is to see how these concepts are linked to a

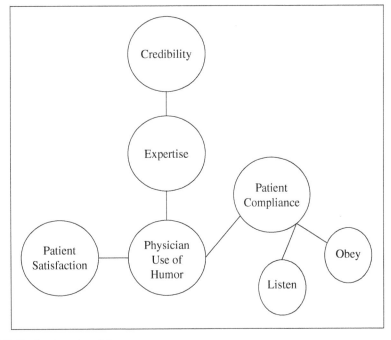

Figure 4.3 Brainstorming Map

doctor's use of humor. It is important to continue generating terms that are synonymous with these key concepts and to include additional terms in the diagram. Suppose when searching for information in the library you discover that the words used in the search return only a few examples of books or articles that have examined the topic. At that point, it is helpful to have the list of related terms to aid in broadening the search. If a search for physician humor and credibility results in only three articles, the terms "doctor" and "expertise" could be included in a subsequent search to see whether more articles can be found. Remember to include communication, messages, and meaning as the central focus of your research.

Step 3: Locating Sources of Information

Once you have identified the initial research question and key concepts, the next task involves searching for information that has already been published on the topic. In Chapter 1, we stated that a primary goal of research is to produce new knowledge that explains the "how" and "why" of communication. To build new knowledge, it is important to search for the information that already exists on a topic. After all, how useful would it be to keep answering the same research question over and over? As you review existing articles on your topic, you will note "gaps" or unanswered questions to help you refine your initial research question.

You are likely to come across two basic types of sources while looking for previous literature: primary and secondary. Hairston and Ruszkiewicz (1996) define **primary sources** as "materials on a topic upon which subsequent interpretations or studies are based, anything from firsthand documents such as poems, diaries, court records, and interviews to research results generated by experiments, surveys, ethnographies, and so on" (p. 547). Although the first part of this definition is not useful for our discussion, the second part specifically relates to research results generated by experiments and surveys. In other words, primary research reports the results of a study actually conducted by the author(s).

Secondary sources, by contrast, are restatements or analyses of the primary research. For example, when you read an academic article, the first section is the review of literature. Within this review, the new article's author(s) summarizes preexisting research on a subject. This summarization of preexisting research is secondary because the new article's author did not conduct the research found in the literature review. Conversely, when the new article then explains what the author actually did in the study, the author is generating primary research because he or she is describing what was done in the current project. We want to make this distinction clear because many students fall into the trap of citing secondary sources from an author's literature review within the student's literature review without ever reading the original source.

Furthermore, using secondary sources can actually be a form of plagiarism. One common problem that we have seen over the years is a student author finding a great citation or series of references that would be useful for her or his research. For example, imagine you are reading an article and you read the following quotation: "More recently researchers have started becoming interested in the after-effects of detected deception in a variety of interpersonal relationships: coworkers (Aunne, Metts, & Ebesu Hubbard, 1998; Dunleavy, Chory, & Goodboy, 2007), customers (Jehn & Scott, 2008), friendships (Aunne et al., 1998), and romantic relational partners (Aunne et al., 1998; Jang, Smith, & Levine, 2002; McCornack & Levine, 1990)." You read this sentence and think the information from Jehn and Scott (2008) and Dunleavy, Chory, and Goodboy (2007) would really help you build your argument. If you lift those citations (and corresponding references) from the article and place them into your own paper without ever actually reading those articles, you are plagiarizing. If you think those articles could be useful for your paper, you should always go back and read them yourself. In fact, we often recommend to our students to look in the reference sections of published papers as a launching point for finding more sources. We call this process **backtracking** because you are taking one article and using that article's references to track down other articles and books that have been published.

We always recommend going back to the original source whenever possible because you may find something in the primary source that is more helpful to your research than what is discussed by the secondary source. Avoiding the use of secondary sources within your own writing does not mean that secondary sources are not useful. Often if we read a secondary source written on a given topic at the beginning of the research process, we can greatly decrease the amount of time we must spend looking for literature because the secondary source can help us get an understanding of the breadth of information on a given topic. In essence, secondary sources are useful when starting the research process because they help you quickly grasp the general research subject area before you delve into the primary research. There is one notable exception to the above-mentioned qualifications for use of secondary sources. If the primary source exists in a language that you do not read, then citing the secondary source's translation of the primary source is appropriate. Now that we have explained the differences between primary and secondary sources, we can look at the types of primary sources that exist.

TYPES OF INFORMATION SOURCES

Although it may be easy to turn on the computer and use a popular search engine such as Google or Yahoo! to compile a list of resources, scholarly research involves searching a variety of sources for relevant information. The best place to begin a quest for information is your campus library. Remember—librarians are our friends, so treat them well. Librarians enjoy being asked to assist students in locating sources of information if you do it nicely! Think of the librarian as a tour guide. There are literally thousands of sources and strategies that can be used to search for existing literature. In fact, some of our former students have said that they avoid the library because they suffer from "information overload." There are so many sources of information that they are not sure where to begin the search. A librarian can help navigate the options available to make your search more efficient and effective. Information about your research topic can come from a variety of sources. Of course, the sources you select for information will depend on the question you are trying to answer. The most common sources of information are books, magazines, scholarly journals, magazines, newspapers, encyclopedias, handbooks, and the World Wide Web.

A summary of the different types of information sources is included in Figure 4.4. The type of information needed will dictate the selection of the information source. Remember—research projects require you to conduct a review of existing scholarly literature on your topic. Students often flock to popular magazines and websites for information on a topic. After all, they are familiar with various magazines and they are fairly easy to locate. Students express reluctance about reviewing scholarly sources. The language used in journal articles is sometimes foreign to beginning researchers. But there are shortcuts that can help you sift through scholarly articles to locate information you can understand. We recommend reviewing the abstract first, which will provide an overview of the article. Next, skim the review of literature to see what key concepts the researchers examined in the project. Finally, look at the discussion section. What conclusions did the researcher make as a result of the study? As you progress through this book, we will provide you with more tools for interpreting and writing scholarly research, but for the time being it is important to note the differences between magazines and scholarly journal articles so that you can understand what each has to offer when conducting your review of literature. A summary of their differences is provided in Figure 4.5.

Source Type	When to Use	Examples
Books	• To searching for comprehensive coverage of a topic. • To locate historical information on the topic. • To find summaries of research conducted on the topic.	• McGhee, P.E. (1999). *Health, healing and the amuse system: Humor as survival training.* Dubuque, IA: Kendall Hunt. • Robinson, V. (1991). *Humor and health professions* (2nd ed.). Thorofare, NJ: Slack.
Magazines	• To examine information or opinions on topics related to popular culture. • To locate current, up-to-date information on a topic. • To review articles written in general "layman" terms.	• Patients pleased; doctors surprised. (1998, June). *Physician's Management, 38*(6), 12. • Laugh it off. (2005, June). *Prevention,* 58(6), 55.
Scholarly Journals	• To search for scholarly research articles. • To identify what research has already been conducted on a topic. • To review reference lists of existing research to assist in locating other potential sources.	• Wanzer, M., Booth-Butterfield, M., & Booth-Butterfield, S. (1995). The funny people: A source orientation to the communication of humor. *Communication Quarterly, 43,* 142–154. • Wolf, M.H., Putnam, S.M., James, S.A., & Stiles, W.B. (1978). The medical interview satisfaction scale: Development of a scale to measure patient perceptions of physician behavior. *Journal of Behavioral Medicine, 1,* 391–401.
Newspapers	• To identify the most current information on topic of interest. • To review editorial and commentaries on a topic of interest.	• Howlett, D. (2003, March 4). It hurts not to laugh. *USA Today,* p. D9.
Encyclopedias & Handbooks	• To locate comprehensive summaries or background information on a topic. • To identify key concepts, authors or dates.	• Nature Encyclopedia of Life Sciences • Encyclopedia of Rhetoric • Handbook of Health Communication
World Wide Web	• To locate statistics and quick facts. • To identify opinions of others on a topic. • To connect to library resources.	• http://www.hnu.edu/ishs/ISHSbibs/MEDICINE.doc. Retrieved December 21, 2011. • http://www.doaj.org – Directory of Open Access Journals

Figure 4.4 Types of Information Sources

	Scholarly	Popular
Author	Written by experts in a specific field. Institutional affiliation is typically included.	Written by staff members, freelance writers, or anonymous sources.
Audience	Readers familiar with discipline's terminology and research history. Typically professors, researchers, and students.	General audience
Documentation	Extensive citations to reference other research studies. Typically include a reference page.	Includes little or no documentation outside of quotes by "witnesses."
Writing style	Scholarly and formal	Informal, casual language designed to inform or entertain.
Review process	Peer-reviewed	Not peer-reviewed
Publication	Published less frequently (quarterly, annually)	Published frequently (weekly, monthly)
Appearance	Plain. Graphics typically include charts, tables, and graphs.	Appealing to the eye. Colorful with several pictures and advertisements.
Examples	*Communication Quarterly* *Journal of Applied Communication*	*Time* *Sports Illustrated* *US News and World Report*

Figure 4.5 Distinctions Between Scholarly Journals and Popular Magazines

Scholarly journals are fairly easy to identify based on the title alone. Many of them contain the word "journal" in the title, or they may contain a reference to the frequency of publication (e.g., "Quarterly" "Annual"). Another clue can be found by flipping through the pages of the publication. Although popular magazines are designed to grab the reader's attention with their glossy pages and use of color and photographs, the appearance of scholarly journals tends to be plain. You will rarely find photographs in these publications; rather, you will note the use of graphs, tables, and charts depicting the results of data analysis. Scholarly journals should always be at the top of your list of information sources to consult when conducting a research study. Figure 4.6 contains a list of many of the major journals in which communication research is published. Although this list is long, it is in no way exhaustive. In fact, communication-related work is often published in a wide range of journals, so do not think that the list provided is complete.

LOCATING INFORMATION SOURCES

Just as a variety of information sources exist to assist you in conducting a review of existing literature on a topic, a variety of search tools exists to assist you in locating the specific sources of information. Often students comment that "I searched for books on the library home page and there are no sources on my topic." Although this could be because the topic is unique or recent and there may not be any books dedicated to the specific topic, as a researcher you should not stop the quest for existing literature! Just as it is important to know which tools are most beneficial for fixing or building something, understanding which sources are the best "tools" to use in your search for sources is essential to a successful research project. A common mistake made by beginning researchers is that they experience "tunnel vision" when searching for sources. Remember the earlier example where we expanded the list of key terms to include in our search for information on physician use of humor? Just as we broadened our scope of concepts to explore, we must broaden our scope of resources or tools to use in the search for literature. Three excellent tools for beginning the search include handbooks and subject encyclopedias, electronic databases, and the World Wide Web. The fourth item on your Research Planning Worksheet (Figure 4.1) asks you to identify examples of each of these tools to assist you in beginning your search for information.

Handbooks and Subject Encyclopedias

The first step in any research project should involve examining printed resources that provide comprehensive coverage of topics in a given subject area. Two excellent resources for locating general sources of information are handbooks and subject encyclopedias. Using your key concepts, a search of general reference resources can direct you to bibliographies and summaries of research that has been conducted on your topic. As you search these sources, take careful notes about any additional key terms and concepts used to describe your topic.

Handbooks provide a comprehensive summary of past research and often include commentaries or recommendations for future research directions. The handbook is an excellent starting point for identifying the themes that have been used to examine a topic. Although they provide a broad look at communication, the fact that many handbooks focus on specific contexts makes them useful for examining the historical foundations of a specific topic area. Examples of handbooks include the following:

- ASTD Handbook for Workplace Learning Professionals
- Handbook of Attitudes
- Handbook of Closeness and Intimacy

Academy of Management Journal	*Journal of Experimental Psychology*
American Anthropologist	*Journal of Experimental Social Psychology*
American Behavioral Scientist	*Journal of Family Communication*
American Journal of Psychology	*Journal of General Psychology*
American Journal of Sociology	*Journal of Health Communication*
American Political Science Review	*Journal of Homosexuality*
American Psychologist	*Journal of Intercultural Communication Research*
American Sociological Review	*Journal of Intergroup Relations*
Archives of Psychology	*Journal of International and Intercultural*
Argumentation and Advocacy	* Communication[2]*
Asian Journal of Communication	*Journal of International Communication*
Atlantic Communication Journal	*Journal of Marketing Research*
Audio-Visual Communication Review	*Journal of Marriage and the Family*
Australian Journal of Communication	*Journal of Media and Religion*
Basic and Applied Social Psychology	*Journal of Nonverbal Behavior*
Behavioral Science	*Journal of Personality and Social Psychology*
Behavior	*Journal of Popular Culture*
British Journal of Psychology	*Journal of Popular Film and Television*
British Journal of Social and Clinical Psychology	*Journal of Psychology*
British Journal of Sociology	*Journal of Social and Personal Relationships*
Business Communication Quarterly	*Journal of Social Issues*
Canadian Journal of Behavioral Science	*Journal of Social Psychology*
Canadian Journal of Communication	*Journal of Speech and Hearing Research*
Central States Speech Journal	*Journal of Verbal Learning and Verbal Behavior*
Child Development	*Journal of Written Communication*
Chinese Journal of Communication	*Journal of Public Relations Research*
Columbia Journalism Review	*Journalism Educator*
Communication and Cognition	*Journalism Monographs*
Communication and Critical/Cultural Studies	*Journalism & Mass Communications Quarterly*
Communication and Research	*Language and Speech*
Communication Book Notes Quarterly	*Language and Society*
Communication, Culture, and Critique1	*Learning and Motivation*
Communication Education[2]	*Management Communication Quarterly*
Communication Law and Policy	*Management Science*
Communication Methods and Measures	*Mass Communication Review*
Communication Monographs[2]	*Media, Culture, and Society*
Communication Quarterly[4]	*Memory and Cognition*
Communication Reports6	*Middle East Journal of Culture & Communication*
Communication Research	*Newspaper Research Journal*
Communication Research Reports[4]	*New Jersey Journal of Communication*
Communication Studies[3]	*Ohio Journal of Communication*
Communication Teacher[2]	*Open Communication Journal*
Communication Theory[1]	*Organizational Behavior and Human Performance*
Communication Yearbook	*Personality and Social Psychology Bulletin*
Critical Studies in Mass Communication[2]	*Personal Relationships*
Cyber Psychology	*Personnel Psychology*
Current Directions in Psychological Science	*Philosophy and Rhetoric*
Editor and Publisher	*Political Behavior*
Electronic Journal of Communication	*Political Communication*
ETC: A Review of General Semantics	*Political Communication Review*
European Journal of Communication	*Political Science Quarterly*
European Journal of Social Psychology	*Politics and Society Popular Communication*
Family Process	*Progress in Communication Science*
Family Relations	*Psychological Bulletin*
Gender and Communication	*Psychological Record*
Group and Organization Management	*Psychological Reports*
Health Communication	*Psychological Review*

Figure 4.6 Partial List of Communication Journals

Continued

Howard Journal of Communication	*Psychological Science*
Human Communication	*Psychological Science in the Public Interest*
Human Communication Research[1]	*Psychology of Women Quarterly*
Human Organization	*Public Administration Review*
Human Relationships	*Public Opinion Quarterly*
HUMOR	*Public Relations Journal*
Intermedia	*Public Relations Quarterly*
International Journal of Listening	*Public Relations Review*
International Journal of Psychology	*Qualitative Research Reports in Communication*[4]
Journal of Science Communication	*Quarterly Journal of Speech*[2]
International Journal of Strategic Communication	*Risk Analysis: An International Journal*
International Organization	*Science Communication*
International Political Science Review	*Semiotica*
International Social Science Journal	*Sex Roles: A Journal of Research*
Journal of Abnormal and Social Psychology	*Signs: Journal of Women in Culture and Society*
Journal of Advertising Research	*Small Group Research*
Journal of Advertising	*Social Forces*
Journal of Anthropological Research	*Social Science Research*
Journal of Applied Behavior Analysis	*Sociological Inquiry*
Journal of Applied Communication Research[2]	*Sociological Methods and Research*
Journal of Applied Psychology	*Sociological Quarterly*
Journal of Asian Pacific Communication	*Sociology: Journal of the British Sociological*
Journal of Black Studies	*Association*
Journal of Broadcasting and Electronic Media	*Sociometry: Social Psychology Quarterly*
Journal of Business	*Southern Communication Journal*[5]
Journal of Business Communication	*Studies in Communication*
Journal of Business and Technical Communication	*Television Quarterly*
Journal of Business Research	*Text and Performance Quarterly*[2]
Journal of Clinical Psychology	*The Review of Communication*[2]
Journal of Communication[1]	*Vital Speeches of the Day*
Journal of Communication and Religion	*Washington Journalism Review*
Journal of Computer Mediated Communication	*Western Journal of Communication*[6]
Journal of Conflict Resolution	*Women's Studies*
Journal of Consumer Research	*Women's Studies in Communication*
Journal of Cross-Cultural Psychology	*Women's Studies International Quarterly*
Journal of Educational Psychology	*World Communication*

[1] Journal Sponsored by the International Communication Association.
[2] Journal Sponsored by the National Communication Association.
[3] Central States Communication Association.
[4] Eastern Communication Association.
[5] Southern States Communication Association.
[6] Western States Communication Association.

- Handbook of Communication and Instruction
- Handbook of Communication and Social Interaction Skills
- Handbook of Communication Ethics
- Handbook of Communication Science
- Handbook of Conflict Communication
- Handbook of Family Communication
- Handbook of Gender and Communication
- Handbook of Group Communication Theory and Research

- Handbook of Health Communication
- Handbook of Intergroup Research
- Handbook of International and Intercultural Communication
- Handbook of Instructional Communication: Rhetorical and Relational Perspectives
- Handbook of Interpersonal Communication
- Handbook of Language and Intercultural Communication
- Handbook of Language and Social Interaction
- Handbook of Media Studies
- Handbook of Nonverbal Communication
- Handbook of Organizational Communication
- Handbook of Organizational Justice
- Handbook of Personality Development
- Handbook of Political Communication
- Handbook of Public Relations
- Handbook of Risk and Crisis Communication
- Handbook of Sexuality in Close Relationships
- Handbook of Visual Communication
- IABC Handbook of Organizational Communication
- Media Handbook
- Work and Family Handbook

Subject encyclopedias are a bit different from the *Encyclopedia Britannica*, with which most of us are familiar. The *International Encyclopedia of Communication* was published in 1989 and most recently in 2007 and is the first communication subject encyclopedia of its kind. Bibliographies and articles covering a variety of communication contexts are included. The index of this source is particularly useful for building your list of key terms and concepts.

Electronic Databases

Considering the prevalence of computers in our lives, it should come as no surprise that the most efficient and comprehensive searches for sources are conducted using electronic databases. Your professors have probably shared stories of the "good old days" when they had to search for sources using tools called "card catalogs" and "periodical indexes." Listen to their stories (trust us, they are telling the truth!), hug your computer, and be thankful that search strategies have come a long way! A task that used to take researchers many hours can now be accomplished in a fraction of the time. With the list of key concepts identified in Step 2 in hand, it is time to begin the journey.

Electronic databases (also referred to as "computerized" or "online" databases) can be thought of as a virtual library index where you can search for articles and books. Have you ever looked in the index of a book to find a specific topic or concept? It is much easier to find the term "paralanguage" in a 300-page textbook with the assistance of the index. Electronic databases serve as an enormous index. They search through literally thousands of records in seconds to help you find books and articles containing the key words you use to search. There are literally hundreds of databases to choose from, so the most difficult task may be selecting the one that best suits your research needs. Most libraries list databases both alphabetically and according to subject or content area for ease of searching. Figure 4.7 includes a sample list

Database	Type of Information
Academic Search Complete	• Full text articles and abstracts for more than 13,000 different publications. • Social sciences, humanities, education, language/linguistics, and ethnic studies.
Business Source Complete	• Full text articles and abstracts. • Management, economics, finance, and international business. • Cited references are provided for more than 1,300 journals.
Child Development and Adolescent Studies	• Full text articles and abstracts. • This is the go to database for information on individuals under the age of 21. • Has over 350,000 citations.
Communication Abstracts	• Full text articles and abstracts. • Interpersonal, mass, organizational, and small group communication; journalism; and public relations. • Has over 244,000 references.
Communications and Mass Media Complete	• Full text articles and abstracts. • Access to bibliographic references, reviews, encyclopedias, and handbooks. • Communication Studies and Media Studies • The database includes indexing and abstracts for more than 770 journals and includes full text for over 450 journals.
Educational Research Complete	• Full text articles and abstracts. • Topics covered include all levels of education from early childhood to higher education, and all educational specialties, such as multilingual education, health education, and testing. • Provides indexing and abstracts for more than 2,100 journals, as well as full text for more than 1,200 journals, and includes full text for nearly 500 books and monographs.
ERIC	• Citations from journals and reports • Field of education and related areas. • Sponsored by the U.S. Department of Education • Has more than 1.3 million links with further links to over 300,000 papers and articles.
Family & Society Studies Worldwide	• Full text articles and abstracts. • Coverage spans from traditional academic journals to government publications and working papers. • Indexes articles from a wide range of social science disciplines: anthropology, sociology, psychology, demography, health sciences, education, economics, law, history and social work.
Gender Studies Database	• The database covers the full spectrum of gender-related scholarship inside and outside academia. • This database includes more than 921,000 records with coverage spanning from 1972 and earlier to the present.
LGBT Life	• Full text articles and abstracts • Includes text for more than 120 of the most important and historically significant lesbian, gay, bisexual, transgender/transsexual journals, magazines and regional newspapers. • Contains more than 150 full-text monographs and books.
LexisNexis Academic	• Full text and abstracts • Popular, scholarly, trade, and professional periodicals.

Figure 4.7 Types of Databases

Continued

Continued

Medline with Full Text	• Full text and abstracts • Medline is the number one database for health and medical related information • Provides full text for more than 1,470.
Newspaper Source	• Selected full text articles, indexes and abstracts • Over 180 regional U.S. newspapers, international newspapers, newswires, newspaper columns and other sources • Full text television & radio news transcripts are provided from CBS News, FOX News, NPR, etc.
Psychology and Behavioral Sciences Collection	• Full text and abstracts • This is the world's largest full text psychology database offering full text coverage for nearly 400 journals
PsychArticles	• Abstracts, citations and some full-text articles • Contains full-text articles from over 40 journals published by the American Psychological Association. • Contains other smaller journals from the field of psychology from other publishers.
Papers First	• Full text and abstracts • Papers presented at conferences worldwide, covering every congress, symposium, exposition, workshop and meeting
Proceedings First	• Tables of contents of papers • Papers presented at conferences worldwide.
Social Science Citation Index	• Abstracts and citations • Coverage from nearly 50 social science disciplines.
Vocational and Career Collection	• Full text and abstracts • This collection provides full text coverage for nearly 340 trade and industry-related periodicals.

of electronic databases that are useful for locating resources specific to communication and related areas. Included in the right-hand column is information about the format of information in the database as well as a general description of the types of articles included. An excellent starting point to search for articles on any communication topics is the Communication and Mass Media Complete database located in EBSCOhost. It contains abstracts, citations, and some full-text articles. It is important to note that libraries may not be able to provide access to all the databases included on this list. Many electronic databases require a subscription to allow access, so your ability to search particular databases is dependent on whether your library subscribes to them. Suppose that your research topic is on teacher use of humor in the classroom. Although the Communication and Mass Media Complete database is an excellent starting point for locating articles that have focused specifically on communication, be sure to search the ERIC (Education Resource Information Center) database, which includes articles that have been published by scholars in the field of education. Figure 4.7 contains a list of a wide variety of databases that your college or university may have access to online. If you do not know whether your library has access, ask your friendly research librarian for help.

Once you have identified the database that best suits your research needs, the next step involves selecting the type of search you wish to conduct. There are a variety of fields or criteria that can be used to search for articles. These include the following:

- **Subject search**—searches for key terms that the author has submitted to the subject field to describe the article or book.
- Keyword search—searches for a specific keyword or a set of keywords a researcher is attempting to find.
- **Title search**—searches the title field for words included in the title of an article or book.
- **Author search**—searches for the author's name in the author field.

We recommend conducting a subject search first. For example, the key terms "humor" and "physician" could be used to conduct a subject search. But suppose that only a few results are returned from this search. Remember that the subject search only includes the key terms provided by the author to be entered into the subject field, and the terms you entered must match those that the author supplied exactly. Suppose that the author described an article using the term "doctor" instead of "physician." It is likely that your initial subject search would not retrieve this article.

Attempt the search again by entering the same phrase into a "key word" or "word" search. A key word search looks for a term anywhere in the library record. Essentially, a key word search tells the computer to look for any instances in which the words appear in the title or abstract rather than limiting the search to only those words that the author has supplied as subject descriptors.

What if your search of key terms results in only one or two articles? Or worse yet, suppose that the results include more than 500 articles. Two tools—**Boolean logic** and **truncation symbols**—are available to help you expand or narrow your search. Using these tools will increase your search flexibility and maximize your research effectiveness.

First, Boolean operators can be used in situations such as these to help narrow or expand the search. Three of the most commonly used operator terms are "AND," "OR," and "NOT." When searching for articles that focus specifically on the use of humor in health contexts, it is beneficial to use the Boolean operator AND to narrow the focus. Doing so will return only a list of articles that include both terms. An example of the AND Boolean operator can be seen in the first example in Figure 4.8. In this example, we are looking for instances that involve the words "humor" and "health" at the same time.

The Boolean operator "NOT" can also be used to limit a search. This operator will exclude search terms from your search that might otherwise be included. When searching for articles about communication apprehension, you might want to exclude any articles that include the term "shyness." Using NOT will help limit the results to those that focus specifically on apprehension. An example of the NOT Boolean operator can be seen in the second example in Figure 4.8. In this example, we are looking for instances that where the term "communication apprehension" exists but the word "shyness" is not also present.

In some cases, a researcher might discover that the topic must be expanded. To do so, the Boolean operator "OR" can be used to conduct a search of all articles that include either one of the search terms or the other. Suppose that you were conducting a search for information about biased broadcast news coverage of the 2004 U.S. presidential election and want to include all media types that people use as sources of information. The Boolean operator OR could be used to tell the computer to search for any articles that contain at least one of the key terms included. An example of the OR Boolean operator can be seen in the last example in Figure 4.8. In this example, we are looking for instances where either the word "television" or the word "radio" is present.

The second flexibility aspect available in key work searches involves truncation symbols. Have you ever searched for something only to discover that you forgot to explore some of your options or look in some places? Truncation symbols are used to ensure that your search looks for every possible version of a word. Although the symbol used to truncate a word will differ

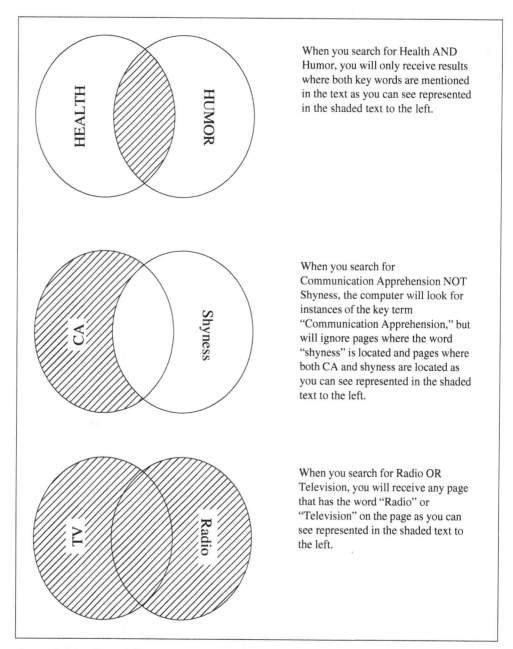

When you search for Health AND Humor, you will only receive results where both key words are mentioned in the text as you can see represented in the shaded text to the left.

When you search for Communication Apprehension NOT Shyness, the computer will look for instances of the key term "Communication Apprehension," but will ignore pages where the word "shyness" is located and pages where both CA and shyness are located as you can see represented in the shaded text to the left.

When you search for Radio OR Television, you will receive any page that has the word "Radio" or "Television" on the page as you can see represented in the shaded text to the left.

Figure 4.8 Boolean Operators

from library to library, the one most commonly used is the asterisk (*). Suppose that you are searching for articles on the topic of children and divorce. In your list of key terms, you have identified "child" as a concept to explore. However, a search for the term "child" would overlook other versions of the word that might be used in subject fields. This search would not pick up articles that use the word "children" or "child's." To ensure that your search grabs all versions of a word, include a truncation symbol with your key term. Entering "child*" would return a list of articles with any versions of the word "child."

Search Engine	URL
General Search Engines	
Ask	http://www.ask.com/
Bing	http://www.bing.com/
Dogpile	http://www.dogpile.com/
Google	https://www.google.com
Yahoo	https://search.yahoo.com/
Specialty Search Engines	
Creative Commons	http://search.creativecommons.org/
Find Law	http://www.findlaw.com/
Library of Congress (multiple search engines)	http://www.loc.gov/
Medline Plus	http://www.nlm.nih.gov/medlineplus/
USA.gov	http://www.usa.gov/
Wolfram Alpha	http://www.wolframalpha.com/

Figure 4.9 Popular Web Search Engines

The World Wide Web

Although electronic databases are the best tool for locating scholarly articles on a topic, the World Wide Web (WWW) can also assist in finding sources of information. In instances where the topic has generated recent attention, it is essential that the researcher conduct a web search to obtain the most current information. After all, it can take anywhere from 6 months to 2 years for scholarly articles to be published. That means that a significant period of time has elapsed before the article is listed in an electronic database. If you need to search for more current information, the Internet is the best tool for the job because it offers a multitude of research benefits. In addition to searching for current information, it can be used to locate scholarly articles that are housed in databases that your campus library does not have available. Some of the most commonly used search engines are listed in Figure 4.9. The first part of the list covers search engines that will yield general results across the WWW. The second part of the list are what are called specialty search engines that focus on more narrowed topics of focus. For example, USA.gov is a great search engine to search across state and federal governments' various websites looking for specific information.

Some professors may advise students against using the web to search for information for a project. However, it is important to obtain clarification as to how they define "using the web." Most often, instructors prefer that students refrain from citing only information from websites as sources for a research paper. However, that does not mean that you should not use the Internet to assist you in locating research articles. After all, searches of electronic databases are conducted using the computer, and the articles are often retrieved in electronic format rather than going to the printed version of the journal or newspaper. We will discuss special methods for citing sources that are retrieved electronically later in this chapter. You would not want to write a research paper on the topic of organizational culture and only cite information that you found through a Yahoo! search. However, you can locate scholarly articles on a topic using popular search engines if you take a few moments and search in the correct locations.

Google Scholar

Did you know that Google has a section dedicated to searching for scholarly articles? Google Scholar is a database of scholarly research articles and texts that can be utilized

Continued

Google Scholar   Continued

to find academic, peer-reviewed information (http://scholar.google.com/). To visit the Google Scholar page, just click on the hyperlink. On the next screen, you will see an option titled "Scholar." All you have to do to conduct a search is to type in a key word or key term in to the search bar and click "OK." For example, type in the key term "communication apprehension" and you will find nearly 7,000 web sources (almost triple what was found when we ran this search for the first edition of this book in 2008—2,500). You will see that many of the initial results have J. C. McCroskey's name listed, which is a good sign because he is the originator of the term "communication apprehension." Conducting a search in this section will return lists of articles and books that have been included in scholarly publications. Many of these articles can be downloaded in full-text format, whereas others will include online access.

We do have some words of caution about using Google Scholar. First, many of the citations listed in Google Scholar will take you to for-profit academic databases that will try to get you to pay money for access to the research article. From our experience using Google Scholar, most of those "for-pay" websites contain information you should have access to through your college or university's library. As such, you should never assume that you need to pay for information or that you cannot get access to information because the link through Google Scholar takes you to a "for-pay" website.

Our second word of caution comes in the form of type of manuscripts found on Google Scholar. Although many of the articles you can find through Google Scholar will be reproductions of physical articles (in the form of PDF documents), others may be preprints or .html files of research information. If an article is a scanned copy of the original article, you do not have to worry about the article because it will look exactly the same as if you picked up the printed version in the library. However, when an article is a preprint copy, which should be clearly indicated on the first page, the article may look distinctly different than the final version. As such, you must follow the APA guidelines on citing a preprint publication. For articles found in .html, you must realize that there are not page numbers in a typical .html file, so you will need to cite information according to the paragraph number. We warn you about both of these problems because Google Scholar will present you with a variety document types that will need to be cited differently according to APA style.

Other Online Research Databases

Beyond various Internet search engines that can help you find scholarly information, a number of research organizations online are also helping to catalog available scholarly journals that have full-text access online. One such open-access database is the Directory of Open Access Journals (DOAJ) (http://www.doaj.org/). The DOAJ's goal is to provide scholarly information to both scholars and the general public at no cost. The DOAJ had cataloged more than 7,000 full-text journals at the time this textbook was published (again, this number has more than tripled since 2008, when DOAJ cataloged around 2,000 journals) and includes a number of publications on the list in Figure 4.6, for example, the *American Communication Journal*; *Conflict and Communication Online*; *Communication and Culture Online*; *Journal of Intercultural Communication*; *Journal of Literature, Culture, and Media Studies*; *Journal of Science Communication*; *Open Business Journal*; and *The Jury Expert*.

For information pertaining specifically to communication, the Communication Institute for Online Scholarship (CIOS; http://www.cios.org/) is a not-for-profit service that has a searchable database of communication abstracts. Although some of the functions of CIOS are free to the public, many functions require a small annual fee. CIOS also has houses the online journal the *Electronic Journal of Communication* and a number of open-access communication books including *Communication, Affect, and Learning in the Classroom* (3rd edition) written by Virginia Peck Richmond, Jason S. Wrench, and Joan Gorham. If you are going to be completing a lot of research, joining CIOS can be cost-effective. Furthermore, CIOS also features open-access books and journals on the website.

Working with Librarians

One invaluable resource researchers have up their sleeves is the research librarian. Sadly, many people do not know the value of a librarian today. For some reason, there is a growing feeling among the general public that librarians are becoming antiquated because of the Internet and search engines. However, the reality is quite different. If anything, because of the sheer abundance of information at our disposal today, librarians are more important than ever before because they are trained in helping researchers weed out the rubbish and find the material most appropriate for their research. Although a librarian will not do the research for you, he or she can help point you in directions that you never would have considered. Librarians at colleges and universities generally have a Master's degree, and sometimes even a doctorate, in library and information sciences, so librarians are a highly trained and specialized group of individuals. In today's rapidly evolving information landscape, librarians keep on top of the newest trends in information delivery while ensuring that they understand how to utilize older models.

In a book that one of our coauthors wrote (Wrench, Goding, Johnson, & Attias, 2011), he sent an e-mail to research librarians across the country asking them for tips and strategies for students working with librarians. Sadly, there is little information for students on working with research librarians. After receiving responses from librarians around the country working at all shapes and sizes of academic institutions, 18 general recommendations for student researchers emerged:

1. Your librarian is just as knowledgeable about information resources and the research process as your professor is about his or her discipline. Collaborate with your librarian so that you can benefit from his or her knowledge.
2. Try to learn from the librarian so that you can increase your research skills. You will need these skills as you advance in your academic coursework, and you will rely on these skills when you are in the workplace.
3. When we are in our offices, we are not on reference desk duty. Whether an office door is open or closed, please knock first and wait to be invited in. With that said, if we are at the reference desk, we are there to help you. Please ask! You are not interrupting. Helping students does not bother us. It is our job and profession, and we like doing it.
4. I am here to teach you, not go to bat for you. Please do not expect me to write a note to your instructor because the materials (reference, reserve, or whatever) were not available.
5. Please, please, please do not interrupt me when I am working with another student. This happens regularly and we work on a first-come, first-serve basis. Wait your turn.
6. If we help you find sources, please look at them, so we will be more likely to want to help you in the future.

Continued

Working with Librarians   Continued

7. Research is a process, not an event. If you have not allocated enough time for your project, the librarian cannot bail you out at the last minute.

8. Do not expect the librarian to do the work that you should be doing. It is your project and your grade. The librarian can lead you to the resources, but you must select the best sources for your particular project. This takes time and effort on your part.

9. Reference librarians are professional searchers who went to graduate school to learn how to do research. Reference librarians are here to help no matter how stupid a student thinks her or his question is.

10. Good research takes time and, although there are shortcuts, students should still expect to spend some time with a librarian and to trawl through the sources they find.

11. Students should also know that we ask questions like, "Where have you looked so far?" and "Have you had a library workshop before?" for a reason. It may sound like we are deferring the question, but what we are trying to do is gauge how much experience the student has with research and to avoid going over the same ground twice.

12. Students should approach a librarian sooner rather than later. If a student does not find what they need within 15 minutes or so, they must come find a librarian. Getting help early will save the student a lot of time and energy.

13. If you do not have a well-defined topic to research or if you do not know what information resources you are hoping to find, come to the reference desk with a copy of your class assignment. The librarian will be glad to help you to select a topic that is suitable for your assignment and to help you access the resources you need. Having at least a general topic in mind and knowing what the assignment entails (peer-reviewed only, three different types of sources, etc.) helps immensely.

14. Most academic librarians are willing to schedule in-depth research consultations with students. If you feel you will need more time and attention than you might normally receive at the reference desk or if you are shy about discussing your research interest in a public area, ask the librarian for an appointment.

15. Students should be as specific as possible in what they ask for, if they know their topic. Students who are struggling with identifying a narrow topic should seek help from either their professors or librarians. We cannot help you find sources if your topic is not clear.

16. Students must learn that many questions do not have ready-made or one-stop answers. Students must understand that an interface with a reference librarian is a dialog and part of a recursive, repetitive process. They must make time for this process and assume an active role in the exchange.

17. Students should understand that information can come in a variety of formats. If a student asks for a "book about" something without providing any other details about the information needed, that student could come away empty handed. Instead, students should get in the habit of asking for "information about" something first.

18. "Gee thanks!" every now and then will win every librarian's heart! (pp. 103–104)

EVALUATING WEB SOURCES

Let's revisit our earlier statement about professors discouraging students from using web sources for research projects. This is not because they fear a conspiracy against libraries.

Typically, instructors will discourage the use of web sources because of the difficulty in evaluating the quality of information located on sites. There is no peer review process for publishing information on the Internet. Anyone can post information on the web. A 14-year-old can create a website for a class project on media coverage of the recent election and include a personal commentary. If you fail to evaluate the credibility of the source, you could end up quoting a 14-year-old as an expert source for your persuasion research project. Four criteria should be used to examine the credibility and quality of web sources. These include accuracy, authority, currency, and objectivity.

Accuracy of a site can be evaluated by taking a closer look at its content. Is the information free of errors? If you notice spelling and writing errors on the site, this should be a signal that the author of the information has not taken care to proofread the material before publishing it on the web. Look to see whether an editor for the site is listed. Unlike printed publications, web sources rarely go through any type of editorial process to check for errors.

To assess the authority of web sources, you should first look to see whether the page is "signed." Who is the author? What credentials are listed on the site? If the site is sponsored by a credible organization, this lends credibility to the source of information. Suppose the site does not include any information about the author or sponsoring organization. Clues about the authority of the source can sometimes be identified by examining the web address (or URL) for the site. For example, suppose you are conducting a research project on the topic of assessing the credibility of web resources. During your search, you locate a link to the following site: http://lib.nmsu.edu/instruction/eval.html/. By examining the web address more closely, you notice that the article is published by someone at New Mexico State University, as identified by the ".edu" extension in the URL. Because the information is from an academic institution, you can be fairly confident that it is a credible source. Other extensions that could signal credible sources include ".gov" (which are government sites) and ".org" (which are organization sites). Be careful of information found on ".com" sites because often these websites are used for advertising, not to provide unbiased information to the public.

Currency of web resources can be determined by looking for dates that indicate when the site was created and when it was last updated. Dates will ensure that the information cited in a research paper is current. The dates of websites are typically included at the bottom of the page. Always check whether links to sites are still active. Do not include links to sites in your paper that are no longer in existence. Doing so indicates that you have not checked the currency of information you are citing.

Last, but certainly not least, the objectivity of the site should be assessed. Look for links on the site to sections titled "About," "Philosophy," or "Background" to provide information about the goal or mission of the site. As you browse the site, be sure to ask yourself whether there is a hidden bias or purpose to including information on the page. If it does appear that there is a bias, ask yourself how this biased information could be useful to your project if you decide to include the information, or at least mention in your paper that the information may be biased because of the biases of the source.

The Wikipedia Problem

By this point in your academic career, you have undoubtedly come into contact with information from Wikipedia. Wikipedia is an open-source online encyclopedia that allows anyone to edit its entries. In essence, anyone can add information to Wikipedia that may or may not be actually factual. When we look at the four criteria for evaluating websites, Wikipedia only excels at one—currency. Yes, Wikipedia is great for current information and allows for new information to be added constantly. However, it does have three huge problems: (1) entries in Wikipedia consistently contain inaccurate information, (2) there is a lack of clear authority of the authors of the entries, and (3) there is no way to ascertain the author(s)' objectivity. In other words, Wikipedia may be a good launching point for getting a basic grasp on information, but it should never be considered a useable source for academic research. In essence, Wikipedia is a highly problematic secondary source of information. As we discussed earlier in this chapter, researchers should mainly use primary sources unless there is clear justification to use a secondary source. In an article by Read (2006), he recalls an interview he had with Jimmy Wales, one of the cofounders of Wikipedia:

> I get an e-mail every week from some college student who says, "Help me; I cited you and I got an F on my paper." I always say the same thing: "For God's sake, you're in college now!" People really need to be educated not just about whatever topic they're looking for, but about the meta-question of, "How do you decide what to trust?" (p. A36)

In other words, even one of the cofounders of Wikipedia realizes that it should not be used for academic research purposes.

Step 4: Organizing and Evaluating Information

At this point in the research process, we must emphasize the importance of maintaining a working bibliography. After all, why spend hours conducting research on a topic if you do not have a game plan for organizing the sources and information you locate? The bibliography is simply a list of sources that you have located and reviewed in conducting the review of literature. Trust us—eventually you will need this information as you cite sources of information in your "Review of Literature" and "References." It is much easier to record the information now than to recreate the list later. Nothing is more frustrating than beginning to put together a reference list only to discover missing information such as the year the source was published or the page numbers of an article.

Maybe you are not a fan of working with index cards, so try the sticky-note method instead. The sticky-note method requires you to print out all of the articles you plan on using within a research project. As you go through the articles, look for big ideas and mark them within the article, along with your immediate thoughts. Additionally, write down those ideas (along with the page numbers) on a sticky note. When you are done with an article, place the sticky note directly on top of the article. By doing this, you will be able to find your ideas (along with the relevant page numbers) within journal articles and books more effectively.

Docear

One piece of software that we recommend is called Docear; it is freely available and can be downloaded for multiple operating systems (http://www.docear.org/). Docear allows you to organize your thoughts electronically. (and back them up to the cloud). Unlike the previous two methods, Docear assumes that you will be working completely electronically, so it works in conjunction with Adobe Acrobat Reader (http://get.adobe.com/reader/). Adobe Acrobat Reader allows you to read portable document formats (PDFs). When you are reading PDFs, you save them to your hard drive and highlight the articles and even make notes electronically within the program. When you are done reading the articles, you can then import the PDF files (including all of your highlights and annotations) right into Docear. You also have the ability to highlight and annotate documents in Docear. Once you have all of the research articles you think you will need, you can then start organizing your articles into a visual mind map. For people who like to think through things visually, Docear is a great tool. Go ahead, check it out! It is free, so you have nothing to lose and everything to gain.

| SOURCE: | Book | Journal | Text Journal | Webpage | Magazine |

Newspaper

Title:_____

Article Title (for journal, magazine or newspaper)

_____

Author(s) _____

Copyright Date OR if web site, date you used website_____

Publisher of book OR Sponsor of website_____

Place of Publication OR Web URL _____

NOTES:
_____
_____
_____
_____
_____

Figure 4.10 Source Record Card

Effective library searches and organization strategies include the following steps:

- Step 1: Using your list of key terms, begin searching general reference materials. Review handbooks, subject encyclopedias, electronic databases, websites, or other reference sources.

- Step 2: As you locate potential sources of information, complete a source record card (see Figure 4.10) for each source. Be sure to include all required information—this will save the work of going back and looking for it later. The type of source will dictate the information that must be included in citations and references. Figure 4.11 provides a summary of the pieces of information needed to correctly cite sources.

- Step 3: Review the abstract as you locate each source. Next, review the discussion section if the article comes from a scholarly journal. If the source is a book, glance at the table of contents and index. This will be useful in determining whether the source contains information that is relevant to your study.

- Step 4: Read through the bibliographies of sources that you locate. You might discover that the author has cited articles that would be useful for your study!

Step 5: Citing Sources of Information Using the APA Format

Given the wide variety of communication contexts (e.g., rhetoric, interpersonal, media studies), scholars may adopt diverse writing styles when reporting on the research in their

Source	Citation Elements Needed
BOOK	• Author's Name (may be more than one) • Date of Publication/Copyright • Title · • Publisher • City/State where published
PRINT JOURNAL ARTICLE	• Author's Name (may be more than one) • Publication Date • Title of Article • Title of Journal • Volume Number • Issue Number • Page numbers of article • Digital Object Identifiers (doi)
ELECTRONIC FULL-TEXT VERSION OF A PRINT JOURNAL ARTICLE	• Same info as for Print Journals • Database name or access path • Date the article was accessed • NOTE: Some electronic versions of articles may not include page numbers
WEBPAGE	• Author's Name • Title or description of the page • URL • Date the page was accessed
MAGAZINE ARTICLE	• Author's Name • Publication Date • Title of Article • Title of Magazine • Volume Number • Issue Number • Page numbers of article
NEWSPAPER ARTICLE	• Author's Name (if available) • Publication Date (Month/Day/Year) • Title of Article • Title of Newspaper • Page Number
Interviews with People	• Interviewee's Name • Date of Interview

Figure 4.11 APA Information

particular area. Consider the fact that each student in this class has a unique writing style. If your professor did not provide any guidelines for how the paper should be written, sources that should be included, or page length, chances are each paper written in your class would be vastly different in terms of format. The same is true for research that is published in academic journals. Guidelines exist to provide standards for how sources and references should be cited and how papers should be formatted.

Any researcher who is writing an article for publication is required to adhere to publication guidelines. Although a host of different style manuals exist (e.g., MLA, *The Chicago Manual of Style*), the preferred format for most communication journals is **APA style**. APA is a style of writing that was developed and is revised by the APA. Every detail of the format required for research papers is described in the *Publication Manual of the American Psychological*

Association (APA, 2010). Most libraries keep a copy of the manual at the reference desk, and numerous online sites provide summaries for quick reference (http://www.apastyle.org/). To correctly adhere to format guidelines, it is important to understand what information must be referenced in a research paper and how sources of information should be cited. Figure 4.12

Section of Paper	Citation Elements Needed
General Format of Paper	• 1 inch margins top, bottom, left & right • 12 point font (Times Roman or Courier) • Double space throughout paper • Align along left margin • Paragraph indentions 5 spaces • Page number located 1 inch from right edge of paper on first line of every page (including title page) • Running head on every page located five spaces to the left of the page number on every page • Use active voice
Page Order	• Title • Abstract • Body of Paper • References • Appendices • Footnotes • Tables • Figures
Title Page	• This is always page 1 • Include Running Head, Paper Title, Author, Institutional Affiliation, and Author Note. • All text is double-spaced • The Words "Running head:" should be followed by the Running head in All Capital Letters.
Abstract	• One paragraph summary of highlights of paper • Begins on page 2 • 120 words or less • Heading "Abstract" centered and bolded on first line below header • Body of abstract in block format, left justified • From this point forward, the words "Running head:" are no longer needed, but the running head itself should still be left justified with the page number right justified.
Body	• Begins on page 3 • Tile of paper centered on first line below header • Main headings (i.e., Methods, Results, Discussion) are centered using upper and lowercase letters • Subheadings are italicized and left justified using upper and lowercase letters
Reference Page	• Begins on a separate page • Heading "References" is centered and bolded on first line after header • Names in alphabetical order of last name
Appendices	• Begins on a separate page • Heading "Appendix" is centered on first line below header • For more than one appendix use "Appendix A" "Appendix B" and so forth
Tables	• Begins on a separate page • Heading "Table 1" (or Table 2, etc.) is left justified on the fist line below the header. • Double space after the title "Table x" and type the table title left justified

Figure 4.12 APA Style Checklist

shows a checklist of format guidelines to refer to when preparing a research paper for submission to a conference or journal. Information about general formatting issues (such as margins, font size, and spacing) as well as details about the layout of subsequent pages and sections in the paper is included. It is important to note that this list is by no means comprehensive. Rather, it is designed to provide a quick check to avoid falling into the APA style traps.

WHAT INFORMATION MUST BE REFERENCED?

As a general rule, all work done by other researchers that you wish to include in your own study must be referenced and cited. Any instance in which you include the exact words of another author must be quoted. Not giving proper credit to their work is considered plagiarism. Typically, any information you do not reference will be interpreted to be general knowledge or your own work. Information that is considered general knowledge does not need to be referenced. For example, it is common knowledge that George H. W. Bush was the president of the United States, so it is unnecessary to cite a source for that particular fact.

A good strategy to use when writing your paper is to build your reference list as you work on the text of the paper. As you include a source in the paper, scroll down to a reference page and list the source using APA format. This is where the information included on your source record cards (Figure 4.10) will come in handy. As a general rule, the reference page should begin on a separate page. The title "References" should be centered on the first line below the running head. All sources included in the references should be alphabetized by the first author's last name. Each reference includes four primary elements: the author(s) name, year of publication, title of book and or article, and retrieval information. In Figure 4.13, you can see a sample of what many journal articles published in the field of communication look like on the title page. An example of a reference for a journal article would look like the reference in Figure 4.14.

Journal of Generic Communication, Volume 9: 1–11, 2012
Copyright # Name of Publisher,
ISSN: 1081-07xx print/1087-04xx online
DOI: 10.1090/108107304902714xx

6th Edition of the APA Style Manual: New Trends & Changes

Jason S. Wrench

SUNY New Paltz

Candice Thomas-Maddox

Ohio University Lancaster

Figure 4.13 Sample Article

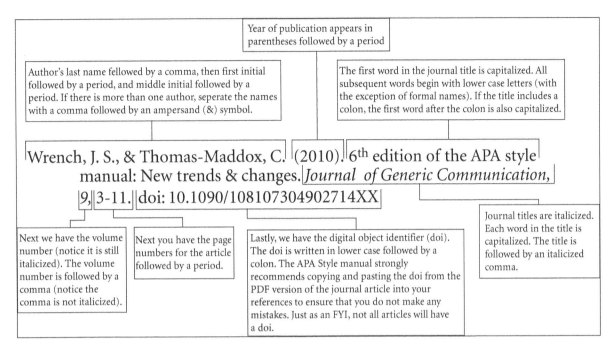

Figure 4.14 APA Reference

Figure 4.15 includes information for citing a variety of sources. If you have a source that is not included on this list, please consult your librarian, the APA style manual, or an online APA style guide. Finally, Figure 4.16 provides the various ways articles should be cited within the text of a paper. Note that different types of author combinations will lead to different requirements for your in-text **citations**.

CITING SOURCES OF INFORMATION

There are four general guidelines to consider when including citations. First, citations should be included for all sources of information that you have directly quoted in the paper. Second, citations should be included when summarizing or paraphrasing information from another source. Although you are not directly quoting the source, it is still important to let your reader know where you located the original information. Third, citations should be used when you want to direct your reader's attention to relevant research or important facts or information. Finally, citations are not required for information that is common knowledge. We will discuss each of these in the sections that follow.

Parenthetical Citations

Parenthetical citations (also referred to as internal citations) are used when you are including information taken directly from another source. This enables the reader to identify where information was obtained, and it lends credibility and authority to your research. Citing sources of information is often one of the most difficult aspects of research writing for some students because they are reluctant to use the words of others. We have all received information from our instructors warning us about the penalties for plagiarizing the work of others. But do not forget that the very nature of scholarly research *requires* you to use the work of

Research Article in a Journal—One Author, No doi	Wrench, J. S. (2010). Development and validity testing of the Risk Communicator Style Scale. *Human Communication, 13*, 233–257.
Research Article in a Journal—Two to Five Authors with a doi	Teven, J. J., Richmond, V. P., McCroskey, J. C., & McCroskey, L. L. (2010). Updating relationships between communication traits and communication competence. *Communication Research Reports, 27*, 263–270. doi:10.1080/0882 4096.2010.496331
Book – One Author	Kasssing, J. (2011). *Dissent in organizations*. Malden, MA: Polity Press.
Edited Book	Daly, J. A., McCroskey, J. C., Ayres, J., Hopf, T., Ayres Sonandré, D. M., & Wongprasert, T. K. (Eds.). (2009). *Avoiding communication: Shyness, reticence, and communication apprehension* (3rd ed.). Cresskill, NJ: Hampton Press.
Chapter in an Edited Book – One Author	Chory, R. M. (2010). Media entertainment and verbal aggression: Content, effects, and correlates. In T. A. Avtgis & A. S. Rancer (Eds.), *Arguments, aggression, and conflict: New directions in theory and research* (pp. 177–197). New York, NY: Routledge.
Chapter in an Edited Book – Two or More Authors	Bryant, E. M., Marmo, J., & Ramirez, A., Jr. (2011). A functional approach to social networking sites. In K. B. Wright & L. M. Webb (Eds.), *Computer mediated communication in personal relationships* (pp. 3–20). New York, NY: Peter Lang.
Newspaper Article	Richtel, M. (2011, December 18). Reframing the debate over using phones behind the wheel. *The New York Times*, p. A25.
Magazine Article	Spenner, P. (2010, December). Why you need a new-media "ringmaster". *Harvard Business Review, 88*(12), 78–79.
Preprint Version of an Article	Regazzi, J. J. (in press). Constrained? – An analysis of U.S. academic library shifts in spending, staffing and utilization, 1998–2008. *College and Research Libraries*. Retrieved from http://crl.acrl.org/content/early/2011/09/21/crl-260.full.pdf
Blog	Wrench, J. S. (2011, October 28). Stand Up, speak out: The practice and ethics of public speaking [Web log post]. Retrieved from http://www.jasonswrench.com/blog/blog1.php/stand-up-speak-out-the
Vlog	Wrench, J. S. (2009, May 15). Instructional communication [Video file]. Retrieved from http://www.learningjournal.com/Learning-Journal-Videos/instructional-communication.htm
Discussion Board	Wrench, J. S. (2009, May 21). NCA's i-tunes project [Online forum comment]. Retrieved from http://www.linkedin.com/groupAnswers?viewQuestionAndAnswers
E-mail List	Wrench, J. S.. (2009, June 19). Communicast [Electronic mailing list message]. Retrieved from http://lists.psu.edu/cgi-bin/wa?A2=ind0906&L=CRTNET&T=0 &F=&S=&P=20514
Podcast	Wrench, J. S. (Producer). (2011, December 21). *Communication apprehension* [Audio podcast]. Retrieved from http://www.communicast.info/CA.mp3
Electronic-Only Book	Richmond, V. P., Wrench, J. S., & Gorham, J. (2009). *Communication, affect, and learning in the classroom* (3rd ed.). Retrieved from http://www.jasonswrench.com/affect
Electronic-Only Journal Article	Holton, A. E., & Lewis, S. C. (2011). Journalists, social media, and the use of humor on Twitter. *Electronic Journal of Communication, 21*(1&2), Retrieved from http://www.cios.org/www/ejcmain.htm

Figure 4.15 Sample APA References

Continued

Electronic Version of a Printed Book	Wood, A. F., & Smith, M. J. (2004). *Online communication: Linking technology, identity & culture* (2nd ed.). Retrieved from http://books.google .com/books
Online Magazine	Lachlan, K.A. (2011, December). Using institutions of faith to communicate about crises and emergencies. *Communication Currents, 6*(6). Retrieved from http://www.communicationcurrents.com
Online Newspaper	Clifford, S. (2011, November 2). With an app, your next date could be just around the corner. *The New York Times*. Retrieved from http://www.nytimes.com
Entry in an Online Reference Work	Viswanth, K. (2008). Health communication. In W. Donsbach (Ed.), *The international encyclopedia of communication*. Retrieved from http://www .communicationencyclopedia.com. doi: 10.1111/b.9781405131995.2008.x
Entry in an Online Reference Work, No Author	Communication. (2009). In *Collins English dictionary* (10th ed.). Retrieved from http://dictionary.reference.com/browse/communication
E-Reader Device	Lutgen-Sandvik, P., & Davenport Sypher, B. (2009). *Destructive organizational communication: Processes, consequences, & constructive ways of organizing.* [Kindle version]. Retrieved from http://www.amazon.com

	Citation Listed in the Text		Citation Set Apart from the Text	
Type of Citation	*First Time*	*Subsequent Times*	*First Time*	*Subsequent Times*
One work by one author	Wrench (2012)	Wrench (2012)	(Wrench, 2012)	(Wrench, 2012)
One work by two authors	Wrench and McCroskey (2012)	Wrench and McCroskey (2012)	(Wrench & McCroskey, 2012)	(Wrench & McCroskey, 2012)
One work by three to five authors	Wrench, Thomas-Maddox, Richmond, and McCroskey (2012)	Wrench et al. (2012)	(Wrench, Thomas-Maddox, Richmond, & McCroskey, 2012)	(Wrench et al., 2012)
One work by six or more authors	Wrench et al. (2012)	Wrench et al. (2012)	(Wrench et al., 2012)	(Wrench et al., 2012)
Groups (readily identified through abbreviation)	National Communication Association (NCA, 2012)	NCA (2012)	(National Communication Association [NCA], 2012)	(NCA, 2012)
Groups (no abbreviation)	Generic University (2012)	Generic University (2012)	(Generic University, 2012)	(Generic University, 2012)
Author (no date)	Wrench (n.d.)	Wrench (n.d.)	(Wrench, n.d.)	(Wrench, n.d.)
Author with manuscript in press	Wrench (in press)	Wrench (in press)	(Wrench, in press)	(Wrench, in press)

Figure 4.16 APA Parenthetical Citations

others to build a rationale for your own work. After all, the foundation for research is built on the unanswered questions or weaknesses of previous studies.

Parenthetical citations include three primary elements of information. These include the author's last name, the date of publication, and page number if a direct quote from the source is included in the text of the literature review. The format used to cite sources depends on the goal of the reference. If your goal is to highlight a specific concept or idea, typically the parenthetical citation information would be included at the end of the sentence. Suppose your goal is to highlight the scholarship of a particular researcher. The parenthetical citation should begin with the researcher's last name, followed by the year of the article you are citing in parentheses. When the goal is to follow a chronological order when citing information, the year of the source should appear first, followed by the author's name. Examples of how to cite information for these three goals are included in Figure 4.17.

Quotations and Paraphrases

Quotations involve the use of another author's exact words in your study. It is important to give credit where credit is due. After all, not citing a source is considered plagiarism. As a general rule, use direct quotations only if you have a good reason for doing so. Including numerous quotations from sources causes the author's own voice and ideas to become "lost" in the project. Ensure proper credit is given to sources by using the author's exact words, including the quotations in quotation marks (unless you are citing a long source, in which case it should be included in an indented block), and indicating the page number where the quotation is published.

Paraphrasing refers to including another author's ideas in your own words and involves summarizing or highlighting one or two important points from the author. Consider the following example:

ORIGINAL

"It is important to recognize that no single artifact, value, or assumption is, or can create, an organization's culture." (Keyton, 2005, p. 28)

PARAPHRASE

Keyton (2005) emphasizes that one cannot simply examine only one dimension of an organization and understand the creation or current culture. Rather, a researcher must be willing to examine multiple facets of the organization to gain a comprehensive understanding of the history and factors that have led to the existing culture.

Remember that paraphrases should always include the author's name and the year of the publication from which the information was retrieved. Typically, paraphrases are not enclosed within quotation marks or indented. After all, these words represent your interpretation of the source's work and are not words taken directly from the article. Some find paraphrasing to be difficult at first. We recommend reviewing several examples of published work to increase your familiarity and comfort with the style used to cite information from other sources.

Use quotations to highlight strategically selected information. You have probably been told by teachers to provide as much evidence as possible in support of your thesis. But packing your paper with quotations will not necessarily strengthen your argument. The majority of your paper should still be your original ideas in your own words (after all, it is your paper). And quotations are only one type of evidence. Well-balanced papers may also make use of paraphrases, data, and statistics. The types of evidence you use will depend in part on the conventions of the discipline or audience for which you are writing.

One of the biggest mistakes novice researchers make is including excessive direct quotations. Remember, the goal is to be original, so if more than 5 percent of your paper is directly

Focus of Citation	Sample Citation
Conceptual/Idea	Physicians and other medical professionals personally use humor as a means of coping with the uncertainty that surrounds the medical profession (Bosk, 1996; Wanzer, Booth-Butterfield, & Booth-Butterfield, 1997).
Researcher	Fitzpatrick (1993) described patient satisfaction as an "emotional link to healthcare."
Chronology	In 1991, Booth-Butterfield and Booth-Butterfield identified the concept of humor orientation, otherwise referred to as HO.

Figure 4.17 Internal Citations

quoted from other sources, you are not really being original. A good general rule of thumb is you should probably not have more than one direct quotation for a single section of a paper.

You should never have just a string of quotations in a paper. When you use quotations, you should (1) provide a clear context for the quotation, (2) attribute the quotation to its original source, (3) explain the significance of the quotation, and (4) provide the correct parenthetical citation. Note that there are four steps to using quotations, and none of those steps involves just stringing a series of quotations together with no explanation or context.

Using Direct Quotations

There is no great single rule for explaining when to use direct quotations. However, there are some pretty good questions to help you decide if that direct quotation is actually necessary:

1. Does the quotation contain exact wording needed for technical accuracy (e.g., definition, law, regulation, theory, etc.)?
2. Does the quotation clearly show that a recognized authority supports your argument?
3. Does the quotation contain a contested or critical claim?
4. Does the quotation contain moving or historically important language?
5. Does the quotation include a term or expression coined or created by the author?
6. Does the quotation explain a difficult or complex concept in a concise manner?

APA Paper Formatting

The last part of this chapter will discuss how to format your paper using APA style. Although the next chapter will discuss what goes in each section of a paper, there are a few formatting issues we must discuss first. In this section, we will look at formatting issues related to the title page, abstract, first page, and reference page.

CREATING A TITLE PAGE

The title page is the page that goes on top of your actual document when you are getting ready to either turn in your paper to a professor or send it off to a conference or journal for possible publication. There are a number of unique parts of an APA title page that may be tricky if you are not used to working with APA style. Figure 4.18 shows what a title page should look like.

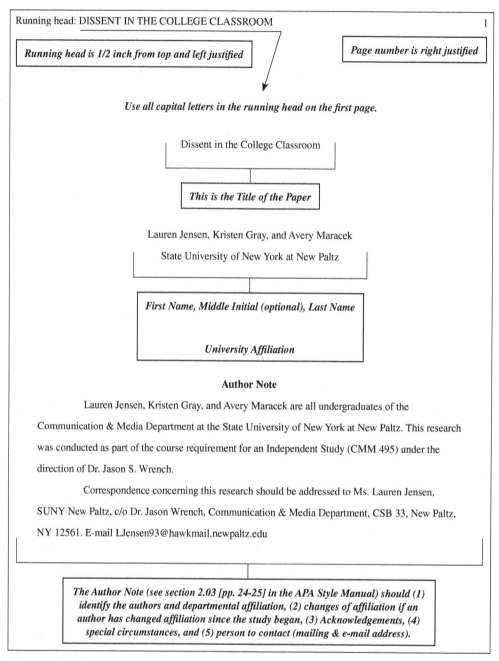

Running head: DISSENT IN THE COLLEGE CLASSROOM   1

Running head is 1/2 inch from top and left justified   *Page number is right justified*

Use all capital letters in the running head on the first page.

Dissent in the College Classroom

This is the Title of the Paper

Lauren Jensen, Kristen Gray, and Avery Maracek

State University of New York at New Paltz

First Name, Middle Initial (optional), Last Name

University Affiliation

Author Note

Lauren Jensen, Kristen Gray, and Avery Maracek are all undergraduates of the Communication & Media Department at the State University of New York at New Paltz. This research was conducted as part of the course requirement for an Independent Study (CMM 495) under the direction of Dr. Jason S. Wrench.

Correspondence concerning this research should be addressed to Ms. Lauren Jensen, SUNY New Paltz, c/o Dr. Jason Wrench, Communication & Media Department, CSB 33, New Paltz, NY 12561. E-mail LJensen93@hawkmail.newpaltz.edu

The Author Note (see section 2.03 [pp. 24-25] in the APA Style Manual) should (1) identify the authors and departmental affiliation, (2) changes of affiliation if an author has changed affiliation since the study began, (3) Acknowledgements, (4) special circumstances, and (5) person to contact (mailing & e-mail address).

Figure 4.18 APA Cover Page

The first thing you may notice about an APA cover page is that it has something called a "running head." A running head is a series of words that is placed on every page, followed by a page number so a reader knows that all of the pages with that running head on it belong to the same document. Often people who review manuscripts for conferences or publications will read 20–50 manuscripts at a time, so the running head prevents pages from getting misplaced or attached to the wrong document. A good running head should be distinct and relate to the overarching topic of your paper. A running head can be no longer than 50 characters counting letters, characters, and spacing between words. You will notice that on the first line of the cover page you type the words "Running head," followed by your actual running head in all capital letters. By doing this, you enable your reader to quickly see what your running head is. You will also notice that your cover page contains your running head in the upper right-hand corner, down half an inch from the top of the page. Your running head is then followed by five spaces and then the page number. Most computer programs have header programs built in to enable you to place your running head and page numbers automatically rather than attempting to do it by hand.

Next on a cover page, you will find the paper's title. A title should sell a reader on what the overarching topic of your paper is going to be about, so your reader can see whether he or she wants to read further. APA recommends that your title be approximately 10–12 words, but this is only a guideline. Some titles are considerably longer and some are shorter—it all depends on what you need so your intended audience will realize that your paper relates to a topic they are interested in reading. Titles should also avoid using abbreviations, opting instead for spelling out technical acronyms. Titles are often used for cataloging research articles and papers, so ensuring that your title contains all of the appropriate key terms and words makes for a more efficient title.

The last part of the title page consists of the author's name and university/professional affiliation or the authors' names and university/professional affiliations. Authors in academia are not listed alphabetically on a paper. Generally speaking, author names are listed according to who contributed the most to a specific project. Although many articles have one author, other projects have listed as many as 900 authors. Admittedly, most papers rarely have more than 5 authors, but some projects will have more people who have actually contributed to the success of the research project. Ultimately, the lead author on a project is the person who has contributed the most to the conceptualization and enactment of the research project itself and is listed as the first author. Often, the first author then makes the determination of who shall be the second author, third author, and so on, on the cover page. In addition to listing the authors' names on a project, each author's university/organizational affiliation is also listed below her or his name.

CREATING AN ABSTRACT

The second page in an APA styled paper is an **abstract**. Although what goes into an abstract will be discussed in the next chapter, we do want to discuss the basic formatting of an abstract here. Figure 4.19 contains an example abstract.

Abstracts should have one-inch margins all the way around (except for the running head, which is still half an inch from the top of the page). The word "Abstract" is centered on the first line, which should be one inch from the top of the page. The abstract should be double spaced and left justified. "Left justified" means that there is not an indention or tab on the first line of written text.

CREATING THE FIRST PAGE

The third page of your paper is your first page of actual text and contains the text related to the actual paper you plan on writing. However, there are still a few important formatting issues that you should be aware of when creating your first page.

Figure 4.20 shows the first page of the paper by Jensen, Gray, and Maracek that we have been examining in the past few figures. You will see that the first few lines of the paper contain the same title that you have listed on the cover page. The reason that your title is listed

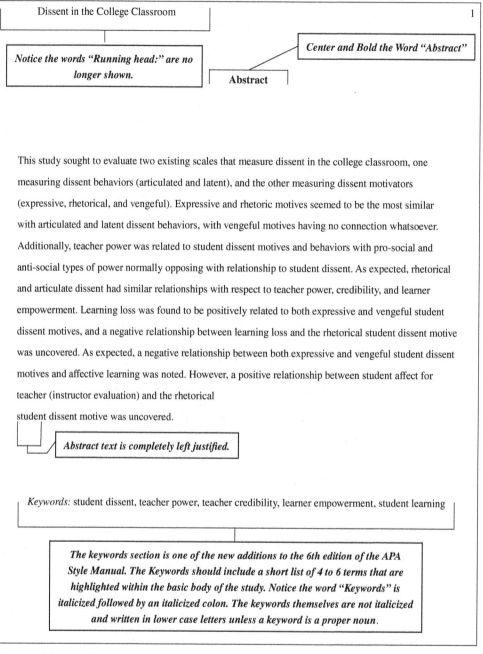

Dissent in the College Classroom   1

Notice the words "Running head:" are no longer shown.

Abstract

Center and Bold the Word "Abstract"

This study sought to evaluate two existing scales that measure dissent in the college classroom, one measuring dissent behaviors (articulated and latent), and the other measuring dissent motivators (expressive, rhetorical, and vengeful). Expressive and rhetoric motives seemed to be the most similar with articulated and latent dissent behaviors, with vengeful motives having no connection whatsoever. Additionally, teacher power was related to student dissent motives and behaviors with pro-social and anti-social types of power normally opposing with relationship to student dissent. As expected, rhetorical and articulate dissent had similar relationships with respect to teacher power, credibility, and learner empowerment. Learning loss was found to be positively related to both expressive and vengeful student dissent motives, and a negative relationship between learning loss and the rhetorical student dissent motive was uncovered. As expected, a negative relationship between both expressive and vengeful student dissent motives and affective learning was noted. However, a positive relationship between student affect for teacher (instructor evaluation) and the rhetorical student dissent motive was uncovered.

Abstract text is completely left justified.

Keywords: student dissent, teacher power, teacher credibility, learner empowerment, student learning

The keywords section is one of the new additions to the 6th edition of the APA Style Manual. The Keywords should include a short list of 4 to 6 terms that are highlighted within the basic body of the study. Notice the word "Keywords" is italicized followed by an italicized colon. The keywords themselves are not italicized and written in lower case letters unless a keyword is a proper noun.

Figure 4.19 APA Abstract Formatting

here as well as on your cover page is that often editors and conference reviewers do not ever see your cover page because academics use what is called "blind review." Blind review is the process where an editor or conference program planner sends out papers anonymously to other scholars and has them evaluate the scholarly quality of the paper. Because editors and conference program planners want honest feedback about the quality of the paper, papers should have no identifying marks on them that would let a reviewer know who the author is.

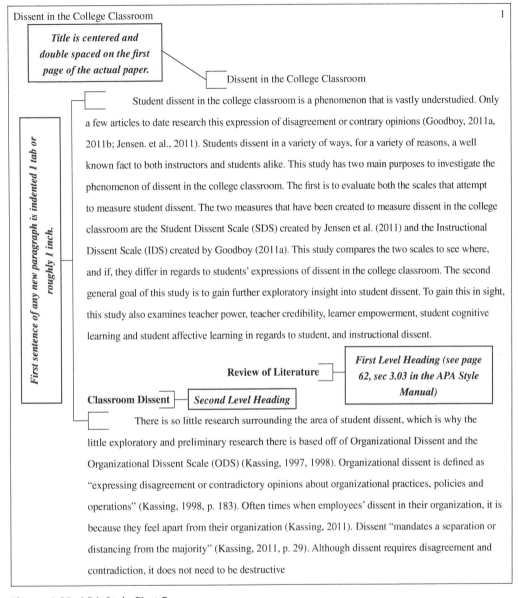

Figure 4.20 APA Style First Page

For this reason, cover pages are taken off papers when they are sent out to reviewers, so it is important to have the title of your paper on the first page of the actual manuscript.

After the title on the first page of your written manuscript, you always indent new paragraphs using the tab function on your word processor. If you do not have a fancy word processor, one tab is approximately 10 spaces on your average keyboard. Although this section gives you some basic information on how to format a paper, you should really buy a copy of the most recent version of the APA style manual because there are so many other formatting issues that we cannot go into in this textbook. Everything from politically correct language to formatting tables is covered in the APA style manual, so make sure you buy a copy if you have not already done so.

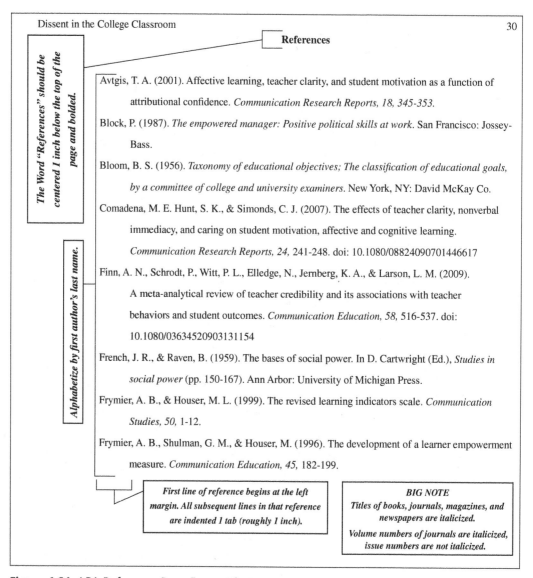

Figure 4.21 APA Reference Page Formatting

CREATING THE REFERENCE PAGE

The aspect of APA formatting we will discuss in this section is how to format a **reference page** using APA style. Although you may have formatted works cited pages, a reference page is distinctly different. Figure 4.21 shows a brief reference page.

The first thing you will see on a reference page is the running head in the upper right-hand corner, like it has been on every page of your manuscript. Next, you will have the word "References" centered one inch from the top of the page. From here, place all of your references for every source that is cited within your manuscript alphabetically by the first author on the source. The first line of the citation is left justified, but the rest of the citation is aligned to the right one tab (or 10 spaces). Also, note that the reference page is double spaced.

There are many different problems you can run into when creating a reference page, so we strongly urge you to buy a copy of the APA style manual because our brief help section here is simply not adequate to explain every citation you may face.

Conclusion

In this chapter, we have examined how to pick a topic, how to find research materials using a variety of different tools, and how to use basic APA style. In the next chapter, we will examine the various parts of a research paper, with special attention paid to how to write literature reviews, how to write a rationale section (research questions and hypotheses), and writing method sections.

KEY TERMS

Abstract	Citation	Reference page
APA style	Electronic database	Secondary source
Author search	Paraphrase	Subject search
Axiom	Parenthetical citations	Title search
Backtracking	Primary source	Truncation symbols
Boolean logic	Quotation	

REFERENCES

American Psychological Association. (2010). *Publication manual of the American Psychological Association* (6th ed.). Washington, DC: American Psychological Association.

Berger, C., & Calabrese, R. (1975). Some explorations in initial interaction and beyond: Toward a developmental theory of interpersonal communication. *Human Communication Research, 1*, 99–112.

Keyton, J. (2005). *Communication and organizational culture: A key to understanding work experiences.* Thousand Oaks, CA: Sage.

Read, B. (2006, October 27). Students flock to an easy-to-use reference, but professors warn that it's no sure thing. *Chronicle of Higher Education, 53* (10), A36.

Thomas, C., Booth-Butterfield, M., & Booth-Butterfield, S. (1995). Perceptions of deception, divorce disclosures, and communication satisfaction with parents. *Western Journal of Communication, 59*, 228–245.

West, R., & Turner, L. H. (2006). *Introducing communication theory: Analysis and application* (3rd ed.). Boston, MA: McGraw–Hill.

Wrench, J. S., & Booth-Butterfield, M. (2003). Increasing patient satisfaction and compliance: An examination of physician humor orientation, compliance-gaining strategies, and perceived credibility. *Communication Quarterly, 51*, 482–503.

Wrench, J. S., Goding, A., Johnson, D., & Attias, B. (2011). *Stand up, speak out: The practice and ethics of public speaking.* Irvington, NY: Flat World Knowledge.

FURTHER READING

American Psychological Association. (2020). *Concise rules of APA Style: The official pocket style guide from the American Psychological Association* (6th ed.). Washington, DC: American Psychological Association.

Anderson, C. E., Carrell, A. T., & Widdifield, J. L., Jr. (2007). *What every student should know about citing sources with APA documentation*. Boston, MA: Allyn & Bacon.

Frey, L., Botan, C., & Kreps, G. (2000). *Investigating communication: An introduction to research methods* (2nd ed.). Englewood Cliffs, NJ: Prentice Hall.

Girden, E. R., & Kabacoff, R. I. (2011). *Evaluating research articles: From start to finish* (3rd ed.). Los Angeles, CA: Sage.

Hairston, M., & Ruszkiewicz, J. J. (1996) *The Scott, Foresman handbook for writers* (4th ed.). New York, NY: HarperCollins.

Hocking, J. E., Stacks, D. W., & McDermott, S. T. (2003). *Communication research* (3rd ed.). Boston, MA: Allyn & Bacon.

Salkind, N. J. (2004). *Statistics for people who (think they) hate statistics* (2nd ed.). Thousand Oaks, CA: Sage.

Singleton, R. A., Jr., & Straits, B. C. (1999). *Approaches to social research* (3rd ed.). New York, NY: Oxford University Press.

CHAPTER 5

Research Structure and Literature Reviews

CHAPTER OBJECTIVES

1 Understand the different sections of a research paper.
2 Understand the basic information that one should include in a study abstract.
3 Explain how to effectively write an introduction to a paper.
4 Apply the different methods for laying out a literature review.
5 Describe the different parts of a methods section.
6 Explain the basic purposes for both results and discussion sections.
7 Describe techniques for reading academic research articles.
8 Explain some basic tips associated with writing a first draft.

Organization is one of the most important processes in any endeavor we undertake. Many people try to jump right into the writing process without making sure all of the necessary tools, safeguards, and supplies are readily at hand. Have you ever tried to build something, only to realize halfway through your project that you do not have a tool you need? Have you ever known someone who bought a do-it-yourself building project only to finish the project and realize that they have a number of leftover parts? Being organized helps people to see deficiencies and prepare for future success. Whether you are building a bridge or writing an article for a communication journal, you must be organized in your thinking and layout to achieve success.

Many authors do not organize their research articles in an effective manner, only to realize halfway through the writing process that they are missing a key point. Other people finish writing a paper and realize that the paper has serious gaps in logic. Being an organized writer means selecting and arranging the appropriate ideas and materials for the paper into a logical and discernible pattern. In other words, an organized writer has thought out her or his paper and created a clear pattern that readers can follow. Additionally, if a reader can understand a paper, the reader will recall the information more easily.

Although most of the information in this chapter is similar to the information that students receive in basic public speaking courses every year, there are some specific aspects to organizing a research paper that are unique. This chapter will focus on how to organize an article into a format that will ultimately help readers retain information. To examine organization, this chapter will discuss the major parts of a research paper (abstract, literature review, methods, results, and discussion) in separate sections. Furthermore, this chapter will dissect portions of an article by Jason S. Wrench and Melanie Booth-Butterfield (2003) to aid in your understanding of the concepts discussed here. To read the entire article by Wrench and Booth-Butterfield, see the textbook's website.

The Abstract

You may have heard the old adage, "You never get a second chance to make a good first impression." This statement is undeniably true. No matter how hard we try, people will always remember the first time they met us. Although writing a research paper is not exactly like meeting someone, the paper's abstract is just as important as an introduction is when meeting a person. For example, if you bore someone the first time you meet them, the chances that the two of you will become friends is not likely. Similarly, if you bore someone in your abstract, you will turn that person off to your paper immediately and possibly even turn that person off to your topic in general. If you are an interesting person to talk to when you first meet someone, people will be drawn to you as a person. Likewise, if your paper has a good abstract, people will be drawn to you as an author and ultimately to your topic. An abstract, simply defined, is a short paragraph at the beginning of a scholarly paper that concisely and comprehensively explains the contents of the paper. In other words, an abstract is a snapshot of the overall paper.

According to the *Publication Manual of the American Psychological Association* (APA, 2010), an abstract should be accurate, self-contained, and concise/specific. First, an abstract should be accurate, or correctly reflect what occurs in the paper itself. If your paper is about public speaking and your abstract discusses football, your abstract is not reflecting what actually occurs in the paper. Second, an abstract should be self-contained; it should not need any specialized information for the reader to understand what it is communicating. To be self-contained, an abstract should clearly define any abbreviations and acronyms, spell out names of tests and/or drugs, define any unique terms, and accurately cite any relevant research without directly quoting the source. Finally, a good abstract should be concise and specific. An abstract is not a complete retelling of your entire paper, but should give as much information as needed to help a potential reader understand what your paper is discussing. According to the APA manual, an abstract should not be more than 120 words in length. Although that may sound like a lot of words, it is not. An abstract should explain to your readers your basic purpose for writing the paper and any relevant results and conclusions. However, many research projects can have more than 10–20 results or major conclusions, so it is usually best to limit your number of conclusions in the abstract to the five most important findings.

One note should be made about the abstract. Although we are presenting the abstract at this point in this text to present the parts of a paper according to APA style in the order in which they are read, an abstract is written after everything else is complete. You cannot write a meaningful abstract until you have completed a study. Your abstract is like a quick snapshot of everything you did in your study.

Look at the abstract in Figure 5.1. Note how the abstract explains in a brief manner what is actually discussed in the rest of the paper. Often when researchers are conducting literature

This study examined the impact that patients' perceptions of a physician's humor orientation, credibility, and compliance gaining strategies had on their satisfaction and compliance. Perceived physician humor orientation positively related to perceived physician credibility, physician compliance-gaining strategies, and patient satisfaction. Other positive relationships among perceived physician credibility, physician compliance gaining strategies, and patient satisfaction emerged. Compliance did not relate significantly to physician humor orientation and perceived credibility. Aspects of patient satisfaction and physician use of compliance-gaining strategies affected compliance. Additionally, this study revealed minimal differences among data collection methods (undergraduate ($N = 44$), graduate ($N = 48$), general public ($N = 66$), and online participation ($N = 26$)).	General sentence explaining the overall purpose of the study. Goes into specific detail related to the various findings in this study. Lastly, the abstract mentions a secondary analysis examining the different data collection methods employed in this study.

Analysis	
Accurate	If you read the actual article completely, you will notice that the basic purpose discussed at the beginning of the abstract correctly explains what occurs throughout the study.
Self-contained	Although the abstract may be confusing if you do not know what the terminology means (e.g., perceived credibility, physician humor orientation, etc.), notice that no acronyms are used and tests were not specifically referred to by name. For example, instead of referring to a Physician's HO the authors specifically call it a physician's humor orientation.
Concise and specific	If you compare the results section with the results described above, you will notice that the results discussed above are the major results discussed in the article itself.

Figure 5.1 Article Abstract

searches, they will read only the abstract to see whether the article contains useful information. In essence, understanding the purpose of an abstract can actual greatly reduce the time it takes to complete a full literature search.

The Introduction

Now that we have discussed the first part of a paper, we can focus on the "traditional" **introduction** of a research paper. A good introduction should have six basic components: an attention-getter, a link to the topic, a statement of the topic's significance, an espousal of credibility, a thesis statement, and a preview (McCroskey, Wrench, & Richmond, 2003).

ATTENTION-GETTER

The first part of an introduction is referred to as an attention-getter because this portion of an introduction should be able to grab your reader's attention. After the abstract, the first words in your paper are probably the most important in your document. If you are able to grab your reader's attention in a unique or captivating way, your reader will continue to read what you have to say. There are a number of attention-getters that writes can use to successfully capture the reader's interest.

Using Statistics or Claims

One way to get the reader's attention is to alarm her or him with the use of a startling statistic or claim. People have a tendency to respond to information that has a statistical assessment attached. Although statistics can be useful to demonstrate the extent to which there is a problem or the occurrence of a phenomenon, statistics can also be misleading and come back to haunt a writer. When using statistical information, knowing how the statistic was generated can add credence to your message. Consider the following statement: "According to a new study, 50 percent of the people exposed to a new drug will develop liver cancer" (Hause & Botner, 2000). If in this drug trial only two people had been exposed to the drug, repeating the results from this study as an attention-getter would be misleading.

Likewise, startling claims can be made to grab a reader's attention. "You have a greater chance of dying in your car on the way to the airport than you do once you have entered the terminal" (Smith, 2000) could be a startling claim to begin a paper on air safety. The same concerns that apply to startling statistics apply to startling claims; you must know the validity of the claim you are making.

When deciding whether a startling statistic or claim is a useful attention-getting device for a research paper, ask yourself three important questions. First, will this statistic or claim cause some readers to become interested in my research topic? If you start your research paper with a dull statistic or claim, readers are not likely to go beyond the introduction. Second, is the statistic or claim so outrageous that it could prevent someone from believing what I have to say? You must be careful to avoid offending the reader's logic with a statistic or claim. If an author wrote that "100 percent of Americans who travel in trains die," people would laugh at the author and think he or she was nuts. If an author actually used this outlandish statement, it would not matter whether the author had a citation for her or his statistic; people would be highly skeptical and simply dismiss the paper based on this one simple fact. Lastly, is there a better way of grabbing the audience's attention? Always ask yourself this question when deciding on an attention-getting device. Often our first idea for an attention-getting device is not ultimately the best device we can use.

Posing a Rhetorical Question

A **rhetorical question** asks the reader to simply ponder the question internally without audibly responding to it. Many research papers begin by stating right off the bat the overall theme of the study by posing a rhetorical question. For example, if an author was planning on studying communication apprehension across the life cycle (children, teenagers, young adults, and retirement age), he or she might ask, "Although the importance of communication apprehension to communication scholars is clear, how does communication apprehension affect people across the life cycle?" From this question, the author could discuss various articles that have examined communication apprehension in various populations or various age groups.

Using an Acknowledged Fact

The next way to grab an audience's attention is to start with a widely acknowledged fact and build on it. To use an acknowledged fact as an introduction, the fact must be fairly universal so that anyone who reads it will have the ability to quickly understand and agree with what has been written. For example, in the article by Chesebro (1999), he began by saying the following:

> Most people have encountered different types of listeners. Some people seem quite responsive and notice even the slightest of our nonverbal cues. Others carefully scrutinize and analyze our

messages. Some people can't wait until we just get to the point. Others look at their watches with the hope that we will recognize that they would rather be somewhere else. The way in which our interaction partners listen is important to us when we are the ones doing the talking. (p. 234)

In this attention-getter, Chesebro has clearly identified common problems that everyone experiences and notices when communicating with other people.

Using a Story or Illustration

The next way that an author can grab a reader's attention is to tell a story that relates to her or his topic. For example, if you are writing a paper about how test anxiety affects student performance in the classroom, you could start your paper off by explaining how once there was a student who missed every test day because of her or his apprehension, which ultimately caused the student to fail. Another possible way to grab your audience's attention is to use an illustration.

Whereas stories are the telling of real or pseudo-real events that relate to your topic, **illustrations** are more general stories that can be applied to a variety of different contexts. For example, one famous illustration is the story of the frog that agrees to transport a scorpion on its back across the river on the condition that the scorpion will not sting him. During the trip, the scorpion stings the frog. While the scorpion and frog are drowning, the frog asks why the scorpion broke his promise, to which the scorpion responds, "I'm a scorpion; I sting things." This short illustration can be applied to a number of contexts. You could use this illustration to begin a paper on how humans have innate personalities that cannot be changed, on the problems of being too trusting, or on how organizations change. Ultimately, the usefulness of an illustration lies in an author's clear connection from the illustration to the topic at hand.

Quoting or Acknowledging a Source

The last, and most common, way of introducing a paper is to directly quote or acknowledge another source. As discussed in the previous chapter, directly quoting a source is when author A copies the exact text of author B's document and places it verbatim into author A's new work. For example, in the article by Brummans and Miller (2004) the authors started by quoting a chunk of text from Schumacher that read

> Ortega y Gasset once remarked that "life is fired at us point-blank." We cannot say: "Hold it! I am not quite ready. Wait until I have sorted things out." Decisions have to be taken that we are not ready for; aims have to be chosen that we cannot see clearly. (Schumacher, 1995, p. 15)

From this quotation, Brummans and Miller then discuss how in the information age life moves quickly and our lives are earmarked by constant change.

The second way to grab an audience's attention is simply by acknowledging a source. As discussed in the previous chapter, acknowledging a source is when an author paraphrases specific information and then gives credit for that information to the scholars who are actually responsible for it. For example, in the article by Weber, Fornash, Corrigan, and Neupauer (2003), the authors started with, "Much of the research conducted in the instructional realm has dealt with the effect of affective variables on cognitive learning (Wanzer & Frymier, 1999)." In this attention-getter, the authors did not directly quote from Wanzer and Frymier; they paraphrased what Wanzer and Frymier wrote in their study.

LINK TO TOPIC

The next major part of the introduction is the link from the attention-getter to the actual topic of your paper. Some attention-getters are easy to link directly to your topic. For example, the attention-getter used by Chesebro (1999) discussed previously spends an entire paragraph explaining in common terms how he perceives the link between an individual's listening style and conversational sensitivity, which is the goal of his overall study. However, other attention-getters take more creativity to make a clear link to the topic. Of the examples listed in the previous section on attention-getting devices, the hardest one to directly link to a topic is usually an illustration (e.g., the scorpion and the frog), because an illustration is a metaphor for the topic itself, and not all metaphors are clearly seen by people reading them.

SIGNIFICANCE OF TOPIC

The third major step in the introduction of a paper is demonstrating why the topic is significant enough for your reader to care. If you are writing a paper about a communication phenomenon seen only by tribesmen in a remote tribe in South America, you are going to have a hard time demonstrating why academics in the United States should care about your topic. However, if you can demonstrate that this communication phenomenon is similar to something we do in the United States or contradicts something we think is communication fact, then you can help others see why your topic is significant. One of the hardest facts to get new researchers to understand is that research for research's sake is not significant. Every researcher should be able to clearly answer the "Why should we care?" or "So what?" question in a couple of sentences.

ESPOUSAL OF CREDIBILITY

The fourth major component of the introduction of a paper is the espousal of one's credibility to write a paper on the subject. Although in public speaking we talk about espousing one's credibility in terms of your personal qualifications for speaking on a subject, in writing papers credibility is less about explaining how one is credible and more about supporting one's assertions through the citation of empirical research. If you have not completely researched a concept, a trained reader will clearly see gaps in your literature that are extremely important. Within your introduction, you must start integrating literature appropriately both to help build your case for significance and to demonstrate that you have examined previous research and are not just stating your opinions. Even the number one researcher in the field of communication must demonstrate that a paper is thoroughly researched and is supported by the literature. For example, look at the article by McCroskey, Richmond, Johnson, and Smith (2004) to see how McCroskey and his colleagues thoroughly cite substantial previous research before starting the literature review.

THESIS AND PREVIEW

The fifth component of a good introduction is the thesis statement. A **thesis** is a short, declarative sentence that explains to a reader the purpose of the paper itself. If you are writing a paper on how cults use thought reform (brainwashing) to influence their victims, for example, your thesis may be, "The process of thought reform, although often misunderstood, is not difficult when a person is unknowingly vulnerable to outside influences." After the thesis, an author generally transitions into a brief preview of what will be examined in the literature review.

In a **preview**, the author lists the specific sections that he or she is planning on covering in the literature review of the paper. For example, to preview the thought reform paper, one could say, "To understand how thought reform occurs, an analysis of the history of thought reform research, common thought reform tactics, and how cults use these tactics will be examined in this literature review, followed by a series of hypotheses and research questions for the current study." In this case, each of the phrases mentioned in the preview would be a single distinct subsection written in the literature review.

Overall, the introduction portion of a paper is extremely important and truly focuses a reader's attention and helps a reader understand the scope and focus of a paper. This section has used a number of the articles from the textbook's website to illustrate various aspects of an introduction; an introduction by Wrench and Booth-Butterfield (2003) is shown in Figure 5.2.

At the end of visits to a personal physician, the physician generally will prescribe some sort of medication, treatment, or lifestyle change to help patients recover from, or cope with, medical problems. Since physicians reportedly have high credibility as healers in our society, one might assume that patients would follow their physician's directions. Yet, nearly 50% of all patients do not follow the prescribed treatment from their physicians (Stone, 1979). This statistic has not changed much in the last twenty years (Bullman, 1996). Such data link to a number of negative outcomes, not only for noncompliant patients, but others in the community as well. People who do not comply may contribute to higher medical costs and insurance rates because they are often subject to re-treatment as a result of therapeutic failures, recurring, or lingering infections, which can ultimately lead to surgical interventions and hospitalizations that initially are not necessary (Baskin, 1998). Surprisingly, noncompliance rates are as high for individuals suffering from severe chronic pain as they are for those having symptomless diseases (Tamaroff, Festa, Adesman, & Waco, 1992; Turk & Rudy, 1991). One possible way to rectify this lack of compliance is through better patient–physician interactions (Fitzpatrick, 1991). Therefore, it is useful to examine variables that may indicate whether one will follow a physician's directions.	Notice in the first two sentences how the purpose of this article is foreshadowed. An introductory discussion of the problem of patient noncompliance is initiated here. Transition to thesis statement.
Our study concerned how a physician's perceived humor orientation, credibility, and communication competence relate to patients' levels of satisfaction and their compliance. We begin this report by examining scholarly literature concerning patient compliance, patient satisfaction, and medical humor.	Thesis statement. Preview.

Analysis	
Attention-getter	This attention-getter was a statement of fact. Most people expect to be told about a medication, treatment, or lifestyle change at the conclusion of a medical interview.
Transition to topic	"Since physicians reportedly have high credibility as healers in our society, one might assume that patients would follow their physician's directions."
Significance of topic	Discussion of how noncompliance affects cost of medical care for everyone.
Espousal of credibility	Consistent citation of both primary and secondary sources throughout the introduction paragraph.
Thesis	"Our study concerned how a physician's perceived humor orientation, credibility, and communication competence relate to patients' levels of satisfaction and their compliance."
Preview	"We begin this report by examining scholarly literature concerning patient compliance, patient satisfaction, and medical humor."

Figure 5.2 Article Introduction

Literature Review

One of the most important parts of a research paper, and often the largest, is the literature review section. A **literature review** is the selection of available documents (published and unpublished) on a given topic that contain information, opinions, data, and evidence written from a particular point of view that aid in a reader's understanding of pertinent review prior to examining the results in a new study. For most people, the literature review is the easiest section to write and the one they are most familiar with writing. In many ways, a literature review is like a series of brief research papers about various related topics.

In an article by Rocca and Vogl-Bauer (1999) looking at sports fans' perceptions of appropriate fan communication, the researchers examined three major areas of literature. First, the authors discussed some background on the popularity and known behavior of sports enthusiasts, then discussed verbal aggression, and finally discussed how individuals identify with various teams. By clearly explaining the research previously completed in the three subcategories, Rocca and Vogl-Bauer were able to help the reader gain a full understanding of the current state of research in each area and how the three separate research areas could be studied together in the "Rationale for Research Questions" section of their article.

FIVE REASONS FOR LITERATURE REVIEWS

First, a literature review provides and explains necessary vocabulary for readers. One of the fundamental aspects of a literature review is that it is educational and definitional. A literature review must clearly explain all technical terms related to that research paper. In academia, we often create terms that have slightly different meanings than they do when used by the general public. For example, to communibiologists the term "psychoticism" refers to the degree to which an individual believes that society's rules pertain to her or him. If you ask people in the general public what psychoticism means, you will probably get definitions related to psychological disturbances such as antisocial personality disorder, schizophrenia, or borderline personality disorder. Even scholars in different subfields of the same discipline can examine the same term in slightly different ways, so it is always important to clearly specify what you mean by various terms in a literature review to ensure everyone is on the same page. Also, having clear definitions helps a researcher to "operationalize" her or his variables. Operationalizing variables is when a researcher determines how to measure a specific variable, which will be discussed in detail in Chapter 7.

The second reason we have literature reviews in academic research papers is because literature reviews place our current research into a historical context, which helps readers synthesize existing research in a concise manner. One of the basic goals of the literature review is to provide enough historical and conceptual information about a research topic so readers of the research will be able to adequately judge the merits and usefulness of a new research study. For example, if you were to write a literature review section about the variable *communication apprehension* and only mentioned articles written in the past year, you limit the type of information your readers will receive, and they will not have enough information to adequately judge your new study. This does not mean that you must include every article that has ever been written on the subject. In fact, the term *communication apprehension* appeared in more than 400 journal article titles, and this does not even include the journal articles that utilized communication apprehension within the study but did not include the term in the title. There is no way you can attempt to talk about each of these different articles in a literature review. In fact, there are actually around 15 different books that take on the concept of communication apprehension alone. Ultimately, when creating the historical context for a new study, it is important to find the most important pieces of research directly related to your study. Ultimately, if you find the best research sources, your reader should be able to understand where your new study fits into the history of research within a specific research area.

The third reason academics write literature reviews is because they aid in the explanation and rationalization for why specific variables have been chosen as an object of study in a research project. In quantitative research, scholars are never just studying one variable like communication apprehension. Instead, scholars examine a variety of variables together to gain an understanding of how those variables relate to or differ from each other. For example, the articles that accompany this text examine a wide array of different variables: Boiarsky, Long, and Thayer (1999)—children's television shows, content pacing, sound effects, and visual pacing; Brummans and Miller (2004)—organizational ambiguity and organizational effects; Chesebro (1999)—listening style and conversational sensitivity; Punyanunt (2000)—behavior alteration techniques, humor orientation, and humor effectiveness; McCroskey et al. (2004)—organizational orientations, job satisfaction, communication apprehension, nonverbal immediacy, sociocommunicative orientation, credibility, and human temperament; Rocca and Vogl-Bauer (1999)—verbal aggression, fan identification, and appropriate fan communicative messages; Thomas, Richmond, and McCroskey (1994)—nonverbal immediacy, sociocommunicative style; Weber et al. (2003)—cognitive learning, learner empowerment, and nonverbal immediacy); Wrench and Booth-Butterfield (2003)—humor orientation, credibility, compliance-gaining strategies, patient satisfaction, and patient compliance. As you can see from the short list of articles we present along with this text, a large variety of communication variables are studied in these 10 articles. More important, no one article utilizes the same combination of variables. Some studies include only a couple of variables, like Brummans and Miller (2004), who only study two variables. Other studies will examine a large number of variables; for instance, McCroskey et al. (2004) studied seven different variables. Ultimately, it is the job of a literature review to demonstrate why a researcher is studying only two variables or seven variables in a specific project.

The fourth major reason for writing a literature review is to help demonstrate what has been done in research and what still must be accomplished. We will never get to the point where there is no more research to be accomplished in the field of communication. A literature review should demonstrate that you have examined the literature closely enough to know that there are still avenues to be explored. Although there are some studies that replicate or reconduct previously completed studies, most research completed is new. Whether you are researching previously studied variables in a new context (political, educational, romantic relationships, physician–patient relationships, etc.) or researching variables that have never been examined together at all, literature reviews aid in explaining what has not been studied yet and why it should be studied at all.

The last reason scholars write literature reviews is to help establish the argument being tested in the study. In every study there is some argument being made. Like giving a persuasive speech, a literature review ends with a persuasive argument for either a hypothesis or a research question. Although these hypotheses and research questions will be discussed in more detail later in this chapter, we will introduce the two concepts here. First, a hypothesis is defined as a statement about the relationship between independent and dependent variables, whereas a research question is an explicit question researchers ask about variables of interest. Ultimately, whether one is able to form a hypothesis or research question is dependent on whether a researcher has the literature to support making a clear argument or hypothesis.

Now that we have examined the five main reasons academics write literature reviews, we can examine the two main sections of a literature review: previous research and study rationale.

PREVIOUS RESEARCH

The first major part of a literature review consists of an examination of pertinent previous research about the variables in your study. The previous research section of a literature review is what most people generally think of when they think about a literature review. This is the section where authors actually discuss previous research about the variables to be studied in the current paper or article. First, if you have completed your literature search in the way we discussed in the previous chapter, this section will be easy to write. Writing the previous research section is the part of the research process with which most people are familiar. In fact, you have probably been writing traditional "research papers" since you were in junior high or middle school. After you have done your literature search, you simply must determine how to organize the primary and secondary sources into a cohesive new product that clearly defines all key concepts, demonstrates the history of those concepts, and links those concepts together in your new research study to form your argument.

When organizing the previous research section in a literature review, there are two aspects to be considered (McCroskey et al., 2003). The first aspect to organizing the previous research section relates to the overall organization and style. Many people, when writing the previous research section of a literature review, will have one organizational pattern they start with and keep throughout the entire section. In essence, an author can pick one organizational pattern and then use that pattern to tell a story within the literature review. However, other people will break their previous research section of the literature review into different subsections or groupings and then use similar or different organizational patterns for each subsection within the literature review.

Chronological

The first pattern for arranging main ideas is what is referred to as the chronological pattern. The **chronological order** places the main ideas in the order in which they appear in history—whether backward or forward. For example, if you were writing a literature review section that contains both communication apprehension and humor assessment, you would start off writing about communication apprehension, which has been around since the 1970s. You would start by only writing about communication apprehension until 2001, which was when the humor assessment was first published, and then you would continue writing the literature review from 2001 to the most current research incorporating information about both communication apprehension and humor assessment. In essence, you would cover 30 years of communication apprehension in your literature review before you integrated information about humor assessment. In this first instance of the chronological organizational pattern, the author would have used one organizational pattern to create one constant story throughout the previous research section of the literature review. Now we will see how the chronological organizational pattern can be used if a literature review is broken into subsections.

If an author decided to chunk pieces of information within a previous research section of a literature review, he or she could also easily use the chronological organizational pattern. Using the same example of communication apprehension (CA) and humor assessment as the variables being studied in a research project, in one section the author would explain the history of CA starting in the 1970s and continuing through the most recent research about CA. This historical perspective on CA would then be followed by a historical telling of the origins of humor assessment. Although the history of humor assessment only dates back to 2001, a variety of research projects, both published and unpublished, have been written about the variable humor assessment, so a clear history of the concept does exist—even if it is much shorter.

Cause and Effect

The **cause-and-effect** organizational pattern is used to explain what causes a specific situation and what the effect of that situation is. For example, if you are writing a study about the use of a new miracle drug that can help individuals with high levels of communication apprehension, you could start your previous research section of your literature review by explaining how neurochemical processes may be a strong root cause of communication apprehension. After explaining the cause of communication apprehension, you could then explain the various effects of having elevated levels of communication apprehension (lower self-esteem, less likely to be called on by a teacher, more likely to be fired, fewer friends, lower grades in school, etc.). Ultimately, this organizational pattern helps you establish why your study should take place. In other words, you demonstrated what researchers think causes communication apprehension and what happens if you have high levels of communication apprehension, so a new drug that can help lower people's levels of communication apprehension (or your new study) would be beneficial to highly communicative apprehensive people.

If you were studying multiple variables within a study, the cause-and-effect organizational format can also be useful. If a researcher were examining racism and sexism, he or she may decide to write two separate sections on the causes and effects of both racism and sexism. If both the causes and the effects of racism and sexism are similar, the researcher can then assert that the two concepts should be highly related to one another, which could be the purpose of the study.

Compare and Contrast

Another method for creating main points is the **compare-and-contrast** method. Comparing (showing how information is similar) and contrasting (showing how information is different) is a tool we have all used on a number of occasions to help us analyze chunks of information. If you want to arrange the whole previous research section of your literature review using a compare-and-contrast organizational pattern, you could compare and contrast two similar but different variables using existing literature. For example, in communication, researchers try to differentiate between argumentativeness (discussing ideas and issues in a debate) and aggressiveness (attacking the other person). However, these two terms are often confused with one another by both scholars and laypeople. A literature review containing both communication variables could first show how the two variables are similar (compare) and then show how the variables are different (contrast). Although this organizational pattern often consists of two main points (one section on comparing and one section on contrasting), an author can easily create an introduction point where basic information about the two variables is initially discussed. For example, you could spend a subsection of the previous research section of your literature review discussing what argumentativeness is and what aggression is. This subsection would be followed by a subsequent subsection where you talk about the similarities of argumentativeness and aggression and finally a subsection where you examine how these two communication variables are different.

An author can also use the compare-and-contrast organizational pattern as an independent subsection. Maybe one of the major research variables you are studying in a project is sociocommunicative orientation. To discuss sociocommunicative orientation using compare and contrast, you could discuss Richmond and McCroskey's (1990) concepts of sociocommunicative orientation (assertiveness and responsiveness) and compare and contrast them with Sandra Bem's (1974) concepts of masculinity and femininity. In essence, by the time this subsection of your literature is written, your audience would have a general understanding of sociocommunicative orientation and how it is functionally different from Bem's concepts of masculinity and femininity.

Problem–Cause–Solution

Another format for creating distinct main points is the **problem–cause–solution** format. In this specific format, you discuss what a problem is, what is causing the problem, and finally what the solution could be to correct the problem. Maybe a researcher wants to study whether a new training program helps people communicate better on a first date. The researcher can start her or his previous research section of the literature review by discussing the problems that many people face when dating (shyness, anxiety, not knowing what to say, etc.). The problems with first dates could be followed by a discussion of what causes these problems with first dates to occur (lack of dating experience, bad previous dating experiences, poor communication skills, etc.). Finally, the researcher could explain how to solve the problems that occur with first dates. Ultimately, the researcher could run a study to see whether her or his "solution" to the first date problem actually works.

Psychological

The next way to organize your main ideas within a previous research section of a literature review is through a **psychological order** organizational pattern, or "a" leads to "b" and "b" leads to "c." In most behavioral genetics research, researchers start with the premise that our genetics causes humans to have specific temperaments, and these temperaments cause humans to behave in specific ways. In other words, genetics (a) leads to temperament (b) and temperament (b) leads to human behavior (c), or "a" leads to "b" and "b" leads to "c." When using the psychological organizational pattern, a researcher must clearly show how previous literature has established causal relationships. However, if a researcher does not need to explain causal relationships, this organizational pattern is probably not useful.

Categorical/Topical

The last organizational pattern for arranging the previous research subsection of the literature review is using various categories or topics to lay out your main points. The **categorical/topical pattern** is the organizational pattern used most often by researchers. To use this organizational pattern, a researcher simply separates her or his main concepts or variables being explored in a study into separate subsections within the literature review. For example, if you are conducting a study and want to examine organizational orientations (upward mobile, ambivalent, and indifferent), sociocommunicative orientation (assertiveness and responsiveness), and workplace satisfaction, you could organize your previous research section into three main sections, one for each variable.

You can also use this organizational pattern for your subsections if you have a section that has clearly delineated parts. In other words, you could organize your section on organizational orientations into three subsections, or one for each orientation (upward mobile, ambivalent, and indifferent). You could organize sociocommunicative orientation into two subsections (assertiveness and responsiveness). Whereas the first two variables can easily be sectioned off into their respective parts, workplace satisfaction would probably need to be organized using a different organizational pattern than those discussed previously. For this reason, there are three specific organizational patterns that can be used when organizing a subsection: general to specific, specific to general, and known to unknown.

General to Specific

The first subsection organizational pattern is **general to specific**. Think of this organizational pattern as a funnel. The brim is wide at the top (general) and then gets narrow at the bottom (specific). This type of organizational pattern is useful when an author wants to start off writing about anything and everything about a topic and then narrow her or his way down to an aspect of that topic that relates to the current study. For example, if you are writing a subsection on communication apprehension for an article about workplace communication apprehension, you could start off by explaining what communication apprehension is, followed by some specific studies related to communication apprehension in general, and end with a discussion of any studies that have examined communication apprehension in the workplace.

Specific to General

The second subsection organizational pattern is **specific to general**. You can also think of this organizational pattern in terms of a funnel, but you must turn that funnel upside down to get the effect. The brim is narrow at top (specific) and then gets wide at the bottom (general). Use this organizational pattern if you are trying to extrapolate some general ideas from specific information. Although it seems backward (and often is), this organizational pattern can be useful if you are trying to see the large picture instead of a more narrow one. If you were to use this organizational pattern, you could start your subsection on communication apprehension by talking about communication apprehension in the workplace, followed by a discussion of some specific studies related to communication apprehension in general, and end with a general discussion of communication apprehension.

Known to Unknown

The last organizational pattern specifically for subsections of your previous research is **known to unknown**. In this organizational pattern, an author discusses what we know about a specific topic or variable and then leads the reader to what we do not know. What we know is based on what has been studied in the previous research, and what we do not know is based on what seems to be a big hole in the literature. For example, maybe you are studying talkaholism and you note when doing your literature search that talkaholism has never been studied in intimate relationships. When you organize your subsection of talkaholism, you would start off with all the information researchers have found about talkaholism and then lead into a discussion of the fact that research has never examined how talkaholism affects intimate relationships.

Now that we have examined a number of different ways that researchers can organize previous research when writing a literature review, we will switch our attention to the Wrench and Booth-Butterfield (2003) article to see how these researchers laid out their literature review. Figure 5.3 shows a subsection from their literature review examining "Humor in the Medical Context"—read this subsection now. You will note that this subsection of the literature review is categorical with regard to what is discussed in each paragraph. To see how this subsection fits into the overall scheme of the article, read the previous literature section from the article on the textbook's website.

Study Rationale

After you have developed the background information for your study in the previous research section of the literature review, you are ready to explain to your readers why you have decided to perform the current study. The **rationale** section of the literature review is the subsection where you explain why and how you are going to perform your analysis of the variables you have described in your literature review (Figure 5.4). More important, the study rationale section of a literature review is where a researcher introduces her or his specific hypotheses and

Humor in the Medical Context

In a recent study in the *Journal of American Medical Association*, Levinson, Roter, Mullooly, Dull, and Frankel (1997) reported that physicians who used humor and laughed more during patient–physician interactions were less likely to engender malpractice suits. The use of humor as a variable in medical research has proved to be positive for both patients and their caregivers. Patients exposed to humorous messages have lower levels of stress-related hormones (Berk, 1989); increased immunoglobulin rates (Lambert & Lambert, 1995; McClelland & Cheriff, 1997); increased helper T-cells (Berk, 1993); lower levels of pain (Adams & McGuire, 1986; Cohen, 1990; Pasquali, 1991); lower blood pressure (Fry & Savin, 1982); and faster recovery rates from illnesses (McClelland & Cheriff, 1997). A patient's sense of humor and the degree to which he or she actively seeks humorous messages are predictive of her or his perceived health and morale (Simon, 1990). In a study conducted by Gaberson (1991), patients exposed to humorous messages had lower levels of anxiety before operations and higher post operation recovery rates. The inclusion of humorous messages in the patient–physician relationship can reduce fear while promoting trust (Robinson, 1991). Overall, humor in the medical environment appears to have an overwhelmingly positive effect and seems likely to increase positive perceptions of caregivers and subsequently compliance with their directions (James, 1995).

Physicians and other medical professionals personally use humor as a means of coping with the uncertainty that surrounds the medical profession (Bosk, 1996; Wanzer, Booth-Butterfield, & Booth-Butterfield, 1997). The use of humor appears to allow doctors and other medical personnel to ease tension (Ditlow, 1993). Medically speaking, the enactment of humor causes us to laugh, which physiologically increases endorphin levels, which, in turn, are associated with decreased anxiety levels (McGhee, 1996).

Despite the benefits of integrating humor into the medical office, humor should not be unskillfully used. Mulkay (1988) mentions that humor has the potential to create a language of domination and opposition rather than collaboration. Misinterpretation of humorous language could force the individuals interacting to see each other as foes instead of collaborators (Witkin, 1999). Hence communicators must be aware of potential negative effects of poorly enacted or misperceived humor, as well as the potential of positive outcomes. It may be diagnostic that highly humor-oriented individuals spend more time rehearsing jokes when compared to minimally humor-oriented individuals (Honeycutt & Brown, 1998). Hopefully, a portion of this rehersal time involves considering the possible positive and negative implications of enacted humor. Honeycutt and Brown (1998) suggest that people who use humor well probably have a contingency plan if the first one fails to have the desired impact or leads to a negative outcome.

Right off the bat you should notice that this is clearly categorical. The other major categories in this literature review are patient compliance, patient satisfaction, perceived credibility, and compliance gaining strategies.

The first part of this subsection explains the biological benefits of humor.

The second part of this subsection examines the psychological benefits of humor in the medical environment.

Here we have a discussion of physician use of humor in the medical environment.

This section discusses problems and suggestions for using humor in the medical environment.

Figure 5.3 Literature Review Segment

Recently, communication researchers have begun examining humor from an enactment perspective to see how individuals differ in the production of humorous messages (Booth-Butterfield & Booth-Butterfield, 1991; Punyanunt, 1997, 2000; Wanzer, Booth-Butterfield, & Booth-Butterfield, 1995, 1996a, 1996b, in press; Wanzer & Frymier, 1999). Booth-Butterfield and Booth-Butterfield (1991) identified the concept of humor orientation (HO), or an individual's predisposition to enact humorous messages in interpersonal situations. Research has shown humor orientation to be a positive trait among nurses (Wanzer et al., 1996b, 1997), in supervisor–subordinate relationships (Rizzo, Wanzer, & Booth-Butterfield, 1999), and in teacher–student relationships (Punyanunt, 1997, 2000; Wanzer & Frymier, 1999). Although no research has directly examined the effects of humor orientation in physician–patient interactions, the link is readily made to satisfaction and compliance.	This paragraph functions as the quick version of a study rationale. You'll notice that the beginning part explains that humor has been studied in a variety of different types of interpersonal situations, but it has not been studied in physician–patient interactions.
Fitzpatrick (1993) described patient satisfaction as an "emotional link to healthcare." And since humor creates a positive emotional state (Wrench & McCroskey, 2000), those patients who find their physicians humorous presumably would also be more satisfied than those patients who do not find their physicians humorous. Hence: H1: Physicians with higher levels of perceived humor orientation will also have higher levels of patient satisfaction.	Starting here the authors make the link between emotion, humor, and satisfaction to generate a clear hypothesis.

Analysis

This hypothesis is a very clear series of two If statements followed by a Then statement:

If (a):   Patient satisfaction is an emotional link to healthcare.
If (b):   Physician humor creates a positive emotional state in their patients.
Then: Physician humor will cause patients to be satisfied.

Figure 5.4 Rationale

research questions. In Chapter 2 we discussed in great detail how researchers go about creating arguments utilizing the findings of previous research. In empirical research, we must be able to form clear arguments before we can pose a hypothesis. As mentioned in Chapter 2, a hypothesis is a tentative statement about the relationship between two or more variables. This tentative statement occurs at the end of a logical argument. Unfortunately, researchers often have questions they want to ask in research, but a logical argument simply cannot be created to offer support for a hypothesis. When a researcher cannot create a hypothesis, he or she may ask a research question. The difference between a hypothesis and a research question is the ability to form an argument for the proposed relationship or difference. In a hypothesis, we use the previous research to make a prediction that is logical, whereas in a research question the previous research cannot help us make a prediction, so we must simply ask a question. To aid in the clarification of the purpose of a study rationale, we will examine both hypotheses and research questions separately.

Method Section

The **method section** helps readers understand who the participants were in a study and how the study was conducted. The purpose of the method section is twofold. First, it enables readers to see exactly what you did and either agree with or question your research strategies when your readers are attempting to determine the overall significance of your research. Second, the method section allows future researchers to replicate what you have done in a consistent manner. According to the American Psychological Association (2010), the method section can be broken down into four basic areas: participants, apparatus, procedure, and instrumentation.

PARTICIPANTS

First, when writing a method section you want to give as much detail about your participants as necessary. We call this the **participant section**. Although there are countless demographic questions you can ask participants, not everything is actually necessary when writing a literature review. The two most common demographic questions asked are sex and age. When reporting sex, it is best to do a simple frequency report followed by a percentile for the total population, for example, 50 females (50%), 48 males (48%), and 2 (2%) participants who did not indicate their biological sex. Note that we did report missing data in this answer. Often when people are filling out surveys they will accidentally miss one of the questions or opt to not answer a specific question; you should report these as missing data. When you are reporting a sample's mean age, it is important to also report the standard deviation. When writing articles using the APA style, report the sample age using the notation M (mean) and SD (standard deviation), both of which will be discussed in greater detail in Chapter 15. For example, when reporting the mean you could write, "Overall, the sample consisted of 245 participants with a mean age of 23.45 ($SD = 5.25$)," or "The 245 participants represented a typical college age sample ($M = 23.45$, $SD = 5.25$)." Whether you choose the first or the second way does not matter; it is ultimately a matter of personal writing style.

Whether you need to report other demographic characteristics such as ethnicity, sexual orientation, hair color, social economic status, and so on will depend on the overall purpose of your study. If you are running a study on the impact of hair color on perceived physical attractiveness, then identifying your participants' hair colors could be extremely important. However, if you are running a study on the impact of verbal aggression on political campaigns, hair color is clearly not a useful demographic characteristic. Look at Figure 5.5 to see how Wrench and Booth-Butterfield (2003) described their participants. Note that the researchers actually had four different subsamples about which they reported demographic characteristics.

APPARATUS

The second part of the method section is the **apparatus** subsection. In this subsection, researchers briefly describe any special equipment (apparatuses) or materials they used in the course of a specific study. According to the APA (2010), standard laboratory equipment furniture, stopwatches, screens, pencils, paper, scantrons, and so on do not need to be mentioned. However, if you are running a study and use a magnetic resonance imaging or computed tomography scan, then you must elaborate on the equipment. Some researchers go so far as to add ordering instructions in an appendix if the equipment is specialized. Also, if you build or have equipment built for you, it is often necessary to provide schematics or at least technical drawings of the equipment for your readers.

PROCEDURE

In the **procedure** section, you describe the exact procedures that were used in your study in a step-by-step fashion. The last paragraph in Figure 5.5 is the procedure paragraph. This

Participants

To maximize external validity, participants for this study represented four groups. Some participants were diverse undergraduates enrolled in communication courses at a large Middle Atlantic public university. This portion included 25 (56.8%) males and 19 (43.2%) females and constituted 16.9% of the total sample. The second segment of participants consisted of graduate students in an applied master's degree program. Individuals in this program are all adult students who primarily focus on their occupations while taking courses throughout the year in educational cohorts. This portion of the sample consisted of 7 (14.6%) males and 41 (85.4%) females and was 18.4% of the total sample. The third group included individuals from the general public, shopping at a mid-Atlantic mall. Trained student interviewers conducted surveys in the mall. The mall was attractive because its patrons represent a diverse community, not just people associated with the university. This portion of the sample consisted of 76 (53%) males and 66 (46%) females and constituted 54.8% of the total sample.

The final portion of the sample was the product of fifty Internet postings in AOL chat rooms asking for volunteers. The postings occurred over a two-day period in order to reach a wide range of individuals. Individuals in the chat rooms were also asked to forward the call for participants to any friends and family members. Those who decided to participate in the study received information concerning the World Wide Web site where they could participate. This portion of the sample consisted of 6 (23%) males and 20 (77%) females, or 10% of the total sample.

The overall sample included 146 females (55.5%) and 114 (43.3%) males. Mean ages were: undergraduate students, $M = 22$; master's students, $M = 38.6$; general public, $M = 38.7$; and Online, $M = 37.3$. The overall mean age of 35.7. The ethnic breakdown was: 46 (17.5%) African Americans, 189 (71.9%) Anglos/Caucasian, 9 (3.4%) Middle Eastern, 15 (5.7%) Asian, 6 (2.3%) Hispanic/Latino, 10 (3.8%) Native American, and 1 (.4%) other. A final demographic category, highest level of education, showed the following statistics: 46 (17.5%) high school/ GED, 70 (26.6%) some college, 12 (4.6%) associate's degree, 79 (30%) college degree, 40 (15.2%) graduate/professional degree, and 15 (5.7%) postgraduate. Thus, the sample was quite diverse in background representing a wide variety of perspectives.

Procedure

Participants completed the Humor Orientation Scale, Compliance-Gaining Questionnaire, Perceived Credibility Scale, and Patient Satisfaction Scale, with their personal physician as the object of focus. If they did not have a personal physician, they were instructed to think of the most recent physician with whom they had interacted. Participants then indicated on a 0–100 scale the extent to which they had followed their physician's prescriptions and/or treatments after their last visit.

The first part of the method section clearly explains where the sample came from in this study. This study had four different population groups.

Here the number and percentages of females and males for each subsample is given.

The overall sample is discussed here including demographic characteristics (biological sex, age, ethnicity, and education level). Notice that the Standard Deviations for the mean ages were not given. Generally speaking, it is always best to report Standard Deviations with means.

The procedure section explains what the study participants actually did during their participation.

Figure 5.5 Method Section

paragraph explains to the reader that participants were asked to fill out a questionnaire while thinking about their primary-care physician. The paragraph is short and not overly technical. In some studies, this paragraph could be expanded to three or four pages, depending on how technical your procedures are. In the article by Boiarsky et al. (1999), the researchers go into great detail describing how the children's shows were selected for inclusion in the study; how the sample of episodes from each show was selected, and how the selected episodes were then coded for the study. A lot of technical information was necessary to share in case any future researchers decided to replicate this specific study.

INSTRUMENTATION

The last part of the method section is the **instrumentation** or measurement section. The instrumentation or measurement section is where a researcher explains which research measures were used to measure the specific study variables. For example, if you were running a study examining the time it takes a talkaholic's heart rate to slow down after giving a public speech, you would need to explain how you measured talkaholism and her or his heart rate. Did you randomly observe people in public and then choose people to participate in your study who you thought talked a lot, or did you give them a scale that measures a person's trait talkaholism and then select your sample? Did you use an electrocardiogram to measure heart rate, or did you just use fingers on the wrist or neck to measure heart rate? Ultimately, how we go about measuring things is extremely important. Chapter 7 will go into detail regarding how we measure variables. For now, we can explain the basic components of what you must write down in this specific section by examining how to write up the measurement part for a scale. First, an author must explain what the scale is attempting to measure and who wrote the scale. For example, in the article by Rocca and Vogl-Bauer (1999), they wrote a measurement section for verbal aggression:

> The Verbal Aggression Scale (VAS) has been found to be both valid and reliable in assessing verbal aggression (Infante & Wigley, 1986; Rubin, Palmgreen, & Sypher, 1994). The VAS is a 20-item Likert-type scale with response categories ranging from (1) *almost never true* to (5) *almost always true*. This measure includes 10 positive worded and 10 negatively worded items. The reliability has been .80 or above in several studies (Infante & Wigley, 1986; Rubin et al., 1994). Obtained reliability for the verbal aggression scale in this study was .81. The mean for the VAS was 50.73 out of a possible 100 (*SD* = 9.93).

The first sentence explains that the verbal aggression scale (VAS) is a research measure that has been used in previous research and has been shown to be both reliable and valid. After reading the next two sentences, a reader can tell that the VAS has 20 items (10 positively worded and 10 negatively word) and uses a 5-point Likert scale ranging from "*almost never true*" to "*almost always true*." The next two sentences examine the scale's reliability (reliability will be discussed in greater detail in Chapter 8). The first of the two reliability sentences explains the level of reliability that is typically seen by the VAS, and the second sentence reports the obtained reliability for the VAS in the researcher's study. In the last sentence, the researchers report the mean and standard deviation for the VAS as seen in the study. This paragraph is a quick way of reporting the necessary information a reader needs about any scale to be used in research. For another example of how to write up a scale in the measurement section, see Figure 5.6. Wrench and Booth-Butterfield (2003) included a section on the scale's validity, which will be discussed in greater detail in Chapter 8. Although it is always important to explain the validity of a scale, some journals and editors will require more information about a scale's validity than others. It is our recommendation to attempt to add as much validity information about a scale as possible up front and then take it out at a later time

Measurement This study incorporated three measures of patient perceptions of their physician's communicative behavior (Humor Orientation, Physician Credibility, and Physician Compliance Gaining) and two others relating to perceptions of themselves (Satisfaction and Compliance).	This sentence is a very general introduction to the measurement section listing the scales used in the entire study.
Humor Orientation Scale. The Humor Orientation (HO) Scale is a 17-item, self-report measure that uses a 5-point Likert format ranging from "strongly disagree" to "strongly agree." Booth-Butterfield and Booth-Butterfield (1991) developed the HO to permit an encompassing look at an individual's overall propensity to use humorous communicative messages in interpersonal situations. An adapted version of this instrument permitted examination of the perceived humor orientation of a physician in a format similar to that in studies by Wanzer and Frymier (1999) and Rizzo, Wanzer, and Booth-Butterfield (1999) involving teachers and supervisors. Previous research examining humorous communication in the classroom has shown that perceived humor enactment enhances teacher evaluations (Bryant, Cominsky, Crane, & Zillmann, 1980; Javidi, Downs, & Nussbaum, 1988); student learning (Gorham & Christophel, 1990); perceptions of teacher nonverbal immediacy (Gorham & Crhistophel, 1990); and affect in the classroom (Wanzer & Frymier, 1999), suggesting criterion validity for HO.	Notice that the scale is named, format explained (Likert), author identified, and what the scale purports to measure is explained. The authors then explain that the scale is used in a variety of contexts and relate some of the previous findings associated with the scale. Authors explain validity of the scale.
The Humor Orientation scale demonstrates predictive validity in that it has specifically been related to enhanced perceptions of social attractiveness (Wanzer et al., 1996a), greater skill in humorous presentation of information (Wanzer et al., 1995), and heightened perceptions of liking for supervisors (Rizzo et al., 1999), all of which would be expected outcomes for someone who enacts humor effectively. Scores for the HO can range from 17 to 85. For this sample, the HO had a Cronbach's alpha of .91 ($M = 52.74$; $SD = 10.47$).	Authors explain overall scoring and then the scale's reliability.

Figure 5.6 Instrumentation or Measurement

if it is deemed unnecessary or extraneous to the research project. It is always faster to take material out than to try to add material at a later point.

Results Section

At this point we will mention the results section only briefly because most of the last part of this book is devoted to running statistics and writing up **results** sections. The results section is the part of a research article that untrained individuals pass over completely because it contains the bulk of the statistical information in the article. A general idea for a results section is that you will have one to two paragraphs for each hypothesis or research question unless one statistical device is able to analyze multiple hypotheses or research questions simultaneously. Either way, one should always explain in the first line of a paragraph what results are analyzed in that paragraph. It is often helpful to say up front, "In this paragraph, hypothesis three will be analyzed, which stated . . ." Being up front about what is in a paragraph keeps you focused while writing and makes your writing easier for others to read. Overall, the results section is not a place to write fancy treatises on life or research. The results section is simply that—a place to present the statistical results from the study you have

The first hypothesis was that a physician's perceived humor orientation would relate to her or his patient's level of satisfaction. Testing this hypothesis occurred by means of a series of bivariate linear regression analyses involving three dimensions of the patient satisfaction variable (cognitive, affective, and behavioral), with physician's humor orientation as the dependent variable. The regression equation for the first analysis was as follows: *Cognitive Satisfaction = .26 Humor Orientation +* 21.22, $F (1, 260) = 36.66$, $p < .0001$. As hypothesized, the stronger the physicians' humor orientation, the more likely their patients were to report cognitive satisfaction. This equation suggests that accuracy in predicting the overall cognitive satisfaction would be moderate. The correlation between physician humor orientation and patient cognitive satisfaction was .35. Approximately 12% of the variance of cognitive satisfaction was accounted for by its linear relationship with physician humor orientation.

The resulting regression equation for the second analysis was as follows: *Affective Satisfaction = .30 Humor Orientation +* 18.19, $F (1, 261) = 57.52$, $p < .0001$. As hypothesized, physicians with a more pronounced humor orientation tended to have patients who were more affectively satisfied. With this equation, accuracy in predicting affective satisfaction would be moderate. The correlation between physician humor orientation and patient affective satisfaction was .43. Approximately 18% of the variance of affective satisfaction was accounted for by its linear relationship with physician humor orientation.

The regression equation for the last analysis relating to Hypothesis 1 was as follows: *Behavioral Satisfaction = .19 Humor Orientation +* 19.53, $F (1, 261) = 31.38$, $p < .0001$. As physicians' humor orientation increased, patients were more behaviorally satisfied. The predictive accuracy of humor orientation for the behavioral satisfaction measure was moderate. The correlation between physician humor orientation and patient behavioral satisfaction was .33, which accounts for 11% of the variance of behavioral satisfaction from its linear relationship with physician humor orientation.

Notice how the first line of the results section explains what the first hypothesis was.

To avoid making you more confused at this point, just trust us when we say that the rest of this section explains the statistical processes that were used to examine the first hypothesis in the Wrench and Booth-Butterfield (2003) study.

Figure 5.7 Results

conducted. Figure 5.7 presents an example of a portion of a results section from Wrench and Booth-Butterfield (2003).

Discussion Section

The **discussion section** of a research study is broken into three major parts: the results discussion, the limitations, and future research. The first part of a discussion section provides a researcher space to explain her or his interpretation of the basic results found within a study, which is sometimes referred to as the discussion of the results. The purpose of the results discussion is to interpret results in light of the study outcomes and explain how readers can understand the study variables differently than they could at the onset of the study. The discussion section should be connected to the literature review by way of the hypotheses and research questions posed and the literature cited. However, a discussion section should not be a retelling of the arguments made when forming hypotheses in the rationale. Instead, a results discussion explains how a study has moved knowledge of the study variables forward from where the arguments were made during the rationale.

One of the primary reasons for having a discussion section is for an author to provide her or his reasoning for the why the results turned out the way they have. Specifically, an author must give reasons for why hypotheses were either supported or not supported and for why research questions were able to detect relationships and differences. One important note is that your results did not prove or disprove anything. In academic writing, when discussing one's results, it is important to avoid language that makes it sound like you discovered or proved anything; instead you can support or not support hypotheses based on your research. At the same time, make sure you always tackle the results that are directly related to your hypotheses and research questions first and then discuss any interesting features in the results that are worthy of explanation. Furthermore, the discussion section is not the place to attempt to introduce new findings and results. Although you might occasionally include in the discussion section tables and figures that help explain a result you are discussing, the tables and figures must not contain new results.

When interpreting your results, you should also find yourself comparing your results with those found in the past literature. It is extremely important to integrate sources from your literature review to help in your explanation of your results. Your literature will help you determine whether your results are in line with previous research or are breaking new ground. If your results are consistent with previous research, you may feel your task is complete. However, the ultimate challenge is not reiterating research, but demonstrating how your findings actually add to the ever-growing body of research on your subject. In Figure 5.8, Wrench

The primary goal of this study was to determine how physicians' humor orientation, credibility, and use of compliance-gaining strategies relate to patient satisfaction and compliance. The findings revealed significant relationships suggesting that better physician communication skills were associated with improved patient perceptions of physician credibility and patient satisfaction. The following paragraphs focus on the relationship that a physician's humor orientation has on patient satisfaction and physician credibility, the relationship between patient satisfaction and physician credibility, the relationship of compliance-gaining strategies with physician–patient interactions, and the post hoc analysis of the data sources used.	The first sentence re-explains the basic reason for this study.

This sentence explains how the discussion section will be laid out (it's basically an easy-to-follow preview). |
| The first major area of emphasis was patients' perceptions of physician humor orientation and how these perceptions related to patient satisfaction and physician credibility. Results for the first hypothesis indicated that a physician's humor orientation accounted for a moderate portion of the variance in each of Wolf et al.'s (1978) three dimensions of patient satisfaction (cognitive, affective, and behavioral). These results indicate that a physician's enactment of humor as an interpersonal communication tool, in general, positively relates to a patient's level of satisfaction. Although a physician's humor orientation accounts for some of the variation in a patient's satisfaction, the low coefficients of determination indicate that it is not the primary variable determining what ultimately causes patient satisfaction. This finding is similar to the one that Fitzpatrick (1991) reported in looking at patient satisfaction and physician friendliness and previous research that has also linked humor orientation with friendliness (Wanzer, Booth-Butterfield, & Booth-Butterfield, 1996a). | This part explains actual findings that occurred in the results section related to physician humor orientation, patient satisfaction, and physician credibility.

Notice how the result is explained and previous research is integrated to aid in the reasoning for why this finding actually occurred in this study. |

Figure 5.8 Discussion

and Booth-Butterfield (2003) analyze one part of their results. In the first paragraph the authors establish how the whole section will be laid out, followed by a quick preview. Writing your discussion section in this manner is primarily about organization and making it easy for your reader to follow where you are going with your findings.

The second part of the discussion section is the limitations subsection. When organizing a limitations subsection it is important to include discussions of both design flaw and procedural problems. A design flaw is an oversight that does not come to the surface until the data have been collected. In cases where a flaw in the design of the experiment is the cause or possible cause of a peculiar data pattern, the design flaw must be brought to the attention of your readers. One of the most common design flaws is that much research, ours included, often relies on college student samples, which may or may not be representative of the general public. Although a college student sample may not change many results in research studies, it is also possible that college students could be systematically different from the general public. For example, if you are conducting a study on the amount of alcohol being consumed in a given week, it is possible that college students could consume more or less alcohol than the general public. If you do not attempt to correct this problem, you could end up with skewed results. Ultimately, when writing a discussion section it is important to admit when you have an actual or potential design flaw.

The second type of problem that you will want to discuss in your limitations is a procedural problem. A procedural problem is usually a mistake made by an experimenter (or experimenters), through either carelessness or ignorance, which resulted in the data being collected in a way not intended in the design of the experiment. For example, maybe you are conducting a study examining heart rates during impromptu speeches. If immediately prior to the study you are offering your participants cookies and coffee while they are waiting (sugar and caffeine are stimulants), your results may be altered because of the stimulants and not the impromptu speeches. If this kind of problem occurs, it is best to be forthright about the problem in your discussion section. In Figure 5.9, Wrench and Booth-Butterfield examine two possible limitations to their study.

Limitations. No matter how rigorously a study is conducted, there are always limitations. Measurement issues are of concern. First, using a single perception-oriented answer to determine whether or not a patient would comply with her or his doctor's medication/treatment may not be the best way to measure compliance. Although this was the method devised by Dillard and Burgoon (1985) and also used by Burgoon et al. (1987), the results could be enhanced by taking into account more situational variables that conceivably affect compliance.	This limitation is a form of a design flaw.
The second major limitation in this study is the online sample used. Although individuals on AOL and in the general public samples were randomly selected to participate in the study, the completed sample was still admittedly self-selected. In addition, the small number of individuals who did participate in the online version was somewhat unsettling. New and more accurate attempts at getting online participants should be developed. At the same time, contrary to Sheehan and Hoy's (1999) fear that online samples are not generalizable to a larger and more diverse population, the lack of a meaningful significant difference between the online sample and those involving the other means of data collection does show the promise of online samples. As use of the Internet becomes more prevalent, concerns about skewed online samples should recede.	This limitation is a form of a procedural problem.

Figure 5.9 Limitations

The last part of the discussion section is the future directions of research subsection. The directions for research section is a paragraph or series of paragraphs explaining your ideas for where future research should go as a result of your study. The goal of all new research is to gain knowledge. However, when we gain knowledge, new questions will always surface, so good research should lead to both an increase in knowledge and new questions that can be posed for future research. When creating your future research subsection, make sure you are specific about future developments and do not write statements like "this needs more research" or "in the future, more research should be done." The purpose of this section is for you as a researcher to explain how you see future research in this area being conducted. Provide constructive and specific instructions to your readers about how they can further your study and answer some of the questions left unanswered. For example, maybe your research found an odd relationship or difference that should be replicated. Or maybe someone should examine your variables in a different communication context to see whether the same results appear. Any possible future avenues of research that came about as a result of your study should be discussed.

Conclusion. This study clearly linked communication variables (humor orientation, credibility, and compliance gaining) to patient satisfaction and compliance. It also demonstrated why physicians need to think consciously about how they are using communication during patient–physician interactions. Although the results may seem to be intuitively obvious to communication researchers, further explanation of communication concepts in unique professional and social contexts helps to validate our theoretical conceptualizations of human communication in applied settings. Additionally, information concerning patient–physician communication has the potential for improving patient compliance, minimizing malpractice claims, and improving patient satisfaction.	Notice that the first sentence clearly summarizes the major results. The rest of this paragraph is explaining the benefits of research in the area of patient–physician communication.

Figure 5.10 Conclusion

The Conclusion

The last part of a research project is the concluding section. When reading a research article, it is common to find that the concluding section does not exist. Like a speech, a research paper must have a solid concluding device. The concluding section should briefly summarize the main finding(s) from your study and demonstrate that the main arguments made in your study are all clearly explained. Think of the concluding section as the dinner mint after eating a five-course meal. It should be brief, contain no new information, and neatly wrap up the paper. It is often helpful to end your paper by reexamining the attention-getter you used in the introduction of your paper, if appropriate. In Figure 5.10, Wrench and Booth-Butterfield (2003) demonstrate how a conclusion can be easily written.

Research Outside the Walls of Academia

Although research outside of academia may not necessarily be presented in a traditional research paper, there are common conventions for writing about such research. Remember, research is only as good as the utility of that research in the hands of people who need the information. As such, we must ensure that we present our research in a format that is commonly suited for different contexts. Although an academic paper may be appropriate for a research conference or peer-reviewed journal, O'Shea (1986) recommends breaking a professional research report into nine distinct sections:

1. *The executive summary.* An executive summary is a short, one-page (or less) explanation of the major findings from the study itself.

2. *Project background.* The project's background includes an explanation for the reason(s) that the project was undertaken in the first place. You should include the project's original goals. You can also include any relevant literature that helps support the basic reasoning for the study or if there are concepts or terms that a lay audience may be unfamiliar with.

3. *Objectives and scope.* Next, explain what the specific objectives of the research study were. You should also clearly articulate the study's basic aim. Business people appreciate someone explaining how what was originally discussed was actually achieved.

4. *Methods.* The methods section in a business report are identical to that in a more formal research study. One major difference is that in a business report it is appropriate to include graphs and charts to more clearly explain one's participants.

5. *Analysis.* The analysis section should be as complete as it is in a traditional research paper. However, after conducting a statistical test you should also provide a short explanation of what the test means and what the findings indicate. You should not try to extrapolate meaning from the findings at this point, but you do want to explain the purpose of the results and how to interpret the results for novices.

6. *Findings and conclusions.* Next, you want to clearly articulate what the basic findings of the study were and what conclusions can be drawn from the study. Unlike a discussion section in a traditional research paper, the findings and conclusions section should be explicit and is not designed to enhance theory. Instead, the findings and conclusions should be clearly stated and relate back to the objectives of the original study.

7. *Recommendations.* In the recommendations section of a business report a researcher explains what he or she thinks an organization should do based on the results of the study. In academic research, we often avoid making specific recommendation statements, but in applied business research, it is expected that a research study will be followed by recommendations.

8. *Expected benefits.* In addition to making recommendations, you should explain in your report what benefits an organization can expect to gain if your recommendations are followed. These should be realistic benefits, so do not promise something you cannot actually deliver to your organization.

9. *Implementation guide.* The last part is where you explain to your business audience how they can implement your recommendations within their organization. These last three parts force you, as a researcher, to function as a consultant and not just someone conducting research.

Reading and Critiquing Academic Literature

Now that you have a general idea about the setup of quantitative research articles, we will discus reading and critiquing academic literature. Academic articles are not always the easiest or fastest reads. Anyone who thinks that he or she can quickly scan an article and come away with a good conceptualization of what occurred within the study is going to have problems.

As such, it is important to think through strategies that will make your reading experience easier. For our purposes, here are 16 questions we think you should consider when reading an academic article:

1. Are there any key terms that are defined?
2. What did the authors state as the purpose of their study?
3. Do the authors have a clear summary of previous research?
4. Do the authors provide a clear critique of previous research?
5. Do the authors clearly identify a gap in the research? Do you note any gaps in the literature that the authors did not identify?
6. What is the rationale for the current study?
7. What are the explicit hypotheses and/or research questions in this study?
8. What was the sample used in this study?
9. How was the sample recruited in this study? Are there any known flaws to this method?
10. Are the demographics of the sample generalizable?
11. What was measured in this study and how? Are there any flaws that you see in how the authors went about measuring?
12. What are the results in this study? What statistical methods were used to achieve these results? Do the statistical methods make sense in the context of this study?
13. Are there any results that seem to be missing?
14. Do the authors explain how the results are consistent with existing literature? Do the authors explain how the results are inconsistent with existing literature?
15. What limitations did the authors mention to their study? Do you note any additional limitations not discussed by the authors?
16. Do the authors discuss any future directions for this line of work? Do you see any additional lines of research that could stem from this study?

One common way of using these questions is to go through an article and answer these questions as you go along. By answering these questions, you force yourself to really delve into the literature itself and see what is written.

Preparing a First Draft

So you have been asked to write a literature review. We cannot attempt to discuss all of the ins and outs of writing a literature review in one section of a chapter, but the "Further Reading" section at the end of this chapter includes a number of books that focus specifically on the topic of writing a literature review. Here are 12 basic steps to help you write an effective literature review.

STEP 1: IDENTIFY YOUR GENERAL TOPIC

Before you can start doing anything with regard to a literature review, you must have a general topic. In Chapter 4 we discussed creating a topic, so we will not reiterate that here. What we will add is that searching for literature before you have a clear idea of what you are interested in studying will waste a lot of valuable time.

STEP 2: DETERMINE THE TYPE OF STUDY YOU ARE CONDUCTING

Once you have a general topic, it is important to start thinking about what type of study you will be conducting. We will go into more detail later in this book discussing the four primary methods quantitative researchers use (e.g., survey, content analysis, experiments, and Big Data), so for now we will just mention that it is important to have a general direction. One of the primary reasons this becomes important is because it can help you narrow down your literature search in some ways.

STEP 3: DETERMINE WHAT VARIABLES YOU WILL EXAMINE

In the next chapter we will discuss the idea of variables in detail, but for now we will say that a variable is anything that can change from person to person within the confines of an ordered structure. For example, you can have the variable biological sex, which has two basic categories: female and male. Students' GPAs are another type of variable because GPAs vary from person to person. Before you can really start searching for literature, it is important to know what you need to be looking for, so having a clear idea of what your variable will be is important.

STEP 4: SEARCH FOR PRIMARY SOURCES

Once you have your topic and a list of the variables you plan on having in your study, it is time to start looking for articles and books related to those areas. Now, because we are talking about academic literature reviews here, it is important to remember that we are primarily looking for academic sources and not popular press materials (newspapers, magazines, and books written in a jargon-free language for a general audience who has little to know technical knowledge on a given subject that are written by professional journalists whose publishers provide varying degrees of control for the accuracy or validity of the content).

STEP 5: OBTAIN FULL TEXT REFERENCES

Part of searching for primary sources is obtaining the full text references you will be using within your literature review. It is important to keep yourself organized during this process. Whether you want to download all of the PDF files to your hard drive or you decide to print everything out, you must do this in a mindful manner. It is easy to forget where you found an article, so write down the full APA style reference to ensure you have the information you need when you use the article later on in your literature review.

STEP 6: LOOK FOR OTHER REFERENCES IN OBTAINED MATERIALS

As we discussed in the previous chapter, one way to locate relevant sources is through a process called backtracking. Backtracking is when you look at the references of articles you have found and then use those references to find new ones. When you start reading through your articles, look at other authors' literature reviews for possible relevant references. If you find one, grab the article and read it for yourself. You should never take a reference from an author's literature review and place it inside your own because it is unethical. As we always say, if you do not lay your own eyes on it, you should not be using it.

STEP 7: NARROW YOUR LIST OF REFERENCES

All of the articles and books you find will not be useful. Novice researchers feel that any and every article they find should be used. Some do this because they do not want to spend the appropriate amount of time searching for relevant articles. Others simply have problems distinguishing between relevant and irrelevant information. If you fall into the first camp, keep searching for relevant research that will help you make the case for your study. If you fall into the second category, look through your articles and ask yourself, "Does this article help me build the case for my study?" If the article does not help you, then it may not be something that is necessary for your literature review.

STEP 8: ORGANIZE REFERENCES BY MAJOR AND SUBTOPICS

Once you think you have the requisite set of references you need to adequately discuss the relevant literature, it is time to start organizing your references into major topics and subtopics. Say that you are writing a literature review on the effectiveness of social media. You may have articles that define what social media is. You may have other articles that explain the history of social media. You may also have articles that discuss the effectiveness of social media in differing contexts (e.g., health, job searches, relationships). At this point, start organizing these references into the relevant categories. However, a single article may cross over into multiple areas, so it is always important to make note of that.

STEP 9: LOOK FOR GAPS IN YOUR REFERENCES

Once you start narrowing your down your list of references into major topics and subtopics, see whether the areas within your study are equally balanced. Say you are conducting a study on two public relations campaigns. The goal of the study is to see whether fear appeals work with public relations. After reviewing the different sources you have found, you may note that you have many articles on fear appeals, fear appeals in health communication, fear appeals in advertising, etc., but you do not have any specifically looking at fear appeals and public relations. For this reason, you should probably start a specific search to fill in this gap.

STEP 10: FIND REFERENCES TO FILL GAPS

Once you have noted any specific gaps, you must start plugging the holes in your argument. It is possible that there is not relevant research on a specific topic, but this is rare. You may need to consider using an array of synonyms to help you find relevant literature, but your literature review must be balanced. We hope you are beginning to see that you really cannot research and write an effective literature review overnight. Often the references you need may not be located on your college or university campus. Thankfully, colleges and universities participate in a program called interlibrary loans that allows you to get materials from other colleges and universities. Librarians are amazing at what they do, but you cannot expect them to find the one rare article you need at the last minute. The rarer something is, the longer it may take to find another library willing to loan the material.

STEP 11: CREATE A LITERATURE REVIEW OUTLINE

One of the biggest mistakes novice literature review writers make is to forget everything they have learned about the basics of writing. Although social-scientific writing is different in tone from the types of writing you learned in English classes, the basic writing process is still the basic writing process. One of the fundamental steps of any good piece of writing is a clear organizational structure. Whether you are writing the next great American novel or a quantitative research paper, you must have a clear organization before you start. As such, you will still have all of the basic parts of traditional writing: introduction, thesis statement, preview of main ideas, major body points, and conclusion. At the beginning of this chapter, we discussed multiple ways that you can organize your literature review. Ultimately, you must pick which outline format is going to work best for your literature review. Whatever format you choose, list your APA citations within the outline to again ensure your different sections are balanced with regard to the amount of research you are discussing.

STEP 12: WRITE

Finally, the time has come to begin writing your literature review. Some authors prefer starting with the introduction and going from there. Others prefer working on the different main points and then writing the introduction and conclusion once they have the full body of the literature review written. The method you choose is not as important as making sure you have all of the necessary parts.

Common Pitfalls to Literature Reviews

1. Not having a clear thesis statement in your introduction.
2. Not clearly previewing the body of your literature review.
3. Not including transition sentences between the major parts of your literature review.
4. Not defining important key terms for your readers.
5. Using dictionary definitions for key terms (stick to academic ones).
6. Writing about a single article across multiple paragraphs or pages.
7. Each paragraph discusses a separate research study with no links between the paragraphs (these are annotations, not a literature review).
8. Using flowery language to make the literature review longer.
9. Not having enough research to adequately write a thorough literature review.
10. Missing important or seminal articles or books related to the literature review.

Conclusion

This chapter has focused on the basic parts of a research paper: abstract, introduction, literature review, method section, results, discussion, and conclusion. Although this style of writing is clearly not a format that most people learn in their formative school years, the tricks and tools you have learned for writing will greatly benefit you as you attempt to write your own research papers. The best piece of advice we can give you from our years of writing research articles is to write, edit, rewrite, edit again, and keep on writing. Most research articles barely resemble their first drafts by the time they are published in a scholarly journal. Although the writing process is arduous and complex, the impact that you can have on the academic world and the rewards you get when you see your name in print are worth the process.

KEY TERMS

Abstract
Alternative hypothesis
Apparatus
Cause-and-effect order
Chronological order
Comparison-and-contrast
  order
Directional research
  Questions
Discussion section
General-to-specific order
Hypothesis

Illustration
Instrumentation
Introduction
Known-to-unknown order
Literature review
Method section
Nondirectional research
  Question
Null hypothesis
One-tailed hypothesis
Participant section
Preview

Problem–cause–solution
  order
Procedures
Psychological order
Rationale
Research question
Results section
Rhetorical question
Specific-to-general order
Thesis
Topical order
Two-tailed hypothesis

REFERENCES

American Psychological Association. (2010). *Publication manual of the American Psychological Association* (6th ed.). Washington, DC: American Psychological Association.

Bem, S. L. (1974). The measurement of psychological androgyny. *Journal of Consulting and Clinical Psychology, 47,* 155–162.

Boiarsky, G., Long, M., Thayer, G. (1999). Formal features in children's science television: Sound effects, visual pace, and topic shifts. *Communication Research Reports, 16,* 185–192.

Brummans, B. H. J. M., & Miller, K. (2004). The effect of ambiguity on the implementation of a social change initiative. *Communication Research Reports, 21,* 1–10.

Chesebro, J. (1999). The relationship between listening styles and conversational sensitivity. *Communication Research Reports, 16,* 233–238.

McCroskey, J. C., Richmond, V. P., Johnson, A. D., & Smith, H. T. (2004). Organizational orientations theory and measurement: Development of measures and preliminary investigations. *Communication Quarterly, 52,* 1–14.

McCroskey, J. C., Wrench, J. S., & Richmond, V. P., (2003). *Principles of public speaking.* Indianapolis, IN: College Network.

O'Shea, T. J. (1986). Presentation of results. In S. W. Barcus & J. W. Wilkinson (Eds.), *Management consulting services* (pp. 235–252). New York, NY: McGraw–Hill.

Punyanunt, N. M. (2000). The effects of humor on perceptions of compliance-gaining in the college classroom. *Communication Research Reports, 176,* 30–38.

Richmond, V. P., & McCroskey, J. C. (1990). Reliability and separation of factors on the assertiveness-responsiveness measure. *Psychological Reports, 67,* 449–450.

Rocca, K. A., & Vogl-Bauer, S. (1999). Trait verbal aggression, sports fan identification, and perceptions of appropriate sports fan communication. *Communication Research Reports, 16,* 239–248.

Thomas, C. E, Richmond, V. P., & McCroskey, J. C. (1994). The association between immediacy and sociocommunicative style. *Communication Research Reports, 11,* 107–115.

Weber, K., Fornash, B., Corrigan, M, & Neupauer, N. C. (2003). The effect of interest on recall: An experiment. *Communication Research Reports, 20,* 116–123.

Wrench, J. S., & Booth-Butterfield, M. (2003). Increasing patient satisfaction and compliance: An examination of physician humor orientation, compliance-gaining strategies, and perceived credibility. *Communication Quarterly, 51,* 482–503.

FURTHER READING

Cooper, H. (1998). *Synthesizing research: A guide for literature reviews* (3rd ed.). Thousand Oaks, CA: Sage.

DeWine, S. (2001). *The consultant's craft: Improving organizational communication* (2nd ed.). Boston, MA: Bedford/St. Martin's.

Fink, A. (1998). Conducting research literature reviews: From paper to the Internet. Thousand Oaks, CA: Sage.

Girden, E. R., & Kabacoff, R. I. (2011). *Evaluating research articles: From start to finish* (3rd ed.). Los Angeles, CA: Sage.

Hart, C. (1998). *Doing a literature review: Releasing the social science research imagination.* Thousand Oaks, CA: Sage.

Pan, M. L. (2008). *Preparing literature reviews: Qualitative and quantitative approaches* (3rd ed.). Glendale, CA: Pyrczak.

Salkind, N. J. (2012). *100 questions (and answers) about research methods.* Los Angeles, CA: Sage.

Variables

1 Explain the concept of a variable.

2 Distinguish between abstract and concrete variables.

3 Understand the four units of analysis (individuals, dyads, groups, and organizations).

4 Distinguish between variable attributes and variable values.

5 Differentiate between positive, negative and neutral relationships.

6 Explain two types of differences (kind and degree)

7 Distinguish between independent and dependent variables.

8 Differentiate among the four levels of variables (nominal, ordinal, interval, and ratio).

9 Explain the four basic types of interval scales (Likert, semantic differential/bipolar, Staple, and scalagram).

10 Understand the purpose of the book's dataset and how the data were collected.

11 Identify the variable levels for measures included in this book's dataset.

12 Describe how personality traits influence human communication.

13 Differentiate among trait, context, audience, and situational behavior.

14 Apply information from this chapter to write an APA format method section.

Ask a researcher how a particular research project was developed and you will likely hear a fascinating story. Sometimes the stories about how projects were conceptualized are almost as intriguing as the research itself. Recall our discussion in Chapter 4 of the methods for conceptualizing a research topic—some topics evolve from personal experiences and others may be the result of current events or unanswered questions from previous studies. Once the idea for a study has been identified, the real task is in creating a "recipe" for the research project.

Just as a chef is responsible for identifying the food ingredients necessary for a gourmet dish, a researcher creates a list of research "ingredients" (more commonly referred to as "variables") that will be used to conduct a study. In this chapter we identify the research variables necessary for a successful project and discuss various methods of analysis.

How Are Research Projects Developed?

Ideas for a project can come from a variety of sources—a conversation, other research articles, or media examples. Once the conceptual idea has been identified, the next task involves writing a specific research question and identifying key terms or concepts. Remember the list of key concepts that we discussed in Chapter 4 to assist you in conducting library research on the topic? The same list can be used to help you identify potential variables to include in your study and to narrow your research topic. Specific questions that may be beneficial to ask when determining the overarching research question could include the following:

- How is communication related to the topic?
- What specific communication behaviors are involved?
- Are there other factors that could potentially influence the behavior?

Answers to these and other questions involve identifying the specific "things" that should be examined in a study. Returning to our earlier analogy of the recipe, the answers to the questions often require a researcher to identify the research "ingredients" that will be included in the study to find answers.

Variables: Units of Analysis

Variables are the ingredients of research projects. A **variable** can be defined as any entity that can take on a variety of different values. The manipulation, measurement, and control of variables is the primary mission of research. In essence, it is a concept or construct that varies. Examples of variables include age, sex, or level of public speaking anxiety (or fear of public speaking). Each of these variables will take on a different value for different people at a given time. One participant in a study could be a 32-year-old female with low public speaking anxiety and another could be a 19-year-old male with moderate public speaking anxiety. **Concrete variables** are stable or consistent. Examples might include characteristics such as biological sex or birth order (e.g., first born, middle child, or the last-born). **Abstract variables** are those that change or differ over time or across situations or contexts. Examples of abstract variables could include communication satisfaction or self-disclosure.

Researchers identify the specific variables or elements to compare differences between individuals and groups. For example, we might compare the level of parent–child communication satisfaction for first-born, middle-born, and last-born children. In this instance, birth order is a concrete variable that remains constant. Communication satisfaction is classified as an abstract variable. Differences could emerge when asking a participant to report on the level of communication satisfaction with one's mother versus one's father. Let's look at another example. Suppose you wanted to compare the self-disclosure of men and women. In this study, biological sex would be considered a concrete variable—it does not change. Self-disclosure would be classified as an abstract variable. An individual may engage in different patterns of disclosure with friends compared to family members. As you can see from these examples, the next task when determining the research question to guide the project involves identifying the types of units that will serve as the focus of the study.

Units of Analysis

Once a researcher has determined the specific communication behaviors to include in a study, the next step involves determining the unit of analysis for the project. Most communication research examines communication in one of four units of analysis: individuals, dyads, groups, and organizations.

Communication studies examining individuals as the unit of analysis may focus on an individual's temperament, personality, or communication traits, or the research could focus on specific communication strategies or behaviors selected by a person. In their study of sports fans (located on http://www.oup.com/us/wrench/), Rocca and Vogl-Bauer (1999) selected the individual as the unit of analysis. Data were collected to identify an individual's level of verbal aggressiveness (attacking the self-concepts of people instead of attacking the positions they espouse, e.g., "only an idiot would think that," "what kind of moron are you?") and its relationship to perceptions of the appropriate communication at sporting events. Verbal aggressiveness and perceptions of appropriate behavior use the individual as the unit of analysis.

Research on dyads focuses on collecting information about two people involved in an interpersonal relationship. Barbato, Graham, and Perse's (2003) study asked 202 parent–child pairs to complete questionnaires assessing perceptions of the family communication climate and interpersonal communication motives for interacting with one another. Results indicated that the communication climate had a significant influence on the motives selected for communicating in the dyad.

Sometimes the communication dynamics change when individuals are placed together in groups to accomplish a goal. Tim Kuhn and Marshall Scott Poole (2000) focused on 11 groups in two major corporations as the unit of analysis in their examination of the effects of group conflict management styles on decision making. They found that groups that were more integrated in their conflict styles and addressed conflict openly were more effective in decision making than groups that engaged in conflict avoidance or confrontational styles.

If a researcher is interested in identifying the ways in which organizational members interact with one another and the resulting impact on task completion, efficiency, satisfaction, or a host of other variables, the organization becomes the unit of analysis. Coombs and Holladay (2004) designed the Workplace Aggression Tolerance Questionnaire (WATQ) to identify perceptions of appropriateness of workplace verbal aggression. Although at first glance it may appear that the unit of analysis is an individual's perceptions, the core of the research focuses on appropriateness of behavior in the organizational context.

Identifying the unit of analysis is essential to maintain focus during the research project and to enable researchers to generalize results to similar units. However, it is important to resist the temptation to make inferences about individuals based on their group membership. The concept of ecological fallacy is similar to stereotyping and occurs when researchers assume that because a participant is a member of a specific group (such as a culture), he or she possesses all the same communication characteristics as the group. Similarly, assuming that one organization is similar to all others would lead to erroneous conclusions. It is important to keep in mind that units of analysis possess unique characteristics—after all, this is what makes communication research an exciting venture!

Aspects of Variables

Once the researcher has identified the unit of analysis for a particular study, the next step involves revisiting the list of variables that will be examined to identify the specific aspects associated with each variable. We will examine two aspects of variables—attributes and values—in more detail.

VARIABLE ATTRIBUTES

Variable **attributes** refer to the specific categories of a variable. For example, the variable "biological sex" includes the attributes of male or female, whereas the variable "sociocommunicative orientation" has the attributes of assertiveness, responsiveness, and versatility. To ensure that you have included all relevant information for your own research study, consider the various categories or attributes for each variable you will be examining.

VARIABLE VALUES

Whereas attributes identify the categories for variables, variable **values** refer to the numerical designation assigned to each variable to allow for statistical analysis. Some variables, such as age, possess a numerical value on their own because the value of the variable already exists. Other variables may require a researcher to assign a number to represent each attribute of the variable. If biological sex of the respondent is a variable being examined, numerical values must be assigned to designate male and female respondents. In this instance, values are arbitrarily assigned by the researcher. The number "1" can be used to represent males, and the number "2" can be used to represent females, or vice versa. As you assign values to each variable, it is important to write down this information because it will be important in the data-analysis phase.

UNDERSTANDING RELATIONSHIPS AND DIFFERENCES

Beyond attributes and values, all variables in statistical research enable researchers to generally understand two basic phenomena: relationships and differences.

Relationships

Just as the concept of interpersonal relationships refers to the connection between two people, "**relationship**" as a research concept refers to the correspondence or connection between two variables. The vast majority of communication studies are designed with the goal of identifying connections or relationships between variables. Michael Beatty (1988) set out to examine the relationship between an individual's level of public speaking anxiety and one's level of conspicuousness (feeling like you are under a giant spotlight and everyone is watching) and one's level of perceived similarity with one's audience. Relationships between variables typically fall into one of three categories: positive, negative, or neutral.

Positive Relationship
Positive relationships exist when an increase in one variable produces an increase in the other variable, or a decrease in a variable corresponds with a decrease in the other variable. Beatty found that an individual's level of public speaking anxiety was positively related to an individual's level of conspicuousness. Increases in one variable (an individual's level of conspicuousness) correspond to increases in the other (level of public speaking anxiety). In other

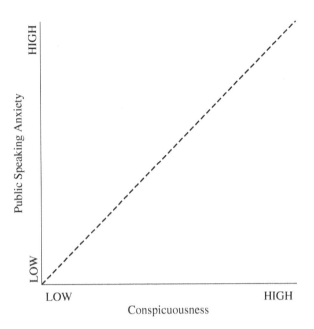

Figure 6.1 Positive Relationship

words, the more conspicuous a person feels, the more anxious he or she will be while engaging in public speaking. The opposite is also true—the less conspicuous a person feels, the less anxious he or she will be while engaging in public speaking. This relationship is visually represented in Figure 6.1.

Negative Relationship

A **negative relationship** exists when a decrease in one variable corresponds to an increase in the other variable or vice versa. Beatty (1988) also found a negative relationship between public speaking anxiety and perceived similarity with one's audience. Increases in one variable (perceived similarity) correspond to decreases in the other variable (level of public speaking anxiety). In other words, the more a speaker perceives an audience as being similar to her or him, the less anxious he or she will be while engaging in public speaking. However, the converse is also true. The more dissimilar a speaker perceives her or his audience to be, the more anxious he or she will be. Figure 6.2 depicts a negative relationship.

Neutral Relationship

In some instances, a researcher may discover that the variables selected for a study are not related to one another. **Neutral relationship** is another term used to refer to this lack of relationship, or when the change of one variable does not correspond with a change in another variable. Figure 6.3 provides a visual representation of two variables that have no relationship to one another. As you can see, no pattern in the data is evident when the points are plotted on the diagram. Hence, changes in one variable do not produce consistent changes in the other variable being studied. Examining the relationship between the amount of pizza one consumes and an individual's level of public speaking anxiety would likely result in a neutral relationship.

Differences

In addition to looking at relationships, statistics enables researchers to examine differences. A **difference** can be referred to as the degree to which one person or a group of people are

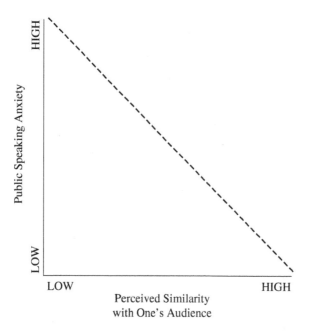

Figure 6.2 Negative Relationship

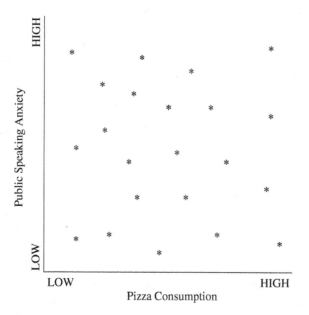

Figure 6.3 No Relationship

dissimilar from another person or group of people. In research, differences fall into one of two categories: differences in kind and differences in degree.

Differences in Kind

Differences in kind occur when two or more groups do different things associated with their groups. For example, football players play football and cheerleaders lead the crowd in cheers. The two groups (football players and cheerleaders) are fundamentally different and exhibit different behaviors. Although it may be entertaining to some, we really do not want to see a 90-pound cheerleader being tackled by a 350-pound defensive lineman, nor would we want to see the 350-pound lineman trying to do a flip or toe touch. Although differences in kind are interesting, they really do not relate to statistics except in that differences in kind create grouping variables (or nominal variables, which will be discussed soon).

Differences of Degree

Instead, quantitative researchers are often interested in **differences of degree**, or when two groups have differing degrees of a variable that they both display. For example, perhaps we wanted to determine whether females and males differed in their levels of verbal aggression. We may give each group a survey to fill out and then look at the averages of the two groups. Statistical difference tests would then allow a research to determine whether the two groups have different averages on verbal aggression. Figure 6.4 shows two curves representing theoretical scores on a test of verbal aggression. The curve to the left represents female verbal aggression scores and the curve to the right represents male verbal aggression scores. Although eyeballing the two curves may make it appear that males have higher verbal aggression scores, researchers cannot use the eyeballing technique, which is why we use difference tests to determine whether the two groups are really different.

Statistical Differences

However, difference tests only tell us half of the story. Let's pretend that the two curves seen in Figure 6.4 represent a difference between the male and female levels of verbal aggression. The curves can be "statistically different," but the difference between the female and male average could only be a matter of four or five points. For this reason, researchers are also interested in the magnitude of the difference (effect size), not only the fact that a difference exists. For example, look at the two curves in Figure 6.5. In the two curves, the difference between the male and female verbal aggression averages is much greater than that in the two curves seen in Figure 6.4.

   This section introduced you to the basic concepts of relationships and differences; much of the rest of this book will examine these two concepts in greater detail.

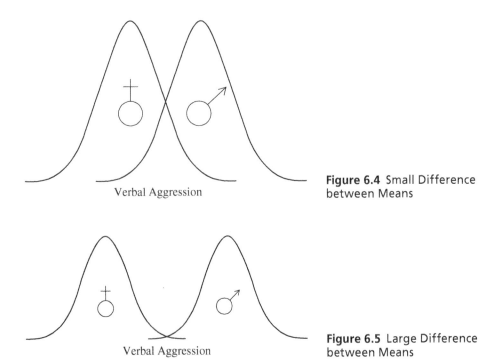

Verbal Aggression

Figure 6.4 Small Difference between Means

Verbal Aggression

Figure 6.5 Large Difference between Means

Types of Variables

To answer the research question or hypothesis, the next step in the process involves identifying the two types of variables identified as the focal points of the study. Variables can be classified as being independent or dependent. Independent variables are the part of the research environment that are manipulated or changed. More specifically, the **independent variable** is what we are studying with respect to how it impacts a dependent variable.

Dependent variables, by contrast, are not manipulated. They are recorded or measured, but they are not exposed to any type of alteration. Researchers look for any change in the dependent variable as a result of the manipulation of the independent variable. In essence, the goal of the research is to find out whether there is a change in the dependent variable in response to the change or manipulation of the independent variable. Although the distinction between dependent and independent is fairly easy when variables are used in an experimental situation, identifying the variables can be confusing in nonexperimental situations. Because of this, the term "criterion" variable is sometimes used to refer to the dependent variable.

So how can you determine which variable is the independent variable and which is the dependent variable in a study? Consider the following hypothesis from Weber, Fornash, Corrigan, and Neupauer's (2003) study on the effect of student interest in a topic on recall of information:

H: Lectures utilizing interest-based examples should result in participants with higher scores on subsequent tests of cognitive recall.

The independent variable in this hypothesis is lecture examples. Lectures were manipulated by showing students two different versions of videotapes: (1) lectures that incorporated current examples and (2) lectures using standard examples. Cognitive recall of information serves as the dependent variable. The researchers are trying to explain the difference in information recall as a result of the types of examples used in lectures.

Some studies examine variables that the researcher does not manipulate. Rather, the differences in a variable may be naturally occurring. Consider the following research question from a 1995 study examining communication satisfaction of children from divorced families (Thomas, Booth-Butterfield, & Booth-Butterfield, 1995):

H: Communication satisfaction with parents will be lower among children from divorced families than children from intact families.

At first glance, it may be difficult to distinguish between the dependent and independent variables in this hypothesis, but recall the definitions for both concepts. The study wanted to examine the level of communication satisfaction of children from divorced and intact families. Thus, family status (divorced or intact) is the independent variable for the hypothesis. The goal is to determine whether differences in family status affect the dependent variable or communication satisfaction.

Our third example is more difficult. Consider the following research question:

RQ: What is the relationship between parents who engage in verbally aggressive behavior at sporting events and a child's verbal aggressiveness?

According to this research question, we simply want to ascertain a possible relationship between the two variables. In other words, there is not a dependent variable and an independent variable in this example. However, if we proposed that a parent's level of verbally aggressive behavior at sporting events caused her or his child's level of verbal aggression, then we could say that the parents' level of verbal aggression is the independent variable attempting to predict the child's level of verbal aggression.

If we were only dealing with independent and dependent variables in research, our task would be fairly simple. But we know that nothing in life can ever be as easy as it looks. Sometimes there are additional variables whose presence may impact the relationship between the dependent and independent variables. **Intervening variables** are often included in a study to determine whether the effects of a change in the independent variable in turn cause a change in the dependent variable. If you wanted to examine the effect of teacher feedback on student motivation, it might be beneficial to consider the variable of self-esteem as a potential intervening variable. Positive feedback from a teacher may boost a student's level of self-esteem, which in turn may impact the level of motivation.

Antecedent variables also have the potential to affect the relationship found between the independent and dependent variable. These variables answer the question, "What happened prior to the time data were collected?" and shed light on some of the differences that could emerge between the independent and dependent variables. A study examining the impact of conflict (independent variable) on marital satisfaction (dependent variable) should take into consideration possible antecedent variables that could potentially impact the results. For example, if both partners had incompatible personalities before marriage, this could lead them to experience or view conflict in their relationship differently than those who are deemed to be compatible. Similarly, if a person comes from a family where parents frequently engaged in conflict, the impact of conflict on marital satisfaction may be a result of the predetermined expectations for conflict.

Variable Levels

Another integral part of the research design process involves selecting variables to examine that will answer the proposed research question or hypothesis. Each variable selected for a study will be directly associated with identifying the particular statistical method appropriate for answering the research question. Variables can possess qualitative or quantitative characteristics. Variables with qualitative characteristics involve assigning items to groups or categories to describe the population. No quantitative value is implied with these variables. In contrast, quantitative variables are easily identified because they represent differences in quantity or amount. A research variable can be classified into one of four levels. These levels, listed in order of precision in measuring variables, are nominal, ordinal, interval, and ratio.

NOMINAL VARIABLES

Nominal variable data make up the variable level that is identified by its qualitative characteristics. To categorize nominal level data, simply name each characteristic using categories that are mutually exclusive. It is important to remember that a characteristic can only be represented by one category of a variable. No logical order is followed for creating the categorization, and values cannot be assigned quantitative values or rank ordered.

There are three primary rules for categorizing nominal level data. First, the categories used to classify the attributes must be mutually exclusive. Second, all categories used to represent the data must be equivalent. Remember the old adage, "Don't compare apples to oranges!" The same principle applies in developing nominal categories. Finally, all categories used to classify nominal level data must be exhaustive. Examples of nominal level data include political affiliation (a person can be a Democrat, Republican, other, or not registered) and sex (a participant is either a male or a female). As you can see from the categories created to describe each characteristic, a participant can only "fit" into one category. Thus, the categories established meet the first criteria of being mutually exclusive. Further, the categories used to represent the participants are exhaustive. A person can only be male or female, and the categories of "other" and "not registered" are included to capture all participants who are not registered Republicans or Democrats.

Descriptive statistics and frequency distributions are the primary method of data analysis for nominal level data from the data disk included with your text. The nominal variable "sex" can be described in terms of percentages of males (56.8%) and females (43.2%) or in terms of frequencies representing the number of participants that fall into each category (males = 183, females = 139). Although a researcher would typically assign values to the categories of "male" and "female" for data entry purposes (perhaps a "1" to represent males and a "2" to represent females), it is important to note that these numbers have no relationship to the categories they represent. It would make no sense to try to compute a mean score for sex. Because the categories are mutually exclusive (a participant is either a male or a female), calculating a mean of 1.3 for sex would have no meaning. Instead, the mode is the typical statistic employed to describe nominal level data. It is meaningful to say that most participants were males. In instances in which a researcher wants to examine the differences between two nominal level variables, a chi-square test is the most appropriate method of statistical analysis. This statistic will be discussed in more detail in Chapter 16.

ORDINAL VARIABLES

Ordinal variables allow us to rank order attributes with regard to which has less versus which has more of a characteristic. Ordinal variables have both qualitative and quantitative characteristics. Ordinal variables are qualitative because people are placed into categories that are used to represent characteristics; however, these categories have real numerical associations, so the variables are also quantitative. Although there is a logical order to the creation of categories used to represent characteristics, it is important to note that the researcher is not able to make comparisons with regard to the magnitude of difference between categories. Examples of ordinal level data include socioeconomic status (lower, middle, or upper class), education level (elementary, junior high, high school, or college), or letter grades (A, B, C, D, or F). It is evident that there is a distinct difference between each of the levels, and there are quantitative differences between them, but we are unable to specify an amount or quantify the differences that exist. Suppose we know that the category of "middle class" is used to represent individuals with an income between $30,000 and $50,000. "Upper class" is the category used to represent those earning more than $50,000 per year. The difference between middle and upper class could be one penny (or the difference between $50,000 and $50,000.01) or millions of dollars.

There are three primary properties for categorizing ordinal variables. First, the categories must be mutually exclusive. That is, a participant can only "fit" into one of the categories. Second, the researcher must follow a logical ordering of the categories. Consider the ordinal variable of military rank. As a participant achieves status within the organization, a higher level of rank is awarded. Finally, each category must be balanced to represent the amount of a characteristic possessed by a participant.

To quantify ordinal level data for statistical analysis, numerical values are assigned to represent each category. However, the numbers used to represent each quality of the variable must increase such that higher numbers are used to represent high values. For example, a "1" could be assigned to represent lower class, "2"for middle class, and "3" for upper class. It is important to remember that the intervals between the numbers used to represent each category are not necessarily representative of equal distances or quantities, nor does a zero point exist.

INTERVAL VARIABLES

Interval variables are quantitative and are classified in a logical order that represents equal distances between levels within each category. Examples of interval variables include levels of people's public speaking anxiety, levels of perceived similarity, and levels of perceived conspicuousness (to use the earlier example in this chapter when we discussed relationships). Interval variables enable a researcher to rank order items and to compare the magnitude of differences between each category. For example, McCroskey (1970) created the Personal Report of Public Speaking Anxiety (PRPSA) to measure an individual's level of public speaking anxiety, and scores on the scale range from 34 to 170, with higher scores indicating higher levels of anxiety when delivering a speech. We can say that a PRPSA score of 160 is higher than a PRPSA score of 80. However, we cannot state that an individual with a PRPSA score of 160 is twice as anxious as someone who has a PRPSA score of 80. This is because PRPSA does not have a zero as the scale's absolute starting point. Four types of scales are used to measure interval level variables: Likert, semantic differential, Staple, and scalagram scales.

Likert

In a **Likert scale** participants are presented with a number of statements and then asked to respond to those statements based on a preexisting scale. Figure 6.6 shows an example of a short Likert scale called the Homonegativity Short Form, created by Wrench (2005). This scale has 10 scale items, all generally measuring an individual's perception of gay and lesbian people. The scale is measured using a five-step system ranging from 1 (*strongly disagree*) to 5 (*strongly agree*). Each participant who fills out this scale only has five possible choices for each item on the scale: 1, 2, 3, 4, or 5. The scores for each individual item can be added together to achieve a composite score, which can then be used in various statistical analyses. McCroskey's (1970) PRPSA is another example of a Likert scale.

Semantic Differential

The second type of research scale commonly used to examine interval level measurements is the **semantic differential/bipolar scale**. The semantic differential scale consists of a series of adjectives that are oppositely worded (good/bad, happy/sad, eventful/uneventful, positive/negative, etc.). There then exists a continuum of possible choices between the adjectives, and participants are asked to select the number that most represents their perception between the two adjectives. For example, we may ask participants to rate the movie *Charlie and the Chocolate Factory* using the adjectives "good" and "bad," with a choice of 1 to 7 between the two words. Numbers 1 and 7 indicate a very strong feeling. Numbers 2 and 6 indicate a strong feeling. Numbers 3 and 5 indicate a fairly weak feeling. Number 4 indicates you are undecided. If you thought the movie was good but not amazing, you might give the movie a rating of 2 or 3 because these are closest to the word "good," whereas if you thought it was the worst movie you had ever seen, then you might rate the movie a 7 because it is closest to the word "bad." Figure 6.7 is another example of a bipolar scale. In this example, we see the job motivation scale, which is a retooling of Virginia Richmond's (1990) student motivation scale. The scale asks people to respond to how they feel about work using five adjective pairs. When you add up the responses from all five adjective pairs, you can then use this number in a variety of statistical tests.

Homonegativity Short Form

Instructions: Below are several descriptions of how you may feel. Please use the scale below to rate the degree to which each statement applies to you. Remember, we want you to be completely honest and we appreciate your cooperation.

Strongly Disagree	Disagree	Neutral	Agree	Strongly Agree
1	2	3	4	5

_____ 1. Gay and lesbian people make me nervous.
_____ 2. Homosexuality is perfectly normal.
_____ 3. I wouldn't want to have gay or lesbian friends.
_____ 4. I would trust a gay or lesbian person.
_____ 5. I fear homosexual persons will make sexual advances towards me.
_____ 6. I would have no problem living with someone who is gay or lesbian.
_____ 7. Homosexual behavior should be perfectly legal.
_____ 8. I would have a serious problem if I saw two men or women kissing in public.
_____ 9. I think that gay and lesbian people need civil rights protection.
_____ 10. When I see a gay or lesbian person I think, "What a waste."

SCORING: To compute your scores follow the instructions below:

1. How to Score:
   Step One: Add scores for items 1, 3, 5, 8, & 10.
   Step Two: Add scores for items 2, 4 6, 7, & 9.
   Step Three: Add 30 to Step One.
   Step Four: Subtract the score for Step Two from the score for Step Three.

Source:

Wrench, J. S. (2005). Development and validity testing of the homonegativity short form. *Journal of Intercultural Communication Research, 34*, 152–165.

Figure 6.6 Likert Scale

Staple's

As an offshoot of the semantic differential scale, Jan Staple, co-director of the Netherlands Institute of Public Opinion, devised a different way to measure people's opinions (Crespi, 1961). The scale is designed to measure individual attitudes toward a topic by providing participants with a set of adjectives and then having them rank those adjectives from –5 (words are not an accurate portrayal of something) to +5 (words are an accurate portrayal of something). Imagine we wanted to create a Staple scale for evaluating anxiety; it could look something like Figure 6.8. Items 3 and 4 (calm and relaxed) are oppositely worded, so they would have to be recoded to reflect the opposite score to achieve a composite score for this measure.

Scalogram

The last scale that is used to create an interval variable is called the Guttman or **scalogram** scale. Although scalogram scales are interesting, they are rarely actually employed in communication research. The goal of a scalogram scale is to ascertain an individual's belief about

---

Work Motivation Scale

Instructions: The following scale is designed to examine how you currently feel about work. Only think about this one class when filling out the following scale. Numbers 1 and 7 indicate a very strong feeling. Numbers 2 and 6 indicate a strong feeling. Numbers 3 and 5 indicate a fairly weak feeling. Number 4 indicates you are undecided.

Unmotivated	1	2	3	4	5	6	7	Motivated
Excited	7	6	5	4	3	2	1	Bored
Interested	7	6	5	4	3	2	1	Uninterested
Involved	7	6	5	4	3	2	1	Uninvolved
Dreading it	1	2	3	4	5	6	7	Looking forward to it

Scoring:

To determine your level of work motivation, add your scores for each question together.

Source:

Richmond, V. P. (1990). Communication in the classroom: Power and motivation. *Communication Education, 39*, 181–184.

Figure 6.7 Semantic Differential/Bi-Polar Scale

Staple Scale

Below are a series of adjectives that indicate how you may currently feel. For each adjective, circle the number that most closely corresponds to how you feel from –5 (this does not at all explain how I feel) to +5 (this is exactly how I feel).

+5	+5	+5	+5	+5
+4	+4	+4	+4	+4
+3	+3	+3	+3	+3
+2	+2	+2	+2	+2
+1	+1	+1	+1	+1
Anxious	Nervous	Calm	Relaxed	Agitated
–1	–1	–1	–1	–1
–2	–2	–2	–2	–2
–3	–3	–3	–3	–3
–4	–4	–4	–4	–4
–5	–5	–5	–5	–5

Figure 6.8 Staple Scale

a given topic. A perfect Guttman scale would consist of a set of unidimensional items that respondents rank in order from the least extreme to the most extreme position (Guttman, 1944). For example, maybe you want to determine how much homework is too much for high school students. You give them a list of 10 possible time frames ranging from zero to 10 hours of homework. You then have your participants answer yes or no next to each time frame: "No Homework to 1 Hour" up to "10 Hours or More of Homework." The goal of a scalogram scale is that at some point along the way you will hit a cutoff point beyond which people will not go. For example, maybe someone believes that "4 to 5 hours of homework" is legitimate, but thinks "5 to 6 hours of homework" is unreasonable. If someone marks that "5 to 6 hours of homework" is unreasonable, we would not expect her or him two questions later to state that "7 to 9 hours of homework" is okay. In essence, a scalogram scale attempts to determine where people cut themselves off in relation to a specific belief. Figure 6.9 contains an example of a scalogram scale created to examine environmentalism. As this scale progresses, each statement becomes slightly more radicalized with regard to an individual's perception of environmentalism.

Environmentalism Scale		
Instructions: For each phrase circle whether you agree with that statement by circling YES or disagree with the statement by circling NO.		
1. I never throw trash on the ground because it hurts our environment.	YES (1)	NO
2. I think recycling is a noble endeavor.	YES (2)	NO
3. I always participate in recycling in my city.	YES (3)	NO
4. My friends and family know my commitment to the environment.	YES (4)	NO
5. I would send a letter to a company that willfully hurts the environment.	YES (5)	NO
6. I vote for politicians based on their environmental policies and voting behaviors.	YES (6)	NO
7. I would picket a company that is hurting the environment.	YES (7)	NO
8. I would organize a campaign against a corporation that is polluting the environment.	YES (8)	NO
9. I would participate in tree spiking to prevent companies from destroying our environment.	YES (9)	NO
10. Bombing a company that hurts the environment is completely justifiable.	YES (10)	NO
Scoring:		
To score this measure, add the numbers under each YES answer selected. Scores can run from 0 to 57. Higher scores indicate a more radical environmental stance.		

Figure 6.9 Scalogram Scale

RATIO VARIABLES

Ratio variables are similar to interval variables with one notable exception—ratio variables have an absolute zero starting point to represent the absence of the characteristic. Examples of ratio variables include income, exam scores, temperature (when measured by the Kelvin scale, which has an absolute 0), and speed. Whereas we could not make statements regarding the magnitude of difference between categories of interval level data, we can make statements such as "An exam score of 50 is two times more than an exam score of 25." Since most statistical analysis procedures view interval and ratio characteristics in the same way, the same statistical tests are used to describe and compare both types of variables.

A variety of statistical tests can be used to analyze interval and ratio level variables. The *t* test (comparing two groups) and one-way analysis of variance (comparing two or more groups) are the appropriate difference tests when analyzing interval/ratio variables. We will discuss *t* tests in Chapter 17 and one-way analysis of variance in Chapter 18. To describe linear relationships between two or more interval variables, correlations (Chapter 19) or regression analyses (Chapter 20) are most appropriate.

Choosing the Right Test

Figure 6.10 summarizes the appropriate statistical tests to be used when analyzing each type of variable. For example, if a researcher wanted to test for differences on public speaking anxiety (an interval scale) between females and males (two groups), the researcher would need to conduct a *t* test. In this example we started off with our interval scale and realized we had two groups we were testing (female and male), so the only choice of statistical test was the *t* test. If we had two or more ordinal variables and wanted to test for a relationship, what test would we use? According to our chart, if we have two ordinal variables, the only test available for examining relationships is a correlation (specifically a Spearman rho correlation). Figure 6.10 will become *very* important later in this book.

Interval/Ratio	Differences	Two groups	*t*-Test
		More than two groups	ANOVA
	Relationships	Two variables	Correlation
		More than two variables	Regression
Ordinal	Differences	Two groups	Mann-Whitney or *t*-Test
		More than two groups	ANOVA
	Relationships		Correlation
Nominal	Differences		Chi-square
	Relationships		Percentage differences

Figure 6.10 Summary of Appropriate Statistical Tests for Variable Levels

Communication Variables

Earlier in this chapter, we introduced the major levels of variables that social science researchers are concerned with: nominal, ordinal, interval, and ratio. The authors of this book believe that the best way to really learn how to conduct quantitative research is to actually conduct quantitative research on real variables. For this reason, we decided to put together a study using some common communication variables and then supply you, the reader, with the actual data gathered from real research participants.

In the spring of 2005, the authors of this book recruited 325 undergraduate students to participate in a research study and in the fall of 2011 they recruited an additional 328 participants, for a total of 654 participants. The data from these 654 participants are made available to the readers of this book. Not only will we discuss these data at various parts of the book, but also you have access to the datasets located on the textbook's website. These datasets can be analyzed using your favorite statistical software package. The goal of this data collection was to provide the readers of this text an actual dataset that can be used to ask real research questions. The questionnaire distributed can be seen in Appendix B (see textbook's website) exactly as we distributed it to the participants. Since the goal of this dataset is to enable you to use real participant data to ask real research questions, we made sure that we had variables from each level (nominal, ordinal, interval, and ratio) in the dataset. The rest of this chapter will explain each of the variables we collected.

NOMINAL VARIABLES

For the purposes of this book, we decided to include two nominal variables. The first variable was a common nominal variable included in most research studies, biological sex. Biological sex, as a variable, has only two possible attributes (female and male). For a variable to be nominal, the categories must be equivalent (the categories of female and male are equivalent), the categories must be mutually exclusive (you cannot be both female and male), and the categories must be exhaustive (there is not a third or fourth biological sex).

The second nominal variable we included in this study was political affiliation. The concept of political affiliation is tricky, so ultimately how participants will respond when asked "What is your political affiliation?" will depend on the categories a researcher provides her or his participants. We could have listed different political parties like Communist Party, Democratic Party, Green Party, Independent, Libertarian Party, Natural Law Party, Republic Party, and so on until we had listed every known political party in the United States, which would be a long list. Instead, we opted to use the two prominent parties (Democratic and Republican) as two categories and then add a category for "Other" parties for anyone who belonged to one of those political parties outside the mainstream political process. However, on further contemplation, we realized that those three categories were not completely exhaustive. Not everyone in this country belongs to a political party or sees her- or himself as an independent voter. In fact, many people are simply not registered to vote at all. For this reason, we decided that our fourth category should be "Not Registered to Vote." Everyone who filled out the survey should fall into one of the categories provided (Democrat, Republican, Other, or Not Registered to Vote). Not only are the categories exhaustive, but also someone who is not registered to vote is not someone who belongs to the Democratic Party because registering to vote is how people join political parties in our country. Furthermore, someone who is a Republican cannot also be an Other, so our categories are mutually exclusive as well. And all of the categories relate to political affiliation (even Not Registered to Vote), so our categories are equivalent.

ORDINAL VARIABLES

For the purposes of the study conducted for this textbook, we created two ordinal variables for analysis: university classification and time spent on the Internet. The first ordinal variable we used in this study was university classification. We created a variable with five levels (freshman, sophomore, junior, senior, and graduate student). You may be wondering why these are ordinal and not nominal; the reason they are ordinal is the same reason someone is labeled as upper class as opposed to middle class—there is no true indication of magnitude. In college, these categories are based on the numbers of hours taken and passed, not on the number of years someone has been in school. For example, one of the authors of this textbook was 1 hour shy of being a sophomore at the beginning of his second year in college, but he was still classified as a freshman according to the university. On the flip side, how many of us have known people who are 8- or 9-year seniors?! In essence, the labels associated with university classifications represent a difference between the classification levels, but we do not get any indication of the magnitude of this difference.

The second ordinal variable that we selected for inclusion in this book's dataset was the amount of time someone spent online. Specifically, we asked the study participants to disclose how much time they spend online during a given week. We then provided the participants a series of categorical answers: 0–½ hour, ½–1 hour, 1–2 hours, 2–5 hours, 5–10 hours, 10–15 hours, 15–20 hours, and 20+ hours. With each categorical level we increase the magnitude of the difference, but the exact magnitude is not known. Someone who spends 80 hours a week online would fall into the 20+ hour group, as would someone who spends 21 hours a week online. In the same vein as university classification, the difference in how one classifies her- or himself can be a matter of minutes. Maybe someone spends 9 hours and 45 minutes online on average, so he classifies himself as spending 5–10 hours online. However, another participant spends 10 hours and 15 minutes online on average, so she classifies herself as spending 10–15 hours online. All in all, this gradient of 30 minutes cannot be taken into account when dealing with the categorical nature in this ordinal variable.

INTERVAL VARIABLES

Most interval variables studied by communication researchers measure traits, behaviors, beliefs, and attitudes. Luckily, the study that we compiled for this measured all of those, so we will look at each category separately.

Common Interval Variable Measures

Personality Traits and Communication

Personality is the total psychological makeup of an individual, which is a reflection of her or his experiences, motivations, attitudes, beliefs, values, and behaviors, derived from the interaction of these elements with the environment external to the individual. Thus, personality can be defined as the sum of an individual's characteristics that make him or her unique (Hollander, 1976). If everyone had the same personality, we would all communicate the same way all the time in every situation. Thankfully, we do not all communicate the same way, and these differences in our communicative behaviors can be observed.

Ultimately, Hollander (1976) noted that personality consists of two basic dimensions that are important to communication researchers. The first dimension of personality distinguishes the external level (observable characteristics of an individual) of personality from the internal level (individual's attitudes, values, and beliefs, interests and aspirations, and motivations). We often use an individual's external personality to determine an individual's internal personality during interpersonal interactions. We may watch someone shake and turn red while giving a speech and surmise that the individual is experiencing a great deal of anxiety. However, the person could just be ill, which could cause the shaking and red flushing during the speech.

The second feature of personality distinguishes its dynamic aspects (the degree to which a personality trait can change over time or during certain contexts or situations) from its consistent aspects (the degree to which a personality trait does not change over time or during certain contexts or situations). In essence, we have a continuum of personality traits ranging from consistent to dynamic. Many external and internal factors can cause personality traits to change. For example, getting married, moving to another country, experiencing a crisis, losing a job, and so on can change how a person looks at life (internal level) and how he or she behaves (external level). There are, however, many aspects of our individual personalities that do not alter over time. Elements of the internal level of personality that are least likely to undergo change are those that comprise the consistent aspect of personality (e.g., values). Another reason why some personality traits are resistant to change is human genetics. There is an increasing body of research examining how our genetic code affects various personality traits. Although this textbook is outside the purview of examining how genetics affects human behavior, we recommend reading Dean Hamer and Peter Copeland's (1998) *Living with Our Genes: Why They Matter more Than You Think* to examine how genetics influence various personality traits and Michael Beatty, James McCroskey, and Kristin Valencic's (2001) *The Biology of Communication: A Communibiological Perspective* to examine how genetics influence human communication specifically.

As humans, we expect people to behave according to the way they think and feel. In other words, we expect the external behavior to be a window into the internal reality. So when we see someone shaking and turning red during a speech, we reach the conclusion that he or she is experiencing anxiety brought on by the speech itself. In reality, however, the internal and external personalities are not always in sync with each other. We may feel that someone who is shaking and flushing during a speech has anxiety, but there could be many other reasons that the specific behavior is being exhibited.

The perceptions we have about people based on their exhibited behaviors also affect how we view that person. In our daily interactions with others, we constantly assume that because an individual is exhibiting a particular behavior, he or she is "that kind of person." We make these assumptions because we expect internal and external personality traits to be consistent. Imagine you watch that same flustered speaker over an entire semester. Every time he or she speaks, you see the same shaking and turning red. After watching an individual shake and turn red every time he or she spoke, we would begin to see this anxiety as characteristic of her or his personality. As Hollander (1976) notes, it is only a short time until you begin to view this characteristic in others as a *trait*, or the way he or she "typically" behaves. There are four different ways that personality characteristics can be exhibited by specific individuals: traits, contexts, audience, and situational.

Trait

In the psychology of personality, "traits" or **trait behavior** refer to individual characteristics that are not found in all people, only in relatively few. Traits are an individual's predispositions for responding in a certain way to various situations. A given trait will exhibit itself in almost any situation responded to by the individual. For example, if our anxious speaker from above was later seen talking in a meeting and was turning red in that communicative situation as well, we might conclude that this individual's communicative anxiety is clearly trait based because it is seen across multiple contexts.

Context

The second way that personality characteristics can be demonstrated by individuals is within specific contexts. The basic contexts that communication scholars examine are interpersonal, group, meeting, public, and mediated. Contexts are specific modes where behavior can be different, which leads to contextual behavior. For example, maybe our anxious speaker only gets anxious when having to give a public speech (public context), but experiences no anxiety while communicating interpersonally, in groups, in a meeting, or when talking online. In this case, we can say that her or his speech anxiety is context based.

Audience

The third way that personality characteristics surface is dependent on the audience with whom an individual is communicating, or **audience-specific behavior**. Different audiences have differing perspectives of how interactions should occur, so we tend to act differently based on the type of audience we are interacting with. Maybe our anxious speaker is fine while giving a speech to her or his Rotary Club, but gets anxious in front of someone who is giving her or him a grade. In this case, a teacher grading the student could cause the student to experience audience-based speech anxiety.

Situational

The final way in which personality characteristics surface depends on the situation, which can lead to **situational behavior**. There are times when we start communicating in a manner that is not normal for us because of the situation. We refer to this behavior as situational because it is not generally replicated. In the case of our nervous speaker, it is possible that this person has never before in her or his life experienced any kind of anxiety while giving a speech, but during this speech was overcome with anxiety. Sometimes, out of nowhere, we alter our normal communication patterns as a result of the situation, or our "odd" communicative behavior happens only within a specific situation.

Overall, personality differences manifest themselves in variations in communicative behavior. To take this concept one step further, we can examine the notion of a specific type of personality trait—a communication trait. A **communication trait** is a hypothetical construct that accounts for certain kinds of communication behaviors. Researchers in the field of communication have examined numerous communicative patterns that are traitlike because in some people they are not alterable, whereas in other people they can be situationally based. For the remainder of this chapter it is useful to think of all of the communication traits we examine as existing along a four-point continuum (see Figure 6.11). Starting at one extreme

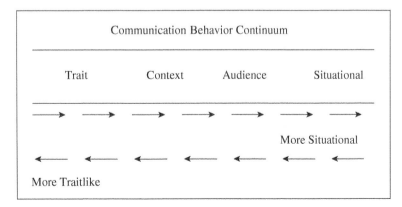

Figure 6.11 Communication Trait Continuum

end of the continuum and moving to the other extreme, the four points are communication behavior: (1) as a trait, (2) in a generalized context, (3) with a specific audience, and (4) within a specific situation.

Now that we have examined what personality and communication traits are, we can look at the various communication traits measured in this book using an interval scale. The interval variables that were selected for inclusion in this chapter are communication apprehension, ethnocentrism, humor assessment, nonverbal immediacy, sociocommunicative orientation, willingness to communicate, generalized belief, and generalized attitude.

Communication Apprehension

Before we discuss the nature of this first communicative trait, please fill out the Personal Report of Communication Apprehension–24 (PRCA-24) in Figure 6.12. **Communication apprehension** (CA) is defined as the fear or anxiety associated with either real or anticipated communication with another person or persons. Let's break this definition down into its various parts. First, CA is about fear and anxiety. People exhibit fear and anxiety differently. Some people are generally fearful and anxious about almost everything, whereas other people are more focused in their fear and anxiety. People that are said to be high CA (scores between 80 and 120 on the PRCA-24) will experience fear and anxiety in every context when having to communicate (actual or real communication). However, people who are high CA do not stop having anxiety just because they do not have to engage in communication at that moment. In fact, people who are high CA experience apprehension and anxiety even when they *think* about having to communicate with another person (anticipate communication). High-CA people often experience severe anxiety while practicing a public speech alone in their house, thinking about having to interact with someone interpersonally, or thinking about having to talk in a group or meeting the next day. Research has shown that approximately one in five people, or 20 percent of the general population, suffers from high CA.

Scores on the PRCA-24 should be between 24 and 120. If your score is between 24 and 50, you are among those in our society who experience the least communication apprehension, to whom we refer as low-CA individuals. You are apt to be a higher talker and may actively seek out opportunities to interact with others. Few, if any, communication situations cause you to be fearful or anxious. If your score is somewhere between 50 and 60, you experience less CA than most people. However, you are likely to feel some fear or anxiety about a few situations. If your score falls between 60 and 70, your level of CA is similar to that of most people. There are some communication situations that may cause you to feel anxious or tense; in others you will feel quite comfortable. If your score is between 70 and 80, you experience more CA than most people. Probably many communication situations cause you to be fearful and tense, but some do not bother you. If your score falls between 80 and 120, you are among those who experience the most CA. You are likely a low talker, one who actively avoids many communication situations because you feel much anxiety and tension in those situations.

Although having high levels of CA (trait CA) will impact a person's social life, having high levels of CA has also been shown to impact other areas of a person's life. Research has shown that high CA individuals tend to have low self-esteem and are more prone to depression than low CA individuals. High-CA individuals are perceived as having low intelligence by peers, teachers, and supervisors although there is no research to support any difference in IQ levels based on an individual's CA. Research has shown that people with high levels of CA are less likely to visit their physicians, and when they do go to their physicians, they are less likely to ask questions about medical treatment and medication. Overall, CA impacts an individual in every aspect of her or his life. People who have high levels of CA can be truly crippled in our society.

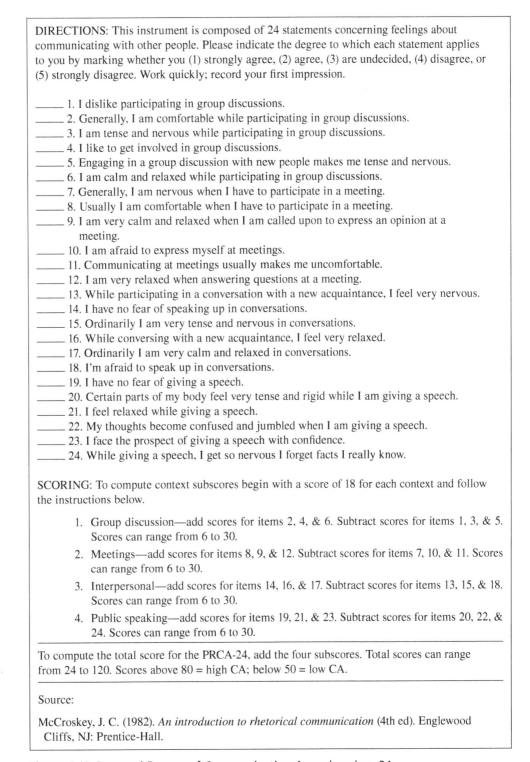

DIRECTIONS: This instrument is composed of 24 statements concerning feelings about communicating with other people. Please indicate the degree to which each statement applies to you by marking whether you (1) strongly agree, (2) agree, (3) are undecided, (4) disagree, or (5) strongly disagree. Work quickly; record your first impression.

_____ 1. I dislike participating in group discussions.
_____ 2. Generally, I am comfortable while participating in group discussions.
_____ 3. I am tense and nervous while participating in group discussions.
_____ 4. I like to get involved in group discussions.
_____ 5. Engaging in a group discussion with new people makes me tense and nervous.
_____ 6. I am calm and relaxed while participating in group discussions.
_____ 7. Generally, I am nervous when I have to participate in a meeting.
_____ 8. Usually I am comfortable when I have to participate in a meeting.
_____ 9. I am very calm and relaxed when I am called upon to express an opinion at a meeting.
_____ 10. I am afraid to express myself at meetings.
_____ 11. Communicating at meetings usually makes me uncomfortable.
_____ 12. I am very relaxed when answering questions at a meeting.
_____ 13. While participating in a conversation with a new acquaintance, I feel very nervous.
_____ 14. I have no fear of speaking up in conversations.
_____ 15. Ordinarily I am very tense and nervous in conversations.
_____ 16. While conversing with a new acquaintance, I feel very relaxed.
_____ 17. Ordinarily I am very calm and relaxed in conversations.
_____ 18. I'm afraid to speak up in conversations.
_____ 19. I have no fear of giving a speech.
_____ 20. Certain parts of my body feel very tense and rigid while I am giving a speech.
_____ 21. I feel relaxed while giving a speech.
_____ 22. My thoughts become confused and jumbled when I am giving a speech.
_____ 23. I face the prospect of giving a speech with confidence.
_____ 24. While giving a speech, I get so nervous I forget facts I really know.

SCORING: To compute context subscores begin with a score of 18 for each context and follow the instructions below.

1. Group discussion—add scores for items 2, 4, & 6. Subtract scores for items 1, 3, & 5. Scores can range from 6 to 30.
2. Meetings—add scores for items 8, 9, & 12. Subtract scores for items 7, 10, & 11. Scores can range from 6 to 30.
3. Interpersonal—add scores for items 14, 16, & 17. Subtract scores for items 13, 15, & 18. Scores can range from 6 to 30.
4. Public speaking—add scores for items 19, 21, & 23. Subtract scores for items 20, 22, & 24. Scores can range from 6 to 30.

To compute the total score for the PRCA-24, add the four subscores. Total scores can range from 24 to 120. Scores above 80 = high CA; below 50 = low CA.

Source:

McCroskey, J. C. (1982). *An introduction to rhetorical communication* (4th ed). Englewood Cliffs, NJ: Prentice-Hall.

Figure 6.12 Personal Report of Communication Apprehension–24

Other people are likely to have contextually based CA, or they experience apprehension in one of the communicative contexts (interpersonal, meeting, group, or public). For example, an individual may experience CA while interacting with someone on a one-on-one basis but have no problem standing up before an audience of 1,000 people and giving a speech. Yet other people experience CA more based on the audience with whom they must communicate. Almost everyone experiences CA at some point with a specific audience. Whether you are giving a presentation in front of your peers or your boss can impact the degree of anxiety you may feel.

The last type of CA that can occur is referred to as situationally based CA. Sometimes the uniqueness of a specific situation may cause you to experience anxiety. One of the authors of this text has given countless numbers of public speeches. During one particular speech, our colleague looked down and noticed that his hand was visibly shaking. He had never before in his life had a shaking hand while giving a speech. His outward nervousness made him even more anxious, and before he knew it he had no idea what he was saying because he was focusing on his own anxiety.

Ethnocentrism

We all know that people around the world believe that "The United States is the best country on the face of the planet. Without the United States, the world would be less artistic, less moral, and less intelligent. In fact, if everyone would be more like the United States, this world would be much better off." Yes, people from around the world say this exact sentence—they just plug in their own country of origin in place of "the United States." The Russians, Chinese, Australians, South Africans, Finns, Brazilians, Egyptians, Singaporeans, Puerto Ricans, and Japanese all feel their country is the best and that if everyone would just behave like people in their country, the world would be much better off. Few things have been found to be truly **pancultural** (the same across all cultures), but this view that an individual's own culture is superior to all the rest is pancultural. The view that the customs and practices of one's own culture are superior to those of other cultures is known as ethnocentrism. People in all cultures are ethnocentric to varying degrees. Neuliep and McCroskey (1997) created an ethnocentrism scale to measure this phenomenon. Before we start discussing the nature of ethnocentrism, please fill out the ethnocentrism scale in Figure 6.13.

The term "**ethnocentrism**" comes from the combination of two Greek words: *ethnos* (nation) and *kentron* (center). In combination, *ethnos* and *kentron* suggest that an individual's nation is the center of the universe. When one holds ethnocentric views, as virtually everyone does, an individual's culture is used as the standard by which all other cultures are evaluated. In fact, any deviation from an individual's culture is most likely (but not always) seen as negative, which indicates the inferiority of the *other* culture and the people from that culture. Although ethnocentrism may sound innately bad, it is not inherently bad to have some level of ethnocentrism. In fact, ethnocentrism can be positive.

One way in which ethnocentrism is positive is that it gives the people in a culture an identity and helps make them more cohesive, which helps promote positive and effective communication among members of the culture. For a short period after September 11, 2001, people in the United States truly functioned as Americans. During this time period, Americans were welcoming of all Americans, but wary of anyone who was not an American citizen. At the same time, in New York on 9/11 people saw everyone around them as New Yorkers despite the amazing cultural diversity that exists in New York City. You may be thinking to yourself that these are just examples of patriotism, and you are right. Patriotism is innately ethnocentric. Wars are often fought in cultures because one culture views their way of life as something ultimately moral and worth fighting for.

Instructions: Below are items that relate to the cultures of different parts of the world. Work quickly and record your first reaction to each item. There are no right or wrong answers. Please indicate the degree to which you agree or disagree with each item using the following five-point scale:

Strongly Disagree	Disagree	Neutral	Agree	Strongly Agree
1	2	3	4	5

_____ 1. Most other cultures are backward compared to my culture.
_____ 2. My culture should be the role model for other cultures.
_____ 3. People from other cultures act strange when they come to my culture.
_____ 4. Lifestyles in other cultures are just as valid as those in my culture.
_____ 5. Other cultures should try to be more like my culture.
_____ 6. I am not interested in the values and customs of other cultures.
_____ 7. People in my culture could learn a lot from people in other cultures.
_____ 8. Most people from other cultures just don't know what's good for them.
_____ 9. I respect the values and customs of other cultures.
_____ 10. Other cultures are smart to look up to our culture.
_____ 11. Most people would be happier if they lived like people in my culture.
_____ 12. I have many friends from different cultures.
_____ 13. People in my culture have just about the best lifestyles of anywhere.
_____ 14. Lifestyles in other cultures are not as valid as those in my culture.
_____ 15. I am very interested in the values and customs of other cultures.
_____ 16. I apply my values when judging people who are different.
_____ 17. I see people who are similar to me as virtuous.
_____ 18. I do not cooperate with people who are different.
_____ 19. Most people in my culture just don't know what is good for them.
_____ 20. I do not trust people who are different.
_____ 21. I dislike interacting with people from different cultures.
_____ 22. I have little respect for the values and customs of other cultures.

SCORING: To compute your scores follow the instructions below:

1.   How to Score Drop questions 3, 6, 12, 15, 16, 17, 19

Step One: Add scores for items 1, 2, 5, 8, 10, 11, 13, 14, 18, 20, 21 & 22.
Step Two: Add scores for items 4, 7, & 9.
Step Three: Add 18 to Step 1.
Step Four: Subtract the score for Step two from the score for Step Three.

The result is your Ethnocentrism score. Higher scores = higher levels of ethnocentrism.

Interpretation:

Scores should be between 15 and 75. Most people score between 20 and 40. Scores over 32 are considered high.

Source:

Newuliep, J. W., & McCroskey, J. C. (1997). The development of a U.S. and generalized ethnocentrism scale. *Communication Research Reports, 14*, 385–398.

Figure 6.13 Ethnocentrism Scale

Humor Assessment

Have you ever noticed that people who are able to get everyone around them laughing tend to have more friends and are invited to more parties? The ability to effectively use humor is a trait that many people wish they could have, but only some people seem to have that extra spark that makes their humor usage appear flawless. In an attempt to measure the extent to which an individual uses humor during interpersonal interactions, Wrench and Richmond (2004) created the humor assessment instrument. Before we start discussing the nature of an individual's **humor assessment**, please fill out the humor assessment instrument in Figure 6.14.

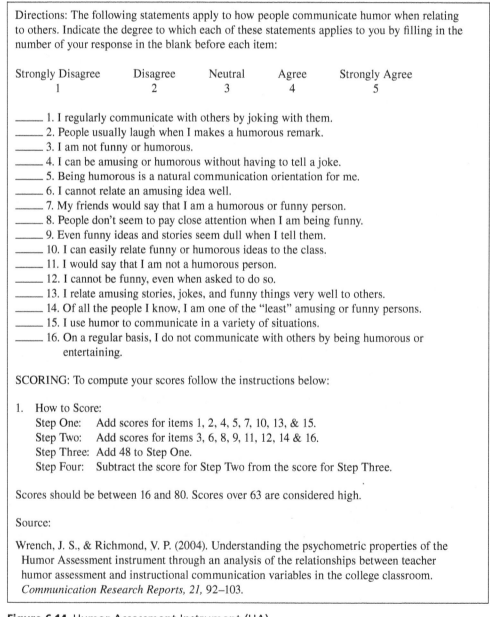

Directions: The following statements apply to how people communicate humor when relating to others. Indicate the degree to which each of these statements applies to you by filling in the number of your response in the blank before each item:

Strongly Disagree	Disagree	Neutral	Agree	Strongly Agree
1	2	3	4	5

_____ 1. I regularly communicate with others by joking with them.
_____ 2. People usually laugh when I makes a humorous remark.
_____ 3. I am not funny or humorous.
_____ 4. I can be amusing or humorous without having to tell a joke.
_____ 5. Being humorous is a natural communication orientation for me.
_____ 6. I cannot relate an amusing idea well.
_____ 7. My friends would say that I am a humorous or funny person.
_____ 8. People don't seem to pay close attention when I am being funny.
_____ 9. Even funny ideas and stories seem dull when I tell them.
_____ 10. I can easily relate funny or humorous ideas to the class.
_____ 11. I would say that I am not a humorous person.
_____ 12. I cannot be funny, even when asked to do so.
_____ 13. I relate amusing stories, jokes, and funny things very well to others.
_____ 14. Of all the people I know, I am one of the "least" amusing or funny persons.
_____ 15. I use humor to communicate in a variety of situations.
_____ 16. On a regular basis, I do not communicate with others by being humorous or entertaining.

SCORING: To compute your scores follow the instructions below:

1. How to Score:
   Step One: Add scores for items 1, 2, 4, 5, 7, 10, 13, & 15.
   Step Two: Add scores for items 3, 6, 8, 9, 11, 12, 14 & 16.
   Step Three: Add 48 to Step One.
   Step Four: Subtract the score for Step Two from the score for Step Three.

Scores should be between 16 and 80. Scores over 63 are considered high.

Source:

Wrench, J. S., & Richmond, V. P. (2004). Understanding the psychometric properties of the Humor Assessment instrument through an analysis of the relationships between teacher humor assessment and instructional communication variables in the college classroom. *Communication Research Reports, 21,* 92–103.

Figure 6.14 Humor Assessment Instrument (HA)

Humor is a fascinating variable to study because of the dramatic effects that humor can have on people's everyday lives. The ability to use humor as a tool for interpersonal communication has consistently been shown to be useful whether you are in the health-care setting, classroom, or boardroom. In research that has examined humor in health-care settings (Wrench & Booth-Butterfield, 2003 [see textbook's website for this article]), physicians who are more humorous are perceived by patients as being more credible. Patients are also more satisfied with physicians who are funny and are less likely to sue a physician who uses moderate levels of humor during a medical interview. In the area of educational research, teachers who are more humorous are also perceived as more trustworthy and credible by their students when compared to teachers who are not perceived as humorous by their students. Students also like humorous teachers more than nonhumorous teachers and even like the content more from humorous teachers than from nonhumorous teachers. In fact, teachers who are humorous in the classroom actually have students who learn more in the class. In the organizational setting, many businesses actually hire humor consultants to come in and "liven things up" around the office because a humorous work environment has been shown to increase productivity levels. Furthermore, employees who perceive their superiors as being humorous experience higher levels of job satisfaction and are less likely to quit their job, which ultimately saves an organization lots of money.

When you examine the results from research on humor in different contexts, it points in one direction—humor is a good thing. Although what people find humorous is culturally based, the ability to enact it appears to be more biologically based. When we talk about a cultural basis for what we find humorous, think about the types of stand-up comedians you like versus the type of comedians your parents or grandparents would like. What people within a different culture or co-culture enjoy as humorous is dependent on what they are taught is funny. If you are taught that farting in public is rude and obnoxious, you will not find a "fart joke" funny, although other people will think the joke is hysterical.

Nonverbal Immediacy

Have you ever noticed that you are drawn to some people and not to others? One reason for this is an individual's level of nonverbal immediacy. **Immediacy**, as a general concept, refers to the degree of perceived physical or psychological distance between people in a relationship. An immediate relationship is one in which the people in the relationship see themselves as close (both physically and mentally) to one another. When we talk about physical closeness, we are not talking about intimacy—just a perception that the other person is physically near you. Have you ever noticed how some people can make themselves look unapproachable just by the way they hold their bodies and look at you? Although these people may be in the same physical environment as you are, you probably will not perceive yourself to be close to these people. On the flip side, many people experience a certain feeling of closeness with a public speaker although they are 100 yards away during the speech. All of us communicate a certain presence to other people. How we hold our bodies and look at people will determine whether we start, continue, or terminate interactions with other people. Whom we desire to communicate with is communicated to that other person through both our verbal and our nonverbal messages. Thus, the verbal and nonverbal messages we send and receive in a relationship will define the level of immediacy that develops in that relationship. Figure 6.15 shows the Self-Report of Nonverbal Immediacy.

As mentioned earlier, immediacy is created through both verbal and nonverbal messages. **Verbal immediacy** is created through comments such as, "I see what you mean," "Tell me more," "That is a good point," and "I think so too." Contrast these comments with the following: "Oh, shut up," "I do believe a village lost its idiot," "I thought of that years ago,"

DIRECTIONS: The following statements describe the ways some people behave while talking with or to others. Please indicate in the space at the left of each item the degree to which you believe the statement applies to (**fill in the target person's name or description**). Please use the following 5-point scale:

1 = Never; 2 = Rarely; 3 = Occasionally; 4 = Often; 5 = Very Often

_____ 1. I use my hands and arms to gesture while talking to people.
_____ 2. I touch others on the shoulder or arm while talking to them.
_____ 3. I use a monotone or dull voice while talking to people.
_____ 4. I look over or away from others while talking to them.
_____ 5. I move away from others when they touch me while talking.
_____ 6. I have a relaxed body position when talking to people.
_____ 7. I frown while talking to people.
_____ 8. I avoid eye contact while talking to people.
_____ 9. I have a tense body position while talking to people.
_____ 10. I sit close or stand close to people while talking with them.
_____ 11. My voice is monotonous or dull when talking to people.
_____ 12. I use a variety of vocal expressions when talking to people.
_____ 13. I gesture when talking to people.
_____ 14. I am animated when talking to people.
_____ 15. I have a bland facial expression when talking to people.
_____ 16. I move closer to people when talking to them.
_____ 17. I look directly at people while talking to them.
_____ 18. I am stiff when talking to people.
_____ 19. I have a lot of vocal variety when talking to people.
_____ 20. I avoid gesturing while talking to people.
_____ 21. I lean toward people when talking to them.
_____ 22. I maintain eye contact with people when talking to them.
_____ 23. I try not to sit or stand close to people when talking with them.
_____ 24. I lean away from people when talking to them.
_____ 25. I smile when talking to people.
_____ 26. I avoid touching people when talking to them.

SCORING: To compute your scores follow the instructions below:

Step One: Add scores for items 1, 2, 6, 10, 12, 13, 14, 16, 17, 19, 21, 22, & 25.
Step Two: Add scores for items 3, 4, 5, 7, 8, 9, 11, 15, 18, 20, 23, 24, & 26.
Step Three: Add 78 to Step One.
Step Four: Subtract the score for Step Two from the score for Step Three.

Scores should be between 26 and 30. Scores over 112 for females and over 104 for males are considered high.

Source:

Richmond, V. P., McCroskey, J. C., & Johnson, A. D. (2003). Development of the nonverbal immediacy scale (NIS): Measures of self- and other-perceived nonverbal immediacy. *Communication Quarterly, 51*, 504–517.

Figure 6.15 Nonverbal Immediacy Scale–Self-Report (NIS-S)

and "Frankly, I don't care what you think." The first series of phrases helps to increase the perceived physical and psychological closeness between two people, whereas the second series of phrases only increases the perception of distance. **Nonverbal immediacy**, by contrast, consists of communicative behaviors like leaning in toward the person while talking to her or him, maintaining eye contact, smiling, nodding your head, not folding your arms in front of you while talking, and many other behaviors. Nonimmediate nonverbal behaviors would be the opposite of the immediate ones: leaning away from the person while talking, avoiding eye contact, frowning or scowling, not moving your head at all (looking rigid), folding your arms in front of you, and many other behaviors. The Nonverbal Immediacy scale (Figure 6.15) was designed to examine an individual's tendency to employ different nonverbally immediate behaviors while avoiding communicative behaviors that are not nonverbally immediate.

You may be wondering why nonverbal immediacy is so important that we need to research it as a variable. Nonverbal immediacy has been linked to a number of important communication outcomes. First, immediacy will usually lead to an increase in communication between participants and interactants. When someone feels that another person is either physically or psychologically close to her or him, he or she becomes more relaxed and open to communication. Second, immediacy will lead to increased attentiveness by the receiver. If we perceive someone is immediate, we naturally focus attention on that person. So if you want someone to listen to what you are saying, employing nonverbally and verbally immediate behavior is a trick that can be used to get and maintain that person's attention. Third, immediacy will increase the likelihood that listening will improve between the interactants. People are more open to listening to what another person is saying to them when they perceive that the person is immediate. Fourth, immediacy leads to increased liking between interactants. If you perceive that someone is physically and psychologically close to you, you are simply going to like that person more. Overall, these four outcomes lead to more effective communication.

Sociocommunicative Orientation

Psychologist Sandra Bem (1974) started researching the concepts of masculinity and femininity and created a scale she called the Bem Sex-Role Inventory (BSRI). The BSRI was originally constructed by having different groups of participants read a list of adjectives and determine which characteristics on the list were seen as more desirable in the United States for one biological sex or the other. After participants rated these lists, Bem determine that 20 items were ranked by females and males to be more desirable for a man (masculine scale) and 20 items were ranked by females and males to be more desirable for a woman (feminine scale). A number of researchers examined the BSRI and realized that what Bem thought she was measuring really was not a scale of maleness and femaleness, but a scale of how people interact with each other. For this reason, Richmond and McCroskey (1985) created a scale to measure how people communicate either assertively (Bem's masculinity) or responsively (Bem's femininity), and called the scale the Sociocommunicative Orientation Scale. Figure 6.16 illustrates the Sociocommunicative Orientation Scale; please fill out the scale.

In the Sociocommunicative Orientation Scale, two factors are measured: assertiveness and responsiveness. **Assertiveness** is the capacity to make requests, actively disagree, express positive or negative personal rights and feelings, initiate, maintain, or disengage from conversations, and stand up for oneself without attacking another. Bem's research originally suggested that these communicative behaviors were only enacted by males, but we all know many women who are equally adept at all of the assertive behaviors. Although many women employ assertive communication behaviors, many societies stereotype appropriate male communication behavior as being closely associated with these behaviors. Conversely,

DIRECTIONS: The questionnaire below lists 20 personality characteristics. Please indicate the degree to which you believe each of these characteristics applies to YOU, as you normally communicate with others, by marking whether you (5) strongly agree that it applies, (4) agree that it applies, (3) are undecided, (2) disagree that it applies, or (1) strongly disagree that it applies. There are no right or wrong answers. Work quickly; record your first impression.

_____ 1. Helpful
_____ 2. Defends own beliefs
_____ 3. Independent
_____ 4. Responsive to others
_____ 5. Forceful
_____ 6. Has strong personality
_____ 7. Sympathetic
_____ 8. Compassionate
_____ 9. Assertive
_____ 10. Sensitive to the needs of others
_____ 11. Dominant
_____ 12. Sincere
_____ 13. Gentle
_____ 14. Willing to take a stand
_____ 15. Warm
_____ 16. Tender
_____ 17. Friendly
_____ 18. Acts as a leader
_____ 19. Aggressive
_____ 20. Competitive

Items 2, 3, 5, 6, 9, 11, 14, 18, 19, & 20 measure assertiveness. Add the scores on these items to get your assertiveness score. Items 1, 4, 7, 8, 10, 12, 13, 15, 16, & 17 measure responsiveness. Add the scores on these items to get your responsiveness score.

Source:

Richmond, V. P., & McCroskey, J. C. (1990). Reliability and separation of factors on the assertiveness-responsiveness scale. *Psychological Reports, 67*, 449–450.

Figure 6.16 Sociocommunicative Orientation Scale

responsiveness is the capacity to be sensitive to the communication of others, to be a good listener, to make others comfortable in communicating, and to recognize the needs and desires of others. Terms commonly used to describe a person who engages in responsive communication behaviors include helpful, sympathetic, compassionate, sensitive to needs of others, sincere, gentle, warm, tender, friendly, understanding, and (of course) responsive to others. Although such terms do describe the stereotypical perception of how females communicate in the United States, in a broader sense these terms describe any person who is open to the communication of others and empathetic with those others.

At this point we should note that **sociocommunicative orientation**, which is a self-report scale, is only half of the puzzle when examining this variable. The scale seen in Figure 6.15 can easily be retooled to examine someone else's behavior in what is called the sociocommunicative style scale using the following instructions: "Please indicate the degree to which you believe each of these characteristics applies to the [place name here] by marking whether you (5) *strongly agree that it applies*, (4) *agree that it applies*, (3) *are undecided*, (2) *disagree that it applies*, or (1) *strongly disagree that it applies*." A lot of research has examined how an individual's **sociocommunicative style** impacts people's perceptions of other behaviors. For example, research in instructional communication has found that highly assertive and responsive teachers are perceived as more nonverbally immediate, more trustworthy, and more humorous. In fact, teachers who are highly responsive have been shown to have students who learn more, are more satisfied with their teacher, and are more likely to talk to their teacher outside of class. Sociocommunicative style has also been examined in the health-care setting examining a patient's perception of her or his physician's sociocommunicative style. In the health-care setting, physician assertiveness and responsiveness were both shown to relate to patient perceptions of her or his physician's credibility. Furthermore, patients who perceived their physicians as responsive were more satisfied and believed they received good medical care compared to patients who did not perceive their physicians as responsive. These results were also seen in subordinate supervisor relationships in organizations. Subordinates who perceived their supervisors as assertive and responsive also perceived their supervisors as credible. And subordinates who perceived their supervisors as assertive and responsive also reported higher levels of job satisfaction and motivation. Overall, sociocommunicative orientation/style has been shown to be an extremely important communication variable.

Willingness to Communicate

The next interval variable is the variable willingness to communicate (WTC). Communication research has found that some people are more likely to initiate communicative interactions than others. Judee Burgoon (1976) initiated this line of research by examining the construct she labeled as "unwillingness to communicate," which she described as a "chronic tendency to avoid and/or devalue oral communication" (p. 60). McCroskey and Richmond (1987) retooled the concept to examine an individual's general attitude toward communicating with other people. McCroskey (1992) wrote that "the construct is that of an orientation toward communication which we have referred to previously as a predisposition to avoid communication . . . a behavioral tendency regarding talking frequency" (p. 21). In essence, **willingness to communicate** can be defined as the tendency of an individual to engage in communication with other people. Please complete the WTC scale in Figure 6.17. Carefully read the directions on this scale because it is not a Likert-type scale and can throw off some participants because it asks for percentages.

WTC, as previous mentioned, examines the extent to which an individual initiates or avoids communication. Look at your scores for WTC. Do you have any areas in which you exhibit a low WTC? Maybe you have a high WTC in public speaking situations but a low WTC in meetings? You may have a high WTC score in every context, but a low WTC with strangers. Your individual WTC is deeply rooted and has been shown to have a large genetic basis.

Research has shown that an individual's level of CA is probably the best predictor of a person's level of WTC. If someone is high CA, then he or she is probably low WTC and vice versa. WTC is generally thought of as a trait-based predisposition that determines the degree to which people communicate in a variety of contexts (interpersonal, meeting, group, and public). Whether a person is willing to communicate with another in a given interpersonal example (e.g., student–teacher, parent–child, subordinate–supervisor) is often affected by situational constraints within the encounter such as the nature of the relationship of the interactants. Someone may be willing to talk to a teacher, but less willing to talk to her or his supervisor. Although WTC is dependent on the situation, people usually exhibit regular WTC tendencies across situations, contexts, and audiences.

When people talk about WTC, they often mistake it for the term shyness, which is not the same thing. Shyness is the behavioral tendency to not initiate communication and/or respond to the initiatives of others. Shyness stems from a preference for noncommunication by the individual—a reduced WTC. WTC may be considered an attitude toward initiating communication or, as some prefer, the person's intent or disposition toward the behavior of initiating communication. This notion of shyness is similar to CA, previously defined in this chapter as

DIRECTIONS: Below are 20 situations in which a person might choose to communicate or not to communicate. Presume you have *completely free choice*. Determine the percentage of times you would *choose to initiate communication* in each type of situation. Indicate in the space at the left what percent of the time you would choose to communicate. Choose any numbers between 0 and 100.

_____ 1. Talk with a service station attendant.
_____ 2. Talk with a physician.
_____ 3. Present a talk to a group of strangers.
_____ 4. Talk with an acquaintance while standing in line.
_____ 5. Talk with a salesperson in a store.
_____ 6. Talk in a large meeting of friends.
_____ 7. Talk with a police officer.
_____ 8. Talk in a small group of strangers.
_____ 9. Talk with a friend while standing in line.
_____ 10. Talk with a waiter/waitress in a restaurant.
_____ 11. Talk in a large meeting of acquaintances.
_____ 12. Talk with a stranger while standing in line.
_____ 13. Talk with a secretary.
_____ 14. Present a talk to a group of friends.
_____ 15. Talk in a small group of acquaintances.
_____ 16. Talk with a garbage collector.
_____ 17. Talk in a large meeting of strangers.
_____ 18. Talk with a spouse (or girl/boyfriend).
_____ 19. Talk in a small group of friends.
_____ 20. Present a talk to a group of acquaintances.

SCORING: The WTC permits computation of one total score and seven subscores. The range for all scores is 0–100. Follow the procedures outlined below.

1. Group discussion—add scores for items 8, 15, & 19; divide sum by 3. Scores above 89 = high WTC, scores below 57 = low WTC in this context.
2. Meetings—add scores for items 6, 11, & 17; divide sum by 3. Scores above 80 = high WTC, scores below 39 = low WTC in this context.
3. Interpersonal—add scores for items 4, 9, & 12; divide sum by 3. Scores above 94 = high WTC, scores below 64 = low WTC in this context.
4. Public speaking—add scores for items 3, 14, & 20; divide sum by 3. Scores above 78 = high WTC, scores below 33 = low WTC in this context.
5. Stranger—add scores for items 3, 8, 12, & 17; divide sum by 4. Scores above 63 = high WTC, scores below 18 = low WTC with these receivers.
6. Acquaintance—add scores for items 4, 11, 15, & 20; divide sum by 4. Scores above 92 = high WTC, scores below 57 = low WTC with these receivers.
7. Friends—add scores for items 6, 9, 14, & 19; divide sum by 4. Scores above 99 = high WTC, scores below 71 = low WTC with these receivers.

Source:

McCroskey, J. C. (1992). Reliability and validity of the willingness to communicate scale. *Communication Quarterly, 40,* 16–25.
Richmond, V. P., Wrench, J. S., & McCroskey, J. C. (2013). *Communication apprehension, avoidance and effectiveness* (6th Ed.). Boston: Allyn & Bacon.

Figure 6.17 Willingness to Communicate

the fear or anxiety associated with either real or anticipated communication with another person or persons.

Ultimately, when one examines the interrelationships among CA, WTC, and shyness, the three constructs can appear similar. However, with regard to how communication researchers utilize the terms, they do not overlap in definition: CA is what a person feels (they feel fear or anxiety); shyness is the degree to which one refrains from actual communication; and WTC is one's inclination to talk.

Although research has shown that there are a number of possible causes (both nature and nurture) for an individual's WTC level, WTC as a variable is interesting in how it relates to other communication variables in research. Previous research in WTC has primarily occurred in classrooms, health-care, and organizational settings. Research has found that students with low WTC levels participated less in the classroom than students with high scores. Students who have high WTC scores have also been shown to be perceived as more communicatively competent by others than students with low WTC scores.

In essence, not every person you run into who is quiet has the same reasons for being quiet; however, the consequences of being perceived as quiet are similar. As we discussed earlier in this chapter, people who are quiet are generally perceived as less intelligent, lazy, and unfriendly, so quiet people have a number of stereotypes they must battle simply based on their degree of willingness to talk.

Beliefs and Attitudes

Generalized Belief Scale

Unlike the previous interval variables discussed in this section, the next two variables are different because they are designed to be utilized in a wide variety of contexts. The Generalized Belief scale was created by McCroskey (1966) as a tool for examining the strength of an individual's belief on a given topic. **Beliefs** concern our perception of reality about whether something is true or false. The scale in Figure 6.17 is designed to be a general scale that can be utilized in a number of different situations. In essence, the scale in Figure 6.18 could be used to measure a person's belief about abortion, euthanasia, capital punishment, or, as we have in this case, the belief that "everyone should be required to take public speaking in college."

Generalized Attitude Measure

The second scale in this section that has the ability to measure different things every time it is employed is the Generalized Attitude Measure. Like the Generalized Belief Scale, it is designed to measure a range of different attitudes depending on what needs to be analyzed by a researcher. An **attitude** is defined as a predisposition to respond to people, ideas, or objects in an evaluative way. When we define an attitude as a predisposition, we define an attitude as an individual's tendency to do something. Here it is a tendency to *evaluate* people, ideas, or objects. The word "evaluative" in this definition means making judgments of good or bad, desirable or undesirable, likable or unlikable, etc. In essence, there are countless numbers of attitudes that an individual could measure using the Generalized Attitude Scale. For example, you could use it to measure an individual's attitude about sex, broccoli, public speaking, or, as we have in this book, higher education. Figure 6.19 contains the Generalized Attitude Measure retooled to measure an individual's attitude about higher education.

We believe that studying beliefs and attitudes is extremely important for communication researchers. By using the word "believe," we imply that for us (not necessarily for everyone else) the study of beliefs and attitudes is a true, correct, appropriate set of variables to study. We "believe" in the studying of beliefs and attitudes by communication researchers. We also think that studying beliefs and attitudes is good, so we have a positive attitude toward it. Belief has to do with our perceptions of reality; whereas attitude has to do with our evaluation of that reality.

Instructions: On the scales below, please indicate the degree to which you believe the following statement **"Everyone Should Be Required to Take Public Speaking in College."** Numbers "1" and "7" indicate a very strong feeling. Numbers "2" and "6" indicate a strong feeling. Numbers "3" and "5" indicate a fairly week feeling. Number "4" indicates you are undecided or do not understand the adjective pairs themselves. There are no right or wrong answers. *Only circle one number per line.*

1.   Agree   7 6 5 4 3 2 1   Disagree
2.   False   1 2 3 4 5 6 7   True
3.   Incorrect   1 2 3 4 5 6 7   Correct
4.   Right   7 6 5 4 3 2 1   Wrong
5.   Yes   7 6 5 4 3 2 1   No

* To compute your score, simply add up the numbers you circled.

Sources:

McCroskey, J. C. (1966). *Experimental studies of the effects of ethos and evidence in persuasive communication.* Unpublished doctoral dissertation. Pennsylvania State University.

McCroskey, J. C., & Richmond, V. P. (1989). Bipolar scales. In P. Emmert & L. L. Barker (Eds.), *Measurement of Communication Behavior* (pp. 154–167). New York: Longman.

Figure 6.18 Generalized Belief Scale

Instructions: On the scales below, please indicate your feelings about **"Higher Education."** Numbers "1" and "7" indicate a very strong feeling. Numbers "2" and "6" indicate a strong feeling. Numbers "3" and "5" indicate a fairly week feeling. Number "4" indicates you are undecided or do not understand the adjective pairs themselves. There are no right or wrong answers. *Only circle one number per line.*

1.   Good   7 6 5 4 3 2 1   Bad
2.   Wrong   1 2 3 4 5 6 7   Right
3.   Harmful   1 2 3 4 5 6 7   Beneficial
4.   Fair   7 6 5 4 3 2 1   Unfair
5.   Wise   7 6 5 4 3 2 1   Foolish
6.   Negative   1 2 3 4 5 6 7   Positive

* To compute your score, simply add up the numbers you circled.

Sources:

McCroskey, J. C. (1966). *Experimental studies of the effects of ethos and evidence in persuasive communication.* Unpublished doctoral dissertation. Pennsylvania State University.

McCroskey, J. C., & Richmond, V. P. (1989). Bipolar scales. In P. Emmert & L. L. Barker (Eds.), *Measurement of Communication Behavior* (pp. 154–167). New York: Longman.

Figure 6.19 Generalized Attitude Measure

In this section, we have examined six interval variables using a Likert scale (communication apprehension, ethnocentrism, humor assessment, nonverbal immediacy, sociocommunicative orientation, and willingness to communicate) and two variables using a bipolar scale (belief that everyone should take public speaking in college and attitude toward higher education). In the next section, we will examine the ratio variable we collected data on in this study.

RATIO VARIABLES

For the dataset collected for this book, we decided to include one ratio variable. For a variable to be seen as ratio, the distance between attributes has real quantitative meaning and has an absolute zero. Age is the only variable that has a scale with attributes that have real quantitative meaning and an absolute zero. We know for a fact that someone who is 12 years old is exactly twice as old as someone who is 6 years old. You cannot say the same thing with interval variables. We could not say that someone with a CA score of 80 is twice as apprehensive as someone with a CA score of 40 because the ranges do not have real quantitative meaning. Furthermore, age does have an absolute zero. Of course, with humans the absolute zero for age is birth.

Writing Up Scales Using APA Style

To this point, we have discussed the variables collected for this text's real-world dataset. Being able to identify the different variables and the different measurement levels is only part of the picture when conducting a research project. Once a researcher has determined which variables should be examined in a research study, he or she must clearly explain the variables in the method section of the research paper in a clear and concise fashion. For this reason, this section will walk you through how to more clearly write a method section than originally discussed in Chapter 4.

PARTICIPANTS

According to Chapter 4, the first part of a method section should report who the participants were. You must report basic demographic characteristics (sex and age) of the participants along with how you were able to attract them. All of the numbers we will need for this section will be calculated in the next chapter, so for now trust us that these numbers do come from somewhere and have a legitimate purpose. Here is an example of how this might appear in APA:

Participants for this study were undergraduate students taking both lower and upper division courses at a variety of colleges and universities. The sample can be broken into two man groups. First, in spring of 2005, 325 undergraduate students agreed to participate in this project. In the study sample, there were 139 (42.8%) females, 183 (56.3%) males, and 3 (0.9%) who did not respond to the biological sex question. The age of this sample ranged from 18 to 48 with a mean of 21.68 ($SD = 3.69$). Second, in Fall 2011, 328 undergraduate students agreed to participate in the continuance of this project. In the study sample, there were 182 (55.5%) females, 137 (41.8%) males, and 9 (2.7%) who did not respond to the biological sex question. The age of this sample ranged from 18 to 52 with a mean of 22.48 ($SD = 5.90$).

Further demographic variables were also collected to examine school classification and political affiliation of the entire sample. Our sample contained 52 (8.0%) freshman, 107 (16.4%) sophomores, 231 (35.3%) juniors, 244 (37.3%) seniors, 4 (0.6%) other, and 16 (2.4%) who did not respond to the question. The recorded political affiliations of the study participants are as follows: 220 (33. %)

Democrats, 220 (33.6%) Republicans, 131 (20.0%) others, 64 (9.8%) participants who are not registered to vote, and 19 (2.9%) who did not respond to the question.

PROCEDURES

Once you have explained who your sample is, you must explain the apparatus used in the research if you used one discussed in Chapter 5. Because this study did not use an apparatus, we can move on and discuss the procedures. When discussing the procedures, you should be as brief as possible while giving all of the appropriate and necessary information about what you did. For example, here is how you could describe the procedures for this project:

> The study participants were approached during their communication class and asked to participate in the study. All participants were handed a copy of the survey instrument that contained a cover letter explaining the purpose of the study. Participants were asked to sign and detach the cover page if they consented to filling out the questionnaire. All students who participated received extra credit for their participation. An alternative extra credit assignment was available to students who did not opt to participate in the study.

In this example, we start by explaining that all students were approached during class and asked to participate in the study. We then specified that we obtained consent, which is required by law (see Chapter 3), from the participants indicating their desire for participation. We also informed our potential readers that all students who participated in the project were given extra credit, but we did not coerce anyone into filling out the survey because we had an alternative extra credit assignment that participants could choose to complete if they were uncomfortable with the study.

INSTRUMENTATION

Once you have finished with the first three parts of a method section, you must explain all of the measurement tools employed in your study. In this study, we had all eight interval scales plus one ordinal scale that must be explained. To explain a scale, start by telling your audience who the creator of the scale was and what the scale is supposed to measure. Then explain how the scale is formatted, including a discussion of type of scale (Likert, bipolar, Stapel, or scalogram), numerical scale used (5 steps, 7 steps, or 10 steps), range possible on the scale, range received on the scale, and how to interpret scale results. For example:

> The Personal Report of Communication Apprehension-24 (PRCA-24) was created by McCroskey (1982) to measure an individual's level of fear or anxiety associated with either real or anticipated communication with another person or persons. The scale consists of 24 Likert-type items ranging from 1 (*strongly agree*) to 5 (*strongly disagree*) with a range of scores from 24 to 120, which was seen in this study. Higher scores are designed to indicate higher levels of communication apprehension.

In this example, we wrote about the PRCA-24. The first sentence explains that McCroskey (1982) wrote the PRCA-24 to measure CA. The second sentence explains that the scale consists of 24 scale items that were written in a Likert-type format with five steps: 1 *strongly agree*, 2 *agree*, 3 *neutral*, 4 *disagree*, and 5 *strongly disagree*. Note that you only have to give the first step and the last step because researchers who see those two will immediately understand how to interpret the scores. The second sentence also contains the range of possible scores available on the PRCA-24 and mentions that the range was found in the study. The last sentence then explains how the scores can be interpreted. Specifically, the higher someone's PRCA-24 score is, the higher her or his level of CA is. Figure 6.20 shows the complete list of variable write-ups using APA style.

PRCA-24. The Personal Report of Communication Apprehension–24 was created by McCroskey (1982) to measure an individual's level of fear or anxiety associated with either real or anticipated communication with another person or persons. The scale consists of 24 Likert items ranging from (1) *strongly agree* to (5) *strongly disagree* with a range of scores from 24 to 120, which was seen in this study. Higher scores are designed to indicate higher levels of communication apprehension.

Ethnocentrism. The Ethnocentrism Scale was created by Neuliep and McCroskey (1997) to measure an individual's tendency to feel that her or his culture is the center of the universe. The revised version of the scale employed here (Neuliep & McCroskey, 2000; McCroskey, 2001) consists of 22 Likert items ranging from (1) *strongly disagree* to (5) *strongly agree*. Fifteen of the items are scored; the remaining items are used as distracters. This scale has a possible range of 15–75; however, the range seen in this study was 16–61. Higher scores are designed to indicate higher levels of ethnocentrism.

Humor Assessment. The Humor Assessment (HA) was created by Wrench and Richmond (2004) to measure an individual's use of humor as a communicative device in interpersonal relationships. The scale was originally published in Richmond, Wrench, and Gorham (2001) as a tool for teachers to assess their own use of humor in the classroom. The HA was then validated by Wrench and McCroskey (2001), who found that it functioned distinctly different from M. Booth-Butterfield and S. Booth-Butterfield's (1991) Humor Orientation scale. The HA consists of 16 Likert type items range from 1 *strongly disagree* to 5 *strongly agree* with a range of scores from 16 to 80, which was seen in this study. Higher scores on the HA indicate a higher extent to which an individual uses humor while communicating interpersonally.

Nonverbal Immediacy Scale. The Nonverbal Immediacy Scale was created by Richmond, McCroskey, and Johnson (2003) to measure a receiver's perceived nonverbal immediacy between her- or himself and a source. The scale consists of 26 Likert-type items ranging from (1) *strongly disagree* to (5) *strongly agree*. This scale has a possible range of 26–130; however, the range seen in this study was 63–130. Higher scores are designed to indicate higher levels of nonverbally immediate behavior.

Sociocommunicative Orientation. The Sociocommunicative Orientation scale was created by Richmond and McCroskey (1985) as an instructional tool to examine the extent to which individuals use assertive or responsive communication. The instrument was first utilized in research by Thompson, Ishii, and Klopf (1990) and Ishii, Thompson, and Klopf (1990) to examine cultural differences in assertive and responsive communication. After the publication of these two articles, Richmond and McCroskey (1990) demonstrated the reliability and dimensionality of the measure itself. The sociocommunicative orientation scale consists of 10 items on each factor for a total of 20 items. Participants are asked to respond to short descriptive phrases that range from one to five words in length that indicate ways in which they may communicate. The measure asks a participant to respond in terms of how well the item applies to her or him using a Likert scale from (1) *strongly disagree that it applies* to (5) *strongly agree that it applies*. Each factor can range from 10 to 50. In the current study, assertiveness had a range from 19 to 50 and responsiveness had a range from 20 to 50. Higher scores on each factor are designed to represent either higher assertive or responsive communicative behaviors.

Willingness to Communicate. The Willingness to Communicate (WTC) scale was devised by McCroskey (1992) to measures a person's willingness to initiate communication with another person or persons. The scale consists of 20 items. Each of the items is designed to measure whether an individual would initiate communication in a specific situation or with a specific individual. Eight of the items are fillers and 12 are scored as part of the scale. Using a 101-point range from 0 (*never*) to 100 (*always*), participants are asked to indicate the percentage of time they would choose to communicate in each type of situation. Ultimately, the scores on the 12 items are added together to create a composite score, with higher scores indicating a higher

Figure 6.20 APA Write-Ups for Scales   *Continued*

Continued

> willingness to communicate. Scores on the WTC scale can range from 0 to 100; however, scores in the current study ranged from 18.25 to 100. Higher scores on the WTC scale are designed to indicate stronger likelihoods to initiate communicative interactions.
>
> *Generalized Belief Scale.* The Generalized Belief Scale was created by McCroskey (1966) and validated by McCroskey and Richmond (1996). The Generalized Belief Measure was created by McCroskey (1966) as a way to measure beliefs about specific concepts. By attaining an individual's general belief about a given topic, the researcher can measure the degree to which an individual believes in a given statement. The statement measured in this study was "Everyone Should Be Required to Take Public Speaking in College." The belief statement is then measured using a five-item semantic differential scale with seven steps. The Generalized Belief Scale has a range of 5 to 35, which was seen in this study. Higher scores on the Generalized Belief Scale indicate stronger beliefs.
>
> *Generalized Attitude Measure.* The Generalized Attitude Measure was a scale originally created by McCroskey (1966) and later validated by McCroskey and Richmond (1989) as a tool for determining someone's overall attitude about a specific subject. The Generalized Attitude Measure is measured using a six-item semantic differential scale with seven steps. For the purposes of this study, the Generalized Attitude Measure was utilized to determine the attitude of participants about higher education. The Generalized Attitude Measure has a range of 6–42; however, a range of 19–42 was seen in this study. Higher scores on the Generalized Attitude Measure indicate more positive attitudes.
>
> *Time on the Internet.* In addition to the above interval variables, one ordinal variable was also collected in this study to examine the amount of time an individual spends communicating using the Internet. In response to the question how much time they spend online during a given week, participants were given the following categories to select from: 0–½ hour, ½–1 hour, 1–2 hours, 2–5 hours, 5–10 hours, 10–15 hours, 15–20 hours, and 20+ hours. This is similar to the method used by Wrench, Fiore, and McCroskey (2005) to examine the same construct.

Conclusion

In this chapter, we have examined a wide variety of communication variables that were collected for inclusion in this book's accompanying dataset. The variables discussed in this chapter will be used numerous times throughout the rest of this book, so ensure you understand them: how they function in the world, how they are measured, and what they mean to communication researchers. In the next chapter we will go further into how each of the above scales was made by talking about the important issue of measurement.

KEY TERMS

Abstract variable
Antecedent variable
Assertiveness
Attitudes
Audience-specific behavior
Beliefs
Communication
   apprehension
Communication trait
Concrete variable

Dependent variable
Difference
Differences of degree
Differences of kind
Ethnocentrism
Humor assessment
Immediacy
Independent variable
Interval variable
Intervening variable

Likert scale
Negative relationship
Neutral relationship
Nominal variable
Nonverbal immediacy
Ordinal variable
Pancultural
Personality
Positive relationship
Ratio variable

Relationships	Situational behavior	Variable attributes
Responsiveness	Sociocommunicative	Variable values
Scale	Orientation	Verbal immediacy
Scalogram	Sociocommunicative style	Willingness to
Semantic differential/	Trait behavior	communicate
bipolar	Variable	

REFERENCES

Barbato, C. A., Graham, E. E., & Perse, E. M. (2003). Communicating in the family: An examination of the relationship of family communication climate and interpersonal communication motives. *Journal of Family Communication, 3*, 123–148.

Beatty, M. J. (1988). Situational and predispositional correlates of public speaking anxiety. *Communication Education, 37*, 28–39.

Beatty, M. J., McCroskey, J. C., & Valencic, K. M. (2001). *The biology of communication: A communibiological perspective.* Cresskill, NJ: Hampton Press.

Bem, S. L. (1974). The measurement of psychological androgyny. *Journal of Consulting and Clinical Psychology, 47*, 155–162.

Burgoon, J. K. (1976). The unwillingness-to-communicate scale: Development and validation. *Communication Monographs, 43*, 60–69.

Coombs, W. T., & Holladay, S. J. (2004). Understanding the aggressive workplace: Development of the workplace aggression tolerance questionnaire. *Communication Studies, 55*, 481–497.

Crespi, I. (1961). Use of a scaling technique in surveys. *Journal of Marketing, 25*(5), 69–72.

Guttman, L. (1944). A basis for scaling qualitative data. *American Sociological Review, 9*, 139–150.

Hamer, D. H., & Copeland, P. (1998). *Living with our genes: Why they matter more than you think.* New York, NY: Doubleday.

Hollander, E. P. (1976). *Principles and methods of social psychology* (3rd ed.). New York, NY: Oxford University Press.

Kuhn, T., & Poole, M. S. (2000). Do conflict management styles affect group decision making? *Human Communication Research, 26*, 558–591.

McCroskey, J. C. (1966). *Experimental studies of the effects of ethos and evidence in persuasive communication.* Unpublished doctoral dissertation, Pennsylvania State University.

McCroskey, J. C. (1970). Measures of communication-bound anxiety. *Speech Monographs, 37*, 269–277.

McCroskey, J. C. (1982). *An introduction to rhetorical communication* (4th ed.). Englewood Cliffs, NJ: Prentice Hall.

McCroskey, J. C. (1992). Reliability and validity of the willingness to communicate scale. *Communication Quarterly, 40*, 16–25.

McCroskey, J. C., & Richmond, V. P. (1987). Willingness to communicate. In J. C. McCroskey & J. A. Daly (Eds.), *Personality and interpersonal communication* (pp. 119–131). Newbury Park, CA: Sage.

Neuliep, J. W., & McCroskey, J. C. (1997). Development of a US and generalized ethnocentrism scale. *Communication Research Reports, 14*, 385–398.

Richmond, V. P. (1990). Communication in the classroom: Power and motivation. *Communication Education, 39*, 181-195.

Richmond, V. P., & McCroskey, J. C. (1985). *Communication: Apprehension, avoidance, and effectiveness.* Scottsdale, AZ: Gorsuch Scarisbrick.

Rocca, K. A., & Vogl-Bauer, S. (1999). Trait verbal aggression, sports fan identification, and perceptions of appropriate sports fan communication. *Communication Research Reports, 16*, 239–248.

Thomas, C., Booth-Butterfield, M., & Booth-Butterfield, S. (1995). Perceptions of deception, divorce disclosure, and communication satisfaction with parents. *Western Journal of Communication, 59,* 228–245.

Weber, K., Fornash, B., Corrigan, M., & Neupauer, N. (2003). The effect of interest on recall: An experiment. *Communication Research Reports, 20,* 116–123.

Wrench, J. S. (2005). Development and validity testing of the homonegativity short form. *Journal of Intercultural Communication Research, 34,* 152–165.

Wrench, J. S., & Booth-Butterfield, M. (2003). Increasing patient satisfaction and compliance: An examination of physician humor orientation, compliance-gaining strategies, and perceived credibility. *Communication Quarterly, 51,* 482–503.

Wrench, J. S., & Richmond, V. P. (2004). Understanding the psychometric properties of the Humor Assessment instrument through an analysis of the relationships between teacher humor assessment and instructional communication variables in the college classroom. *Communication Research Reports, 21,* 92–103.

Measurement

When you hear the word "measurement," what comes to mind? Maybe you think of pulling out a ruler and seeing how long a line is or pulling out a tape measure to measure the inseam of a pair of pants. In many ways, communication researchers define measurement in the same way as using a ruler or a tape measure. **Measurement** is the process of systematic observation and assignment of numbers to phenomena according to rules. The first part of this definition suggests that measurement is a process. The word process can be defined as a set of progressive, interdependent steps. In other words, when we measure something, there is a series of steps that we must go through. According to the definition, this series of steps helps us systematically observe a phenomenon and then assign numbers to that phenomenon. First, let's look at what we mean by "observe." To examine a phenomenon we must have the ability to see or perceive that phenomenon. If we cannot see or perceive a phenomenon, there is no way for us as researchers to measure it. Once a researcher has a general idea of what the phenomenon is, he or she can then assign numbers to it based on some set of established rules. In essence, when we know what the phenomenon is, we can then determine a way to quantify it, but we must be systematic in our quantification, so we must have some form of established rules.

Let's take the process of measuring a line as an example to walk us through this definition. First, we must define what the phenomenon is that we are attempting to measure. In the case of a line, we are attempting to measure the length of something, or in mathematics speak, we are attempting to measure the greatest dimension of a plane or solid figure. In essence, length must have a beginning and it must have an end. Once we know what the phenomenon is, we can attempt to determine how we are going to assign numbers to that phenomenon. In the case of length, many different numerical categorizing systems have been created. In ancient Greece, one may have measured the line in daktylos, which was roughly equivalent to 1.8–2 centimeters. Centimeters are part of a measurement system for distance called the metric system, which is the international system of units created by French scientists at the request of Louis XVI in the late eighteenth century. In fact, in most countries around the world, the metric system is the measure of choice for measuring distance. However, in the United States we have our own system for measuring length called the U.S. customary units, or English units. Whereas the metric system is based on millimeters, centimeters, meters, and kilometers, the U.S. customary units are based on the inch, foot, yard, and mile. This is not to say that the metric system and U.S. customary units are not related to each other, because 1 centimeter is equivalent to 0.3937 inches; however, each has its own specific rules for how measurement works. When we measure phenomena like distance, we do not combine the two systems of measurement because they have separate measurement rules. For example, we would not tell someone to drive 6 kilometers and 5 miles because your average driver would need a calculator to figure out how far that actually is.

The two important considerations in all measurement are the procedures employed in observation and the rules employed in assignment of numbers. Suppose that we wanted to know how many cars passed a certain intersection on any given day. We might ask several people who we know are frequently near that intersection how many cars they think pass the intersection in a given day. Person A might tell us he thinks about 300 or 400 cars pass. Person B might say he figures between 100 and 200 and person C might suggest there are between 700 and 800 cars that pass in a given day. We cannot say, however, that we have engaged in measurement. We have not "systematically" observed the passing cars at the intersection. Rather, our observation has been chaotic. A better way to determine how many cars pass an intersection would be to station a person at the intersection with a pencil and paper and each time a car drove by, he or she would mark down a "1." If we followed this procedure, we would be engaged in the two essential activities involved in measurement: systematic observation and assignment of numbers to objects according to rules. For some purposes, such low-level measurement might be adequate—if, for example, we were interested in determining the probability that we would be able to "hitch a ride" at that intersection. For many other purposes, such low-level measurement would be inadequate. If we happen to be employed by the state highway department and wanted to estimate how long it would take for the road surface to wear out at that intersection, we would need to know how heavy the cars were.

Numbers and Things

In measurements, numbers are assigned to represent "things." It is important if our measurement is to be of any value that the numbers and the things are *isomorphic*. **Isomorphism** means identity or similarity of form. The question we are asking when we are concerned with whether our measurement is isomorphic with the thing being measured is, "Are our rules for numerical assignment tied to reality?" Let us presume, for example, that we wish to estimate the level of anxiety felt by a public speaker. As the speaker is speaking before us, we may rate her on a scale from 1 to 5 (*low anxiety* to *high anxiety*) on the basis of the distracting mannerisms she evidences in speaking. Such ratings would be isomorphic with anxiety if distracting mannerisms are positively related to anxiety, but if, as is actually the case, distracting mannerisms are more a product of habit and lack of experience in public speaking than they are a product of an internal state of anxiety, then our ratings are nonisomorphic. As such, the ratings are useless and we have "measured" nothing.

In many cases, we are forced to assume that our assignment of numbers is isomorphic with reality. The reason that this problem is so important is the fact that it is not legitimate to do anything with numbers that could not be done (if it were physically possible) with the thing that the number represents. Numbers do not know what we can do with them. We know that we can add them, subtract them, multiply them, or divide them. Sometimes we are justified in engaging in all of these operations, and sometimes we are not.

Review of Measurement Levels

The mathematical operations that are legitimate for a given set of participant scores depend on the level of measurement that has been achieved. There are four levels of measurement, as discussed in the previous chapter: nominal, ordinal, interval, and ratio. Before we discuss different methods for creating scales, we will reexamine these four levels just to reinforce how important it is for you to understand them.

NOMINAL

Nominal measurement is a simple classification. When we assign a person a number because he is a member of a certain classroom, we are engaged in nominal measurement. The numbers are arbitrarily selected and meaningless in themselves. For example, if we wish to measure the sex of the students in a class, we may choose to classify men as "1" and women as "2." Therefore, each male in the class is labeled a "1" and each female in the class a "2." The selection of "1" and "2" is arbitrary. We could just as easily employ "469" and "932." None of the normal mathematical operations may be applied to the numbers assigned at this level of measurement. All that is permissible is to extend our measurement slightly and count up the number of people who were assigned "1" or "2." Thus, we could determine that in our classroom there were 48 men and 40 women.

This is the lowest level of measurement and is seldom desired by the social scientist. In some cases, it is the only level of measurement that would be isomorphic. In the example above, to think of measuring sex more precisely than "female" or "male" is somewhat ludicrous. If we wish to talk about something such as the "degree of maleness" or "degree of femaleness," we are talking about something more than sex, so we would measure something other than biological sex. Sex in human beings is only measurable at the nominal level, and a more "precise" measure would be nonisomorphic and meaningless.

ORDINAL

Ordinal or rank-order measurement assigns numbers to things in such a way as to reflect relationships among the things. Whereas nominal measurement merely indicates the things that are different from one another, ordinal measurement indicates the direction of the difference in some meaningful way. Typical relationships among things are more favorable, more difficult, more preferred, higher, and so on. In ordinal measurement, we may assign something at the lowest level "1," the thing that is just above it we may assign "2," and so on. For example, in most institutions of higher education, seniors receive the nominal categorization of "4," juniors "3," sophomores "2," and freshmen "1." The way that these numbers are customarily assigned is arbitrary. We could assign seniors "940," juniors "623," sophomores "212," and freshmen "5." Ordinal measurement only indicates the direction of the relationship between two things. If a sergeant wears three stripes, a corporal two stripes, and a private one stripe, this merely establishes a hierarchical relationship among the three military personnel. The sergeant could just as well wear seven stripes, the corporal two, and the private one. The relationship, as measured at the ordinal level, would still be exactly the same. Ordinal measurement, then, can tell us that the sergeant is more important (presuming that the number of stripes indicates importance) than the corporal and that the corporal is more important than the private. Ordinal measurement does not tell us how much more important the sergeant is than the corporal or the corporal is than the private. Even on the day a private is being promoted to corporal, he or she would still be classified as a private. People do not say that someone in the military is an almost corporal or has 1.9 stripes; he or she either has the rank of corporal or the rank of private—there is no in between. In other words, ordinal measures allow us to see the hierarchical level between groups, but do not allow us to determine the degree to which people belong within these groups.

INTERVAL

Interval measurement has all of the characteristics of ordinal measurement and one crucial addition. Interval measurement identifies the distance between any two things that are measured. We assign numbers to things in such ways that the distance between things assigned "1" and "2" is equivalent to the distance between two things assigned "4" and "5." This assignment on the basis of equal intervals is essential to establish an isomorphic relationship between our use of numbers in measurement and the mathematical operations of many statistical tests.

The numbers that we use to indicate the distance of an interval are arbitrary. If the interval of distance is, for example, 36 inches, we may measure that interval by employing the numbers 36, 72, 108, and so on, or we may use the numbers 1 (36), 2 (36 + 36), 3 (72 + 36), and so on. The important consideration is that the difference between levels be consistently noted in our numerical scheme. The same degree of difference may be alluded to as "1" unit, "2" units, or "200" units. The numbers, in themselves, have no meaning, but the relationships between the numbers do. The most common example of interval measurement is the way we measure temperature (excluding the Kelvin scale). Typically, nonphysical scientists discuss temperature using both a centigrade and a Fahrenheit system. Both measure exactly the same thing—temperature—but the scaling systems they employ are different. For example, on the centigrade thermometer water freezes at 0 degrees, but on the Fahrenheit thermometer water freezes at 32 degrees. The important thing on interval scales, such as measurement of temperature, is that they are internally consistent in their assignment of numbers. The difference between 80 degrees and 78 degrees is exactly equivalent to the difference between 20 degrees and 18 degrees. The two degrees of difference must mean the same thing at any point on the scale.

Interval measures (Likert, semantic differential/bipolar, and scalogram scales) are probably the most common measures taken by social scientists because most scales created for examining various variables are interval oriented.

RATIO

A ratio scale has all of the characteristics of an interval scale, but in addition it has a true zero point as its origin. As we noted in the measurement of temperatures, zero could mean different things on the two different measures. In ratio measures, zero has an absolute value of its own. One deviation from the prior discussion examining temperature is the Kelvin scale, which emphasizes that there is a point where atomic movement stops completely and is called absolute zero, so the Kelvin temperature scale would be a ratio scale because it has an absolute zero. Two common ratio measures are the measures employed for distance. We may use the metric system or the common system of inches, feet, and yards. In each case, zero means no distance. Zero meters and zero inches are exactly equivalent; they indicate the absence of distance. On interval scales it is not meaningful to compare the absolute numbers assigned in terms of their geometric relationships with each other. Such comparisons are possible with ratio scales. For example, a person who scores 60 on an intelligence measure is not necessarily precisely half as intelligent as a person who scores 120, but a city 500 miles away is precisely twice as far away as a city that is 250 miles away.

By this point you may be wondering, *I know how to measure distance, but what does this have to do with measuring communication?* This is a good question. To help us answer that question we must first look at the history of measurement with regard to human behavior.

A History of Measurement

As discussed in Chapter 1, the history of the social sciences is dependent on the scientific community's understanding of quantitative methods. Darwin, in his book *Origin of Species*, published in 1859, was the first to truly draw attention to variation, or the idea that certain traits and attributes are selected to be passed from one generation to the next, whereas others are not. Ultimately, some traits and attributes thrive, whereas others die out. Darwin's work on genetic variation spurred the drive to measure individual differences. The first person to really set out to accomplish this task was Darwin's half cousin Francis Galton in 1892 in his text *Hereditary Genius: An Inquiry into Its Laws and Consequences*. In *Hereditary Genius*, Galton wanted to apply Darwin's ideas to humans by showing "that a man's natural abilities are derived by inheritance, under exactly the same limitations as are the form and physical features of the whole organic world" (p. 1). Galton realized that he needed to develop a way to assess an individual's genius, so he decided to examine an individual's fame in his career and see how his children fared in their careers. Ultimately, Galton demonstrated that individuals who were famous in their careers had children who were also famous in their careers. Based on this evidence, Galton noted "[Hereditary Genius] has been advocated by a few writers in past as in modern times. But I may claim to be the first to treat the subject in a statistical manner, to arrive at numerical results, and to introduce the 'law of deviation from an average' into discussions of heredity" (p. vi). Ultimately, this publication led to the proliferation of quantitative differential psychology, or the study of how individuals or groups differ. Galton went on to become one of the foremost scientists of his day and a large collection of his research articles, book chapters, pamphlets, and books can be accessed for free at http://www.galton.org. Galton also wrote extensively on the use of statistics in social scientific research.

Psychologist James McKeen Cattell was one of many people influenced by Galton's work. In fact, Cattell ultimately traveled to England to work with Galton and see how he was using statistics to understand humans. In 1890, Cattell was the first social scientist to develop measurements for nonphysical attributes. Cattell began to measure simple mental processes like the time it took subjects to perform simple mental acts like naming objects in a sequence or colors (Baldwin, Cattell, & Jastrow, 1889; Cattell, 1890, 1895). While at the University of Pennsylvania, Cattell began to administer newly developed measures to students, which he ultimately labeled "mental tests." Ultimately, mental tests became labeled **mental measures**, or any tool used for the measurement of mental functions like attitudes, beliefs, cognitive knowledge, perceived knowledge, and personality/behavioral traits. Basically, any achievement test, personality test, aptitude test, intelligence test, or career choice test qualifies as a mental measure (Salkind, 2006). Mental measures are more colloquially known as research scales, so in the next few chapters we use these terms interchangeably. By the time the twentieth century rolled around, mental measurement began to pick up steam both in the United States and around the world.

In 1905, Alfred Binet, a French psychologist, was commissioned to create the first test to determine whether children were functioning at lower than normal levels. Binet, along with his doctoral student Theodore Simon, ultimately created the Binet–Simon scale, which measured a child's adeptness at completing various age appropriate tasks (Binet, 1905). In essence, this became the first known intelligence test of its kind. Binet's research was then furthered by a Stanford University professor named Lewis Terman (1916). Of course, intelligence testing quickly turned to academic achievement testing when in 1937 the Stanford Achievement Test (SAT) became required for entry into Ivy League schools. E. L. Thorndike is credited with creating the multiple-choice test, but its popularity and widespread use began in 1914 when the U.S. Army asked Frederick J. Kelly to develop a way to measure recruit abilities that could be quickly and easily scored by anyone without needing specialized scoring knowledge (Sokal, 1987). Another test developed around the same time as the multiple-choice test was Arthur Gates's (1921) true-or-false test. The first three decades of the twentieth century radically changed how educational assessment was completed. These new advancements in educational testing led to more and more high school students taking the SAT and other college entrance examinations (the SAT is still the most prominent). The Educational Testing Service (ETS) was created in 1947 to oversee numerous tests including the SATs, GREs, TOFELs, and PRAXIS tests, to name a few.

In addition to achievement tests, a new breed of measurements were also on the horizon as the United States went into World War I. Although the notion of personality had been around since the time of Hippocrates, measuring personality really was not feasible until the early 1900s. The first modern personality test was created in 1920 by Robert Woodworth. Woodworth had been commissioned by the APA on behalf of the U.S. military to create a measure of emotional stability that could be used to test new recruits. Woodworth eventually created the Woodworth Personal Data Sheet, which contained a series of 116 "yes" or "no" questions. Unfortunately, the test was developed too late in World War I to be used in the screening of new recruits, but the test did become the forerunner of future personality tests (Segal & Coolidge, 2003). Another test developed around the same time was Pressey and Pressey's (1919) Cross-Out Test. The Cross-Out Test had respondents cross out any words on a list that the respondent considered wrong, inappropriate, unpleasant, or worrisome. Pressey and Pressey believed that the resulting pattern of crossed-out and un-crossed-out words could be used to help categorize respondents' emotional states.

Beyond traditional personality testing, further methods for measuring attitudes became increasingly important during the early 1900s. One of the most important figures in early measurement was Emory S. Bogardus, who was a prominent figure in sociology. He created a scale called the Bogardus Social Distance Scale, which was the first scale to attempt to measure people's willingness to interact with different types of people. The Social Distance Scale attempts to measure degrees of tolerance or prejudice between social groups (Bogardus, 1925). The Bogardus Social Distance Scale is considered the oldest attitudinal research scale still in use today. Beyond Bogardus's research, modern social scientific research has been transformed by the development of two specific measurement devices: Likert scales and semantic differential scales.

LIKERT SCALES

Another researcher interested in understanding attitudes named Rensis Likert hoped to develop a measure for attitudes, the Likert scale. In 1932, Likert published a monograph based on his dissertation in which he developed a new attitude-scaling technique. The basic premise of the Likert scale was simplistic, but it revolutionized social scientific research. Likert started off with the idea of presenting respondents with a declarative statement of some kind (e.g., "Cold pizza is a good breakfast), and then he offered them a range of possible choices: *strongly disagree, disagree, neither agree nor disagree, agree,* or *strongly agree.* Respondents only have five choices, so people must select one of the categories. Because these categories have weighted distances, the answer on a single Likert item is considered ordinal because researchers cannot assume that respondents perceive the difference between the different levels evenly. However, if multiple Likert items are summed together, the summed total may be treated as interval data that actually measure a latent variable.

A **latent variable** or **hypothetical variable** is a variable that a researcher cannot directly observe, but is inferred from other variables that are observable and measured directly. For example, the statement "I dislike participating in group discussions" when measured using Likert's five steps (*strong disagree, disagree, neither agree nor disagree, agree,* or *strong agree*) is an ordinal variable. However, when we combine this statement with the other 23 statements on the PRCA-24, we end up with an interval variable that measures the latent variable "communication apprehension."

Although the five-step Likert scale going from 1 (*strongly disagree*) to 5 (*strongly agree*) is probably the most commonly used Likert scale in all measurement, those anchors (*strongly disagree/strongly agree*) are hardly the only anchor types that exist. Figure 7.1 contains a wide range of Likert-type anchors ranging from simplistic to more complex. Each of these anchors has been utilized over the years by a variety of researchers to help measure various attitudes, beliefs, values, and personality traits. Here is a quick side note about writing anchors in APA style: according to the APA Style Manual, any time you write about an anchor within your text you should always italicize the anchor name.

The first comprehensive discussion of the use of Likert scales in communication research was in 1967 by Arnold, McCroskey, and Prichard, who wrote a short introductory essay to the use and creation of Likert scales in *Today's Speech.* Likert scales have become common in communication research. We will discuss creating Likert scales in much more detail later in this chapter. Now that we have discussed the history and purpose of the Likert scale, we can discuss the next major development in research measurement: semantic differential scaling.

SEMANTIC DIFFERENTIAL

The next major breakthrough in the area of attitudinal measurement came from Osgood (1952) and Osgood, Tannnenbaum, and Suci (1957). A semantic differential scale asks respondents to rate their opinions on a linear scale between two endpoints that have opposite meanings (e.g., *good/bad, dirty/clean, slow/fast, weak/strong, light/heavy, moral/immoral,* etc.). Between these two oppositely worded adjectives, there exists a series of steps. The most common number of steps in a semantic differential scale is seven, so instructions for a semantic differential test read like this: "Circle the number between the adjectives which best represents your beliefs. Numbers 1 and 7 indicate a very strong feeling. Numbers 2 and 6 indicate

1	2	3	4	5
Strong disagree	Disagree	Neutral	Agree	Strongly Agree
Never	Rarely	Sometimes	Often	Always
Definitely not possible	Very unlikely	Don't know	Somewhat likely	Extremely likely
Not at all	To a little extent	To some extent	To a great extent	To a very great extent
Not concerned at all	Not really concerned	Somewhat concerned	Concerned	Very concerned
Definitely false	Possibly false	Don't know	Possibly true	Definitely true
None	Very mild	Mild	Moderate	Severe
Lacking or ineffective	Below average	Average	Above average	Excellent
Very unrealistic	Unrealistic	Not sure	Realistic	Very Realistic
NO	no	?	yes	YES
Poor	Fair	Good	Very good	Excellent
Not important	Somewhat important	Important	Very important	Extremely important
Substantially worse	Somewhat worse	About the same	Somewhat better	Substantially better
Very dissatisfied	Dissatisfied	Neither dissatisfied nor satisfied	Satisfied	Very satisfied
1–20%	21–40%	41–60%	61–80%	81–100%
Definitely did not use	Rarely used	Used moderately	Above average use	Great use
Absolutely do not agree	Do not agree	Neither agree nor disagree	Agree	Absolutely Agree
Not at all like me	Not really like me	Neither like me nor dislike me	Somewhat like me	Definitely like me

F	D	C	B	A
Not at all	Somewhat	Moderately	Quite	Extremely
No Chance	Very little chance	Not sure	Good chance	Certain to happen
Far below expected level	Below expected level	At expected level	Above expected level	Far above expected level
Extremely negative	Moderately negative	Neither positive nor negative	Moderately positive	Extremely positive
Have not	Have slightly	Have moderately	Have mostly	Have fully
Very bad	Rather bad	Neutral	Good	Very good
Never	Occasionally (once or twice altogether)	Regularly (once or twice a year)	Often (several times a year)	Very often (about weekly)
Not at all	Slightly	Moderately	Markedly	Extremely
Very much a loner	Moderately a loner	Average	Somewhat socially sought after	Very socially sought after
None	Slightly	No opinion	Moderately	Extensively
Definitely would not do this	Might not do this	Not sure whether I would do this	Might do this	Would definitely do this
I reject this	I am inclined to reject this	I neither reject nor accept this	I accept this as important	I accept this as of the greatest importance
Extremely Conservative	Conservative	Moderate: Middle of the road	Progressive	Extremely progressive
–	–	0	+	++
Infrequently	Fairly infrequently	No opinion	Fairly frequently	Frequently

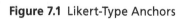

Figure 7.1 Likert-Type Anchors

a strong feeling. Numbers 3 and 5 indicate a fairly weak feeling. Number 4 indicates you are undecided or do not understand the adjectives themselves." For example, maybe we want respondents to tell us whether they believe capital punishment is good or bad. We would place the adjectives "good" and "bad" on opposite sides of a continuum with seven steps like this:

Good   1   2   3   4   5   6   7   Bad

or

Good   __   __   __   _   _   __   __   __   Bad

Whether we actually have the physical numbers present in a semantic differential is not important as long as we, as the researchers, know that we have direct quantifiable distances between each step. Because these steps are weighted distances, the answer on a single semantic differential item is considered ordinal because researchers cannot assume that respondents perceive the difference between the steps evenly. However, if multiple semantic differential items are summed together, the summed total may be treated as interval data that actually measure a latent variable.

As discussed earlier, a *latent variable* is a variable that a researcher cannot directly observe but can infer from other variables that are measured directly. For example, respondents can be asked to rate their supervisor using the following bipolar adjectives:

Good   7   6   5   4   3   2   1   Bad

This single semantic differential item is ordinal; however, when we combine this item with the five other semantic differential items on McCroskey's (1966) Generalized Attitude measure, we end up with an interval variable that measures the latent variable—attitude toward a specific target. Heise (1970) did have one major warning when constructing semantic differential scales: the adjectives must be relevant and understandable for respondents. For example, if you want to have respondents rate their interaction with someone, using the adjectives sweet/sour would not be as useful as the adjectives helpful/unhelpful. You should also avoid using jargon-loaded language that may be too specialized for nonscientists, such as *extraverted/introverted*; you should opt to use more common adjectives like *talkative/quiet*.

The first real discussion of the use of semantic differential scales in communication research was in 1966 by Arnold, McCroskey, and Prichard, who wrote a short introductory essay about the use and creation of semantic differential scales in *Today's Speech*. Since then, semantic differential scales have become common in communication research. We should note that many researchers use the terms semantic differential scales and bipolar adjective scales interchangeably.

Measuring Communication

In 2004, James McCroskey, Virginia Richmond, Aaron Johnson, and Heather Smith wanted to create research instruments to help measure the concept of organizational orientations theory, which stated that different people view their relationships with their jobs in different ways (this article can be found on the textbook's website). Some people see work as a central focus of their life, whereas other people see work as a means to an end—their social life. Ultimately, organizational orientations theory proposes that how people see their relationships with their jobs will impact various job-related outcomes. Although this theory sounds reasonable and some early research seemed to support it, the question that McCroskey et al. found problematic was how one goes about determining one's organizational orientation.

Also in 2004, Jason Wrench and Virginia Richmond were talking about yet another measurement-oriented problem. They noted that a scale that had been previously developed by Melanie Booth-Butterfield and Steven Booth-Butterfield (1990) had a problem. This scale was called the Humor Orientation Scale and allegedly measured the degree to which an individual used humor as a communicative tool in interpersonal relationships. However, when one looks at the Humor Orientation Scale, all of the questions were centered on an individual's ability to tell jokes or funny stories. Is humor only about jokes and funny stories? If this were the case, comic legends such as Mr. Bean and Charlie Chaplin would not even be considered humorous because they relied greatly on nonverbal forms of humor.

In both of the above examples, researchers were faced with a problem in measurement. McCroskey et al. (2004) needed to determine how to measure an individual's organizational orientation, and Wrench and Richmond (2004) needed to determine how to measure a person's use of humor in interpersonal interactions without relying on joke and storytelling as the only form of humor. Although both groups of authors could have outside observers watch people over an extended period of time to determine either their organizational orientation or their tendency to use humor in communicative interactions, this process would take a long time and many hours of observation, which is unrealistic in most research circumstances. For this reason, research scales are often created to enable a researcher to ask participants about their personality traits/states, beliefs and attitudes, and knowledge. Let's look at each of these three categories separately.

PERSONALITY TRAITS/STATES

We first visited the concepts of traits and states in Chapter 6 when we introduced the variables in the dataset that accompanied this textbook. To refresh your memory, we will discuss these two concepts again briefly. Trait behavior is behavior that that is assumed to be consistent across contexts and specific situations within particular constructs. For example, an individual's level of CA is fairly trait oriented. People with high levels of CA tend to be anxious about communication in any situation, in any communicative context, or with any audience. State behavior, by contrast, is behavior that varies from one situation to another within the same context. Some people tend to be more state-oriented in their CA. People that are not high CA, but rather more moderate in their CA, may only experience apprehension in one of the four major contexts (group, meeting, interpersonal, or public), or they may experience CA differently depending on the audience they are in front of at a given moment. Although the first case is clearly more trait CA and the second case is state CA, we are able to measure this personality trait using the PRCA-24 scale. In essence, when researchers discuss personality traits or communication traits, they are discussing the measurement of hypothetical constructs that accounts for certain behaviors. In the case of CA, the hypothetical construct is anxiety associated with either real or perceived communication. The hypothetical construct must be clear; if it is not clear, there can be serious measurement issues (see Chapter 8). Research has shown that the hypothetical construct CA can help account for a wide variety of communicative behaviors, ranging from the tendency to sweat while giving a speech to the likelihood of being hired for a job or promoted within one's current employment situation.

Personality traits/states can also be classified in terms of psychological and behavioral traits/states. Behaviorally oriented trait/state research scales involve both perceptions of one's own behavior and other individual's perceptions of one's behavior. For example, it would be difficult to answer the PRCA-24 for another person because the questions are designed to measure an individual's internal psychological state while communicating with other people. However, we could ask people to look for observable signs of anxiety while giving a speech (lack of eye contact, discoloration of the skin, fidgeting, hand shaking, voice quivers, etc.).

For example, the Nonverbal Immediacy Scale–Self Report is designed to measure an individual's perception of her or his own tendency to exhibit nonverbal behaviors that increase the feelings of immediacy in other people (I use my hands and arms to gesture when talking to people). However, the scale can be retooled to be Other Report, and then an individual can report the tendency of another person's use of nonverbal behaviors that increase feelings of immediacy (my teacher uses her or his hands and arms to gesture while talking to people). In both cases, the intent of the scale is not changed; the object of measurement is shifted from the first person (my behavior) to another person (someone else's behavior).

BELIEFS AND ATTITUDES

The second classification of things that can be measured by a research scale are beliefs. As we discussed in Chapter 6, a belief is our perception of reality about whether something is true or false, whereas an attitude is a predisposition to respond to people, ideas, or objects in an evaluative way. In Chapter 6 we introduced two scales that can be employed to measure beliefs (Generalized Belief Scale) and attitudes (Generalized Attitude Measure). Although these two scales are easy to employ to measure any belief or attitude, other scales can also be created to measure a belief.

One type of scale designed to measure a set of beliefs is called a scalogram scale. The purpose of a scalogram scale is to create a series of beliefs about a single topic starting very weak (I never throw trash on the ground because it hurts our environment) and moving to very strong (bombing a company that hurts the environment is completely justifiable). The environmentalism scale discussed in Chapter 6 measured different beliefs that can people can have about environmentalism. With each new belief statement, a person answers either "yes" or "no." If the scalogram scale is accurate, if a person says "no" to the first question, then he or she will say "no" to every item on the scale. If the person says "yes" to the first three questions and then says "no" to the fourth question, then questions 5 through 10 should also be answered "no.' In essence, a scalogram scale is designed to measure a series of beliefs and how strong a person holds those beliefs. Although the authors of this book all think recycling is a noble endeavor, not all of us actually recycle regularly.

KNOWLEDGE

The history of measuring an individual's cognitive knowledge of a subject goes back to the earliest formation of schools. Even Socrates tested his students, but he measured his students' learning through their abilities to orally defend and explain themselves. There is even evidence of a basic form of testing of Chinese public officials by the emperor around 2200 BCE. In other words, the idea of testing has been around for 4,000 years. However, the first multiple-choice test did not appear until 1914, when Frederick J. Kelly was asked by the U.S. Army to develop a way to measure recruit abilities (Sokal, 1987). Another test developed around the same time as the Kelly multiple-choice test was the true-or-false test (Gates, 1921). Since this time, a variety of different types of measures of cognitive knowledge have been created, including fill-in-the-blank, word completion, matching, and many others.

The last major type of variable that can be measured by a scale is real and/or perceived knowledge. All of us are familiar with scales that attempt to measure perceived knowledge. A multiple-choice or true–false test is a simple example of a scale that is designed to measure knowledge. Maybe you want to measure the effect that a teacher's choice of clothing has on retention of a lecture. The easiest way to determine retention of a lecture is to test participants about information that was in the lecture after the fact. In education, we constantly survey students' acquisition of **cognitive knowledge** in a class. A good teacher will understand that a test basically lets us know two different things: (1) how well every student understands the material and (2) how well our teaching methods are working for student understanding as a whole. Some people in education believe that if all students fail a test, then the teacher has done a good job weeding out the bad students. However, what is more likely the case is that the testing mechanism was not appropriate or the teaching strategies were not working. Although this is outside the purview of the current text, we should mention that there is an entire field of educational psychometrics or the creation and analysis of cognitive tests. Although many of us hate standardized tests, substantial time and politics goes into their creation. After students have taken a standardized test, psychometricians spend a lot of time analyzing the statistical properties of the test to make sure the test is effective and appropriate.

The second type of knowledge that can be measured is **perceived knowledge**. Although understanding what a person knows is important, it is also important to be able to measure what a person thinks he or she knows. Figure 7.2 shows the Risk Knowledge Index.

Instructions: Below are several descriptions dealing with the extent to which you are aware of the risks involved in bungee jumping. Please use the scale below to rate the degree to which each statement applies to your perceptions about your knowledge of the risk(s):

Strongly Disagree	Disagree	Neutral	Agree	Strongly Agree
1	2	3	4	5

_____ 1. I know the risks involved.
_____ 2. I do not feel knowledgeable about the risks involved.
_____ 3. The risks involved are very clear to me.
_____ 4. I do not know the risks involved.
_____ 5. I do not comprehend the risks involved.
_____ 6. My knowledge of the risks involved is limited.
_____ 7. I completely understand the risks involved.
_____ 8. I feel knowledgeable about the risks involved.
_____ 9. I comprehend the risks involved.
_____ 10. The risks involved are not clear to me.

SCORING: To compute your scores follow the instructions below:

Step One: Add scores for items 1, 3, 7, 8, & 9.
Step Two: Add scores for items 2, 4, 5, 6, & 10.
Step Three: Add 30 to Step One.
Step Four: Subtract the score for Step Two from the score for Step Three.

Interpreting Your Score:

Scores on the Risk Knowledge Index should be between 10 and 50. Individuals with scores above 40 are considered to have a high perceived understanding of a risk, and individuals with scores below 40 are considered to have a low perceived understanding a risk.

NOTE: The mean for risk knowledge tends to be fairly high.

Source:

Wrench, J. S. (2007). The influence of perceived risk knowledge on risk communication. *Communication Research Reports, 24,* 63–70.

Figure 7.2 Risk Knowledge Index

The Risk Knowledge Index was originally created by Wrench (2007) as a way to measure the degree to which an individual believed he or she understood the risk associated with a specific hazard (something that could cause loss of life or limb). In Figure 7.1, the scale is designed to measure an individual's perception of her or his knowledge of the risks associated with bungee jumping. We could have determined a person's perception of her or his perceived knowing by asking the question, "How much do you know about the risks of bungee jumping from the range of 0 (*I know nothing about the risks*) to 9 (*I know about all of the risks involved*)?" However, a one-shot question can be problematic because it does not allow for a statistical way to determine whether your sample's response to this question was random or consistent.

In this section, we have examined the three primary variable types that can be analyzed through research scales (personality traits/states, beliefs and attitudes, and perceived and real knowledge). However, before one can measure anything at all, he or she must have a clear idea of what the variable is that he or she is attempting to measure.

Developing Your Operationalization

In the two scale examples discussed in this section (organizational orientations and humor assessment), both scales started with what we call a **germinal idea**. A "germinal idea" is a term for that spark that causes an individual to realize that something new can be measured. We often get the ideas for new scales because we face real events in our lives that cause us to wonder about some communication phenomena, or maybe when reading a book you will read what an author says and wonder, "*Has anyone ever really studied this concept?*" Recently, two of our authors were having a late-night discussion about organizational communication that led to the realization that there was a huge gap in the organizational communication measurement literature, which led to the creation of nine new scales. Although a germinal idea can help you get the initial push to create a scale, it is the conceptualization of that germinal idea that allows you to start the measurement process.

CONCEPTUALIZATION

Conceptualization is defined as the development and clarification of concepts or your germinal idea. Conceptualization is basically when you take a germinal idea and determine what it is that you want to measure and whether you can realistically measure something. One of the biggest problems many researchers have when creating research scales is that they attempt to measure too much. For example, maybe you wanted to create a scale to measure an individual's perception of health communication. What part of health communication are you interested in? Are you looking at communication between patients and physicians, patients and nurses, clients and therapists, clients and pharmacists, or what? In essence, a scale should be designed to measure a single concept or a set of concepts that are closely related to each other. For example, Richmond and McCroskey's (1990) sociocommunicative orientation scale measures the two related constructs of assertiveness and responsiveness. Realistically, each of those concepts could be measured separately by a single scale, but since the two concepts work together so closely, it makes sense to develop a single scale where both concepts could be analyzed together. However, you would not want to create a scale that attempts to measure assertiveness and conflict management because these are two separate concepts. Although you could examine both of these concepts in a single research study, you would need to create two different scales: one for assertiveness and one for conflict management strategies.

OPERATIONALIZATION

Once you have determined the basic concept you are actually planning on measuring, you must operationalize your concept. **Operationalization** is the detailed description of the research operations or procedures necessary to assign units of analysis to the categories of a variable to represent conceptual properties. The concept of operationalization applies to all forms of measurement, not just working with scales. For example, if you want to create a study where you are going to analyze the types of clothing people have on and their likelihood of spending money in a department store, you would need to create an a priori (before the fact) coding scheme for how you will classify clothing choices. So, if a woman comes in wearing a Gucci business suit and carries a Prada handbag, she would not be classified into the same category as a male wearing cutoff shorts and a tank top. This first form of operationalization is referred to as manipulation into categories. In essence, you operationalize that dress is some sort of nominal/categorical variable, and you purposefully classify people into different groups based on what they are wearing when they enter the store.

The second way that we can operationalize a concept is to estimate the category either by observing existing records or by asking people. The observation of existing records is how Boiarsky, Long, and Thayer (1999) operationalized their concept in their article about children's science television (included on the textbook's website). Boiarsky et al. examined a variety of mediated characteristics (sound effects per minute, cuts per minute, fades/dissolves per minute, wipes per minute, and topic shifts per minute) in a series of children's television shows (*Beakman's World*, *Bill Nye the Science Guy*, *Magic School Bus*, and *Newton's Apple*). Each of these shows was preexisting, so the researchers had to determine what it was they wanted to examine in the show and then operationalize how they would go about analyzing these mediated characteristics. By clearly spelling out the operationalization of coding procedures, future researchers can more accurately understand the findings of the study and replicate the research in the future, either in this genre or in a different genre of television. Using preexisting sources of information for the collection of data can be beneficial when doing research. However, as we discussed in the previous paragraph, you must have a clear idea of what you are looking for before you can truly operationalize your measurement process.

The last form of operationalization is asking for verbal/nonverbal reports of a phenomenon through either interviews or traditional survey techniques. For example, maybe you want to determine the effect of a new political attack advertisement on the public. What kinds of questions would you want to know to determine "the effect"? Maybe you would want to ask questions about the target of the attack ad's credibility or about the attractiveness of the target of the attack ad after viewing it. Whereas this first part is clearly more in line with the conceptualization part of the measurement process, the development of questions is part of the operationalization process. Operationalization is in essence the procedures we go through to place someone in a variable category. When Wrench and Richmond (2004) were first writing a new scale for measuring interpersonal humor, the two fell into the same trap that the Booth-Butterfields had fallen into when developing the humor orientation scale. It was not until a colleague read the initial version of the scale and noted that they had also included a number of items about jokes and humorous storytelling that the two researchers realized that the scale needed to avoid such language altogether if it was to truly be a general humor measure. This process where you narrow the focus of the scale and really try to get at the basic concept being measured is the operationalization of the concept.

Now that we have discussed the initial steps necessary when creating a germinal idea for a scale, conceptualizing the scale, and then operationalizing the scale, we can turn our attention to the actual construction of research scales.

Constructing Questions

Writing research measures that will stand the test of time is not a task to underestimate. Too many people who are not familiar with the psychometric process of creating reliable and valid research measures think that creating a new scale is simply writing down a series of questions. Writing scale questions can be problematic because even the slightest conjecture or ambiguity in an item can cause people to inaccurately respond to the item, which makes your scale's purpose and meaning highly suspect. Once you have determined what you really want to measure (through the conceptualization and operationalization processes), you can then begin to actually write a research scale. The following discussion is focused primarily on the creation of Likert-type scales because they are most often used by communication researchers. Although some of the concepts may not directly apply to semantic differential/bipolar or scalogram scales, most of this discussion can be cross-applied to those scales as well. We will now examine 15 extremely important guidelines creating reliable and valid Likert-type research scales.

1. Start with twice as many items as you will need. When you are first developing a scale, you must begin with nearly twice as many items as you think you will need in the long run. For example, if you want to have a 15-item scale to measure sibling communication satisfaction, you must start off with 30 items because some of your items will be problematic and will eventually be discarded from your scale because they either do not help the reliability of your scale or do not measure the actual construct you are attempting to measure (these will be discussed in Chapter 8). Because you must write a considerable number of items for each scale you create, you will often find redundancy a necessity. One easy way to do this is to oppositely word each item you create later in the scale. For example, if you have a scale that you are writing 20 items for, you may want to have item 1 as "I like potatoes" and item 11 as "I do not like potatoes." In the long run, this will provide you with a healthy balance between positively worded and negatively worded items in your scale. The reason we have positively and negatively worded items in a scale is to make sure that a person is not randomly answering the questions without reading the questions. In other words, if we have both of those questions being answered by a Likert scale ranging from 1 (*strongly disagree*) to 5 (*strongly agree*), we would expect that if someone answers "5" to question 1, he or she should also answer "1" to question 11 since the two questions are oppositely worded. This concept will be discussed in greater detail in the next chapter.

2. Every item should reflect the construct. As a scale writer, ensure that every item that you write on a scale clearly (at least in your mind) reflects the construct you are attempting to measure. Again, you want to make sure that you do not have items on a scale that are supposed to be measuring physician use of storytelling to contain items about patient apprehension while talking to her or his physician. Although both scales could be important, the concepts should be operationalized separately into two different scales.

3. Use concise, clearly worded, unambiguous items. One of the problems that people have early on when creating scales is that they write survey items that are complex. Unfortunately, when working with the general public, the more simplistic a question is, the more likely you will get an accurate response from your survey participants. You also want to make sure that the language you use in a scale item is simplistic enough for a wide audience. To avoid the pitfall of complicated language, always try to pilot test your scale with a group of people prior to mass distributing the scale to determine whether there are any problem areas in the wording itself. If you know the test pilot group well, you may even ask them why they responded to specific questions in ways that you feel are opposite to how they should have scored based on their other answers. This will enable you to determine whether any ambiguity has crept into your scale by accident.

4. Construct relatively short items (e.g., 20 words or less). As an extension of the previous concept, not only do you want to avoid ambiguity, but also you want to have items that are fairly short on a scale. The more text an individual must read on a scale item, the more likely he or she will become confused and end up responding in a manner that is disjointed, which will skew your results. Although we suggest that a single item on any given Likert scale should not exceed 20 words, the shorter you can make a scale item, the easier your scale will be to read and respond to by participants.

5. Pay attention to terminology in the item. Another extremely important problem to look out for when writing a scale is any jargon or discipline-specific terminology in the scale. Recently, some of the authors of this book were writing a scale to measure an individual's perception of an interactant's verbal and nonverbal communication during a specific type of romantic interaction. On further thinking about some of the scale items, we realized that not everyone may completely understand what is meant by verbal and nonverbal communication because communication researchers have specific meanings associated with the two terms. Ultimately, the researchers opted to provide a concise definition of the two terms before the scale to aid in the understanding of the two concepts by participants.

6. Avoid emotionally loaded items. Unless you are attempting to measure an individual's emotional state, emotionally loaded items should be avoided. What do we mean by emotionally loaded items? An emotionally loaded item is a scale item designed to assess an individual's emotional response instead of her or his belief, attitude, or behavior. Suppose that you want to create a scale for assessing a subordinate's perception of her or his supervisor's coaching and teaching on the job. You may have items like, "My supervisor makes sure I understand what I'm doing" or "My supervisor makes sure I understand what I did wrong when I make a mistake." In this scale, you would not want to have an item like, "I hate it when my supervisor corrects my mistakes." Having items that cause people to respond to emotions in otherwise nonemotional scales can result in participants responding to the whole scale in an emotional state skewing your results.

7. Avoid leading items. Another trap you want to avoid when writing scale items involves leading items. A leading item is an item on a scale that clearly informs a person about the answer you are hoping to receive. For example, if you are creating a scale to measure the extent to which a teacher uses humor in a classroom, an item such as "Good students always think their teachers use humor in the classroom" would be extremely inappropriate. Instead, you would want general items (e.g., "My teacher uses humor in the classroom") that avoid leading anyone to believe that they should answer the scale item in a specific socially desirable way.

8. Avoid loaded items. A loaded item is similar to a leading item, just generally in the opposite direction. For example, if you are creating a scale about verbal aggression, you would not want an item to say something like "only an idiot cannot tell the difference between aggression and debate." Basically, if a person agrees with the statement, he or she is saying that there are many people who are idiots in the world, and if he or she disagrees with the statement then he or she is setting her or himself up to being labeled an idiot for not seeing the difference between aggression and debate for her/himself.

9. Avoid double questions. One common problem that is often seen in scale items occurs when an individual attempts to write a scale item with two actual questions involved. For example, "I believe that all students should go to college, and I believe that all students should get a master's degree." Although these two statements may both be true for some, they are not necessarily true for everyone. The best thing to do in this case would be to separate both statements out and ask them separately as two different items on the scale. When reading items on a scale, always double-check to see whether a scale item is asking only one question.

10. Avoid questions with false premises. Often people will attempt to write scale items based on premises that simply are not factual. For example, if you are attempting to measure the degree to which one believes in the current president, you may ask a question such as, "Because people generally support the president, I believe the president is doing a good job." The premise of this item can be hotly contested, since many people do not support the president (any president). So if a question starts with a statement that is not factual, then the rest of the question will be ambiguous at best or unanswerable at worst.

11. Avoid using always, never. Using the words "always" and "never" often confuses people and can cause some participants to avoid answering an item at the extremes (like strongly agree/disagree on a 5-step Likert scale). If you had the item "I always communicate competently" on a scale, you could have problems because no one can honestly say they *always* communicate competently. On the flip side, if you substituted the word always for never, you would run into the same problem because no one can honestly say that they *never* communicate competently either.

12. Avoid double negatives/positives. As a whole, people find double negatives and double positives to be confusing. You would not want to have items like, "Religious groups should not, not have to pay taxes." In this case, streamlining the question and simply making it "Religious groups should have to pay taxes" makes the statement more direct and easier to understand.

13. Avoid hypothetical questions. If you ask people to respond to a hypothetical question, then you are going to get a hypothetical (i.e., made-up) answer. For example, if you create a scale on people's perceived interaction with extraterrestrial life forms, you are going to have people randomly answering your scale because interaction with extraterrestrials can only be speculated on, so no real answers can be given (except by a few people in New Mexico). As a researcher, it is best to keep scales and what you are measuring as concrete as possible.

14. Avoid ambiguous pronoun references. When writing scales, you do not want to include pronouns that make the participant unsure of what you are asking in a scale item. For example, if you included the item "I would rather it not happen to me" on a scale about euthanasia, people would be highly suspect of what "it" actually is in this scale item. Instead, you would want to be as concrete as possible and reword the scale to read "I would rather not be euthanized" to avoid the ambiguous pronoun.

15. Consider recall issues for certain types of items. The last major concept to keep in mind when writing a scale is the concept of recall. In essence, when we ask people to recall information about an attitude, belief, or behavior, we must know whether what we are asking someone to remember can be remembered. We would not want to ask someone to recall the color of the tie a male physician was wearing 3 months earlier. We also need to think about whether the items on the scales we are creating force people to recall information that is unrealistic to be recalled at a later point. For example, if you are creating a scale on the posture one uses while standing, the scale may be difficult for people to accurately fill out if the target of the participants' observations has not been seen in a while.

Overall, we hope that you now understand that scale creation is not simply about writing a series of sentences and attaching several Likert scales to those sentences. The art and science of research measurement is complex and takes substantial time and effort to scientifically perform. Now that we have discussed how to create scales, we can examine how to put together a survey-based study.

One Measure, Multiple Factors

Before we continue, we must discuss one common area of confusion for people when it comes to measurement (and specific research measures specifically). Often a single research measure can actually measure multiple different (albeit related) concepts. Figure 7.3 contains a

Instructions: Below are several oppositely worded adjective pairs that represent how you may feel about the United States President. Circle the number between the adjectives which best represents your beliefs. Numbers "1" and "7" indicate a very strong feeling. Numbers "2" and "6" indicate a strong feeling. Numbers "3" and "5" indicate a fairly weak feeling. Number "4" indicates you are undecided or do not understand the adjectives themselves. There are no right or wrong answers.

1.	Unintelligent	1	2	3	4	5	6	7	Intelligent
2.	Untrained	1	2	3	4	5	6	7	Trained
3.	Doesn't care about me	1	2	3	4	5	6	7	Cares about me
4.	Dishonest	1	2	3	4	5	6	7	Honest
5.	Doesn't have my interests at heart	1	2	3	4	5	6	7	Has my interests at heart
6.	Untrustworthy	1	2	3	4	5	6	7	Trustworthy
7.	Inexpert	1	2	3	4	5	6	7	Expert
8.	Self-centered	1	2	3	4	5	6	7	Not self-centered
9.	Not concerned with me	1	2	3	4	5	6	7	Concerned with me
10.	Dishonorable	1	2	3	4	5	6	7	Honorable
11.	Uninformed	1	2	3	4	5	6	7	Informed
12.	Immoral	1	2	3	4	5	6	7	Moral
13.	Incompetent	1	2	3	4	5	6	7	Competent
14.	Unethical	1	2	3	4	5	6	7	Ethical
15.	Insensitive	1	2	3	4	5	6	7	Sensitive
16.	Stupid	1	2	3	4	5	6	7	Bright
17.	Phony	1	2	3	4	5	6	7	Genuine
18.	Not understanding	1	2	3	4	5	6	7	Understanding

Source: McCroskey, J. C., &Teven, J. J. (1999).Goodwill: A reexamination of the construct and its measurement. Communication Monographs, 66, 90–103.

Figure 7.3 Source Credibility Measure

measure that was originally created by James McCroskey and Jason Teven (1999) to analyze a participant's perception of a specific target's credibility (in this case, the U.S. president's credibility). Researchers dating back to Socrates have written and attempted to discuss what "credibility" is. Through a series of different research studies, McCroskey paired down his own measure of credibility (with the help of Teven) to consist of three distinct but closely related concepts. Here is what we want you to do before progressing further. In Figure 7.3, see whether you can find three sets of items that appear to be measuring a similar concept. Yes, there are only three concepts being measured by this scale and each concept has six items, so see whether you can detect the six items that go along with each of the three subscales (or factors).

A **subscale** is a hypothetical subdivision of a mental measure. In the case of the Source Credibility Measure, there are three distinct hypothesized subscales. Each subscale measures a specific aspect of credibility. No one subscale encapsulates the whole concept of credibility, which is why all three subscales are necessary.

A factor, by contrast, is derived through a statistical test called a factor analysis. A **factor analysis** looks for patterns among your participants' responses to each scale question in an effort to determine whether participants respond in any discernable patterns. The goal of a factor analysis is to see whether any specific items tend to be answered in a consistent fashion by participants, whereas other items are answered in a different, yet consistent, fashion by your participants. Think of the term "subscale" as the hypothesis and the term "factor" as the observance (through statistics) of the subscale. Often researchers propose a subscale that is later not confirmed when they conduct a factor analysis, so the research measure must be tweaked to reflect the observed factor structure.

In the case of the source credibility measure, research has shown us that the three subscales are distinctly different factors. This means that research participants tend to answer six of the items in a similar fashion, the second six items in a similar fashion, and the last six items in a similar fashion (these three groupings do not correspond to the numbers next to the individual items in Figure 7.2). Only after a researcher utilizes a factor analysis can he or she be sure that hypothesized subscales are distinctly different factors. You can label anything a subscale, but only a factor analysis can statistically determine whether there are unique factors within a specific mental measure.

If you have not done so by this point, please see whether you can find the three distinct subscales/factors in the Source Credibility Measure (Figure 7.2). If you want to check your answers, the groupings of the three factors can be found at the end of the chapter. Also, see whether you can label the three distinct subscales/factors within the Source Credibility Measure.

Ultimately, it is important to remember that a single scale can measure multiple concepts in an effort to more fully understand the larger hypothetical construct. However, an ethical researcher should not say that a set of items has multiple subscales in a published research article unless he or she conducts a factor analysis to support the presence of subscales (more on this in the next chapter). Many pop-science measures have been created over the years purporting to measure a wide range of phenomena, and researchers should be leery of using these measures at face value because they often pretend to measure subscales when those subscales do not statistically exist. For more information on factor analyses, check out Chapter 21 on advanced statistical tests.

Finding Mental Measures

Survey-based research is prevalent in communication research. Thankfully, we do not have to spend all of our time creating new scales to conduct survey-based research. In fact, most studies do not attempt to reinvent the measurement wheel at all and instead rely on combining previously existing scales in new ways that have not been explored. Literally thousands of research scales already exist, so there are millions of variable combinations that have yet to be explored. The more time you spend conducting survey research, the larger your collection of interval scales will ultimately become. If you are just starting out in research, you may not know where to turn to find scales. Here are five books that may be useful for finding communication scales:

Manusov, V. (Ed.). (2005). *The sourcebook of nonverbal measures: Going beyond words.* Mahwah, NJ: Erlbaum.

Rubin, R. B., Palmgreen, P., & Sypher, H. E. (Eds.). (2004). *Communication research measures: A sourcebook.* Mahwah, NJ: Erlbaum.

Rubin, R. B., Rubin, A. M., Graham, E. E., Perse, E. M., & Seibold, D. R. (2009). *Communication research measures II: A sourcebook.* New York, NY: Routledge.

Wrench, J. S., Jowi, D., & Goodboy, A. (2010). *The directory of communication related mental measures.* Washington, DC: National Communication Association. (Only available through the NCA online store: http://www.natcom.org/.)

Wrench, J. S., McCroskey, J. C., & Richmond, V. P. (2007). *Human communication in everyday life: Explanations and applications.* Boston, MA: Allyn & Bacon.

Continued

Finding Mental Measures   Continued

These next six books may be useful for finding variables outside of the field of communication relating to communication phenomena:

Davis, C. M., Yarber, W. L., Bauserman, R., Schreer, G., & Davis, S. L. (Eds.). *Handbook of sexuality-related measures.* Thousand Oaks, CA: Sage.

Fields, D. L. (2002). *Taking measure of work: A guide to validated scales for organizational research and diagnosis.* Thousand Oaks, CA: Sage.

Goldman, B. A., & Mitchell, D. F. (2003). *Directory of unpublished experimental mental measures* (Vol. 8). Washington, DC: American Psychological Association. (See also Vols. 1–7.)

Hill, P. C., & Hood, R. W., Jr. (Eds.). (1999). *Measures of religiosity.* Birmingham, AL: Religious Education Press.

Robinson, J. P., Shaver, P. R., & Wrightsman, L. S. (Eds.). (1991). *Measures of personality and social psychological attitudes.* San Diego, CA: Academic Press.

Robinson, J. P., Shaver, P. R., & Wrightsman, L. S. (Eds.). (1993). *Measures of political attitudes.* San Diego, CA: Academic Press.

There are also two online databases that can be useful when searching for mental measures. By 1938, so many new mental measures were being developed that Oscar K. Buros decided to publish the first volume of the *Mental Measures Yearbook*. The *Mental Measures Yearbook* attempts to locate and provide descriptions of the test, one or two reviews of the test, and references for how to find the test. The Buros Center for Testing (http://www.unl.edu/buros/) is still an active research center for mental measures, and the 18th volume of the *Mental Measures Yearbook* came out in 2010 (Spies, Carlson, & Geisinger). Your local library may have access to the *Mental Measures Yearbook* database through EBSCOhost. If you do not have access, the cost for a single copy is $15, but this is just the cost for the measure review and does not include a copy of the measure itself. The Educational Testing Service (http://www.ets.org/) also has started compiling mental measures. If you are on ETS's website, click on the link that says "Tests and Products." You will be taken to the Tests and Products homepage. You will need to scroll down until you find the link to "ETS Test Link," which is a database of more than 25,000 mental measures. In fact, in a simple name search there are more than 150 mental measures with the word "communication" in the title alone.

Measurement and Statistical Analysis

Because of the other chapters in this book, we will neither assume sophisticated knowledge of statistics nor attempt to explain statistical matters in any detail. However, it is important that a student studying measurement have elementary knowledge of statistics so that he or she may be better able to evaluate the measuring instruments he or she chooses or develops.

There are essentially two types of statistical tests: parametric and nonparametric. A **parameter** is a value of a population. For example, if we administered an intelligence test to all of the people in the world, we might then add all of their scores together and divide by the number of people and obtain the "mean" or average score for all people on this measure of intelligence. This "mean" would be a parameter of the population. Because in most cases we are unable to apply any measure to all of the people to whom it might be applied, we are forced to employ samples from a population. All statistical tests make certain assumptions, but **nonparametric** statistical tests make no assumptions about parameters of the population from which the research sample was drawn, whereas **parametric** tests do make such assumptions. The important distinction between parametric and nonparametric statistical tests, for our purposes, is that parametric tests assume that the level of measurement employed in obtaining the data was at least the interval level. Nonparametric tests make no such assumption. Parametric tests are normally considered more powerful, that is, they are precise and less subject to error than nonparametric tests. Thus, social scientists normally wish to employ parametric statistical procedures.

If we rigidly adhere to the characteristics required for the achievement of interval scales, we would be forced in many instances to employ nonparametric statistical tests although we might prefer to employ parametric ones. In some cases, this is a particularly difficult problem because some parametric analyses have no equivalent nonparametric approach, for example, factor analysis (see Chapter 21 for a brief explanation of factor analysis). Within the nominal, ordinal, interval, and ratio scaling category systems, most attitude measures fall in the ordinal or interval categories. It is highly unlikely to affect general results whether one treats the data as ordinal or interval, but a much wider range of techniques is available with interval measures.

Research Outside the Walls of Academia

Whether you are attempting to measure someone's trait level of CA or someone's level of customer satisfaction within your organization, measurement is a static process. Maybe you have been asked to put together a short web survey for your company about customer satisfaction with the latest website. Creating or finding good measures is an art and a science that should be taken seriously. Thankfully, there are a variety of useful sources that you can lean on for finding measures commonly used in the business world.

If your goal is to locate measures that relate to any aspect of marketing, we recommend looking at the books edited by Gordon Bruner (Bruner, 2009; Bruner, Hensel, & James, 2001). The 2001 book by Bruner et al. has full-text versions of 654 measures ranging from people's attitudes toward television advertising to communication about purchasing products between parents and adolescents. The 2009 book is similar in fashion to the 2001 book, but it is available only electronically through Bruner's website (http://www.marketingscales.com/). The 2009 book has 716 unique measures published within its pages. Overall, these two books are great sources for anyone interesting in surveying people about products and services.

If your goal is to measure communication within an organization, we recommend reading Cal Downs and Allyson Adrian's (2004) book *Assessing Organizational Communication: Strategic Communication Audits.* This book focuses specifically on the applied work communication consultants can engage in within modern organizations. The book discusses numerous ways to conduct communication research within an organization and provides access to both proprietary and public domain measures consultants can utilize.

Conclusion

In this chapter, we have discussed a number of extremely important factors involved in measurement. We started by reviewing the purpose of measurement and the different levels of measurement (nominal, ordinal, interval, and ratio) and then examined the history of social scientific measurement that led to the creation of Likert scales and semantic differential/bipolar adjective scales. Next, we talked about how we measure phenomena in communication, concluding with a discussion of how to write Likert-type items effectively. Finally, we discussed where one can find mental measures and how mental measures are used in statistical research. However, our discussion of measurement is not over yet. In the next chapter, we will discuss two extremely important concepts related to measurement: reliability and validity.

KEY TERMS

Attitudes	Likert scale	Perceived knowledge
Beliefs	Lurker/hypothetical variable	Semantic differential/bipolar
Cognitive knowledge	Measurement	scale
Conceptualization	Mental measure	Subscale
Factor analysis	Nonparametric	Trait behavior
Germinal idea	Operationalization	
Isomorphism	Parametric	

REFERENCES

Arnold, W. E., McCroskey, J. C., & Prichard, S. (1966). The semantic differential. *Today's Speech, 14(4)*, 29–30.

Arnold, W. E., McCroskey, J. C., & Prichard, S. V. O. (1967). The Likert-type scale. *Today's Speech, 15*, 31–33.

Baldwin, J. M., Cattell, J. M., & Jastrow, J. (1889). Physical and mental tests. *Psychological Review, 5*, 172–179.

Binet, A. (1905). New methods for the diagnosis of the intellectual level of subnormals. *L'Année Psychologique, 12*, 191–244.

Bogardus, E. S. (1925). Measuring social distance. *Journal of Applied Sociology, 9*, 299–308.

Boiarsky, G., Long, M., & Thayer, G. (1999). Formal features in children's science television: Sound effects, visual pace, and topic shifts. *Communication Research Reports, 16*, 185–192.

Booth-Butterfield, M., & Booth-Butterfield, S. (1991). Individual differences in the communication of humorous messages. *Southern Communication Journal, 56*, 208–218.

Bruner, G. C., II. (2009). *Marketing scales handbook: A compilation of multi-item measures for consumer behavior and advertising* (vol. V). Carbondale, IL: GCBII Productions.

Bruner, G. C., II, Hensel, P. J., & James, K. E. (2001). *Marketing scales handbook: A compilation of multi-item measures for consumer behavior and advertising* (Vol. IV). Chicago, IL: American Marketing Association and Thomson Southwestern.

Buros, O. K. (Ed.). (1938). *The 1938 mental measurements yearbook.* Lincoln, NE: University of Nebraska Press.

Cattell, J. M. (1895). Measurements of the accuracy of recollection. *Science, 2*, 761–766.

Cattell, J. M. (1890). Mental tests and measurements. *Mind, 15*, 373–381.

Darwin, C. (1859). *On the origin of species by means of natural selection.* London: Murray.

Downs, C. W., & Adrian, A. D. (2004). *Assessing organizational communication: Strategic communication audits.* New York, NY: Guilford Press.

Galton, F. (1869). *Heredity genius: An inquiry into its laws and consequences.* New York, NY: Macmillan. Retrieved from http://galton.org/books/hereditary-genius/

Gates, A. I. (1921). The true–false test as a measure of achievement in college courses. *Journal of Educational Psychology, 12*, 276–287.

Heise, D. R. (1970). The semantic differential and attitude research. In G. F. Summers (Ed.), *Attitude measurement* (pp. 235–253). Chicago, IL: Rand McNally.

Likert, R. (1932). A technique for the measurement of attitudes. *Archives of Psychology, 140*, 1–55.

McCroskey, J. C. (1966). *Experimental studies of the effects of ethos and evidence in persuasive communication. Unpublished doctoral dissertation.* Pennsylvania State University.

McCroskey, J. C., Richmond, V. P., Johnson, A. D., & Smith, H. T. (2004). Organizational orientations theory and measurement: Development of measures and preliminary investigations. *Communication Quarterly, 52*, 1–14.

McCroskey, J. C., & Teven, J. J. (1999). Goodwill: A reexamination of the construct and its measurement. *Communication Monographs, 66*, 90–103.

Osgood, C. E. (1952). The nature and measurement of meaning. *Psychological Bulletin, 49*, 197–237.

Osgood, C. E., Tannenbaum, P. H., & Suci, G. J. (1957). *The measurement of meaning.* Urbana, IL: University of Illinois Press.

Pressey, S. L., & Pressey, L. W. (1919). Cross-out test, with suggestions as to a group scale of the emotions. *Journal of Applied Psychology, 3*, 138–150.

Richmond, V. P., & McCroskey, J. C. (1990). Reliability and separation of factors on the assertiveness-responsiveness measure. *Psychological Reports, 67*, 449–450.

Salkind, N. J. (2006). *Tests & measurement for people who (think they) hate tests & measurement.* Thousand Oaks, CA: Sage.

Segal, D. L., & Coolidge, F. L. (2003). Objective assessment of personality and psychopathology: An overview. In M. J. Hilsenroth, D. L. Segal, & M. Hersen (Eds.), *Comprehensive handbook of psychological assessment: Volume 2: Personality assessment* (pp. 3–13). New York, NY: Wiley.

Sokal, M. M. (Ed.). (1987). *Psychological testing and American society, 1890–1930.* New Brunswick, NJ: Rutgers University Press.

Spies, R. A., Carlson, J. F., Geisinger, K. F. (2010). *The eighteenth mental measurements yearbook.* Lincoln, NE: University of Nebraska Press.

Terman, L. M. (1916). *The measurement of intelligence.* Boston, MA: Houghton Mifflin.

Woodworth, R. S. (1920). *Personal data sheet.* Chicago, IL: Stoelting.

Wrench, J. S. (2007). The influence of perceived risk knowledge on risk communication. *Communication Research Reports, 24*, 1–8.

Wrench, J. S., & Richmond, V. P. (2004). Understanding the psychometric properties of the Humor Assessment instrument through an analysis of the relationships between teacher humor assessment and instructional communication variables in the college classroom. *Communication Research Reports, 21*, 92–103.

FURTHER READING

DeVellis, R. F. (1991). *Scale development: Theory and applications* (Applied Social Research Methods Series, Vol. 26). Newbury Park, CA: Sage.

Dillman, D. A. (2000). *Mail and Internet surveys: The tailored design method* (2nd ed.). New York, NY: Wiley.

Fowler, F. J., Jr. (1993). *Survey research methods* (2nd ed.). Newbury Park, CA: Sage.

Linn, R. L., & Grolund, N. E. (2000). *Measurement and assessment in teaching* (8th ed.). Upper Saddle, NJ: Merrill.

Salkind, N. J. (2012). *100 questions (and answers) about research methods.* Los Angeles, CA: Sage.

Singleton, R. A., Jr., & Straits, B. C. (1999). *Approach to social research* (3rd ed.). New York, NY: Oxford University Press.

Wrench, J. S., Jowi, D., & Goodboy, A. (2010). *The directory of communication related mental measures.* Washington, DC: National Communication Association.

SCORING THE SOURCE CREDIBILITY MEASURE

Competence Factor (1, 2, 7, 11, 13, and 16)   _____
Caring/Goodwill Factor (3, 5, 8, 9, 15, and 18)   _____
Trustworthiness Factor (4, 6, 11, 12, 14, and 17)   _____

Reliability and Validity

The purpose of this chapter is to explore two important characteristics in measurement: reliability and validity. We will begin by discussing reliability.

Reliability

When people think about the word *reliability*, numerous synonyms come to mind: dependable, accurate, honest, trustworthy, consistent, and so on. Although the word *reliability* is used in a specific manner by quantitative researchers, those adjectives still hold true. **Reliability** for this text is defined as the accuracy that a measure has in producing stable, consistent measurements. The first part of this definition relates to the information we talked about in the previous chapter examining measurement, so ultimately reliability is about making sure our tools for measuring a phenomena are accurate. And we are dealing with whether the measurement has the ability to find consistent results. One of the authors of this book has an unreliable cell phone—the clock on the cell phone is constantly changing. At one point in time you will look down and the cell phone will say that it is 6:45, and you will look down 5 minutes later and the cell phone will say that it's 10:15. Obviously, this particular cell phone is not a reliable tool for telling the time because a clock should not indicate that 3½ hours have passed in 5 minutes. Admittedly, social scientists do not generally sit around watching clocks and watches to ascertain their reliability as tools for measuring time, so we must determine whether our tools for measurement are as reliable as a good clock.

In the social sciences, we often use research scales to conduct studies. Because research scales are a common form of measurement, social scientists must ensure that these scales are reliable measurements of the constructs they claim to measure. One of the first things a researcher must determine when he or she has collected data is whether people have consistently filled out a research scale or completed the scale haphazardly. Imagine you just handed out the Generalized Attitude Scale about Higher Education to 300 people. How can you tell whether people randomly filled out the scale or whether the participants put in the time and effort into their participation in a research project?

As stated earlier, reliability of a measuring instrument *whether a measure produces stable, consistent values.* In other words, if I give you the same measure under the same conditions multiple times, your score should not change significantly. A perfectly reliable instrument would produce the same score every time it is administered, even if it were administered an infinite number of times. In measuring human beings it is impossible to measure an infinite number of times. Thus, we never know the precise reliability of our measures. Rather, we must estimate that reliability.

SCALAR RELIABILITY

Scalar reliability (the reliability of individual research scales) is the most common form of reliability assessed in quantitative research in communication. Almost every quantitative research study will employ at least one research scale, and we must have a way to determine whether people are consistently filling out the scale. In Figure 8.1, we present a copy of the Generalized Attitude Measure used in this book.

In this scale some of the adjective pairings are positively worded and some are negatively worded. For example, in the first pairing (good/bad) the word "good" to the left receives a lower score (1) and the word "bad" to the right receives a higher score (7), whereas in the second pairing (wrong/right), the word "wrong" to the left receives the lower score (1) and the word "right" to the right receives the higher score (7). In this scale, is "good" an equivalent to "wrong"? Not at all! When researchers create scales, we often do so with items that are oppositely worded to determine whether people are just randomly answering the scale.

Imagine you had a participant in your study who filled out the scale like you see in Figure 8.2. You will note that in this case someone just went through and circled almost all 7's on the scale. In essence, this person perceives higher education to be bad, right, beneficial, unfair, foolish, and positive. Does this make sense to you? Well, do not worry—it does not make sense to us either. If a person consistently filled out the Generalized Attitude Measure, it might look like either option in Figure 8.3.

In the first case in Figure 8.3, you have someone who has a strong, positive attitude toward higher education, with a score of 42. In the second case, you have someone who has a

Instructions: On the scales below, please indicate your feelings about "**Higher Education**." Numbers "1" and "7" indicate a very strong feeling. Numbers "2" and "6" indicate a strong feeling. Numbers "3" and "5" indicate a fairly week feeling. Number "4" indicates you are undecided or do not understand the adjective pairs themselves. There are no right or wrong answers. *Only circle one number per line.*

1.	Good	1	2	3	4	5	6	7	Bad
2.	Wrong	1	2	3	4	5	6	7	Right
3.	Harmful	1	2	3	4	5	6	7	Beneficial
4.	Fair	1	2	3	4	5	6	7	Unfair
5.	Wise	1	2	3	4	5	6	7	Foolish
6.	Negative	1	2	3	4	5	6	7	Positive

To compute your score:

Step One: Add the scores from items 2, 3, & 6.
Step Two: Add the scores from items 1, 4, & 5.
Step Three: Add 24 to Step One.
Step Four: Subtract Step Two from Step Three.

Scores should be between 6 and 42.

Sources:

McCroskey, J. C. (1966). *Experimental studies of the effects of ethos and evidence in persuasive communication.* Unpublished doctoral dissertation. Pennsylvania State University.

McCroskey, J. C., & Richmond, V. P. (1989). Bipolar scales. In P. Emmert & L. L. Barker (Eds.), *Measurement of Communication Behavior* (pp. 154–167). New York: Longman.

Figure 8.1 Generalized Attitude Measure

1.	Good	1	2	3	4	(5)	6	7	Bad
2.	Wrong	1	2	3	4	5	6	(7)	Right
3.	Harmful	1	2	3	4	5	6	(7)	Beneficial
4.	Fair	1	2	3	4	5	6	(7)	Unfair
5.	Wise	1	2	3	4	5	6	(7)	Foolish
6.	Negative	1	2	3	4	5	6	(7)	Positive

Figure 8.2 Generalized Attitude Measure Scored Inconsistently

moderately negative attitude, with a score of 36. Although this example was completed looking only at a bipolar adjective scale, the same principle holds true for a Likert scale as well. If you have two questions ("I like public speaking" and "I dislike public speaking") on a Likert scale with five steps running from 1 (*strongly disagree*) to 5 (*strongly agree*), a consistent

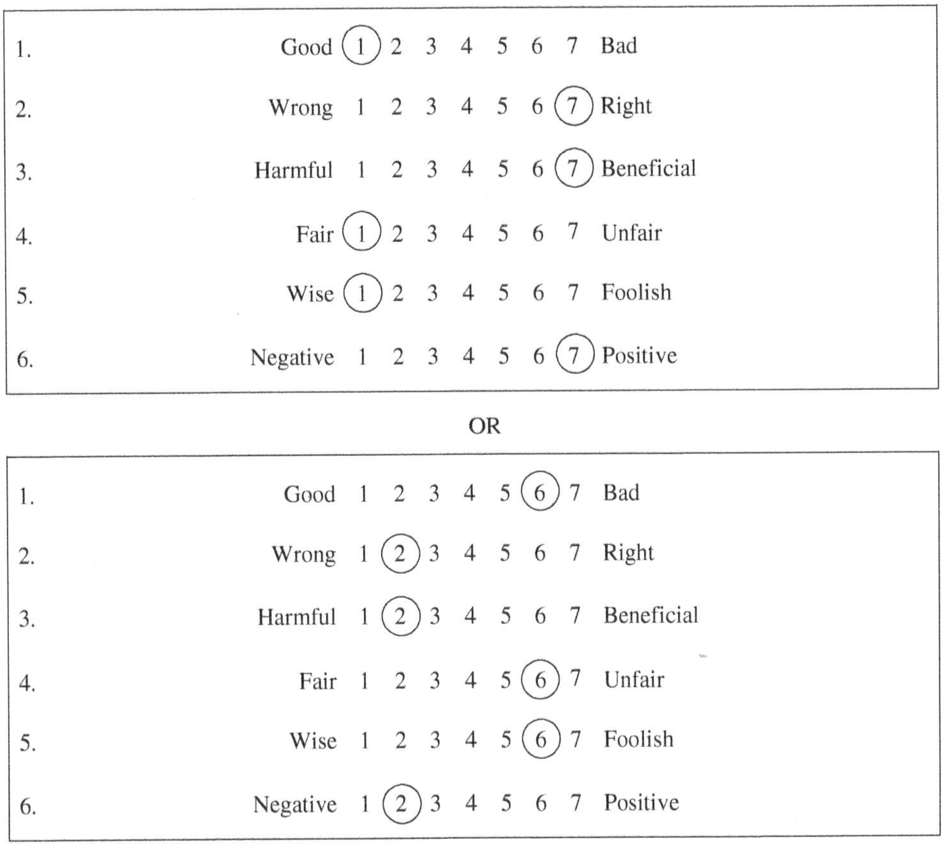

Figure 8.3 Generalized Attitude Measure Scored Consistently

participant may score the first question with 5 and the second question with 1. However, if a participant scored the first question as a 1 and the second question as a 1, we have a problem with the participant's consistency. Although we have talked about how an individual responds to a scale in this section, when looking at the overall picture of reliability in a study we look at a sample's responses to a scale collectively, not individual participant scores.

Now that we have looked at some of the basic principles behind the concept of reliability, we will turn our attention to a number of statistical tests that can be used to examine reliability. Specifically, we will discuss the test–retest, alternate forms, split-half, Hoyt, and Cronbach forms of reliability.

Test–Retest Reliability

One of the most obvious methods for testing the reliability of an instrument is to measure the same thing on more than one occasion and see whether you get the same score, which is the essence of the **test–retest reliability** approach. If we presume that the thing we are measuring does not change, our measure should produce the exact same score the second time we use it as it did the first time. Test–retest reliability for attitude measures is estimated by administering the instrument to the same group of people on two occasions, separated by some given amount of time. The subjects' scores at "Time 1" and "Time 2" are then subjected to statistical analysis to obtain a correlation coefficient. This correlation coefficient is referred to as a reliability coefficient, or an estimate of the degree of association between the scores at Time 1 and Time 2. Reliability coefficients may vary to the same degree that correlation coefficients signify consistent measurement. Good attitude-measuring instruments normally produce test–retest reliability coefficients of 0.70 or above, and many coefficients are 0.90 or above. If a researcher finds a test–retest reliability below 0.70, then her or his participants are not responding to the scale in a consistent manner. Conversely, test–retest reliability coefficients of about 0.90 indicate that people are filling out the scale at Time 1 and Time 2 in almost identical fashions.

Alternate Forms Reliability

The logic and procedure for **alternate forms reliability** estimation are essentially the same as that for test–retest reliability. In many cases, we can develop two attitude-measuring instruments to measure the same attitude. We may then administer the first instrument at Time 1 and the second at Time 2. We may then obtain the reliability coefficient for the two forms. Reliability coefficients for the alternate forms are normally somewhat lower than reliability coefficients developed through the test–retest procedure. The reason for this is that with the test–retest procedure there is no variety in the items administered from Time 1 to Time 2. No matter how carefully two forms of the same test are developed, there is always some variability in the items from Time 1 to Time 2. Thus, slightly lower reliability estimates should be expected.

Split-Half Reliability

In many instances, it is impossible or economically infeasible to administer instruments to the same people on two occasions. Therefore, we must be able to estimate the reliability of our measuring instrument with only one administration. The **split-half reliability** approach is similar to the test–retest and alternate forms procedures except that there is only one measurement period, so there is no time delay that could be accompanied by changes in the subjects, which would be reflected in lower reliability estimates. The split-half reliability procedure involves computing two scores for each participant on the basis of one administration of the test. One of the scores comes from one half of the test and the other score comes from the other half.

Several methods can be employed to divide the test in half to obtain the two scores. A common one is to have all the odd-numbered items compose one half of the test and the even-numbered items the other half. Alternatively, if we had 20 items in our test, we could take the first 10 items as one half of the test and the last 10 items as the other half of the test. A somewhat less frequently employed method is to randomly select half of the items on the test to compose the first half and employ the remainder to represent the second half. The reliability coefficients that are produced by correlating the two scores of the two halves of the test must be corrected before they are interpreted. In essence, we have the reliability for only half of the test; for example, if we administered half of the items at Time 1 and the other half at Time 2 we would be presuming that we had a 10-item test at each time, but we have a 20-item test.

CRONBACH'S ALPHA RELIABILITY

The type of scalar reliability most commonly used by social scientists is the single administration reliability, and the most popular single administration reliability test is the **Cronbach alpha reliability** test (Cronbach, 1951). The Cronbach alpha reliability test is probably the most consistently reported reliability test in the social sciences, including communication. Because Cronbach's alpha is the most commonly used form of reliability testing, we will discuss how to go about determining a scale's Cronbach alpha and how you report alpha in a research project.

For the purposes of this analysis, we will use the Generalized Attitude Measure data gathered for this book. As we saw in Figure 8.1, the Generalized Attitude Scale has six bipolar items with a 7-step scale between the two adjectives. To determine the alpha reliability, all of the items must be recoded so that all of the positively worded items with low scores (*good*, *fair*, and *wise*) are scored with a 7 instead of a 1. For example, if a participant circled a "2" on the first row (*Good*), that number would be reflected as a "6." We do this recoding so that all of the positive words (*good*, *right*, *beneficial*, *fair*, *wise*, and *positive*) receive high scores of "7" and all of the negative words (*bad*, *wrong*, *harmful*, *unfair*, *foolish*, and *negative*) receive low scores of "1." You cannot determine the alpha reliability of a scale until this recoding has occurred.

There are two basic statistical packages commonly used by communication researchers: SPSS and Excel. We should note that both SPSS and Excel have different methods for recoding items, so please read the individual instruction books for each software package to learn how to recode items for your own research purposes. On the dataset on the textbook's website, all of the recoding has already been conducted.

COMPUTER PRINTOUTS OF CRONBACH'S ALPHA

Most researchers no longer compute statistics by hand. Computing statistics by hand is dangerous because humans make errors easily when handling large quantities of data. To avoid simple computational mistakes, a variety of computer programs have been created to aid in this process. The two most commonly used statistical software packages used by communication researchers are SPSS and Excel. If you look on the textbook's website, you will find the "Book Datasets" section. In this folder, you will find folders for SPSS datasets, Excel datasets, and Note Pad datasets. If you do not have SPSS or Excel but have a different statistical software package, you can use the SPSS dataset in either PSPP or R or you can use the Note Pad datasets to import the data into whatever program you prefer to use. However, we will only be discussing how to read and interpret results from SPSS and Excel in this book. To calculate your own alpha reliability, open the file called "Recoded Dataset." The "Recoded Dataset" has already recoded all of the scales using the coding schemes discussed in Chapter 6.

SPSS and Cronbach's Alpha

After opening SPSS, a window will pop up called "SPSS for Windows." In this window, the "Open an Existing Data Source" button is preselected, so you can either scroll through a list of previously used data files or select "More Files . . ." to find the data file you are attempting to open. Once you have selected either the correct data file or the "More Files" option, click "OK." If you chose "More Files" before you clicked "OK" in the previous box, the "Open File" window will appear on your screen. At this point you just need to search your computer hard drive to find the data file you are attempting to use. If you do not know how to look for a file on your hard drive or textbook's website, you may want to pick up a simple MS Windows manual at your local bookstore.

If you are looking on the textbook's website, you will find a folder called "Book Datasets." You can then select the SPSS Datasets folder. Once you are inside the SPSS Datasets folder, you will find a number of different SPSS files that are designed to be used with your textbook. The "Main SPSS Dataset" is the collected dataset without any changes or alterations to the data itself. The file marked "Recoded Dataset" is the file with the data that has already been recoded for your convenience, so the data can be easily manipulated in SPSS. To save the file to your hard drive, right click on the file hyperlink, choose "save as," and then save the file to your hard drive in a desired location or just run the dataset from the textbook's website. When you finally open the file you want to work with, your computer will import the data into the SPSS window. If you encounter a problem opening the data file, go back to the beginning and repeat the steps or consult your computer's owner's manual for further instructions.

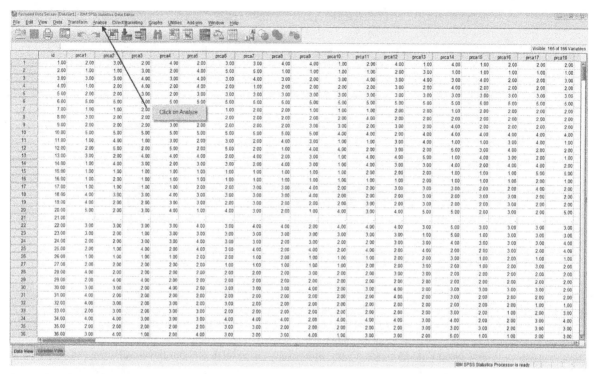

Figure 8.4 SPSS Dataset Recoded Image

To conduct Cronbach's alpha, click on the drop-down menu under the word "Analyze" (Figure 8.4). Then scroll over the word "Scale." When you scroll over "Scale," a menu will pop out to the left. Click on the word "Reliability Analysis" (Figure 8.5). At this point, a window will open called "Reliability Analysis" (Figure 8.6a). If you did not get this window, backtrack

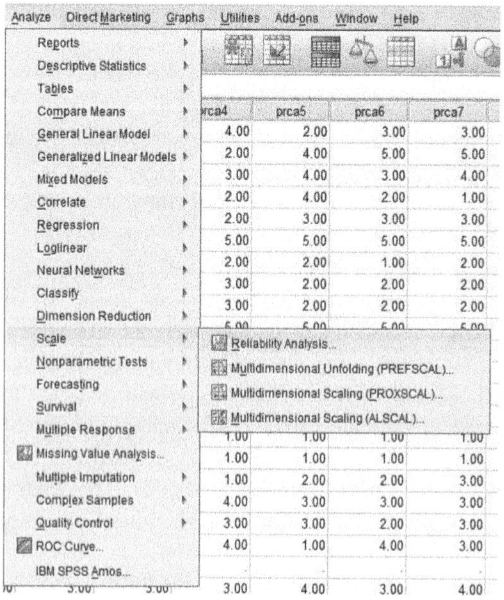

Figure 8.5 Reliability Analysis Menu

and try to find out what went wrong. In the "Reliability Analysis" window, there are three major scroll- or drop-down boxes. On the upper left, you will find a scrolling box with all of the variables in the dataset, and on the right you will see a scrolling box with nothing in it labeled "Items." Underneath the box with all of your variables is a drop-down box with different types of reliability formats. The screen comes up with Cronbach's alpha reliability preselected for use (Figure 8.6b). To run Cronbach's alpha, simply highlight the scale items that you are wanting to analyze. So, to run Cronbach's Reliability for the Attitude Scale you must scroll down the list of variables until you find the variables listed as ATT1–ATT6. Depending on which version of SPSS you are using, ATT1 may come up as "Attitude about Higher Education" in the variable list. To highlight more items than can be seen at one time, click the first item and hold your "shift" button on your keyboard. Then scroll down to the last item and (still holding your shift button) click the last item, which will allow you to highlight all six attitude items (Figure 8.6c).

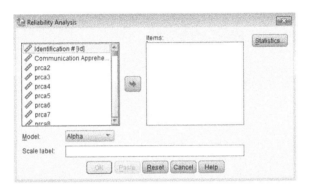

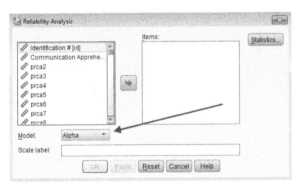

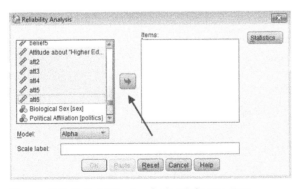

Figure 8.6 Reliability Analysis Dialogue Box

Continued

Continued

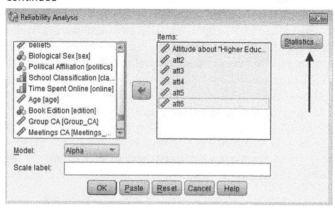

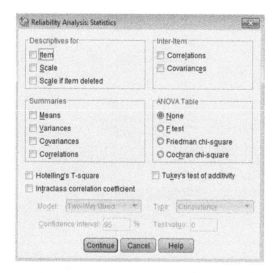

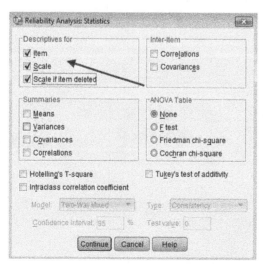

Scale: ALL VARIABLES

Case Processing Summary		N	%
Cases	Valid	625	95.6
	Excluded[a]	29	4.4
	Total	654	100.0

[a] Listwise deletion based on all variables in the procedure.

Reliability Statistics	
Cronbach's Alpha	N of Items
.909	6

Figure 8.7 SPSS Cronbach's Alpha Reliability

Now simply send the six items to the "Items" box by clicking the arrow in between the two boxes. If this has been done correctly, you will now see all six attitude variables in the box on the right-hand side of the screen (Figure 8.6d). At this point you can do one of two things: you can click OK and get a simple printout of reliability (Figure 8.7) or you can click on the "Statistics" button at the bottom of the screen. We will click on the Statistics button.

When you click on the Statistics button in the "Reliability Analysis" window, the "Reliability Analysis: Statistics" window will appear (Figure 8.6e). You will see many different types of tests that can be conducted. Most of these qualify as advanced statistical tests, so we will not explain what they mean in this book. However, in the upper left-hand corner, you will find the "Descriptives For" box. These statistics give basic information about each item, the overall reliability of the scale, and the reliability of the scale if we deleted one item. Once you have selected these three options (Figure 8.6f), simply hit the Continue button. Once you have finished with the "Reliability Analysis: Statistics" window, you will be taken back to the "Reliability Analysis" window, and you are ready to run your Cronbach's alpha reliability test, so simply hit OK on the right-hand side of the window. You will be given two different sets of information. You will see the same reliability information that was given to you in Figure 8.7, plus you will be given the information you asked for about the descriptive statistics for the scale and the alpha reliability if the scale is deleted (Figure 8.8).

In Figure 8.7, you will find two boxes. The first box is the Case Process Summary box, which tells you how many participants have scores for the Generalized Attitude Measure that were used in the calculating of Cronbach's alpha ($N = 625$). The second box is the box with the reported reliability, 0.909, and the number of scale items ($N = 6$) that were used in the calculation of the reliability. Using the following information, the scales reliability can be interpreted:

0.90 +	Excellent
0.80–0.90	Good
0.70–0.80	Respectable
0.65–070	Minimally acceptable
0.60–0.65	Undesirable
0.60	Unacceptable

Item Statistics

	Mean	Std. Deviation	N
Attitude about "Higher Education"	6.2144	1.25401	625
att2	5.9952	1.29036	625
att3	6.1104	1.31155	625
att4	5.4128	1.51779	625
att5	5.9296	1.38496	625
att6	6.0672	1.27298	625

Item-Total Statistics

	Scale Mean if Item Deleted	Scale Variance if Item Deleted	Corrected Item-Total Correlation	Cronbach's Alpha if Item Deleted
Attitude about "Higher Education"	29.5152	32.494	.733	.895
att2	29.7344	31.625	.776	.889
att3	29.6192	31.428	.775	.889
att4	30.3168	31.611	.623	.914
att5	30.3408	30.606	.785	.887
att6	29.6624	31.224	.823	.883

Scale Statistics

Mean	Variance	Std. Deviation	N of Items
35.7296	44.547	6.67435	6

Figure 8.8 SPSS Cronbach's Alpha Reliability–Other Statistics

In Figure 8.8, you are also presented with three boxes: Item Statistics, Item-Total Statistics, and Scale Statistics. The Item Statistics box presents you with the basic descriptive statistics (mean, standard deviation, and number of participants) for each individual scale item. The Item-Total Statistics box enables you to see what would happen to the overall scale if a single item from the scale was left out of the scale. The most important column in this box, for this discussion, is the last column (Cronbach's Alpha if Item Deleted), which is the column that lets us see whether our alpha reliability can be helped if we drop an item from the scale. For example, if we dropped the first item from the scale, which would be the good/bad item, the alpha reliability would drop to 0.901, which is below the overall scale reliability of 0.915. In the world of reliability, the higher the reliability (the closer your score is to 1), the more consistent your participants have been when filling out the scale. So, when examining Figure 8.8, are there any items that, if we dropped them from the scale, would increase our overall reliability? The answer is yes. If you look in the Cronbach's Alpha if Item Deleted column next to Item 4, you will see that the overall reliability of the scale would increase from 0.909 (overall reliability with 6 items) to 0.914 (with item 4 dropped from the scale). Overall, the slight bump up in reliability is not going to be that meaningful, so the item should be kept. However, often you will find that if you drop one item you will get a significant bump in your reliability (e.g., 0.65 to 0.89), so dropping an item from a scale can often be necessary.

APA Write-Up for SPSS

The Generalized Attitude Measure is a scale originally created by McCroskey (1966) and later validated by McCroskey (2006) as a tool for determining someone's overall attitude about a specific subject. The Generalized Attitude Measure is measured using a six-item bipolar adjective scale with seven steps, which gives the scale a range from 6 to 42. For the purposes of this study, the Generalized Attitude Measure was utilized to determine the attitude of participants about higher education. The scale is coded so that higher scores represent more positive attitudes about higher education. The alpha reliability found for the Generalized Attitude Measure in the current study was 0.91 ($M = 35.73$, $SD = 6.67$).

Excel and Cronbach's Alpha

Unfortunately, there is not an easy way to calculate Cronbach's alpha in Excel. As such, you must use a variety of formulas for the calculations of alpha. Thankfully, a psychometrician at the University of Leicester in the United Kingdom named Professor Glenn Fulcher has created an easy-to-use Excel template to conduct an alpha reliability (http://languagetesting.info/statistics/excel.html/). When you download the alpha reliability file, it will open with all of the calculations in place, but there will be no actual data within the file yet. The Excel file is built for up to 200 scale items and 3,005 individual cases (Figure 8.9). Note that there are two tabs to this Excel file. The one currently selected in Figure 8.9 is where the data will be pasted. The arrow in Figure 8.9 is pointing to the tab where you can see the alpha reliability after you have pasted the data.

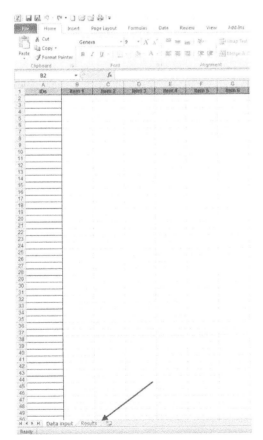

Figure 8.9 Fulcher's Excel File

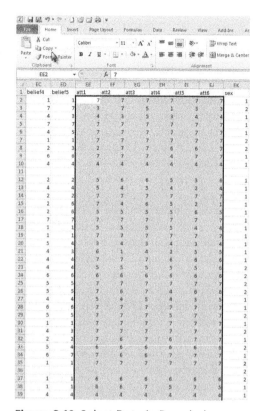

Figure 8.10 Select Data in Recoded Dataset

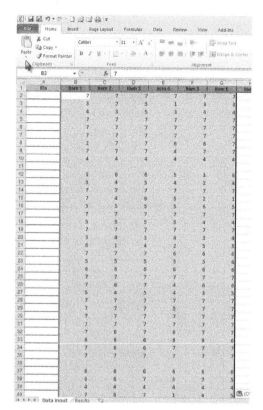

Figure 8.11 Pasted Scale Items into Excel

To paste the data, find the data you want to include in the alpha reliability test in the Recoded Dataset (Figure 8.10). Note that you do not select the variable names at the top of each column. Then go to copy function and click "copy" (note the pointer in Figure 8.10). Once you have copied the data, you can then go to the Alpha Reliability Excel File and paste that copied data into the file. Select the square located at B2 and paste the data (Figure 8.11). Once you have pasted the data, just click on the "Results" worksheet at the bottom of the screen and you can view the alpha reliability calculated (Figure 8.12). Please note that it is using a slightly different formula for calculating alpha reliability than the one used by SPSS, which has resulted in a slightly elevated alpha reliability. To learn more about the specific calculations utilized in this alpha reliability test, check out Fulcher's discussion on conducting alpha reliability in Fulcher and Davidson (2007) or Fulcher (2010).

APA DISCUSSION

The first part of the APA write-up is a simple description of the scale itself. In this case, the scale was originally created by McCroskey in 1966 as part of his dissertation, but was then later validated and used in more research by McCroskey (2006). The second part of the APA write-up clearly explains what kind of scale is being used. In this case, the scale consists of six bipolar items with a 7-step scale between the adjectives (1, 2, 3, 4, 5, 6, 7). The next part of the write-up explains to the reader that higher scores represent more positive attitudes about higher education. This step is often skipped by researchers and can end up leading to

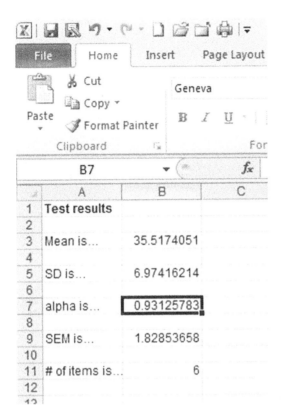

Figure 8.12 Excel Alpha Reliability Results

results that are extremely confusing to interpret. Finally, the scale's reliability is presented to the reader. Immediately after the reliability is presented, the mean (*M*) and standard deviation (*SD*) are presented as well. (Note that "*M*" and "*SD*" are italicized, but the equal signs and numbers are not.)

ALPHA RELIABILITIES FROM THIS BOOK

Now that we have looked at the reporting of attitude scale used in the creation of the dataset for this book, you might be wondering what all of the reliabilities are for the various scales. Figure 8.13 has all of the alpha reliability information for every scale used in the creation of the dataset that accompanies this book, along with the means and standard deviations. In Figure 8.14, you will see the corresponding APA write-ups for each scale.

RELIABILITIES IN THE REAL WORLD

The textbook's website has a number of different research articles on it published in *Communication Research Reports* and *Communication Quarterly* to help you further understand how research actually happens. Figure 8.15 contains the alpha reliabilities for every scale used in any of the articles on the textbook's website.

You will note that not all of the reported reliabilities are either good (0.80–0.90) or excellent (0.90+). In fact, if you look at the Cheseboro (1999) article reliability results, the listening style scale clearly has a reliability problem. On this scale, the content factor is below 0.60, so it is unacceptable; people and action are between 0.60 and 0.65, so they are undesirable; and

Variable	Alpha Reliability	Mean	Standard Deviation
Communication Apprehension			
Group CA	.87	15.04	5.04
Meeting CA	.87	15.56	4.99
Interpersonal CA	.85	14.42	4.53
Public CA	.87	18.61	5.72
Total CA	.94	63.66	17.00
Ethnocentrism	.89	31.74	9.10
Humor Assessment	.91	63.24	9.53
Nonverbal Immediacy Scale – Self Report	.90	96.52	13.35
Sociocommunicative Orientation			
Assertiveness	.83	35.33	6.31
Responsiveness	.90	40.33	6.28
Willingness to Communicate			
Contexts			
Group WTC	.52	73.49	17.36
Meeting WTC	.68	65.34	21.60
Interpersonal WTC	.68	73.33	17.12
Public WTC	.48	65.01	20.91
Audience			
Stranger WTC	.85	45.76	25.63
Acquaintance WTC	.78	74.59	20.00
Friend WTC	.68	87.58	14.01
Overall WTC	.87	68.95	15.71
Belief that Every College Student Should take Public Speaking	.96	23.38	9.20
Attitude Towards Higher Education	.91	35.73	6.67

Figure 8.13 Reliabilities for Book Dataset Variables

time is 0.66, which is minimally acceptable. In essence, people are not consistent when filling out this scale, so the scale clearly has some problems and is not reliable.

Improving Reliability of Measurement

We measure things because we want to know what they "are." Reliability is crucial to our measurement. If we measure something on several different occasions and never get anywhere near the same score, there are only two conclusions that we may draw: either the thing we are measuring is constantly changing or our measuring instrument is worthless. Presuming that we are attempting to measure a reasonably stable characteristic, the latter conclusion is probably the most appropriate. Reliability is absolutely crucial to measurement. Because there are excellent methods of estimating the reliability of our measuring instruments and because there are ways of improving instruments that lack reliability, there is no excuse for the social scientist to employ measures that lack adequate reliability. Let us consider a few of the ways in which reliability may be increased.

PRCA-24. The Personal Report of Communication Apprehension-24 was created by McCroskey (1982) to measure an individual's level of fear or anxiety associated with either real or anticipated communication with another person or persons. The scale consists of 24 Likert items ranging from (1) *strongly agree* to (5) *strongly disagree*. This scale has a range from 24 to 120 with higher scores indicating stronger levels of anxiety associated with communication. The alpha reliability found for the PRCA-24 in the current study was .94 (*M* = 63.66, *SD* = 17.00).

Ethnocentrism. The Ethnocentrism Scale was created by Neuliep and McCroskey (1997) to measure an individual's tendency to feel that her or his culture is the center of the universe. The revised version of the scale employed here (Neuliep & McCroskey, 2000; McCroskey, 2001) consists of 22 Likert items ranging from (1) *strongly disagree* to (5) *strongly agree*. Fifteen of the items are scored; the remaining items are used as distracters. This scale has a range from 15 to 75 with higher scores indicating stronger ethnocentric attitudes. The alpha reliability found for the Ethnocentrism scale in the current study was .89 (*M* = 31.74, *SD* = 9.10).

Humor Assessment. The Humor Assessment instrument was created by Wrench and Richmond (2004) to measure an individual's use of humor as a communicative device in interpersonal relationships. The scale was originally published in Richmond, Wrench, & Gorham (2001) as a tool for teachers to assess their own use of humor in the classroom. The HA was then validated by Wrench and McCroskey (2001) who found that it functioned distinctly different from M. Booth-Butterfield and S. Booth-Butterfield's (1991) Humor Orientation scale. The HA consists of 16 Likert type items range from 1 *strongly disagree* to 5 *strongly agree*. This scale has a range from 16 to 80 with higher scores indicating higher usage of humor as a communicative tactic. The alpha reliability found for the HA in the current study was .91 (*M* = 63.25, *SD* = 9.53).

Nonverbal Immediacy Scale. The Nonverbal Immediacy Scale was created by Richmond, McCroskey, & Johnson (2003) to measure a receiver's perceived nonverbal immediacy between a her or himself and a source. The scale consists of 26 Likert type items ranging from 1 *strongly disagree* to 5 *strongly agree*. This scale has a range from 26 to 130 with higher scores indicating stronger degrees of nonverbal immediacy. The alpha reliability found for the Nonverbal Immediacy Scale in the current study was .90 (*M* = 96.52, *SD* = 13.35).

Sociocommunicative orientation. The Sociocommunicative Orientation scale was created by Richmond and McCroskey (1985) as an instructional tool to examine the extent to which individuals use assertive or responsive communication. The instrument was first utilized in research by Thompson, Ishii, and Klopf (1990) and Ishii, Thompson, and Klopf (1990) to examine cultural differences in assertive and responsive communication. After the publication of these two articles, Richmond and McCroskey (1990) demonstrated the reliability and dimensionality of the measure itself. The sociocommunicative orientation scale consists of ten items on each factor for a total of twenty items. Participants are asked to respond to short descriptive phrases that range from one to five words in length that indicate ways in which they may communicate. The measure asks a participant to respond in terms of how well the items applies to her or him using a Likert scale from (1) *strongly disagree that it applies* to (5) *strongly agree that it applies*. Each subscale has a range from 10 to 50. The alpha reliability found for assertiveness in the current study was .83 (*M* = 35.33, *SD* = 6.31), and the alpha reliability for responsiveness was .90 (*M* = 40.33, *SD* = 6.28). Higher scores for each subscale represent higher levels of that concept.

Willingness to Communicate. The Willingness to Communication instrument was devised by McCroskey (1992) to measures a person's willingness to initiate communication with another person or persons. The scale consists of 20 items. Each of the items is designed to measure whether an individual would initiate communication in a specific situation or with a specific individual. Eight of the items are fillers and twelve are scored as part of the scale. Using a 101 point range from 0 (never) to 100 (always), participants are asked to indicate the

Figure 8.14 APA Write-Ups for Reliabilities

Continued

percentage of time they would choose to communicate in each type of situation. Ultimately, the scores on the twelve items are added together to create a composite score with higher scores indicating a higher willingness to communicate. The alpha reliability found for Willingness to Communicate Scale in the current study was .91 ($M = 68.95$, $SD = 15.71$).

Generalized Belief Scale. The Generalized Belief Scale was created by McCroskey (1966) and validated by McCroskey & Richmond (1996). The Generalized Belief Measure was created by McCroskey (1966) as a way to measure beliefs about specific concepts. By attaining an individual's general belief about a given topic, the researcher can measure the degree to which an individual believes in a given statement. The statement measured in this study was "Everyone Should be Required to take Public Speaking in College." The belief statement is then measured using a five-item semantic differential scale with seven steps, which gives the scale a range from 5 to 35. The scale is coded so that higher scores represent stronger beliefs. The alpha reliability found for Generalized Belief Scale in the current study was .96 ($M = 23.38$, $SD = 9.20$).

Generalized Attitude Measure. The Generalized Attitude Measure was a scale originally created by McCroskey (1966) and later validated by McCroskey and Richmond (1989) as a tool for determining someone's overall attitude about a specific subject. The Generalized Attitude Measure is measured using a six item semantic differential scale with seven steps, which gives the scale a range from 6 to 42. For the purposes of this study, the Generalized Attitude Measure was utilized to determine the attitude of participants about higher education. The scale is coded so that higher scores represent more positive attitudes about higher education. The alpha reliability found for Generalized Attitude Scale in the current study was .91 ($M = 35.73$, $SD = 6.67$).

1. *Item construction.* Nothing contributes more to unreliability in a measuring instrument than bad items. If an item is ambiguous, it will produce variable responses both among people and with the same person on different occasions. At this point, we will merely suggest that the best way to improve reliability is to improve your items using the suggestions for scale item writing from the previous chapter.

2. *Length of the instrument.* Reliability is directly associated with the number of items included in the measuring instrument. Other things being equal, a 20-item test will be more reliable than a 10-item test. If everything possible has been done to improve the quality of individual items and the reliability is still somewhat below the level desired, creation of more items of the same type should increase the reliability of the instrument. Obviously, there are limitations normally imposed on the length that an instrument may be. Extreme increases in the length of the instrument may actually increase unreliability because subjects may become fatigued and merely record responses at random.

3. *Administration of the test.* Measures should always be administered under standard, well-controlled conditions. If the instructions that are given to the subjects are ambiguous, the subjects may interpret how they are supposed to respond differentially and thus contribute to unreliability. Similarly, if the psychological conditions surrounding the subjects differ, this may influence the way the subjects respond. For example, one group of subjects may be in a friendly environment and do their best to record accurate responses, whereas another group of subjects may take a dislike to the person administering the instrument and give random responses. In such cases, the reliability of the instrument will be estimated at much below what the actual reliability of the instrument could be.

Scale tested	Alpha reliabilities
McCroskey, Richmond, Johnson, & Smith (2004)	
Study #1 (Organizational Orientations Scales)	
Ambivalent	.91
Indifferent	.79
Upward Mobile	.66
Study #2 (Initial Validation)	
Job Satisfaction	.97
Personal Report of Communication Apprehension–24	.95
Self Report of Immediacy Behaviors	.84
Assertiveness	.86
Responsiveness	.88
Study #3 (Measurement Improvement)	
Upward Mobile	.84
Ambivalent	.89
Indifferent	.79
Study #4 (Etiology and Outcomes)	
Organizational Orientations	
Upward Mobile	.85
Ambivalent	.88
Indifferent	.80
Job Satisfaction	.96
Source Credibility	
Competence	.89
Caring/Goodwill	.94
Trustworthiness	.93
Eysenck's Big Three	
Extraversion	.78
Neuroticism	.82
Psychoticism	.65
Thomas, Richmond, & McCroskey (1994)	
Perceived Nonverbal Immediacy Behavior Scale	.83
Assertiveness	.90
Responsiveness	.91
Wrench & Richmond (2004)	
Humor Assessment	.95
Student Affective Learning	
Teacher Evaluation	.87
Affective Learning	.81
Nonverbal Immediacy Measure	.81
Student Motivation	.89
Teacher Credibility	
Competence	.80
Trustworthiness	.86
Caring/Goodwill	.86
Weber, Fornash, Corrigan, & Neupauer (2003)	
7-Item Multiple Choice Quiz	.73
Learner Empowerment Scale	
Impact	.71
Competence	.85
Meaningfulness	.85
Nonverbal Immediacy Scale	Not reported

Figure 8.15 Article Alpha Reliabilities

Continued

Continued

Scale tested	Alpha reliabilities
Cheseboro (1999)	
Listening Style	
People	
Action	.61
Time	.61
Content	.66
Conversational Sensitivity	.54
	.85
Punyanunt (2000)	
Behavior Alteration Techniques	
Effectiveness of Humor	.92
Uses of Humor	.94
	.95
Wrench & Booth-Butterfield (2003)	
Humor Orientation	
Source Credibility	.91
Competence	
Trustworthiness	.86
Caring/Goodwill	.90
Compliance Gaining Questionnaire	.88
Expectancies/Consequences	
Relationship/Identification	.69
Values/Obligations	.82
Patient Satisfaction	.74
Cognitive	
Affective	.89
Behavioral	.92
	.85
Rocca & Vogl-Bauer (1999)	
Verbal Aggression Scale	
Sports Spectator Identification Scale	.81
Sports Identification Behavior Scale	.93
Fan Display	
Verbal Response	.78
Violent Response	.93
	.85

Validity

In the first part of this chapter, we introduced the concept of reliability; in the last half of this chapter, we will discuss another extremely important concept in measurement, validity. **Validity** is the degree to which the instrument measures what it is intended to measure. For example, would you look at a clock and say, "It's 50° outside"? Of course not, because a clock is a measurement of time, not a measurement of temperature. If you want to know how hot it is outside, you look at a thermometer. In social scientific research, we must be equally concerned with whether our measuring instruments actually measure what they are intended to measure. Let's look at a Likert-type item (1, *strongly disagree*, to 5, *strongly agree*), "Children should be seen and not heard." Would you expect to see this item on a scale intended to measure happiness? Of course not. However, this item could be on a scale designed to measure people's traditional views of children. Ultimately, when researchers talk about a scale's validity, we are discussing whether a created scale actually measures what we say we are measuring. Now that we have explained the general concept of validity, we will look at some examples of validity issues in communication research.

A communication researcher is in the process of creating a new measure to examine individuals who experience apprehension during social settings. Because she wants to assess the efficacy of helping people who experience this form of CA, she creates a physiological tool that can measure blood pressure, heart rate, and galvanic skin responses. She then takes some participants to a bar and grill whom she knows experience CA and some people who do not. If her new device is valid, the participants who are most afraid of communicating in social settings should register the highest ratings (increased blood pressure, heart rates, and galvanic skin responses) on her new device.

Another researcher is in the process of creating a new test for measuring nonverbal responses during greetings. Rather than creating a survey and asking people how they interact with people when they greet them, he develops an observational checklist for measuring greeting behaviors. He believes that greeting behaviors will be distinctly more intimate depending on the length of time people have known each other. He then trains a few coders to use the checklist and brings pairs of people (strangers, acquaintances, friends, family members, and romantic partners) into a lab. After separating the pairs for an hour, he brings the two people back together in a room with a one-way mirror, and the coders watch how the two people interact when they see each other again using the newly design observational checklist.

A third research team, Sandy and William, are in the process of trying to create a new scale to examine different forms of communicative humor in the classroom. Based on research by Wanzer and Frymier (1999), Sandy and William know that students perceive humor as either appropriate or inappropriate. Wanzer and Frymier designated appropriate classroom humor as content-related humor, humor not related to content, impersonation, nonverbal behaviors, disparaging humor, humorous props, sarcasm, and unintentional humor; inappropriate classroom humor was designated as humor that makes fun of a student, humor-based stereotypes, failed humor, sexual humor, irrelevant humor, sarcasm, swearing, joking about serious issues, personal humor (inside jokes), and sick humor. Sandy and William used this typology of humor behaviors from Wanzer and Frymier (1999) to create a new scale to measure appropriate and inappropriate classroom humor and then distribute the scales to a large group of undergraduates, asking them to rate a professor in whose classroom the students had been that day or the day before.

The question that you may be asking by this point is, "How good will these new measures be?" Are they accurate measures for examining anxiety, nonverbal greetings, and classroom humor? What if the anxiety measure ends up measuring sexual attraction or drinking behavior, of which there is a lot in a bar setting? Maybe the greeting checklist is incomplete and only has a handful of behaviors on it, like hand shaking, hugging, and kissing, which are predominant greeting patterns in the United States, but it may not include greeting patterns between people who come from other cultures. Maybe the new classroom humor scale ends up measuring quantity of humor used and not appropriate versus inappropriate humor in the classroom setting. In essence, how can we determine whether a new measure employed in research is actually measuring what it alleges to be measuring? Social scientists have been examining these types of questions for years and have devised a number of strategies for combating these problems. Ultimately, these questions concern what researchers call a measure's validity.

As important as reliability is to measurement, validity is even more important. Validity may be defined simply as the degree to which the measuring instrument measures what it is intended to measure. If we wish to measure the number of apples produced in a county, it will do us no good whatsoever to count the number of oranges produced in that county. Similarly, if we want to know a person's attitude toward rap music, it will probably do us little good to ask him questions about his relationship with his mother. There are three primary approaches to validity: face or content validity, predictive or concurrent validity, and construct or factorial validity. Let us consider each in turn.

FACE OR CONTENT VALIDITY

Face or content validity does not involve the use of correlation coefficients. Rather, it is a subjective type of validity criterion. The researcher or someone he or she employs for the task examines the content of the measuring instrument to see whether on its "face" it appears to be related to that which the researcher wished to measure. In addition, it is asked whether the items on the measure are reasonably representative of the universe of possible items that could be included. Unfortunately, because of its inherently subjective nature, face or content validity is the validity approach most commonly employed by researchers. In some circumstances this is not as serious a drawback as in others. As long as her or his measure is susceptible to influence as a result of the message manipulations, the instrument is "valid" for her or his purposes. However, when the social scientist is concerned with predicting behaviors, there is no true test of validity except how well it predicts those behaviors.

CRITERION VALIDITY

Criterion validity is concerned with how accurately a new measure can predict a well-accepted criterion or previously validated concept. For example, if we wanted to test a newly developed anxiety tool, we could have people fill out the PRCA-24 and then give a speech. People who register the highest on our new anxiety tool should also have higher scores on the PRCA-24. To determine whether the anxiety tool corresponds with scores on the PRCA-24, we calculate the correlation between the two measures, and the end result would be a correlation coefficient. The coefficient estimates the degree to which a measuring instrument will predict a value on some outside criterion. That criterion might be the behavior of the person whose attitude was measured, or it might be some other measure of attitude. If our theory suggests that a high attitude score should be accompanied by a given behavior whereas a moderate score would be less associated with that behavior and a low score would not be associated with that behavior, then we can obtain a correlation between the attitude score obtained by subjects on our instrument and their subsequent behaviors. That correlation coefficient is referred to as a validity coefficient, and if it is reasonably high, we may suggest that our measure is a valid one. By contrast, if there is no correlation or low correlation, we have an indication that our instrument is invalid for making this kind of prediction. Few attitude-measuring instruments are actually submitted to the test of predictive validity. This is because, in most cases, we are not interested in predicting a specific behavior. If the scores are highly correlated, we have an indication that one is to the degree of the correlation as valid as the other. There are three subtypes of criterion validity that we should discuss briefly: predictive, concurrent, and retrospective.

Predictive

Predictive or prospective validity is a subset of criterion validity and is concerned with whether a person's score on a new measure can be used to predict future scores on another measure. For example, maybe we have 10 teachers all teaching the same class and using the same textbook, syllabus, and tests. We measure students' perceptions of teacher use of appropriate and inappropriate humor utilizing our new measure. Previous research has shown that the use of humor in the classroom can lead to higher levels of learning. If our new tool is truly measuring the use of appropriate and inappropriate humor in the classroom, we could predict that teachers who use the most appropriate humor and the least amounts of inappropriate humor should have students who perform better on the final examination. In essence, we are using our newly created scale to predict scores on a future scale.

Concurrent

An alternative to predictive validity when examining criterion validity is to examine a measure's concurrent validity. In **concurrent validity**, a researcher obtains the score for the new measure and the score for the criterion measure at the same point and then determines how strongly the two scores correlate. For example, if we are testing our new apprehension-measuring tool, we could have people fill out the State Communication Apprehension Measure, a previously validated scale for examining state levels of communication apprehension, while wearing the new apprehension-measuring tool in a social setting. In essence, if our new apprehension-measuring tool is an accurate measure, it should strongly relate to an individual's score on the State Communication Apprehension Measure.

Retrospective

The last way to examine criterion validity is to examine a newly developed scale's **retrospective or postdictive validity**. Retrospective validity occurs when a researcher has previously measured the criterion and then attempts to relate it to a newly developed measure at a later point. Maybe a researcher wants to determine whether a person's level of CA as a child correlates with her or his level of CA as an adult, so the researcher looks through old report cards looking for incidents of "doesn't talk," "is very shy," or "is very quiet" in report card notes. The researcher then quantifies these messages to correlate them with an adult measure of CA.

CONSTRUCT OR FACTORIAL VALIDITY

An important property of all hypothetical constructs is that they are a result of theoretical development. In Chapter 7, we discussed the development of theoretical constructs, and **construct validity** therefore is a validity test of the theoretical construct itself. If we theorize, for example, that people with highly intense attitudes are less subject to influence by a persuader than are people with moderately intense attitudes, we must develop an attitude measure that taps the intensity dimension. We may then engage in an experiment in which we administer a persuasive treatment to subjects with an intense attitude and to subjects with only a moderately intense attitude. If the predicted difference in amount of attitude change is observed on our measure, we not only have confirmed our theory, but also have an indication that our measuring instrument validly taps the intensity dimension. The difficulty with this approach to validity is that if our predicted effects are not obtained, we do not know whether it is because of our faulty theory or because our instrument is invalid.

Another approach to construct validity that is less susceptible to the confounding with theory than the approach just mentioned is the measurement of known groups. If we are trying to develop an instrument to measure ethnic intolerance, we may administer that measure to members of the Ku Klux Klan (a group known for intolerance) and members of B'nai B'rith (a Jewish organization that fights anti-Semitism, racism, and bigotry while striving for human rights and peace throughout the world). If our measure is reasonably valid, we should observe large differences in the scores between these two groups, unless the former group was much more tolerant or the latter group is much less tolerant than is customarily presumed.

A third approach to construct validity that almost deserves a category to itself is factorial validity. Factorial validity is based on the statistical technique known as "factor analysis." Factor analysis is a highly sophisticated statistical technique for examining a series of items to see which items correlate well with one another but are not highly correlated with other items or groups of items. Simply put, factor analysis can tell us how many groups of items, or factors, there are in our instrument. This approach to validity was employed by McCroskey (1966) in the development of measuring instruments to tap source credibility (the attitude of communication receivers toward communication sources). At the outset, McCroskey presumed that this attitude was like other attitudes, that is, unidimensional. He therefore developed a set of items to measure this attitude. However, when he subjected these items to factor analysis, he found that there were two dimensions to this attitude rather than one. More simply put, he thought he was measuring "apples," but he found that he was measuring "Granny Smith apples" and "Red Delicious apples." In essence, there were two parts (competence and trustworthiness) that created participants' perceptions of credibility, just like Granny Smith and Red Delicious are two different types of apples. As a result, he was forced to develop two separate measures to measure these two new constructs. The only serious problem with the approach to validity through factor analysis is that it is a strictly negative approach. That is, factor analysis can tell someone that she is not measuring her construct, but cannot tell her that she is at least independent of other considerations.

In a more recent study, Richmond, McCroskey, and Johnson (2003) worked with the Nonverbal Immediacy Scale to improve reliability and validity. Since nonverbal immediacy is such a strong concept in the field now and was not 30 years ago, it was determined that the 14-item scale did not have high enough reliability and validity to continue using it. Thus, Richmond, McCroskey, and Johnson completed a study in which the reliability and validity of the Nonverbal Immediacy Scale was substantially improved.

In conclusion, many social scientists are concerned with which approach to validity they should employ in the development of measuring instruments. The answer to this is simple. Do not choose among the approaches to validity. Rather, we should employ all of the approaches to validity that can be employed in the given case. If any one of the approaches indicates that the instrument is invalid, this is sufficient ground for substantial revision in the instrument that has been developed.

Validity Threats

A number of problems can occur when one is attempting to determine whether a newly developed measure is valid. In this section we will examine seven categories of threats to a newly developed measure's validity.

1. Inadequate preoperational explication of concepts. The first threat that can befall a new measure's validity can occur when an individual really has not determined what a scale was supposed to measure in the first place. For example, if a researcher wants to create a scale about humor but has questions about CA thrown in the scale, the scale is going to have validity problems. Would you use a wrist watch to tell you how hot it is outside? Too often researchers write countless numbers of scale items and then throw them against a statistical wall to see what sticks, which is not a good practice when writing a research scale. The more concrete your purpose is for creating a scale from the onset, the more valid your scale can be in the long run.

2. Mono-operation bias. Another problem that can affect the validity of a newly developed measure can occur when you only administer the measure once known as the **mono-operation bias**. If you only measure something once, it is hard to determine whether you are truly measuring the variable you intend to or just a portion of the variable. It is also possible that there will be some form of error that prevents you from accurately testing a newly developed measure's validity the first time you use it, so multiple administrations will enable you to get a much clearer picture of your scale's overall validity.

3. Interaction of different treatments. Often in research we want to determine whether a newly developed treatment for something is effective. For example, maybe we create a new way to reduce students' levels of public speaking anxiety. To determine whether our treatment is effective, we must know whether the measure we are using to determine public speaking anxiety is valid. Unfortunately, there are intervening variables that could prevent you from getting an accurate measure of the effectiveness of your treatment. For example, maybe one of your participants has hired a speech coach, and the individual attention has helped the participant lower her or his level of public speaking anxiety with no change occurring from your treatment. It is also possible that one of your participants could have a horrible public speaking experience that causes her or his public speaking anxiety to rise despite your treatment. In essence, one threat to validity is whether the results you are seeing are real or whether they are the result of multiple treatments by yourself and others.

4. Interaction of testing and treatment. Often the combined effect of being measured multiple times along with receiving a treatment can cause someone to be more aware of the measurement process and alter her or his scores as a result of this awareness and not the treatment itself. When participants are aware of what is going on in an experiment, they are often more sensitive and/or receptive to future measures of a particular variable.

5. Restricted generalizability across constructs. Another threat to the validity of a newly developed measure is how restricted that measure is across differing constructs. In the example given at the beginning of this chapter about the newly developed scale for examining appropriate and inappropriate humor in the classroom, is this measure generalizable to elementary school teachers, junior high/middle school teachers, high school teachers, and college professors, or is this tool only useful in the college classroom? It is possible that Wanzer and Frymier's (1999) appropriate and inappropriate categories of humor are only true in the college setting, so the scale could not be applied to lower levels of education and the results from the newly developed scale found in college classrooms could not be cross-applied to elementary, junior high/middle school, and high school classrooms.

6. Confounding constructs and levels of constructs. Another problem that can affect the validity of a measure is whether you are measuring a single construct, multiple constructs, or multiple levels of one construct in a given measure. Often one of the biggest problems with newly developed measures is that they are measuring more than one construct at a time or multiple levels of the same construct. For example, in the PRCA-24, the overall construct of CA has been found to have four basic subconstructs (or subscales) within it: meeting, group, interpersonal, and public. Statisticians often call subconstructs factors, as discussed earlier in this chapter. Unfortunately, a researcher often does not know which subconstructs or even multiple constructs exist in a set of scale items until he or she has collected the appropriate data to examine the validity of the scale.

7. Social threats to validity. In addition to the above threats to validity, there are four social threats that can affect a measure's validity. The first social validity threat is hypothesis guessing. Participants will guess what a researcher is attempting to measure and then respond to a measure accordingly. When a person guesses your hypothesis (either correctly or incorrectly), it can skew how he or she responds to your survey. A second social validity threat is evaluation apprehension. Many people experience anxiety when they know they are being evaluated, which can cause them to give responses that they might not have normally. A third social threat to validity involves experimenter expectancies. Experimenters may unknowingly influence a participant's scores when the experimenter encourages the participant to respond in a specific manner. Experimenters should be trained to avoid influencing a participant's answers and behaviors as much as possible to prevent this validity threat. Finally, social desirability bias can be a threat to a measure's validity. **Social desirability bias** is the term used by researchers for when a participant changes how he or she scores on a measure to be perceived in a "better light" than her or his actual scores would reveal. For example, maybe you are asking your participants how often they drink alcohol and a participant who normally drinks a case a day says he or she drinks a couple of beers a week for fear of being perceived as an alcoholic. Although social desirability bias cannot be completely avoided, explaining that responses are confidential or ensuring anonymity should lessen social threats to a measure's validity.

Now that we have examined some threats to a measurement's validity, we will examine some general problems with measurement as a whole.

Problems with Measurement

The two most commonly discussed problems of measurement are reliability and validity, which are actually parts of one problem. Researchers are only concerned with reliability because of its implications for validity. A measure can be perfectly reliable and have absolute zero validity for the purpose for which a researcher created the measure. By contrast, a measure cannot be valid unless it is also reliable. This may be better understood if we think in terms of reliability and validity coefficients for a moment. Presume we have two separate measures and are concerned with the ability of one measure to predict scores on the other measure. Through our research we obtain a Cronbach alpha reliability coefficient for the first measure of 0.65 (minimally acceptable) and a Cronbach alpha reliability coefficient for the second measure of 0.30 (unacceptable). To obtain the maximum possible validity coefficient for the predictability of one of these measures for the other, we can multiply the two reliability coefficients by each other ($0.30 \times 0.65 = 0.195$). This does not give us the actual validity coefficient; rather, it indicates the *absolute maximum* validity coefficient that we could obtain. Thus, if either of our measures is unreliable, we will have little or no validity. In the example we have just considered, one measure is minimally acceptable (0.65) and the other is simply unacceptable (0.30). Even if we increase the reliability of our most reliable instrument to the point of perfection, the highest validity coefficient we could obtain would be 0.30. Thus, we should not be overly concerned about the lack of high validity coefficients between our attitude measures and overt behaviors in the real world. This probably does not indicate that our attitude measure in itself is invalid. Rather, this is influenced by the extremely unreliable methods we have developed to measure behaviors in the real world. These measures tend to have two major problems accompanying them: the difficulty in obtaining agreement among observers and the low level of potential measurement, seldom even ordinal, of such behaviors. Thus, even with a perfectly valid measure we are unlikely to get a high validity coefficient because of the unreliability of our criterion measure. We must be extremely concerned with reliability and the less precise estimates of validity such as content and construct validity rather than predictive validity. For example, it may be that attitudes toward federal finance of education and federal control of education are related to federal assistance to our local schools. These two attitudes may not simply add together to produce our behaviors—more likely they interact. Thus, to predict that particular behavior, we must be able to measure these two attitudes separately. The two procedures most commonly employed to determine whether a measure is tapping more than one variable are factor analysis, as previously discussed, and "scalogram analysis," as described by Guttman (1945).

A third problem to which measurement is particularly susceptible is what we shall call "faking." This is actually a broad title for several types of problems. **Faking responses** refers to any circumstance in which a respondent to our instrument deliberately attempts to alter the results in some specific way. Whenever faking is present, the validity of our instrument is not. One type of faking can be referred to as **acquiescence**. The acquiescent individual wishes to cooperate with the investigator and give her or him what she or he wants. Thus, the respondent tries to determine the kind of response the investigator wishes and produce it. Another type of acquiescence that is somewhat different is produced by a personality type that merely tends to say "yes" to anything.

A second type of faking is produced by the influence of perception of social desirability. Often a respondent will not indicate his true beliefs, but will indicate beliefs that he thinks society accepts. This is particularly a problem when we are attempting to measure socially sensitive attitudes toward racial intolerance and morality. For example, a woman may indicate that she strongly disapproves of premarital intercourse because society opposes it. Her private behavior, however, may be contrary to this response. This type of faking can be overcome to a considerable extent by ensuring the respondent that her or his responses will be anonymous.

A third type of faking has been referred to by researchers by several colorful terms. For the sake of propriety, we shall refer to it as the "nuts-to-you" response, or as Joseph Masling (1966) described it, the "screw-you" effect. This is the almost exact opposite of acquiescence. Rather than attempting to give the researcher what he wants, the individual engaging in "nuts-to-you" behavior may attempt either to give him the exact opposite of what he wants or to give a completely random response.

All of these faking behaviors have implications for reliability, but their main impact is on validity. Whenever faking is present, validity is not.

The fourth problem that affects measurement, unless carefully avoided, is response set. A **response set** is any tendency that causes a person to give different responses to test items than he or she would if the item was presented in a different form. Response set, although severely reducing the validity of any instrument, may actually increase the obtained reliability estimate for the instrument. Response set is more often observed when all of the items in an instrument are worked in much the same way. For example, if all of the items are worded positively or negatively, response set is likely to be present. In such cases, if the subject indicates the fifth response to the first question, he or she is likely to continue to make the fifth response to the rest of the questions. This problem may be overcome by including an equal or nearly equal number of positively and negatively worded items and then arrange the items in random order.

The fifth and final major problem that affects measurement we have saved until last because it is the worst. This is the problem of bad items on the measure. In the development of any measure it is almost certain that some bad items will be included, but there is no excuse for them continuing to be included. A technique known as item analysis can be employed that will help to identify bad items in a group of items. Simply put, item analysis produces a correlation between an individual item and a total score across all items. A bad item will have a negative or low positive correlation, whereas a good item will tend to have a high positive correlation. The solution to the problem of bad items is simple—identify them, throw them out, and develop good items.

Within the notable exception of the semantic differential as developed by Osgood (1957), almost all of the techniques for attitude measurement that have been developed employ the use of declarative statements or questions as items. The most important part of attitude scale construction is creating items that reflect both a balanced and a representative set of opinions about the issue at hand. The question of which scaling technique to use is of secondary importance despite the emphasis that differences in these techniques have received in the professional literature over the years. Using essentially the same set of items, researchers have found that the various techniques place individuals at the same locations on attitude scales relative to each other (i.e., individual A is more liberal than B, but only slightly more liberal than C). That is, there is little statistically one can gain from reliability or validity beyond what is already inherent in item content. A number of elements must be taken into consideration when developing items to reduce sources of spurious response, and these will be considered in another chapter.

Research Outside the Walls of Academia

Many researchers working outside the walls of academia simply forget to think through issues related to measurement reliability and/or validity. We realize that reliability is difficult to calculate and validity is a complicated subject, but measures that are not reliable or valid will lead people to conclusions that are simply not true. If your goal is to conduct research that is useful for an organization, then the research should conform to the basic practices of good measurement.

Imagine you have been asked to conduct a survey of people who call a medical insurance company's help line. After a phone call ends with a customer service representative, customers are redirected to your survey. If you utilize just one Likert question, "what was your level of satisfaction with the customer representative" (1 = *satisfied*; 5 = *not satisfied*), you will not be able to tell whether the information you are being provided with is actually a measure of someone's attitude at all because one item is ordinal data and not useful for inferential purposes. As such, you would need to develop a measure that has enough items on it to help you get a more holistic score of satisfaction to ensure that the new measure is reliable. Next, you would have to figure out whether the measure is valid using the strategies discussed earlier in this chapter.

Conclusion

This chapter has focused on how we can be sure that people answer our research scales consistently and how to make sure we are measuring what we say we are measuring. Reliability and validity are extremely important for researchers because if your measures are not reliable and valid, your results are not meaningful. Now that we have discussed the measurement process, reliability, and validity, we will examine how research is conducted using three research techniques—survey, content analysis, and experimental—in the next three chapters.

KEY TERMS

Acquiescence	Face/content validity	Retrospective validity
Alternate forms reliability	Faking responses	Screw you effect
Concurrent validity	Mono-operation bias	Social desirability bias
Construct validity	Predictive validity	Split-half reliability
Criterion validity	Reliability	Test–retest reliability
Cronbach's alpha reliability	Response set	Validity

REFERENCES

Cheseboro, J. (1999). The relationship between listening styles and conversational sensitivity. *Communication Research Reports, 16*, 233–238.

Cronbach, L. J. (1951). Coefficient alpha and the internal structure of tests. *Psychometrika, 16*, 297–333.

Fulcher, G. (2010). *Practical language testing.* London, UK: Hodder Education.

Fulcher, G., & Davidson, F. (2007). *Language testing and assessment: An advanced resource book.* London, UK: Routledge.

Guttman, L. (1945). A basis for analyzing test–retest reliability. *Psychometrika, 10*, 255–282.

Masling, J. (1966). Role related behavior of the subject and psychologist and its effects upon psychological data. In D. Levine (Ed.), *Symposium on motivation* (pp. 67–103). Lincoln, NE: University of Nebraska Press.

McCroskey, J. C. (1966). *Experimental studies of the effects of ethos and evidence in persuasive communication.* Unpublished doctoral dissertation, University Park: Pennsylvania State University.

McCroskey, J. C. (2006). Reliability and validity of the Generalized Attitude Measure and Generalized Belief Measure. *Communication Quarterly, 54*, 265–274.

Osgood, C. E. (1957). *The measurement of meaning.* Urbana, IL: University of Illinois Press.

Richmond, V. P., McCroskey, J. C., & Johnson, A. D. (2003). Development of the nonverbal immediacy scale (NIS): Measures of self- and other-perceived nonverbal immediacy. *Communication Quarterly, 51*, 504–517.

Wanzer, M. B., & Frymier, A. B. (1999, April). *Being funny in the classroom: Appropriate and inappropriate humor behaviors.* Paper presented at the Eastern Communication Association's Convention, Charleston, WV.

FURTHER READING

DeVellis, R. F. (1991). *Scale development: Theory and applications* (Applied Social Research Methods Series, Vol. 26). Newbury Park, CA: Sage.

Dillman, D. A. (2000). *Mail and internet surveys: The tailored design method* (2nd ed.). New York, NY: Wiley.

Fowler, F. J., Jr. (1993). *Survey research methods* (2nd ed.) (Applied Social Research Methods Series, Vol. 1). Newbury Park, CA: Sage.

Green, S. B., & Salkind, N. J. (2004). *Using SPSS for Windows and Macintosh: Analyzing and understanding data* (4th ed.). Upper Saddle River, NJ: Prentice Hall.

Grimm, L. G., & Yarnold, P. R. (Eds.). (2000). *Reading and understanding more multivariate statistics.* Washington, DC: American Psychological Association.

Singleton, R. A., Jr., & Straits, B. C. (1999). *Approach to social research* (3rd ed.). New York, NY: Oxford University Press.

Tabachnick, B. G., & Fidell, L. S. (2007). *Using multivariate statistics* (5th ed.). Boston, MA: Allyn & Bacon.

CHAPTER 9

Survey Research

1   Distinguish among surveys, questionnaires, and interview schedules.
2   Identify four questions a researcher should ask to determine whether a survey is the most appropriate research method.
3   Describe Fink's (2006) five steps for conducting a survey.
4   Explain the purpose of open-ended questions in survey research.
5   Distinguish among cross-sectional, longitudinal, and accelerated longitudinal survey designs.
6   Explain the guidelines for pilot testing a survey.
7   Be able to explain the positive and negative aspects of the different ways to disseminate questionnaires.
8   Define response rate.
9   Distinguish between unit and item nonresponses and discuss how they affect surveys.
10 Explain some general ways to increase response rates.
11 List the three types of equivalence one must consider when translating survey items from one language to another.
12 Understand the five different ways a research can translate a survey from one language to another.

Chances are, by this point in your academic career, you will have participated in some form of survey research. Whether filling out a questionnaire in class or being interviewed about our political views by a pollster, we are constantly completing surveys. You cannot even register a recently purchased product these days without filling out a questionnaire. Since the moment James Cattell (1890) started discussing the notion of mental measures and using them to examine college students, the art and science of surveying has become a mainstay of our cultural reality. Before we can really discuss what a survey is, we first must distinguish among three terms that often prove confusing for people: survey, questionnaire, and interview schedule. A **survey** is a social scientific method for gathering quantifiable information about a specific group of people by asking the group members questions about their individual attitudes, values, beliefs, behaviors, knowledge, and perceptions. There are two basic types of survey a researcher may conduct. First a researcher may conduct a **descriptive survey**, which is designed to find out how common a phenomenon is within a given group of people. For example, a researcher investigating how widespread communication apprehension (CA) is across the United States would be an example using a survey to examine a specific phenomenon within a given group of people (people living in the United States). The second type of survey is an **analytical or explanatory survey**. The purpose of analytical surveys is "to explain why people think or act as they do by identifying likely causal influences on their attitudes and behavior" (Buckingham & Saunders, 2004, p. 13). A **questionnaire**, by contrast, is a form containing a series of questions and mental measures that is given to a group of people in an attempt to gain statistical information about the group as part of a survey. In other words, a questionnaire is a tool that a researcher who is conducting a survey uses to get data from the group of interest. The third term we use when discussing surveys in this chapter is interview schedule. An **interview schedule** is the list of survey questions an interviewer reads an interviewee when conducting an oral survey. Although some people will discuss interview schedules as questionnaires, we prefer to differentiate between the two terms: paper-and-pencil methods (questionnaire) and oral interviewing (interview schedule). Later in this chapter, we will discuss specific issues related to survey formation, but for now we are going to focus on when a survey is appropriate.

When to Use a Survey

People utilize surveys for a number of different projects, but you should never just jump into a survey project without knowing why you are conducting the survey in the first place. Buckingham and Saunders (2004) believe there are four questions a researcher must ask before conducting a survey.

DO YOU KNOW WHAT YOU WANT TO ASK?

First, does a researcher know what he or she wants to ask? Because of the physical need to generate a questionnaire or list of interview questions before a survey can occur, a researcher must know what he or she wants to study. Whether the researcher wants to conduct a descriptive survey or an analytical survey, he or she must have some kind of a priori (before the fact) notion of what is being studied. Qualitative and rhetorical researchers have the ability to conduct exploratory research where they go in and start organically observing a phenomenon without any preconceived notions, but quantitative researchers simply do not have this luxury because of the nature of quantitative information.

DO YOU REALLY NEED TO COLLECT NEW DATA?

Second, researchers must ask themselves whether they really need to collect new data on a specific phenomenon. In certain types of research, performing a survey would be meaningless, if not impossible. For example, we cannot exactly conduct a survey of Irish American immigrants during the potato famine, because they are all dead, and for some reason, dead people do not like filling out questionnaires. If the lives of immigrants during the potato famine is your research topic, conducting a survey is not going to help you get at anything. Although there are research methods to study the lives of Irish immigrants during the potato famine, they are beyond the scope of this book.

A second reason why a researcher may not need to conduct a survey occurs when an observational method is available that does not interfere with how people live their daily lives. For example, one common type of research conducted, often without your knowledge, pertains to shopping behavior. Retail stores often hire consulting firms to study shopping behaviors within a store for the purpose of determining the best way to lay out the store to maximize profits. Although some scholars say this research is unethical because it invades your privacy, others say that it is perfectly ethical because the researcher is unobtrusively watching a shopper's behavior without direct contact or interference.

A third reason why a researcher may not need to collect data is if existing data are available. There are many organizations devoted to the collection and dissemination of information about people. In these cases, it is not that a survey was not conducted—it is that the survey was conducted by a third party for the purpose of disseminating the data to other researchers. *The Journal of Statistics Education* (http://www.amstat.org/publications/jse/) has numerous datasets that people can use to learn statistics, and many of them are based on actual collected survey data. The dataset provided with this textbook is another example of a preexisting dataset that could be used for analysis. Furthermore, check out organizations such as the Centers for Disease Control and Prevention (http://www.cdc.gov/) and USA Gov (http://www.usa.gov/) to find a wide variety of datasets at your fingertips.

DO YOUR PARTICIPANTS KNOW ANYTHING OR WILL THEY EVEN TELL YOU?

Third, researchers must ask themselves how much their group of interest will know about what the researchers are interested in analyzing and whether the group members will even tell the researcher. Let's break this one down into some simple chunks. First, as a researcher you must ask yourself whether your future participants will even know about the topic you are studying. For example, if you want to examine the lasting impact of memorable messages after the *Challenger* explosion, using a group of college freshmen probably would not be useful since your typical freshman was born after the accident in 1986. Furthermore, the types of questions you are interested in may also be problematic. Say you are interested in the media's effect on perceptions of terrorism, so you ask a group of participants how many news stories about terrorism they remember seeing the week after the 9/11 attacks. If you are like us, we could not even tell you how many news stories on terrorism we saw in the last week, let alone more than a decade ago. Asking people questions about events that have happened in the past is always problematic. However, the closer you can get to the event in question, the stronger your data will actually be.

The flip side of this issue deals with whether participants will be willing to tell you information about themselves. There are some issues that frankly make people antsy, and they often will not want to discuss these issues openly. There are three basic reasons people may have for not wanting to disclose information. First, some people may simply be embarrassed by certain information. For example, researchers who study issues involving sexual communication often find that people are embarrassed by some of the questions asked on a questionnaire or during an interview. For some people, filling out a questionnaire about human sexuality is as close to openly discussing sexuality as they will ever get, so this could really make them feel embarrassed, which could lead to **socially desirable responding**. Socially desirable responding occurs when a participant fills out a questionnaire or responds to interview questions in a way that the participant thinks makes her or him look better.

The second reason some people may be hesitant to disclose information is shame. In research that has been conducted looking at people who are victims of violent crimes, especially sex crimes, many victims feel shame for having been violated. When people experience deep shame, they are much less likely to open up about the topic that is causing the shame.

The third reason some people may be hesitant to disclose information during a survey is because they fear some kind of retribution for their answers. For example, if a manager hands out a survey to subordinates on her or his managerial skills and then has the subordinates turn the survey back into the manager, people are going to be hesitant to say anything negative for fear that the manager will hold their responses against them. Other people are simply hesitant to disclose information for fear that their disclosure will get them into legal trouble. Many researchers study illegal behaviors, and many people will either not participate in a study or lie during a study about illegal behaviors for fear that their answers will get them put in jail.

We are not suggesting that you should never use surveys with people who might be embarrassed, shamed, or fearful. In fact, researchers have used survey methods with all kinds of people who experience embarrassment, shame, and fear as a result of the information discussed during a survey. However, it is extremely important that you ensure confidentiality and anonymity. The more certain people feel that their answers will not be used against them or traced back to them, the more honest they are going to be while filling out a questionnaire or answering a series of interview questions.

Is Your Goal Generalizability?

The last question a researcher should ask her- or himself is whether the goal of the study is **generalizability**. When discussing generalizability, there are two important terms to understand: populations and samples. A population is an entire set of objects, observations, or scores that have some characteristic in common. In the case of survey research, a population is everyone that has a specific characteristic in common that a researcher is attempting to study. For example, if you want to examine television-viewing patterns among college females, your population consists of every female who is in college. A sample, by contrast, is a subset of the larger population. Instead of attempting to survey the entire female population on television-viewing patterns, you decide to survey 300 females at a local university. When researchers discuss the concept of generalizability, we are basically questioning whether the results of a sample (the 300 female students at a local college) mirror the results that would be found in the larger population (all college females). To make sure that your end results are generalizable, that is, your sample can be said to reflect the population correctly, you should randomly (i.e., every unit of analysis that exists within your population has an equal chance for inclusion in your sample) select your sample. We will discuss random sampling in more detail in Chapter 13.

Now that we have discussed the four primary reasons researchers have for conducting a survey, we can switch gears and discuss the process one goes through when conducting survey research.

How to Conduct Survey Research

Many young scholars will simply find a series of random scales and throw them together to create a survey research project; this is not only ineffective for hypothesis testing, but also a waste of time. First, randomly throwing scales together with no theoretical reason enables you to find results that may not mean anything. Randomly putting together a survey is like throwing a vat of spaghetti against a wall—something will stick, but you are left with a mess. If you create a large dataset for no other purpose than seeing what relationships and differences might exist, you will most definitely find statistical relationships and differences by chance. But being haphazard in one's approach to research is not science. For this reason, the authors of this textbook have stated from the beginning that you should start with an overarching research question and then determine the most appropriate ways to go about measuring that communication phenomenon. Overall, use previously existing research scales wisely. The temptation to throw a handful of research scales together is great, but the end result is generally substandard research that is not publishable. To make sure that you design a good survey study, you might use Fink's (2006) five steps for conducting a good survey.

STEP 1: PICKING YOUR QUESTIONS

First, there is no single way to go about picking the types of questions to include in a research survey. We wish that we could tell you there was a magic bullet, but there simply is not. Ultimately, the types of questions you will need to ask will be dictated by the hypotheses and research questions you want to examine in your study. As Converse and Presser (1986) wrote, "Every questionnaire must, finally, be handcrafted. It is not only that questionnaire writing must be 'artful'; each questionnaire is also unique, an original. A designer must cut and try, see how it looks and sounds, see how people react to it, and then cut again, and try again" (p. 48). Although Converse and Presser are specifically talking about questionnaire development, the same is also true for developing an interview schedule. In this section, we will discuss a number of commonly used question formats seen on questionnaires by examining the types of variable levels.

Nominal Level Questions

Many questionnaires will have a series of nominal level questions like biological sex, ethnicity, religious affiliation, political party, and so on. These questions are great for determining descriptive statistics of your research sample. When deciding which questions to include on your questionnaire, you must ask yourself which questions are actually related to the current study. If you are not planning on examining your participants' political affiliations, then you have no need to include the variable on your questionnaire. You may also find yourself at some point needing to ask a series of yes/no questions. Often having a "don't know" category is also useful. You may want to ask your participants, "Have you ever lived in a country other than the United States?" In this case, you probably do not need the "don't know" category because some people will ultimately check off "don't know" just to say "screw you." Ultimately, when dealing with nominal level variables on a questionnaire, ensure that you follow the guidelines for creating nominal variables discussed in Chapter 6.

One big question that is difficult to answer is where to place nominal level variables in the overall flow of a questionnaire. We recommend keeping participant demographics until the end because in longer surveys you may end up with participant fatigue and participants can generally recall their own demographic information without much cognitive expenditure. As for other types of nominal level questions, place the questions where they will be the most beneficial for your participants. For example, if you are having participants fill out a questionnaire examining their supervisor's communicative behavior, you may want to start by getting participants thinking about their supervisor before you jump into any mental measures related to the supervisor. To do this, place any nominal level demographic variables related to the supervisor before the more complex measures. Ultimately, when participants have to tell you their supervisor's biological sex up front, it forces the participant to start thinking about that specific supervisor, which will help the participant keep that supervisor in mind as they are responding to the rest of the survey.

However, demographic questions must be thought of in terms of ethics as well. In an often-cited paper working paper by Lynn Sweeney in 2000, the Carnegie Mellon researcher demonstrated that with just three pieces of information (zip code, biological sex, and birthdate), you could correctly identify 87 percent of people living in the United States. For obvious reasons, knowing that people can easily be identified with just three nominal demographic questions raises serious ethical considerations related to anonymity, confidentiality, and privacy. Do not be surprised if an IRB member questions the utility of specific nominal questions because they may make it too easy to identify participants in a supposedly "anonymous" sample. In other words, it is not ethically sound to collect data from extra nominal variables just out of curiosity. All of the data you collect should help you answer your research questions and/or hypotheses.

Ordinal Level Questions

Like nominal level variables, there are numerous ordinal level variables that are commonly used in research (year in school, social economic status group, level of education, etc.). Any time someone uses a single Likert-type question or semantic differential question, those function as ordinal level questions as well. One example of an ordinal variable discussed by Hildebrand, Laing, and Rosenthal (1977) related to political ideology is *left*, *left-center*, *center*, *right-center*, and *right*. Although these categories may not be measurable using a ruler, we can say that the categories clearly differ from each other qualitatively and quantitatively.

When it comes to using ordinal level variables on a survey, the biggest question concerns what statistical tests you plan on conducting. Although it is possible to use ordinal data in both relationship and difference tests, the results are based on one-shot questions, which leads to serious reliability and validity issues. Although an ordinal question may be useful for determining someone's socioeconomic status (lower, middle, upper), an ordinal question would not be useful for measuring someone's level of communication apprehension.

Interval Level Questions

The most common type of question seen on questionnaires involves interval level variables. For example, all of the mental measures discussed in Chapter 6 are interval level variables. All of your Likert and semantic differential/bipolar adjective scales are interval variables, so a great deal of communication research involves interval level variables.

One of the biggest questions involving interval variables is where to place them in your overall questionnaire. Especially if you have multiple interval variables, how should you order the mental measures so that you have a sequence that easily flows from one scale to the next and does not end up confusing your participants? Although there are no steadfast rules on this, here are some general guidelines you may want to consider.

First, group items with like anchors together. An anchor is the technical term used for the words that you give people on a questionnaire and ask them to pick one (e.g., *Disagree, Neither Agree or Disagree, Agree*; *Ineffective, Neutral, Effective*; *Unsatisfied, Neutral, Satisfied*). Many types of anchors exist in mental measures, so group measures that have similar anchors together to avoid confusion. You may also want to indicate in your instructions that you are using multiple anchoring systems so your participants do not think the new anchor is a typo.

Second, do not start a study with the most controversial questions. For example, Wrench, Corrigan, McCroskey, and Punyanunt-Carter (2006) conducted a study examining numerous variables including religious fundamentalism, ethnocentrism, intercultural CA, tolerance for religious disagreements, and homonegativity. In the initial version of the questionnaire the homonegativity scale, which measures negative perceptions people have about bisexual, gay, and lesbian people, was one of the first scales. However, the researchers started discussing whether having that scale up front would actually end up biasing the way the participants might responding to the other questions. People tend to assume that the first scale on a questionnaire reflects what the study is about as a whole. In public speaking we talk about the concept of primacy—people remember the information at the beginning of a speech. People also tend to remember what the first set of scale items were asking, which can slant how they respond to the rest of the study.

Third, keep like questions together. When we say like questions, we are talking about questions asking about the same target (as in a teacher or supervisor). When conducting survey research you may have questions the participant is supposed to respond to about her- or himself (e.g., participant's level of communication apprehension, ethnocentrism, sense of humor, etc.) and questions that the participant is supposed to respond to about a specific target (e.g., supervisor's nonverbal immediacy, teacher's use of humor, physician's credibility, etc.). Our recommendation is to keep questions about the participant together and questions about the target together to avoid confusion. If your survey jumps back and forth between the two, you may end up with some participants responding about themselves when they should be responding about the target and vice versa.

Fourth, keep like contexts together. Often when conducting a survey we may be interested in comparing more than one communicative context. For example, maybe you want to compare participants' reported use of compliance-gaining strategies with both Internet and face-to-face friends. In this example, you would have survey questions relating to both the Internet communicative context and the face-to-face communicative context on your questionnaire. To ensure that your participants are not confusing the two contexts, you should keep them separate on your survey.

Fifth, place sensitive questions toward the end of a survey. If you start by asking for a participant's deepest, darkest secret, the chances that they will either start lying or start answering in a socially desirable manner increase. Asking more benign questions initially allows the participant to become more comfortable with the questions. Ultimately, if your participants are comfortable with the earlier questions, they will be much more willing to divulge more private and personal information later in the survey.

Ratio Level Questions

Overall, there are not many questions a researcher will ask using ratio level questions. The most common ratio level question asked on a survey is a participant's age. However, there are other types of ratio questions that may be asked during a survey that involve a number range that starts with a possible zero. How many visits to your doctor have you made this year? How many times a week do you eat breakfast? How many different sexual partners have you had in the past month? How many children do you have? All of these questions start with a possible zero and then escalate in an actual numerical fashion.

Another common form of ratio level questions that appear on surveys are cognitive-based questions. When creating tests that are designed to measure an individual's cognitive understanding of something, we rely on a number of different measurement mechanisms: matching, multiple choice, and true or false. All of these start with an absolute zero score (the participant got none of the answers correct), and then we can mathematically compare participants' scores as they go up from zero.

Open-Ended Questions

The final type of question commonly asked during a survey is an open-ended question. Open-ended questions are designed to allow respondents to further explore a concept. Instead of limiting the possible number of choices like we do with nominal, ordinal, interval, and ratio level questions, the answers given during open-ended questions are realistically limitless. For example, an open-ended question might ask, "How do you think you can improve your interpersonal communication with your spouse?" This question could receive one-sentence-long answers or pages of information. Open-ended questions can be useful because they often present you with information that you did not expect to receive from your respondents. You may be wondering how an open-ended question can be quantitative, and you are right to ask this question because the responses are not innately quantitative. However, there are quantitative tools that we have at our disposal that can be used to analyze open-ended questions; we will discuss the most common one, content analysis, in the next chapter.

As for placing open-ended questions on an actual questionnaire, the biggest consideration is providing enough space for your respondents to answer. People's handwriting differs in size, so allow the participants enough room to adequately answer a question. We generally recommend at least half a page for an open-ended answer. The more complex your question is, the more space your respondents may need to answer the question.

STEP 2: CREATING CLEAR INSTRUCTIONS

Murphy 's Law: If people can find a unique and creative way for screwing something up, they will. Over the years, all of the authors of this text have received a wide range of unique answers on questionnaires. We have also learned that if our instructions are clear, we can avoid some of the ambiguity people may have while filling out a questionnaire or responding during an interview. One of the easiest ways to avoid ambiguity during the first part of an interview questionnaire is to offer your participants dummy questions and walk them through how to correctly answer the question.

Figure 9.1 presents examples from an actual study that included dummy questions to walk participants through how to fill out the scales correctly. In our experience, college students tend to know how to correctly fill out research surveys, but the general public tends to be more likely to need extra help, probably because they do not fill out as many questionnaires. When looking at your instructions you should ask yourself a simple question: "Will these instructions make sense to my intended participants?" If you want to survey people in a nursing home, you may want to show your instructions to someone who is elderly and get their feedback before moving on to pilot-testing the questionnaire.

STEP 3: STUDY DESIGN

When designing a survey research study, we typically talk about two types of designs: cross-sectional and longitudinal (Fowler, 1993). A **cross-sectional survey design** is used when a researcher wants to get information from a group of participants at a given point in time. For example, maybe you want to conduct a study like Rocca and Vogl-Bauer (1999), who studied sports team identification and verbal aggression. In their study, the researchers asked a series of participants to fill out a scale containing items for sports team identification, verbal aggression, and sports spectator identification. In this study, the researchers simply wanted to get people's perceptions at the time they had filled out the scale. When using a cross-sectional survey design, researchers can examine things like relationships between variables and differences between groups that exist within the research sample, but you cannot study changes that occur over time.

To examine how people change over time, one must employ a **longitudinal survey design**. Although a longitudinal design cannot be used to make causal conclusions about relationships and differences, it can allow you to make statements about variable order. The first type of longitudinal design is a trend design. A **trend design** is used to examine different samples of

Weight Locus of Control

Directions: The following questions are concerned with how you perceive yourself across a variety of issues. For each statement, place an "X" in the box that corresponds with your perception of the item based on the following scale: SD = Strongly Disagree, D = Disagree, N = Neutral, A = Agree, and SA = Strongly Agree.

For example, if given the sentence "I like peanut butter," if you only agree with the statement, but do not strongly agree with the statement, you would place an "X" in the column marked "A" for Agree (See example below).

		SD	D	N	A	SA
Ex.	I like peanut butter.				X	
1.	Being the ideal weight is a matter of luck.					

Generalized Attitude Measure

Directions: On the scales below, please indicate your feelings about **"Restaurant X."** Circle the number between the adjectives which best represent your feelings about **"Restaurant X."** Numbers "1" and "7" indicate a very strong feeling. Numbers "2" and "6" indicate a strong feeling. Numbers "3" and "5" indicate a fairly weak feeling. Number "4" indicates you are undecided or do not understand the adjectives themselves. There are no right or wrong answers. Circle only ONE number per row.

For example, if you were given a pair of adjectives (cheap and expensive) and you felt the program was reasonably priced, you might circle 1 or 2.

Ex.   Cheap   ①   2   3   4   5   6   7   Expensive
1.   Good   1   2   3   4   5   6   7   Bad

Figure 9.1 Sample Questionnaire Questions

people at different points in time. For example, many researchers collected research data within the week before the 9/11 terrorist attacks in the United States. These same researchers were then able to collect data immediately after 9/11 using completely different samples to see whether changes had occurred within that short time period. Although it is possible that preexisting differences between the two groups caused the change to occur, there is no way to know this in a trend design.

Another way to conduct a survey study longitudinally is to employ a **panel design**. A panel design is when a researcher recruits a series of participants who agree to be surveyed periodically over a given period of time. Some researchers have used this type of design to examine marital conflict. Researchers recruit participants when they get married and agree to pay them a certain amount of money if they will agree to be surveyed every 6 months. Then every 6-months the researchers survey the couple about how they are handling conflict and the types of conflicts they are having. By surveying a panel over and over again like this, researchers can see how marital conflict strategies and themes change over time.

The last design is actually a combination of the first two types, which is called an **accelerated longitudinal survey design**. An accelerated longitudinal design is employed when a researcher wants to see how things change over a long period of time during a short period of time. We know this sounds odd, so we will use an illustration for clarification. Maybe a researcher wants to see how perceptions of situation comedies on television change over the course of one's adult life until retirement. In essence, the researcher wants to see how people's perceptions change from age 18 to 65. To complete this study using a traditional longitudinal study, it would take a researcher 47 years, or most of his or her career. For this reason, this type of study is not realistic. Instead, the researcher decides to recruit people in 5-year intervals starting at age 20, so they recruit 20-year-olds, 25-year-olds, 30-year-olds . . . all the way to 60-year-olds. The researcher then tracks these groups for 5 years. The idea here is that we are seeing changes over 5 years from participants who started the project at 20 and ended at 25 to participants who started when they were 60 and ended at 65. Ultimately, this type of design allows researchers to track how time affects the individual age groups over time, as well as how the differing age groups change.

STEP 4: DATA PROCESSING AND ANALYSIS

One of the areas the authors of this book have consistently realized is problematic for new researchers involves making sure the hypotheses and research questions can be answered by the information on the questionnaire. After you are done collecting data is not the time to realize that you should have asked another question(s). For this reason, before you ever set out to distribute your survey, you must ensure that you can statistically answer your hypotheses and research questions based on the questions you actually have on your questionnaire. For example, last year one of the authors of this text had a group of students conducting a project in organizational communication. At the end of the project, the students realized they had measured employee motivation and not employee satisfaction. One of the students said, "Well if they're motivated, they're satisfied, right?" Nope! Although research has shown the two variables to be positively related, they are not synonymous. If a researcher does not measure employee satisfaction, he or she cannot answer hypotheses or research questions about satisfaction.

In other words, you must know exactly how you plan on analyzing your data when you are finished with the study itself. Figure 6.10 (on page 141) contains a chart that helps you determine which tests are most appropriate to conduct. For example, if you have two interval level variables (like CA and ethnocentrism) and you want to find the relationship between these two variables, you would use a correlation to test for a statistical relationship. If you had one nominal variable (female and male), and you wanted to test for a possible difference between these two categories on an interval level variable (willingness to communicate, WTC), the appropriate test would be an independent samples *t* test. The last part of this book will go into more detail examining each of these different types of tests.

STEP 5: PILOT TESTING

The only way a researcher can really ever know how her or his respondents will provide answers to a survey is give it to people and find out directly. You may think your instructions were crystal clear and your survey questions all made sense, but once you give your survey to real people, that can all change quickly. In the study mentioned earlier in this chapter conducted by Wrench et al. (2006) examining religion, the researchers had listed Protestant as one of the possible religious affiliation categories (nominal variable). Protestants are any Christian groups who are not Roman Catholic, Eastern Orthodox, or Anglican. In other words, Baptists, Methodists, Disciples of Christ, and so on are all Protestants. However, the researchers ended up with more people selecting "other" and defining themselves by their individual denominational names instead of as Protestant. Many respondents simply did not know that they were Protestants, so they answered the best way they could. Thankfully, changing the respondents' answers to Protestant in this case was easy, but this could have been a bigger problem. One way to prevent problems like this from occurring is to administer a pilot study. According to Buckingham and Saunders (2004), a **pilot study** is a "small-scale test-run for a planned piece of empirical research" (p. 294). We use pilot studies to make sure our instructions are easy to follow and our survey questions make sense to potential respondents. The following are some basic guidelines to follow when piloting a survey. These guidelines are applicable whether you are piloting a questionnaire or an interview schedule, the series of questions an interviewer asks during an interview.

Use Actual Survey Population Members

First, when you are pilot testing a survey you want to actually use the people you plan on surveying to test the survey. For example, if you are going to be surveying people in a retirement village, you do not want to pilot test your survey instrument on college students because they simply will not respond the same way.

Anticipate Survey Context

When piloting a survey, you should attempt to pilot the survey using the same conditions that people actually responding to the survey items will experience. For example, if you are going to be surveying people using an interview schedule over the phone, you would not want to pilot your survey using college students sitting in a lecture hall. Although you may not be able to anticipate every possible survey context (e.g., person filling out a questionnaire in her or his car), you should at least try to approximate the general conditions under which most of your respondents will be participating.

Test Parts of the Survey

Another idea that can be helpful when developing a survey is to pilot test parts of your survey instead of the whole thing. Often you have used parts of a survey in the past with the same population, so you do not need to retest those sections of the survey. Instead, you may want to test a newly developed section to make sure respondents understand the new instructions or questions.

Determining a Pilot Sample Size

Is there a magical number one should attempt to have in a pilot study? Not really. However, we do recommend that you attempt to pilot your questionnaire or interview schedule using at least 5–10 percent of your target sample size. So if you are planning on surveying 200 participants, you should pilot your questionnaire or interview schedule with at least 10–20 people. The larger your pilot study is, the more likely you will find potential problems with your questionnaire or interview schedule.

Ask Questions after Someone Completes the Survey

One common practice that you can use during the pilot phase of survey testing phase of a survey is to interview the respondents about their experience after they have completed the survey. Ask the respondents whether they found any instructions confusing, were the questions clear, did they guess on any items, was the survey too long, could they physically read the survey (especially important when working with elderly populations)? The more you know about how your participants felt while taking the survey, the more appropriate your revisions will be before disseminating your survey to your target sample. Once you have pilot tested your survey, you are ready to hand out your survey to potential participants.

Disseminating Your Surveys

In the previous section, we discussed the creation of research scales or measures. In this section we will discuss the dissemination of a research survey or questionnaire. Although many different people use all five terms (scale, measure, research instrument, survey, and questionnaire) interchangeably, for the purpose of this book we are delineating a difference between scales/measures/research instruments and surveys/questionnaires. The first group is a single set of items designed to measure a specific variable. Surveys and questionnaires, by contrast, are the putting together of a series of scales/measures/research instruments in an attempt to examine how variables relate to or differ from each other. In essence, a survey or questionnaire is when you place a variety of scales together to examine statistical relationships and differences. For example, maybe you want to put together a survey to examine the variables sociocommunicative orientation, WTC, and humor assessment. To examine these three variables, you put the three scales together in one small packet and have each participant fill out all three scales. You may even include some basic demographic information like biological sex, ethnicity, sexual orientation, and so on. Once you have created a survey/questionnaire, you then need to determine the best way to get your survey into the hands of your target population. There are two primary ways that people can go about disseminating a survey: interviewing and self-administration.

INTERVIEWING

Face-to-Face Interviewing

Face-to-face (FtF) interviewing occurs when an interviewer asks an interviewee a set of questions. There are some clear advantages and disadvantages to FtF interviewing. The first advantage is that you tend to get a high response rate. People have a tendency to tell people "no, I don't want to participate" when they are looking at them. FtF interviews also tend to be beneficial for long surveys where fatigue might be a problem because the interviewer can encourage the interviewee to continue answering questions at a point where they would stop answering them in other formats. The interviewer can also answer questions about the survey items if an interviewee is having problems understanding the questions, which can be important when an interviewee's language skills are not high. FtF interviewing is also the best format in which to ask open-ended questions. In the first part of this chapter we focused on asking closed-ended questions or questions that have a clearly defined set of possible choices. In a Likert scale with a range from 1 (*strongly disagree*) to 5 (*strongly agree*), the person is not given the option of 9. There is a clearly defined set of permissible answers. However, open-ended questions are questions that allow for a wide variety of different answers. For example, maybe you want to know how someone perceives the federal government's propaganda about a new piece of legislation, so you ask, "How would you characterize the information you are receiving from Washington, DC, about this piece of legislation?" This enables the interviewee to express her or his thoughts in an open fashion. Although these open-ended responses can be coded and quantified, open-ended questions typically fall under the heading of qualitative rather than quantitative.

Although there are some clear advantages to completing FtF interviews, there are also some rather important disadvantages as well. First, the cost of FtF interviewing is high. You need teams of trained interviewers who interview people in the sample you are intending to examine. These teams of trained interviewers cost a lot of money, not including the expense of travel, food, and hotels that may be incurred. Another disadvantage is that the interviewer can inadvertently affect how an interviewee responds to the questions. A simple sidewise glance from an interviewer that says "I can't believe you just answered that way" can cause the interviewee to start censoring her- or himself and start feeding responses to the interviewer that the interviewer wants to hear. Another problem caused by interviewers can be slight changes in how the questions are asked with regard to the actual text of the question; how a question is asked can change how people respond to questions either randomly or systematically. Even the biological sex or ethnicity of an interviewer can affect how some people will respond to an interviewer. Although it is impossible to negate the effect that an interviewer can have on an interviewee, training interviewers to deliver questions in a systematic fashion and not outwardly respond to the answers they are given can help prevent interviewer effects from occurring.

One of the most famous social scientists to use interviewing as his primary form of research was a university professor at Indiana University named Alfred Kinsey. Kinsey initiated a line of research in the 1940s examining human sexuality in both females and males (Kinsey, Pomeroy, & Martin, 1948; Kinsey, Pomeroy, Martin, & Gebhard, 1953). Before Kinsey's studies, little research had been conducted about human sexuality in the United States. Kinsey and a group of highly trained interviewers set out to interview a wide variety of different people around the country about their sexual histories. Kinsey realized early on that FtF interviewing enabled people to be more honest and forthright about their current and past sexual behaviors. Based on their research, Kinsey and his team revolutionized the discussion of sexuality in the United States and around the world.

Telephone Interviewing

The second way to disseminate a survey to a specific population is through the use of telephone interviewing. Telephone interviews are similar to FtF interviews in that an interviewer can clarify questions that interviewees have about the survey, and interviewers can ask more probing, open-ended questions. Telephones interviews are also considerably cheaper and quicker than FtF interviews. A researcher no longer needs to send someone to interview a person, so researchers cut down on travel, lodging, and meal expenses, which drastically reduces your overall research budget. In fact, telephone surveys actually enable researchers to include responses from geographically remote locations that they could not afford to visit, which makes a sample more representative of the total population.

Although there are some clear advantages to telephone interviewing, there are some major drawbacks as well. First, a telephone interview cannot be as long as an FtF interview. In fact, a telephone interview that lasts 15 minutes is long. Interviewers are also more likely to have people tell them that they are not interested in participating or to be hung up on altogether, which can randomly or systematically skew a sample. People also tend to trust telephone interviewers less than they do FtF interviewers because there is always the perception in the back on the interviewee's mind that an interviewer is trying to sell something. Unfortunately for academic researchers, there are less than scrupulous people out in the world who do attempt to disguise product sales as telephone research, which confuses the public and makes them less trustworthy of legitimate research endeavors as a whole. As with FtF interviewing, interviewers still run the risk of inadvertently affecting the responses received from an interviewee, so again, training is extremely important to prevent this from occurring. One major limitation with phone surveys is that not everyone has a phone, so a group of people who could be a part of our research sample is not reached. When we exclude people who do not have or have less access to a phone, we bias our sample in the direction of people with phone access. Although the bias caused by the lack of phone service is generally not important, for some research projects this could be problematic. If you wanted to determine people's perceptions of the phone as a communicative tool, you would get a slanted population if you surveying only people you can reach by phone because these people already clearly use the tool for communication purposes.

Self-Administration

The final way to get your survey into the hands of your targeted research sample is through self-administration. Self-administration is when an individual receives the survey and then fills out the survey without the help of an interviewer. There are three basic ways to administer a self-administered survey: mass administration, mailed administration, and Internet administration.

Mass administration

Mass administration occurs when you have a large group of people in a stable environment where you can pass out surveys. For example, if you want to examine religious communication, maybe you would hand out surveys in a large church and have a collection box where people can place the surveys when they are done filling them out. Mass administrations are useful when you have a large group of possible participants in a single location. One group that is consistently used in mass administration surveys are college students because they are conveniently available and do not cost researchers much money to use since college students are most commonly paid for their participation in the form of class credit or extra credit.

Mailed administration

A mailed administration survey is when you mail an individual a survey to fill out and then that individual sends the completed survey back to you. Say that you wanted to survey all of the members of your state government on their use of persuasion during political campaigns. You could get a list of addresses for every elected state official and send them your survey, and when they are done filling it out they could send it back to you. Mailing surveys, however, is extremely expensive, and often people you have asked to participate will not send the survey back.

Some techniques have been shown to help increase the number of participants you can acquire during mail-administered surveys. First, send a postcard to your potential participants letting them know that a survey is coming and why you are conducting your survey. This postcard hopefully will encourage people to participate or at least be on the lookout for the survey packet itself. Second, send the survey packet with a self-addressed stamped envelope. You may even provide some kind of compensation in the envelope to provide incentive to the participant. One of the coauthors of this book remembers receiving a $1 bill in a survey he received in the mail. Even the $1 bill made our coauthor feel somewhat obligated to participate, so he did. Finally, if you have not received a survey packet back from a particular participant, you may want to follow up with a second postcard reminding the individual to participate. Some scholars will even send another copy of the survey packet to the potential participant through certified mail to ensure that the participant is actually receiving the survey. However, the more mailings you send as a researcher, the more costly mail surveys will become.

Internet administration

The Internet-administered survey is the newest form of research and can be used as a replacement for mass-administered and mail surveys or as a unique form unto itself (Best & Krueger, 2004; Dillman, 2000). As a way to replace traditional pen-and-paper surveys, many researchers opt to put surveys online because it saves the killing of many trees on an annual basis. Instead of having church members fill out a survey and turn it in, you ask them to go to the website and fill out the survey there. Or, instead of mailing your survey to the members of your state government, you e-mail them asking them to fill out the survey online instead. These are two examples of how the Internet can replace pen-and-paper studies; however, the Internet can also be used to gain access to populations that you may not be able to reach using traditional means. For example, maybe you wanted to research the impact that image fixation has on female Buddhists. In the United States, finding a large enough sample of female Buddhists may be difficult, but could be considerably easier online. All you would have to do is find a series of Buddhist websites and ask whether they would post your call for research. Many groups will agree to help a researcher if they can sense that what is being studied is not derogatory toward their group and could possibly benefit their group in the long run.

Advantages and Disadvantages of Self-Administered Surveying

Like other forms of surveying, self-administered surveys have basic advantages and disadvantages. First, self-administered surveying is by far the cheapest form of surveying. With the exclusion of mail surveys, which can cost a few thousand dollars as a result of postage, most self-administered surveys do not cost more than a few hundred dollars in photocopying expenses or software and website development. One nice thing about Internet surveys is that once a website has been developed and the software purchased, you can run countless numbers of surveys at one time without any additional expense. Another advantage of self-administered surveys is that you can reach a large cross-section of people in a short period of time. If you have a solid research strategy, getting 200 research participants can be achieved in a short period of time if you utilize a self-administered technique. Furthermore, you do not have to worry about an interviewer affecting your sample inadvertently.

The authors of this book first started online surveying in 1999 and it was much easier to get people to participate because online surveys and research were new. Now, there are hundreds of thousands of surveys constantly being conducted, so making your survey stick out is easier said than done. In a series of studies conducted online under the direction of one of our coauthors, the studies showed the challenges and promises of online surveying. In one study, the students tried posting the survey link on Facebook and other social networking sites thinking the topic would encourage people to participate. Unfortunately, this strategy was wildly misguided. After attempting to collect data for a month, the survey had a grand total of 30 participants, so the study was a bust. In a different study, the researchers examined librarian interactions with their supervisors. One of the student researchers was a medical librarian and had numerous contacts within the librarian community. Using her own network, she sent out requests to participate in the project and ended up with almost 500 responses in a short period of time. These two cases demonstrate that knowledge of a specific population and access to a sample from that population are two important factors when conducting online surveys. If you think the participants will flock to your online survey, you will be disappointed.

There are other clear disadvantages. First, participants do not have the ability to seek clarification when they do not understand a question on your survey. In fact, you may end up with serious problems at the end of a study because you did not see an inherent flaw in the design that could have been picked up on and corrected if you were interviewing people face to face. Second, you also do not have the ability to check to see whether people are randomly answering your survey until the survey is entered into a dataset and your reliability drops. Third, people may not take the survey as seriously if they are filling it out alone as if they are being asked the questions with the interviewer sitting in front of them or on the telephone. This problem is often seen in some of the questionnaire responses given by college students. Some patterns of response clearly fall into the "screw-you" category. For example, if you are using a 5-point Likert scale and you receive a survey that reads "123451234512345" or "12345432123454321," you can be guaranteed that the person just randomly filled out the survey because he or she obviously did not care. When we come across a survey where the respondent randomly filled in responses like this, we consider the survey a unit nonresponse (discussed below) and eliminate the survey from the dataset.

In the past few years, a number of different companies have emerged in an effort to help people (from business owners to academic researchers) conduct surveys. Some of the more common survey companies are Lime Survey (http://www.limesurvey.org/), Survey Monkey (http://www.surveymonkey.com/), and Zoomerang (http://www.zoomerang.com/). All three of these surveys will enable you to administer a short survey for free, but longer surveys (like those seen in academic research) will cost you a fee. However, Lime Survey is an open-source option that you can host on your own website if you have access to your school's web server or can work with your school's information technology department to launch the Lime Survey application. A nice thing about these online survey programs is that they come with a variety of survey item templates including templates for Likert, semantic differential, multiple-choice, open-ended, and other survey question formats. However, there are growing concerns in the research ethics community about the security and confidentiality of some of these services. Before investing time and money on one of these services, you should ask your local IRB about their thoughts and procedures for online surveying.

Problem Areas Associated with Survey Research

As a whole, there are always disadvantages one must be aware of when conducting any specific type of research. This section will discuss a series of situations that can be problematic for researchers.

RESPONSE RATE

One of the biggest questions a researcher must worry about when conducting research is her or his **response rate**. A researcher's response rate is the percentage of surveys returned compared to the percentage of surveys distributed. For example, if you initially hand out 100 surveys and 95 are returned, your response rate is 95 percent. However, in the real world of research it is not unheard of to receive a response rate under 50 percent. One of the authors of this book completed a two-part study examining parent–adolescent conflict. The first part of the study was completed and the researcher had approximately 200 participants. The second part of the study was to be completed 6 months later, and all of the participants in the first part had agreed to participate in the second. Unfortunately, the researcher only received 26 surveys back during the second stage of the research, which is a response rate of only 13 percent. Ultimately, this entire project had to be scrapped because of the low response rate from the participants. This study fell victim to the problem of **nonresponse**. According to Dillman, Eltinge, Groves, and Little (2002), "Nonresponse occurs when a sampled unit does not respond to the request to be surveyed or to particular survey questions" (p. 3). Based on this definition, we can see that there are two types of nonresponse problems that can affect a researcher's survey: unit nonresponse and item nonresponse.

Unit Nonresponse

In this example, which yielded a 13 percent response rate, we can say that the other 87 percent of the sample falls into the category of unit nonresponse. **Unit nonresponse** is defined as the "failure to obtain any survey measurements on a sample unit" (Dillman et al., 2002, p. 6). There are three reasons why people do not participate. First, some participants may not receive the invitation to participate. For example, if you use the National Communication Association's database of members, some people will have moved and not updated their information. If you randomly select any of these people to participate in a study, they may never receive the invitation to participate. The second group of people that does not respond simply refuse to do so. These people actually receive the request and ignore it. The last group that does not respond are people who are either physically or mentally unable to do so. Maybe you send out an e-mail survey, and one of the people you asked to participate is ill in the hospital. He or she may even get the e-mail request, but not be in a physical or mental position to respond.

Now that we have examined why people do not participate, you may be wondering why a participant agrees to participate in a study. Dillman et al. (2002) argue that there are three basic reasons why people will agree to participate in a research survey; this information is also true for getting people to participate in any type of research. First, participants will weigh the potential costs and rewards of participating in the survey. If a respondent sees her or his participation as a waste of time, he or she will be unlikely to participate unless the researcher can adequately entice the respondent to participate. Although some people believe participating in research is part of her or his "civic duty," most people feel the need to be compensated in some way for their participation. This "compensation" can come in many different forms, from monetary incentives to personalized letters asking for cooperation. If the participant feels that the researcher is at least attempting to provide some benefit for participation, the participant is much more likely to participate. This is the real reason why researchers offer college students extra credit to participate in research projects.

Second, the more interesting the topic of research is to the participant, the more likely he or she will want to participate in your study. For example, if a potential participant is not interested in politics, he or she will not be likely to participate in a survey examining political communication. This is especially true in self-administered surveys because respondents can preview the types of questions asked on the survey prior to actually filling out the survey. For this reason, the more mundane a research study is, the more likely it will be that the researcher will need to provide adequate compensation to get participants. However, if you land on a really "sexy" topic, people will be likely to participate without expecting compensation. Unfortunately, as a researcher you often do not know whether your topic is going to be seen as salient to people until after you begin collecting your data.

Finally, many participants are influenced to participate in a research project based on their previous participation in research. This is true for both new projects and continuing projects. For example, if a person feels he or she was treated poorly by a researcher in the past, he or she will be unlikely to participate in future research studies when asked. Also, if a participant feels he or she is being mistreated during a research project, he or she may decide to leave the study. For these reasons, researchers must attempt to make the survey experience as interesting and harmless as possible.

Item Nonresponse

Item nonresponse occurs when an individual participant fails to answer individual or groups of questions on a survey. According to Dillman et al. (2002), there are seven causes of item nonresponse: survey mode, interviewer training, question topics, question structure, question difficulty, institutional requirements and policies, and respondent attributes.

The first reason participants may not respond to specific items on a survey deals with the nature of surveying. In a self-administered survey, individual participants are ultimately responsible for reading and responding to all of the questions on the survey. One of the simplest reasons some people do not respond to an item is that their eyes visually skip an item, whereas during an interview an interviewer is responsible for making sure the participant responds to the survey questions, but an interviewer could accidentally skip a question. In fact, if a participant is hesitant to respond to a question, the interviewer can even encourage the interviewee to answer, which is not possible during a self-administered survey.

The second reason participants may not respond relates specifically to surveys that rely on interviewers. The interviewer can either help foster answers or actually cause participants to not answer survey questions. If an interviewer can develop a positive, friendly relationship with a participant, the interviewer is more likely to get the participant to answer survey questions. If, however, the interviewer is either unfriendly or bland, the interviewee will be more likely to not answer questions. Also, interviewers have the ability to coax answers out of participants who may not otherwise answer a specific question.

The third reason participants may not respond to survey questions relates to the topics of the questions themselves. As discussed earlier in this chapter, many topics make people feel embarrassed, shamed, or fearful. When topics evoke these emotional responses, people may feel the questions are psychologically or physically threatening and avoid answering them altogether.

The fourth reason people may not respond to survey questions involves the actual structure of the survey questions. Certain types of questions are more likely to be answered than other types. For example, in self-administered surveys, open-ended questions are considerably more likely to be left unanswered when compared to closed-ended questions such as Likert and semantic differential/bipolar adjective scales. Also, if you have questions that do not pertain to specific participants, respondents may skip those questions and skip more relevant questions at the same time. Again, if you have properly pilot tested a survey, this is much less likely to be a cause of nonresponse.

The fifth reason some people may not answer questions involves the difficulty of the question itself. Sometimes questions are either too difficult to answer or too confusing for participants to answer. If you follow the general requirements for writing Likert scales in Chapter 7, you are less likely to run into this problem. Other questions may ask participants to recall information they simply cannot remember. For instance, if you ask a participant to recall the number of times he or she communicated with a family member in the past month, this may be impossible for some people to answer, so they leave the item blank. Yet again, if you properly pilot test a study, this problem should take care of itself prior to administering your survey to your entire sample.

The sixth reason some people may not answer questions relates to institutional requirements and policies. First, some participants will not respond to items because they are not legally allowed to answer all of the questions. Institutional review boards will generally require researchers to include statements indicating that participants do not have to answer all of the questions on the questionnaire and that participants may stop participation at any time. Other participants may not answer specific questions because they consider the information private or proprietary. An example of information that may be considered private is someone's salary, whereas information that is proprietary is information over which an individual or group exercises private ownership. For example, if you are surveying organizational members about organizational coaching practices, some may see you as trying to steal their organization's information, so they will refuse to answer questions. The easiest way to alleviate this problem is to reassure the participants that all information is confidential or anonymous and will not be seen by anyone outside the research team.

The last reason some people do not respond to surveys is more of a personal issue than one the researcher can control. Dillaman et al. (2002) note that "older people and those with less education are less likely to provide answers in many surveys" (p. 14). Mason, Lesser, and Traugott (2002) also found that people who are reluctant participants in the first place are much more likely to not respond to individual items during the study. This is yet another reason to make sure that you attempt to get participants to see their participation as beneficial.

Effects of Nonresponse

Every survey will have some level of nonresponse associated with it. However, the question is whether this nonresponse actually alters the results of your survey in some meaningful way. Ultimately, a researcher must ask, "Are those who are not responding distinctly different in some manner from those who are responding?" Fowler (1993) noted that in mail research "people who have a particular interest in the subject matter or the research itself are more likely to return mail questionnaires than those who are less interested" (p. 41). In other words, if a mail survey has a low response rate, as a researcher you must question the generalizability of your results to the whole population. Low response rates can also cause a specific type of error to enter into your study called nonresponse bias. In essence, the people who did not participate are different enough from the people who did participate that it skews your results.

Although we know that **nonresponse bias** is extremely detrimental to a study, we do not know how much of a bias there actually is. When you cannot get individuals to participate in the first place, it is hard to find out why they did not respond later on. For this reason, we often have no way of quantifying the actual bias within a dataset because of nonresponse. There is no way to prevent nonresponse in survey research. Some people, for whatever reason, simply will either not participate or not answer specific questions in a research study. However, the research can improve the response rate by ensuring the survey, whether a questionnaire or interview, is presented in a clear and logical manner. ·

Improving Response Rates

Now that we have looked at some of the disadvantages to mass-administered surveys, here are some suggestions for how you can overcome some of these problems.

1. Make the survey easy to fill out. The more confusing a survey is for a participant, the more likely that participant is going to quit. Make sure that your font is large enough to be read by an average audience. Make sure your directions are clear. We even suggest adding sample questions that clearly illustrate how items in your study should be answered. For example, if you have a Likert scale, add a fake item and explain how the item could be answered. In our experience, the survey format that is often the most confusing is the bipolar adjectives format. Too many people believe they need to select a step on the scale for each adjective. For example, if your adjectives are "Yes 1, 2, 3, 4, 5, 6, 7 No," many people will circle 2 for "yes" and 6 for "no." It does not matter whether you boldface, italicize, or underline the phrase "circle only one number per adjective pair"; people will still make mistakes filling out your survey. Having a sample question has been shown to alleviate some of the more common mistakes.

2. Keep it short. Short surveys will always result in more participants, but longer surveys give you more information to analyze. Although there is no magic formula, it is recommended that a pen-and-paper survey be no longer than three to four pages in length. It does not matter whether your survey is single or double sided. In essence, people tend to view four single-sided pages and four double-sided pages as being equal in length because they are still four pages. You should also vary the types of questions you have on a survey. Too often people will have page after page of Likert scale items, which can cause people to become bored and tired and not complete the study.

3. Include an SASE. This particular hint is primarily for mail-administered surveys. SASE is the acronym for self-addressed stamped envelope. If you do not include an SASE and put postage on the envelope, people will likely not return your survey. People generally believe that they are doing you a favor by filling out your survey, so the least you can do is make the filling out and returning experience as easy as possible.

4. Include a good cover letter. The cover letter should explain to potential participants who you are and why you are conducting the research along with any legal notifications related to compliance as established by both the federal government and your university. Although the goal of the cover letter is to first convince people that they want to participate in your project, the letter is also a legal notification to participants of their rights as a participant. Some universities have simple guidelines for what must be in a cover letter, and other universities have specific guidelines. If you have any questions about what your university wants to see in a cover letter, contact your institutional review board.

5. Use multiple administration techniques. The concept of multiple administration techniques can be broken down into two categories: (1) options of survey method and (2) multiple contacts. The first multiple administration technique is to allow participants the option to fill out a survey by pen and paper or by Internet. When you allow people this option, people who may not be likely to fill out the pen-and-paper survey may go online and fill out the survey. The second aspect of the multiple administration technique is to use the multiple contact method. In essence, you contact a potential participant about your study through a quick e-mail or postcard to let them know you are sending them a survey. Next, you send them your survey. Two or three weeks later, you send a follow-up letter or e-mail either thanking them for participating or reminding them that you still need their participation. Some scholars even suggest sending a final survey through certified mail, but this can get expensive in the long run.

Translating Surveys into Other Languages

One area in which researchers conducting survey research may have substantial trouble occurs when they conduct surveys using samples from multiple intercultural groups. Often researchers want to conduct surveys of people who do not speak English as their native language or even speak English at all. For this reason, researchers have had to devise a range of different techniques for translating surveys into other languages. However, translating a survey into another language is easier said than done. Translating surveys into different languages involves three key equivalence issues: semantic, conceptual, and normative (Behling & Law, 2000; Gudykunst, 2002).

SEMANTIC EQUIVALENCE

The first major issue involved in translating surveys into other languages involves issues of **semantic equivalence**. The simple fact is that languages are semantically different from each other. Semantics is the study of meaning. So when we say that there is a problem with semantics, we are describing a language problem where a word in one language may not have an equivalent word with the same meaning in a different language. Words that exist in English may have no direct translation in Mandarin, which is going to cause problems if you attempt to translate a survey from one language to another.

CONCEPTUAL EQUIVALENCE

Often when we create mental measures that are designed to measure one specific construct in one culture, the construct will not hold true in another culture, which is referred to as **conceptual equivalence**. In other words, does the basic concept a researcher is attempting to study in one culture even exist within another culture? For example, one area where we tend to see conceptual problems is family communication. In some cultures, the notion that a child would be allowed to speak her or his mind to elders is absurd. If you have a mental measure that examines openness of ideas shared within the family, the basic concept will not translate to some other cultures. In other words, just because we can study a concept in the United States does not mean that the concept is able to be studied within other cultures. Zhang (2005a, 2005b, 2006) has examined the notion of nonverbal immediacy and how U.S. students and Chinese students perceive nonverbal immediacy different. In this case we have a concept that has been regularly studied within the United States that Zhang has shown does not translate for Chinese students. For this reason, Zhang (2006) has created a new mental measure specifically designed to measure Chinese students' perceptions of teacher nonverbal immediacy.

NORMATIVE EQUIVALENCE

Every cultural group has its own set of norms or social conventions. These norms do not translate from one culture to the next because they are culturally dependent. For this reason, survey questions are often culturally specific. Behling and Law (2000) note that this issue of **normative equivalence** includes three behaviors that can impact the translating of research instruments: willingness to discuss certain topics, manner in which ideas are expressed, and treatment of strangers.

The first behavior that can impact the translating of research instruments is whether people in a specific culture are open to discussing certain topics. Different cultures have different norms when it comes to discussing specific topics. Although the U.S. culture has no problem gossiping about the sex lives of our political figures, other cultures tend to be less likely to discuss sexuality as a general concept (Frayser, 2002). For this reason, if you are conducting a survey on sexual communication in another culture, you may find that your nonresponse rate escalates because your participants do not like openly discussing the subject.

The second behavior that can affect the translating of research instruments deals with how participants may respond to questions. In some cultures, people are less likely to engage in self-aggrandizement or to make themselves appear better or greater than they actually are. For instance, if you are conducting a study on WTC, you may find cultural differences. Barraclough, Christophel, and McCroskey (1988) found that American students reported having higher levels of WTC and higher levels of self-perceived communication competence when compared to Australian students. When results like this are found, we could be looking at actual differences between cultures or just differences in how people in different cultures rate themselves on mental measures. Lonner and Ibrahim (1996) note that it is common for people in different cultures to respond to mental measures differently. In essence, Lonner and Ibrahim believe that people in different cultures have different positional response styles; that is, people within cultures respond to scales in similar patterns that are representative of cultural test taking and not the differences on the measures themselves. In other words, people may be more or less likely to use the extremes on mental measures, or they are more likely to go for the neutral option on mental measures, based on their culture rather than their actual perceptions of their own attitudes, behaviors, beliefs, cognitive knowledge, personality traits, and values.

The final behavior that can impact the translating of research instruments deals with different cultures' handling of strangers. As noted by Behling and Law (2000), "Reactions to strangers—particularly to strangers asking questions—also vary from society to society" (p. 6). Different people in different cultures will have widely different reactions to people attempting to conduct research. Some people may attempt to give answers to a researcher that they perceive the researcher wants. Or the respondent may simply go along with the survey out of politeness, but not actually give the researcher any useful information. For this reason, we always recommend having at least one person on your research team who is from the target culture. If you are going to conduct research in Zimbabwe, you should have at least one researcher on your project who is from Zimbabwe to prevent the issue of being a stranger conducting research in another culture.

Now that we understand some of the problems researchers face when translating surveys from one language to another, we must discuss the ways in which researchers can successfully complete a survey translation. Behling and Law (2000) expanded on Guthery and Lowe's (1992) original ideas for translating surveys and came up with five unique methods researchers can employ for translating surveys.

SIMPLE DIRECT TRANSLATION

The first method that a researcher can employ for translating scales from one language to a secondary language is the **simple direct translation**. In this method of translating, a researcher recruits a bilingual individual, who takes the original survey and then translates this survey from the primary language to the secondary language. However, there are some problems with this method. First, when conducting a simple direct translation, the translator is only paying attention to semantic issues of translation. In essence, the translator is making sure the survey can be read and understood by people in the secondary language, but does not pay attention to conceptual or normative issues. Furthermore, the translator is not really being double checked. We already know that people make mistakes, so relying on one person to conduct a translation automatically opens your research projects to translation errors.

MODIFIED DIRECT TRANSLATION

The second method a researcher can employ for translating scales from one language to a secondary language is the **modified direct translation**. In this version of survey translation, a translator performs the same translation he or she did in the simple direct translation, but with the addition of one step. After the translation process is completed, the translation is given to a panel of experts who know the primary and secondary languages, and the group decides whether the individual item translations are appropriate. Although this sounds better than a simple direct translation, this method also opens itself up to a number of problems. First, the panel may be no more knowledgeable about translating information from one language to another language than the original translator is. Second, this method is time consuming and does not provide the researcher any information that he or she could not get from the original translation about the quality. If anything, the translation may end up making less sense after a group of people attempt to translate the survey.

TRANSLATION/BACKTRANSLATION

The third method a researcher can employ for translating scales from one language to a secondary language is the **translation/backtranslation** method. In this method, a researcher has a translator complete the same steps he or she would complete in the simple direct translation. After the initial translation is complete, the researcher then provides the new translation to another bilingual individual who has not seen the original survey, and then the second translator attempts to translate the work back into the first language. If the original survey and the retranslated survey are similar, then the translation is semantically successful. If, however, the two translations are different, the original and secondary translator can discuss possible problematic areas and a new translation can be completed. Although this provides great semantic verifiability, the researcher cannot be sure that the translator is actually paying attention to conceptual or normative issues. Furthermore, utilizing two translators can be quite expensive if they must be hired for the study.

PARALLEL BLIND TECHNIQUE

The fourth method that a researcher can employ for translating scales from one language to a secondary language is the **parallel blind technique**. In this method of translation, a researcher has two independent translators translate the survey in the same way as described in the simple direct translation. After both researchers complete their independent translations, the two translators then compare their translations and ultimately agree on a third translation that is given to the researcher. Ultimately, the researcher must trust her or his translators in this technique. However, the researcher cannot be sure that the translation is actually paying attention to conceptual or normative issues. Again, two translators can be expensive. On the plus side of this method, it tends to be fast.

RANDOM PROBE

The fifth method that a researcher can employ for translating scales from one language to a secondary language is the **random probe translation**. In this method, a researcher has a translator complete the same steps he or she would complete in the simple direct translation. After the researcher has the translation in hand, he or she then pilot tests the translation with a group of bilingual participants. After the participants complete the survey, the researcher then asks a series of open-ended questions examining why the participants answered questions in a specific manner. The goal of this process is to ascertain whether the participants understand the questions in a manner that is similar to the researcher's own understanding of the mental measure. This method can actually help a researcher test for conceptual and normative issues of translating during the open-ended question interview portion of the pilot test. Behling and Law (2000) suggest using this approach in combination with the modified direct translation, translation/backtranslation, or the parallel blind technique to ensure that the survey's translation is equivalent on all three levels (semantic, conceptual, and normative).

Using the Research Project Worksheet

The last part of this chapter contains what we call the Designing a Research Project Worksheet (Figure 9.2). This worksheet was originally designed by Dr. Jason Wrench (one of the text's coauthors) while he was working for a medical school and teaching biostatistics. This worksheet is useful when either planning your own research projects or analyzing someone else's study. This worksheet contains components from this chapter and the next two chapters (content analysis and experimental research). The rest of this chapter is going to walk through a sample survey research project and demonstrate how you could fill out the Designing a Research Project Worksheet. You can find an MS Word document file containing this worksheet on the textbook's website in the Workbook folder.

QUESTION

The first section of the Designing a Research Project Worksheet asks a researcher to explain in a single sentence what he or she would like to know when the project is done. Researchers must have the ability to concisely explain the purpose of a research project, so forcing yourself to explain the project in one sentence will help keep you focused as you design your project.

Question (In a single sentence, what would you like to know when your project is done?)

Design
(Check one):   ( ) Survey   ( ) Content Analysis   ( ) Data Mining   ( ) Randomized Study   ( ) Nonrandom Study

If a self-administered survey, how?	( ) Mass Administered	( ) Mail	( ) Web Based	
If an interview-based survey, how?	( ) Phone	( ) In Person		
If a content analysis, what type?	( ) Mediated	( ) Interactional	( ) Microlevel	( ) Macrolevel
If using preexisting data?	( ) Personally Collected	( ) Governmental Agency	( ) Other Records	( ) Other
Type of randomization?	( ) Nonblind	( ) Single Blind	( ) Double Blind	
Type of nonrandomized study?	( ) Case-Control	( ) Cohort		

Type of Experimental Design:

Quasi-Experimental Design			
( ) Pretest–Posttest	( ) Time Series	( ) Multiple Time Series	( ) Switching Replications

True Experimental Design			
( ) Pretest–Posttest	( ) Two-Group Posttest Only	( ) Randomized Switching Replications	( ) Solomon Four-Group

Setting (Where will the survey/study be conducted?)

Participants
1. Do your participants need to possess any specific characteristics (high levels of communication apprehension, users of instant messaging, relational partner, age grouping, biological sex, etc.)?
   ( ) YES ( ) NO
      If Yes, explain:

2. How are you going to select/acquire participants?

3. Do you need a letter of consent for participation? (NOTE: All survey and experimentally based studies must have a letter of consent.) ( ) YES ( ) NO
      If No, explain why not:

Variables (What are your IVs/DVs, how are they measured, and what level of measurement are they?)
1. Independent Variables (label as nominal, ordinal, interval, or ratio):

Figure 9.2 Designing a Research Project Worksheet

Continued

Continued

---

2. Dependent Variables (label as nominal, ordinal, interval, or ratio):

Hypotheses/Research Questions

Statistical Testing (Using the above Hypos/RQs, what statistical tests will you use to answer each question?)

Tentative Study Title:

Principal Researcher(s):

For our example study, we will look for a possible difference between females and males in their levels of CA and WTC and for a relationship between CA and WTC. Therefore, our one-sentence question could be, "Do females and males differ in their level of CA and WTC, and is there a relationship between CA and WTC?" This sentence is short, sweet, and to the point.

DESIGN

The second section of the Designing a Research Project Worksheet is concerned with the basic study design. The design section has components for surveys, content analysis, and experimental designs. Depending on which type of study you are planning on conducting, you should focus on those design aspects.

For our example study, we are planning on conducting a survey, so we would place an "X" next to Survey. Once you have determined that you are conducting a survey, you must decide whether this survey will be self-administered (mass, mail, or Web) or interview based (phone or in person). For our study, we will use a mass-administered survey, so put an "X" next to Mass Administered. This is the last thing we must check in the Design section, since the rest of this section is either for content analysis studies or experimental studies.

SETTING

The third section of the Designing a Research Project Worksheet is concerned with the physical location you plan to use for your study. Although this section is not useful for a content analysis study, it is extremely important when conducting both survey research and experiments.

For our example study, we will pretend that we have gotten permission to hand out questionnaires at a local business club. For our setting, we may include information like where the club meets, what time the meeting is, and the appropriate dress. When thinking about the setting, you must think about the context of the setting (a business club) and how this context will affect how you should present yourself as a researcher. If you are studying a sports team, you may present yourself in a different manner than you would at a business club. Your goal for this section is to be as detailed as possible. Here is an example of what you might end up writing: "We will be handing out questionnaires at the local American Business Club meeting, which meets in Civic Center room 3-A on Mondays at noon. The researchers should be in professional dress since most of the potential participants are at the meeting during their lunch hour."

PARTICIPANTS

The fourth section of the Designing a Research Project Worksheet is concerned with the actual participants you are planning to recruit during your study. Typically, there are three basic items you should know when thinking about potential participants: specific characteristics, how to recruit, and how to gain consent.

Specific Characteristics

The first question you must ask yourself as a researcher is whether there are any specific characteristics your participants should have for recruitment into a study. For example, if you are conducting a survey of physicians, one of the characteristics your participants must possess is an MD or DO. For our example study, we really have no specific characteristics in mind, so place an "X" next to the word NO.

Recruitment

The second question to ask yourself related to participants is how you are going to get your participants. Throughout this chapter, we have discussed many ways you can recruit participants, whether in the college classroom, by random phone surveying, or asking people at a business club meeting. The clearer your recruitment plan is up front, the easier it will be to actually recruit participants later on in your study. Also, if you have a unique group you want to study, you will have more time to determine how to best target those participants.

Consent

The next question you must think about is whether you will need to attach a cover letter explaining consent. You should also decide whether the consent form needs to be signed. Of course, these are decisions that you cannot ultimately make yourself because you must get approval from the IRB to conduct any survey research study.

VARIABLES

Independent Variables

The next thing you want to have for your study is all of your independent variables. In our study, the only truly independent variable is biological sex.

Dependent Variables

Next, you want to list all of your study-dependent variables. For our study, we have two dependent variables: CA and WTC. If you are testing for relationships, you can list the variables where most appropriate for your study. This will be discussed further in Chapter 20 when we talk about regressions.

HYPOTHESES/RESEARCH QUESTIONS

In the next section, you should list any hypotheses and research questions. These should relate directly to your independent and dependent variables. Remember, if you do not list a variable on your independent variable or dependent variable list, you cannot have a hypothesis or research question that involves that variable. In our sample study we list three variables (biological sex, CA, and WTC); therefore, I could not have a hypothesis that predicts that people who have been in their jobs longer will have lower levels of CA because we are not measuring how long someone has been in her or his job. If you find you want to measure a variable not listed as an independent or dependent variable, you should add that variable to your study.

STATISTICAL TESTING

Once you know what your hypotheses and research questions are going to be, you can decide which statistical tests will be the most appropriate tests to conduct. Although we will discuss how to determine which statistical tests to use in Chapters 14 through 20, you can always go back and use the chart in Chapter 6 (Figure 6.9).

For our current study, we know we are examining a difference between two groups (female and male participants) on one interval variable (CA/WTC), so we would use a *t* test to analyze this hypothesis. Our second hypothesis tests for a relationship between two interval/ratio level variables, so we would use a correlation to analyze this hypothesis.

TENTATIVE STUDY TITLE

Every study must be called something. Although the title you create at this stage in your research project will probably not be the title at the end of your project, you should give your study a title just so you have something to call the study while you're working. There is no clear-cut way to title a study. The only real rule is that your title relate to your study itself. Our example study may be titled "Sex Differences and Communication Apprehension and Willingness to Communicate."

PRINCIPAL RESEARCHER(S)

The last part of the Designing a Research Project Worksheet is a list of all those involved in your project. Make sure you list all of the principal investigators and your advisor, if you have one, for this study. If you need to remember the appropriate method for listing authors for a study, reread the section in Chapter 3 on ethics related to authorship.

A completed version of the Designing a Research Project Worksheet can be seen in Figure 9.3.

Measurement Outside of Academia

As a quick caveat to conducting surveys in nonacademic settings, researchers should carefully attend to the length of survey they try to administer. We know that people are more likely to answer a lengthy survey if the survey is being conducted for academic or intellectual pursuits,

Question (In a single sentence, what would you like to know when your project is done?)

Do females and males differ in on their level of CA & WTC, and is there a relationship between CA and WTC?

Design   (**X**) Survey   ( ) Content   ( ) Data   ( ) Randomized   ( ) Nonrandom
(Check one):   Analysis   Mining   Study   Study

If a self-administered survey, how?	(**X**) Mass Administered	( ) Mail	( ) Web Based	
If an interview based survey, how?	( ) Phone	( ) In Person		
If a content analysis, what type?	( ) Mediated	( ) Interactional	( ) Microlevel	( ) Macrolevel
If using preexisting data?	( ) Personally Collected	( ) Governmental Agency	( ) Other Records	( ) Other
Type of randomization?	( ) Nonblind	( ) Single Blind	( ) Double Blind	
Type of nonrandomized study?	( ) Case-Control	( ) Cohort		

Type of Experimental Design:

Quasi-Experimental Design			
( ) Pretest–Posttest	( ) Time Series	( ) Multiple Time Series	( ) Switching Replications
True Experimental Design			
( ) Pretest–Posttest	( ) Two-Group Posttest Only	( ) Randomized Switching Replications	( ) Solomon Four-Group

Setting (Where will the survey/study be conducted?)

We will be handing out questionnaires at the local American Business Club meeting, which meets in Civic Center room 3-A on Mondays at noon. The researchers should be in professional dress since most of the potential participants are at the meeting during their lunch hour.

Participants
1. Do your participants need to possess any specific characteristics (high levels of communication apprehension, users of instant messaging, relational partner, age grouping, biological sex, etc.)?
( ) YES (X) NO
    If Yes, explain:

2. How are you going to select/acquire participants?

Participants will be recruited during the American Business Club meeting. Participants will be handed a questionnaire as they arrive to the luncheon and asked to turn the questionnaires back in to one of the researchers at the end of the luncheon.

Figure 9.3 Completed Project Worksheet

Continued

Continued

3. Do you need a letter of consent for participation? (NOTE: All survey and experimentally based studies must have a letter of consent.) (X) YES ( ) NO
  If No, explain why not:

Variables (What are your IVs/DVs, how are they measured, and what level of measurement are they?)

3. Independent Variables (label as nominal, ordinal, interval, or ratio):
  Biological Sex (Nominal Variable)

4. Dependent Variables (label as nominal, ordinal, interval, or ratio):
  Communication Apprehension (Interval Variable)
  Willingness to Communicate (Interval Variable)

Hypotheses/Research Questions
  H1: There will be a difference between men and women in their levels of communication apprehension.
  H2: There will be a difference between men and women in their willingness to communicate.
  H3: There will be a negative relationship between communication apprehension and willingness to communicate.

Statistical Testing (Using the above Hypos/RQs, what statistical tests will you use to answer each question?)
  H1: There will be a difference between men and women in their levels of communication apprehension.
    A t-test will be conducted using biological sex as the independent variable and communication apprehension as the dependent variable.
  H2: There will be a difference between men and women in their willingness to communicate.
    A t-test will be conducted using biological sex as the independent variable and willingness to communicate as the dependent variable.
  H3: There will be a negative relationship between communication apprehension and willingness to communicate.
    A correlation will be conducted between communication apprehension and willingness to communicate.

Tentative Study Title:
  Sex Differences and Communication Apprehension and Willingness to Communicate

Principal Researcher(s):
Jason S. Wrench, Candice Thomas-Maddox, Virginia Peck Richmond, & James C. McCroskey

but people are less likely to answer a lengthy survey for an organization (unless they have highly involved with that organization). As such, we recommend keeping surveys in nonacademic settings to the bare essentials. Ultimately, the shorter your survey is, the more likely participants will respond and complete the whole survey.

If you are conducting a survey (or any type of study for that matter) in someone's place of work, you must take extra precautions to guarantee that person's confidentiality or anonymity. Imagine you are conducting a survey on someone's satisfaction with communication in her or his division. If a participant's manager reads that participant's survey, the participant could actually be in jeopardy of retaliation if the manager does not like the responses. For this reason, especially on surveys that involve controversial matters in the workplace, researchers must have a strict policy in place for how surveys will be handled and who has access to the raw data. As a consultant, it is important to ensure that who will have access to what kind of data is clearly spelled out in a contract or proposal before beginning the study.

Conclusion

This chapter has examined some of the basic concepts related to survey research. In the next chapter we will discuss a second research method technique called content analysis.

KEY TERMS

Accelerated longitudinal survey design
Analytical survey
Conceptual equivalence
Cross-sectional survey Design
Descriptive survey
Generalizability
Interview schedule
Item nonresponse

Longitudinal survey design
Modified direct translation
Nonresponse
Nonresponse bias
Normative equivalence
Panel design
Parallel blind technique
Pilot test
Questionnaire
Random probe translation

Response rate
Semantic equivalence
Simple direct translation
Socially desirable responding
Survey
Translation/backtranslation
Trend design
Unit nonresponse

REFERENCES

Barraclough, R. A., Christophel, D. M., & McCroskey, J. C. (1988). Willingness to communicate: A cross-cultural investigation. *Communication Research Reports, 5(2),* 187–192.

Behling, O., & Law, K. S. (2000). *Translating questionnaires and other research instruments: Problems and solutions.* Thousand Oaks, CA: Sage.

Best, S. J., & Krueger, B. S. (2004). *Internet data collection.* Thousand Oaks, CA: Sage.

Buckingham, A., & Saunders, P. (2004). *The survey methods workbook: From design to analysis.* Malden, MA: Polity Press.

Cattell, J. M. (1890). Mental tests and measurements. *Mind, 15,* 373–381.

Converse, J. M., & Presser, S. (1986). *Survey questions: Handcrafting the standardized questionnaire.* Thousand Oaks, CA: Sage.

Dillman, D. A. (2000). *Mail and Internet surveys: The tailored design method* (2nd ed.). New York, NY: Wiley.

Dillman, D. A., Eltinge, J. L., Groves, R. M., & Little, R. J. A. (2002). Survey nonresponse in design, data collection, and analysis. In R. M. Groves, D. A. Dillman, J. L. Eltinge, & R. J. A. Little (Eds.), *Survey nonresponse* (pp. 3–26). New York, NY: Wiley.

Fink, A. (2006). *How to conduct surveys: A step-by-step guide* (3rd ed.). Thousand Oaks, CA: Sage.

Fowler, F. J., Jr. (1993). *Survey research methods* (2nd ed.). Newbury Park, CA: Sage.

Frayser, S. G. (2002). Discovering the value of cross-cultural research on human sexuality. In M. W. Wiederman & B. E. Whitley, Jr. (Ed.), *Handbook for conducting research on human sexuality* (pp. 425–453). Mahwah, NJ: Erlbaum.

Gudykunst, W. B. (2002). Issues in cross-cultural communication research. In W. B. Gudykunst & B. Mody (Eds.), *Handbook of international and intercultural communication* (2nd ed., pp. 165–177). Thousand Oaks, CA: Sage.

Guthery, D., & Lowe, B. A. (1992). Translation problems in international marketing research. *Journal of Language and International Business, 4*, 1–14.

Hildebrand, D. K., Laing, J. D., Rosenthal, H. (1977). *Analysis of ordinal data.* Newbury Park, CA: Sage.

Kinsey, A. C., Pomeroy, W. B., & Martin, C. E. (1948). *Sexual behavior in the human male.* Philadelphia, PA: Saunders.

Kinsey, A. C., Pomeroy, W. B., Martin, C. E., & Gebhard, P. H. (1953). *Sexual behavior in the human female.* Philadelphia, PA: Saunders.

Lonner, W. J., & Ibrahim, F. A. (1996). Appraisal and assessment in cross-cultural counseling. In P. B. Pedersen, J. G., Draguns, W. J. Lonner, & J. E. Trimble (Eds.), *Counseling across cultures* (4th ed., pp. 292–322). Newbury Park, CA: Sage.

Mason, R., Lesser, V., & Traugott, M. W. (2002). Effect of item nonresponse on nonresponse error and inference. In R. M. Groves, D. A. Dillman, J. L. Eltinge, & R. J. A. Little (Eds.), *Survey nonresponse* (pp. 149–161). New York, NY: Wiley.

Rocca, K. A., & Vogl-Bauer, S. (1999). Trait verbal aggression, sports fan identification, and perceptions of appropriate sports fan communication. *Communication Research Reports, 16*, 239–248.

Sweeney, L. (2000). Simple demographics often identify people uniquely. *Data Privacy Working Paper 3.* Pittsburgh, PA: Carnegie Mellon University.

Wrench, J. S., Corrigan, M. W., McCroskey, J. C., & Punyanunt-Carter N. M. (2006). Religious fundamentalism and intercultural communication: The relationships among ethnocentrism, intercultural communication apprehension, religious fundamentalism, homonegativity, and tolerance for religious disagreements. *Journal of Intercultural Communication Research, 35*, 23–44. doi:10.1080/1745740600739198.

Zhang, Q. (2005a). Immediacy, humor, power distance, and classroom communication apprehension in Chinese college classrooms. *Communication Quarterly, 53*, 109–124. doi:10.1080/01463370500056150.

Zhang, Q. (2005b). Teacher immediacy and classroom communication apprehension: A cross-cultural investigation. *Journal of Intercultural Communication Research, 34*, 50–64.

Zhang, Q. (2006). Constructing and validating a Teacher Immediacy Scale: A Chinese perspective. *Communication Education, 55*, 218–241. doi:10.1080/03634520600566231.

FURTHER READING

Groves, R. M. (2004). *Survey errors and survey costs.* Hoboken, NJ: Wiley.

Lee, E. S., & Forthofer, R., N. (2006). *Analyzing complex survey data* (2nd ed.). Thousand Oaks, CA: Sage.

Patten, M. L. (2001). *Questionnaire research: A practical guide* (2nd ed.). Los Angeles, CA: Pyrczak.

Punch, K. F. (2003). *Survey research: The basics.* Thousand Oaks, CA: Sage.

Rea, L. M., & Parker, R. A. (2005). *Designing and conducting survey research: A comprehensive guide* (3rd ed.). San Francisco, CA: Jossey–Bass.

Singleton, R. A., Jr., & Straits, B. C. (1999). *Approach to social research* (3rd ed.). New York, NY: Oxford University Press.

CHAPTER 10

Content Analysis

CHAPTER OBJECTIVES

1 Explain the basic principles underlying the use of content analysis.
2 Describe the different types of research studies that can be conducted using content analysis methods.
3 List the basic steps necessary to conduct a content analysis.
4 Explain the relationship among conceptualization, operationalization, and unit of analysis.
5 Describe the types of units of analysis often studied in content analysis.
6 Define coding and explain how one creates a codebook and coding form.
7 Explain the process for training and evaluating coders.
8 Define intercoder reliability and calculate it using Cohen's kappa.
9 Identify four problems a researcher may encounter with coders (coder misinterpretations, coder in attention, coder fatigue, and recording errors).

In Chapter 9, we discussed how communication researchers go about studying a communicative phenomenon (surveying). In the next two chapters, we will focus on two other methods that communication researchers can use to learn about human communication: content analysis and experimental research. Before delving into how communication researchers actually use content analysis, we will first explain what content analysis is and how it can be applied to a variety of communicative contexts.

According to Neuendorf (2002), **content analysis** is a "summarizing, quantitative analysis of messages that relies on the scientific method (including attention to objectivity–intersubjectivity, a priori design, reliability, validity, generalizability, replicability, and hypothesis testing) and is not limited as to the types of variables that may be measured or the context in which the messages are created or presented" (p. 10). When we look at this definition there are a number of important parts to understand. First, content analysis attempts to quantitatively summarize different messages. These messages may be verbal (e.g., types of jokes told by comedians), nonverbal (e.g., incidence of facial expressions during conversations), or mediated (e.g., portrayal of global warming in magazines). In each of these three cases, a researcher using content analysis would attempt to understand how various messages function.

Second, Neuendorf's (2002) definition of content analysis is dependent on the scientific method. Although we are not going to rehash our discussion of the scientific method here (see Chapter 2 to refresh your memory), we do want to emphasize that the empirical use of content analysis should conform to the traditional norms of scientific research. In other words, researchers should not randomly opt to use content analysis, but should have specific reasons for believing that content analysis is the most appropriate method to examine communicative phenomena.

Finally, Neuendorf (2002) notes that content analysis can be applied to a wide range of differing communicative contexts: "Content analysis may be conducted on written text, transcribed speech, verbal interactions, visual images, characterizations, nonverbal behaviors, sound events, or any other type of message" (p. 24). Neuendorf does acknowledge that the notion of content analysis started by specifically examining textual works. One of the earliest examples of a content analysis occurred during the 1770s in Sweden. In Sweden, a hymnal entitled *Songs of Zion* was published and republished in multiple editions. At first, the Swedish authorities granted permission to publish the volume of songs, but then fear that the songs contained unorthodox (i.e., not approved by the Swedish Church) teachings began to arise. A well-read orthodox clergyman named Kumblaeus attempted to solve the debate through a simple textual analysis of the hymnal itself. Kumblaeus counted various orthodox themes in the hymnal, compared them to the number of unorthodox themes, and "concluded on the basis of his analysis that the exclusion of certain Christian themes and emphasis on certain others tended to create new conceptions which threatened the doctrine of the established church" (Dovring, 1954–1955, p. 392). Overall, Kumblaeus was able to quantitatively examine the text and determine that the hymnal was indeed a clear source of unorthodox teachings. Not only did Kumblaeus complete a quantitative analysis of the themes within the text, but also he further suggested that these themes indicate that the editor of the volume clearly had an underlying motivation to spread unorthodox themes in the hopes of converting more followers. This example clearly illustrates how content analysis can be used to show how sources of messages construct messages and have motivations underlying the messages sent and how a source's message is intended to influence a specific receiver.

In modern scholarship, content analysis has been used to examine a wide range of different communication phenomena. In the context of mass-mediated messages, content analysis has been used to examine advertisers' use of product pricing (Howard & Kerin, 2006), physical attributes of violent video game characters (Lachlan, Smith, & Tamborini, 2005), candidate blogs during a presidential election (Bichard, 2006), differences in television reporting between embedded and nonembedded journalists in the Iraq war (Pfau et al., 2005), coverage of the SARS outbreak in Chinese newspapers (Zhang & Flemming, 2005), portrayals of models more than 50 years old in the United Kingdom (Simcock & Sudbury, 2006), types of advertising found in New York City newspapers after 9/11 (McMellon & Long, 2006), portrayals of Muslims in American media (Cagle, Cox, Luoma, & Zaphiris, 2011), and the types of merchandise sold by Evangelical Christians (Hirdes, Woods, & Badzinski, 2009). This list of content analyses in mass-mediated communication represents only a small selection of studies published in 2005 and 2011, but it gives a general portrayal of the types of studies being conducted in this area. Overall, media researchers have historically been the primary group to utilize content analysis methods (Riffe, Lacy, & Fico, 2005), but they are not the only communication researchers to do so.

Many communication scholars conduct research that falls under the content analysis umbrella related to nonmediated messages. Some nonmediated messages have asked participants to write out how they perceived interactions would go: parent–adolescent conflict (Comstock & Buller, 1991), young adults' views of intergenerational communication (Harwood, 1998), and heterosexuals' perceptions of interactions with gay, lesbian, and bisexual people (Hajek & Giles, 2005, 2006). Other studies have attempted to code actual human interaction: communication strategies between patients and physicians (Roter, Lipkin, & Dorsgaard, 1991), gesturing (Feyereisen & Havard, 1999), dominance and control between husbands and wives (Ayres & Miura, 1980; Courtright, Millar, & Rogers-Millar, 1979), facial expressions (Ekman & Rosenberg, 2005), self-disclosure (Shaffer, Pegalis, & Cornell, 1991), and speech rate (Feyereisen & Havard, 1999). When we use the word "code" in content analysis, we simply mean to group one's findings in a consistent way. For example, maybe you are conducting a study on the incidence of biological sex in speakers at political conventions. For every speaker who speaks at the Democratic and Republican national conventions, you code the speakers as being either female or male. Overall, content analysis can be used in a variety of unique and interesting ways.

Conducting a Content Analysis

Now that we have explained what content analysis is and how the technique can be used in a variety of different research studies, we can focus our attention on the process one goes through when completing a content analysis. For this analysis, we will pretend that we want to conduct a study examining the level of physical attraction of lead characters in situation comedies during prime-time television. According to Neuendorf (2002), there are nine steps that a content analyst must complete to correctly conduct a content analysis: (1) theory and rationale, (2) conceptualization, (3) operationalization, (4) coding schemes, (5) sampling, (6) training and pilot reliability, (7) coding, (8) final reliability, and (9) tabulation and reporting. To help us understand the content analysis process, we will examine each of these areas individually.

THEORY AND RATIONALE

Like previous research we have discussed in this book, research in content analysis should be conducted using the scientific method. For this reason, a good content analysis should be theoretically based. The only way to make sure that you can create a strong rationale for your study is to do the necessary library legwork.

In Chapter 2 and Chapter 5 we discussed how to create a rationale for hypotheses and research questions, and this discussion cross-applies when conducting a content analysis as well. If you are going to conduct a content analysis, your hypotheses and research questions must stem from the work previously conducted by other researchers.

For our example of attractiveness of sitcom actors, there is a wealth of information about body shapes, facial characteristics, and even clothing choices. There is no lack of information to help you formulate theoretically based hypotheses and research questions about this topic.

CONCEPTUALIZATION

In Chapter 7, we defined conceptualization as the development and clarification of concepts of your germinal idea (the spark that causes an individual to realize that something new can be researched or measured). This definition is also relevant to our discussion of content analysis. When we conceptualize something, we must determine what variables we want to study and how we can define those variables combining all the necessary characteristics or particulars. There are many ways a researcher can go about defining a specific concept, so you must ensure that your definition is clear from the beginning. The more ambiguous your attempt to define your research variables, the more likely you will finish conducting a study only to realize that you have ended up with nothing to show for your work.

For our example study (attractiveness of sitcom actors), one of the primary concepts a researcher must define is "attractiveness." Should a researcher rate individual actors on a scale of 0 (Someone hit every branch on the ugly tree) to 100 (Oh wow, baby!!!!), which would be a ratio variable? Or should a researcher create more of an ordinal variable where people are separated into three categories: *unattractive*, *average*, *very attractive*? Ultimately, whichever conceptualization a researcher decides to utilize, he or she must be clear about how an actor is categorized. Furthermore, in a study examining the attractiveness of television personalities, one must realize that all sitcom stars are fairly attractive by society standards. Let's face the fact; television networks are not going to be starring Quasimodo in the fall lineup anytime soon. For this reason, your conceptualization of attractiveness may be a little skewed because of the context itself. In essence, you must determine what "attractiveness" means in the context of television sitcoms. More traditional ways of defining attractiveness cannot be used in this study because everyone would fall into the upper end of attraction. So a conceptualization of attractiveness of sitcom actors must take into account that everyone is attractive, but some actors are more attractive than others.

OPERATIONALIZATION

In Chapter 7, we defined operationalization as the detailed description of the research operations or procedures necessary to assign units of analysis to the categories of a variable to represent conceptual properties. When we operationalize a variable in a content analysis, many different questions must be asked. First, a content analyst must determine whether her or his operationalization is consistent with her or his conceptualization of the variable itself. If a researcher's operationalization and conceptualization differ, then he or she will have problems with internal validity, as discussed in Chapter 8. Second, researchers must determine their unit of analysis or the major phenomenon that is being analyzed within a study. In a content analysis, the **unit of analysis** is generally the specific message(s) that a content analyst is coding. There are many different typical units of analysis that a content analyst may opt to use. Keyton (2006) notes that words or phrases; complete thoughts or sentences; themes or a single assertion about some subject; paragraphs in text; message sources (both real and actors); communication acts, behaviors, or processes; advertisements; and television programs, films, or scenes have all been used in mediated research as units of analysis (p. 237). For studies that are more focused on interactional analysis, it is possible that a variety of units of analysis are also going to be utilized: nonverbal behaviors, turns in a conversation, an entire interaction sequence. Ultimately, when determining the appropriate unit of analysis, you must think about how your operationalization determines which unit of analysis is the most appropriate for your specific hypotheses and research questions. For example, maybe you are coding videos of marital conflicts. Do you code each sentence of the conflict, or do you code each spouse's turn during a conflict? Ultimately, if you want to look at micro-level functions of conflicts (i.e., how people interact on a moment-to-moment basis during a conflict), coding each sentence or turn may be useful. However, if you want to code macro-level themes (more overarching themes about conflict in general, not specific behaviors), coding each conflict interaction as one unit of analysis may be useful. Overall, determining your unit of analysis is all part of successful operationalization. You also need to determine which level of measurement (nominal, ordinal, interval, or ratio) is the most appropriate for your conceptualization. Whichever level of measurement you decide to use, you must be clear about how the rating process occurs.

For example, maybe you will define "unattractive" as someone who is overweight, is sporting out-of-date or plain clothing, and/or looks messy or dirty. Although we are not suggesting that people who are overweight are unattractive, we will argue that the lack of portrayals of overweight people in Hollywood indicates that there is this perception among entertainment executives. You may define someone who is "average" as someone who is physically in shape and healthy looking, wears normal clothing, and is clean and kept. Finally, you may define someone who is "very attractive" as someone who has clear muscular definition, wears high-end fashions, and is meticulously groomed (i.e., not a hair is out of place, eyebrows perfectly plucked, and cuticles cut). Once you have a working operationalization of your variable (attractiveness), you can move on to the next stage of a content analysis—creating coding schemes.

CODING SCHEMES

Previously in this chapter, we defined **coding** as the process a researcher goes through to group one's variable of interest in a consistent way. Your coding scheme should stem directly from your operationalization. As a content analyst, you will need to create two products to help you with your content analysis: a codebook and a coding form. A **codebook** is a book that a researcher creates to explain the operationalization in a clear and succinct way. The codebook should be so clear that even a stranger could pick it up and accurately code the phenomenon of interest. Second, you must create a coding form. A **coding form** is a form that contains all of the information in the codebook in a simple check-off sheet to make it easier for coders to code information quickly.

In our example of sitcom attractiveness, Figure 10.1 represents what our codebook may look like. Our codebook has the operationalization discussed in the previous step to help coders understand exactly what we are looking for in our coding of sitcom actors' attractiveness. The codebook also asks for the show's identification number (we will discuss this in more detail in the next step) and for the coder's ID. When conducting a content analysis, it is always important to have multiple coders looking at a set of data. Multiple coders will help you determine whether your codebook is actually useful when coding the communicative phenomenon of interest. Often the coders will read your codebook and have wildly different perceptions of the communicative phenomenon because your codebook is not clear, so you may need to spell some things out more clearly and revise the codebook, which is why we have a training stage in content analysis (more on this in a moment).

The blank coding form (Figure 10.2a) quickly summarizes the information in the codebook. In this case, we have spots for the Show ID, Coder ID, Character Name, and the coding of attractiveness (unattractive, average, and very attractive). Each coding form will look different depending on the codebook used in a given study. Some content analysis codebooks could contain 15–20 pages of information being coded, so the corresponding coding forms could be 5–8 pages in length as well. Because our example study is simple, the coding form is also short. In Figure 10.2b and 10.2c, we see two completed coding forms. In both cases, the coders indicate the Show ID (in this case 3 for *How I Met Your Mother*); the coders indicate their individual coder numbers; the coders indicate the lead actor (Neil Patrick Harris); and the coders rate Neil's level of attractiveness. This example illustrates how a coding form is used. In the long run, coding forms make entering data into a statistical software program much faster.

Sitcom Attractiveness Study

Unit of Data Collection: Each individual who is the lead in a situation comedy.

Show ID: Fill in the show's ID number, as indicated on the television show list provided.

Coder ID: Each coder has received an individual number, please write this number on every sheet.

Character Name: Please provide the name of the character you listed as the lead in each television show.

Character Attractiveness: Please rate each character's physical attractiveness using the following rating scheme:

1. Unattractive: Someone who is overweight, sporting out-of-date or plain clothing, or looks messy or dirty.

2. Average: Someone who is physically in-shape and healthy looking, wears normal clothing, and is clean and kept.

3. Very Attractive: Someone who has clear muscular definition, wears high-end fashions, and is meticulously groomed (i.e., not a hair is out of place, eyebrow not teased, or cuticle uncut).

Figure 10.1 Codebook

a) Coding form

Sitcom Attractiveness Study			
Show ID: _____	Coder: _____		
Character Name	Attraction Level		
	Unattractive	Average	Very Attractive

b) Coder 1

Sitcom Attractiveness Study			
Show ID: _____3_____	Coder:_____1_____		
Character Name	Attraction Level		
	Unattractive	Average	Very Attractive
Neil Patrick Harris			X

c) Coder 2

Sitcom Attractiveness Study			
Show ID: _____3_____	Coder: _____2_____		
Character Name	Attraction Level		
	Unattractive	Average	Very Attractive
Neil Patrick Harris		X	

Figure 10.2 Coding Form

SAMPLING

One of the hardest tasks for content analysts is determining the sample necessary to conduct a study. Although we will discuss the nature of sampling in much greater detail in Chapter 13, we do want to discuss some pertinent sampling issues related to content analysis here. When discussing sampling, there are two important terms to understand: populations and samples. A population is an entire set of objects, observations, or scores that have some characteristic in common. For example, in our example study, the population would include every sitcom on television, whereas a sample is a subset of the larger population. For example, maybe there are 20 sitcoms on television (whole population) and you want to only analyze half of those sitcoms, so you would need to take a sample of 10 sitcoms for your study. Although there are numerous methods for sampling, there is no one way that is the best. However, to ensure that your end results are generalizable, that is, your sample can be said to reflect your population correctly, you should randomly (i.e., every unit of analysis that exists within your population has an equal chance for inclusion in your sample) select your sample. We will discuss random sampling in much more detail in Chapter 13.

TRAINING AND PILOT RELIABILITY

Researchers use **coders** for a wide variety of different reasons, but primarily because it helps maintain objectivity within the study. As researchers, we often spend many hours working on a study prior to the point where we start coding our data. For this reason, we may get to the point where we have spent so much time working on the project that we lose sight of some of the more simple aspects of the project. In other words, we may be so focused looking at the forest (our overall study) that we completely miss the trees (individual pieces of data). For this reason, researchers use coders to look at the data for them. If you have completed the previous step (codebook and coding form) accurately, training your coders should be easy. However, just because we train our coders to examine individual pieces of data does not mean that our data will be coded correctly; for this reason the training process should always include some specific steps: introduction to coding book, sample coding, coding of initial data, initial reliability, retraining, final coding, and final reliability.

Introduction to Coding Book

The first part of coder training is to introduce your coders to the codebook and coding form. You should make sure that you go through the codebook, explaining how each part of the codebook should be used on the coding form. This process should be comprehensive because you want to make sure that your coders will be able to use the codebook accurately.

Sample Coding

Once you have completed your codebook and coding form instruction, it is time to let your coders practice. We recommend having a number of sample pieces of data prepared prior to the coding session that can be used to allow your coders to practice using the coding form. For example, in our sitcom study, maybe you will bring in snippets from dramatic shows instead of sitcoms and have the coders rate the dramatic actors' levels of attraction. Once your coders have completed the sample coding, it is time to go over the results from the sample coding and determine whether everyone is coding the data the same way. For example, if someone codes *White Collar's* Matt Bomer as "very attractive" and someone codes him as "unattractive," you must discuss which one you (as the researcher) would classify him as according to the information in the codebook. These practice sessions are important because it allows the researcher to see where any misunderstandings in the coding process are occurring and correct them.

Coding of Initial Data

Once everyone has coded the practice data, it is time to let your coders work on some real data. However, you do not let them code all of the data initially. You should tell your coders to code a specific number of pieces of data and make sure that they are coding the same pieces of data. Depending on how large your sample is, you may need to have your coders code a few hundred pieces of data initially or as few as 10.

Initial Reliability

Once your coders have had a chance to code some of the initial pieces of data, you must determine whether they are coding the data in a reliable way. In Chapter 8, we focused on the concept of reliability and on determining whether participants fill out a survey in a consistent fashion, but reliability is equally important in determining whether coders are consistent. In content analysis we must determine whether multiple coders are actually perceiving the data in the same way, what researchers call **intercoder reliability**.

Your two research assistants are asked to rate the same sitcom actors as being unattractive, average, or very attractive. As shown in Figure 10.2, Neil Patrick Harris could be rated by one coder as "very attractive" and by the other coder as "average." How do you determine whether the two coders are using the same coding system to determine attractiveness? If the first coder only finds redheads attractive and the second coder does not find redheads attractive, then you will end up with vastly different perspectives on attraction. Although some problems may be corrected during training and practice coding, some issues will only surface once actively coding begins. For this reason, researchers have created a range of different statistical devices to help us determine whether coders are coding information in consistent ways.

So, you ask your two coders to code 10 sitcom actors using the coding form. In Figure 10.3, you can see that your coders coded each of the 10 sitcom actors people as either "V" for very attractive, "A" for average, or "U" for unattractive. The first sitcom actor was coded as "V," very attractive, by Coder 1 and Coder 2, so you have agreement. If both coders find someone very attractive, then we have a match and we can count that as one match on our tally board (seen in Figure 10.3. in the 3 × 3 matrix).

Here are our results from the study. U = Unattractive, A = Average, and V = Very Attractive.

Person:	1	2	3	4	5	6	7	8	9	10
Coder 1:	V	U	A	A	U	U	V	A	V	U
Coder 2:	V	U	A	U	V	U	V	A	U	U

Coder 2	Coder 1		
	Unattractive	Average	Very Attractive
Unattractive			
Average		1	
Very Attractive			1

Figure 10.3 Coding Example

Unfortunately, our coders did not always agree with each other. In fact, the fourth sitcom actor was rated as "A" by Coder 1 and "U" by Coder 2. In this case, you must mark that as a miss in the appropriate box. To do this, you would go to Coder 1 (the columns) and find the "A" column, then go to Coder 2 (the rows) and find the "U" row, and where the two intersect you count that as one occurrence. Ultimately, you will have placed all 10 of the matches or mismatches in the appropriate places on the 3 × 3 grid, which can be seen in Figure 10.4.

Step 1
Once you have all of the matches and mismatches in place, you are ready to calculate the intercoder reliability. Start by adding the columns separately. In the first column (Coder 1 "Unattractive"), Coder 1 agreed with Coder 2 three times about people who were "unattractive," Coder 1 found no one "unattractive" that Coder 2 found "average," and Coder 1 found one person "unattractive" that Coder 2 found "very attractive." In other words, 3 + 0 + 1 = 4 is the column total. You can then repeat this process for all of the columns and then for the rows as well. After you have done the simple addition, you should have a chart that looks like Figure 10.5.

Step 2
Next you must compute the total number of times your two coders agreed, or down the center diagonal (3, 2, 2).
Based on this, the percent of agreement would be 7/10, or 70 percent. If you only use the percentile agreement, then you are using an inflated agreement because it does not take into account the possibility that some of those agreements occurred by chance. To find out what is occurring by chance, you must use the formula in Figure 10.6.

This formula is easy to compute. First, take the row total and then multiply it by the column total. For the first column total (5) and first row total (4), simply multiply the totals by each other (5 × 4 = 20), and then divide that number by the overall total or N(10), so: 20/10 = 2. This process than can then be repeated for the second column total (3) and second row total (2), so: (3 × 2)/10 = 0.6. Repeat the process for the third column total (3) and third row total (3), so: (3 × 3)/10 = 0.9. Finally, simply add the three values together to get the "sum of expected frequencies" (Σef) value, so: $\Sigma ef = 2 + 0.6 + 0.9 = 3.5$.

	Coder 1		
Coder 2	Unattractive	Average	Very Attractive
Unattractive	3	1	1
Average	0	2	0
Very Attractive	1	0	2

Figure 10.4 Coder Totals

	Coder 1			
Coder 2	Unattractive	Average	Very Attractive	SUMS
Unattractive	3	1	1	5
Average	0	2	0	2
Very Attractive	1	0	2	3
SUMS	4	3	3	TOTAL 10

Figure 10.5 Coder Totals

$$\text{Expected Frequency (ef)} = \frac{\text{Row Total} \times \text{Column Total}}{\text{Overall Total}}$$

Figure 10.6 Expected Frequency Formula

Step 3

Once you have obtained your sum of expected frequencies value, you can simply plug everything into the formula in Figure 10.7.

Earlier in this section we calculated the sum of a (Σa) as being 7, we have calculated the sum of expected frequencies (Σef) as 4.1, and we know that the number of participants observed (*N*) in this study was 10. At this point, we have all of the parts we need to complete the formula:

$$\kappa = \frac{\sum a - \sum ef}{N - \sum ef}$$

$$\kappa = \frac{7 - 3.5}{10 - 3.5}$$

$$\kappa = \frac{3.5}{6.5}$$

$$\kappa = 0.5384615385 \text{ or } 0.54$$

So, for this study the consistency to which the two coders rated the attractiveness of situation comedy actors was 0.54. According to Cohen (1960, 1968) if **Cohen's kappa (κ)** is greater than 0.70, the intercoder reliability is satisfactory, and if κ is less than 0.70, the intercoder reliability is not satisfactory. In this example, Cohen's kappa = 0.54, so the intercoder reliability is not considered satisfactory. Here is how you would write up this result using APA.

APA WRITE-UP

Two coders were asked to rate a series of television situation comedy leads using the categories not attractive, average, and very attractive. A total of 10 observations were made. To determine whether our two coders were assessing attraction uniformly, Cohen's kappa was calculated, $\kappa = 0.54$, which is not considered satisfactory.

If you get an initial Cohen's kappa that is unsatisfactory, there could be a number of problems causing this to occur. First, your codebook could be flawed at either the conceptual or the operational level. If this is the case, you should rethink how you are conceptualizing and/ or operationalizing your variables in the study. Second, your codebook could be confusing your coders, which could be causing them to miscode specific communicative behaviors. If this is the case, you may need to revise the codebook to make it clearer for your coders. Third, one of your coders could not be following the codebook or misusing the coding form. If your low intercoder reliability results from either the second or the third problem, retraining is probably necessary.

$$\text{Cohen's Kappa (K)} = \frac{\Sigma a - \Sigma ef}{N - \Sigma ef}$$

Figure 10.7 Cohen's Kappa Formula

Retraining

Once you have determined where the coding problem is occurring (if you have a low inter-coder reliability), you must retrain your coders to correct any mistakes. If one of your coders is simply refusing to follow the codebook, you may want to consider simply removing the coder from the project. During the retraining, you should go through all of the data that have been coded and discuss why the coders coded the data the way they have. In other words, ask Coder 1 why he finds Neil Patrick Harris "very attractive," and then ask Coder 2 why she finds Neil Patrick Harris only "average." Often during the retraining phase you will realize that there could be legitimate reasons why your coders disagree. If you end up in a situation where your coders disagree about a coding, you may need to utilize a third coder to break the tie. Often, the researcher functions as the third coder. Once you have everyone back on the same track, it is time to let your coders finish coding all of the data.

Final Coding

The final coding of the data should be overseen closely by the researcher to ensure the most accurate results. Neuendorf (2002) warns that four problems may surface during coding: coder misinterpretations, coder inattention, coder fatigue, and recording errors. First, despite all of your training and the exactness of your codebook, it is always possible that a *coder may misinterpret a piece of data.* Although you do not want to influence a coder's decision about her or his coding, you may want to have them recheck the data to see whether they coded it accurately without telling the coder where you think the problem lies. Second, a *coder may simply wander off mentally while coding,* which can cause errors in her or his coding. We all have moments when our minds wander for a second. If a coder is coding long, detailed conversations, he or she may miss something because he or she simply stops paying attention. Coder inattention often goes along with *coder fatigue,* when a coder gets so tired from coding that he or she starts to simply lose track of what he or she is doing. You may walk into the room where your coders are hard at work and see one of your coders coding the same piece of data for the third time. Coders often wish to finish the coding more than they desire to do the coding correctly. As the researcher, you may have to tell your coder to stop coding for the day or at least take a break and get some caffeine. Finally, all *coders will make mistakes when coding.* The mistake could be as simple as placing their coder number in the spot where the episode number should be. Other coders may skip a question on the coding form, which

Coding Tested	Reliability
Brummans & Miller (2004)	
Independent Variable (High vs. Low Ambiguity)	
Dependent Variable (Effects of Ambiguity on Initiative Success)	Cohen's Kappa = 0.86 Cohen's Kappa = 0.70
Boiarsky, Long, & Thayer (1999)	
Content Pacing (Existence of a topic shift)	
Sound Effects (Counted number of effects)	Cohen's Kappa = 0.77–0.87
Visual Pacing (Counted number of cuts, wipes, and fads/dissolves)	Pearson Correlation = 0.83 − 0.97 Pearson Correlation = 0.85 − 1.0

Figure 10.8 Cohen's Kappa in Articles

throws off all of their codes by one question. As the researcher in charge, your job is to make sure that the coding is done as consistently as possible.

Final Reliability

Once your coders have coded all of the data in your study, it is time to find the final intercoder reliability. To find the intercoder reliability, follow the steps utilized for Cohen's kappa discussed earlier in this chapter. In this chapter, we have used Cohen's kappa, which is useful if you have two coders with no missing data. However, often researchers will opt to use more than two coders, so they would want to use Krippendorff's alpha (Hayes & Krippendorff, 2007).

On the textbook's website there are two articles that utilized forms of content analysis (Boiarsky, Long, & Thayer, 1999; Brummans & Miller, 2004). Although only two articles relied on coding observations, both articles reported Cohen's kappa to demonstrate that the people who were coding behaviors were coding these behaviors consistently. Figure 10.8 is the reporting of Cohen's kappas from the articles on the textbook's website.

You will note that all of the reported Cohen's kappas fall into the satisfactory range, so you can say that the coders in both studies consistently coded the same observations. You will also note that Boiarsky et al. (1999) reported Pearson correlations for sound effects and visual pacing, since those were not categorical observations but the number of times those occurred. We will discuss how to interpret correlations in detail in Chapter 19.

TABULATION AND REPORTING

Once a researcher has completed her or his basic reliability analysis, he or she is ready to summarize the information and place it into a statistical program such as SPSS or Excel. There are many different ways that information can be presented, which will depend largely on the types of variables that you have collected. The last part of this book includes information on how to properly analyze statistical information. All of these different statistical techniques can be used to examine the data collected in a content analysis. To see how various types of content analyses analyze data, look at the various examples discussed in the early part of this book.

Conclusion

Overall, content analysis is one of the most unique and interesting methodologies communication scholars have developed. Whether you are using content analysis to answer questions related to mass communications or human communication, the technique can be telling about how communication occurs. In the next chapter we will look at the third type of quantitative study design, the experiment.

KEY TERMS

Codebook
Coder
Coding
Coding form

Cohen's kappa (κ)
Conceptualization
Content analysis
Intercoder reliability

Operationalization
Unit of analysis

REFERENCES

Ayres, J., & Miura, S. Y. (1981). Construct and predictive validity of instruments for coding relational control communication. *The Western Journal of Speech Communication, 45*, 159–171.

Bichard, S. L. (2006). Building blogs: A multi-dimensional analysis of the distribution of frames on the 2004 presidential candidate web sites. *Journal of Mass Communication Quarterly, 83*, 329–345.

Boiarsky, G., Long, M., & Thayer, G. (1999). Formal features in children's science television: Sound effects, visual pace, and topic shifts. *Communication Research Reports, 16*, 185–192.

Brummans, B. H. J. M., & Miller, K. (2004). The effect of ambiguity on the implementation of a social change initiative. *Communication Research Reports, 21*, 1–10.

Cagle, A., Cox, L., Luoma, K., & Zaphiris, A. (2011). Content analysis of the portrayal of Muslims in American media. *Human Communication, 14*, 1–16.

Cohen, J. (1960). A coefficient of agreement for nominal scales. *Educational and Psychological Measurement, 20*, 37–46.

Cohen, J. (1968). Weighted kappa: Nominal scale agreement with provision for scaled disagreement of partial credit. *Psychological Bulletin, 70*, 213–220.

Comstock, J. M., & Buller, D. B. (1991). Conflict strategies adolescents use with their parents: Testing the cognitive communicator characteristics model. *Journal of Language and Social Psychology, 10*, 47–59.

Courtright, J. A., Millar, F. E., & Rogers-Millar, E. (1979). Domineeringness and dominance: Replication and expansion. *Communication Monographs, 46*, 179–192.

Dovring, K. (1954–1955). Quantiative semantics in 18th century Sweden. *Public Opinion Quarterly, 18*, 389–394.

Ekman, P., & Rosenberg, E. L. (Eds.). (2005). *What the face reveals: Basic and applied studies of spontaneous expression using the Facial Action Coding System (FACS)* (2nd ed.). New York, NY: Oxford University Press.

Feyereisen, P., & Havard, I. (1999). Mental imagery and production of gestures while speaking in younger and older adults. *Journal of Nonverbal Behavior, 23*, 153–171.

Hajek, C., & Giles, H. (2005). Intergroup communication schemas: Cognitive representations of talk with gay men. *Language and Communication, 25*, 161–181. doi:10.1016/j.langcom.2005.01.002

Hajek, C., & Giles, H. (2006). On communicating pride, crying in moves, and recruiting innocent bystanders: The effect of sex on communication schemas activated with gay and heterosexual targets. *Communication Research Reports, 23*, 77–84. doi:10.1080/08824090600668873

Harwood, J. (1998). Young adults' cognitive representations of intergenerational conversations. *Journal of Applied Communication Research, 26*, 13–31.

Hayes, A. F., & Krippendorff, K. (2007). Answering the call for a standard reliability measure for coding data. *Communication Methods and Measures, 1*, 77–89.

Hirdes, W., Woods, R., & Badzinski, D. M. (2009). A content analysis of Jesus merchandise. *Journal of Media & Religion, 8*, 141–157. doi:10.1080/15348420903091030

Howard, D. J., & Kerin, R. A. (2006). Broadening the scope of reference price advertising research: A field study of consumer shopping involvement. *Journal of Marketing, 70*, 185–204.

Keyton, J. (2006). *Communication research: Asking questions, finding answers* (2nd ed.). Boston, MA: McGraw–Hill.

Lachlan, K. A., Smith, S. L., & Tamborini, R. (2005). Models for aggressive behavior: The attributes of violent characters in popular video games. *Communication Studies, 56*, 313–329. doi:10.1080/10510970500319377

McMellon, C. A., & Long, M. (2006). Sympathy, patriotism, and cynicism: Post-9/11 New York City newspaper advertising content and consumer reactions. *Journal of Current Issues and Research in Advertising, 28*, 1–18.

Neuendorf, K. A. (2002). *The content analysis guidebook.* Thousand Oaks, CA: Sage.

Pfau, M., Haigh, M. M., Logsdon, L., Perrine C., Baldwin, J. P., Breitenfeldt, R. E., . . . Romero, R. (2005). Embedded reporting during the invasion and occupation of Iraq: How the embedding of journalists affects television news reports. *Journal of Broadcasting & Electronic Media*, *49*, 468–487.

Riffe, D., Lacy, S., & Fico, F.G. (2005). *Analyzing media messages: Using quantitative content analysis in research* (2nd ed.). Mahwah, NJ: Erlbaum.

Roter, D., Lipkin, M. Jr., & Dorsgaard, A. (1991). Sex differences in patients' and physicians' communication during primary care medical visits. *Medical Care*, *29*, 1083–1093.

Shaffer, D. R., Pegalis, L., & Connell, D. P. (1991). Interactive effects of social context and sex role identity on female self-disclosure during the acquaintance process. *Sex Roles*, *24*, 1–19.

Simcock, P., & Sudbury, L. (2006). The invisible majority? Older models in UK television advertising. *International Journal of Advertising*, *25*, 87–106.

Zhang, E., & Flemming K. (2005). Examination of characteristics of news media under censorship: A content analysis of selected Chinese newspapers' SARS coverage. *Asian Journal of Communication*, *15*, 319–339. doi:10.1080/01292980500261639

Experimental Design

1   Explain the basic reasons researchers conduct experiments.
2   Explain the basic parts of an experiment (random assignment, manipulation of the independent variable, measurement of the dependent variable, and control).
3   Describe the different ways a researcher can go about manipulating an independent variable.
4   Explain different measurement options for the dependent variable.
5   List and explain the four issues researchers must be aware of when attempting to control an experiment (threshold effects, experimenter effects, Hawthorne effect, and intervening variables).
6   Differentiate among the three types of confounding variables (suppressor, reinforcer, and lurker).
7   Describe six external threats to validity associated with experiments (historical flaw, maturation, testing flaw, regression to the mean, selection threat, and attrition).
8   Recognize and explain preexperimental designs.
9   Recognize and explain true experimental designs.

Whether the experiment consisted of adding two chemicals together in a chemistry class to see what would happen or you attempted to make a trash bag float using straws, tape, and birthday candles, we all conducted experiments in our physical science classes in grade school, but most people are not as familiar with the purpose of experiments. The general reason scientists perform experiments is to establish **time order**, or the idea that researchers can establish an exact order to when things occur—T_1 occurred and then T_2 occurred. For example, in a chemistry class you must first combine baking soda and vinegar together (T_1) to get the "volcanic reaction" (T_2) we all remember as children. If you set the box of baking soda and the bottle of vinegar on the counter side by side without combining the two, you will never get the volcanic reaction. Although the social sciences may not be as exact as the physical sciences, social scientists also use experiments in research, so this chapter will examine how communication researchers can use experiments. Time order for experimental research is akin to the age-old question, "Which came first, the chicken or the egg?" Imagine you are a researcher who took on this question. If at the end of your study you have a chicken and you have an egg, would you know which came first? Nope! If, however, you can show scientifically that it is a necessity for an egg to exist prior to a chicken's existence, then you can establish the "time order" of events—first egg, then chicken.

Communication researchers may not be interested in chickens and eggs, but we are interested in whether specific phenomena must occur prior to exhibited communication behaviors. For example, imagine that you wanted to find out whether children playing violent video games will exhibit increased antisocial behavior. In essence, you want to find a time order between playing violent video games (first instance of time) and its effect on antisocial behaviors (second instance of time). Although you could ask for self-reports of video game playing and antisocial behavior, these reports may not be completely accurate and could only show a relationship between the two variables, not a time order between the two variables. For this reason, techniques beyond surveying (as discussed in Chapter 9) have been created to help researchers answer causal relationship questions. In this chapter we will examine what experiments are and why we do them and explore a series of common experimental designs.

What Are Experiments and Why Do We Do Them?

An **experiment** occurs when a researcher purposefully manipulates one or more variables in the hope of seeing how this manipulation affects other variables of interest. In the physical sciences, manipulating a variable is easy. If I want to see the effects of liquid nitrogen on a blown-up balloon, I simply submerge the inflated balloon in liquid nitrogen and watch what happens. Although some communication experiments can be designed in this fashion (placing doughnuts in a room full of people and watching what happens), most require considerably more complicated methods. In this section we will explore three important aspects of experiments: rationale, experimental design aspects, and experimental process.

RATIONALE FOR EXPERIMENTAL RESEARCH

Researchers use experimental research for a variety of reasons, all of which come back to one basic notion: experiments allow for demonstration of causal relationships. In essence, a researcher will conduct an experiment because it allows her or him to establish whether an independent variable causes a change in the dependent variable. In survey-based research, researchers essentially examine differences and relationships that individuals perceive, whereas in experimental research, researchers can examine differences and relationships that they manipulate. This process of examining how independent variables affect dependent variables is called "time order." As discussed earlier, time order is the idea that researchers can establish an exact order as to when things occur. For example, to determine whether playing violent video games leads to antisocial behavior, a researcher could use two groups. One group, the control group, plays a video game that does not contain violence. In the experimental group, the researcher has the participants play a video game that has notable amounts of violence within the game. If the control group's antisocial behavior does not change from a pre- to a posttest but the experimental group's antisocial behavior increases from a pre- to a posttest, then we can ascertain that a time order occurred (first test of antisocial behavior, playing a violent video game, and then second test of antisocial behavior).

Experiments also allow researchers to rule out alternative explanations for their research findings. By having a baseline score (or pretest), the researchers in our video game study are able to know whether the playing of the violent video game led to violence. If the researchers did not have an initial score of antisocial behavior, the antisocial behavior seen after playing the video game could occur for a number of reasons. If the children placed in the nonviolent video game condition have already been exposed to many violent video game images, the results of antisocial behavior between those playing violent versus nonviolent video games may not be different at all. Furthermore, exposure to other violent media could also cause a difference in antisocial behavior. All in all, experiments enable researchers to control what occurs within the testing situation in a way that allows the researchers to either prevent or rule out other explanations for changes seen.

Another reason for performing experiments is to determine whether intervening and antecedent variables are influencing the results. An antecedent variable is a variable that occurs prior to the experiment and may impact the way an independent variable or dependent variable functions. For example, maybe you want to determine whether the type of school a student went to in college affects her or his earning potential after college. Although this may seem straightforward, what you may forget is that an individual's socioeconomic status could impact both her or his choice in colleges and her or his earning potential after college. In other words, there is a third variable that exists outside the simple linear model of how college affects earning potential. As mentioned previously, another variable that can influence the results is an intervening variable. An intervening variable occurs between an independent variable and a dependent variable. We will discuss these in more detail later in this chapter. Since life is often complex and requires complex questions and answers, experiments allow researchers to attempt to find underlying antecedent and intervening variables. If a researcher thinks that socioeconomic status may affect choices of colleges and earning potentials, then he or she could control for socioeconomic status to see how much impact the variable actually has.

The last reason we conduct experiments is to determine whether phenomena happen for some underlying reason or simply by chance. Often when researchers rely solely on survey research, they will find relationships between variables that simply do not mean much. For example, maybe a researcher found a relationship between a physician's use of touch and a patient's perception of that physician's physical attractiveness. In other words, a patient finds a physician more physically attractive if the physician touches them (in a nonsexual way). When another researcher reads these results, he or she may be puzzled as to why such a relationship exists. To determine whether this relationship truly exists or occurred by chance, the researcher may perform an experiment to determine causal relationships. The researcher could train a series of physicians to randomly use touch with some patients (condition 1) and not use touch with other patients (condition 2). The researcher could have participants rate the physicians' physical attractiveness and test whether physicians' use of touch during medical interviews increases patients' perceptions of the physician's physical attractiveness.

ASPECTS OF EXPERIMENTAL DESIGN

When looking at experimental designs, there are a number of aspects that a researcher must constantly attend to while doing research: random assignment, manipulation of the independent variable, measurement of the dependent variable, and control.

Random Assignment

Imagine that we want to determine whether an individual's use of verbal aggression affects an interaction partner's perception of the verbally aggressive person's likability. We may train a group of people called **confederates** (individuals who pretend to be researchers or research participants but are really part of the experimental manipulation) to use or not use specific verbal aggression strategies and then have the confederates interact with the study participants in one-on-one interactions to see whether the participant perceives highly verbally aggressive people differently than people who are not verbally aggressive. If we let people choose whether they wanted to interact with a high versus low verbally aggressive person, we may see some outcomes that are not real. Maybe participants who are verbally aggressive themselves enjoy other verbally aggressive people, so they would flock to the higher verbally aggressive interactant and purposefully rate these people highly likeable. People who are not verbally aggressive may avoid the verbally aggressive condition completely. For this reason, randomly placing participants into experimental conditions becomes extremely important for research to enable an accurate time order of experimental events.

156	675	878	553	748	187	979	592
443	930	530	144	612	638	365	615
523	180	420	666	633	808	839	688
451	487	355	478	604	877	144	810
231	108	790	870	788	805	167	356
607	673	294	674	718	590	892	805
159	326	996	778	216	801	521	598
915	355	275	590	703	315	729	886
221	558	220	223	442	400	993	434
218	780	463	153	399	337	790	619
597	732	240	793	764	807	954	845
773	939	452	524	304	466	291	522
652	256	655	250	574	892	347	835
977	155	481	867	946	533	605	998
865	950	104	605	418	251	439	479
577	107	187	761	410	607	521	481
417	622	607	583	242	995	363	891
510	992	583	246	804	998	134	942
536	437	126	679	619	865	184	315
347	417	879	336	628	375	734	845
499	629	470	452	804	840	814	361
142	486	621	947	128	137	231	478
844	745	872	866	725	297	945	494
543	988	471	207	857	746	694	636
722	978	611	283	907	233	769	442
238	633	576	305	947	105	439	420
505	387	572	733	419	793	170	938
596	302	436	307	674	764	411	940
435	911	107	756	596	211	782	383
612	423	877	240	995	263	586	710
686	811	164	154	924	999	784	539
713	184	310	935	562	328	309	917
303	873	700	393	672	170	490	538
439	301	662	684	898	742	699	149
912	462	111	334	546	271	545	682
706	308	792	134	461	985	330	576
326	797	652	678	743	565	277	354

Figure 11.1 Random Number Table

Random assignment comprises the procedures experimenters use for placing participants into a research condition that ensures that every participant in the sample has an equal chance to be in a research condition. For example, in this case everyone in our sample would have an equal chance of interacting with a highly verbally aggressive partner or a minimally verbally aggressive partner, and it is the experimenter's job to make sure that this randomization occurs.

So, how does one randomly assign people into experimental conditions? There are a number of ways. Maybe for each participant you flip a coin—participants who land on heads interact with the verbally aggressive individual, and participants who land on tails interact with the nonverbally aggressive individual. Maybe you have participants draw a condition out of a hat. You have equal numbers of pieces of paper in a hat labeled "A" for the verbally aggressive condition and "B" for the nonverbally aggressive condition. If a person draws the letter "B," he or she is taken to the room where a nonverbally aggressive interactant is waiting. A third possible way is to use a random number generator or a random number table. Figure 11.1 was created using a random number generator located at http://www.random.org/.

One way to use a random number generator is to create a single column of random numbers and place the estimated number of participants needed in each experimental condition next to the same number of random numbers. For example, if I needed 20 participants in the first condition (verbally aggressive interactant) and 20 participants in the second condition (nonverbally aggressive interactant), then I would place a VA (verbally aggressive) next to the first 20 random numbers and an NVA (nonverbally aggressive) next to the second 20 random numbers (Figure 11.2).

1	156	VA	21	499	NVA
2	443	VA	22	142	NVA
3	523	VA	23	844	NVA
4	451	VA	24	543	NVA
5	231	VA	25	722	NVA
6	607	VA	26	238	NVA
7	159	VA	27	505	NVA
8	915	VA	28	596	NVA
9	221	VA	29	435	NVA
10	218	VA	30	612	NVA
11	597	VA	31	686	NVA
12	773	VA	32	713	NVA
13	652	VA	33	303	NVA
14	977	VA	34	439	NVA
15	865	VA	35	912	NVA
16	577	VA	36	706	NVA
17	417	VA	37	326	NVA
18	510	VA	38	984	NVA
19	536	VA	39	675	NVA
20	347	VA	40	930	NVA

Figure 11.2 Random Number Table

1	142	NVA	21	543	NVA
2	156	VA	22	577	VA
3	159	VA	23	596	NVA
4	218	VA	24	597	VA
5	221	VA	25	607	VA
6	231	VA	26	612	NVA
7	238	NVA	27	652	VA
8	303	NVA	28	675	NVA
9	326	NVA	29	686	NVA
10	347	VA	30	706	NVA
11	417	VA	31	713	NVA
12	435	NVA	32	722	NVA
13	439	NVA	33	773	VA
14	443	VA	34	844	NVA
15	451	VA	35	865	VA
16	499	NVA	36	912	NVA
17	505	NVA	37	915	VA
18	510	VA	38	930	NVA
19	523	VA	39	977	VA
20	536	VA	40	984	NVA

Figure 12.3 Randomized Conditions

If I then took the random numbers and ordered them numerically, I would effectively randomize the order in which we assign people into one of the two conditions. In our example, the first participant in the study is placed in the nonverbally aggressive condition (as seen in Figure 11.3), and then the next 5 are randomly assigned to the verbally aggressive condition. This trend continues until we have placed 40 participants into one of the two conditions.

Manipulation of the Independent Variable

The second major component of experimental design is the **manipulation of the independent variable**. Before defining what we mean by "manipulation of the independent variable," let's look at an example. In Chapter 2, we discussed an experiment conducted by Wrench, Millhouse, and Sharp (2007). In this study, the researchers wanted to see whether the inclusion of humor in preflight safety briefings influenced how people saw the flight attendants. To determine whether humor had an effect on people's perceptions of flight attendants, the researchers created two preflight safety briefing scripts—one with humor and one without humor. In the experiment itself, participants were exposed to either one script or the other and then asked about their perceptions of the flight attendant. We will break this experiment down for you. In this study, Time 1 occurs when the participants are exposed to the preflight safety briefing (humorous vs. standard), and Time 2 occurs as the participants responded to a series of survey questions about the flight attendants.

Ultimately, experimental designs involve manipulating an independent variable and seeing how that manipulation affects a dependent variable. By manipulating we mean that a researcher purposefully alters or changes the independent variable to see whether this alteration in the independent variable has an effect on the dependent variable. In our example in the previous paragraph, the researchers "altered" a standard preflight safety briefing to include humor. By creating one preflight safety briefing with humor and one without humor (manipulation of the independent variable), the researchers could see whether the inclusion of humor could affect people's perceptions of their flight attendants (dependent variable). The goal of this experiment is to test for differences between the two experimental conditions (humorous preflight safety briefing and standard preflight safety briefing). Now that we have introduced you to the basic components of independent variable manipulation, we will look at a number of ways that communication researchers can manipulate an independent variable.

First, researchers can provide some participants a specific stimulus or phenomenon (**experimental group**) and not give the same stimulus or phenomenon to the other participants (**control group**). In a study conducted by Tamborini, Eastin, Skalski, Lachlan, Fediuk, and Brady (2004), the researchers wanted to examine the effect that video games had on hostile thoughts. At the beginning of the semester, participants completed a self-report questionnaire designed to measure prior video game use and hostile thoughts. Participants were then randomly assigned to one of four conditions: (1) playing a violent virtual reality video game, (2) playing a standard violent video game, (3) observing a violent video game, and (4) observing a nonviolent video game. Ultimately, people in the first three conditions all experienced elevated hostile thoughts after engaging with or watching violent video games, but not in the fourth condition, where a nonviolent video game was observed.

Second, researchers can rely on written materials to manipulate people. For example, Stewart (1994) wanted to examine whether an individual's expressed religious identity would add credibility to a speaker. To examine this research question, Stewart used written texts to introduce participants to a potential speaker. In one of the texts, Stewart mentioned that the speaker was "a regular churchgoer, is very active in church functions, and often publicly expresses his belief that prayer is important in achieving one's professional goals," whereas in the second introduction no mention of religion was made at all. Stewart ultimately found that participants perceived the potential speaker whose introduction contained religious content as more credible.

A third way of manipulating an independent variable in communication research is similar to the written method, but instead of using a written text, you record (using either audio or video) the manipulation. In the article by Weber, Fornash, Corrigan, and Neupauer (2003) contained on the textbook's website, the researchers recorded two public relations lectures. In the first lecture (the control), the researchers used examples that are traditionally found in public relations textbooks. In the second lecture (the experimental condition), the researchers used more modern examples of public relations that are not typically found in textbooks. The goal of this study was to determine whether the use of more modern, updated examples helps students score higher on a quiz.

Another prominent way of manipulating an independent variable is the use of confederates. A confederate is an individual who, without the participants' knowledge, is actually part of the experiment being conducted. An example of confederate use was found in a study conducted by Guéguen and De Gail (2003). Guéguen and De Gail had eight confederates (four females and four males) randomly walk by 800 customers in a supermarket (400 females and 400 males) and randomly smile or not smile at the person. Immediately after this interaction, a second confederate (who was blind to whether smiling or not smiling had occurred) holding a portfolio and package of computer disks would "accidentally" drop the disks. Ultimately, the study wanted to determine whether the smiling of the first confederate would lead the participant to help the second confederate. Overall, this study did find that smiling led to an increase in helping behavior.

The last major way in which communication researchers manipulate independent variables is through hypothetical scenarios and role-playing activities. In this type of manipulation, researchers give the participants a scenario and then the participants are asked to role-play a situation as if they actually were taking part in the fictionalized scenario. In a study by Wiener and Doescher (1994), the researchers wanted to determine the effect that expectation would have on willingness to comply with a request. The researchers placed 84 undergraduates into one of two conditions—high expectation or low expectation. The scenario given to the participants was the need to put an energy-regulating device on their apartment air-conditioning unit. In the high-expectation group, the participants were told that 70 percent of the people within their state had already indicated a willingness to add the energy-regulating device to their air conditioning units; the low-expectation group was told that only 15 percent would add the device. The participants were then asked whether they would be willing to add the device to their air conditioners. Of the participants in the high-expectation condition, 84 percent said they would add the device, compared to only 59 percent of the participants in the low-expectation group.

Typically, when people think about independent variable manipulation it is easy to think of putting people into either an experimental condition or a control condition. However, as we have seen in these examples, a wide variety of different experimental forms are possible. Some experiments have more than two levels (control vs. experimental), and other experiments manipulate more than one independent variable. When an individual attempts to manipulate more than one independent variable, he or she is using a **factorial experiment design**. In the study by Guéguen and De Gail (2003), the researchers examined one dependent variable, smiling versus nonsmiling, but they also examined the impact of the biological sex of the confederate who smiled and the biological sex of the confederate who dropped her or his portfolio and disks. In this case, we have what is called a 2 × 2 × 2 factorial experimental design. Each variable in this study (smiling, confederate who smiles biological sex, and confederate who drops materials biological sex) is represented by one of the 2's in the factorial design. The numeral 2 is used because each variable only has two levels (smiling vs. not smiling, female vs. male for confederate 1, and female vs. male for confederate 2). If we broadened this study to examine the impact that a third smiling characteristic, frowning, has on the study, then the study would become a 3 × 2 × 2 factorial experimental design because the smiling variable would be manipulated three different ways (frowning, smiling, and nonemotion). If this had been the case, our experimental design would look like Figure 11.4.

	Female Confederate Smiling Condition		Male Confederate Smiling Condition	
	Female Confederate Dropping Condition	**Male Confederate Dropping Condition**	**Female Confederate Dropping Condition**	**Male Confederate Dropping Condition**
Smile at Participant				
Frown at Participant				
Show no Emotion Towards Participant				

Figure 12.4 Factorial Design

In essence, we end up with 12 experimental conditions being compared to each other. The more independent variables a researcher utilizes, the more participants he or she must have in a study. For statistical purposes, each experimental condition should have no fewer than 10 participants, but it is safer to have closer to 50 participants in each condition. The more factors (independent variables) a researcher wants to examine, the more complicated the design will become and the more participants a researcher will ultimately need to complete the experiment. For example, if we then decide to add another independent variable to the study (participant's biological sex), we now have 24 experimental conditions in this example. For this reason, most experiments are greatly limited in the number of independent variables studied because it is not always realistic to recruit enormous samples for research.

Measurement of the Dependent Variable

The third major component of experimental design is the measurement of the dependent variable. In all three of the previous experiments discussed in this chapter (video game violence and antisocial behavior; verbal aggression and likability; and medication and communication apprehension (CA)), the dependent variable could easily be measured by having a participant fill out a research scale. In the impact of violent video games on antisocial behavior, after a participant is exposed to the video game we could have the participant fill out a research measure examining levels of desire to engage in antisocial behavior. In the impact of verbal aggression on likability, after a participant interacted with the verbally aggressive or the nonverbally aggressive person the researchers could have the participant fill out a scale measuring their interactant's likability. By doing this, researchers can measure the extent to which participants like both verbally aggressive and nonverbally aggressive people. In the third example, the dependent variable is CA and can easily be measured by having participants fill out the PRCA-24 before the participants take the medication or placebo and then fill it out again after they have been on the medication or placebo for a month. In all three of these studies, the dependent variable was measured by having the participants fill out a pen-and-paper scale.

However, there are other, more observational ways to measure dependent variables. In the first example, after exposing a group of children to both violent and nonviolent video games, we could place all of them in a room together and watch for antisocial interaction behaviors. If the participants exposed to the violent video games are more likely to initiate antisocial behavioral patterns than those participants exposed to nonviolent video games, we would establish a time order between exposure and outcome. If you wanted to measure likability of verbally aggressive versus nonverbally aggressive interactants, you could watch the participants' nonverbal communicative behavior during the interaction. Participants who are attracted to their interaction partners will exhibit more nonverbally immediate behaviors than those participants who are not attracted to their interaction partners. Finally, maybe you want to examine whether being on an antianxiety medication or a placebo changes a person's heart rate while giving an impromptu speech. In this case, you would hook a person up to a heart monitor and record her or his heart rate while giving the impromptu speech before and after the manipulation of the independent variable. Ultimately, when determining how to measure a dependent variable, a researcher must ask her- or himself what the basic purpose of the study is and what would be the most efficient way to determine whether the independent variable manipulation is causing a change in the dependent variable.

One extremely important concept must be discussed with reference to measuring dependent variables. If a dependent variable is to change as a result of time order, the manipulation of the independent variable must be substantial enough to cause a change. For example, some people may argue that video games such as *Frogger* and *PacMan* are violent. However, will exposing children to *Frogger* and *PacMan* lead to increases in antisocial behavior? Probably not. If exposing children to *Frogger* and *PacMan* are not adequate independent variable manipulations to cause a change in the dependent variable, exposing children to more obviously violent games such as *Doom*, *Grand Theft Auto*, *Call of Duty*, and *Mortal Combat* may be necessary to see changes in the dependent variable. Ultimately, if the manipulation of the independent variable is not substantial, the experiment will fail to see changes in the dependent variable that may actually exist.

Controlling an Experiment

One of the most difficult aspects of conducting experiments is attempting to make sure that what a researcher is examining with an experiment is actually being examined. For example, what if you are trying to manipulate the types of conflicts a married couple engages in only to find out that you are actually manipulating the compliance-gaining strategies a couple uses instead? For this reason, researchers must be careful to avoid influencing an experiment in a way not being measured in the experiment itself. Researchers must be aware of a number of different issues that can affect the outcome of an experiment: threshold effects, experimenter effects, the Hawthorne effect, and intervening variables.

Threshold Effects
The first issue that researchers must be keenly aware of is the possibility of threshold effects. A **threshold effect** occurs when changes in a specific dependent variable are only seen after an independent variable reaches a certain level. For example, maybe a person only decreases her or his perception of an interactant's likability when the interactant becomes absurdly verbally aggressive, so low levels of verbal aggression do not impact the interactant's likability. Maybe high levels of antianxiety medication decrease an individual's level of CA but low dosages change nothing. In both of these examples there is a threshold or minimum level that the independent variable must meet before it will affect the dependent variable.

Experimenter Effects
The second, and often the most problematic, issue that can affect the outcome of an experiment is experimenter effects. **Experimenter effects** are effects caused unknowingly by the experimenter on the participants. Experimenters often will accidentally influence research results without even knowing that they are doing so. For example, in the placebo versus antianxiety medicine study, it is possible that a researcher actually informs the participants slightly differently. This is not to say that the experimenter is purposefully trying to slant the results in one way or the other, but people often unconsciously change their behavior in ways that can affect the results of an experiment. For this reason, a technique has been developed by researchers called the double-blind study. In a double-blind study, neither the researcher nor the participant knows whether the participant is receiving the actual manipulation (antianxiety medication) or a fake manipulation (placebo).

Hawthorne effect
The third problematic area researchers must be aware of is called the Hawthorne effect. The **Hawthorne effect** gets its name from a series of experiments conducted at the Hawthorne Works of Western Electric Company in Chicago from 1924 to 1932. In this set of studies, the researchers initially determined whether the level of lighting in an electric company affected the productivity level of the employees. In the original study, the researchers manipulated the lighting in the electric company (independent variable) to see whether it influenced worker output (dependent variable). Ultimately, the researchers were astonished when they

determined that their manipulation of the lighting did nothing to affect productivity because worker output increased in all of the lighting conditions. When the experiment was complete, the researchers realized that the lighting had not changed the worker output, but hovering over the workers and watching what they were doing had increased the worker output. This same problem can exist in other experiments as well, so researchers have adopted a number of safeguards to help prevent the Hawthorne effect from occurring in an experiment. First, researchers will often try to observe participants through video monitoring systems or one-way mirrors, so the participants do not know when they are being watched. Researchers will also deceive participants about the actual nature of the study being conducted. Whereas there clearly are ethical issues that must be addressed (in Chapter 3), deception can be useful when used in a fashion to help a researcher attain clear and consistent results. Other researchers will throw in blank or dummy experiments to throw a participant off the actual nature of the study. In the verbal aggression study, maybe the researcher will have the participants fill out a wide range of scales about the personality of the confederate interactant. Although the researcher is attempting to look at likability, the researcher may also ask questions about the use of humor, immediacy, and so on.

Extraneous variables

The last problem that must be overcome when conducting experiments is to be aware that other variables may be influencing the outcome of your experiment. In any experiment there can be a series of what are called **extraneous variables**—variables not being measured in your study but affecting your results. There are two major categories of extraneous variable: intervening and confounding. Intervening or mediating variables, often called latent variables, are variables that intervene between the independent variable and the dependent variable. For example, if you want to determine the effects of drinking in college on grades, it is possible that the two variables are not going to tell you the complete picture. While it is true that there may be a negative relationship between alcohol consumption in college and grades, it is also possible that what is really being seen is that alcohol consumption is a measure of partying at school, which means that a person is spending less time going to class and studying. As a result of spending less time in class and studying, the participants' grades may start to suffer. In other words, alcohol consumption does not necessarily cause grades to slip in college, but it may create the circumstances (not going to class and not studying) that lead to slipping grades. In this example, the variables identified as not going to class and not studying are examples of intervening variables.

Confounding variables, by contrast, are variables that obscure the effects of your independent variable. There are three types of confounding variables that often occur in research: suppressor, reinforcer, and lurker. **Suppressor variables** are variables that suppress or reduce the effect of the independent variable on the dependent variable. For example, research has shown us that introverts are more likely to have higher scores of CA than extraverted people. One cause of this could be that introverts are less likely to communicate innately, so they do not end up gaining as much experience communicating with other people. This lack of experience could be a factor in causing introverts to be anxious when interacting with people. The variable "lack of experience" could be seen as a suppressor variable.

The second category of confounding variable is a **reinforcer variable**. For example, research has shown that extraverted people are more communicatively competent. Does this mean that extraverts are born with more information on how to communicate in a competent way than introverts? Probably not. However, extraverted people do probably have more experience interacting with other people, so they have more opportunities to develop competent communicative behaviors. In this case, experience is seen as a reinforcer variable.

The final type of confounding variable is a **lurker variable**, or a variable that explains both the independent variable and the dependent variable. For example, maybe a study finds that there is a relationship between CA and the number of friends a person has. However, it is possible that a third variable, introversion, is actually causing the other two variables to occur in the first place. In this example, introversion is a lurker variable because it is not a variable being directly studied, but is ultimately responsible for the scores of both the independent variable (CA) and the dependent variable (number of friends).

CONDUCTING AN EXPERIMENT

Now that we have examined the key components of experiments and the rationale for experiments, we can focus on the basic process of performing an experiment. The basic process that all researchers go through when conducting an experiment is as follows: introduce the experiment to the participant and obtain consent, randomly assign people to different conditions, manipulate the independent variable, measure the dependent variable, and debrief the participants when the experiment is completed.

Introducing the Experiment and Obtaining Consent

The first part of any actual experiment involves explaining to a participant what an experiment will actually entail. Although researchers may use deception to prevent the participants from knowing what the researcher is actually examining, some cover story will be given to the participants. One reason researchers use deception when explaining what an experiment is examining is to prevent what Joseph Masling (1966) calls the "screw-you" effect. When participants know what a researcher is looking for, many participants will try to answer questions contrary to how they feel to throw off the experiment. We will talk more about the ethical issues of deception in Chapter 13.

The second part of the initial part of an experiment is obtaining consent. In the United States, the federal government has mandated that anyone who participates in a research experiment should give her or his consent. If someone cannot give consent (e.g., children or mentally impaired individuals), a legal guardian is needed to give consent. Obtaining consent entails explaining any actual risks involved in a study. For the most part, communication research does not involve physical risks, but many researchers examine sensitive topics that could cause people psychological distress. To avoid putting participants in a situation that would make them feel uncomfortable, participants must be informed of their legal rights (e.g., ability to leave the experiment at any time) and the risks involved with the study. As discussed in Chapter 3, every university has an IRB that researchers must comply with to carry out research of any kind (both experimental and nonexperimental).

Random Assignment

The second part to conducting an experiment is to randomly assign people to a treatment group. Earlier in this chapter, we discussed in much greater detail a number of ways to randomly assign people to different treatment groups. Once the participants are in a group, any pretesting of the dependent variable that is necessary for the experiment will be conducted.

Manipulate the Independent Variable

Once participants have been placed into the different conditions of an experiment, a researcher will manipulate the independent variable. All of the experimental examples discussed in this chapter thus far have involved manipulating an independent variable. Whether studying interactions with verbally aggressive or nonverbally aggressive persons or the effects of being given a placebo or antianxiety medication, a researcher will attempt to alter the independent variable in a way that could cause a change in the dependent variable. One way to ensure that the participants are actually seeing the manipulation of the dependent variable is to perform a manipulation check.

A **manipulation check** is a procedure where a researcher inserts a quantitative measurement into a study to determine whether different conditions portray the independent variable differently. For example, in a study that had participants interacting with confederates who did or did not communicate verbally aggressively, a researcher could have the participants fill out the verbal aggression scale on the confederates. If the researcher found that the participants did not perceive the verbal aggression and nonverbal aggression interactants differently with regard to the verbal aggression levels, then the results of the study will be flawed. If, however, your participants rate the verbally aggressive confederate as being more verbally aggressive than the nonverbally aggressive confederate, then you can say that your manipulation of verbal aggression was good.

For example, in the Wrench et al. (2007) study examining humorous versus standard preflight safety briefings, the researchers created the two scripts, but how do they know people perceive the humorous script as actually humorous? The three authors of the study could all have the same sense of humor, which could differ from their participants' senses of humor. To ensure that the participants perceived the humorous script as funny and the standard script as not funny, the researchers asked a single question that participants answered at the end of the survey, "On a scale of '0' not humorous to '9' very humorous, indicate how humorous you found the flight attendant's preflight briefing." By including this question, the researchers could then determine whether the two groups actually viewed the humorousness of the script differently. By checking to see whether the manipulation occurred, the researchers are able to know whether the results they receive are actually a result of their manipulation of the independent variable (in this case the preflight safety briefing).

Measure the Dependent Variable

Once you have manipulated the independent variable, the next step in performing an experiment is to measure the dependent variable. As mentioned previously, there are a number of ways to measure a dependent variable, and a researcher must be careful when measuring a dependent variable that the measure is both reliable and valid (as discussed in Chapter 8).

Debriefing

The last part of an experiment occurs after a dependent variable has been measured for the last time. In the **debriefing** part of an experiment, a researcher first corrects any deception that was used at the beginning of an experiment. Researchers realize that it is unethical to let a research participant complete a study and not know what was done to them. In addition to correcting deception, researchers should also reaffirm the value of the research study and the participants' addition to the research process. Finally, a researcher may ask a couple of pointed question to determine whether a participant knowingly changed her or his results based on what he or she thought the experiment was testing. After a participant has been debriefed, participants are usually open to admitting that they may have slanted their answers in a particular direction because they thought it was what the researcher actually wanted to know ("demand characteristics"). Another problem that can also be noted during an experimental debriefing is whether a participant was more anxious than usual because he or she knew that the researcher was evaluating her or his behavior. Many people behave abnormally as a result of the contrived evaluation situation that many research projects create (remember the Hawthorne effect). By listening to participants' thoughts about the research process after the fact, a researcher can determine whether either of these problems has occurred.

Threats to Experimental Validity

In this section, we will examine six threats to the validity of an experiment, derived from the work by Campbell and Stanley (1963): historical flaw, maturation, testing flaw, regression to the mean, selection threat, and attrition.

HISTORICAL FLAW

The first validity threat that can affect an experiment is the historical flaw. When a **historical flaw** occurs, some historical event has caused the sample to change in a way that is not measurable. For example, in a study conducted after September 11, 2001, terrorist attacks in the United States, a researcher who wanted to see how attuned participants were to crisis communication could have a sample more attuned to crisis communication than would have occurred normally. Often historical flaws can be mentioned as a limitation, but other times the historical flaw may not even be known to the researcher.

MATURATION

A second threat to a study's validity is called maturation. **Maturation** involves changes to a sample that occur naturally as a result of time. In essence, the maturation threat occurs because it is possible that a portion of the estimated change is not a result of our independent variable manipulations, but a result of the passage of time between the first measure of a dependent variable and following measures. Many experiments can last for decades as a researcher collects pertinent data. If a researcher has a sample over a long period of time, some natural changes may occur that are outside the scope of the experiment. For example, many studies that involved large-scale pharmaceutical variables last 5 to 10 years. In a 10-year period, people naturally change. A person who was active and fit at 30 may have gained weight and be a couch potato at 40 and skew the results of the study. Overall, researchers must collect a number of data indicators at the beginning of a study to determine whether the participants have drastically changed by the time they reached the end of the study.

TESTING FLAW

The third threat to validity that can exist in an experiment is what is called a **testing flaw**. As we have discussed previously in this chapter, one way to determine whether an independent variable alters a dependent variable is to get a **baseline** score of the dependent variable at Time 1, manipulate the independent variable, and then get a second score of the dependent variable at Time 2. Unfortunately, changes in the score at Time 2 can occur simply because a score was taken at Time 1. So a researcher must be concerned with whether a score on a dependent variable occurs as a result of multiple administration of the dependent variable. We will look at a couple of experimental designs that attempt to control for this problem later in this chapter.

REGRESSION TO THE MEAN

The fourth validity threat that can occur in an experiment is referred to as a regression to the mean. A **regression to the mean** is the tendency for extreme scorers on one measurement to move (regress) closer to the mean on a later measurement, causing a change that would normally not happen in the population. For example, imagine you are teaching a class; you have 10 students take a midterm examination (Time 1) and you get the following scores: 0, 84, 85, 79, 89, 85, 86, 87, 82, 100. You would have a mean of 77.7 and a standard deviation of 27.86. If you then gave the test a second time a week later (Time 2), you may naturally see a shift in the scores toward the mean (72, 85, 86, 79, 89, 86, 86, 88, 82, 100), which would give you a mean of 85.3 and a standard deviation of 7.20. Note that from Time 1 to Time 2 the standard deviation got smaller; this occurs because the scores on the test started to clump more around the mean, or regressed to the mean.

In Figure 11.5 you can see the example in graph form. In the first graph, the sample is left skewed, whereas the second graph looks more bell shaped. The first time the students took the test, their scores were further apart from the mean and regressed toward the mean the second time they took the test.

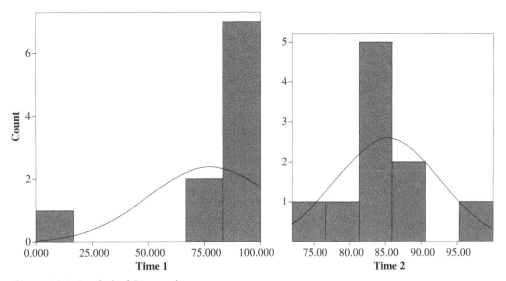

Figure 11.5 Statistical Regression

SELECTION THREAT

The fifth threat to experimental validity is the selection threat. The **selection threat** asks whether the participants who have selected to participate in an experiment have some characteristic that could slant the findings of the study. For example, a lot of researchers rely on college students in need of extra credit for participation in research studies. Are people who desperately need extra credit the most accurate sample when trying to make generalizations about the general population?

ATTRITION

The last validity threat that experiments can have is called attrition. **Attrition** is simply the number of participants who have left a study since it began. Although short-term studies are not generally affected by attrition, long-term studies often can be greatly affected by the drop-out rate of the participants. One of the authors of this book started a study with 200 participants at Time 1 and was only able to get 36 participants to continue the study at Time 2. A researcher cannot generalize results from 36 participants accurately because only 16 percent of the initial sample still agreed to participate at Time 2. Attrition is one of those factors that cannot be accurately predicted, but can have a devastating impact on the overall outcome of a study. One of the major problems with attrition occurs if the participants who dropped out of a study are systematically different from those participants who remained in the study.

Although these six validity threats are specifically related to experimental procedures, we should remind you that we discussed a number of other validity threats in Chapter 8. All of the major threats to validity discussed in Chapter 8 (inadequate preoperational explication of concepts, mono-operation bias, interaction of different treatments, interaction of testing and treatment, restricted generalizability across constructs, confounding constructs and levels of constructs, and social threats to validity) are also validity threats to experiments. Now that we have explored some of the validity threats experiments can face, we will focus our attention on some common experimental designs.

Replication

At times researchers may identify a study with potential validity problems or a study that produced results inconsistent with other studies or apply a theory to new contexts or populations to determine the generalizability to other groups or settings. **Replication** involves conducting additional research on an existing topic for one of several reasons: (1) to determine whether the original results were by error or remain constant; (2) to examine the variable using new population characteristics; (3) to apply results from previous studies to new situations; and (4) to combine the results of two or more previous studies in developing new research directions.

Four primary types of replication are conducted. Each is distinguished by the researcher's decision to alter instrumentation or methods, samples, and data analysis procedures. **Literal replication** involves duplicating a previous study by keeping the instrumentation, experimental procedures, and the sample as similar as possible to the original study. In **operational replication**, the researcher maintains similar samples and methods, but the instrumentation or surveys used in the study are changed. **Instrumental replication** involves measuring the dependent variable the same way as in the initial study, but changes in the independent variable are made to see whether a different operationalization of experimental procedures will yield similar results. Finally, **constructive replication** refers to a researcher's decision to use entirely new instrumentation, methods or procedures, sample, and data analysis techniques to duplicate the conceptual foundation of a previous study.

Replication is essential for testing and supporting various communication theories. Recall the discussion of central limits theorem earlier in this chapter. We pointed out that data collected from multiple samples will yield results that are more generalizable to the population. The sample principle of probability applies to replication. Repeated studies focusing on the same variable or phenomenon assist communication scholars in building strong theoretical foundations for our discipline. Authors often provide suggestions for ways in which their studies can be replicated when discussing the limitations. However, few researchers attempt to replicate original studies. As students of research methods, you may want to consider ways in which you can replicate and build on previous research as you define your own interests.

Common Experimental Designs

We can now examine the three types of experimental designs that researchers work with (preexperimental, quasi-experimental, and true experimental). However, we must introduce a few notation devices that researchers commonly use to aid a discussion of research designs. Over the next few pages, you will be shown a series of characters that look like mathematical formulas followed by a paragraph example. The characters in the "formula" are there to help illustrate how a specific experimental design is conducted. The characters we will use to illustrate the experimental designs are "O," "X," "R," "N," and "C." When you see the letter "O" in an illustrated experimental design, the "O" is an observation of the dependent variable being made by a researcher. When you see the letter "X" in an illustrated experimental design, the "X" is any time a researcher has manipulated the independent variable. You will often see "X" followed by a subscript 1 or 0. If the X is followed by a subscript 1 (X_1), then the independent variable has been manipulated and that line represents an experimental condition. If the X is followed by a subscript 0 (X_0), then the independent variable has not been manipulated. When you see the letter "R" in an illustrated experimental design, the "R" illustrates the fact that people within that experimental design have been randomized into the different treatment conditions. When you see the letter "N" in an illustrated experimental design, the "N" illustrates the fact that people within that experimental design have not been randomized into the different treatment conditions. Finally, when you see the letter "C" in an illustrated experimental design, the "C" represents the idea that participants have been placed into groups based on a cutoff score. For example, everyone above the mean is in group one and everyone below the mean is in group two (this could also be done using the median). Now that we have the basic terminology necessary for examining the different experimental designs, we can start by looking at the preexperimental designs. We will demonstrate how each different design can be used to answer one common research question in many different ways. The example used in the next few pages will be as follows: a researcher wants to find out whether attending a 6-hour workshop on using humor in the classroom will affect how students perceive their teacher's communication competence.

PREEXPERIMENTAL DESIGNS

One-Shot Case Study

$$N\,X_1 \rightarrow O$$

In the one-shot case study design, a researcher uses a nonrandomized sample (N), manipulates the independent variable (X_1), and then measures how people score on the dependent variable (O). In this first example, the researcher would send a group of teachers to a 6-hour workshop on using humor in the classroom (X_1) and then have the teachers' students fill out a communication competence scale on the teachers (O). The problem with this design is that we can never say with complete confidence that our manipulation of the independent variable caused the measurement of the dependent variable.

One-Group Pretest Posttest Design

$$N \, O_1 \rightarrow X_1 \rightarrow O_2$$

In the one-group pretest–posttest design, a researcher uses a nonrandomized sample (N), gives the sample a pretest (O_1), manipulates the independent variable (X_1), and then gives the sample a posttest (O_2). In this example, a researcher would have a teacher's students fill out the communication competence (O_1), then send the teacher to the 6-hour workshop on how to use humor in training (X_1), and then resurvey the students to see if their perception of the teacher has changed (O_2). This design is also somewhat problematic because it is easy for a researcher to miss intervening and confounding variables in this design of testing effects.

Static Group Comparisons

$$N \, X_1 \rightarrow O$$

$$N \, X_0 \rightarrow O_1$$

In the static group comparisons design, a researcher uses a nonrandomized sample (N), manipulates the independent variable (X_1), and then measures how people score on the dependent variable (O). Furthermore, the researcher does not manipulate the independent variable of a second group or the control group (X_0), but does measure the dependent variable (O_1).

In this example, a researcher has two groups: an experimental group and a control group. The researcher would send one teacher through the 6-hour workshop on using humor in the classroom (X_1) and not send another teacher through the 6-hour workshop (X_0). After the teacher in the first group has gone through the workshop, the researcher has the students in both groups fill out a communication competence scale on both teachers (O_1). This manipulation is called a static group comparison because the two groups already exist and were not created for the experimental purpose. The problem with this design is that there exists the possibility of prior relationships between the teacher and students, a history of maturation, and other experimental flaws that could prevent a researcher from attaining clear, useful results. For example, if the teacher sent to the workshop was more communicatively competent to begin with, there would be no way to determine whether one uses this preexperimental design.

QUASI-EXPERIMENTAL DESIGNS

A **quasi-experimental design** mirrors an experimental design but lacks randomization (Cook & Campbell, 1979). The next four types of designs are different perspectives on how to design a quasi-experiment.

Pretest–Posttest Design

$$N\,O_1 \rightarrow X_1 \rightarrow O_2$$

$$N\,O_1 \quad O_2$$

The purpose of this design is to determine whether the effect of a pretest can account for the scores a person may achieve on a posttest. In this design, a researcher either creates two groups or uses two stagnant groups. In the manipulation group, a researcher measures the dependent variable (O_1), followed by a manipulation of the independent variable (X_1), and follows that by another measurement of the dependent variable (O_2). In the control group, a researcher measures the dependent variable (O_1) and then measures the dependent variable (O_2) a second time without any kind of manipulation in between.

In the first group, the researcher measures the student perceptions of the teacher's communication competence (O_1), sends the teacher to the 6-hour workshop on humor (X_1), and retests the student perceptions of the teacher's communication competence (O_2). In the control group, the teacher is not sent to the workshop on humor. After the teacher in the first group has gone through the 6-hour workshop, the researcher has the students in the control group fill out a communication competence scale again on the teacher (O_2) who had not attended the workshop. These are all issues previously discussed in this chapter on the validity of a study.

Time Series

$$N\,O_1 \rightarrow O_2 \rightarrow O_3 \rightarrow X_1 \rightarrow O_4 \rightarrow O_5 \rightarrow O_6$$

The time-series design is a way for researchers to establish a clear baseline score on a specific dependent variable and then determine whether the manipulation of the independent variable has lasting effects. In the time series design, one group is nonrandomly established. The researcher measures the dependent variable the first time (O_1), measures the dependent variable a second time (O_2), and measures the dependent variable a third time (O_3). The researcher then performs the manipulation of the independent variable (X_1). After the manipulation of the independent variable, the researcher then measures the dependent variable a fourth time (O_4), followed by a fifth measurement of the dependent variable (O_5), and then followed by a sixth measurement of the dependent variable (O_6). A time-series experimental design is not limited to six measurements of the dependent variable—it could just as easily have been eight or ten measurements of the dependent variable. Multiple measurements of the dependent variable are useful because they help decrease the chance of a statistical regression to the mean validity threat by stabilizing outliers (participants with extreme scores).

In our example experiment, a researcher could measure a group of students' perceptions of the teacher's communication competence three times, then send the teacher to the six-hour workshop on how to use humor during training, and then measure the students' perception of the teacher's communication competence three more times. All in all, the teacher's communication competence would be measured six times. The major problem with this experimental design is that the researcher cannot determine whether the use of the same method for measuring the dependent variable (communication competence scale) is causing a change or the manipulation of the independent variable.

Multiple Time Series

$$N\,O_1 \to O_2 \to O_3 \to X_1 \to O_4 \to O_5 \to O_6$$

$$N\,O_1 \to O_2 \to O_3 \to X_0 \to O_4 \to O_5 \to O_6$$

The multiple time-series design is a way for researchers to establish a clear baseline score on a specific dependent variable and then determine whether the manipulation of the independent variable has lasting effects while controlling for multiple testing effects. In the multiple time-series design, two groups are nonrandomly established (N). In the first group, the researcher measures the dependent variable the first time (O_1), measures the dependent variable a second time (O_2), and measures the dependent variable a third time (O_3). The researcher then performs the manipulation of the independent variable (X_1). After the manipulation of the independent variable, the researcher then measures the dependent variable a fourth time (O_4), followed by a fifth measurement of the dependent variable (O_5), and then followed by a sixth measurement of the dependent variable (O_6). In the second group, the researcher simply measures the dependent variable six separate times (O_1, O_2, O_3, O_4, O_5, O_6), but does not attempt to manipulate the independent variable (X_0).

In our example experiment, a researcher could measure the experimental group of students' perception of the teacher's communication competence three times, then send the teacher to the 6-hour workshop on how to use humor during training, and then measure the students' perception of the teacher's communication competence three more times. In the control group, the researcher simply measures the students' perception of the teacher's communication competence six different times. The purpose of the control group in this design is to determine whether the effect of measuring the dependent variable six different times causes any of the changes noted in the dependent variable. However, because this design is not random, it is always possible that the two groups had preexisting characteristics that could lead to a change seen in the experiment.

Switching Replications Design

$$N\,O_1 \to X_1 \to O_2 \qquad O_3$$

$$N\,O_1 \qquad O_2 \to X_1 \to O_3$$

The switching replications design solves one of the basic problems that many people have with experimental designs—the need to exclude some participants from the independent variable manipulation. For example, maybe you find a treatment for public speaking anxiety. You would not want to turn down people who could benefit from the treatment, would you? Although the new treatment clearly needs to be researched, you could give one half of your participants the treatment to begin with and then give the other half the treatment later, but both groups would still receive the treatment. In this design, researchers create two nonrandom groups. The researcher starts off by observing the dependent variable in both groups (O_1), followed by a manipulation of the independent variable in the first group (X_1) while doing nothing in the second group, followed by an observation of the dependent variable a second time for both groups (O_2). At this point, the researcher switches gears and manipulates the independent variable for the second group (X_1) while doing nothing in the first group. This is followed by a third observation of the dependent variable for both groups (O_3).

In our experimental example, we could use two groups that we create or that are previously established. To start our experiment, we would measure how the students in both groups perceive their teachers' communication competence. We then send the first teacher to the workshop on how to use humor in the classroom. After the workshop, we then measure perceived teacher communication competence for both groups. At this point, we send the second teacher to the workshop on how to use humor in the classroom. After the workshop, we then measure perceived teacher communication competence for both groups for the third, and final, time. This design is good and can determine whether changes in the dependent variable are happening by chance or as a result of the researcher's manipulation of the independent variable. Although this is a strong design, because of its lack of randomization it still can succumb to the validity threats discussed earlier in this chapter.

TRUE EXPERIMENTAL DESIGNS

True experimental designs are considered such because participants in the study are randomly placed into an experimental condition and the independent variable is actively manipulated (not just observed). In this section we will examine four different experimental designs.

Pretest–Posttest Design

$$R\, O_1 \to X_1 \to O_2$$

$$R\, O_1 \qquad\qquad O_2$$

The purpose of this design is to determine whether the effect of a pretest can account for the scores a person may achieve on a posttest. In this design a researcher randomly assigns a larger group of participants into two groups (R). In the first group, a researcher measures the dependent variable (O_1), followed by a manipulation of the independent variable (X_1), and then by another measurement of the dependent variable (O_2). In the control group, a researcher measures the dependent variable (O_1) the first time and then measures the dependent variable (O_2) a second time without any kind of manipulation in between.

In our example experiment, a researcher would recruit a sample of research participants and then randomly assign the participants to one of two training conditions (use of humor or control). In the first group, you measure the student perceptions of the teacher's communication competence (O_1), then send the teacher to the 6-hour workshop on humor (X_1), and then retest the student perceptions of the teacher's communication competence (O_2). In the control group, the teacher is not sent to the workshop on humor. After the teacher in the first group has gone through the workshop, the researcher has the students in the control group fill out a communication competence scale again (O_2). There still exists a possibility of a threat to the validity of the study caused by the pretest. Theoretically, the effect of the independent variable could be different when a pretest is present compared to when it is not.

Two-Group Posttest-Only Design

$$R\, X_1 \to O_1$$

$$R \qquad O_1$$

In the two-group posttest-only design, a researcher uses a randomized sample (R), manipulates the independent variable (X_1), and then measures how people score on the dependent variable (O_1). Furthermore, the researcher only measures the dependent variable (O_1) for the second group. In this example, a researcher has two groups: an experimental group and a control group.

Using our example, the researcher would send one teacher through the six-hour workshop on using humor in training sessions (X_1) and not send another teacher. After the teacher in the first group has gone through the workshop, the researcher would then have the students in both groups fill out a communication competence scale on both teachers (O_1). This experimental design is economical, which is why it is often used in research. This experiment also eliminates the possibility of pre- and posttest interactions. However, without a baseline observance of the dependent variable, you always run the risk that the two groups were different to begin with.

Randomized Switching Replications Design

$$R\ O_1 \rightarrow X_1 \rightarrow O_2 \qquad O_3$$

$$R\ O_1 \qquad O_2 \rightarrow X_1 \rightarrow O_3$$

The randomized switching replications design solves one of the basic problems of experimental designs—the need to exclude some participants from the independent variable manipulation. In this design, researchers randomly place participants into one of two groups. In this design, the researcher starts off by observing the dependent variable in both groups (O_1), followed by a manipulation of the independent variable in the first group (X_1) while doing nothing in the second group, and then by an observation of the dependent variable a second time for both groups (O_2). At this point, the researcher switches gears and manipulates the independent variable for the second group (X_1) while doing nothing in the first group. This is followed by a third observation of the dependent variable for both groups (O_3).

In our experimental example, we could use two groups that we create or that are previously established. To start our experiment, we found how the students in both groups perceive their teachers' communication competence. We then send the first teacher to the workshop on how to use humor in the classroom. After the workshop, we measure perceived teacher communication competence for both groups. At this point, we send the second teacher to the workshop on how to use humor in the classroom. After the workshop, we then measure perceived teacher communication competence for both groups for the third and final time. This design is good and can determine whether changes in the dependent variable are happening by chance or as a result of the researcher's manipulation of the independent variable.

Solomon Four-Group Design

$$R\ O_1 \rightarrow X_1 \rightarrow O_2$$

$$R\ O_1 \qquad O_2$$

$$R \qquad X_1 \rightarrow O_2$$

$$R \qquad O_2$$

The Solomon Four-Group Design is considered the "granddaddy" of all experimental research designs because it attempts to control for any major experimental flaws. In the Solomon Four-Group, a researcher separates her or his participants into a series of four different groups (R). In the first group, the research measures the dependent variable (O_1) at Time 1, manipulates the independent variable (X_1), and then measures the dependent variable (O_2) at Time 2. In the second group, the researcher observes the dependent variable (O_1) at Time 1 and then measures the dependent variable (O_2) at Time 2, but does not manipulate the independent variable. In the third group, the researcher does not measure the dependent variable at Time 1. Instead, the researcher starts the third group by manipulating the independent variable (X_1) and then measuring the dependent variable at Time 2 (O_2). In the fourth and final group, the research does not measure the dependent variable at Time 1 or manipulate the independent variable. The only thing the researcher receives from the fourth group is a measure of the dependent variable (O_2) at Time 2. In essence, the first group in the Solomon Four-Group Design measures the traditional pre- and posttest experimental design. The second group helps a researcher know whether there is a difference between a pretest and posttest score in general. The third group determines whether a pretest influences the outcome of the posttest. And the final group helps to determine whether a maturation effect is occurring and the change is a result of time and not the independent variable manipulation.

Ex Post Facto Design

Sometimes you may want to see the effects of an independent variable on a dependent variable, but manipulating that independent variable may be impossible (e.g., changing someone's height, changing someone's sight) or highly unethical (e.g., changing someone's weight, life experiences, sexual orientation). For example, maybe you want to see whether someone's weight causes changes in how he or she reacts to a marketing campaign of dietary supplements. Although this design mirrors true experimental designs, it is not an experimental design in the strictest sense of the term. First, there is no random assignment of participants into control and tests groups. Second, there is manipulation of the independent variable because the participants already exist in the categories prior to the beginning of the study. For example, in our hypothetical marketing study, you could easily classify people based on the general body mass index (BMI) categories: underweight, normal weight, overweight, obese, and morbidly obese. As such, when we assign people to one of these categories, we are doing so based on events that have happened in the past, which is where the name ex post facto (after the fact) comes from.

Although researchers can look for differences between the different groups within an ex post facto design (e.g., the BMI weight categories), researchers cannot establish time order because they are not manipulating anything. Instead, we can only examine differences that exist between or among the different groups. So yes, a researcher may find that participants in the different BMI groups view the dietary supplement marketing materials differently, but one must be careful not to over interpret these results saying that weight *causes* differences in how people view the marketing materials because we cannot establish time order.

Final Thoughts on Experiments

Experiments are useful and can help researchers determine the time effects or causal relationships between two variables. However, there are some problems with the experimental process in general. First, a researcher can only examine a small number of independent variables in any given experiment. The more independent variables a researcher attempts to manipulate, the more complex the design must become and the more participants a researcher will need. We suggest a minimum of 30 participants in each experimental condition. All of the experimental designs examined above were for one independent variable manipulation with two nominal levels. If an experimenter is conducting a factorial experimental design (e.g., a 2 × 3 design), the experimental design becomes even more complex and cumbersome. Furthermore, the more advanced the statistical tests a researcher wants to use, the more participants a researcher needs. For example, it is recommended that a researcher have a minimum of 300 participants to run multivariate statistical tests or statistical tests that use more than one dependent variable.

A second major problem that occurs with experimental designs relates to the overall generalizability of the findings in an experiment. One of the basic questions that all researchers must ask themselves is whether their results can be generalized to the larger population. Can the results from one study be generalized to similar subject areas, time periods, or contexts? If an experiment is so finite in its generalizability, then its usefulness and meaning can be seriously called into question. Three factors have been shown to limit the generalizability of experimental research. First, researchers in every social scientific field have overly relied on college students as participant populations. Everyone will admit that college students are easy for researchers to get their hands on and are fairly cooperative (especially when extra credit is offered). For this reason, college students are the single most overstudied population in the United States. This is not to say that college students should not be studied, but researchers must think outside of the box and find participant populations outside the university walls.

Second, there exists an overreliance on laboratory settings when conducting experiments. There is a long-held belief that participants being studied in a laboratory environment will act differently than they would in a more natural environment. For this reason, researchers must start creating more experimental designs employing natural environments instead of laboratory ones.

The third reason many experiments have generalizability problems is that many experimental tasks are low in mundane realism. In one rather famous study, participants were asked to persuade people to sit in a room and turn pegs on a pegboard clockwise 25 degrees. As far as we can tell, there is no practical application of this experimental task. Although the finding from this study demonstrated that people commit to the persuasion task differently based on how much they were being paid to persuade someone to turn the pegs, the task cannot be generalized to any other task in the "real" world. Researchers must create experimental tasks that are similar to real tasks a participant could face in her or his daily life.

We have looked at three ways in which generalizability is limited, and we can now discuss two ways to enhance generalizability. First, more researchers should attempt to conduct field experiments. Field experiments happen in the real world outside the confines of a laboratory. They are much more likely to reveal real behavior than laboratory experiments. Also, researchers should use more complex studies examining multiple independent variable manipulations. In most real-world phenomena, the effect of a single independent variable manipulation will not be that big. For this reason, researchers must develop more complex research designs to enable researchers to develop better understandings of how human communicative behavior occurs. Ultimately, complexity in research design is a matter of sample size. Researchers and statistical tests can handle complex designs, but as designs become more complicated, additional research conditions are needed, which requires an ever-increasing sample size.

Conclusion

In this chapter, we have examined what experiments are and why we do them while exploring a variety of preexperimental, quasi-experimental, and true experimental study designs. In the next chapter, we will explore how to best sample a population to attain the most generalizable results possible.

KEY TERMS

Antecedent variable	Experimenter effects	Maturation
Attrition	Extraneous variable	Quasi-experimental design
Baseline	Factorial experimental design	Random assignment
Confederate	Hawthorne effect	Regression to the mean
Confounding variable	Historical flaw	Reinforcer variable
Control	Intervening variable	Selection threat
Control group	Lurker variable	Suppressor variable
Debriefing	Manipulation check	Testing flaw
Experiment	Manipulation of independent	Threshold effect
Experimental group(s)	Variables	Time order

REFERENCES

Campbell, D. T., & Stanley, J. C. (1963). *Experimental and quasi-experimental designs for research.* Skokie, IL: Rand McNally.

Cook, T. D., & Campbell, D. T. (1979). *Quasi-experimental design and analysis issues for field settings.* Boston, MA: Houghton Mifflin.

Guéguen, N., & De Gail, M. A. (2003). The effect of smiling on helping behavior: Smiling and good Samaritan behavior. *Communication Reports, 16,* 133–140.

Masling, J. (1966). Role-related behavior of the subject and psychologist and its effects upon psychological data. In D. Levine (Ed.), *Nebraska symposium on motivation* (pp. 67–103). Lincoln, NE: University of Nebraska Press.

Stewart, R. A. (1994). Perceptions of a speaker's initial credibility as a function of religious involvement and religious disclosiveness. *Communication Research Reports, 11,* 169–176.

Tamborini, R., Eastin, M. S., Skalski, P., Lachlan, K., Fediuk, T. A., & Brady, R. (2004). Violent virtual video games and hostile thoughts. *Journal of Broadcasting & Electronic Media, 48,* 335–357.

Weber, K., Fornash, B., Corrigan, M, & Neupauer, N. C. (2003). The effect of interest on recall: An experiment. *Communication Research Reports, 20,* 116–123.

Wiener, J. L., & Doescher, T. A. (1994). Cooperation and expectations of cooperation. *Journal of Public Policy & Marketing, 13,* 559–270.

Wrench, J. S., Millhouse, B., & Sharp, D. (2007). Laughing before takeoff: Humor, sex, and the preflight safety briefing. *Human Communication, 10,* 381–399.

FURTHER READING

Brown, S. R., & Melamed, L. E. (1990). *Experimental design and analysis.* Thousand Oaks, CA: Sage.

Field, A., & Hole, G. J. (2003). *How to design and report experiments.* Thousand Oaks, CA: Sage.

Levin, I. P. (2004). *Relating statistics and experimental design: An introduction.* Thousand Oaks, CA: Sage.

Ryan, T. P. (2007). *Modern experimental design.* New York, NY: Wiley.

Shadish, W. R., Cook, T. D., & Campbell, D. T. (2002). *Experimental and quasi-experimental designs for generalized causal inference.* Boston, MA: Houghton Mifflin.

Singleton, R. A., Jr., & Straits, B. C. (1999). *Approaches to social research* (3rd ed.). New York, NY: Oxford University Press.

Spector, P. E. (1981). *Research designs.* Newbury Park, CA: Sage.

Big Data

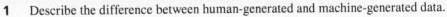
Imagine that you could live in a world where all of the following can happen:

• Your local department store could predict when you are pregnant based on your buying patterns.
• Your watch could let you know when you are having a heart attack.
• A website could determine what fashion trends, colors, and styles are going to be "in" this season to help clothiers prepare for the season.
• Your video game could predict when you are attempting to cheat.
• Your phone knew your frequent locations and remembered them.

Sound like a far-fetched world? All of these things are happening right now as a result of a new quantitative tool called Big Data.

First, Target has actually created a predictive model based on buying patterns that can fairly accurately predict when a woman is pregnant. Second, one of the eventual goals of Apple's smart watch is to be able to predict and tell when someone is having a heart attack. This predictive capability will be based on large studies examining precursors to heart attacks. There is already a computer program that can diagnose a heart attack up to four hours before a cardiologist. A company called Editd has won awards for the real-time analytics it has been using to help fashion houses, designers, and corporate buyers prepare for changing trends. In fact, their corporate slogan is "how the world's best apparel retailers, brands & suppliers have the right product, at the right price, at the right time." If you play video games, you probably know the number one video game on the planet is *Call of Duty*. Quantitative researchers who work for Activision, the company that owns *Call of Duty*, have been working on predictive analytics to determine when someone is boosting. Their analytics are based on a similar premise that credit card companies use to predict credit card fraud. So yes, Activision is working to ensure that everyone who plays *Call of Duty* will be on equal footing in the near future. Finally, your smartphone (i.e., Android, iPhone, etc.) tracks and remembers your every move. Your smartphone keeps track of the places you go and how often you visit each place. Your phone then "learns" which places are important to you and will provide you with personalized services such as predictive traffic routing to help you arrive more efficiently to your frequently visited locations.

All of these examples demonstrate the new and powerful world of quantitative research in the twenty-first century. More specifically, these are all part of a particular type of quantitative research called "Big Data." The notion of Big Data has graced the covers of magazines from the traditionally technical (e.g., *Nature, Popular Science, Cosmos*) to the more general (e.g., *Time, The Economist, Harvard Business Review*). This chapter explores the new and fascinating world of Big Data.

So what is "Big Data"? Big Data is a term that has been used by a range of different people in slightly different ways. Furthermore, the term "Big Data" is often misconstrued with other, closely related concepts that can confuse the picture. Specifically, **Big Data** are data that is simply too large to store on a single computer and are beyond the scope of traditional statistical research software. Saying that something is big is not enough to really make it Big Data, but we will revisit this idea in a moment.

In the three previous chapters, we showed you how to conduct surveys, content analyses, and experiments; however, this chapter is going to be less about showing you how to conduct Big Data studies and more about what these studies are. Because Big Data is a fairly recent concept, the majority of the writing on the subject is extremely technical and not written on the introductory level at all. As such, the goal of this chapter is to help you understand how Big Data is being used all around you every day to make a wide range of decisions that impact your life. Many of the examples we use in this chapter were designed to help researchers predict phenomenon, and many of these examples were designed by corporate entities and not for the sake of academic research.

As we explore Big Data, we will define what Big Data is, explain the intersection of cloud computing and Big Data, explore common analytical techniques used to examine Big Data, examine some recent research studies using Big Data in communication, and discuss some of the real ethical issues related to Big Data research today. Before we go any further, we really do must define what we mean by Big Data.

What is the Data in Big Data?

Before we break down the definition of "Big Data," we will have a brief conversation of what is meant by "data." Earlier in this book, we defined **data** as the collected measures of independent and dependent variables that can be used for statistical calculations. However, in the traditional research process, data is something that is often specifically collected for the purposes of research. For example, when you conduct an experiment and have a participant fill out a survey, the survey is being collected explicitly for that experiment. The data used in Big Data are not generally collected in the same way. To help us understand what we mean by this, we must talk about two important factors related to data: types of data generated by humans and types of data generated by machines.

HUMAN-GENERATED DATA

Humans produce data all the time without thinking twice about it. You go on Facebook and click the iconic "thumbs-up" symbol: you just generated data. You make a purchase from iTunes: you just generated data. You text your best friend where to meet you: you just generated data. Humans generate a ton of data in the twenty-first century. Every purchase, like, webpage view, etc. is a piece of data that we are creating. We may not always think of these behaviors as generating data, but they are. We call this intentional data because the data result from our direct behavior that creates the data. We may not realize that the data are being stored in any fashion, but our behavior allows for the generation of that data. Think about your average day. You wake up in the morning and check your e-mail: data generated. You then listen to Pandora or Spotify while in the shower: data generated. You plug your iPhone into your car and listen to iTunes: data generated. And so on and so on. We go through our days amassing tons of data about ourselves, our habits, our personalities, etc.

Metadata

Not all data generated by humans are intentional, however. In fact, much of the data we generate on a daily basis is called metadata, or information that provides context for other pieces of data generated. For example, you take a photo with your iPhone and post it to Instagram. Unbeknown to you, that picture contains a range of data that has nothing to do with the image itself: GPS coordinates of where the picture was taken (altitude, latitude, longitude, etc.), the date the picture was taken, model of phone used to take the picture, and a range of factors related to photography (aperture, brightness, focal length, lens model, shutter speed, etc.). There are even other apps out there that allow you to take the metadata from an image file and locate the exact location where the photo was taken. Thankfully, there are other apps that will allow you to clean or alter the metadata from an image before you post or share that image. It is even possible to control some metadata in the systems setting of your phone by controlling location services.

Do not be fooled, however; images are not the only pieces of data we create that contain metadata. In fact, every 140 character tweet someone sends contains more than 2,150 pieces of metadata including tweet content, geographic location, author's biography, author's URL, creation date of account, number of followers, number of tweets ever sent, etc. (Dwoskin, 2014). That is more pieces of metadata than you have characters in your tweet.

MACHINE-GENERATED DATA

In addition to humans, machines also create tons of data in what is called machine-to-machine data. Think about your house right now. How many devices do you currently have connected to your Internet? In my house, I have a cloud storage drive, an iPad, an iPhone, a laptop, a Surface, and a desktop, which are all on the more normal side. However, I also have my DVR, television, and stereo system linked to the Internet. At any given moment, these devices are interacting with each other and with the Internet, where they are interacting with large computer mainframes that are collecting data. My stereo system is the Amazon Echo, which connects to the Internet and has access to my digital music archive, but it also can tell me the weather and time and even keep me up to date on breaking news. My "stereo" can even tap into my household lights with an adaptor that gives it control over specific light fixtures. I do not tell you all of this to sell you an Echo, but rather to explain that each of these functions requires the device to constantly interact with the world outside of my house without me paying attention and telling it what to do. Furthermore, with each of these activities, the device is communicating with other devices and amassing massive quantities of data in the process.

This process of connecting a wide variety of our lives together through the Internet is commonly called the **Internet of things**. In fact, more and more of our basic devices are now being embedded with microchips that help them collect data in an effort to perform better. There are already more devices connected to the Internet than people connected to the Internet. In a 2014 report, Hewitt Packard examined 10 of the most common Internet of things devices: televisions, webcams, home thermostats, remote power outlets, sprinkler controllers, hubs for controlling multiple devices, door locks, home alarms, scales, and garage door openers. Of these different devices, 90 percent of them collected at least one piece of personal information that was transmitted. Admittedly, you probably only have one or two of these devices (if any) right now. In the future, you can expect everything to be connected and collecting data. Imagine that your printer can detect when it is running low on ink, so it orders more ink on its own. Imagine a car that can drive itself while you are able to enjoy the ride and catch up on sleep or finish getting ready in the morning. Imagine a situation where a major car accident causes traffic delays on your normal route, so your alarm clock wakes you up early and even gets your coffee started earlier as well. These may seem far-fetched right now, but these are just a few of the technologies researchers are looking to create in the near future. In fact, it is predicted that the overwhelming majority of data created in the near future will be machine-to-machine data that is never witnessed by the machine's users.

Big Data?

When people start talking about this idea of "Big Data," most of the time it is in reference to the world of business. Early on, business realized that the massive amounts of data they were collecting could help them be more productive and efficient, which, of course, leads to higher profit margins. However, businesses are not the only people who are using Big Data. In fact, Big Data can be used for a wide range of different purposes, as we saw in the introduction of this chapter.

BIG DATA EXPLAINED

As mentioned at the beginning of the chapter, a common definition of Big Data involves data that are too large for traditional statistical software packages. However, this definition is not overly descriptive. As such, it is important to differentiate Big Data from a number of closely related terms: machine learning, data science, and data analytics. Without going into too much detail on each of these terms, we will differentiate each of them from Big Data. The first commonly heard term involving Big Data is machine learning. **Machine learning** is an interesting branch of science involving the creation of algorithms that enable a computer to learn and make decisions when exposed to new data. Machine learning is a type of artificial intelligence. Let's say that you are shopping at Amazon.com. You've been purchasing DVDs, .mp3 files, clothing, food, etc., for a while and Amazon.com starts making recommendations of what it thinks you will enjoy and may want to purchase. No one has to explain to Amazon.com's computer network what your recommendations will be. Instead, Amazon.com's computers learn over time about your varied interests and buying patterns and use that information to make individualized recommendations to you. In essence, the computer has learned about you and is using that information to market specific products tailored for your tastes. Is this process always perfect? Of course not. However, the more interaction you have with their system, the more specific and accurate these predictions can become over time.

The second common term used in conjunction with Big Data is data science. For our purposes, we are going to define **data science** as the emerging field that attempts to extract knowledge from data through advanced mathematical analyses, computers, and databases. Obviously, then, data scientists are the individuals who are working to combine these three fields into unique processes for analyzing data using the intersection of these three fields.

According to data scientist Drew Conway (2010), data science is the intersection of three primary skill sets: hacking skills, substantive expertise, and math and statistics knowledge (Figure 12.1). With regard to hacking skills, we are not talking about the illegal types of hacking commonly associated with "black hat" activities. Instead, data hackers must have the ability to manipulate text files using an array of programing skills. As for substantive expertise, Conway argues that data scientists must understand the scientific research process. Everything we have discussed in this book is information that a good data scientist should know. Finally, data scientists must understand how to extract information from data using appropriate statistical methods and a variety of different statistical software packages when necessary.

Last, **data analytics** are a set of tools used to make predictions about the future based on information from the past. For example, if you want to predict how much your organization is going to spend on paper this year, you can analyze how much paper has been purchased over the past five years and make a decent prediction about what will probably happen in the future. When you rely on past data to make predictions, you are engaging in predictive analytics. However, researchers can also engage in descriptive and prescriptive analytics as well.

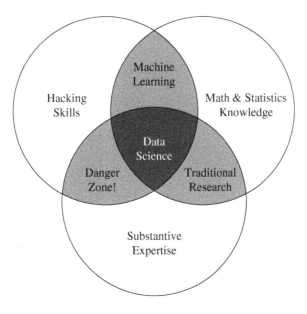

Figure 12.1 Data Science (Used with permission by Drew Conway, http://drewconway.com/)

Descriptive analytics involve describing the data, for example, how many people are viewing a website, how many people make a purchase, how many likes you have on Facebook, etc. In fact, a great deal of the information generated from Big Data is ultimately descriptive. Last, we could have prescriptive data analytics. **Prescriptive analytics** are the newer of the three. The goal of prescriptive analytics is to use data to determine possible courses of action and what the ramifications would be of these different courses of action. In essence, data analytics is a set of tools one can use to analyze Big Data.

In the past few pages we have introduced a number of terms that are often clustered together with the notion of Big Data. With all of this in mind, we will turn our attention to trying to understand what data scientists mean when they talk about Big Data.

Algorithms in Big Data

An algorithm can be simply described as a series of necessary steps to accomplish a task. In the case of Big Data, we are dealing with necessary mathematical computations to help us analyze data. Algorithms are important in anything involving computers. For this reason, data scientists often use algorithms to investigate and make predictions. Imagine that you are a nonverbal researcher examining facial expressions. If you got a hold of a large database of faces (with facial expressions), how would you create a program that could analyze millions of faces and place names with those faces? AT&T started doing this back in the early 1990s and have made such a database openly available for people: http://www.cl.cam.ac.uk/research/dtg/attarchive/facedatabase.html/. The AT&T facial database contains images for 40 different people. Each person has 10 different facial expression pictures. Two researchers, Alex Rodriguez and Alessandro Laio (2014), created a new algorithm that enabled a computer to look for similarities among pictures and determine how many people existed when given the 400 different images without any other information. As you can imagine, algorithm involved here was complex and involved many different mathematical equations and models all running together to help correctly identify that there were only 40 people represented by the 400 pictures.

Reference

Rodriguez, A., & Laio, A. (2014). Clustering by fast search and find of density peaks. *Science, 344*(6191), 1492–1496. doi:10.1126/science.1242072

LANEY'S 3V'S

In 2001, Doug Laney wrote a white paper (authoritative report) examining the concept of data and the future it would play for businesses. Specifically, Laney predicted that businesses were on the precipice of a period of time when data would become an increasingly larger part of day-to-day operations. To help explain the forthcoming new world of data science, Laney differentiated this new data from previous data. As such, Laney recommended three specific characteristics to describe this new type of data: volume, velocity, and variety.

Volume

In our basic definition of "Big Data," we said that it comprises data that are too large for a traditional computer or statistical software package. With that said, calling something "too large" is a problem in its own right. I remember buying my first laptop computer. The internal hard drive at that time was ridiculously large and there was no way I would ever need something larger. That amazing internal hard drive had 6 gigabytes of space. Now I have a 2-terabyte primary hard drive with a 6-terabyte backup hard drive in my computer. The idea of "big" can change rapidly.

In 1965, Gordon E. Moore wrote an article specifically focusing on this issue of size. In his article, he discussed what is now commonly called Moore's law. Basically, the physical capacity and performance of a computer doubles every two years. This doubling has been amazingly predictive of the state of computing since Moore's law originally gained traction. As such, what we call "Big Data" today might not be that big tomorrow. For example, we will look at a computer program we discussed in this book already, Microsoft Excel. In Excel 2003, the maximum sized spreadsheet was 65,536 rows by 256 columns. With the 2013 version of Microsoft Excel, the spreadsheet size is now 1,048,576 rows by 16,384 columns.

We mention all of this to show you that the idea of "volume," or the pure amount of data that we are dealing with, does change over time. If you look at Figure 12.2, you will see a history of data. From the good old days of the 1.44-MB floppy disk to the petabyte hard drives that all of us will see fairly soon, our idea of data volume has changed. Today's "Big Data" may be tomorrow's small data as our computer processors and hard drives keep on doubling every two years. As such, just looking at the volume of data is not enough for something to be truly considered Big Data.

Bit (b)	1 or 0	A big stands for a binary digit and is always represented as a 1 or 0. Bits are the basic foundation of all computers.
Byte (B)	8 bits	In computer code, a byte is just enough to create a single letter or number.
Kilobyte (KB)	1,0001 bytes	Roughly ½ of a page of typed text.
Megabyte (MB)	1,000 kilobytes	One of the old 3 ½ floppy disks was 1.44 MBs. Your average .mp3 song is approximately 4 MBs.
Gigabyte (GB)	1,000 megabytes	1 GB is about a 90 minute long standard definition movie.
Terabyte (TB)	1,000 gigabytes	1 TB is the equivalent of 1,500 CD-ROMS. 1 TB can hold 1 million minutes of .mp3s.
Petabyte (PB)	1,000 terabytes	1 PB is enough to play .mp3 files continuously for 2,000 years. 1 PB is the equivalent of 20 million 4-drawer filing cabinets of text.
Exabyte (EB)	1,000 petabytes	It is estimated that 5 EBs would be the equivalent to every spoken word from a human throughout history. 1 EB is roughly the equivalent of 36,000 years of nonstop streaming HD movies.
Zettabyte (ZB)	1,000 exabytes	Global internet traffic is approximately 1.1 ZBs per month. The entire amount of information available on the internet is expected to reach over 400 ZBs by 2018.

¹ Some argue that a KB is actually 1,024 bytes, a MB is 1,024 kilobytes, etc...

Figure 12.2 Understanding Volume

In terms of Big Data, keeping accurate records of how much data are being generated is almost impossible on a day-to-day basis. However, IBM has been widely cited as saying that in 2012 approximately 2.5 exabytes of data were generated daily (Wall, 2014; Ward & Barker, 2013).

Velocity

The second 'V" in Laney's 3 V's of Big Data is velocity, or the speed and continual onslaught of data activity. In traditional research, we often collected what are called "static" datasets, or datasets that, once they are collected, stay the same. For example, Dawson (1995) put together a simple dataset examining the sinking of the Titanic. In this dataset, he has four variables: class (crew, first, second, or third), age (adult or child), sex (male or female), and survived (yes or no). Is this dataset going to evolve over time? No. These data are set in stone and how they exist today is how they will exist 100 years from now, assuming some radical information about the sinking of the Titanic's survivors is not discovered. We have known this information for a long time, and we will continue to know this information. Of course, you can still use this information to make some interesting assessments about who survived and who did not. Survey data, content analysis data, and experimental data are generally examples of static datasets.

Velocity, on the other hand, refers to datasets that are not as easy to capture because the data are continuously being recorded over time and/or space. If a pristine lake is an example of a static dataset, then Niagara Falls is an example of Big Data. Where a 7.5-acre lake has 2.5 million gallons of water standing still and can be watched from day to day, Niagara Falls has 150,000 gallons of water rushing over its ledges every second. Niagara Falls reaches the same amount of water in that static lake in about 17 seconds. So, you may be wondering, what does this have to do with quantitative research? Well, your average research may collect data from 200 participants over the course of a one-year study, and then the researcher analyzes this static data. Big Data researchers, on the other hand, look at data that are coming in at much higher volumes much faster.

Imagine you want to examine how people in the world are using Twitter. Twitter admits to tracking who is tweeting, the GPS location of those tweets, networks used to access Twitter, and many other pieces of metadata. For one user, this would not seem like much information; however, when you have 8,872 tweets per second, that is a lot of data being collected quickly. Currently, the Twitterverse sends more than 1 billion tweets in under 2 days. Want to see how much data are being generated via social media per second, today, or this year? Check out http://www.internetlivestats.com/ to see this information live. The speed at which these data are generated causes problems for most of our traditional statistical software (e.g., Excel, SPSS). These software programs are designed for fairly large static datasets. As such, new data-management techniques have been created to help us analyze these data in real-time.

Variety

The last "V" in Laney's 3 V's of Big Data is variety. In the other research methods we have discussed, all of these data can be easily input into a traditional spreadsheet for analytic purposes (e.g., Excel, SPSS). Other traditional data can be used in a traditional relational database (e.g., Access, FileMaker). Whether you want to create an employee database containing contact information, photos, and summaries of annual reports or you want to handle the reservation system for a multi–million dollar hotel chain, a database is the most effective tool to help you. Although most people just call them databases, there are a number of different types of databases that can exist. The most common one is a relational database. Edgar Codd (1970)

Fields

Employee Name	Tenure at Company	Department	Salary
Rebecca Smith	8 Years	Human Resources	$75,000
Donald Praeger	17 Years	Management	$225,000
Candice Flayhan	3 Years	Marketing	$100,000
Joan Johnson	17 Years	Management	$225,000
Jessie Attias	8 Months	Public Relations	$60,000

Figure 12.3 Relational Database

coined the term relational database while working at IBM in the late 1960s. The basic part of a relational database is a single table that consists of rows (records) and columns (fields). Figure 12.3 is an example of a basic relational database. These databases are called relational because of the ability to establish mathematical relationships across multiple tables. The relationships between rows in these databases are sometimes described as parent and child. Your average database may have 10 different tables that it creates various relationships between. Advanced databases could have up to 1,000 different tables.

The "variety" of Big Data comes into play because the statistical techniques associated with Big Data can analyze traditional structured data (e.g., spreadsheets and databases), but it can also handle semistructured and nonstructured data that come in the forms of audio, images, text, video, etc. For example, most social media sites enable people to post some kind of text in addition to photos and videos that are shared, along with links to other websites. To understand how people are truly using social media, you cannot ignore these other forms of data ust because they do not easily fit into the more traditional data management box. Some information scientists have argued that 80 to 85 percent of the data being analyzed today are unstructured data, especially in the form of text; however, these numbers do not always have actual data to support them (Grimes, 2008). Whether you believe that 80 to 85 percent of data being analyzed are unstructured is not as relevant as the reality that unstructured data comprise a huge part of Big Data today.

FOUR MORE V'S

In addition to the original 3 V's proposed by Laney (2001), van Rijmenam (2014) has proposed an additional four V's.

Veracity

Data are only good when you can trust the data. When your data are bad, you will make decisions based on that data that are simply invalid. This is especially true when much of the decision making is automated by computers. For example, on Tuesday, April 23, 2013, the Associated Press sent out the following tweet at 12:07 PM: "Breaking: Two Explosions in the White

House and Barack Obama is injured." The U.S. stock market took a $200 billion nose dive after this tweet was sent. Of course, the tweet was fake and was corrected within minutes. So how did the stock market dive so quickly? One of the main reasons is that many stock trading companies have super computers constantly analyzing data across the net (including Twitter). When those computers received the tweet from a predetermined trusted source like the Associated Press, the computers went into a selling frenzy automatically without any human actually telling them to do so. As you can see, when you have bad data, you will have bad decisions.

Variability

Variability refers to data in which meaning is always changing. For example, imagine I tweet "Lacey's Coffee shop is great," and another customer responds to my tweet saying, "Lacey's Coffee Shop is great if you like bad customer service." Although data analysts who are studying tweets about Lacey's Coffee Shop might search the data for the word "great," they would need to have sophisticated algorithms that look at the surrounding pattern of words to truly understand the meaning of great in this tweet. Thus, great is the piece of data under analysis, but the meaning of great is variable. Context does matter. As van Rijmenam (2014) explains, "Variability is often confused with variety. Say you have bakery that sells 10 different breads. That is variety. Now imagine you go to that bakery three days in a row and every day you buy the same type of bread but each day it tastes and smells different. That is variability" (p. 11).

Visualization

The third of van Rijmenam's V's is visualization, or taking a large amount of data and putting it into some kind of easy-to-read format. van Rijmenam warns against thinking of visualization as simple barographs and pie charts. Visualization is designed to help people quickly see and understand what the data are saying. Although visualization may seem simple, it can actually be one of the hardest parts of the Big Data process. For example, imagine you want to display a history of the use of various terms in printed books going back to the 1800s. You could spend the rest of your natural life going through books trying to accomplish this task, or you could rely on the Big Data set created through the Google Books Library Project. Google has been scanning massive number of books dating back to the 1800s in an effort to create a digital knowledge base. One of the fascinating parts of this process involves being able to analyze the text within these books in a way that could never have been dreamed of before.

Going back to our example, when we analyze the use of the words elocution, speech, communication, media, and nonverbal in books dating back to the 1800s, an interesting trend starts to emerge. When you look at Figure 12.4, you can see how the inclusion of these words has changed over time. Although "speech" was the preferred term for a long time, "communication" has usurped "speech" as the more commonly written term. The other three terms (elocution, media, and nonverbal) hovered fairly close together toward the lower end of the spectrum. The first recorded inclusion of the word "nonverbal" by Google happened in 1806, but you really do not see its use take off until the 1960s. As for the word "media," we saw steady increased use from the 1800s into the 1900s, but the real takeoff of the term did not happen until the 1930s. Now the term "media" is more common in books than the term "speech." As for the word "elocution," it was never as common as speech and communication, but it was used more commonly at the beginning of the 1800s than it was by the 1900s.

The one simple chart was created using massive amounts of data that could not have been completed back at the turn of the twenty-first century. Although you could make some

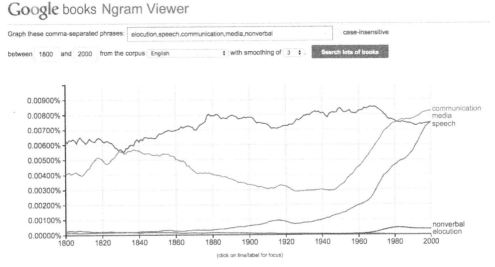

Figure 12.4 Google Books Library Project

interesting conjectures about the use of those terms over time based on the data, for our purposes we want you to look at how the data were visualized in a simple chart to help you understand massive quantities of books for more than 200 years. If you want to play with this tool on your own, you can go to their website at https://books.google.com/ngrams/.

Value

The last of van Rijmenam's (2014) four additional V's is value, or the ability to turn Big Data into information that helps generate knowledge and wisdom. For the professional world, this knowledge and wisdom means ensuring that people using the data can make decisions based on the data that will help the organization competitively. In academia, we want these data to tell us something about how humans behave, interact, and communicate with one another. If you are going to take the time and expense to use Big Data, you want to ensure that the end result has value.

Big Data and the Cloud

As we discussed in the previous section, one of the biggest factors that makes Big Data "big" is that it cannot be stored on a single personal computer, which Laney (2001) referred to as the volume of the data. In fact, even adding an extra external hard drive to your computer will not help you handle the amount of data that is being produced. We will give you a simple example. Imagine you want to analyze the data that a company like Facebook produces in a single day. You are looking at sifting through around 700 terabytes of data. Your average computer may have a 1-terabyte hard drive, so you would need 700 average PCs to store all of the data necessary. That 700 terabytes is just storage space, so it does not include any software that you would must run your computer or statistical software. In this section, we are going to explore what is meant by "the cloud," the relationship between the cloud and data, and the intersection of Big Data and the cloud.

UNDERSTANDING THE CLOUD

The idea of needing access to data at ever-increasing sizes is not new. As we mentioned earlier in this chapter, in the good old days when you needed your data to go with you, you put it in a floppy disk that contained about 1.44 MB of memory. These quickly became obsolete with the need to carry ever-increasing amounts of data with you. The first major player in this space game was the zip drive. Most of you reading this text probably have never seen a zip drive because it was introduced in 1994 and was gone by 2000. These zip drives originally stored around 250 MB and eventually grew to 750 MB before the writeable CD-ROM became the norm. The CD-ROM came in a few different sizes as well, ranging from 650 MB to 900 MB. Next in our series of special increases was the DVD-ROM, which could hold 4.7 GB of data. One interesting technology that changed storage capacities was the USB flash drive, which was first introduced by IBM and Trek Technology. The original USB flash drive (also called a thumb drive because of their size) only contained 8 MB of data. Unlike some of the other technologies discussed above, the USB flash drive is the only one that has grown with the ever-increasing need to handle larger amounts of data. Today you can purchase a 1terabyte USB drive. Admittedly, the current cost is close to $850, so it is priced out of the range of most people for a simple thumb drive, but you can be assured that this price will be dropping.

You may be wondering why this brief history of the size of portability of data is important to the world of Big Data, but it is actually essential to understanding where we are today. In recent years, instead of taking a USB drive with you when you must carry data, many of us rely on Internet-based storage. Internet-based storage is like a giant filing cabinet of your data kept on the Internet so you can access it from anywhere you need. Of course, we call this giant filing cabinet on the Internet the cloud. "The cloud" makes it sound like our data are stored in some magical place, but in all actuality our data gets stored on servers that are hosted by cloud storage companies. These servers are actually housed in extremely large data storage centers (or data farms). It is not uncommon to see many of the top names in social networking or cloud storage having servers located within a single data storage center just rows from each other. Some companies, like Facebook, have opted to stop leasing space in a data storage center and open multiple facilities of their own. The ultimate purpose of these large data storage facilities is to allow these massive servers to have easy, direct access to the Internet so users can access their information without ever knowing the necessary computing power behind what is happening.

We will use one basic company as an example (we are not promoting this company). Dropbox was founded in 2007 by Drew Houston and Arash Ferdowsi, two former MIT computer science graduates. The idea behind Dropbox was simple. Houston was tired of having to save work to a flash drive that was taken between home, school, and work. Flash drives, although great devices, can fail. As such, Houston started creating a way to access his files through the Internet in an effort to ditch the flash drive. So, how does Dropbox work? Simply put, when you sign up for a free 2-GB membership, you save files into a Dropbox folder on your computer that is automatically synced to a storage server at a data storage center. When you want to access those folders on a different computer or device, the Dropbox application is able to locate your content on the server and give you access to those files. Voilà! You have now used cloud computing.

THE CLOUD AND DATA

The cloud has enabled a wide range of businesses to have almost unlimited amounts of storage capacity online because of massive data storage centers. One of the biggest names in cloud storage is actually Amazon Web Services. Amazon's S3 data storage has more than 50 regional data storage centers around the world. In fact, if you have ever watched Netflix, then you have accessed data that were streamed from an Amazon storage facility. When it comes to partnering with a storage center, there are three important characteristics to consider: scalability, redundancy, and speed.

Scalability refers to the ability of the data storage center to grow as you grow. Can it meet the demands that you have when you have them? As organizations amass more and more data, they often must increase the amount of data storage they have available. In the past, organizations had their own data storage servers, but these could either quickly become obsolete because more storage capacity was needed or they purchased too much that was never utilized.

Second, *redundancy* involves how many backup copies of your data can be made. Data can even have problems in the cloud, so having redundancies built into data storage prevents any data from getting corrupted or lost. Dropbox is a great example of redundancy. When someone uses Dropbox, copies of the files are kept on that person's hard drive, any other hard drive where that individual installs Dropbox and syncs files, and by Dropbox itself on multiple servers. In fact, Dropbox stores copies of every file uploaded to Dropbox (including multiple versions of files and deleted files) for up to 30 days. If someone accidentally deletes a file, Dropbox's redundancy is right there to help her or him get the data back.

Last, *speed* refers to how quickly you want to be able to access your data. If you are working with a program like Dropbox, you want fast access to the files that you have stored with Dropbox. However, there are other instances where immediate access to your data may not be as important. Imagine you are a college or university that has just digitized all of its student records since the school opened. This amount of digitization will create a lot of data, but do you need quick, immediate access to all of these data? Probably not. Many data storage centers have repositories for what is called "cold data," or data that are not needed often but must be stored somewhere. Amazon's cold data program is called Glacier. It is cheap (about $.01 per GB) and can grow as an organization needs more data space; however, getting access to these data could take a few hours when a request is made. Obviously, as scalability, redundancy, and speed increase, so does the cost of the cloud service.

BIG DATA IN THE CLOUD

Now that we have explained how the cloud works, it is also important to discuss the notion of cloud computing, or computer services that are delivered to your computer via the cloud. There are four basic types of common services delivered: infrastructure as a service (IaaS), platform as a service (PaaS), software as a service (SaaS), and data as a service (DaaS). IaaS is really what we have been talking about with regard to data storage centers. IaaS involves access to storage, hard drives, servers, etc. PaaS is a service that allows application creators to develop, test, and deploy their apps at a much faster rate. As an end user of all of these tools, SaaS is where most of us really experience cloud computing. When you interact with a website software like Google Docs, Microsoft OneDrive, or iWork for iCloud, you are experiencing SaaS.

Last, we have DaaS, which enables individuals to purchase access to data. According to Pringle (2014), DaaS can be defined "as the sourcing, management, and provision of data delivered in an immediately consumable format to organizations' business users as a service" (p. 3). DaaS providers realize that in the twenty-first century data are a commodity, so collecting and selling that data to others is a profitable business. Maybe you want access to every tweet that has ever been sent. You could start scrolling through all of that information or you could purchase access to that information from a DaaS provider who has already done the legwork. Some of the more common sources of this type of data are Factual (http://www.factual.com/), Gnip (https://gnip.com/), Infochimps (http://www.infochimps.com/), Opera Solutions (http://operasolutions.com/), and Oracle (https://www.oracle.com/cloud/daas.html/).

Type of Data	Data Source
Amazon Web Services Public Data	
List of various publicly available datasets.	http://aws.amazon.com/datasets
Data.gov	
Source of open data created by the U.S. government.	http://www.data.gov/
Data.gov.UK	
Open data compiled and available from the United Kingdom Government.	http://data.gov.uk/
European Union Open Data Portal	
Range of data collected by various institutions within the European Union.	http://open-data.europa.eu/en/data/
HealthData.gov	
125 years of public health data collected within the U.S.	https://www.healthdata.gov/
Million Song Database	
This database contains metadata for over one million songs.	http://aws.amazon.com/datasets/6468931156960467
Pew Research Center	
Downloadable datasets from PRC research projects. Not all are necessarily Big Data.	http://www.pewinternet.org/datasets
WikiData	
Centralized, structured database of content from other Wikimedia sites.	https://www.wikidata.org/
Yelp's Academic Dataset	
Data and reviews of the 250 closest businesses for 30 universities (maybe your university is on the list).	https://www.yelp.com/academic_dataset

Figure 12.5 Free Sources of Big Data

Thankfully, not all accessible data must be gathered by yourself or purchased. There are a number of great sources of data that can be freely used. Figure 12.5 lists some good, publicly available sources of Big Data.

Big Data Analysis

Before we begin our discussion of Big Data analysis, we want to make it clear that we are introducing you to the basic ideas of Big Data analysis and are not going to be showing you the ins and outs of Big Data analysis because it would take many volumes of information to even begin that discussion. In this section we are going to discuss some of the common analytic methods used with Big Data: data mining and monitoring and anomaly detection.

DATA MINING

Next, we have a term that is often confused with Big Data, data mining. **Data mining** is the process of examining data for new, useful information. The concept of data mining became popularized in the 1990s and has been a commonly used set of techniques to look for information in large datasets. For our purposes, data mining is a technique that data scientists can use to analyze Big Data. In fact, data mining techniques can lead to all kinds of interesting findings related to business and health care. There have been a number of cases where prescription drugs were pulled from the market after they were found to cause significant risks to users that had not been discovered using the traditional research process.

Unfortunately, data mining can lead to some interesting and spurious relationships. A researcher can overexamine a dataset looking to find anything that may exist, which is often called data dredging or data fishing (looking for relationships between variables that happen only by chance), which, to all kinds of statistical outcomes, have no place in actual reality. According to Milloy (1995), data dredging is akin to a sharpshooter who shoots his gun at the broadside of the barn and then goes up to the barn and draws his target on the side, ensuring that all of his shots are right in the bullseye.

One of the most notorious cases of data dredging was conducted by Peters et al. (1994). In this study, Peters and colleagues were using data mining techniques to fish for relationships in one's diet and childhood leukemia. This group of researchers tested everything from fruits and vegetables to processed meats. The only finding that indicated any kind of statistical relationship was hot dogs. Yes, Peters et al. found that if a child ate 12 or more hot dogs a month, he or she had an increased risk of childhood leukemia. At the time, some newspapers took the risk seriously, reporting it as sacrosanct scientific law, but many others scoffed at the study and drew criticism to the data-mining methods used. Marian Burros (1994) in the *New York Times* wrote, "HO-HUM. Another month, another scare. The latest is about a possible connection between the high consumption of hot dogs and childhood leukemia" (¶ 1). Eventually, a more empirically structure study did examine this issue and determine that the finding was not accurate (Kwan, Block, Selvin, Month, & Buffler, 2004). However, there are still many websites out there that tout the original Peters et al. (1994) study as evidence of the harm of hot dogs in general.

Although data dredging or data fishing can be highly problematic, data mining is a useful and valid set of statistical techniques if someone follows the scientific method and has a clear purpose for analyzing data. However, most data-mining experts will argue that there can be times when exploring one's data can be meaningful (LaRose & LaRose, 2014).

MONITORING AND ANOMALIES

Two common analyses that Big Data are used for are monitoring and anomalies. *Monitoring* is a form of Big Data analysis where individuals have a general idea of what they are looking for in the first place. In the beginning of this chapter we discussed two examples of monitoring: Target being able to predict when someone is pregnant and Call of Duty predicting when people are cheating. In each of these cases, data scientists have created predictive models designed to monitor an individual's behavior. When a certain number of variables are triggered, then the data scientist is notified that the event has potentially occurred. Of course, we say that the data scientist is notified, but more often than not the positive monitoring automatically triggers a response to occur (e.g., an individual receives coupons for baby furniture, toys, and products in the mail or a user has her or his account suspended for cheating).

Big Data analysis can also be used to help people find *anomalies*. Anomalies occur when something within the data falls outside of normal activity. When looking for anomalies, you often have no idea what these anomalies may look like so there is no way to monitor for them.

Instead, anomaly detection attempts to look for patterns within the data that are outside of the norm. When these boundaries are crossed, a data scientist is notified that an anomaly has occurred. A data scientist is informed that an anomaly has occurred because you still need a human set of eyes to look at the results and attempt to make sense of them. Although not necessarily used for research purposes, anomaly detection is often useful. For example, if you work for a stockbrokerage firm you may want to know when stock trading patterns suddenly jump outside the traditional trading patterns. Although this anomaly may mean nothing, the anomaly could be a huge red flag that something drastic and unexpected is occurring. For example, a colleague worked on a research study where an automated phone system monitored the symptoms of heart-failure patients. When a patient reported gaining more than 3 pounds in 3 days, this was considered an anomaly and a nurse would receive an email. This email triggered the nurse to call the patient to determine whether the weight gain was caused by eating a bag of chips or a worsening of the patient's heart failure.

Both monitoring and anomaly detection are not necessarily new ideas, but Big Data has made the analysis of both stronger. For example, imagine you had data from 1,000 people and you would have 1 anomaly. For traditional research purposes, 1 anomaly of 1,000 is not interesting. However, when you can analyze 1 million cases, now you have 1,000 anomalies occurring, so understanding what is causing the anomaly becomes a fascinating research study. Furthermore, with more than 1,000 cases, researchers have the ability to make better predictive models to start predicting these anomalies and manage them when they occur.

Communication and Big Data

Overall, there has not been a huge amount of research conducted within the field of communication using Big Data. In 2014 the *Journal of Communication* published a special issue to highlight some of the ways researchers are using Big Data within the field. The issue's editor had this to say: "Big Data research is still in its infancy in communication. Relatively little of the work done in this early stage will stand the test of time, but all of it will likely be critical in the ongoing process of conceptual and methodological advance" (Parks, 2014, p. 355). Researchers in communication have focused on a number of interesting areas using Big Data to investigate health communication, mass communication, political communication, and social networking. We expect to see an increase in Big Data research in the near future, but we are writing this chapter while this specific research method is still "in its infancy." In this section, we are not going to look at each of the articles published in this special issue, but we are going to highlight a few of the techniques these researchers utilized.

One of the classic areas of research within media studies has consistently been agenda setting. Agenda-setting theory purports that the media has the ability to set the political agenda discussed within society. If the media finds a topic important and discusses it enough, then the public will likewise also find the topic important. Neuman, Guggenheim, Jang, and Bae (2014) conducted a comparison analysis of political discussions via Twitter versus what the mainstream media was determining as important. The researchers used a third-party vendor to get access to the "Twitter firehose," which is the enormous, real-time stream of tweets. The firehose is also recorded, so it enables researchers to examine past phenomena as well as current ones. Overall, the researchers were able to compare what was important to social media users directly with what the traditional media outlets were broadcasting as news at the same time. Not surprising, social media and modern news outlets were not really in sync with one another. Without this massive amount of Twitter data, this type of research project would have been impossible. When looking at the various articles in the special issue of the *Journal of Communication*, a number of studies used Twitter as a source of information (Colleoni,

Rozza, & Arvidsson, 2014; Emery, Szczypkal, Abrill, Kim, & Vera, 2014; Giglietto & Selva, 2014; Jungherr, 2014; Park, Baek, & Chal, 2014; Vargo, Guo, McCombs, & Shaw, 2014).

Although Twitter is the most popular source of Big Data by communication scholars thus far, it is not the only source of Big Data communication researchers have utilized to understand human communication. Balmas and Sheafer (2014) used 800,000 news items over three decades to examine how political leaders in six countries were represented in international media. These scholars specifically used the news archiving service Lexis Nexus to locate the articles and then performed a giant content analysis of the 800,000 news items they located. In another study, Shaw and Hill (2014) used data from Wikipedia to examine how people collaborate on wikis. The researchers examined 683 different wikis to see how people go about creating and interacting with one another in the collaborative environment. According to Shaw and Hill, "This dataset consists of rich longitudinal records, which include every contribution made to each wiki, recorded with timestamps accurate to within 1 second. It includes 33,278,993 distinct contributions by 469,524 different contributors to 6,167,797 different wiki pages—more than 264 gigabytes of raw data" (p. 222).

As you can see, whether using Twitter, Lexis Nexis, or Wikipedia, communication researchers are making inroads in the field of Big Data. However, there is still more work to be done. One of the biggest hurdles many communication scholars will face with regards to Big Data is access (Parks, 2014). Many of the most dominant social networking sites of our time do not make data available to the public without a price. Even as I am writing this chapter, the Twitter hose that Neuman et al. (2014) used is being turned off to third-party vendors (Goel, 2015). Instead, the Twitter hose will only be accessible through Twitter's data arm, https://gnip.com/, which Twitter recently purchased. Twitter sees these data as a commodity, and people who want access to the data are going to be forced to pay a lot of money to have that access. Unfortunately, without funds to get access to the data, many scholars will simply avoid delving into the Big Data world.

Big Data Ethics

Hopefully by this point, you have begun to realize that Big Data is an amazing analytic approach/paradigm, but there are definitely points where some of it begins to seem a little creepy. Do you really want Target to know when you are pregnant before anyone else (including yourself)? Clearly, Big Data raises some big ethical questions. Unlike traditional academic research, much of the research conducted using Big Data simply does not fall under the traditional ethical oversight that academic research does. As such, we rely on individuals and organizations to treat these data ethically. According to Big Data ethicists, big data ethics involves four primary issues: privacy, identity, ownership, and reputation (Davis & Patterson, 2012; Richards & King, 2014).

PRIVACY

Probably the single biggest concern with regard to ethics and Big Data involves an individual's privacy. We live in a world where information is being collected about us all the time without our knowledge. Most data collectors will argue that the collection of data is completed in a way to maintain an individual's anonymity or confidentiality. However, a number of studies have shown that this simply is not the case. For example, Latanya Arvette Sweeney (2000) was a graduate student when the state of Massachusetts decided to release the medical data for all public employees. The state of Massachusetts did due diligence in its attempt at deidentifying the dataset. The governor at the time, William Weld, promised the public that the data were deidentified and they had no reason to worry that anyone could go about identifying their individual medical data. Sweeney took this challenge and set out to reidentify the governor's data. First, she knew the governor resided in Cambridge, Massachusetts, so for $20 she purchased the voter ID data. The voter ID database included the names, ages, addresses, zip codes, and birthdates of everyone in Cambridge. Sweeney quickly compared the information she learned about the governor to that in the patient database and found that only six people had the governor's birthdate, only three were male, and only one lived in his zip code. With that information, Sweeney was able to correctly identify the governor's health records, including diagnoses and prescriptions he was taking. Sweeney (2000) would later determine that with just three pieces of information (birthdate, sex, and zip code) she could correctly identify 87 percent of people.

In 2002 the implementation of Health Insurance Portability and Accountability Act (HIPAA) did put a few new protections in place with regard to health information. However, deidentifying data in other venues has also become a concern. In 2006, Netflix released a dataset to the general public containing the deidentified movie viewing history of 480,189 users' ratings of 17,770 movies. Overall, the dataset contained 100,480,507 ratings from Netflix users. Netflix released these data in an effort to allow individuals and teams to create new algorithms that could predict an individual's rating of a movie. Researchers Arvind Narayanan and Vitaly Shmatikov (2008) took this dataset and decided to see whether they could reidentify the individuals within the deidentified dataset. The researchers compared the Netflix data with information taken from ratings on the Internet Movie Database (IMDB). The researchers successfully reidentified a Netflix user's movie watching and rating history by comparing similar information on IMDB ratings.

As you can see from both of these examples, privacy is a serious problem in the world of Big Data. When it takes only three pieces of information to correctly identify 87 percent of people, then one must always question the privacy of these data.

IDENTITY

In Walt Whitman's (1871) poem "Song of Myself," he writes, "I am large, I contain multitudes." In this short phrase, Whitman is acknowledging that many of us have varying parts to our individual identities. Social psychologists have argued for years that an individual's identity is a complex and ever-evolving idea. An individual's identity is her or his own conception of who he or she are based on unique individuality and group affiliations. Cohen (2013) asserts, "people are born into networks of relationships, practices, and beliefs, and over time encounter and experiment with others, engaging in a diverse and ad hoc mix of practices that defies neat theoretical simplification" (p. 1910).

Unfortunately, not everyone in the networked world sees people as having this right to create their own identities. One of the biggest concerns related to Big Data is who gets to determine your identity in the twenty-first century. Richards and King (2014) noted "big data analytics can compromise identity by allowing institutional surveillance to moderate and even determine who we are before we make up our own minds" (p. 422). In essence, Big Data can create a picture of who you are to others without you having any real say in the matter. Instead of you determining your own identity, the numbers determine that identity for you and place you in a clearly labeled box.

A secondary identity concern involves the creation of multiple identities in life. We often have differing identities in school, with our friends, with our families, and in the workplace. However, some argue that this kind of pluralistic understanding of identities has no place in the online world. Mark Zuckerberg, founder and chief executive officer of Facebook, was once quoted as saying, "Having two identities for yourself is an example of a lack of integrity"

(Helft, 2011, ¶ 3). Clearly, Zuckerberg sees the world of identity as purely either 100 percent authentic or 100 percent inauthentic, with no room in between.

We should mention that there is a highly symbiotic relationship between issues of privacy and identity. As everything we do online is collected and fed into giant storehouses of information, there is a serious question about how this information is used by others. Calo (2014, 2015) has argued that the next wave of Big Data analytics is going to be targeted less at understanding who we are as people and more on how they can shape us as people. Basically, Calo (2014) argues that Big Data is getting to the point where the information businesses learn about us as individuals will be used to directly influence who we are as individuals. In essence, marketers will attempt to shape our identities based on what they have learned about our identity. Calo (2014) takes this one step further and asks to what extent this same technology could be used against the populace. The idea that politicians could gather "information about individual citizens to better persuade them comes very close to the sort of Orwellian propaganda society has collectively rejected. A related critique of nudging is that it tends to infantilize the citizen by removing the habit of choice. Again, the constant mediation of the citizen by technology could accelerate this effect" (p. 1049).

OWNERSHIP

The third type of serious ethical concern related to Big Data involves ownership. To what extent (if any) do we own the information gathered about ourselves? Do we own basic demographic information about ourselves (e.g., height, weight, eye/hair color, ethnicity/race, birthdate, zip code)? What about family information (e.g., genetic history, family lineage, family health histories)? Do we own data about our hobbies (e.g., video editing, basketball, car mechanic, crafter)? Do we own information about the skills we have (e.g., throwing a free-throw, kicking a field goal, sewing clothing, arranging large events)? What about our own individual personal tastes (e.g., Coke vs. Pepsi, broccoli vs. asparagus, McDonalds vs. Burger King, plastic vs. paper)? A lot of information can (and is) collected about us all the time, but do we have any actual ownership of these data?

Europe has long had much more stringent rules for how companies can collect and use data. In fact, the European Union's website devoted to data protection explicitly states, "Protecting your personal data—a fundamental right!" (http://ec.europa.eu/justice/data-protection/). Furthermore, the European Union has a set of fairly straightforward policies that argue that an individual's data can only be collected for legitimate purposes. In other words, you cannot just collect data on or about people just because you want to collect the data for unspecified reasons to be determined at a later time. However, these same rules do not apply in the United States. Although there have been pushes to create a Consumer Privacy Bill of Rights that tackles issues of data ownership, these legislative pushes have not gone far.

REPUTATION

The last major ethical question related to Big Data involves an individual's reputation, or the extent an individual has to control how others think about her or him. According to Davis and Patterson (2012), "Unless we were famous for some other reason, the vast majority of us managed our reputation by acting well (or poorly) in relation to those directly around us. In some cases, a second-degree perception—that is, what the people who knew you said about you to the people who they knew—might influence one's reputation" (p. 18). You may be wondering what reputation has to do with Big Data by this point. As we discussed earlier under identity, today people have the ability to infer your identity and form opinions about who you are as a person based purely on the data that are collected about you.

The tech industry has not always been understanding of issues related to reputation. Google's chief executive officer, Eric Schmidt, once told a reporter, "If you have something that you don't want anyone to know, maybe you shouldn't be doing it in the first place" (Newman, 2009, ¶3). To put this quotation in context, Schmidt was discussing the amount of data that are kept and tracked for each individual under the U.S. Patriot Act. However, there is an inherent idea behind Schmidt's statement that impacts one's deeper reputation. Most of us have probably seen something on the Internet that we wish we could simply unsee. Should your reputation be based on seeing whatever that was? In fact, online reputation management is becoming a huge business. Just ask the many companies that now profit by helping individuals, groups, and organizations with online reputation management. Brandyourself.com says it all right on their website: "Look great when employers, clients and even dates Google you."

Manage Your Online Reputation

1. Google yourself. It is important to know what information exists on the Internet about you. You may be surprised by some of what you see.

2. Buy your domain name. Part of brand management is purchasing the domain name that corresponds with your name. For example, the first author of this book has his domain name at http://www.JasonSWrench.com/. The last thing you want is someone else to own your domain and have information on that website that is deemed inappropriate.

3. Join social networks. One mistake that some people make is thinking that if they are not on social networks, then it is a good thing. Actually, not being on social networks can be a red flag. Instead, join social networks like LinkedIn, Facebook, and Twitter, but be mindful of the content you post and support.

4. Optimize your presence. You want people to find you. So you want to make it easy for them to do this. For example, our lead author can be found on Facebook, Twitter, LinkedIn, YouTube, Vimeo, SlideShare, and other social networking sites all under the name JasonSWrench. Why does he do this? When you are consistent across your social networking platforms, you can create a brand that tells the story of who you are. Furthermore, when you link these various accounts together, they help you rise in Google's and other search engines. You can also use the free version of http://brandyourself.com/ to help manage this.

5. Keep your private things private.

If you do not want your grandmother, boss, or a future boss to learn it about you, then do not put it online. Admittedly, some younger people have been on social networking sites since they were children and did not think about or care about their reputations. Unfortunately, anything that exists on the Internet about you can come back to harm you.

KEY TERMS

Big Data
Data analytics

Data mining
Data science

Internet of things
Machine learning

REFERENCES

Balmas, M., & Sheafer, T. (2014). Charismatic leaders and mediated personalization in the international arena. *Communication Research, 41*, 991–1015. doi:10.1177/0093650213510936

Burros, M. (1994, June 22). Eating well. *The New York Times.* Retrieved from http://www.nytimes.com/1994/06/22/garden/eating-well.html/

Calo, R. (2014). Digital market manipulation. *The George Washington Law Review, 82*(4), 995–1051.

Calo, R. (2015). Robot-sized gaps in surveillance law. In M. Rotenberg, J. Horwitz, and J. Scott (Eds.), *Privacy in the modern age: The search for solutions* (pp. 41–45). New York, NY: New Press.

Cohen, J. E. (2013). What is privacy for? *Harvard Law Review, 126*(6), 1904–1933.

Codd, E. F. (1970). A relational model of data for large shared data banks. *Communications of the ACM, 13*(6), 337–387.

Colleoni, E., Rozza, A., & Arvidsson, A. (2014). Echo chamber or public sphere? Predicting political orientation and measuring political homophily in Twitter using Big Data. *Journal of Communication, 64*, 317–332. doi:10.1111/jcom.12084

Conway, D. (2010, September 30). *The data science Venn diagram* [Web log post]. Retrieved from http://drewconway.com/zia/2013/3/26/the-data-science-venn-diagram/

Davis, K., & Patterson, D. (2012). *Ethics of big data: Balancing risk and innovation.* Sebastopol, CA: O'Reilly.

Dawson, R. J. M. (1995). The "unusual episode" data revisited. *Journal of Statistics Education, 3*(3). Retrieved from http://www.amstat.org/publications/jse/v3n3/datasets.dawson.html/

Dwoskin, E. (2014, June 6). In a single tweet, as many pieces of metadata as there are characters. *Wall Street Journal.* Retrieved from http://blogs.wsj.com/digits/2014/06/06/in-a-single-tweet-as-many-pieces-of-metadata-as-there-are-characters/

Emery, S. L., Szczypkal, G., Abrill, E. P., Kim, Y., & Vera, L. (2014). Are you scared yet? Evaluating fear appeal messages in tweets about the Tips campaign. *Journal of Communication, 64*, 278–295. doi:10.1111/jcom.12083

Giglietto, F., & Selva, D. (2014). Second screen and participation: A content analysis on a full season dataset of tweets. *Journal of Communication, 64*, 260–277. doi:10.1111/jcom.12085

Goel, V. (2015, April 11). Twitter's evolving plans to make money from its data stream. *The New York Times.* Retrieved from http://bits.blogs.nytimes.com/2015/04/11/twitters-evolving-plans-to-make-money-from-its-data-stream/?_r=0/

Grimes, S. (2008, August 1). Unstructured data and the 80 percent rule. *Breakthrough Analysis* [blog post]. Retrieved from http://www.lakeandpondsolutions.com/helpful-info/acreage-and-volume-calculations/

Helft, M. (2011, May 13). Facebook, foe of anonymity, is forced to explain a secret. *The New York Times.* Retrieved from http://www.nytimes.com/2011/05/14/technology/14facebook.html?_r=0/

Jungherr, A. (2014). The logic of political coverage on twitter: Temporal dynamics and content. *Journal of Communication, 64*, 239–259. doi:10.1111/jcom.12087

Kwan, M. L., Block, G., Selvin, S., Month, S., & Buffler, P. A. (2004). Food consumption by children and the risk of childhood acute leukemia. *American Journal of Epidemiology, 160*, 1098–1107.

Laney, D. (2001, February 6). *3D data management: Controlling data volume, velocity, and variety* (File 949). Stamford, CT: META Group.

LaRose, D. T., & Larose, C. D. (2014). *Discovering knowledge in data: An introduction to data mining.* Hoboken, NJ: Wiley.

Milloy, S. (1995). *Science without sense: The risky business of public health research.* Washington, DC: Cato.

Moore, G. E. (1965, April 19). Cramming more components onto integrated circuits. *Electronics, 38*(8), 114–117.

Narayanan, A., & Shmatikov, V. (2008). Robust de-anonymization of large sparse datasets. *Proceedings of the IEEE Symposium on Security and Privacy, USA,* 111–125. doi:10.1109/SP.2008.33

Newman, J. (2009, December 11). Google's Schmidt roasted for privacy comments. *PCWorld* [Web log post]. http://www.pcworld.com/article/184446/googles_schmidt_roasted_for_privacy_comments.html/

Neuman, W. R., Guggenheim, L., Jang, S. M., & Bae, S. Y. (2014). The dynamics of public attention: Agenda-setting theory meets big data. *Journal of Communication, 64,* 193–214. doi:10.1111/jcom.12088

Park, J., Baek, Y. M., & Chal, M. (2014). Cross-cultural comparison of nonverbal cues in emoticons on Twitter: Evidence from Big Data analysis. *Journal of Communication, 64,* 333–354. doi:10.1111/jcom.12086

Parks, M. (2014). Big Data in communication research: Its contents and discontents. *Journal of Communication, 64,* 355–360. doi:10.1111/jcom.12090

Peters, J. M., Preston-Martin, S., London, S. J. Bowman, J. D., Buckley, J. D., & Thomas, D. C. (1994). Processed meats and risk of childhood leukemia (California, USA). *Cancer Causes Control, 5,* 195–202.

Pringle, T. (2014, July 18). *Data-as-a-service: The next step in the as-a-service journey.* London, UK: Ovum.

Richards, N. M., & King, J. H. (2014). Big Data ethics. *Wake Forest Law Review, 49,* 393–432.

Shaw, A., & Hill, B. M. (2014). Laboratories of oligarchy? How the iron law extends to peer production. *Journal of Communication, 64,* 215–238. doi:10.1111/jcom.12082

Sweeney, L. (2000). Foundations of privacy protection from a computer science perspective. In the *Proceedings of the Joint Statistical Meeting, AAAS,* Indianapolis, IN.

van Rijmenam, M. (2014). *Think bigger: Developing a successful Big Data strategy for your business.* New York, NY: AMACOM.

Vargo, C. J., Guo, L., McCombs, M., & Shaw, D. L. (2014). Network issue agendas on twitter during the 2012 U.S. presidential election. *Journal of Communication, 64,* 296–316. doi:10.1111/jcom.12089

Wall, M. (2014, March 4). Big Data: Are you ready for blast-off? *BBC News.* Retrieved from http://www.bbc.com/news/business-26383058/

Ward, J. S., & Barker, A. (2013, September 20). *Undefined by data: A survey of big data definitions.* Retrieved from arXiv:1309.5821/ [cs.DB]

Whitman, W. (1871). *Leaves of grass* (5th ed.). New York, NY: Redfield.

FURTHER READING

Dean, J. (2014). *Big Data, data mining, and machine learning: Value creation for business leaders and practitioners.* Hoboken, NJ: Wiley.

Granville, V. (2014). *Developing analytic talent: Becoming a data scientist.* Indianapolis, IN: Wiley.

Kitchen, R. (2014). *The data revolution: Big Data, open data, data infrastructures, & their consequences.* Thousand Oaks, CA: Sage.

McArdle, J. G., & Ritschard, G. (Eds). (2014). *Contemporary issues in exploratory data mining in the behavioral sciences.* New York, NY: Routledge.

Weiss, S. M., Indurkhya, N., Zhang, T., & Damerau, F. (2005). *Text mining: Predictive methods for analyzing unstructured information.* New York, NY: Springer.

CHAPTER **13**

Sampling Methods

CHAPTER OBJECTIVES

1   Define the term "sampling" and explain why we use samples instead of populations.

2   Explain the sampling process.

3   Explain the central limits theorem.

4   Differentiate among the different probability samples (simple random samples, stratified random samples, cluster samples, and systematic samples).

5   Describe the importance of sampling error and its relation to probability samples.

6   Differentiate among the different nonprobability samples (convenience samples, volunteer samples, purposive samples, quota samples, and network samples).

7   Explain the general rules discussed in this chapter for determining a necessary sample size.

8   Describe the relationship between confidence intervals and sample sizes.

Selecting participants for a research study is one of the most crucial elements for the success of the project. Suppose a researcher wanted to answer the question, "What is the level of communication satisfaction between teachers and principals?" Who would you suggest that the researcher approach to be included in this study? The obvious answer is teachers and principals. However, there could be other characteristics of these two groups of participants that guide the research design. It would be important to include teachers from private and public schools, as well as those at the elementary, junior high, and high school levels. Perhaps selecting teachers with a variety of years of teaching experience would be important in answering the question. As you can see, there are numerous factors to consider when selecting a sample for your research design.

Consider this: every time you complete an exam for a class, you are responding to questions that address a sample of the information learned in the class. If the instructor were to test you on each and every thing you had learned, the exam might be extremely long. Instead, a sample of concepts is selected to assess your knowledge. In this chapter we will discuss the various sampling methods used to identify who should be included in the research project. Different types of samples will be identified, and questions regarding how many participants to include will be answered.

Why Use a Sample?

Sampling is the term used to refer to selecting people or units for inclusion in a research study. Scholars use samples because including all possible persons or units for a study is virtually impossible. Of course, since it is not possible to include every person or unit in the research project, it is important that the sample chosen be representative of the entire group. To begin our discussion, we will identify some key terms that will guide your understanding of the sampling process.

POPULATION

Population refers to an entire set of objects, observations, or scores that have some characteristic in common. For example, all registered voters between the ages of 18 and 25 could be considered a population. In this instance, all members of the population have two characteristics of interest in common: voter eligibility and age. Suppose the purpose of your research study is to identify the communication motives of college students who have visited their academic advisors. The population for this study would be extremely large. Thus, a sample of the population should be selected for the study to make data collection more manageable.

SAMPLE

Sample is the term used to refer to the people or units that a researcher actually includes in the study. Researchers choose samples because including all members of the population can be costly and time-consuming. Have you ever wondered how the marketers of Trident concluded that four of five dentists whose patients chew gum recommend Trident? They probably did not interview every dentist in the United States, so it is more likely that they contacted a sample from the population of dentists and calculated a statistic that could be generalized. Consider our earlier example of the population of college students who have visited their academic advisors. Since it is impossible to contact all of the college students who have done so, a researcher could select a sample of students and ask them to complete a survey about their communication motives. Furthermore, not all members of your sample will necessarily participate in the study. Sample members may choose to drop out of the study, they may refuse to participate, or they may not respond to every item. At times, the terms "population" and "sample" may be confusing. To review, population refers to all possible people or units that could be included, and sample refers to those people or units who are selected for inclusion in the study. The question becomes: How does a researcher identify the population and select the sample to include in the study?

THE SAMPLING PROCESS

Ask any researcher what her or his ultimate goal is when selecting a sample for inclusion in a study, and he or she will likely respond that he or she wants a sample that will produce results that are generalizable to the population. The term "generalizable" refers to the notion that the results of studying a sample can be assumed to be true of the entire population. To ensure generalizability, the researcher must take specific steps to ensure that the characteristics of the sample closely resemble those of the population. As you can see, the primary task at this stage of the research process involves identifying the appropriate sample. The sampling process involves several steps. Often the population that is the focus of a study is not accessible. For example, conducting a study on the aggressive communication behaviors encountered by women in abusive relationships would be difficult. Because many women in the population are apprehensive about reporting the abuse, although they are members of the **theoretical population** they may not be accessible for the study. So the first step in sampling involves identifying the theoretical population that the researcher would like to generalize the results of the study to and then identifying the actual study population that includes participants that the researcher could realistically contact.

After selecting the study population, the second step involves identifying all members of that group and determining how each one could be contacted for inclusion in the study. Recall our earlier example regarding the communication motives of students who have visited their academic advisors. Suppose a researcher has determined that the accessible population includes students attending Eastern University. Members of the population could be identified by asking all academic advisors on campus to provide a list of the students who had visited their offices during the previous two semesters. The list of all potential participants in the study population (students attending Eastern University) that are accessible to the researcher is referred to as the **sampling frame**. Remember, the sampling frame includes all members of the population accessible to the researcher, not all possible members of the theoretical population.

Say a study requires a researcher to conduct a survey inquiring about citizens' opinions about the credibility of a local politician. The local phone book could be used as a listing of the accessible population. Why couldn't this be considered representative of the theoretical population? Keep in mind that various things could preclude a person from being listed in the phone book. Phone numbers may be unlisted, some members of the theoretical population may only use cell phones, and the listing typically only includes the name of one member of a household. Thus, although the phone book can be used to provide contact information for the accessible population, it does not provide information for the theoretical population.

The final step of the sampling process involves identifying the method that will be used to select members of the accessible population for inclusion in the sample that is contacted for the study. Suppose Eastern University is a large school and the academic advisors provided you with a list of more than 15,000 names. Contacting everyone on the list would be time-consuming, not to mention expensive. Thus, the researcher must identify the sample of students to be included in the study. A variety of sampling designs can be used to determine who will be contacted to participate in the study. Two primary designs involve probability sampling and nonprobability sampling. Each of these designs has a variety of sample methods available for a researcher to use.

SELECTING A SAMPLE DESIGN

When selecting the sample for a study, the researcher must decide whether to use probability or nonprobability designs when choosing participants. **Probability sampling** involves the random selection of participants that guarantees that each member of the population has an equal chance of being selected (as discussed in Chapter 12). Examples of probability methods for selecting participants include simple random samples, stratified random samples, cluster samples, and systematic samples. **Nonprobability sampling** involves selecting members of the accessible population in a nonrandom manner. Examples of nonprobability methods include convenience samples, volunteer samples, purposive samples, quota samples, and network samples.

Your decision of which design to use should consider your desire to predict the sampling error associated with the study. **Sampling error** refers to the random differences that exist between the sample and the population. By selecting a probability design, a researcher can calculate the sampling error or the degree to which the sample might be different from the population it was selected to represent. Nonprobability samples do not enable a researcher to calculate the degree to which the sample differs from the population. We will take a closer look at these sample designs and discuss how a researcher decides which sampling method to use.

PROBABILITY SAMPLING

Probability sampling involves randomly selecting participants from the population so that all potential participants have an equal chance of being selected for the study. Random selection methods eliminate any potential **sampling bias** by ensuring that each person in the population has an equal chance of being chosen. Chances are that you have used probability sampling at various times in your life and not realized it. The strategy of "drawing straws" for a task is one that involves random selection. Because the length of the straws is concealed from view and selection of straws is random, each person who takes a turn at selecting a straw has an equal chance of drawing the short straw.

As we emphasized earlier, probability designs are used in situations where the researcher wants to calculate and report the sampling error. It makes sense that **probability theory** holds true in situations where probability samples are used—the score that occurs most frequently in the sample will also be the score that should occur most frequently in the population. Probability samples produce scores that accurately reflect the most and the least common scores in the population. Recall the normal distribution curve that we discussed in Chapter 7. Probability methods allow the researcher to select a sample whose scores will be distributed in the shape of a normal distribution curve. The central limits theorem is used to explain the relationship between probability samples and the population. According to the central limits theorem, collecting data from repeated samples within the same population will produce a distribution of scores in the shape of a normal curve. More specifically, the **central limits theorem** states that the mean of the scores obtained from the probability sample will be equal to the mean of the scores obtained from the population. Further, the central limits theorem states that the variance of the sample mean is equal to the variance of the population mean divided by the sample size (N). Thus, the more variance that exists between scores in the population, the more variance that will exist between scores in the sample used to represent that population. Finally, the central limits theorem states that the distribution of mean scores from the sample will more closely represent the distribution of mean scores of the population as the sample size (N) increases, which makes sense because probability samples provide equal opportunity for selection, and the results are more likely to reflect the population.

As mentioned earlier, an advantage of probability sampling is that it enables the researcher to calculate sampling error, or how likely it is that the population mean differs from the sample mean. We will address the concept of sampling error in more detail later in this chapter. Once the researcher determines that probability designs are preferred, the next step involves selecting the specific method that will be used to choose participants for the sample.

SIMPLE RANDOM SAMPLES

As discussed in Chapter 12, **simple random samples** are considered by many the "purest" method for collecting a probability sample. This method ensures that each member of the population has an equal chance of being selected for the study. The researcher makes a random decision of who will be included in the sample. Various methods of randomization are used to select sample members, and these methods are selected to ensure the validity of the study. Two forms of randomization can be used in research: random samples and random assignment. "Random sample" refers to the selection of study participants from the population. "Random assignment" is a term used to refer to how the researcher assigns the sample drawn from the population to various groups within the study. Suppose a researcher wants to examine the persuasive effect of language used in fear appeals. To ensure a truly representative sample, a researcher might select a simple random sample of 150 people from the target population. Next, members of the sample would be randomly assigned in groups of 50 to one of three conditions—high-, medium-, and low-intensity fear appeals. Thus, it is possible to design a study that utilizes both random sampling and random assignment. Random sampling allows a researcher to generalize the results to the population, thus enhancing the external validity of the study. Random assignment allows the researcher to strengthen the internal validity of the study by ensuring that participants are randomly assigned to the conditions being examined.

So how do researchers identify a simple random sample for a study? This task is often completed using a table of random numbers or some other computer-generated list that ensures random selection (see Figure 13.1 for an example from http://www.random.org/). Recall our earlier example of students who meet with academic advisors. The first step in securing a random sample requires the identification of the accessible population. To accomplish this, we would ask academic advisors to provide lists of students who had visited their office during the past two semesters. In the next step, we would identify the sample size desired for the project. Sample size will be discussed later in this chapter, but for now we will assume that we want to survey 100 students of the 850 students included on the lists provided by advisors. One method for randomly selecting the participants might involve placing all 850 names in a hat and drawing 100 names to contact. Although this method would ensure that each person had an equal chance of being selected, it would be time-consuming. A more efficient method for randomly selecting participants involves using a table of random numbers. Computers have made the task of random number assignment much easier. In the previous chapter we presented how to use an electronic random number generator—we will now look at an example using a random number table (Figure 13.1).

Using this table of random numbers, we can collect a random sample for our study. Step one involves assigning each student on the list a number between 1 and 850. In step two, refer to the first three digits of each number listed on the chart of random numbers, since 850 is a three-digit number. Step three involves closing your eyes and randomly pointing to a spot on the chart. Suppose you randomly selected 46882 in Figure 13.1. Next, we read the number as 468 (the first three digits). Thus, the student who was assigned the number of 468 is included in our sample list. Continue down the column to the next number, which is 02429. This is interpreted a 024, which means that student 24 is selected for the sample. Our next number on the chart is 85676. However, we only have 850 students on our list. Not a problem—simply

61424	20419	86546	00517
46882	27993	04952	66762
02429	71146	97668	86523
85676	10005	07216	25906
19761	50349	15370	90222
78733	16447	27932	89990

Figure 13.1 Sample Table of Random Numbers

skip that number and continue to the next number in the column. Continue through the chart until 100 students have been randomly selected for the sample.

As you can see, this task can be particularly time-consuming for drawing large samples. Computers have enabled researchers to accomplish this task more efficiently. Yet another method for assigning random numbers to a list generated from the population can be accomplished using Microsoft Excel. For our study of students who visit advisors, we would simply copy and paste the list of names into an Excel spreadsheet. In the column next to the list of names, the formula "=RAND()" is inserted in the cell to instruct Excel to assign a random number between 0 and 1 beside each name on the list. Be sure to copy and paste this formula throughout the entire selection of cells. Next, conduct a sort of both columns by instructing Excel to sort and arrange the list of random numbers from lowest to highest (or vice versa). Once this is completed, you simply select the first 100 names from your list of 850.

So what are the advantages and disadvantages of random samples? The primary advantage is the ability to calculate the statistical sampling error. Disadvantages include the need to have accurate lists representing the entire population and the time involved in the process of random selection. In addition, by sheer luck a researcher may find that the sample selected randomly does not provide an accurate representation of the population. Other probability sampling methods can be used to combat these concerns.

STRATIFIED RANDOM SAMPLES

In some instances in which the population is extremely large, researchers may want to select participants based on criteria chosen specifically for the study. **Stratified random samples** enable researchers to divide the population into specific strata, also known as subsets of the population that have a common characteristic. Participants are randomly selected from the strata that have been identified. Some examples of strata that could be examined in a study include males and females; full-time and part-time students; or Democrats, Republicans, and Independents. Once the strata have been identified, conduct a simple random sample of each group.

Stratified sampling is the preferred method in some studies because it reduces the potential for sampling error. Researchers often use this sampling method in situations where there is unequal representation of one group or stratum of a population compared to other groups. Consider our example of student motives for visiting academic advisors. If the list of names provided by advisors was disproportionate in terms of the number of freshmen, sophomores, juniors, and seniors, the researcher might decide to conduct a stratified random sample to ensure that information is gathered from all class ranks.

Once the strata have been identified, the next task involves determining the sample size for each group. As a general rule, the researcher should ensure that the number of participants selected from each stratum is proportionate to the group's size in the population. Suppose we know that of the 850 students included on the list, 300 are freshmen, 275 are sophomores, 175 are juniors, and 100 are seniors. Since there is a disproportionate amount of seniors in the population, it would be important to conduct a stratified sample to determine whether communication motives of seniors differ from those of freshmen and sophomores. To calculate the proportionate sample size for each stratum, we first must determine what percentage of the overall population is represented by each group. To determine the percentage, you divide the number of people in a group by the total number of students. For example, to find the percentage of freshman we must divide the number of freshmen (300) by the total number of students (850), or 300/850 = 35.29 (when rounded). The population is composed of 35.29% freshman, 30.24% sophomores, 20.59% juniors, and 11.76% seniors. This means that of our sample of 100, we should survey 36 freshmen, 31 sophomores, 21 juniors, and 12 seniors.

The obvious advantage to stratified samples is their ability to ensure that various subgroups in the population are included in the study, which is especially important in instances where there are minority groups who may not be selected for the study if simple random selection methods are used. Disadvantages to stratified sampling include the difficulty in identifying nonoverlapping strata and the additional time needed to organize groups for simple random selection.

CLUSTER SAMPLES

Cluster sampling allows a researcher to identify naturally occurring clusters of participants who have a variable in common within the target population. Suppose in your study of college students you want to collect information from colleges across the country. You would need a lot of time and money to complete the project if you began in California and surveyed students at colleges until you arrived in Maine. An alternative method for ensuring that colleges have an equal chance of being selected would involve using the cluster sample method. This method requires the researcher to first divide the country into regions: West, Southwest, Midwest, East, and so forth. Once all the colleges within each region are selected, the cluster sample method is used to randomly select the region of the country from which to select participants. Once the region is randomly selected, random sampling is conducted within each region to ensure that a probability sample is obtained. Another instance in which cluster sampling could be useful is if a researcher wanted to interview employees of an organization with offices around the nation or the world.

One apparent advantage of cluster sampling is the money and time that can be saved by contacting participants in a few areas rather than gathering data from all possible regions. A disadvantage of the method is that participants in the same geographical area or same organizational region might be similar to one another, and thus they could be less representative of the population than the researcher originally anticipated. A second important disadvantage to cluster samples is that the chance of sampling error (the random differences that exist between the sample and the population) will increase with each step (we will discuss this idea in more detail in a moment).

SYSTEMATIC SAMPLES

A final probability sampling method, **systematic samples**, involves selecting a sample by determining the sample size needed from the population and selecting every "*n*th" person from the population for inclusion in the study. This method is effective as simple random sampling as long as there is no systematic order to the listing of a population. In our earlier example, systematic sampling could be used as long as advisors were not instructed to submit their lists in order of class rank or grade point average. If any of the lists include a method for organizing or ordering population members, systematic sampling cannot be used.

Suppose you want to conduct interviews with 15 employees from a population of 200. Simply divide 200 by 15 and you would discover that every 13th employee on the list should be included in your sample. To ensure that every employee has an equal chance of being chosen, choose a random number between 1 and 15 to determine your starting point. Then select every 13th name on the employee list. If number 7 is the random number selected to start, employees 7, 20, 33, 46, and so forth would be included in the sample.

Systematic samples are often used because they are much easier to conduct compared to simple random samples. However, a potential disadvantage of this method is that results could be biased if there is a hidden order to the list of population members used to generate the sample. For example, say you get a list of addresses and you select every 10th house. If a city block has 10 houses, then you may be selecting every house that is right on a corner. If you want to ask people about noise problems, people living in a corner house may experience more noise than people who live in the middle of the block. In other words, you have actually built into your design error unknowingly.

Sampling Error

As stated earlier, one of the primary advantages of selecting probability sampling methods over nonprobability methods is the opportunity they afford the researcher to calculate the sampling error. Sampling error statistics provide the researcher with an idea of how accurate the sample will be in predicting similar results in the population. When the results of a study produce a low sampling error score, this indicates that there is little range or variability in the sample distribution of scores. A high sampling error score indicates wide variability. How do you know what the sampling error is for the study? You can get a good idea by reviewing the sample standard deviation. The larger the standard deviation score is for the sample, the larger the sampling error that is present. This translates into a greater chance that discrepancies will be found when trying to generalize the results from the sample to the population. Later in this chapter, we will discuss how to calculate sample size. Sample size is directly related to sampling error in that the larger the sample size, the less chance that sampling errors have occurred. It makes sense—the larger the sample size, the greater chance that you have captured the characteristics representative of the population.

Nonprobability Samples

Samples that are not randomly selected are known as nonprobability samples. Because selection is not random, there is a greater chance for bias to exist in the results. Although nonprobability samples do not involve random selection, it is not necessarily the case that nonprobability samples are not representative of the population. Nonprobability samples may represent the population just as accurately as a probability sample. However, a researcher is not able to provide statistical support for the sampling error of a nonprobability sample. As a result, it is difficult to determine whether the results generated from the sample can be generalized to the population. So why would a researcher choose to use nonprobability samples in lieu of a random sample? Several explanations might be offered for such a decision. In some instances a study might be examining a variable or phenomenon that is new. In this situation, it may be difficult to determine which population is most appropriate for the study. Other studies may focus on variables or characteristics that make it difficult to find participants. Recall the earlier example of a study designed to examine the verbal aggressiveness of women in abusive relationships. Finding participants for this sensitive topic may be difficult, and thus a researcher might be forced to engage in nonprobability sampling. A third reason for selecting this sampling method is related to the efficiency of cost and time associated with finding participants. Finally, nonprobability samples are used in instances where the characteristic being studied is not easily found.

Although these are all legitimate reasons for selecting nonrandom methods of sampling, the researcher must be aware of several cautions with their use. As we have already discussed, the chance of sampling error increases with nonprobability sampling. Of course, we can never be sure exactly what the error is because random methods were not employed. As a result of higher sampling error, the ability to generalize results to the population is limited. In these instances, the researcher must pay careful attention to addressing the sampling issues in the discussion section of the research paper when identifying limitations of the study. Finally, sampling bias is often associated with nonprobability samples. This bias is defined as a systematic difference between the population and the sample that results from failing to select representative cases. There are five primary types of nonprobability sampling methods employed by communication scholars: convenience samples, volunteer samples, purposive samples, quota samples, and network samples. We will begin by exploring the selection of convenience samples.

CONVENIENCE SAMPLES

Convenience samples involve the selection of participants for the sample based on their availability. If you have ever been asked to complete a survey during class for a research project, chances are you were part of a convenience sample. Are the results biased using this method? Absolutely! After all, only individuals who are enrolled in the class are included in the sample. Is this necessarily a bad thing? It is not if the variable being examined is only applicable to those who are enrolled in the class.

Although some scholars may perceive results produced by convenience samples with skepticism, there are instances where these samples can produce useful information. In a study designed to examine the nonverbal behaviors displayed in physician–patient interactions, Riddle et al. (2002) used a convenience sample of patients and physicians. Forty-seven patients who sought care at various clinics were approached and asked whether they would be willing to participate in the study. Their medical oncologists also agreed to participate. In this instance, the clinic afforded the researcher the opportunity to solicit a convenience sample of the target population in an environment that ensured they met criteria necessary for inclusion in the study. Soliciting a sample by randomly calling names in a phone book would be less efficient since one criterion for inclusion in the sample was that participants should have engaged in an interaction with a physician.

As stated earlier, the major disadvantage with convenience sampling lies in the inability to generalize the results to the population. However, this method can be particularly useful in exploratory studies when a researcher has limited time or money to compile a random sample.

VOLUNTEER SAMPLES

In some instances, participants may volunteer to participate to be a part of the study sample. **Volunteer samples** are often recruited by offering participants a reward in exchange for their time. Fans who cast their votes each week via phone on *American Idol* or *Dancing with the Stars* are examples of volunteer samples. The participants choose whether to be part of the sample of the population that selects the winner. Many media studies employ this method to obtain feedback from the population. Researchers find that it is often easier to have people volunteer to be a part of the study than to engage in other methods to locate participants.

An obvious disadvantage of this type of sampling method is that only those who are aware of the study would be available to volunteer. There is no mechanism for collecting information from those who are either unaware of the study or who choose not to participate. Advantages to volunteer sampling are that it is efficient to conduct the study in terms of cost and time, and it is more likely that participants who choose to participate have some level of knowledge or interest in the topic.

PURPOSIVE SAMPLES

Purposive sampling involves nonrandomly selecting participants to fulfill or meet a specific purpose the researcher has in mind. The sample is selected based on specific characteristics the researcher is investigating—generally, the participants meet some predetermined criteria that the researcher has used to determine eligibility. Purposive sampling is used in both quantitative and qualitative studies. A primary strength of the purposive sample lies in its ability to select participants or cases who meet the criteria being examined in the study. Suppose that a researcher wanted to explore the perceived communication effectiveness of an organization following a crisis situation. It would make perfect sense to select a purposive sample of workers and businesses in the Gulf Coast region that were displaced from their facilities following Hurricane Katrina.

In a study examining intercultural perspectives taught in public relations courses, Bardhan (2003) used a purposive sample of students enrolled in his public relations course and asked them to provide responses to three open-ended questions. Because the goal was to examine perspectives taught in a public relations class, it is only logical that public relations students would be recruited for the purposive sample. In another study that examined the causes of job satisfaction among public relations practitioners, Grunig (1990) selected a total of 87 practitioners from 48 organizations, which represented one of four structural typologies. These organizations and their members were purposely selected so that there would be 12 organizations representing each of the four types of organization. To ensure that all four organization types would be equally represented in the study, a purposive sample of practitioners and organizations was chosen.

The primary advantage of purposive sampling is that it enables the researcher to collect information from the target sample more efficiently. Furthermore, it ensures that all participants selected for the study have a study variable in common. Disadvantages include the overrepresentation of the sample more easily accessed in the population and the tendency to obtain sample sizes that are not proportionate to the population size.

QUOTA SAMPLES

To obtain a **quota sample**, participants are separated into strata or groups based on a common characteristic or variable, and then participants from each group are selected nonrandomly for inclusion in the study. It is important to note that although both quota and stratified samples identify strata for participant classification, one uses random methods for selecting participants from each group and the other does not.

Quota samples can be proportionate or nonproportionate in relation to the population. **Nonproportionate quota samples** recruit volunteers until the determined number of participants has been recruited. Suppose that you were conducting a study of 100 male and female employees to examine perceptions of their manager's communication style. Although the population of the organization consists of 80 percent females and 20 percent males, a nonproportionate quota sample could be drawn by simply interviewing the first 100 employees who enter the company cafeteria. Doing so may result in a sample population composed of 60 percent females and 40 percent males, but they all meet the group criteria of being an employee in the organization.

Proportionate quota samples are chosen to ensure that the number of volunteers recruited for the study is proportionate or equal to the number of group members in the population. Consider our earlier sample of 100 employees. Because the population consists of 80 percent women and 20 percent men and a total of 100 employees is needed for the sample, the researcher will continue to select participants until the percentage in each group matches the population percentage. In this instance, the researcher will stop interviewing women when 80 have been included in the sample. Even if additional female employees come along prior to soliciting 20 male employees, they will be excluded from the study because a proportionate quota has been met.

The primary distinction between quota and stratified samples is their use of random or nonrandom procedures for selecting participants for the sample. Recall our earlier study of student motives for communicating with their advisor. A total of 100 students were identified as the target sample size for the study. Although stratified sampling methods might utilize a table of random numbers to select students from the list to fill the determined number of participants for each category, quota sampling methods might simply take the first 20 juniors and the first 11 seniors they contacted.

Many communication studies have employed quota sampling methods to identify samples. In a study examining children's comprehension of television advertising, Chan (2000) selected a quota sample of boys and girls to represent each class level from kindergarten to sixth grade. To ensure that each grade level included an equal number of boys and girls, a total of 32 boys and 32 girls were selected from each grade. Thus, participants were selected to participate until the predetermined number in each group was obtained.

An advantage of quota samples is that they enable the researcher to identify a target number for each group or category of a population, thus ensuring that each group is equally represented. Further, this sampling method is less costly and less time-consuming than stratified sampling. The obvious disadvantage lies in the nonprobability methods used for selecting participants. Not everyone has an equal chance of being selected for the study, and thus the study may produce results that are potentially biased.

NETWORK SAMPLE

A final nonprobability sampling method used involves asking participants to refer researchers to other people who could serve as participants. **Network sampling** is often used in instances where a variable or characteristic being studied is rare or difficult to identify in a population. Referrals from participants provide the researcher with a cost- and time-effective method for locating others who meet the study criteria. Earlier, we discussed a study that might examine the verbal aggressiveness of victims of domestic abuse. Because many victims are not willing to openly disclose their situation, a researcher might have to obtain a sample by asking each participant to refer another person who has experienced a similar situation.

Bruess and Pearson (2002) identified participants for their study examining the functions of rituals in friendships and marriages using the network sampling method. They asked undergraduate students to assist them in recruiting married couples to complete questionnaires and participate in interviews. Students volunteered to assist the researchers, resulting in a total of 494 surveys from married individuals and a total of 489 surveys on friendships. Bruess and Pearson would have spent a considerable amount of time soliciting a sample size that large and that diverse without the assistance of network sampling.

One advantage of the network sample is that it enables researchers to recruit members of populations that are not easily identifiable (e.g., gay, lesbian, bisexual, and transgendered people; Internet porn addicts; people with an identical twin; and so on). Another advantage is that it enables researchers to obtain larger sample sizes more quickly. The obvious disadvantage of the network sample lies in the inability to generalize findings to the population.

Determining Sample Size

Perhaps one of the first questions asked by students in research methods classes is, "How many participants should I recruit for my sample?" As we discussed earlier, larger sample sizes typically produce results that are more generalizable to the population. However, it is important to assess your study. Samples that are too large could waste the researcher's time and money. By contrast, a sample size that is too small can produce results that do not accurately reflect the larger population.

A quick analysis of the research design can help answer some initial questions regarding sample size. The more the population varies with respect to the characteristics being examined, the larger the sample size should be to account for the variance. Suppose you wanted to do a study on Internet use in a region of the United States. Chances are that the patterns and motives for use would vary greatly depending on a person's age, sex, and employment or education status. Teens may be more likely to access the Internet than the elderly, and students may use their computers more for class research purposes than do stay-at-home mothers. It is likely that the population will vary greatly, and thus a larger sample size is needed.

The first question a researcher must answer in determining the appropriate sample size is to identify the confidence level with which you want to report your results. Confidence levels tell you how confident or sure you can be that the results are generalizable to the population and not a result of chance. As a general rule, if you want to produce results that are more precise, a larger sample size should be selected. The most frequently used confidence level in research is 95%. This means that the sample results should predict the population results with 95% accuracy.

A **confidence interval** provides additional information to interpret results. Confidence intervals are typically expressed in terms of plus or minus a specific number. Consider the following example. When reporting on election exit poll results, television networks may report that the polls indicate that 62% of the population support Candidate A and cite a confidence interval (also referred to as the margin of error) of plus or minus 3%. This lets the audience know that between 59 and 65% of the population will likely vote for Candidate A. The range (59–65) is the confidence interval. The researchers can be 95% sure that the actual percentage of people voting for Candidate A will fall between 59 and 65%. Obviously, that is good news for Candidate A! It is important to note that the relationship between sample size and confidence interval is not necessarily linear in nature. Simply doubling the sample size will not necessarily reduce the confidence interval by half.

Many online and print resources are available to assist researchers in calculating sample size. Figure 13.2 shows a table for determining the sample size of a given population. To perform online calculations (http://statpages.org/javastat.html/ has many links to online calculators that could be useful), the researcher typically must identify specific criteria: the desired confidence level (typically either 95% or 99%), the desired confidence interval, and an estimate of the population size. It is important to remember that sample size calculators assume that random sampling methods are used in the study. Results obtained from the calculators cannot be used for nonrandom samples. Remember—random samples produce results that enhance the external validity of your study.

Common Sense Sample Recruiting

Recruiting samples can often be difficult and daunting. There is no one way that is the best way to recruit participants. Probably the single most common technique is the mass administration of surveys in a classroom environment. Why do people do this? Because it is fast and you get a lot of data quickly. Unfortunately, you can spend a great deal of time attempting to recruit participants and end up with not much to show for your work. Earlier in this book, one of our coauthors told the story of how he sent out thousands of letters and received less than 50 back. As you can imagine, this was expensive for an endeavor that proved not to

N	*S	N	S	N	S
10	10	220	140	1,200	291
15	14	230	144	1,300	297
20	19	240	148	1,400	302
25	24	250	152	1,500	306
30	28	260	155	1,600	310
35	32	270	159	1,700	313
40	36	280	162	1,800	317
45	40	290	165	1,900	320
50	44	300	169	2,000	322
55	48	320	175	2,200	327
60	52	340	181	2,400	331
65	56	360	186	2,600	335
70	59	380	191	2,800	338
75	63	400	196	3,000	341
80	66	420	201	3,500	346
85	70	440	205	4,000	351
90	73	460	210	4,500	354
95	76	480	214	5,000	357
100	80	500	217	6,000	361
110	86	550	226	7,000	364
120	92	600	234	8,000	367
130	97	650	242	9,000	368
140	103	700	248	10,000	370
150	108	750	254	15,000	375
160	113	800	260	20,000	377
170	118	850	265	30,000	379
180	123	900	269	40,000	380
190	127	950	274	50,000	382
200	132	1,000	278	75,000	382
210	136	1,100	285	100,000	383

N = population size.

S = sample size.

* Confidence Interval = 5 & Confidence Level = 95%.

The entries in this table were computed by the authors.

Figure 13.2 Determining Sample Size from a Given Population

be fruitful. As such, it is important to really think through the best way to recruit your potential sample.

First, you must know who your target population is and how you can possibly recruit them. For example, if you are doing research on college students' perceptions of their teachers, then using a college sample makes perfectly good sense. If, however, you are looking at people's reactions to internal branding in organizations, college students are probably not the best population to tap into. Yes, college students can be easy to access, but this does not mean they should be the only participants we use. When choosing your potential participants, think through how you can get access (or if you can). In the past, we have had students who used professional and volunteer fire fighters, professionals in the New York City theater community, victims of workplace bullying, military personnel, etc. Each of these groups made sense within the context of their individual studies. Furthermore, each of these student researchers had connections that helped them recruit participants.

Second, determine how you will approach potential participants for recruitment. The most common methods are FtF, advertisement, e-mail, letter, and snowball. In the FtF recruitment strategy, you approach potential participants and ask them to participate in your study. I know I have been asked many times to participate in studies when hanging out at the mall. Sometimes the research was being conducted by professional research organizations, but other times college students or academic researchers had gotten permission from the mall to recruit (always remember to get permission). FtF recruitment is probably the best way to recruit potential participants. When conducting an FtF recruitment, approach the potential participant and ask politely whether he or she would participate in an academic research study. It is important to stress that you are a college student conducting an academic research study. We know that potential participants are less likely to say no when they are staring you in the face. At the same time, you must be ready to accept "no" from a potential participant without negatively responding. When a potential participant says "no," thank the individual for her or his time.

The next way to recruit people is through advertisements. Go to any college campus and you will see signs around campus advertising for study participants. The advertisement is often a sound approach to recruiting participants. However, advertisements for research participation are still advertisements, so you should think strategically through the message you want to convey and where you think your potential participants will most likely see the advertisement. In addition to the recruitment poster, some common advertisement venues are newspapers, radio, television, and the Internet. We have known many student researchers who have effectively recruited using Facebook ads. Facebook ads can be short and to the point, but they can be relatively inexpensive, costing around $5 per day. One of our colleagues started using Facebook to recruit for a study. The original ad was bland and just consisted of text. With the permission of her IRB, she changed the ad to include a picture of her son, who is quite attractive. Overnight, her recruitment numbers skyrocketed. Again, advertising for research is still advertising.

Another common approach is to send out targeted letters to potential participants asking for their participation. Maybe you know that you want to recruit physicians in your geographic area for a study on physician responses to pharmaceutical representatives marketing strategies. You could easily find a list of physician addresses in the phonebook and send them letters this way. We should note that recruitment via letter can be difficult. Dillman, Smyth, and Christian (2014) have demonstrated that when a researcher tries multiple avenues of recruitment (send a postcard letting them know a survey is coming, send a follow-up letter with the survey, send a follow-up postcard reminding them to complete the survey, and last send a registered letter with another copy of the survey, etc.) they will increase the overall response rate. However, this process can quickly become expensive and probably is not overly useful as a recruitment method for undergraduate or graduate research.

Many organizations will sell you their member lists complete with e-mail addresses. As such, one other common way of recruiting people is through e-mail. This process is actually quite similar to the letter recruitment strategy. Figure 13.3 shows a possible sample e-mail that you could send to research participants.

The next common recruitment technique is the snowball technique. The snowball technique is called such because it resembles the process of making a snowball. When you make a snowball, you start small, roll the ball in the snow, and it gradually becomes larger and larger until you have the base of a potential snowman. With the snowball technique, the goal is to ask a small number of people to participate in your study and then forward the request for participation to others. You could easily add one sentence to Figure 13.3 to turn that recruitment e-mail into one requesting a snowball: "Please forward this message to any friends and/or family members who may also be interested in learning about this research study."

Dear [Dr. /Mr. / Ms. LAST NAME],

My name is [*name*], and I am a [*undergraduate or graduate student*] from the [*department*] at [*college/university*]. I am writing to invite you to participate in my research study about [describe your research study]. I am conducting this research as part of my degree requirements under the direction of Dr./Professor [*name*]. The survey is an online survey and should not take up more than [*insert time frame*] of your valuable time.

If you decide to participate in this study, you will [*insert description of the study activities*].

Remember, your participation is completely voluntary. If you any questions about the study, please contact me at [*insert contact information*].

Thank you very much.

Sincerely,

[*Principle Investigator*]

[*hyperlink to study*]

Figure 13.3 Sample Recruitment E-mail

Last, and the most recent version of recruitment, involves purchasing samples. Yes, in today's world, you can purchase research samples. In fact, selling research samples is a booming industry. Here is how they typically work. You tell one of these corporations what types of people you are looking for to participate in your study. For example, you could say that you are looking for approximately 300 females and males between the ages of 30 and 50 with children. The company will then charge you a fee to recruit the targeted sample from their database of potential participants. Now, some companies will then offer those participants direct incentives on your behalf for their participation, but often you will also need to consider what types of incentives you can offer potential participants to get them to participate. Other organizations are more general and just allow you to pay individuals a prespecified amount to participants who complete a survey.

ETHICAL RECRUITMENT

First, participant recruiting must be conducted in an ethical manner. If you have already forgotten the main requirements for the ethical treatment of human subjects, reexamine Chapter 3. In this section, we will talk about a few specific ways you can attempt to recruit participants. However, please check with your campus's Institutional Review Board for any specific requirements they may have regarding participant recruitment. Some campuses have strict recruitment policies that go above the minimal requirements set by the Office of Human Research Protections (OHRP), so you must ensure you are always in compliance.

Second, you must make sure that ALL of your recruitment strategies are approved by your IRB. For example, if you tell your local IRB that you are going to recruit female and male students on your campus, then you must only recruit female and male students on your campus. You cannot decide halfway through your project to also include faculty and staff or even students on another campus. If you decide that you need to expand your initial sample, then you must request a modification to your original IRB protocol from the IRB itself. From an IRB perspective, the question becomes one of additional risk if you expand your sample.

Third, you cannot pressure people to participate in your study. Imagine you are a resident assistant in a dorm and you decide to walk around your floor recruiting people. If you do this as a peer and the questions involve nothing overly personnel or damaging, you are probably in a good ethical place. However, if you use your authority as a resident assistant to coerce people into completing your survey, then you are treating your participants in an unethical manner because they feel pressured to consent. We have often heard students say things like, "I just forced all of my friends to fill out the survey" or "I gave them out in my sorority/fraternity and watched to make sure everyone completed it." One of the fundamental parts of research ethics is ensuring that participants can make an informed choice without consequences.

Last, ensure that all of your recruitment materials are honest. You cannot say that a survey will only take 10 minutes when you know that it is going to take 50 minutes for the average person. Lying to get participants is simply not ethical unless there is a legitimate reason for the deception that your IRB has signed off on.

Conclusion

There are many decisions that researchers must consider when identifying which sampling method to use. In this chapter, we have introduced you to a variety of sampling methods that can be used in designing your own research study. Probability and nonprobability sampling methods were discussed. As you decide which of these methods is most appropriate for your own research, it is important to consider the steps you can take to ensure that the results obtained from your sample are generalizable to the target population being examined. An important element in determining the generalizability focuses on the selection of random or nonrandom samples in addition to the size of the sample selected for the study. We concluded this chapter with a discussion of the importance of replication. As you begin studying communication research methods, consider utilizing one of the four methods of replication to build on the research of others and test theories using new populations.

KEY TERMS

Central limits theorem
Cluster samples
Confidence interval
Constructive replication
Convenience samples
Instrumental replication
Literal replication
Network samples
Nonprobability sampling
Nonproportionate quota samples

Operational replication
Population
Probability sampling
Probability theory
Proportionate quota samples
Purposive samples
Quota samples
Replication
Sample
Sampling
Sampling bias

Sampling error
Sampling frame
Simple random samples
Stratified random samples
Systematic samples
Theoretical population
Volunteer samples

REFERENCES

Bardhan, N. (2003). Creating spaces for international and multi(inter)cultural perspectives in undergraduate public relations education. *Communication Education, 52*, 164–172.

Bruess, C. J., & Pearson, J. C. (2002). The function of mundane ritualizing in adult friendship and marriage. *Communication Research Reports, 19*, 314–326.

Chan, K. (2000). Hong Kong children's understanding of television advertising. *Journal of Marketing Communications, 6*, 37–52.

Dillman, D. A., Smyth, J. D., & Christian, L. M. (2014). *Internet, phone, mail, and mixed-mode surveys: The tailored design method* (4th ed). Hoboken, NJ: Wiley.

Grunig, L. A. (1990). An exploration of the causes of job satisfaction in public relations. *Management Communication Quarterly, 3*, 355–375.

Riddle, D. L., Albrecht, T. L., Coovert, M. D., Penner, L. A., Ruckdeschel, J. C., Blanchard, C. G., . . . Urbizu, D. (2002). Differences in audiotaped versus videotaped physician–patient interactions. *Journal of Nonverbal Behavior, 26*, 219–239.

FURTHER READING

Fink, A. (2002). *How to sample in surveys* (2nd ed.). Thousand Oaks, CA: Sage.

Henry, G. T. (1990). *Practical sampling.* Thousand Oaks, CA: Sage.

Kalton, G. (1983). *Introduction to survey sampling.* Newbury Park, CA: Sage.

Thompson, S. K. (2002). *Sampling* (Rev. ed.). New York, NY: Wiley.

Thompson, S. K., & Seber, G. A. F. (1996). *Adaptive sampling.* New York, NY: Wiley.

Hypothesis Testing

HYPOTHESES

A hypothesis is the backbone of modern scientific study, whether it be in the physical or in the social sciences. As defined previously, a hypothesis is a statement about the relationship between independent and dependent variables. Good hypotheses must be testable, compatible with current knowledge, logically consistent, and simple. First, a useful hypothesis is a statement about the relationship or difference between two or more variables that can be tested. A person can say that after watching all science fiction movies he or she believes that all extraterrestrials will speak English, but unless he or she has the ability to sample all extraterrestrials, the statement is not a useful hypothesis because the statement cannot be tested. The key word when examining a hypothesis is "testable." A scientist must be able to perform a test of how two variables or phenomena might be related or differ.

A useful hypothesis also must be compatible with current knowledge about a specific topic. For example, in the study by Weber, Fornash, Corrigan, and Neupauer (2003), the authors examined the effect that student interest has on the college classroom. Previous research had found that if a college student was interested in the examples in a textbook, that student was able to remember more about the material longer than a college student who was not interested in the examples used in a textbook. Although the authors had seen issues of interest in textbooks, no one had examined how interesting examples affect cognitive recall after a lecture. Based on this previous research, the authors hypothesized that if college instructors used examples that were interesting to the students, the students would perform better on a test after a lecture. Note how Weber et al. (2003) used what was previously seen in research to make an argument about what they would expect to see in a new, but related, context.

The Weber et al. (2003) hypothesis contains the words "if" and "then," which are necessary in a formalized hypothesis. But not all if–then statements are hypotheses. For example, "If I gamble, then I will get rich," is not really a hypothesis—it is a simple prediction. In a formalized hypothesis, a relationship or difference is stated. For example, to turn the gambling case into a formalized hypothesis, one could test whether the frequency of winning is related to the amount of time spent playing slot machines. In this case the statement would read something like, "If a person spends more time playing slot machines, then her or his odds of winning goes up." If you always ask yourself whether one thing is related to another, then you should be able to test it.

Many hypotheses are also multilayered and have a number of "if" statements before the "then" statement in the hypothesis. For example, in the Weber et al. (2003) study, you could have the following if statements: (1) If student interest is important to cognitive recall with books and (2) if student interest functions the same way with lecturing and cognitive recall, then (3) student interest should relate to cognitive recall after a lecture. Note that without all three statements together, a clear argument could not be made. An author cannot make a leap in logic without clearly attempting to explain what he or she is thinking when writing a hypothesis.

A third factor of good hypotheses is that they are logically consistent. In other words, a hypothesis cannot contradict itself and actually be a hypothesis. If when examining the literature you find that studies consistently disagree as to whether men or women are more ambivalent in the workplace, you will have problems generating a good hypothesis because your literature is inconsistent. If at any point you find yourself writing a justification for a hypothesis that says "it could be this or it could be that," then you really do not have a strong hypothesis and that hypothesis should probably be rewritten as a research question instead of as a hypothesis.

Finally, good hypotheses are simple. Before each hypothesis is stated in a research study, a short explanation of the relationship between research studies in the literature is given to explain why the hypothesis can be justified. If this explanation becomes too long or too confusing, it is not simple and is more likely to be logically faulty. In the Weber et al. (2003) article, the authors wrote, "Based on what is known about the relationship between affective variables and cognitive learning [citations given in original] coupled with the literature on text-based interest [citations given in original] we could expect that interest would be positively related to recall of lecture material" (p. 118). This short declarative statement clearly outlines the if–then statements and provides the basis for the actual hypothesis, which is "Lectures utilizing interest-based examples should result in participants with higher scores on subsequent tests of cognitive recall" (p. 118). Although this section has introduced what a hypothesis is, we must explain that there are two different types of hypotheses that a person can make when writing a research study.

One-Tailed Hypotheses

The first type of hypothesis is called a **one-tail hypothesis** or a hypothesis that predicts the specific nature of the relationship or difference. In the previous example from Weber et al. (2003), the authors clearly indicated that lectures with interest-based examples would result in participants having higher scores on tests. This hypothesis predicted that students in classrooms where they heard interesting examples during lectures would score statistically significantly higher on cognitive recall (multiple-choice tests) than students in classrooms that did not have interesting examples. Researchers can also write hypotheses to examine the relationship between two variables like Chesebro (1999) did when he wrote, "A positive relationship exists between the People listening style and conversational sensitivity" (p. 235). In this hypothesis, Chesebro is expecting to see a positive relationship between two variables (People listening style and conversational sensitivity).

Two-Tailed Hypotheses

The second type of hypothesis is called a **two-tailed hypothesis**, or a hypothesis that predicts that there is a significant difference or relationship, but does not indicate the specific nature of the difference (which group would have a higher score) or relationship (positive or negative). For example, if we wanted to write the Weber et al. (2003) hypothesis as a two-way hypothesis, it would read "lectures utilizing interest-based examples should result in different participant scores on subsequent tests of cognitive recall when compared to scores of participants who did not hear interest-based examples during lectures." In this case, all we did is take out the direction of the hypothesis and make it more general. To rewrite Chesebro's (1999) hypothesis and make it two way, we could write, "There will be a relationship between the People listening style and conversational sensitivity." In this case, we are no longer saying that we expect the relationship to be positive; rather, we are saying that we expect to see a relationship that could be either positive or negative.

So, how does one choose between one- and two-tailed hypotheses? Ideally, if you have a strong enough argument for the direction of the relationship (positive or negative) or which nominal group will exhibit a variable to a greater degree (males or females; short or tall people; lower, middle, or upper socioeconomic status; etc.), you should make the argument in your hypothesis. However, if you write a hypothesis with a specific direction in mind, it alters the parameters of the statistical tests you will use. For this reason, many scholars argue that you should always be conservative and not write one-tailed hypotheses.

RESEARCH QUESTIONS

As mentioned earlier, a **research question** is an explicit question researchers ask about variables of interest. In other words, researchers often want to see whether there are differences or relationships between variables, so they ask a question about the possibility of that difference or relationship in the rationale section of the literature review. For example, maybe you want to know whether there is a difference between the overall scores of males and females on the PRCA-24. Although you could write your question like we just did, in formal research there are traditional ways of doing so. When preparing to ask a research question, a researcher must thoroughly explain why he or she believes a question should be asked. More importantly, a researcher must demonstrate that there is not enough evidence based on previous research to form a clear hypothesis. Just like a researcher has to explain the rationale for proposing a hypothesis, a researcher must explain her or his rationale for a research question as well. However, this rationale is not a formal argument establishing the possibility of a difference or relationship that is expected, but rather the rationale explains why there could be a difference or relationship between two or more variables. Just like hypotheses, there are two different types of research questions: directional and nondirectional.

Directional Research Questions

Directional research questions occur when a researcher asks whether there is either a specific significant difference between two or more variables or a positive or negative relationship between two or more variables. To test for a difference, you could run a study to see whether females or males consumed more alcohol in social settings by asking this research question: "Do males drink significantly more than females in social situations?" And if you wanted to test for a relationship, you could conduct a study to determine whether there is a relationship between the amount of alcohol consumed and an individual's perceptions of opposite sex attractiveness. For this study you could propose a research question that reads, "Is there a positive relationship between drinking alcohol and individual perceptions of attractiveness?" Most important, both of these statements are questions and not hypothesis statements.

Nondirectional Research Questions

The second type of research question is the **nondirectional research question**—when a researcher asks whether there is a difference or relationship between two or more variables. Most researchers who use research questions in a study will use a nondirectional research question. For example, you can write a nondirectional research question to test for differences in alcohol consumption by males and females: "Is there a difference between consumption of alcohol by females and males during social events?" In this research question, the question was written to determine whether there was a difference between men and women and alcohol consumption during social events. Again, this question does not predict a direction of the difference or that a difference will occur, only that there could be a difference. An example of a nondirectional research question for a relationship can be seen in Rocca and Vogl-Bauer's (1999) study. They asked, "What is the nature of the relationship between trait verbal aggression and sports fans' perceptions of appropriate communicative messages at sporting events?" In essence, this question wants to see how a fan's verbal aggression does or does not relate to her or his perceptions of appropriate communication at a sporting event. Note that no indication of the nature of this relationship is discussed in this research question.

Overall, when determining whether to use hypotheses or research questions, you must first determine whether you have the quality and quantity of previously conducted research to support a hypothesis. If you do not have the literature to form a clear argument for a hypothesis, then create a research question to examine the possible difference or relationship between two or more variables.

ALTERNATIVE AND NULL HYPOTHESES

An **alternative hypothesis** is the prediction that there is a relationship or there is a difference that has not occurred by chance or random error. Although we differentiate between hypotheses and research questions in the creation of theoretical predictions based on previous research, there are no mathematical differences in how they are perceived. For this reason, both of these predictions can be represented as alternative hypotheses:

H_1: There is a negative relationship between communication apprehension and an individual's belief that all students should take public speaking in college.

or

H_1: Females and males differ in their willingness to communicate.

From a research perspective, it is extremely important to understand that in statistics researchers never test an actual alternative hypothesis (or the one listed in a research article as H_1). Instead, researchers always test the **null hypothesis** or the Null Monster!!! The null hypothesis (H_0) is almost always expressed as the "nil" hypothesis—there are zero differences or zero relationships (Cohen, 1994). According to traditional scientific standards, we must assume that the null hypothesis is true until a researcher can provide support to the contrary (or that her or his alternative hypothesis is true). Imagine that your hypothesis is the following:

H_1: There *is* a negative relationship between communication apprehension and an individual's belief that all students should take public speaking in college.

In this case, you are predicting that that people who have higher levels of CA will be less likely to believe that all students in college should take public speaking. If this is your hypothesis (H_1), then your null hypothesis (H_0) must be the following:

H_0: There *is no* relationship between communication apprehension and an individual's belief that all students should take public speaking in college.

So, why then do we test the null hypothesis in statistics? Fisher (1935) posed the first argument for why we test the null hypothesis: we can never really prove anything as true using statistics; however, we can use statistics to prove that something is false. Based on this reasoning, we cannot prove a hypothesis, but we can prove that a null hypothesis is false. Imagine we observed 100 people who all had blue eyes and then made the statement, "everyone has blue eyes." All we would must do is find one person with brown eyes to disprove the statement "everyone has blue eyes." More practically, the null hypothesis provides researchers a more general base to make predictions. If researchers were going to test the hypothesis that females and males differ in their attitudes about the usefulness of public speaking, do you test the hypothesis that females and males differ by a small amount, a medium amount, or a large amount? By testing the null hypothesis, researchers do not have to have a specific magnitude of difference in mind; they just have to test the null hypothesis that there is no difference at all.

In shorthand notation, a null hypothesis is always written as H_0 and a regular hypothesis is written as $H_{1, 2, \ldots, x}$, with x being an infinite number of study hypotheses. For example, in the Weber et al. (2003) study, H_1 is "Lectures utilizing interest-based examples *should* result in participants with higher scores on subsequent tests of cognitive recall" and H_0 is "Lectures utilizing interest-based examples *will not* result in participants with higher scores on subsequent tests of cognitive recall." In the Chesebro (1999) study, H_1 is "A *positive* relationship exists between the People listening style and conversational sensitivity" and H_0 is "*No* relationship exists between the People listening style and conversational sensitivity." Note that the words in bold make it either a hypothesis or the null hypothesis. The null version of Chesebro's hypothesis is not that there will be a negative relationship, but rather that no relationship will exist at all. If you rewrote the Chesebro hypothesis to read that there would be a negative relationship, you are just creating another hypothesis and not the null hypothesis. Remember, the null hypothesis is just the opposite of the actual hypothesis.

You will note here that both hypotheses and research questions that are generated for a study in one's rationale section have null hypothesis counterparts that say either there is not a relationship or there is not a difference. In Chapter 13, we discussed that our goal in research is to be able to determine whether our samples are consistent with their populations. The null hypothesis expresses expectations for what should occur within the population, so the null hypothesis allows researchers to determine the **probability** that the results we find in our samples are consistent with the overall population.

Although we have talked about the null hypothesis as being something generally researchers avoid, this is not always the case. Researchers often hope that there is not a relationship or difference in a study, or they want to accept the null hypothesis. For example, you may theorize that there is no relationship between an individual's CA and her or his IQ and form a hypothesis in a study predicting a lack of relationship. However, the alternative hypothesis always predicts that there is a relationship or difference:

H_1: There is a relationship between an individual's communication apprehension and her or his IQ.

However, the null hypothesis would predict that there is not a relationship:

H_0: There is no relationship between an individual's communication apprehension and her or his IQ.

In this case, the theoretical hypothesis made in our study suggests that we must accept the null hypothesis, which would have us reject the alternative hypothesis. **Hypothesis testing** then is the process a researcher goes through using inferential statistics to determine whether we reject or accept the null hypothesis. Now that we have explained the general concept of hypothesis testing, we will look at a case study to help us further understand the hypothesis-testing process.

Hypothesis Testing Case Study

A team of researchers wanted to determine whether viewing of televangelists positively or negatively influenced nonreligious individuals' perceptions of religion. The researchers used a phone bank that randomly called people in a large city. A large number of potential participants were contacted via telephone and asked whether they would participate in a study, and 80 percent agreed to help. The researchers mailed the participants a series of scales and asked the participants to fill out the scales and return them in the stamped envelope with the researcher's mailing address preprinted on the envelope. The initial survey packet contained a short survey asking the participants about their perceptions of various religious organizations. After completing the initial survey, the participants sent the researchers back the first survey packet.

When the researchers received the first survey packet, the participant was sent a second survey packet (sealed in a secondary envelope) with a set of instructions attached. The researchers asked the participants to refrain from opening the survey packet until the participants watched a televangelist from a religion different from their own on television. Once a participant had watched a televangelist, he or she opened the secondary survey packet and filled out the survey that asked the participants to rate their attitudes toward the religion of the televangelist on the television show they had watched. The participants also supplied information about the television show they had watched. When the survey was completed, the participants sent the survey back to the researchers.

In essence, each participant rated the televangelist's religion two different times. The measurement of the dependent variable (perception of a religion) occurred in the first survey packet, since participants supplied their attitudes about a wide range of religious groups. The second measurement of the dependent variable (perception of religion) occurred more specifically toward the specific religion. However, since attitudes about a religious faith were gathered at both Time 1 (T_1; first survey packet) and Time 2 (T_2; second survey packet), this is a clear experimental procedure. To make sure that the study did not have a time effect on the participants' filling out the surveys, the researchers also had a control group that just filled out the survey packet at T_1 and again at T_2, but were not asked to watch a televangelist from a differing religion. In the control group, the means on the religious attitude scales were virtually identical ($MT_1 = 53.69$; $MT_2 = 53.56$). In the manipulation group (filled out the scales in Time 1, watched the televangelist, and then filled out the survey packet in Time 2), the means are a little different ($MT_1 = 52.9$; $MT_2 = 48.9$). If we were just eyeballing this finding, we might say that there is almost a four-point drop from Time 1 to Time 2, so clearly people end up not liking a religion after viewing a televangelist. However, in statistics we simply cannot eyeball a difference in means and say that the change is statistically meaningful. For this reason, a process has been created called hypothesis testing to determine whether a difference or relationship between two means is meaningful or is occurring as a result of random chance.

HYPOTHESIS TESTING IN THE CASE STUDY

As defined in Chapter 2, a hypothesis is a tentative statement about the relationship between independent and dependent variables. In this chapter, we clump both of these concepts together under the heading of "hypothesis testing" because we are talking about mathematical hypothesis testing, not a hypothesis derived as a result of your literature review. For our case study, the alternative and null hypotheses would be as follows:

H_1: There is a difference between people who view a televangelist and people who do not and their perceptions of a televangelist's religion.

H_0: There is no difference between people who view a televangelist and people who do not and their perceptions of a televangelist's religion.

In this example, we want to determine whether there is a difference between the mean score on the religious attitude scale for Time 1 (before they watched the televangelist) and the mean score on the religious attitude scale for Time 2 (after they watched the televangelist). The mathematical notion for this would then be

$$H_1: \mu_{\text{Time1}} \neq \mu_{\text{Time2}}$$

This statement says that the mean of Time 1 is not equal to (or there is a difference between) the mean of Time 2.

In our example, our null hypothesis would state that the mean score on the religious attitude scale for Time 1 (before they watched the televangelist) and the mean score on the religious attitude scale for Time 2 (after they watched the televangelist) were the same, or no difference exists. The mathematical notion for this would then be

$$H_0: \mu_{\text{Time1}} = \mu_{\text{Time2}}$$

This statement says that the mean of Time 1 is equal to (or there is not a difference between) the mean of Time 2. Note how the alternative hypothesis and null hypothesis would be the same whether you developed a hypothesis or research question out of your literature review.

From Random Samples to a Whole Population

One of the most interesting and complex aspects of empirical social scientific research is that researchers must deal with people and numbers. As a result of dealing with people and numbers, there is a certain amount of error that naturally occurs. Ideally, researchers would be able to gather data from an entire population, but this is not realistic so we must rely on samples as discussed in Chapter 13. When researchers rely on samples, a certain amount of error occurs called sampling error, or the degree to which a sample *probably* differs with respect to a specific variable from a population. For example, imagine our example study in this chapter had only 10 participants. If we attained the mean on the religious attitude scale for each of the 10 participants, we would see that not everyone's score was identical, so we would have what is called a sampling distribution. And as we know, the mean of a sampling distribution can be calculated by adding up all of the 10 individual scores on the religious attitude scale and dividing by 10 (number of participants; $N = 10$). If in our sample we got the 10 following scores—57, 58, 62, 23, 54, 56, 55, 54, 51, and 59 at Time 1 and 55, 57, 60, 20, 50, 52, 53, 55, 48, and 39 at Time 2—you would get means and standard deviations for Time 1 of ($MT_1 = 52.9$, $SD = 10.94$) and for Time 2 of ($MT_2 = 48.90$, $SD = 11.67$). If we wanted to determine how much error was in our sampling distribution (how much our random sample means differ from the overall mean of 52.9), we simply divide the standard deviation by the square root of N (sample size or 10). So first, we must calculate the square root of 10, which is 3.16227766. We can then divide our standard deviation (10.94) by 3.16227766 and we get 3.45953176. In other words, the standard error of the mean (SE_M) in our example is roughly 3.46. In other words, our sample has an inherent amount of error, which is always expected in statistics.

Ultimately, sampling error must be taken into account when attempting to determine whether a statistical difference or relationship exists. Since we calculated that our sample has a standard error of the mean of 3.46 in the first mean, this indicates that we can guess that the actual population mean (everyone who could have participated in the study) should exist between 56.36 and 49.44. We get this interval of possible choices because we take the calculated mean we had in our sample (52.9) and then add and subtract the SE_M (3.46) from that mean. As we will discuss in more detail in Chapter 15, anything that falls within ±1 standard deviation of the mean (10.94 in our example) is said to account for approximately 68.26 % of the individual means in a sample. In other words, using our SE_M of ± 3.46, we know that our population mean will fall between 56.36 and 49.44, but this also means that about 31.74 % of the time the actual population mean will not fall between 56.36 and 49.44. I don't know about you, but I want something that will be accurate more than 65.26 % of the time. For this reason, researchers have decided that for something to be considered statistically significant, an interval of numbers (e.g., 56.36 to 49.44) should be at least accurate 95%of the time. Hence, 95.44percent%t of all sample means will fall between two standard deviations away from the mean or ± SD; the same is also true for the standard error mean (more on this in Chapter 15). In our example, the SE_M is ± 3.46, so if we multiply 3.46 × 2 we get 6.92. If we take this number and add it to and subtract it from our mean, 52.90, we can say that 95 % of all of our scores fall between 45.98 and 59.82, which is a range of 13.84. This range of scores of random sample means associated with a **confidence level** is called a confidence interval, so at the 95 % confidence level (or possibility of 5% chance we are wrong), our population mean would fall between 45.98 and 59.82. So all in all, how confident should a researcher be?

Researchers generally agree that we should be at least 95%confident or have a 95% confidence interval, which means that researchers expect their results to be inaccurate 5% of the time. To achieve a confidence interval of 95 %, we know that the SE_M (3.46) must be multiplied by ±1.96 (see Chapter 15 for a discussion of this), which would be 5.8474. In other words, we can be 95 %confident that the population mean from which our sample mean (the 10 people in the study, $M = 52.9$) will lie between 47.0526 and 58.7474.

You may be wondering whether this is something that only social scientific researchers do—it is not. In fact, most research—from medicine to physics to communication—uses the

95% confidence interval as the standard to judge statistics. Think of it like this: imagine a drug company wants to find out whether their drug kills people. At the 95 % confidence rate, the drug would kill 1 in 20 people. For this reason, occasionally medical studies will increase the confidence rate to 99.99%, which would mean that only 1 of every 10,000 people who take the drug would die as a result. However, the 95% confidence interval is still standard for most statistically based research.

Most research studies do not rely on just one variable's confidence interval, so other techniques have been developed to help us determine how confident researchers are when examining multiple variable means. When researchers are examining multiple variables, researchers pool these individual variables and use them as a single random sample (both Time 1 and Time 2 together) to stand for the large number of random samples that are being examined (both Time 1 and Time 2 separately). By doing this and following the same steps that we performed above looking at the combined $\pm 1.96 SE_M$, researchers can create a confidence interval, and this confidence interval allows researchers to know what kind of sampling error or "margin of error" actually exists. For example, what if we found out that in our example the means for Time 1 (before watching the televangelist) and Time 2 (after watching the televangelist) were different only at a confidence interval of $\pm 20\%$? Would you then be willing to say that these two means were different from each other? If you said a 60%confidence interval is acceptable, then you are saying that 40 times of 100 the findings of your study would be false. In other words, your study's results are meaningless. If, however, we found that the means for Time 1 and Time 2 were different with a confidence interval of $\pm 2.5\%$, then we could say that the two variables were different at a 95%onfidence level.

Testing for Significance

In the previous section, we introduced the concept of confidence intervals and the importance of a 95% confidence level. In this section, we are going to see how we can determine whether a difference or relationship between two variables has occurred by chance. The process to determine whether chance causes a difference or relationship is called "significance testing." In significance testing, the goal is to determine whether our null hypothesis (H_0: $\mu_{Time1} = \mu_{Time2}$) is accurate. As mentioned earlier, in significance testing, we are always concerned with testing the null hypothesis, so significance testing is the process of analyzing quantitative data to determine whether a null hypothesis is probably either true or false. In this definition we are examining whether the null is *probably* true or false, which indicates that there is always a possibility of error occurring when conducting a significance test. **Significance testing**, then, is determining whether you can accept the null hypothesis (there is no difference between the participants' religious attitudes before they watched a televangelist and after they watched a televangelist) or must reject the null hypothesis (there is a difference between the participants' religious attitudes before they watched a televangelist and after they watched a televangelist).

After you have collected data from a sample, the first step in significance testing is determining a significance level. In other words, a researcher must determine how large a relationship or difference must be before it is considered significant. Just as we discussed above in confidence intervals, researchers prefer to be at least 95 percent confident. A 95% confidence in significance testing indicates that a researcher could expect to see a difference or relationship occurring in her or his results by accident as a result of chance about 5 times of 100. Again, that may sound like a lot, but it is the standard used by all scientists when determining whether something is an actual difference or relationship.

In significance testing, we often refer to the "probability level" when discussing how confident we are about our results. To determine the **probability level**, simply take the percentile number (95) and subtract it from 1, or $1 - 0.95 = 0.05$. The probability level is also sometimes called a p value, **probability value**, also referred to by the Greek letter alpha (α). So if you wanted to be 99 % confident, your p value would be 0.01 ($1 - 0.99 = 0.01$), and so on. As a quick side note to the use of the Greek letter α, this is not the same alpha referred to earlier in this book with regard to scale reliability. Often in statistics, statisticians will use the same Greek letter to represent a number of different functions depending on what statistical formula is being discussed.

We should also note that sampling error is also one of the major reasons why replication of studies is important. If a study's findings are accurate 95 % of the time, then there is a 5 % chance that the results obtained in a study happen because of error. For this reason, scientists often will replicate a study or research the same patterns of variables multiple times to make sure the results are consistent. Often researchers find contradictory results even when the research process, measures, and participants are identical. There is an advanced statistical procedure, meta-analysis, that can be used to combine a number of different studies looking at the same phenomenon to achieve stronger support for the existence of a relationship or difference or the lack of a relationship or difference. Now that we have explained what a probability value is, we will examine the steps necessary in significance testing.

STEP 1: SET THE PROBABILITY LEVEL

Before you can perform any statistical tests to determine whether there are differences or relationships in your study, you must first decide how confident you must be. As noted above, the standard probability level is always going to be 0.05, or we are sure that if we ran the same test 100 different times, only 5 tests would yield inaccurate results. If you are researching a study that could have greater chances of killing someone (like many pharmaceutical studies), you may want to be more than 95 % confident in your results. Maybe in a pharmaceutical company you would pick a probability level of 0.0005, indicating that you are 99.95 % confident in the finding of a difference or a relationship between a set of variables. Ultimately, what level of probability you establish for your study will determine whether a difference exists. The lower your p value, the harder it is to be significant at that level. For example, in our study maybe we find out that we are significant at $p < 0.10$ but are not significant at $p < 0.05$. In this case, if we had previously established that for a difference to exist we would have to be 95 % confident that it exists, then the difference found between the pretest (before the participant watched the televangelist) and the posttest (after the participant watched the televangelist) would not be statistically significant. If, however, we had established a 90 % confidence interval, then our study would be significant at $p < 0.10$. Although some researchers will raise their confidence interval to .90, we strongly encourage you not to do this because you increase the probability of type II error (we accept the null hypothesis based on our sample, but the null hypothesis is actually false in the population), which we will examine in the last part of this chapter.

STEP 2: CONDUCT A STATISTICAL TEST

The second part of significance testing is conducting a statistical test. Every statistical test ultimately generates a value called the "**calculated value**," which is simply the end result that a researcher receives when he or she has completed a mathematical formula related to a specific statistical test. This part of significance testing is often the most complicated and time-consuming part if completed by hand. For this reason, researchers often prefer to work with computer packages (e.g., SPSS, Excel) that calculate the calculated value for them.

STEP 3: COMPARING CALCULATED AND CRITICAL VALUES

The third part of conducting a significance test is to compare the calculated value (the answer one achieves through arithmetic) to a **critical value** (a predetermined value calculated by statisticians that a calculated value must be greater than). For example, in the example in this chapter (Is there a difference between an individual's perception of a televangelist's religion after seeing the televangelist in action?), if we obtained a calculated value of 2.176 and the critical value associated with the .05 probability level we had to beat was 2.262, our calculated value is smaller, so it does not beat the threshold. If our calculated value is not greater than the critical value, then we cannot say that we are significant at that level, or the probability of a relationship or difference existing is less than the probability level (less than 95 %). We will spend a lot more time exploring this concept as we look at various statistical tests in the next five chapters.

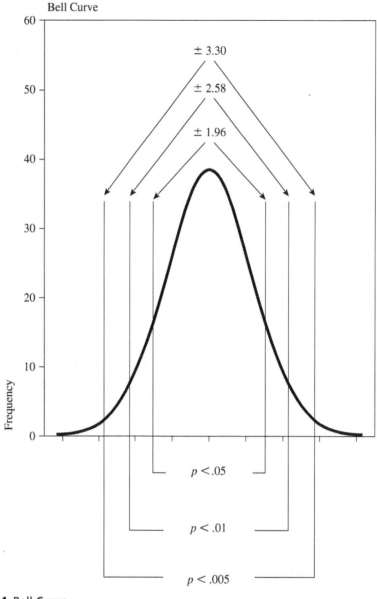

Figure 14.1 Bell Curve

Critical values are determined based on the size of sample a person has, the number of variables being compared, and the type of statistical test. Each statistical test has its own unique set of critical values. These critical values ultimately allow researchers to determine whether a calculated value is greater than a specific critical value that indicates that it is significant at the ±1.96 *SD* away from the mean. Remember that we can be 95 % confident in a result if that result beats the ±1.96 *SD* threshold for determining whether something is confident at that level. Figure 14.1 shows the bell curve with the standard deviation estimates for determining the critical values at the $p < 0.05$, $p < 0.01$, and $p < 0.005$ levels.

As we know from our example, the critical value to beat to obtain a 95 % confidence in our results is 2.262 and the value we calculated was 2.176. (We used a paired *t* test to statistically test for a significant difference between the two means. Paired *t* tests are discussed later in Chapter 18.) Figure 14.2 shows three sets of critical values to beat to obtain significance at $p < 0.05$, $p < 0.01$, and $p < 0.005$. With our calculated value of 2.176, we fall between the mean and the first critical value (±1.96 or 2.262). If, however, we had a calculated value of

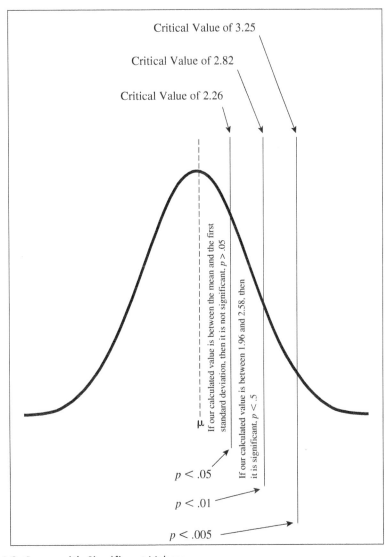

Figure 14.2 Curve with Significant Values

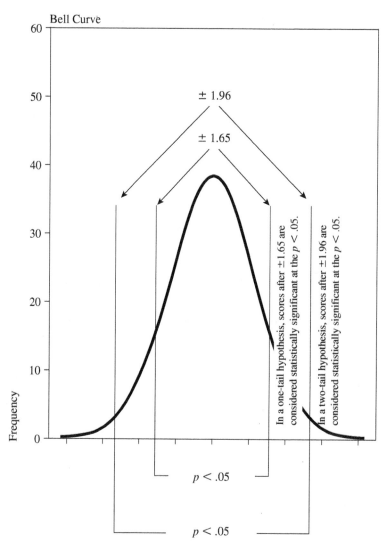

Figure 14.3 One- and Two-Tailed Tests

2.367, we would have fallen between the 0.05 and 0.01 confidence intervals and, thus, would have been significant at $p < 0.05$. Ultimately, this is how significance testing is completed.

Testing for Power

In addition to making sure that a difference or relationship is statistically significant, it is also important to make sure that a statistical test has power. The purpose of statistical **power** is to determine whether a researcher can reject a false null hypothesis. Power allows a researcher to determine how sensitive a statistical test will be in detecting relationships and differences of a specific size. If a study is powerful, then a researcher will be able to correctly find even small differences and relationships, but if a study is not powerful a researcher may miss small differences and relationships. In other words, a researcher could conclude that there is no relationship between an individual's level of CA (anxiety about real or perceived communication) and her or his WTC (desire to initiate communication) based on her or his sample. However, previous research consistently shows that there should be a negative relationship between CA and WTC, or, as someone's CA goes up, her or his WTC goes down. There are three reasons why a researcher may accept a false null hypothesis (i.e., there is no relationship between CA and WTC).

First, the type of test a researcher uses to examine the relationship is relevant. Some tests are less "sensitive," or less likely to note actual relationships or differences even when they do exist. We will talk about some of these issues in the next six chapters.

Second, it is harder to attain statistical differences using two-tailed hypotheses. As we discussed earlier in this chapter, two-tailed hypotheses leave open the direction of a difference or relationship, whereas a one-tailed hypothesis is specific about the direction of the difference or relationship. Figure 14.3 illustrates the problem that can often occur when examining one- and two-tailed hypotheses. To be significant at the 0.05 probability level using a one-tailed test, a calculated value must be greater than a lower critical value (located + or −1.65, but not ±1.65, standard deviations away from the mean); however, to be significant at the 0.05 probability level using a two-tailed test, we test in both directions on the number line so the critical value is higher (±1.96).

If you have a clear reason for using a one-tailed test, it is perfectly appropriate to do so. However, one-tailed hypothesis testing is often misused as a way of gaining significance even when a research question does not warrant the test. In other words, use one-tailed hypothesis testing sparingly, but understand that there are circumstances that do warrant its use.

Finally, small sample sizes often make it impossible for a statistical device to determine when a null hypothesis should be rejected. Many researchers attempt to calculate complicated statistics based on small sample sizes. Much medical and social scientific research is conducted with sample sizes of less than 20 participants. Ideally, no sample should be smaller than 200 unless the entire population from which the sample is drawn is smaller than 200. When a sample has 200 or more participants, the likelihood of finding statistically significant small differences and relationships increases; this decreases the incidence of type II error, as we will see in a moment.

To increase the likelihood that a statistical test will be able to reject a null hypothesis when it should, a researcher should use appropriate statistical tests, use one- and two-tailed tests appropriately, and have a large sample. Power, when it is measured, exists on a continuum from 0 to 1. However, statistical power should never be lower than 0.8, or you risk the chance of missing actual relationships and differences that really exist.

Effect Sizes

Along with power, another extremely important characteristic to understand is the effect size of a statistical finding (as discussed in Chapter 6). An **effect size** is like a thermometer. If there has been a change to one or two degrees cooler, you may not even notice that it has gotten colder. Although there may be a significant difference in the heat, it may not be large enough for it to really matter. If the temperature decreases by 50 degrees, you will be hunting around your house for an electric blanket. In other words, an effect size is the strength of a relationship or the magnitude of a difference occurring between two variables, or the degree to which a null hypothesis is false. There are three types of effect sizes that can be seen in statistics (small, medium, and large). Each difference test discussed in this book has a corresponding effect size that is important to understand, so we will discuss this concept in greater detail later.

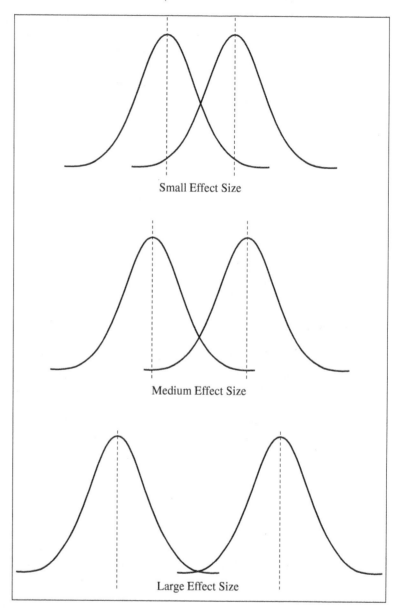

Figure 14.4 Effect Size

In Figure 14.4, the first set of bell curves illustrates what we mean by a small effect size. In this case, we are examining the difference between two means (indicated by the dashed lines). This is similar to the example that we looked at in the first part of this chapter where we wanted to see whether an individual's attitude about a religion changes after he or she sees a televangelist in action (Time 1 = 52.9; Time 2 = 48.9). In the first case, note that the means are closer together. Although the means may be significantly different, researchers cannot conclude that means are drastically different. A lot of research done on sex differences runs into this problem. Basically, little research that examines differences between male and female behavior (if the difference is significant) is beyond a small effect. In case of small effects, researchers must be honest about these effect sizes. Although the difference may be significant, it may not mean much.

The second graph in the chart in Figure 14.4 represents what a medium effect may look like if we graphed it. In this case, the mean differences are further apart than we saw in the first graph, but still closer together than we see in the third graph, which represents a large effect. All in all, it is important to realize that although something may be statistically significant, the effect size associated with that significance is also extremely important.

Understanding Error

The last part of this chapter is going to explore a concept that we have already hinted at in the previous sections in this chapter—error. The chart that we are going to use to explain error is illustrated in Figure 14.5.

✱ KNOW THIS CHART FOR FINAL

In the whole Population → **What** ↓ **We conclude Based on our Sample**	**Null Hypothesis Is True** In reality… • There is no difference or relationship • Our theory is wrong	**Null Hypothesis Is False** In reality… • There is a difference or relationship • Our theory is correct
Accept the Null Hypothesis We <u>say</u>… • There is no difference or relationship • Our theory is wrong	$1 - \alpha$ <u>The Confidence Interval</u> The odds of saying there is <u>no</u> effect or gain when in fact there is none No. of times out of 100 when there is no effect, we'll say there is none	β <u>Type II Error</u> The odds of saying there is <u>no</u> effect or gain when in fact there is one No. of times out of 100 when there <u>is</u> an effect, we'll say there is none
Reject the Null Hypothesis We <u>say</u>… • There is a difference or relationship • Our theory is correct	α <u>Type I Error</u> The odds of saying there <u>is</u> an effect or gain when in fact there is none. No. of times out of 100 when there is <u>no</u> effect, we'll say there is one	$1 - \beta$ <u>Power</u> The odds of saying there <u>is</u> an effect or gain when in fact there is one. No. of times out of 100 when there <u>is</u> an effect, we'll say there is one

Figure 14.5 α and β Errors

To understand this chart, we are going to look at each aspect clearly and then give an example to illustrate each part. Along the top of the chart are two columns: "Null Is True" and "Null Is False." These two columns are referring to what actually happens in the real world. In other words, the "Null Is True" column refers to the notion that in the real world your null hypothesis is true or your hypothesis is false. Maybe you predicted that men and women will have differing levels of humor, but in reality there is no difference between men and women and their use of humor. In this case, the null hypothesis is true in the real world. By contrast, often a null hypothesis is false. If you were examining men and women and differing levels of verbal aggression, men are more verbally aggressive in the real world, so the null hypothesis is false in the real world (or your actual hypothesis—that men have higher verbal aggression scores than women—is true).

As mentioned in both of these examples, often what we expect to happen when we create a mathematical hypothesis is correct and often it is wrong. For this reason, we must understand whether we have accepted the null after we get our results. If we accept the null hypothesis, we are basically saying that our original hypothesis was incorrect. If we had predicted that there would be a positive relationship between nonverbal immediacy and assertiveness and the results indicated that there was not a significant relationship, then we would accept the null hypothesis. By contrast, if we had predicted that there was a relationship between humor assessment and nonverbal immediacy, and we found a significant relationship, then we could reject the null hypothesis (or affirm our actual hypothesis).

We realize that this sounds backward and almost like we are talking out of both sides of our mouths, but remember what we said in the beginning of this chapter—in statistics we are not testing hypotheses; we are testing null hypotheses. For this reason, when we talk about error, many people get confused because it sounds logically backward compared to how most people think. Now that we have looked at what the columns mean and what the rows mean, we can examine the four quadrants indicated by both reality and what we conclude.

THE CONFIDENCE INTERVAL

In the first quadrant, "The Confidence Interval," we have a case where in "reality" (or in the actual population) the null hypothesis is true and through our statistical testing we accept the null hypothesis. Imagine that you predicted there would be a relationship between responsiveness and the attitude people have toward college. However, when you conduct a test with your sample to see whether this relationship exists, you do not find a significant relationship. At the same time, in the larger population this relationship does not exist as well. In other words, first you accepted the null (there is no relationship between responsiveness and attitude toward college) and the null is true (in the real world, there is no relationship between responsiveness and attitude toward college); you get a confidence interval. As discussed earlier in this chapter, a confidence interval lets you know how many times of 100 your results will say there is no effect (difference or relationship) and there is no effect (difference or relationship) in the real world. The confidence interval is represented by $1 - \text{alpha}$ (α). If your alpha reliability (or p value) is 0.0001, then your confidence interval is $1 - 0.0001 = 0.9999$ or a 99.99 % confidence interval. Generally speaking, when reporting alphas it is always important to round up and not down. For example, if you found that a statistical test was significant at 0.052, then this test would not be considered significant at 0.05 because 0.052 is greater than 0.05. Also, it is often best to report alpha levels on half step intervals like 0.05, 0.01, 0.005, 0.001, 0.0005, and 0.0001. So if you found that the calculated value for p was 0.0047, the easiest way to report this alpha would be to say that the test was significant at 0.005, since this is the nearest half-step interval rounded up. To help you think about p values in terms of a number line, see

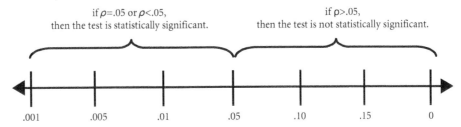

Figure 14.6 Statistical Significance Number Line

Figure 14.6. Remember, the goal is for the probability value (*p* value) to be less than 0.05 to reach statistical significance. In the case of Figure 14.6, those *p* values to the left of 0.05 would be statistically significant and those values to the right of 0.05 would not be statistically significant.

When looking at computer printouts, SPSS and Excel will both provide you with calculated alpha levels. However, there is some disagreement as to how to report alpha levels that are below 0.000. Levine and Atkin (2004) argue that when a computer printout prints a 0.000 alpha level (this occurs with SPSS), it is most correct to report this alpha level as 0.0005 (99.95% confident).

The sixth edition of the APA style manual established some clear-cut guidelines for reporting *p* values in academic research. Here is what the APA style manual says about reporting *p*-values according to the 6th edition guidelines:

> When reporting *p* values, report exact *p* values (e.g., *p* = .031) to two or three decimal places. However, report *p* values less than .001 as *p* < .001. The tradition of reporting *p* values in the form of *p* < .10, *p* < .05, *p* < .01, and so forth, was appropriate in a time when only limited tables of critical values were available. However, in tables the "*p* <" notation may be necessary for clarity (see section 5.16). (p. 114)

For those of you new to APA style, this may not seem like a huge deal, but to those of us who have been using APA style for a few decades (or more), this is a big change in how we report *p* values. Although we are talking about this issue here, you will see where this becomes important in next five chapters as we explore various statistical tests.

POWER

In the quadrant diagonal to "The Confidence Interval" is the quadrant labeled "Power." Power is the odds of saying there is a difference or relationship when in fact there is one. In this case, you reject the null hypothesis based on the results from your statistical analysis and the null hypothesis is actually rejected in the real world. For example, maybe you predicted that there would be a positive relationship between nonverbal immediacy and responsiveness. To test this question, you run a statistical analysis and find out that there is a relationship, and then this relationship actually exists in the real world. In this case, your statistical test rejected the null hypothesis and the null hypothesis should be rejected in the world. When this occurs, the result is called power. In essence, power is the number of times of 100 when there is a relationship or difference in a study and there is a relationship or difference that exists in the real world. Power is represented by 1 − beta (β). If your beta is equal to 0.05, then your power is 1 − 0.05 = 0.95. As we mentioned earlier when we discussed power, power should be greater than 0.80 to successfully reject the null hypothesis when the null hypothesis is rejected in the larger population. These first two quadrants represent what we hope will happen when we use

CHAPTER 14 HYPOTHESIS TESTING

statistics to analyze quantitative data. However, there are two types of errors that occur when people use statistics to analyze quantitative data.

TYPE I ERROR

The first type of error (**type I error** or **α error**) occurs when a researcher rejects a null hypothesis (says their alternative hypothesis was true) based on a sample when the null should be accepted (alternative hypothesis was false in the real world). In other words, you run a test to see whether an individual's level of interpersonal humor (humor assessment) is related to nonverbal sensitivity (ability to pick up on other people's nonverbal behavior). You find a positive relationship between humor assessment and nonverbal sensitivity in your sample, but in the real world this relationship does not exist. When this occurs, you have a type I error. A type I error is the odds of finding a difference or relationship when in fact there is not one. This probability is represented by alpha or your probability value. If a finding is significant at $p < 0.05$, then there is a 5 % chance that you will reject your null hypothesis (or affirming your hypothesis or research question) when in the actual population you would not reject your null hypothesis.

TYPE II ERROR

The second type of error (**type II error** or **β error**) occurs when a researcher accepts a null hypothesis (says their alternative hypothesis was not true) based on a sample when the null should be rejected (says their alternative hypothesis was true in the real world). We can take the flip side of the example discussed under type I error. You run a test to see whether an individual's level of interpersonal humor (humor assessment) is related to nonverbal sensitivity (ability to pick up on other people's nonverbal behavior). You do not find a relationship between humor assessment and nonverbal sensitivity in your sample, but in the real world (or actual population) this relationship exists. When this occurs, you have a type II error. A type II error is the odds of finding there is no difference or relationship when in fact there is one. Type II error is represented by the Greek letter β. If in a study you find that $\beta = 0.05$, then there is a 5 % chance that you will accept the null hypothesis (or reject your hypothesis or research question), when in the actual population you would reject your null hypothesis (or affirming your hypothesis or research question).

One of the basic goals of empirical research is to limit both type I and type II errors as much as possible. To limit type I error, the best thing to do is to increase your confidence interval from, say, 95 % confidence (5 times 100 you are wrong) to, say, 99 % confidence (1 time of 100 you are wrong). However, you might think that this means that researchers should just neglect the 95 % confidence interval for a more conservative 99 % confidence interval all the time. Unfortunately, if you try to protect against type I errors (rejecting a null hypothesis that is probably true, a false positive), you often enable the committing of type II errors instead (accepting a null hypothesis that is probably false, a false negative). In other words, type I errors (alpha errors) and type II errors (beta errors) are inversely related. The more stringent the probability level, the more likely you will commit a type II error, and the more stringent the power, the more likely you will commit a type I error. In an ideal world, a fair balance can be struck between type I and type II errors, but often researchers must err on one side or the other. However, increasing the sample size one obtains does allow a research to achieve both low alpha and high beta values. To prevent both type I and type II errors, researchers are encouraged to recruit fairly large samples (at least 200 participants). Ultimately, the number of participants needed for a study is based on a variety of factors related to how many groups you want to compare and the size of the differences and relationships you hope to obtain.

Conclusion

This chapter has introduced you to three major concepts that will be seen again and again during the next five chapters (significance, power, and effect size). Remember, just because two means may appear different does not indicate that the difference is statistically significant. For instance, we have used an example throughout the entire chapter about 10 participants who agreed to participate in a study to determine whether a difference occurs in an individual's attitude toward a religion after watching a televangelist. Based on the numbers described in the first part of a chapter, there was not a significant difference between Time 1 (before watching the televangelist) and Time 2 (after watching the televangelist). In fact, the calculated p value was 0.052, so the difference was not significant at the 0.05 level. (How this was tested will be discussed in Chapter 17)

KEY TERMS

Alternative hypothesis	Hypothesis testing	Probability value (p value)
Calculated value	Null hypothesis	Sampling error
Confidence interval	One-tailed hypothesis	Significance testing
Confidence level	Power	Two-tailed hypothesis
Critical value	Probability	Type I error (α error)
Effect size	Probability level	Type II error (β error)

REFERENCES

American Psychological Association. (2010). *Publication manual of the American Psychological Association* (6th ed.). Washington, DC: American Psychological Association.

Cheseboro, J. (1999). The relationship between listening styles and conversational sensitivity. *Communication Research Reports, 16,* 233–238.

Cohen, J. (1994). The earth is round ($p < .05$). *American Psychologist, 49,* 997–1003.

Fisher, R. A. (1935). *The design of experiments.* Scotland, Edinburgh: Oliver & Boyd.

Levine, T. R., & Atkin, C. (2004). The accurate reporting of software-generated p-values: A cautionary research note. *Communication Research Reports, 21,* 324–327.

Rocca, K. A., & Vogl-Bauer, S. (1999). Trait verbal aggression, sports fan identification, and perceptions of appropriate sports fan communication. *Communication Research Reports, 16,* 239–248.

FURTHER READING

Chow, S. L. (1997). *Statistical significance: Rationale, validity, and utility.* Thousand Oaks, CA: Sage.

Gravetter, F. J., & Wallnau, L. B. (2000). *Statistics for the behavioral sciences* (5th ed.). Belmont, CA: Wadsworth/Thomson Learning.

Howell, D. C. (1997). *Statistical methods for psychology* (4th ed.). Belmont, CA: Duxbury Press.

Huff, D. (1954). *How to lie with statistics.* New York, NY: Norton.

Keller, D. K. (2006). *The Tao of statistics: A path to understanding (with no math).* Thousand Oaks, CA: Sage.

Lehmann, E. L. L., & Romano, J. P. (2005). *Testing statistical hypothesis* (3rd ed.). New York, NY: Springer-Verlag.

Mohr, L. B., & Lewis-Beck, M. S. (1990). *Understanding significance testing.* Thousand Oaks, CA: Sage.

Salkind, N. J. (2004). *Statistics for people who (think they) hate statistics* (2nd ed.). Thousand Oaks, CA: Sage.

Salkind, N. J. (2012). *100 questions (and answers) about research methods.* Los Angeles, CA: Sage.

Singleton, R. A., Jr., & Straits, B. C. (1999). *Approach to social research* (3rd ed.). New York, NY: Oxford University Press.

Tabachnick, B. G., & Fidell, L. S. (2001). *Using multivariate statistics* (4th ed.). Boston, MA: Allyn & Bacon.

Trochim, W. M. K. (2000). *The research methods knowledge base* (2nd ed.). Cincinnati, OH: Atomic Dog. Retrieved from http://www.socialresearchmethods.net/

Weber, K., Fornash, B., Corrigan, M, & Neupauer, N. C. (2003). The effect of interest on recall: An experiment. *Communication Research Reports, 20,* 116–123.

Descriptive Statistics

Statistics is a term that conjures up many different meanings in the minds of students. Of course, the majority of students we have worked with express a high level of anxiety and apprehension about taking a course in research methods because of a fear of statistics. Be honest—were you excited at the prospect of taking this class? Our guess is that if given the choice, the majority of you would have preferred to take a different course. In fact, this is a good example of a statistic—the "majority."

Imagine we had the ability to have everyone in the world fill out the Personal Report of Communication Apprehension-24 (PRCA-24) scale. The average we would get for the entire world population on the PRCA-24 would be called a parameter because the average would refer to the entire population. However, it is almost impossible to achieve parameters because having an entire population fill out a scale is almost impossible unless the target population is small. Instead, we often use smaller groups from within the entire population called samples. Although we discussed how to get samples in greater detail in Chapter 13, here just understand that a sample is a subset from within the whole population that allows researchers to make generalizations about the whole population. When we calculate information from a sample of data (for example, the sample data's PRCA-24 scores collected for this book), the calculation is referred to as a **statistic**. In essence, the parameter is the real average of communication apprehension in a population, and a statistic is the average of communication apprehension within a sample. In a perfect world, the two numbers would be identical, but there is always a certain amount of error that will exist between parameters and statistics.

The goal of this chapter is to introduce you to the "not-so-scary" side of statistics. We have all seen commercials that say something like this: "Four out of five dentists recommend Chewing Gum Brand X for their patients who chew gum." The advertisement uses a statistic to illustrate that 80 percent of dentists would recommend Chewing Gum Brand X. This is much more effective than simply stating that "most dentists prefer Chewing Gum Brand X." When information is presented using terms like "most," "many," and "substantial," consumers are often skeptical and want to know the exact amount. Generally, we seek proof for claims that are made, and statistics serve as a source that lends credibility. Consider the grades that you earn in your classes. Suppose you take an exam and the instructor simply indicates that you "passed." Typically, the first question asked is, "What percentage did I earn?" Students think statistics are scary, but when you stop to think about it, we encounter them every day of our lives.

THE BENEFITS OF STATISTICS

When considering the usefulness of statistics for communication researchers, three primary benefits are identified. Statistics can be thought of as tools used to describe, organize, and interpret information. First, statistics allow us to summarize or describe data. Statistics enable researchers to make predictions and make sense of the world around us. The ability of statistics to help us summarize data is incredible! For example, the U.S. Census conducted in 2010 collected information from more than 308 million people (http://factfinder2.census.gov/). Statistics are used to summarize massive amounts of information and enable researchers to describe the general U.S. population. For example, we know that 37,253,956 residents who participated in the census live in California. That represents 12.07 percent of the total U.S. population in 2010. Statistics help paint a picture of our nation's population by summarizing data from millions of participants and describing those data in a way that makes sense.

Statistics also enable us to organize information in a meaningful way to make predictions. If information about a sample group is known, those data can be organized and used to make predictions about the general population. For example, in her study of teachers' use of humor to gain student compliance, Punyanunt (2000) found that students were more likely to comply with requests that were humorous (this article is on the textbook's website). By organizing these data, we can predict that if other teachers want to be effective in their compliance-gaining attempts, they should employ a humorous tone. Referring back to the earlier example for Chewing Gum Brand X, you could predict that your dentist will likely recommend Chewing Gum Brand X if you were to ask what brand of gum you should chew.

Finally, statistics assist us in understanding and interpreting the world around us. We doubt that you could go through one day without encountering or using statistics in some way. Sports fans depend on statistics to understand where their favorite team is ranked, and consumers interpret the nutritional values on packages to assist them in making product choices in supermarkets. If you are a frequent reader of *USA Today*, you have probably noticed the "Snapshots" boxes located in the bottom corner on the cover page of each section. Topics explored in these quantitative surveys include everything from favorite food duos (e.g., macaroni and cheese vs. cereal and milk) to sources that influence decisions to purchase products (e.g., word-of-mouth vs. in-store promotions). Daily weather forecasts usually include statistical predictions, such as, "There is a 60 percent chance of scattered thundershowers for the region today." Your existence as a college student revolves around a statistic known as your grade point average. When you stop to think about it, you really know more about statistics than you thought.

Descriptive Versus Inferential Statistics

As stated earlier, one of the benefits of statistics is that they allow us to describe or summarize information. **Descriptive statistics** are used to organize and summarize information or data. Essentially, descriptive statistics allow a researcher to provide a description of what actually "exists" in the data. Data can be defined as any record or observation. Examples of data include the number of years employed, grade point average, annual income, gender, or the number of hours spent watching television each day. Researchers use descriptive statistics to help us reduce large amounts of data to a more manageable size. Perhaps one of the most commonly used descriptive statistics is percentages. Consider the following example—one way a university could use descriptive statistics is to summarize students in a particular class. For example, the class could be%percent females; 4% freshmen, 19 % sophomores, 52 % juniors, and 25 % seniors; or 42 %t traditional students and 58 % nontraditional students. A variety of data can be collected to describe different characteristics of the group. With the individual pieces of information (or data) collected from each student, a summary of the entire class can be calculated. The goal of this chapter is to provide you with statistical tools to assist you in describing groups of data.

Whereas descriptive statistics describe or summarize data, **inferential statistics** are often the next stage in data analysis. Once the researcher has summarized and described the data in terms of percentages or averages, the data can be further analyzed to make inferences from the smaller group of data (also known as the sample) to a larger group of data (also referred to as the population). Inferential statistics are used when a researcher wants to make predictions. To make predictions, researchers often (but not always) take the process of statistical analyses to the next level and use inferential statistics to draw conclusions and make predictions about a larger group based on a smaller group of data. It is important to reiterate the distinction between these two groups—the smaller group of participants that were selected for the study is referred to as the sample. A sample is defined as a subset of the larger population, or all the possible persons who could fall into a particular category. Because it is usually improbable that a researcher would be able to access all possible participants in the population, samples of participants are selected to best represent the entire group. Students in a communication research methods class at a university could be considered a sample of the population of all communication majors currently enrolled at that campus. In Chapter 13, methods for selecting samples are discussed in more detail.

Suppose your university requires all students to complete a public speaking class prior to graduation. To determine whether this requirement is beneficial in preparing students for their careers, they decide to survey a sample of communication alumni from your school. Depending on the size of the school, surveying every graduate might be a difficult and time-consuming task. Instead, a sample of alumni might be used to determine their perceptions of the usefulness of the public speaking requirement. Various statistics could be calculated for this sample of alumni. Suppose you asked alumni the following question: "On a scale of 1 to 10 (1 being lowest and 10 being highest) please indicate how valuable you perceive your public speaking class to be in preparing for your current career." Descriptive statistics could be used to provide an average rating for the perceived value of public speaking as reported by alumni in the sample.

What if you wanted to take your analyses to the next level and compare the results of those graduates who are frequently required to make presentations in their careers with those who do little or no public speaking? Inferential statistics could be used to make comparisons between these two groups and identify whether they differ in their perceptions of the value of the public speaking requirement. The concept of inferential statistics will be discussed in more depth in later chapters. For now, we will focus our attention on using statistics to describe data.

Measures of Central Tendency

One of the first questions typically asked when analyzing data from a group is, "What is the average score?" Recall the last time you received an exam back from an instructor. If you scored a 72 percent on the exam, your initial reaction might be to feel disappointed. However, suppose the instructor announces that the class average on the exam was a 63 percent, so she is going to add points to the grades. Your disappointment turns to elation simply as the result of a statistic that is mentioned. No longer is your score considered "slightly below the average grade" (in this case 75 percent, which typically represents a grade of "C"). Rather, you learn that your grade is now considered well above the average for the class.

To measure the "center" or "middle" score in a group of data, researchers use what are commonly referred to as measures of central tendency. Three **measures of central tendency** that can be examined on a frequency distribution are the mean, median, and mode.

MEAN

The **mean**, or average, is typically defined as the value that represents an entire group of scores. To calculate the mean, add all of the scores in the category you wish to summarize and divide the total by the number of scores. Researchers use two different types of means to describe data. If data have been collected from the entire population, the population mean is the best descriptor of the average score. The formula for calculating the population mean can be seen in Figure 15.1.

Because it is rare that a researcher is able to get data from all possible members of a population, the sample is used to best represent the entire group. Suppose a researcher wants to gauge student satisfaction with campus activities. It is highly unlikely that data could be collected from every student. Instead, a sample of students could be collected by visiting a sample of classes across different majors. The formula used to compute the sample mean is seen in Figure 15.2.

Although the mean is a solid measure of central tendency for datasets that have a relatively normal distribution curve, it can be deceiving for data that are not symmetrically distributed because of extreme scores. Suppose that you want to assess the average level of apprehension of five students who completed the PRCA-24 scale whose scores were 98, 56, 49, 42, and 39. Simply by looking at the list of scores, it is evident that 98 is different from the other four

$$\mu = \Sigma X \div N$$

Figure 15.1 Population Mean

μ = Population mean

ΣX = Sum of all scores within a population

N = Number of scores within a population

$$x = \Sigma x \div n$$

Figure 15.2 Sample Mean

$\bar{x}$ = Sample mean

Σx = Sum of all scores within a sample

n = Number of scores within a sample

scores—thus, it is often referred to as an "extreme" score or outlier. Here we calculate the mean for the sample of PRCA-24 scores.

Step 1: The first step to computing a sample mean is to add all of the numbers of a sample together. In our example, we simply add the five numbers (Σx) together and receive a summed total of 284:

$$98 + 56 + 49 + 42 + 39 = 284$$

Step 2: The second step in computing a sample mean is to take the summed total (Σx) in Step 1 and divide the sum (Σx) by the number of scores in the group (n). In our example, we received a Σx of 284 in Step 1 and we have five participants ($n = 5$), so we divide 284 by 5, or

$$284/5 = 56.8$$

The mean of the five scores is 56.8, which turns out to be higher than the scores reported for four of the five team members. In this instance the mean is not representative of the distribution. In cases where the mean score is biased or skewed by extreme scores, other measures of central tendency may offer a better summary of the data. One statistic that could be used in this instance is the median.

MEDIAN

The **median** is defined as the middle value in a list of data. To calculate the median, first list the data in order from smallest to largest. After you have sorted data in ascending order, identify the number that lies at the exact midpoint of the list. If the list has an odd number of items, the median is the middle entry in the list. If the list has an even number of items, add the two middle numbers and divide by two.

One way of thinking about the median is to consider it a representation of percentile. A score that falls at the 75th percentile will lie at or above 75 percent of all the other scores in the distribution. The median is known as the true "50th percentile" score, or the point at which half of the scores fall above and the remaining half of the scores fall below.

Recall our earlier example, which examined a series of CA scores. In a set of scores where one or more score falls at an extreme end of the distribution, the median is perhaps the best choice for representing the middle value of the dataset. Let's calculate the median for the sample of PRCA-24 scores.

The first step in finding a median in a set of data is to list all the scores in order from smallest to largest:

39   42   49   56   98

Finding the median (if odd number of scores): The first step in finding a median in a set of data is to identify whether the data consist of an even or odd number of scores. If there are an odd number of scores (three scores, five scores, seven scores, etc.), simply find the midpoint of all the scores, which is your median. In our example, we have five scores, which is an odd number, so when we look at the third number in the set of five we have the number "49." In this case, our median is 49.

Finding the median (if even number of scores): Often sets of data will have an even number of scores (two scores, four scores, six scores, eight scores, etc.), so a different technique is needed for determining the median. If there is an even number of scores, add the two middle scores and divide them by the number "2" to find the median score. For example, suppose the dataset from the earlier example looked like this after you rearranged the numbers from least to greatest:

39   42   49   51   56   98

To calculate the median, you would first find the scores in the middle of the data. In this case, we have six data points, so the two middle numbers would be the third and fourth numbers, or 49 and 51. To find the median, we first need to add the two middle numbers:

$$49 + 51 = 100$$

Once we have the summed total, we divide the number by 2 (since there are two numbers involved in the sum total):

$$100/2 = 50$$

In this case the median for this example would be 50.

As mentioned earlier, the median is a better descriptive statistic to use when reporting on the average for data with extreme scores. Often the median will be stated as, "The median income of the average American family is . . ." The median allows for a more accurate representation of the data in situations like this.

Bloomberg and the Mean

When examining descriptive statistics, it is important to examine both the means and medians to get a realistic portrayal of a sample. The mean gives us the general average of a group, whereas the median lets us know the middle most value. For illustrative purposes, imagine you are sitting at a bar with a couple of your friends. Among the three of you, you have the following bank balances: You ($2,100), Friend 1 ($1,692), and Friend 2 ($1,553). Among the three of you, the average current bank account balance is $1,781.67 with a median of $1,692. In this case, the mean and the median are not drastically far away from each other numerically. However, imagine if out of nowhere Michael Bloomberg walks into the bar and sits down and joins you for a drink. In 2013, he was worth approximately $44 billion. Magically, the average net worth for the people sitting at the bar is now $1.1 billion. Would you think this is a great way of representing these numbers? Probably not. In this case, the mean is far from a great tool for understanding the actual net worth of the people in the bar. Instead, the median is going to be considerably more important, which is now $1,896. This little averaging trick is often used by people to inflate the mean incomes of workers.

MODE

Perhaps the least frequently cited descriptive statistic is the mode. The **mode** is defined as the value that occurs most frequently in a dataset. An easy way to remember the definition for mode is to recall the phrase "mode is the most." It is the most general and least precise of all descriptive statistics. To calculate the mode, we will use the data from the even median example discussed earlier.

Step 1: The first step in finding a mode is to create a list of the values that occur in a dataset. Be sure to list each value only once!

39	42	42	49	51	56	98

Step 2: Create a tally of the number of times that each score appears. The number "39" appears once, the number "42" appears twice, the number "49" appears once, the number "51" appears once, the number "56" appears once, and the number "98" appears once.

Step 3: The score or value that appears most often is the mode. In our example, the numbers "39," "49," "51," "56," and "98" appear only one time. However, the number "42" appears twice, so we would consider the number "42" our mode because it is the number seen most often within our data.

Suppose we wanted to examine the dataset examining political affiliation from the first edition of this book. After calculating the frequency of political affiliations, the following data would be reported:

Republicans	144
Democrats	117
Other	39
Not registered	21

What would the mode be for this dataset? Be careful—your first instinct might be to indicate that "144" is the mode, but this is incorrect. "Republican" is the mode for the variable of political affiliation because it is the most frequently occurring value.

As mentioned earlier, a dataset can have more than one mode. In instances where two values occur with equal frequency, the dataset is defined as being bimodal. In the actual dataset that accompanies this text, we ended up with exactly 220 Democrats and 220 Republicans, so our dataset is bidmodal. When a dataset has more than two values that occur with the same frequency, the data are defined as being multimodal. Figure 15.3 provides you with one more look at how the mean, median, and mode compare for a set of scores measuring the level of CA.

Variable	CA	Represented as X
	39	
	42	
	42	Mode (occurs most frequently)
	49	Median (midpoint of data)
	51	
	56	
	98	
n	7	Number of cases
ΣX_i	377	Total or sum of all scores (ages)
$\overline{X}$	53.86	Mean or average score (age)

Figure 15.3 Mean, Median, and Mode for a Sample of PRCA Scores

So which statistic should you use to represent the dataset? Let's use the example of reporting annual salaries for an organization. Suppose an organization employs 10 people who each earn an annual salary of $25,000. The production manager earns $50,000, whereas the supervisor earns $100,000. The mode ($25,000) would be the most accurate statistic to represent the salary that most people in the organization earn. However, if your goal is to make a strong impression on potential employees, you might decide that it is to your advantage to use the mean of $33,333 to attract more applicants. The decision is yours!

Often the decision of which measure of central tendency to use depends on the available dataset. The mode is the best statistic for representing qualitative data such as political affiliation, sex, or class rank. Calculating an average for these types of data would be inaccurate. After all, it would not make sense to say that the average score for biological sex is 1.2—a participant is either female or male. It does make sense to report that "of 325 respondents, most (144) indicated that they are Republican." Unfortunately, SPSS and Excel will not tell if you are running an incorrect statistical test, so you must be smarter than the computer program or you will run statistical tests that mean nothing. Without fail, at least one student every time we teach research methods will fall into this trap. They will think that because the computer will let them run a mean for biological sex that this mean is somehow meaningful, but it is not. Numbers can be computed for almost anything, but not all of these numbers are meaningful. Quantitative data require a researcher to use either the mean or the median to report the measure of central tendency. As stated earlier, the median is best in situations where extreme scores exist so the average score is not misrepresented. The mean is the appropriate statistic for datasets where there are not extreme scores.

FREQUENCY DISTRIBUTIONS

Measures of central tendency are often visually depicted by constructing a frequency distribution. These frequency charts allow researchers to summarize and organize a set of data and enable them to identify trends. To create a **frequency distribution**, simply record the number of occurrences for each value in the dataset. Although the statistics could be computed by hand like we did earlier, it is not time efficient to do so. For this reason, a variety of computer programs have been created to aid in this process. Two commonly used statistical software packages used by communication researchers are SPSS and Excel. The following section expects that you (1) have a statistical software package you prefer to use and (2) know how to find and open files on the textbook's website. If you look on the textbook's website, you will find a section marked "Book Datasets." In this folder you will find SPSS datasets, Excel datasets, and Note Pad datasets. SPSS datasets can easily be opened and used in both PSPP and R (if using R-Commander). The SPSS and Excel datasets can be used only by SPSS and Excel software packages. If you do not have SPSS or Excel but have a different statistical software package, you can use the Note Pad datasets to import the data into whatever program you prefer to use following that program's specific instructions for importing a text file. However, we will only be discussing how to read and interpret results from SPSS and Excel in this book.

SPSS and Frequency Distributions

When using SPSS to calculate frequency distributions, you use the "cross tabs" function. For this example, open the SPSS dataset called "Recoded Dataset" on the textbook's website. Once you open the dataset (Figure 15.4), you must create a frequency table. To get to the "Frequencies" function, go to the menu bar at the top of your screen and click on "Analyze." When you click on "Analyze," a drop-down menu will appear (Figure 15.5). Go to the second category on this menu, "Descriptive Statistics" and scroll over the arrow and another menu

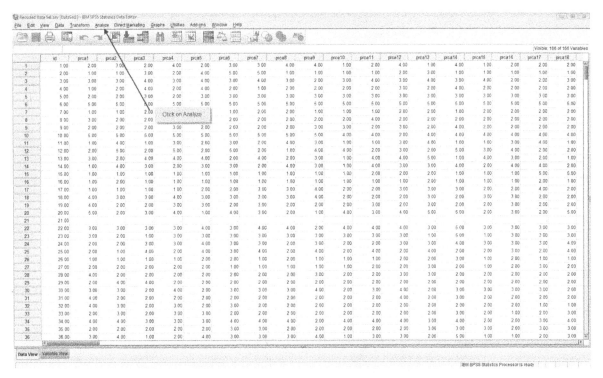

Figure 15.4 Main SPSS Screen Shot

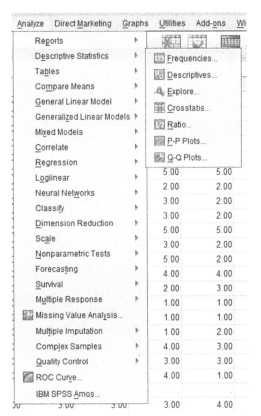

Figure 15.5 Frequencies Drop-down Menu

will appear to the right. In this menu, search for the "Frequencies" option and right click on it. At this point, the Frequencies dialogue box will appear (Figure 15.6a). As previously discussed, a frequency table is a table that lists the numbers and percentages of given answers. For example, maybe you want to find out how many females and males there are in a given sample. To find this out, you would create a frequency table. To create a frequency table in SPSS, first you must select the variable that you want create the table for by highlighting it (click on it once). Scroll through the list of variables in the "Recoded Dataset" and right click on "Biological Sex [sex]." When you right click on "Biological Sex [sex]," the variable is highlighted in blue (Figure 15.6a). You now want to click the arrow button to move "Biological Sex [sex]" to the "Variable(s)" list (Figure 15.6b), which is the list of variables to be analyzed. When you click on the arrow button, the variable "Biological Sex [sex]" will be transferred from the left column (variables in the data set) to the right column (variables you want frequency tables for; Figure 15.6c). At this point, all you need to do to achieve a frequency window is to click "OK" on the right-hand side of the screen because when you initially open the Frequencies dialogue box the frequency tables option is always preselected for you (Figure 15.6d). When you do this, the data in Figure 15.7 will appear.

We have provided all of the frequency information for four of the variables in the "Recoded Dataset" in Figure 15.8 (Biological Sex, Political Affiliation, Year in School, and Time

a) Frequencies Dialogue Box

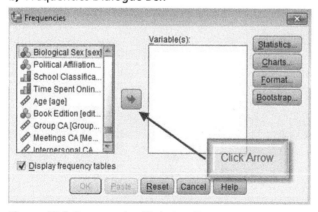

b) Frequencies Dialogue Box

Figure 15.6 Frequencies Dialogue Box

c) Frequencies Dialogue Box

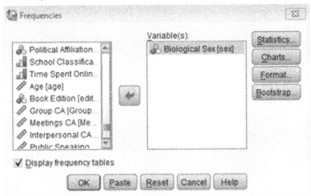

d) Frequencies Dialogue Box

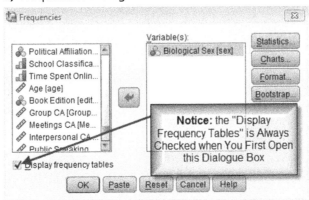

Statistics

Biological Sex

N	Valid	641
	Missing	13

Biological Sex

		Frequency	Percent	Valid Percent	Cumulative Percent
Valid	Male	320	48.9	49.9	49.9
	Female	321	49.1	50.1	100.0
	Total	641	98.0	100.0	
Missing	System	13	2.0		
Total		654	100.0		

Figure 15.7 Frequency Table for Biological Sex

Political Affiliation

		Frequency	Percent	Valid Percent	Cumulative Percent
Valid	Democrat	220	33.6	34.6	34.6
	Republican	220	33.6	34.6	69.3
	Other	131	20.0	20.6	89.9
	Not Registered to Vote	64	9.8	10.1	100.0
	Total	635	97.1	100.0	
Missing	System	19	2.9		
Total		654	100.0		

School Classification

		Frequency	Percent	Valid Percent	Cumulative Percent
Valid	First Year Student	52	8.0	8.2	8.2
	Sophomore	107	16.4	16.8	24.9
	Junior	231	35.3	36.2	61.1
	Senior	244	37.3	38.2	99.4
	Other	4	.6	.6	100.0
	Total	638	97.6	100.0	
Missing	System	16	2.4		
Total		654	100.0		

Time Spent Online

		Frequency	Percent	Valid Percent	Cumulative Percent
Valid	0-.5 hour	15	2.3	2.3	2.3
	.5-1 hour	20	3.1	3.1	5.5
	1-2 hours	58	8.9	9.1	14.6
	2-5 hours	183	28.0	28.6	43.2
	5-10 hours	142	21.7	22.2	65.4
	10-15 hours	93	14.2	14.6	80.0
	15-20 hours	64	9.8	10.0	90.0
	25 + hours	64	9.8	10.0	100.0
	Total	639	97.7	100.0	
Missing	System	15	2.3		
Total		654	100.0		

Figure 15.8 Frequency Table for All Nominal Variables in the Dataset

Spent Online). We will discuss how to calculate means, medians, and modes using SPSS later in this chapter.

Excel and Frequency Distributions

At this point, we will examine how to calculate a frequency chart using Excel as well. Given that Microsoft Excel is readily available to most students, we will include information on using this program to calculate statistics. Although Excel may be a convenient program for analysis, keep in mind that the primary purpose for the program is not statistical analysis. Thus, the process for computing even basic statistics often involves more steps than in other software programs, and the options for post hoc analyses are often more limited than in programs such as SPSS.

Before you begin using Excel, consider the following caveats. First, missing data must be entered as a blank cell in Excel. The program is unable to read any other format for missing data. If you are importing a database that automatically fills an empty cell with data, utilize the "Find and Select" feature to convert all missing data (see Figure 15.9). The imported "Recoded Dataset" file may include several cells with "#NULL!" to represent missing values. To convert the data, click on the "Replace" tab at the top of the screen, type the value that appears in the cells for missing data in the "Find What" box, and leave the "Replace with" box blank. Click on "Replace All" to convert all missing data to empty cells (Figure 15.10).

Second, the steps for calculating statistics may differ depending on the version of Microsoft Excel that you are using (e.g., Excel 2007 vs. Excel 2010). In addition, the data analysis process for statistical computation varies depending on whether you are using a Mac versus a PC for data analysis. Finally, Excel does not come preinstalled with the data analysis tools that are required to complete statistical analyses. However, this is easily remedied with a free

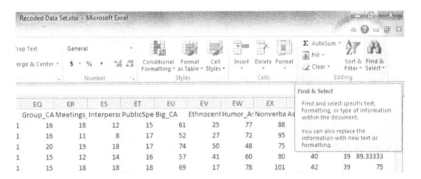

Figure 15.9 Find and Select

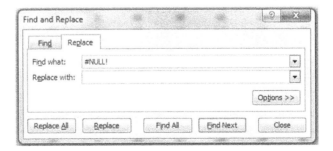

Figure 15.10 Replacing #Null!

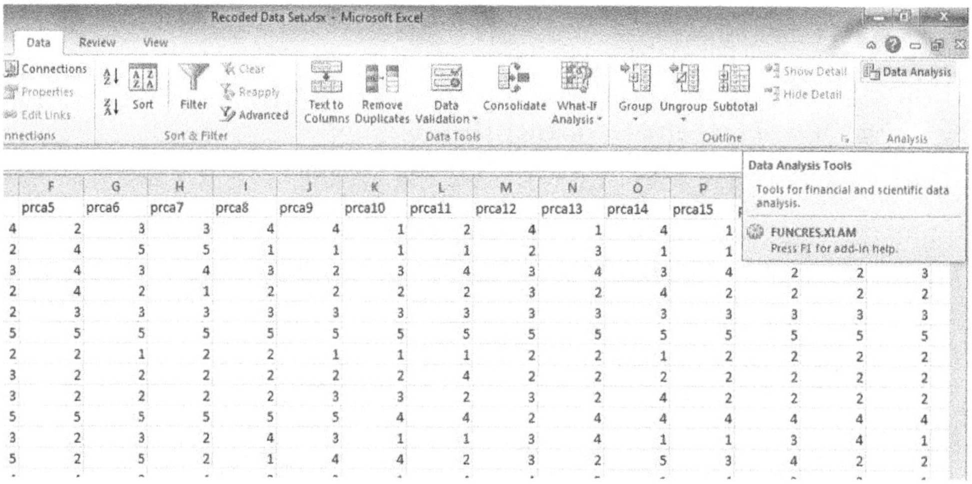

Figure 15.11 Excel Data Menu

download. To determine whether your computer has the data analysis tool kit installed, click on "Help" and type "Data Analysis." If you are using a PC, the Data Analysis ToolPak is available from the Microsoft website (http://www.office.microsoft.com/). The Mac platform will require you to download a program called "StatPlus"(http://www.analystsoft.com/). In this text, we will describe the procedures for calculating statistics using the PC version of Excel 2010.

Once you have downloaded the data analysis package to Excel, you will see a tab on the top of the spreadsheet screen titled "Data." Clicking will provide access to an area labeled "Analysis." This area will enable you to calculate a variety of basic statistics in Excel (Figure 15.11).

To calculate frequencies in Excel, open the data file titled "Recoded Dataset" from the textbook site. Remember—if the dataset contains any missing data, you will need to utilize the "Find and Select" function to convert any data that are used to represent missing values into blank cells. To be able to easily view your data and output, it is recommended that you select and work with one column or variable at a time. To compute the frequency counts for each value, Excel provides the PivotTable and PivotChart options. Begin by highlighting the "Sex" column in the spreadsheet and clicking on the "Insert" tab at the top of the screen. Click on "PivotTable" at the left side of the screen, and the range of values that is highlighted should appear in the box. Check the box for "New Worksheet" and select "OK" (Figure 15.12). A new sheet will open, and you will be asked to indicate the fields that you wish to add to your report. Drag and drop "Age" from the list into both the "Row Labels" and the "Values" boxes. A frequency table with counts for each age reported will appear on the screen. If you would like to add a histogram, select the "PivotChart" option and follow the same process by dragging "Sex" into the "Axis Field" and "Values" boxes. A frequency table and histogram will appear on the new sheet (Figure 15.13).

Frequency Distributions and Charts

Once a frequency distribution has been constructed, the data can be also be graphically represented by creating a histogram. A histogram is a bar chart that represents the frequency with which each value for a variable occurs. Suppose that we wanted to create a histogram for the following scores obtained on a statistics exam. A frequency distribution for the data would look like Figure 15.14. Using this information, a histogram (or bar graph) can be constructed to assist the researcher in identifying the shape of the data, the symmetry, and the presence of

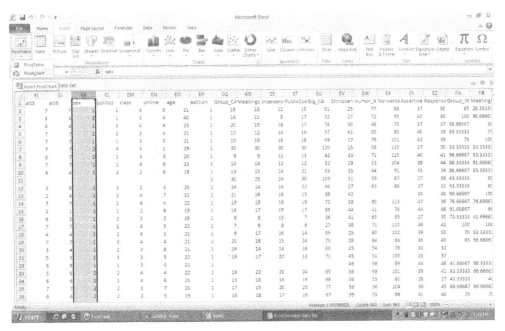

Figure 15.12 Pivot Table

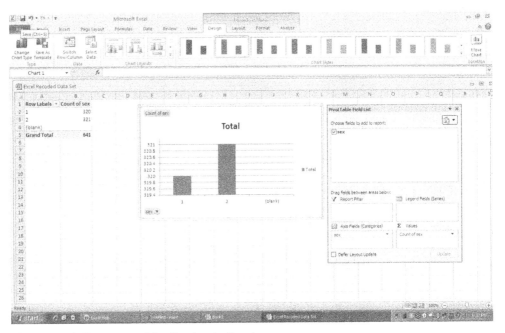

Figure 15.13 Frequency Distribution in Excel

Figure 15.14 Frequency Distribution of Exam Scores

Letter Grade	Score	Frequency
A	90	1
B	80	2
C	70	4
D	60	2
F	50	1

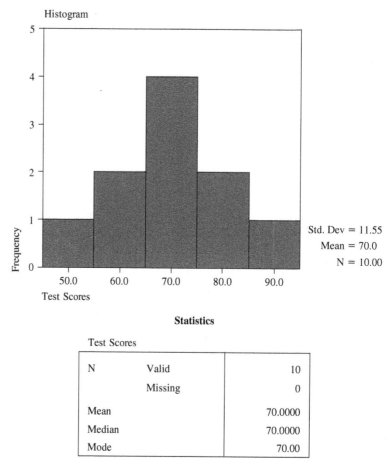

Statistics

Test Scores

N	Valid	10
	Missing	0
Mean		70.0000
Median		70.0000
Mode		70.00

Figure 15.15 Histogram and SPSS Statistics for a Normal Distribution of Exam Scores

outliers (extreme scores). Each test score is included along the *x* axis in ascending order, and the frequency with which each score occurs is plotted on the *y* axis (Figure 15.15).

By glancing at the histogram, the researcher can determine whether the set of data is normally distributed. The score with the highest frequency (in this case 70) falls at the middle of the normal distribution. Scores with lower frequencies are on either side of the mean. If the scores are distributed normally, the curve forms a bell shape. A closer look at the information provided in the SPSS output figure shows that the mean, median, and mode are all the same for this dataset. In fact, statisticians refer to any distribution where the mean, median, and mode are the same as a bell curve.

So why should a researcher be concerned with the shape of the histogram? Normality of data is a condition for certain statistical analyses associated with hypothesis testing, which was discussed in more detail in Chapter 14. Although formal statistical tests can be used to test whether a distribution for a dataset is normal, a simple glance at the histogram can speak volumes. It is important to note, however, that not all distribution curves are normal or bell shaped. Earlier we mentioned that a dataset can have more than one mode. Remember— the mode is the value that occurs most often. If the midpoint in the curve is represented by the mode score, a dataset that is bimodal would produce a shape that resembles an inverted bell curve. Consider the following hypothetical exam scores:

50, 50, 50, 60, 60, 70, 80, 80, 90, 90, 90

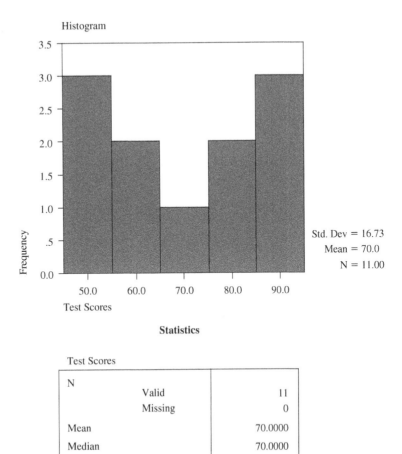

Figure 15.16 Histogram and SPSS Statistics for a Bimodal Distribution of Exam Scores

Note that the scores of "50" and "90" occur with the same frequency—each appears three times in the list. Thus, the dataset is **bimodal**. A histogram for this set of scores would look like Figure 15.16.

A closer look at the information provided in the SPSS output figure shows that the mean and median scores are the same for this dataset, but multiple modes exist. (Note: SPSS only reports the smallest value for the mode.) You will also note that SPSS will report multimodal distributions by placing a superscript letter "a" next to the mode on the SPSS printout.

SKEWNESS AND KURTOSIS

More often than not, the dataset you are analyzing will produce a curve that is asymmetrical, or a dataset's **skewness**. A curve can be either positively skewed or negatively skewed. A positively skewed curve is one in which the tail of the curve is longer on the right side of the distribution. The majority of scores are low, causing the curve to be asymmetrical, with a long tail in the positive direction on a number line. The mean for a sample whose scores are positively skewed will be greater than the median or mode (Figure 15.17).

The opposite is true for a dataset with negatively skewed scores. In this instance, the tail of the distribution curve is longer on the left side. The majority of the scores are high, creating a

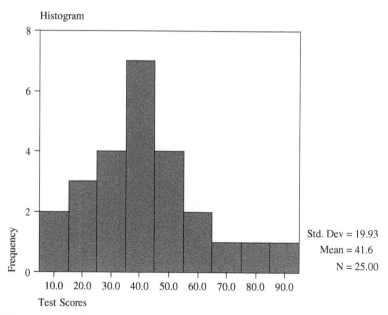

Figure 15.17 Positively Skewed Distribution of Exam Scores

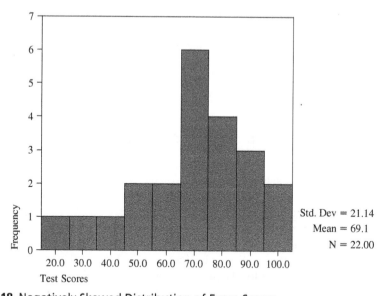

Figure 15.18 Negatively Skewed Distribution of Exam Scores

long tail in the negative direction on a number line. A mean for a sample that is negatively skewed will be less than the median or mode (Figure 15.18).

SPSS can also provide a statistical score regarding the skewness of a distribution. When computing frequencies for a variable, select the "Statistics" button and click on "Skewness." If the sample has a normal distribution, the skewness score will be equal to "0." A positively skewed sample will result in a positive score for skewness, and a negatively skewed score will result in a negative score.

Statistics

Test Scores

N	Valid	21
	Missing	0
Mean		67.6190
Median		70.0000
Mode		70.00
Std. Deviation		20.4707
Skewness		−.766
Std. Error of Skewness		.501
Kurtosis		.289
Std. Error of Kurtosis		.972
Range		80.00
Minimum		20.00
Maximum		100.00

Figure 15.19 SPSS Frequency Distribution with Skewness and Kurtosis Scores

SPSS can also calculate the kurtosis of the distribution curve. **Kurtosis** refers to the degree of peakedness of a distribution of scores. A kurtosis score greater than zero indicates a high, peaked curve with thin tails where the majority of values are in the peak of the curve and few are located in the tails of the distribution. A negative kurtosis score signals that the distribution curve is flat with several cases of scores located in the tails.

If you look at the results in Figure 15.19, you will find a distribution where the mean is 67.62, the median is 70, the mode is 70, the skewness is −0.766, and the kurtosis is 0.289. With reference to skewness and kurtosis, the sample is negatively skewed (skewness is a negative number) and minimally peaked (kurtosis > 0).

Measures of Variability

As previously stated, measures of central tendency are the most commonly used statistics by consumers. However, averages only provide us with half of the information needed to describe the scores in a sample—the other half involves measures of variability. Variability reflects how scores differ from one another. Also referred to as "measures of dispersion," variability refers to how different each score is from the mean score. Four measures of variability can be used to assess the differences in scores: range, sum of squares, variance, and standard deviation.

RANGE

The most general measure of variability is the range. Simply stated, the **range** represents how far apart scores are from another, or the distance between the largest value and the smallest value in the dataset. The range is calculated by subtracting the lowest score in the distribution from the highest score:

$$\text{Range} = X_{max} - X_{min}$$

Suppose that the highest score obtained on an exam was 96 and the lowest score was 53. To find the range, you subtract X_{min} from X_{max} or the smallest score from the largest score. In our example, 53 is the smallest score and 96 is the largest score, so to find the range you subtract 53 from 96, or

$$96 - 53 = 43$$

In this example, our range is 43. Although this score tells us the gap between the high and low score, it does not provide any insight into how each score in the distribution differs from the mean or average score.

SUM OF SQUARES

The sum of squares is a concept seen quite often in both descriptive statistics (statistical tools used to describe a dataset—what we are examining in this chapter) and inferential statistics (statistical tools that allow researchers to make inferences about some unknown aspect of a population from a sample—Chapters 16–20 will examine inferential statistics). In social scientific research, people differ from one another, which makes it impossible for social scientists to make universal statements about all people. These individual differences, however, make up the bulk of what social scientists study. In fact, Thompson (2006) defines the **sum of squares** as the "information about both the amount and the origins of individual differences" (p. 60). Ultimately, the more individual scores in a dataset differ from one another, the greater the sum of squares will become. Overall, the sum of squares is used in the calculating of many statistical tests, so understanding how it is computed is extremely important. Figure 15.20 contains the formula for the sum of squares.

The formula for the sum of squares is easy to compute when you understand what the various parts in the formula mean. The first symbol (Σ) should be familiar to you by this point in the chapter because it stands for the "sum of" something, or all of the numbers added together. The second symbol (X^2) is the squaring of an individual number. Do not confuse this symbol with the next symbol [$(\Sigma X)^2$], which is the sum of all of the numbers added together first and then the sum squared. The last symbol in the equation (N) is the number of people in the population. Because the calculating of the sum of squares is complicated, we will use a small sample in this example. Say we ask four people how many hours they spend watching television daily and we get the following responses: 1 hour, 0 hours, 6 hours, and 1 hour.

Step 1: The first step in computing the sum of squares is to find the numbers that correspond to all of the parts of the equation. First, we want to find what is referred to as the sum of all of the X numbers squared (ΣX^2). To find ΣX^2 we first must find each score's squared value. The first person in our sample indicated that he watched only 1 hour of television daily, and the squared value for 1 is 1 (1 * 1 = 1). The second person in our sample indicated that she watched 0 hours daily, and the squared value for 0 is 0 (0 * 0 = 0). The third person in our sample indicated that he watched 6 hours daily, and the squared value for 6 is 36 (6 * 6 = 36). And the final person in our sample indicated that she watched 1 hour daily, and the squared value for 1 is 1 (1 * 1 = 1). We now have the squared values for each X. To solve for ΣX^2, we simply need to add the four X^2 values together:

$$\Sigma X^2 = 1 + 0 + 36 + 1$$
$$\Sigma X^2 = 38$$

$$SS = \Sigma X^2 - \frac{(\Sigma X)^2}{N}$$

Figure 15.20 Sum of Squares Equation

Step 2: The second step to computing the sum of squares is to determine the sum of all of the X numbers squared $[(\Sigma X)^2]$. To find $(\Sigma X)^2$, we first must determine the value for the sum of X (ΣX), which is just a mathematical way of saying we must add the individual scores together $(1 + 0 + 6 + 1 = 8)$, so $\Sigma X = 8$. Once we know what the ΣX is, we simply square this value to find $(\Sigma X)^2$, so $8 * 8 = 64$.

Step 3: At this point, the complicated math is complete, so we just need to plug the numbers into the equation in Figure 15.15 and compute the formula. We have already determined that that $\Sigma X^2 = 38$, $(\Sigma X)^2$ is 64, and N is 4. Let's complete the part of the formula to the right of the minus sign in the equation, or $(\Sigma X)^2/N$:

$$(\Sigma X)^2/N$$

$$64/4$$

$$16$$

$$\text{So, } (\Sigma X)^2/N = 16$$

We can then perform the subtraction part of the formula, $\Sigma X^2 - [(\Sigma X)^2/N]$. In this case we know that $\Sigma X^2 = 38$ and $[(\Sigma X)^2/N] = 16$, so we just subtract 16 from 38 or $38 - 16 = 22$. At this point we have calculated the sum of square, and the answer is 22.

VARIANCE

Variance measures how wide or spread out a distribution is, or the average distance of the scores for an interval or ratio scale from the mean in squared units. Because our variance is dependent on the sum of squares, we know that as our scores become more different, the variance will increase. The opposite is also true—as the scores become more similar, the variance will decrease. The formula in Figure 15.21 is used to compute the variance of a sample of scores.

When you look at this formula, you will note that to calculate variance you must know two basic pieces of information: the sum of squares (SS) and the number of participants (N). Using the data used in the previous example (1, 0, 6, 1), we have already determined that the sum of squares was 22 and the number of participants was 4, so to calculate the variance we just need to plug the numbers into the appropriate places and solve for s^2:

$$s^2 = SS/(N - 1)$$

$$s^2 = 22/(4 - 1)$$

$$s^2 = 22/3$$

$$s^2 = 7.3333$$

The variance for the sample (1, 0, 6, 1) is 7.3333.

STANDARD DEVIATION

The **standard deviation** of a sample is directly related to the variance of a sample. When we report variance, we are dealing with what is called a "squared metric" because the variance

$$S^2 = \frac{SS}{N-1}$$

Figure 15.21 Variance Equation

$$SD = \sqrt{\frac{SS}{N-1}}$$

Figure 15.22 Standard Deviation Equation

stems from the sum of squares. However, most people are not good at understanding squared metrics by looking at them, so the standard deviation is simply the square root of the variance, which forms the descriptive statistic in a number that can be more easily applied to our sample scores. Ultimately, the standard deviation tells us on average how far each score differs from the average score. A standard deviation score of 3.12 indicates that, on average, each score in the distribution deviates plus or minus 3.12 points from the mean score. The larger the standard deviation score, the greater the distance between each score and the mean and the more different the scores are from one another. The formula for calculating a standard deviation can be seen in Figure 15.22.

If the formula for the standard deviation looks familiar, it is; it can be calculated simply by taking the square root of the variance. In the previous step we determined that the variance for the sample (1, 0, 6, 1) was 7.3333. To determine the standard deviation, we simply take the square root of 7.3333, which is 2.708, or 2.71 after rounding.

Recall our earlier discussion of the normal distribution of scores. If a researcher is able to calculate the mean and standard deviation for a sample that has a normal distribution, a percentile score can be reported for the sample. In a normal distribution, approximately 68 percent of the scores are within one standard deviation of the mean score (Figure 15.23). Overall, nearly 95 percent of the scores fall within two standard deviations from the mean. So in a normal distribution, most scores are relatively close to the mean score.

In the majority of research studies, the sample size is too large to calculate many of the statistics described in this chapter by hand. For this reason, we depend on statistical packages like SPSS and Excel to calculate the variance and standard deviations for us. To calculate the variance and standard deviation using SPSS for the variable communication apprehension, you start by going to the same "Frequencies" dialogue box previously discussed in this chapter and seen in the figures (Figures 15.4 and 15.5). Once you are at the Frequency Dialogue box,

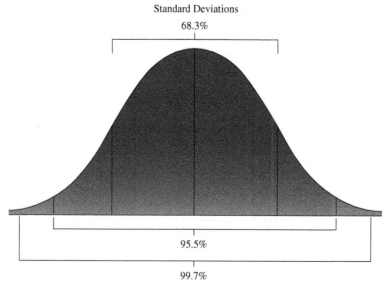

Figure 15.23 Standard Deviations and Percentiles

find the variable "Communication Apprehension" and switch it to the "Variables:" box (Figure 15.24a). Deselect the "Display Frequency Tables" option because you will end up with a list of every score you achieve from 24 to 120, which is not useful for you (Figure 15.24b). Do not be alarmed when the pop-up warning appears (Figure 15.24.c). Just click "OK" and then select the "Statistics" button on the frequencies dialogue box (Figure 15.24d). The "Frequencies: Statistics" dialogue box will appear (Figure 15.24e). Note that you have many different options you can select in this dialogue box. In fact, all of the descriptive statistics discussed in this chapter can be found in this dialogue box. At this point, select the statistics you want to analyze. For our purposes, I selected all of the ones we have discussed in this chapter (Figure 15.24f). Once you have selected your statistics, just click the "Continue" button. When the

a) Highlight Communication Apprehension

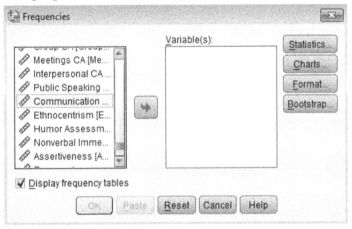

b) Deselect Display Frequency Tables

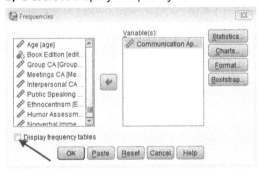

c) Pop-up Warning

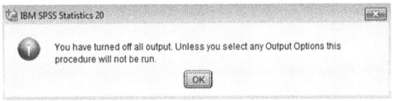

Figure 15.24 SPSS Frequencies Dialogue Box   *Continued*

Continued

d) Select Statistics Button

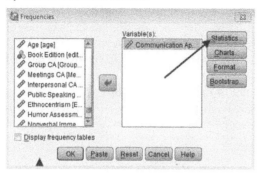

e) "Frequencies: Statistics" Dialogue Box

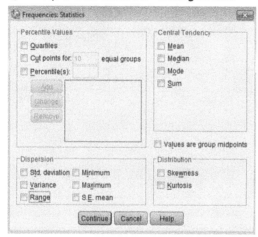

f) Selecting Statistics

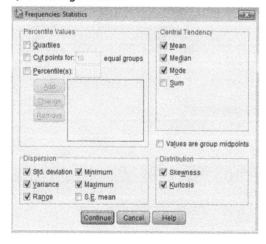

Statistics

Communication Apprehension Total

N	Valid	644
	Missing	10
Mean		63.6630
Median		64.0000
Mode		67.00
Std. Deviation		17.00407
Variance		289.138
Skewness		.203
Std. Error of Skewness		.096
Kurtosis		.335
Std. Error of Kurtosis		.192
Range		96.00
Minimum		24.00
Maximum		120.00

Figure 7.25 Descriptive Statistics for CA

"Frequencies: Statistics" dialogue box disappears, you can click "OK" on the "Frequencies" dialogue box to run the analysis. Follow the steps discussed earlier for calculating the mean, only this time when you are looking at the Frequencies: Statistics window; instead of clicking mean, median, and mode in the Central Tendency box, you want to click on "Std. Deviation," "Variance," "Minimum," and "Maximum" in the Dispersion box. Then you can click "OK" and you will receive the printout seen in Figure 15.25.

To calculate the descriptive statistics for the CA scores for participant, open the "Recoded Dataset" file. Select the "Big CA" field and highlight all values in the column. Click on the "Data" tab at the top of the sheet, select "Data Analysis" from the upper right side of the screen, and choose "Descriptive Statistics" from the menu of options. (Figure 15.26) The range of highlighted values should appear in the "Input Range" box. Select "New Worksheet Ply" to create a new sheet for the output. Select the "Summary Statistics" option and indicate the "Confidence Level for the Mean" in the box provided (Figure 15.27). Click "OK" and the output will appear on a new sheet (Figure 15.28).

If you look in Appendix C (see textbook's website), you can also see how to calculate frequencies using both PSPP and R. We provide this information as a way of introducing you to both statistical packages.

Dataset Variability

In the previous chapter, we introduced you to the variables available in the dataset that accompanies this book. In Figure 15.29, you will see a detailed description for reading descriptive statistics produced in SPSS. In Figure 15.30 you will find the SPSS frequency lists for the nominal and ordinal variables in the data and the measures of variability for the interval and ratio variables.

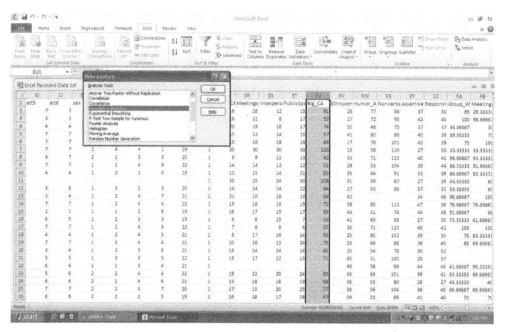

Figure 15.26 Excel's Descriptive Statistics Dialogue Box

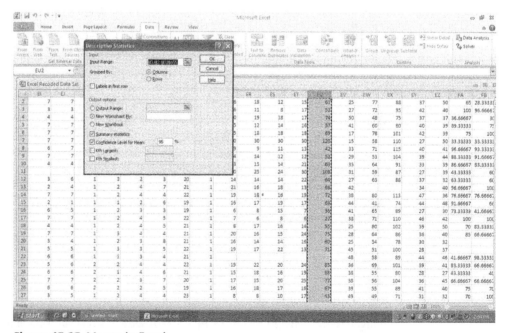

Figure 15.27 Means in Excel

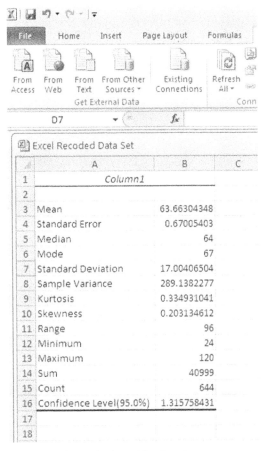

Figure 15.28 Descriptive Statistics Calculated by Excel

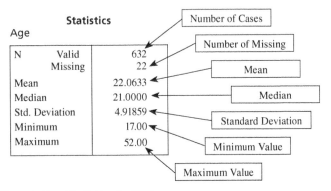

Figure 15.29 Descriptive Statistics in SPSS

Statistics

		Group CA	Meetings CA	Interpersonal CA	Public Speaking CA	Communication Apprehension Total
N	Valid	646	645	645	645	644
	Missing	8	9	9	9	10
Mean		15.0402	15.5628	14.4202	18.6140	63.6630
Median		15.0000	15.0000	14.0000	18.0000	64.0000
Std. Deviation		5.04383	4.98861	4.53303	5.71867	17.00407
Minimum		6.00	6.00	6.00	6.00	24.00
Maximum		30.00	30.00	30.00	30.00	120.00

Statistics

		Ethnocentrism	Humor Assessment	Nonverbal Immediacy	Assertiveness	Responsiveness
N	Valid	650	646	640	645	646
	Missing	4	8	14	9	8
Mean		31.7369	63.2492	96.5188	35.3302	40.3297
Median		31.0000	63.0000	96.0000	36.0000	40.0000
Std. Deviation		9.10274	9.52523	13.35466	6.30570	6.28210
Minimum		15.00	34.00	48.00	16.00	16.00
Maximum		62.00	80.00	130.00	50.00	50.00

Statistics

		Group WTC	Meetings WTC	Interpersonal WTC	Public Speaking WTC	Stranger WTC	Acquaintance WTC	Friend WTC	Willingness to Communicate Total
N	Valid	625	624	625	624	625	624	624	622
	Missing	29	30	29	30	29	30	30	32
Mean		73.4949	65.3446	73.3339	65.0139	45.7556	74.5938	87.5761	68.9518
Std. Deviation		17.36078	21.60458	17.11978	20.90989	25.62502	20.00382	14.00961	15.70704
Minimum		5.00	.00	10.67	.00	.00	.00	25.00	15.45
Maximum		100.00	100.00	100.00	100.00	100.00	100.00	100.00	100.00

Figure 15.30 SPSS Dataset Information

Continued

Statistics

		Everyone should be required to take public speaking in college.	Attitude about Higher Education
N	Valid	623	625
	Missing	31	29
Mean		23.3836	35.7296
Median		25.0000	38.0000
Std. Deviation		9.20395	6.67435
Minimum		5.00	11.00
Maximum		35.00	42.00

Conclusion

For most of you, the initial thought of calculating statistics for a sample was probably overwhelming. Throughout this chapter, we have presented information providing a description of the sample as well as identifying how diverse or spread out those scores are from the average. Statistics such as those discussed in this chapter are often referenced in everyday life. Now you can understand and interpret these statistics with confidence.

KEY TERMS

Bimodal	Measures of central	Sample
Data	Tendency	Skewness
Descriptive statistics	Median	Standard deviation
Frequency distribution	Mode	Statistic
Inferential statistics	Outlier	Sum of squares
Kurtosis	Population	Variance
Mean	Range	

REFERENCES

Punyanunt, N. M. (2000). The effects of humor on perceptions of compliance-gaining in the college classroom. *Communication Research Reports, 176*, 30–38.

Thompson, B. (2006). *Foundations of behavioral statistics: An insight-based approach.* New York, NY: Guilford.

FURTHER READING

Abramson, J. H., & Abramson, Z. H. (2001). *Making sense of data: A self-instruction manual on the interpretation of epidemiological data* (3rd ed.). New York, NY: Oxford University Press.

Bruning, J. L., & Kintz, B. L. (1997). *Computational handbook of statistics* (4th ed.). New York, NY: Longman.

Gravetter, F. J., & Wallnau, L. B. (2000). *Statistics for the behavioral sciences* (5th ed.). Belmont, CA: Wadsworth/Thomson Learning.

Green, S. B., & Salkind, N. J. (2004). *Using SPSS for Windows and Macintosh: Analyzing and understanding data* (4th ed.). Upper Saddle River, NJ: Prentice Hall.

Hocking, J. E., Stacks, D. W., & McDermott, S. T. (2003). *Communication research* (3rd ed.). Boston, MA: Allyn & Bacon.

Howell, D. C. (1997). *Statistical methods for psychology* (4th ed.). Belmont, CA: Duxbury Press.

Huff, D. (1954). *How to lie with statistics.* New York, NY: Norton.

Keller, D. K. (2006). *The Tao of statistics: A path to understanding (with no math).* Thousand Oaks, CA: Sage.

Pyrczak, F. (1999). *Statistics with a sense of humor: A humorous workbook and guide to study skills* (2nd ed.). Los Angeles, CA: Pyrczak.

Salkind, N. J. (2004). *Statistics for people who (think they) hate statistics* (2nd ed.). Thousand Oaks, CA: Sage.

Schmuller, J. (2009). *Statistical analysis with Excel®: For Dummies.* Hoboken, NJ: Wiley.

Singleton, R. A., Jr., & Straits, B. C. (1999). *Approach to social research* (3rd ed.). New York, NY: Oxford University Press.

Trochim, W. M. K. (2000). *The research methods knowledge base* (2nd ed.). Cincinnati, OH: Atomic Dog. Retrieved from http://www.socialresearchmethods.net/

Chi-Square (χ^2) Test of Independence

CHAPTER OBJECTIVES

1   Explain the purposes of a chi-square statistical test.

2   Calculate a chi-square test by hand.

3   Conduct a chi-square test using both SPSS and Excel.

4   Explain the purpose for degrees of freedom (df) within statistics.

5   Interpret the printouts associated with a chi-square test.

6   Conduct and interpret post hoc comparison tests.

7   Explain why a researcher may need to adjust her or his alpha level using a Dunn–Sidak test.

8   Examine a real-world chi-square analysis using the textbook's dataset.

9   Analyze the use of the chi-square test in the article by Brummans and Miller (2004).

10   Explain the purpose of phi (Φ), how one calculates phi by hand, and how to interpret phi.

In this chapter, we will explore the **chi-square** (χ^2) test of independence. The term chi-square actually has two different meanings in statistics, which often leads to confusion for new researchers. First, researchers refer to a specific type of mathematical distribution that occurs without any necessary referent outside of mathematics. Although this distribution is beyond the scope of this textbook, understand that this distribution is important to a number of statistical tests. In this chapter, we are more concerned with the second meaning of a chi-square, which is a specific statistical test. However, this statistical test (χ^2 test of independence) is related to the first definition. In essence, the chi-square test examines whether scores obtained from a group of people is similar to, or different from, the scores expected if the numbers were evenly distributed along the chi-square distribution. Say you want to determine whether females and males differ in their preference for two soft drinks (A and B). In an ideal world, we would have four categories (females who like soft drink A, females who like soft drink B, males who like soft drink A, and males who like soft drink B). Note that both categories (biological sex and soft drink preference) are nominal variables. If we set up a taste test using 200 people (100 females and 100 males), in an ideal world we would expect that there would be 50 people in each of the four categories. Unfortunately, the "ideal world" rarely happens and often scores are not evenly distributed among available categories. Maybe 70 females prefer soft drink A and only 30 females prefer soft drink B. When this lopsidedness happens, the question becomes one of what researchers would expect to see versus what researchers are actually seeing.

The purpose then of a chi-square is to examine the balance between observed frequencies—number of times participants fell into a specific category (how many females and males picked each of the soft drinks)—and expected frequencies—(number of times one would expect participants to fall into a specific category). If the observed and expected frequencies are equal, then the chi-square statistic will always equal zero because there is not a difference between the two numbers. The greater the difference between observed and expected frequencies, the larger the chi-square statistic will be. And as the chi-square statistic increases, so does the likelihood that there is a statistically significant difference between observed and expected frequencies. Now that we have explained the basic purpose of a chi-square statistic, we will examine an example of a chi-square statistic.

Case Study Introduction

For the first part of this chapter, we are going to pretend that you are working in a communication studies department and have been asked to analyze when females and males take public speaking during their academic careers. If you remember back to Chapter 6, female and male is an example of a nominal variable. Remember, nominal variables are categorical or people that can be clearly placed into one category (female) or the other (male), but not both. Your department chair has also given you another variable to examine—school classification. For school classification, your department chair has given you five categories: precollege, first-year student, sophomore, junior, and senior. Yet again, the school classification variable is also a nominal variable because you cannot be a sophomore and a senior at the same time. If you look at Figure 16.1, you will note that if you have two nominal variables, the appropriate statistic to examine differences is a chi-square test for independence.

After discussing this project with you, your department chair hands you a table of when students are taking public speaking in the department (Figure 16.1). In this table, we have what is called a 2 × 5 table. This means that we have two rows (male and female) by five columns (precollege, first-year student, sophomore, junior, and senior). Where a row intersects with a column, we have cells. For example, on row "female" in column "junior" the number 8 appears in the cell. This chapter will illustrate how you can use the chi-square test for independence to determine whether females and males differ in their school classification when they take public speaking.

	Precollege students	First-year students	Sophomores	Juniors	Seniors	*N*
Male	6	8	10	1	25	50
Female	7	20	9	8	6	50

Figure 16.1 When Students Take Public Speaking

Chi-square Background Information

The one-sample chi-square test evaluates whether the proportions of individuals who fall into categories of two or more nominal variables are equal to hypothesized values. In other words, in an ideal world you would have equal numbers of females and males taking public speaking in each school classification category. For example, if you had 50 females and 50 males in a school, you would expect that there would be 10 females and 10 males taking public speaking in the precollege category, 10 females and 10 males taking public speaking in the first-year student category, and so on. However, the real world rarely works this smoothly. Maybe 15 male students were all friends and decided to sign up to take public speaking together during one semester or quarter. If this occurred, then it would prevent our perfect world of 10 females and 10 males in every class.

To be able to use the chi-square test for independence, there are some basic assumptions that must be met before you can use the test:

1. Both variables being analyzed must be nominal in nature (biological sex, school classification, etc.).

2. Participants contributing data should represent a random sample drawn from the population of interest (this is an assumption of most statistical tests—see Chapter 12 for an explanation of the importance of randomization).

3. One participant's appearance in a category (female taking public speaking during her senior year) should not affect the probability of another participant's appearance in another cell (male taking public speaking during his sophomore year).

4. If you have a 2 × 2 table, there should be no fewer than five cases in every cell. However, if you have a larger table (such as the 2 × 5 table like the one in our example), 20 %of the cells should be no fewer than five cases in every cell.

The one-sample chi-square test is more likely to yield significance if the sample proportions for the categories differ greatly from the hypothesized proportions and if the sample size is large. If all the females were able to take public speaking in the first two and half years and all the males took public speaking in the last two and a half years, we would see a large difference. However, as we see in Figure 16.1, there are differences, but whether these differences are truly statistically significant is not known. For this reason, the chi-square test of independence was created to help us determine whether statistically significant differences do exist in examples such as the one we have here.

Before a researcher ever starts calculating a statistical test, he or she must first set the significance level of the test. In Chapter 14, we discussed why researchers set the significance level at 95% confidence level or $p = 0.05$. The reason that we set the significance level prior to conducting the test is ethical. There have been cases where less than scrupulous researchers have lowered their significance level to 90% or $p = 0.10$ because their results were not significant at the 95% confidence level. If you remember back to our discussion of research ethics in Chapter 3, we discussed the problem of post hoc revisions of hypotheses (changing your hypothesis when the study was completed to match the results you found). In many ways, the discussion we had for post hoc revisions of hypotheses is akin to changing our confidence level after the fact. The need for setting your confidence level prior to conducting a statistical test is true for all statistical tests. Once you have set your confidence level, you can then begin calculating your chi-square.

$$\chi^2 = \Sigma \frac{(f_o - f_e)^2}{f_e}$$

Figure 16.2 Chi-square Formula

Look at Figure 16.2, which depicts the mathematical formula for completing the chi-square test of independence. We know this formula looks scary, but it is not hard to understand what it is saying. f_o stands for the frequency observed. "Frequency observed" is the technical term for what was discussed in Figure 16.1. f_e stands for the frequency expected. But before we can discuss frequency expected, we must start going step by step in our computation of the chi-square statistic.

Step-by-Step Approach to the Chi-square Test of Independence

Step 1. The first step in computing the chi-square test of independence is to add the totals from each row separately. For example, to obtain the total for the male row, you must add $6 + 8 + 10 + 1 + 25$, which gives you a row total of 50. You then repeat the same thing for the female row ($7 + 20 + 9 + 8 + 6$), which also gives you a row total of 50. You then repeat this process for each of the five columns (precollege, first-year student, sophomore, junior, and senior) as well. For the precollege column, you will add $6 + 7$, which gives you a total of 13. In Figure 16.3, you can see that we have provided row and column totals for you in an easy-to-use table because we will need these numbers in the next step.

Step 2. The second step is slightly more complicated than the first two steps and requires that you carefully keep track of where you are getting your numbers. As mentioned earlier, the second part of the formula requires us to examine the expected frequency (f_e), so this step is going to help us generate these numbers. The expected frequency is a simple calculation to help define an ideal hypothetical distribution that would be in agreement with the null hypothesis. In other words, based on the data that you have, what is the frequency for upholding the null hypothesis (that there is no difference between females and males and when they take public speaking in college)? To obtain these values, you use the following simple formula:

Expected frequency = (total column $\times$ total row)/overall total

So, let's compute the first expected frequency for males in precollege. The column total for precollege, as seen in Figure 16.3, is 13. The row total for males is 50. And the overall total for the population, or N, is 100. To obtain the expected frequency for males in precollege, we then plug these numbers into the formula: $(13 \times 50)/100 = 6.5$. Based on this result, we can say that to reject the null hypothesis that females and males take public speaking at different points in college, the expected frequency for males in precollege would have to be 6.5. Obviously, you cannot have a 0.5 person, so this number is hypothetical. In reality, we must look at all of the expected frequencies for each biological sex in each school classification to get a full picture of the numbers necessary to reject the null hypothesis. In Figure 16.4, we have computed all of the expected frequencies for you, just repeating the computational process for each category.

	Precollege students	First year students	Sophomores	Juniors	Seniors	TOTAL
Male	6	8	10	1	25	50
Female	7	20	9	8	6	50
Total	13	28	19	9	31	100

Figure 16.3 Adding Row and Column Totals (Step 1)

Step 3. At this point we can once again look at the formula given in Figure 16.2. The basic formula for the chi-square test of independence can be said to be the following:

Chi-square = sum of ((observed frequencies − expected frequencies)² /expected frequencies)

Note that we are looking at the Σ, or sum of the equation. This basically means that we must compute that formula for each and every one of the cells in the table and then add up the values that we obtain. Let's compute the first portion of the chi-square statistic for males in precollege. The observed frequency score for males, as seen in Figure 16.1, is 6. And the expected frequency score for males, as seen in Figure 16.4, is 6.5. So to obtain the portion of the chi-square statistic represented by males in precollege, we then plug these numbers into the formula: $(6 − 6.5)^2/6.5 = 0.038462$. In Figure 16.5, we have computed all of the parts of the chi-square statistic.

Step 4. And since the sigma was in front of the formula, now we just add all of the values from Step 3 together:

0.038462 + 2.571429 + 0.026316 + 2.722222 + 5.822581 + 0.038462 + 2.571429 + 0.026316 + 2.722222 + 5.822581

	Total column		Total row		Overall total		Expected frequency
Males in precollege	13	*	50	/	100	=	6.5
Male first year students	28	*	50	/	100	=	14.0
Male sophomores	19	*	50	/	100	=	9.5
Male juniors	9	*	50	/	100	=	4.5
Male seniors	31	*	50	/	100	=	15.5
Females in precollege	13	*	50	/	100	=	6.5
Female First-year students	28	*	50	/	100	=	14.0
Female sophomores	19	*	50	/	100	=	9.5
Female juniors	9	*	50	/	100	=	4.5
Female seniors	31	*	50	/	100	=	15.5

Figure 16.4 Expected Frequencies

	Observed frequency		Expected frequency			Expected frequency		Chi-square (χ^2) statistic
Males in precollege	(6	−	6.5)	² /		6.5	=	0.038462
Male first year students	(8	−	14)	² /		14.0	=	2.571429
Male sophomores	(10	−	9.5)	² /		9.5	=	0.026316
Male juniors	(1	−	4.5)	² /		4.5	=	2.722222
Male seniors	(25	−	15.5)	² /		15.5	=	5.822581
Females in precollege	(7	−	6.5)	² /		6.5	=	0.038462
Female first year students	(20	−	14)	² /		14.0	=	2.571429
Female sophomores	(9	−	9.5)	² /		9.5	=	0.026316
Female juniors	(8	−	4.5)	² /		4.5	=	2.722222
Female seniors	(6	−	15.5)	² /		15.5	=	5.822581
					χ^2 Calculated value		=	22.362

Figure 16.5 Chi-square (χ^2) Statistics

This sum indicates that the calculated value that we obtained for chi-square is 22.362. However, we still have a couple of steps to go before we can say that we are truly finished with this example.

Step 5. In this step, we must calculate the degrees of freedom for the chi-square computed in this example. The **degrees of freedom** is defined as the number of participant scores in a sample that can or are free to vary. Because this is an important concept, we will think of it in terms of a car lot. Imagine that you are a car salesperson and you have five cars to sell. All of the cars are the same make and model, but are different colors: yellow, blue, green, red, and white. On one day, five customers come to your showroom to buy cars. The first person looks at the five cars and selects the blue one. This person had the ability to choose among five cars, but the next person who comes to the dealership can only choose among four cars (yellow, green, red, and white) because the blue car has already been sold. The second person picks the yellow car. The third person only has three choices then and picks the red car. The fourth person who comes in now only has the freedom to choose between two cars and selects the white car. The fifth person who comes into the showroom now has no ability to vary at all and must select the green car or go elsewhere. Each of these customers had the ability to vary her or his choice until the last customer. Generally speaking, degrees of freedom is seen as the number of options a person has (five cars) minus one, or $5 - 1$.

However, because in the chi-square example we are dealing with two different nominal variables (sex and classification in school), the formula is a little different: $(r - 1)(c - 1)$ or (number of rows $- 1$)(number of columns $- 1$). In this example, we had two rows (male and female) and five columns (precollege, first-year student, sophomore, junior, and senior). So the degrees of freedom for our chi-square example would be $(2 - 1)(5 - 1)$ or $(1)(4)$, which is equal to 4. So in our example, the degree to which the frequencies had the freedom to vary was 4.

Step 6. Figure 16.6 is what is called a critical value table. A critical value table is a table that has been previously created to determine where specific chi-square calculated values are statistically significant (for a discussion of statistical significance, see Chapter 14). On the left-hand side is the column for the degrees of freedom. In our study, our degrees of freedom value, as calculated in Step 5, was 4, so we must compare the number we calculated for the chi-square statistic in Step 4, 22.362, against the numbers in row 4 on this chart. If 22.362 is greater than the number listed in the columns, our chi-square is statistically significant at that p value level (shown at the top of each column). The first column represents $p < 0.10$, which is not statistically significant, as discussed in Chapter 14. The critical value in this column was 7.779, and our calculated chi-square statistic was 22.362, which is greater than 7.779, so we would consider our chi-square significant at the $p < 0.10$ level. However, 0.10 does not meet the 95%t confidence interval discussed in the previous chapter, so we would not consider a chi-square statistically significant at this p value. The second column represents $p < 0.05$, which meets the 95 % confidence interval discussed in the previous chapter, so if our computed value is greater than the critical value, we would consider a chi-square statistically significant at this p value. The critical value in the $p = 0.05$ column was 9.49, and our calculated chi-square statistic was 22.362, which is greater than 9.49, so we would consider our chi-square significant at the $p < 0.05$ level. Our example is clearly larger than the critical value of 9.49 shown in the table, so we can reject the null hypothesis and affirm the claim that female and male undergraduates differ in the year in college when they take public speaking. In fact, if you examine the critical values table further, we can reject the null hypothesis at the $p < 0.01$, $p < 0.005$, and $p < 0.001$ levels as well.

df	0.10	0.05	0.01	0.005	0.001
1	2.71	3.84	6.64	7.88	10.83
2	4.61	5.99	9.21	10.60	13.82
3	6.25	7.82	11.34	12.84	16.27
4	7.78	9.49	13.28	14.87	18.47
5	9.24	11.07	15.09	16.75	20.52
6	10.65	12.59	16.81	18.55	22.46
7	12.02	14.07	18.48	20.28	24.32
8	13.36	15.51	20.09	21.95	26.12
9	14.68	16.92	21.67	23.59	27.88
10	15.99	18.31	23.21	25.19	29.59
11	17.28	19.68	24.72	26.76	31.26
12	18.55	21.03	26.22	28.30	32.91
13	19.81	22.36	27.69	29.82	34.53
14	21.06	23.69	29.14	31.32	36.13
15	22.31	24.99	30.58	32.80	37.70
16	23.54	26.30	32.00	34.27	39.26
17	24.77	27.59	33.41	35.72	40.80
18	25.99	28.87	34.81	37.16	42.32
19	27.20	30.14	36.20	38.59	43.83
20	28.41	31.41	37.57	40.00	45.32

If the observed chi-square is greater than or equal to the tabled value for the desired probability level and degrees of freedom, we should reject the null hypothesis.

The entries in this table were computed by the authors.

Figure 16.6 Probability Values of the Chi-square Distribution

Computer Printouts of the Chi-square Test of Independence

Now that we have examined how the chi-square test of independence can be calculated by hand, we will examine what output from two statistical computer programs, SPSS and Excel, looks like. Most researchers no longer compute statistics by hand. Computing statistics by hand is dangerous because humans make errors easily when handling large quantities of data. In this example, we only had 100 people in the 10 cells in the 2×5 table. Imagine if we had used 4,000 people. Although the statistics could be computed by hand as we did earlier, it just is not time-efficient to do so. For this reason, a variety of computer programs have been created to aid in this process. Two commonly used statistical software packages used by communication researchers are SPSS and Excel. If you look on the textbook's website, you will find a link for "Book Datasets." In this folder you will find folders for SPSS datasets, Excel datasets, and Note Pad datasets. The SPSS and Excel datasets can be used only by SPSS (along with PSPP and R) and Excel software packages. If you do not have SPSS or Excel but have a different statistical software package, you can use the Note Pad datasets to import the data into whatever program you prefer to use. For example, if you would prefer to use STATA, we would recommend reading Acock (2010). However, we will only be discussing how to read and interpret results from SPSS and Excel in this book. We should mention that we specifically used SPSS 20.0 and Excel 2010 in the conducting of the statistical tests in this book. We mention this because previous versions of the software may display more or less information in similar or different ways. Although the steps in conducting the tests will be the same for various versions of the software packages, often the display does get altered. For this reason, if you are utilizing an earlier version (or later version) of either SPSS or Excel, you may want to consult the software guide that accompanied the software package. For the most part, these changes are minor, but for students new to dealing with statistical software packages the changes may be confusing.

SPSS AND CHI-SQUARES

For this section, open the SPSS datasets folder and select the file "Chi-square." *When you select this file, SPSS will automatically import the data into the front page of the software program.* When using SPSS to calculate a chi-square, you use the "Crosstabs" function. To get to the Crosstabs function, go to the menu bar at the top of your screen and click on "Analyze" (Figure 16.7). When you click on "Analyze," a drop-down menu will appear. Go to the second category on this menu, "Descriptive Statistics," and scroll over the arrow and another menu will appear to the right. The last choice on this menu is "Crosstabs"; click on it (Figure 16.8). When you do this, the crosstabs dialogue box appears (Figure 16.9a). On the left side of the screen you will find a box that lists all of the variables in the dataset. If you have opened the chi-square file from the textbook's website, you will see two variables listed (sex and class). To compute a chi-square using SPSS, highlight the sex variable and click on the right arrow to the left of the box labeled "Row(s)" (Figure 16.9b). If you have done this correctly, you will see that the sex variable has not been placed in the "Row(s)" box on the right side of the dialogue box. Next, highlight the class variable and click on the right arrow to the left of the box labeled "Column(s)" (Figure 16.9c). If you have done this correctly, you will see that the class variable has been placed in the "Column(s)" box on the right side of the dialogue box.

At the bottom of the crosstabs dialogue box you will see three buttons: "Statistics," "Cells," and "Format." Click on the "Statistics" button. A new dialogue box called "Crosstabs: Statistics" will appear (Figure 16.9d). In this box, you will see a variety of different

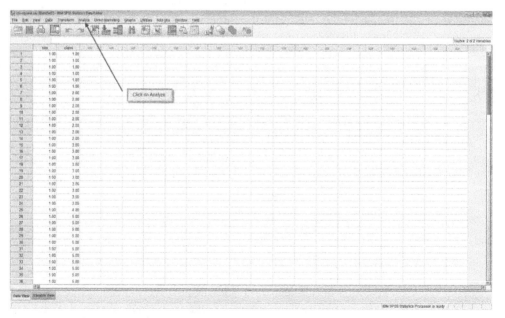

Figure 16.7 Chi-square Main Page

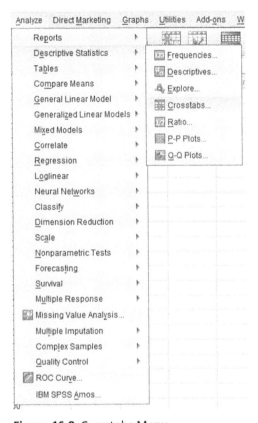

Figure 16.8 Crosstabs Menu

statistical procedures that can be completed using the crosstabs procedure. However, we are only interested in the one on the top left side called "Chi-square." When you click on the white box next to the words "Chi-square," you will see a little black checkmark appear in the box. Do the same for the statistics "Phi and Cramer's V" (Figure 16.9e). Now go click the button "Continue" on the opposite side of the "Statistics" dialogue box.

Next, we are going to go click on the button "Cells." A new dialogue box will open called "Crosstabs: Cell Display" (Figure 16.9f). When this dialogue box first appears, the only box that will have a checkmark in it is next to the word "Observed," which is the same thing as frequency observed. Right under "Observed" is "Expected"; click on this as well (Figure 16.9g), and then click "Continue."

At this point you can click "OK" in the upper right-hand side of the crosstabs dialogue box. Figure 16.10 shows the actual results you will see from SPSS.

When looking at the SPSS printouts, you will see three boxes. The first box is labeled the "Case Processing Summary" box and lets you know how many cases (or participants) were used in this test. Just like when we did it by hand, 100 participants were used in this statistical test. The second box is the "Sex × Class Crosstabultation" box. This box is similar to the box seen in Figure 16.3, but it also has both the observed and the expected values. Note that all of the numbers we calculated by hand match up perfectly to those in this box. The third box in the SPSS printouts, the "Chi-Square Tests" box, is the box that is important for understanding whether the chi-square was statistically significant.

a) Main Dialogue Box

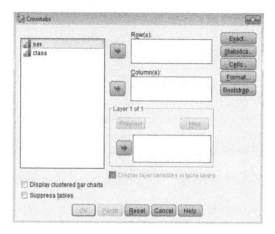

b) Place Variable "Sex" in the Row(s) Box

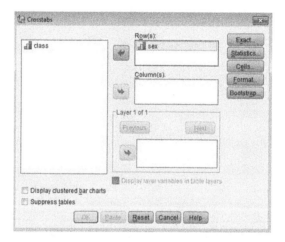

c) Place Variable "Class" in the Column(s) Box

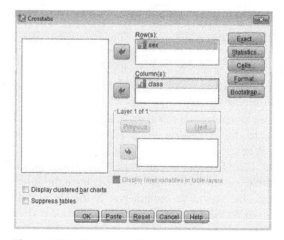

Figure 16.9 Crosstabs Dialogue Box

d) "Crosstabs: Statistics" Dialogue Box

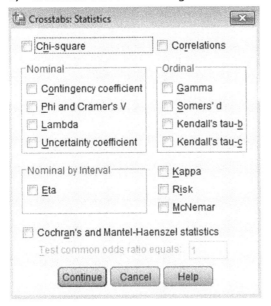

e) Select Statistics to Run

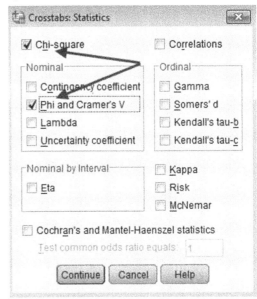

f) "Crosstabs: Cell Display" Dialogue Box

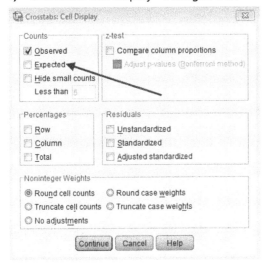

g) Select "Expected"

Although there are three tests represented in this box, the one to be concerned about for a basic chi-square is the first test, the "Pearson Chi-Square." Look at the "Pearson Chi-Square" row, which has been boldfaced, and you will see three columns: "Value," "df," and "Asymp. Sig. (2-sided)." The first column is the calculated value for the chi-square. And just like the calculated value we obtained when we calculated chi-square by hand, the computer also found the calculated value to be 22.362 and the degrees of freedom to be 4. However, the computer is able to obtain a much more exact p value than we could by looking at a critical value chart. In this case, the chi-square was found to be significant at the

Case Processing Summary

	Cases					
	Valid		Missing		Total	
	N	Percent	N	Percent	N	Percent
sex * class	100	100.0%	0	0.0%	100	100.0%

sex*class Crosstabulation

			class					
			Pre-college	First Year Student	Sophomore	Junior	Senior	Total
sex	male	Count	6	8	10	1	25	50
		Expected Count	6.5	14.0	9.5	4.5	15.5	50.0
	female	Count	7	20	9	8	6	50
		Expected Count	6.5	14.0	9.5	4.5	15.5	50.0
Total		Count	13	28	19	9	31	100
		Expected Count	13.0	28.0	19.0	9.0	31.0	100.0

Chi-Square Tests

	Value	df	Asymp. Sig. (2-sided)
Pearson Chi-Square	22.362[a]	4	.000
Likelihood Ratio	24.153	4	.000
Linear-by-Linear Association	9.541	1	.002
N of Valid Cases	100		

[a] 2 cells (20.0%) have expected count less than 5. The minimum expected count is 4.50.

Symmetric Measures

		Value	Approx. Sig.
Nominal by Nominal	Phi	.473	.000
	Cramer's V	.473	.000
N of Valid Cases		100	

[a] Not assuming the null hypothesis.
[b] Using the asymptotic standard error assuming the null hypothesis.

Figure 16.10 Chi-square Results

$p < 0.001$ level. The printout just says that the significance is 0.000; however, this means that the significance is lower than this level, so adding a 5 to the end of it is the most appropriate thing to do (Levine & Atkin, 2004).

One other statistic is also presented here that we have not discussed is **Cramér's phi** (Φ). All a chi-square test of independence can do is tell you that a difference exists; Cramér's phi

$$\Phi = \sqrt{\dfrac{X^2}{N\,(k-1)}}$$

Figure 16.11 Cramér's Phi Statistic

is used to determine how much of the difference in one variable can be accounted for by the variance in another variable (the effect size). In other words, how much an individual's level of the effects of the implementation can be caused by her or his perceptions of the ambiguity of the term "collaborative community health improvement." To obtain Cramér's phi, the formula in Figure 16.11 is used.

To understand this formula, you must have a calculated value for a chi-square (22.362) and remember that N = total number of observations (N = 100) and k = the smaller of the number of rows or columns (k = 2). In other words:

$$\Phi = \sqrt{(22.362/(100\,(2-1)))},$$

$$\Phi = \sqrt{(22.362/(100\,(1)))},$$

$$\Phi = \sqrt{(22.362/(100))}$$

$$\Phi = \sqrt{(22.362/100)}$$

$\Phi = \sqrt{0.22362}$ ← This number is the percent of variability in the dependent variable (effect) accounted for by the independent variable (ambiguity).

$\Phi = 0.472884764$ ← This is the number that is reported in the article.

Cramer's phi in this article was 0.47, and the biological sex of a participant (female or male) accounted for approximately 22 percent of the variability in when a college student takes public speaking in college. Note that this is the same result we see in the previous SPSS results in Figure 16.10. Overall, this article is a good example of how the chi-square test of independence can be used to answer a research question.

EXCEL AND CHI-SQUARES

To calculate the chi-square using Excel, select the Excel file titled "Chi-square" from the textbook's website. Click the "Insert" file tab at the top of the screen and choose the "Pivot-Table" function (Figure 16.12). The data for both the "sex" and the "class" variables should be highlighted. The range for the data will appear in the "Table/Range" box. Select "New Worksheet" from the menu to create a new page for the output (Figure 16.13). Drop and drag "sex" to the section titled "Row Labels" and drag "class" to the box titled "Column Labels." The sum of scores for "sex" should automatically appear in the "Values" section (Figure 16.14). Click on the "X" to close out the dialogue box. The output table includes the total number of responses for each category we identified (e.g., males in the freshman class). Be careful, Excel often does a great job of bringing in the counts for the first row but not for the second row. As such, you may find yourself with a percentage value and not a count value. Look at Figure 16.15. You will note that the first number in the second row is 14 when it should have been 7. To change this, right click on the first number and scroll down to "Summarize Values By." The first one, which will be checked, is Sum. You want

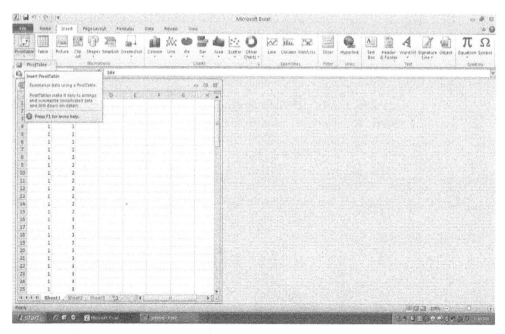

Figure 16.12 Pivot Table

Figure 16.13 New Pivot Table

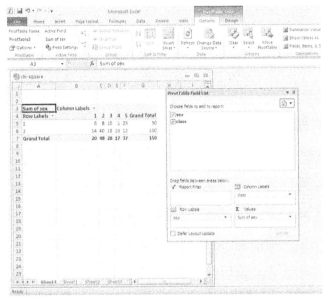

Figure 16.14 Pivot Table Field List Dialogue Box

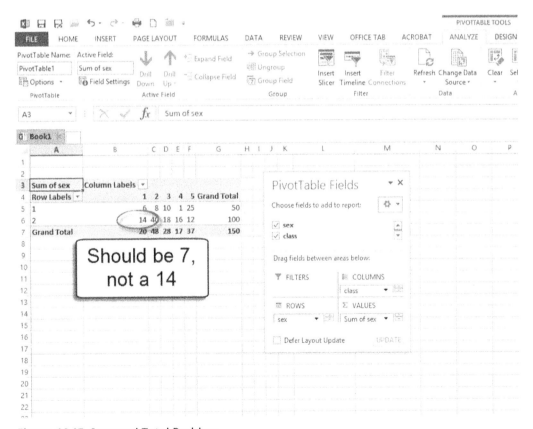

Figure 16.15 Summed Total Problem

Figure 16.16 Summarize Values By

to uncheck Sum and check Count (Figure 16.16). This will correct that row to counts instead of summed totals.

Computing the chi-square statistic involves a couple of steps. First, copy all of the information from the PivotTable. Click on an empty cell below the table, right click, choose "Paste Special," and choose the "Paste Values" option. This will duplicate the table directly below the original PivotTable (Figure 16.17). Doing so will enable you to keep the data separate while you compute the expected values versus the observed values. In the duplicate table of values that you created, highlight and delete the values for each of the cells. Be careful not to delete any of the totals from the table.

To compute the expected values into the table, click on the first empty cell and type the formula "=column total value * row total value/grand total value" (Figure 16.18). Repeat these steps for each empty cell in the table until you have computed the expected values for each cell (Figure 16.19). Finally, select an empty cell below the two tables and click. In the cell, type the Excel formula for a chi-square analysis, which is =CHITEST (actual values, expected values). To enter the range of values, simply highlight the block of expected values from the top table and click Enter (Figure 16.20). Complete the same steps for the expected values in the table below. Click "Enter," and the probability for the chi-square value will appear in the designated cell (Figure 16.21).

Please note that the actual chi-square statistic is not actually calculated by Microsoft Excel. Instead, Excel calculates your p value, so you would still need to calculate the chi-square statistic by hand. Now that we have examined the chi-square test itself, let's see how a researcher would write up this finding using APA style in a results section of an article.

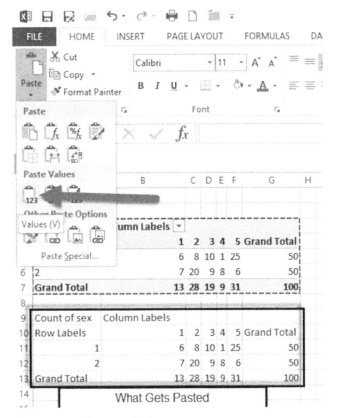

Figure 16.17 Paste as Values

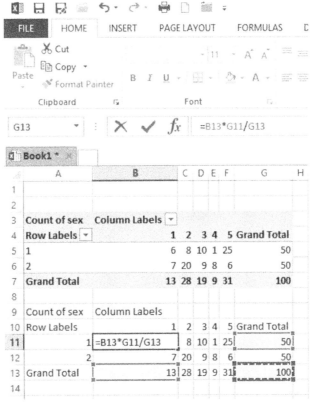

Figure 16.18 Computing Expected Values

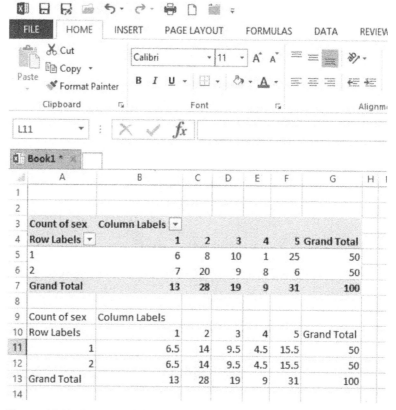

Figure 16.19 Computed Expected Values

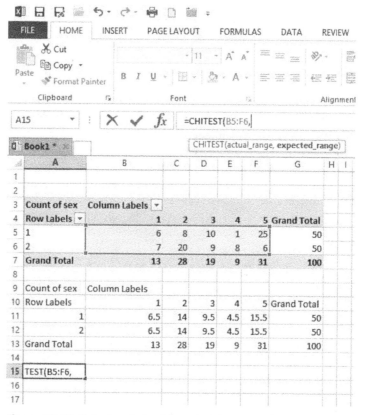

Figure 16.20 Entering Actual Frequencies

Figure 16.21 Chi-square Test Results

APA WRITE-UP

A chi-square was conducted to assess whether females and males take public speaking at different stages in their educational career. The result for this test was significant: $\chi^2(4, N = 100) = 22.36, p < 0.001$. Cramér's phi was 0.47, which indicates that biological sex of a participant (female or male) accounted for approximately 22% of the variability in when a college student takes public speaking in college.

You will note that in this APA write-up, everything is simply stated. The actual statement written is simple: χ^2 = (degrees of freedom, number of people in sample) = calculated value, level of statistical significance. Note that the p value is reported at $p < 0.001$ because the *APA Style Manual* recommends this reporting with p values that are less than 0.001. In the future, when analyzing a chi-square, all you really need to see is this one line to determine what was done and what results were found by the researchers. Also note that APA requires that we round results to the nearest hundredth (two decimal places) for all results except your p value.

DISCUSSION OF FINDINGS

By this point, you are probably wondering what the result actually means. To really grasp what we have found in this chi-square, you must go back to what we said about the chi-square in the beginning of this chapter. A chi-square is a difference test. All you basically get in a chi-square test is whether a difference occurs between the two groups. In this example, based on the basic chi-square, we can say that a statistically significant difference occurs between females and males and when they take public speaking in college. We cannot say exactly when that difference occurs. In other words, we cannot eyeball Figure 16.1 and say that more females take public speaking during their first year in college than men because we did not conduct a test to determine whether this is true. Based on a simple chi-square test of independence, all you can legitimately say is that a difference exists.

To ascertain where this difference exists, you must conduct a multiple comparison procedure. You only need to conduct a multiple comparison procedure if the overall chi-square is significant. Although a chi-square multiple comparison procedure is useful, it is not the most statistically accurate way to obtain results. In a chi-square multiple comparison procedure, you compare all of the parts of the smaller variable (sex) with all of the parts of the larger variable (year in school). Because sex only has two levels (male and female), we do not have to worry about changing anything for sex. However, because year in school has five levels, we have to conduct 10 comparison tests. To determine how many comparison tests are necessary, you can use the following formula: $(K(K - 1))/2$, with K being the number of groups being compared. In this case, we have five groups being compared (precollege, first-year student, sophomore, junior, and senior). So the formula would be solved like this:

$$(5(5 - 1))/2$$

$$(5(4))/2$$

$$20/2$$

$$10$$

To perform a multiple comparison test, you simply select two categories from the larger variable (year in school) you want to compare (e.g., precollege and first-year student) and then compare them by conducting a chi-square. In SPSS, you open the chi-square file and go to the menu bar on the top of your screen and click on "Data." When you click on "Data," a drop-down menu will appear. Scroll down and click on "Select Cases." The "Select Cases" dialogue box will appear. On the left-hand side of the box you will see your variables listed, and on the right-hand side you will see that the radio button "All Cases" currently has a black dot filling the button. Click on the second radio button down, or the radio button that corresponds with the phrase "If condition is satisfied." Next, click on the bottom "If" immediately below. When you click on this button, the "Select Cases: If" dialogue box will appear. In this window, you will see your variables in a box on a left-hand side, an empty box on the top right-hand side, a calculator in the center, and some mathematical expressions on the bottom right. The only box you will need to be worried about at this time is the empty box on the top right-hand side. Type in this empty box *class = 1 or class = 2*. Then click the "Continue" button at the bottom of the "Select Cases: If" dialogue box. Click the "OK" button at the bottom of the "Select Cases" dialogue box. When you do this, a new variable appears called "filter_$". Furthermore, many of your cases now have a slash mark through the case number on the left-hand side of the main SPSS screen. In essence, you have told SPSS that you are only going to pay attention to the first two parts of the "class" variable (precollege and first-year students). You then will compute a chi-square test of independence just like we did earlier. This time, however, the only variables being compared will be a 2 × 2 table or sex (male and female) by class (precollege and first-year students). This process will then be repeated nine more times comparing each set of variables in the chi-square itself (e.g., precollege with sophomores, precollege with juniors, precollege with seniors, sophomores with juniors, etc.). When all 10 chi-square have been calculated, you end up with the results shown in Figure 16.22 and summarized in Figure 16.23.

Based on these results, we can safely say that females and males differ when they take public speaking between precollege and seniors, first-year students and seniors, sophomores

Chi-Square Tests - Pre-College vs. First Year

	Value	df	Asymp. Sig. (2-sided)	Exact Sig. (2-sided)	Exact Sig. (1-sided)
Pearson Chi-Square	1.221[b]	1	.269		
Continuity Correction[a]	.564	1	.453		
Likelihood Ratio	1.196	1	.274		
Fisher's Exact Test				.307	.225
Linear-by-Linear Association	1.191	1	.275		
N of Valid Cases	41				

[a.] Computed only for a 2 × 2 table
[b.] 1 cells (25.0%) have expected count less than 5. The minimum expected count is 4.44.

Chi-Square Tests - Pre-College vs. Sophomore

	Value	df	Asymp. Sig. (2-sided)	Exact Sig. (2-sided)	Exact Sig. (1-sided)
Pearson Chi-Square	.130[b]	1	.719		
Continuity Correction[a]	.000	1	1.000		
Likelihood Ratio	.130	1	.719		
Fisher's Exact Test				1.000	.500
Linear-by-Linear Association	.126	1	.723		
N of Valid Cases	32				

[a.] Computed only for a 2 × 2 table
[b.] 0 cells (.0%) have expected count less than 5. The minimum expected count is 6.50.

Chi-Square Tests - Pre-College vs. Junior

	Value	df	Asymp. Sig. (2-sided)	Exact Sig. (2-sided)	Exact Sig. (1-sided)
Pearson Chi-Square	3.010[b]	1	.083		
Continuity Correction[a]	1.612	1	.204		
Likelihood Ratio	3.298	1	.069		
Fisher's Exact Test				.165	.101
Linear-by-Linear Association	2.874	1	.090		
N of Valid Cases	22				

[a.] Computed only for a 2 × 2 table
[b.] 2 cells (50.0%) have expected count less than 5. The minimum expected count is 2.86.

Figure 16.22 Multiple Comparison Tests   Continued

Continued

Chi-Square Tests - Pre-College vs. Senior

	Value	df	Asymp. Sig. (2-sided)	Exact Sig. (2-sided)	Exact Sig. (1-sided)
Pearson Chi-Square	5.234[b]	1	.022		
Continuity Correction[a]	3.709	1	.054		
Likelihood Ratio	5.006	1	.025		
Fisher's Exact Test				.033	.029
Linear-by-Linear Association	5.115	1	.024		
N of Valid Cases	44				

[a.] Computed only for a 2 × 2 table
[b.] 1 cells (25.0%) have expected count less than 5. The minimum expected count is 3.84.

Chi-Square Tests - First Year vs. Sophomore

	Value	df	Asymp. Sig. (2-sided)	Exact Sig. (2-sided)	Exact Sig. (1-sided)
Pearson Chi-Square	2.773[b]	1	.096		
Continuity Correction[a]	1.848	1	.174		
Likelihood Ratio	2.767	1	.096		
Fisher's Exact Test				.130	.087
Linear-by-Linear Association	2.714	1	.099		
N of Valid Cases	47				

[a.] Computed only for a 2 × 2 table
[b.] 0 cells (.0%) have expected count less than 5. The minimum expected count is 7.28.

Chi-Square Tests - First Year vs. Junior

	Value	df	Asymp. Sig. (2-sided)	Exact Sig. (2-sided)	Exact Sig. (1-sided)
Pearson Chi-Square	1.128[b]	1	.288		
Continuity Correction[a]	.379	1	.538		
Likelihood Ratio	1.272	1	.259		
Fisher's Exact Test				.403	.280
Linear-by-Linear Association	1.098	1	.295		
N of Valid Cases	37				

[a.] Computed only for a 2 × 2 table
[b.] 1 cells (25.0%) have expected count less than 5. The minimum expected count is 2.19.

Continued

Chi-Square Tests - First Year vs. Senior

	Value	df	Asymp. Sig. (2-sided)	Exact Sig. (2-sided)	Exact Sig. (1-sided)
Pearson Chi-Square	16.185[b]	1	.000		
Continuity Correction[a]	14.142	1	.000		
Likelihood Ratio	16.994	1	.000		
Fisher's Exact Test				.000	.000
Linear-by-Linear Association	15.911	1	.000		
N of Valid Cases	59				

[a.] Computed only for a 2 × 2 table
[b.] 0 cells (.0%) have expected count less than 5. The minimum expected count is 12.34.

Chi-Square Tests - Sophomore vs. Junior

	Value	df	Asymp. Sig. (2-sided)	Exact Sig. (2-sided)	Exact Sig. (1-sided)
Pearson Chi-Square	4.414[b]	1	.036		
Continuity Correction[a]	2.845	1	.092		
Likelihood Ratio	4.955	1	.026		
Fisher's Exact Test				.049	.042
Linear-by-Linear Association	4.256	1	.039		
N of Valid Cases	28				

[a.] Computed only for a 2 × 2 table
[b.] 1 cells (25.0%) have expected count less than 5. The minimum expected count is 3.54.

Chi-Square Tests - Sophomore vs. Senior

	Value	df	Asymp. Sig. (2-sided)	Exact Sig. (2-sided)	Exact Sig. (1-sided)
Pearson Chi-Square	4.402[b]	1	.036		
Continuity Correction[a]	3.169	1	.075		
Likelihood Ratio	4.337	1	.037		
Fisher's Exact Test				.056	.038
Linear-by-Linear Association	4.314	1	.038		
N of Valid Cases	50				

[a.] Computed only for a 2 × 2 table
[b.] 0 cells (.0%) have expected count less than 5. The minimum expected count is 5.70.

Continued

Chi-Square Tests - Junior vs. Senior

	Value	df	Asymp. Sig. (2-sided)	Exact Sig. (2-sided)	Exact Sig. (1-sided)
Pearson Chi-Square	14.824[b]	1	.000		
Continuity Correction[a]	11.925	1	.001		
Likelihood Ratio	15.054	1	.000		
Fisher's Exact Test				.000	.000
Linear-by-Linear Association	14.453	1	.000		
N of Valid Cases	40				

[a.] Computed only for a 2 × 2 table
[b.] 1 cells (25.0%) have expected count less than 5. The minimum expected count is 3.15.

Pairwise Comparison	N	df	χ^2	p
Precollege vs. First-Year Student	41	1	1.22	.27
Precollege vs. Sophomore	32	1	1.30	.72
Precollege vs. Junior	22	1	3.01	.08
Precollege vs. Senior	44	1	5.23	.02
First-Year Student vs. Sophomore	47	1	2.77	.10
First-Year Student vs. Junior	37	1	1.23	.29
First-Year Student vs. Senior	59	1	16.19	.0005*
Sophomore vs. Junior	28	1	4.41	.04
Sophomore vs. Senior	50	1	4.40	.04
Junior vs. Senior	40	1	14.82	.0005*

Significant at the .005 level after a Dunn-Sidak correction.

Figure 16.23 Pairwise Comparisons

and juniors, sophomores and seniors, and juniors and seniors. We can make these claims because the chi-square tests of independence were significant for these pairwise comparisons. However, this is a liberal or loose conclusion. With any statistical test, there occurs a certain amount of error, as discussed in Chapter 14. The more statistical tests one runs, the more the error is compounded, and there is an increased chance of type I error. For this reason, statisticians recommend being conservative. One way to be conservative and prevent type I error is to lower the significance level. Although there are many tests to help you lower your significance level, one we commonly use is the **Dunn–Sidak test**. Using the formula $1 - (1 - \alpha)^{1/k}$, where k is the number of comparisons being made (which, as we discussed earlier, is 10 in this case), a lower alpha level can be calculated. Because this hypothesis was examining 10 different chi-square tests, k was equal to 10 and alpha as discussed in Chapter 14 is usually set at $p < 0.05$, so the Dunn–Sidak test would look something like this:

$$1 - (1 - 0.05)^{1/10}$$

$$1 - (0.95)^{1/10}$$

$$1 - (0.9916965052)$$

$$0.0051161969$$

In other words, for the 10 pairwise comparisons to be considered statistically significant, the computed alpha level must now be less than 0.005. For example, by normal standards there is a significant difference between precollege and seniors because alpha was computed at $p = 0.022$; however, at the new alpha level of 0.005, $p = 0.022$ is not considered significant because it is greater than $p < 0.005$. With this more conservative alpha level, only two pairwise comparisons are now significant (first-year students and seniors) and (juniors and seniors). Here is how you would write up this portion of your report in APA:

POST HOC APA WRITE-UP

As a post hoc analysis, 10 pairwise comparisons were calculated to determine where the actual differences are. To correct for type I error in this procedure, a Dunn–Sidak procedure was conducted to correct for possible compounded error resulting from the 10 pairwise comparisons. The new calculated alpha value is $p < 0.005$. Based on the new alpha value, only two pairwise comparisons were found to be statistically significant: first-year students and seniors, and juniors and seniors. Figure 16.22 contains the chi-square statistics for all of the pairwise comparisons.

Now that we have calculated a complete chi-square by hand, we will examine a real chi-square based on data actually collected with a real sample population.

Biological Sex and Book Edition

In this example, we wanted to see whether the numbers female and male participants differed between the first and second editions of this book. In this case, we created a nominal variable for book edition: first edition versus second edition. Figure 16.24 represents the findings from the SPSS results.

Again, note that the results you get from SPSS and Excel are identical. For the most part, the results from these two programs are identical until you get into some of the formulas used for advanced statistical techniques.

APA WRITE-UP

A chi-square was conducted to assess whether the numbers of female and male participants differed between the first and second editions of this book of Wrench, Thomas-Maddox, Richmond, and McCroskey's (2008, 2013) editions of *Quantitative Research Methods for Communication: A Hands-On Approach* (first edition: females [$n = 139$], males [$n = 183$], second edition: females [$n = 182$], males [$n = 137$]). The result for this test was not significant: $\chi^2(1, N = 641) = 12.36, p < 0.001$. Cramér's phi was 0.14, which indicates that the book edition (first or second) accounted for approximately 1.9% of the variability in biological sex within the dataset sample.

We should note that the similarity between the number of females and males from edition to edition was remarkably similar, but flipped. In the first edition we had 139 females and in the second we had 137 males, but in the first edition we had 183 males and in the second we had 182 females. Although these numbers are interesting, they happened by chance. So, what does this result actually tell us? When you look at the basic numbers, we can clearly see that we had significantly more males in the first-edition sample and significantly more females in the second-edition (and vice versa). Overall, however, we had roughly the same number of females ($n = 321$) and males ($n = 320$) when we combine both samples. This

Crosstabs

Case Processing Summary

	Cases					
	Valid		Missing		Total	
	N	Percent	N	Percent	N	Percent
Biological Sex * Book Edition	641	98.0%	13	2.0%	654	100.0%

Count

Biological Sex * Book Edition Crosstabulation

		Book Edition		Total
		1st Edition – 2008	2nd Edition – 2012	
Biological Sex	Male	183	137	320
	Female	139	182	321
Total		322	319	641

Chi-Square Tests

	Value	df	Asymp. Sig. (2-sided)	Exact Sig. (2-sided)	Exact Sig. (1-sided)
Pearson Chi-Square	12.359[a]	1	.000		
Continuity Correction[b]	11.810	1	.001		
Likelihood Ratio	12.399	1	.000		
Fisher's Exact Test				.001	.000
Linear-by-Linear Association	12.340	1	.000		
N of Valid Cases	641				

[a] 0 cells (0.0%) have expected count less than 5. The minimum expected count is 159.25.

[b] Computed only for a 2x2 table

Symmetric Measures

		Value	Approx. Sig.
Nominal by Nominal	Phi	.139	.000
	Cramer's V	.139	.000
N of Valid Cases		641	

[a] Not assuming the null hypothesis.

[b] Using the asymptotic standard error assuming the null hypothesis.

Figure 16.24. SPSS Printout for Sex × Book Edition

balance was not attempted or strived for; it just naturally happened through our data-collecting efforts.

Discussion of Brummans and Miller's Article

To help further your understanding of chi-square tests for independence, the 2004 article by Boris Brummans and Katherine Miller entitled "The Effect of Ambiguity on the Implementation of Social Change Initiative" can be found on the textbook's website in the folder titled "Articles." To view this article, you will need to download a copy of the free Adobe Acrobat Reader (http://www.adobe.com/products/reader.html/) if you do not already have this program installed on your computer. We strongly encourage you to read the article first and then read our analysis of the article. The goal of this process is to make sure you understand how to read and interpret research results related to chi-squares.

ARTICLE PURPOSE

In 1992, the Kellogg Foundation set out to influence health care in three Michigan communities through its Comprehensive Community Health Models Initiative. To do this, the Kellogg Foundatoin sought to "legitimize the problem of community health" and "provide resources and infrastructure for change" (Brummans & Miller, 2004, p. 4). The goal of the Brummans and Miller (2004) article was to see whether people involved with the implementation of the initiative found the ambiguity of the term "collaborative community health improvement" detrimental or beneficial to the implementation of the initiative.

METHODOLOGY

The research team involved in this project interviewed 48 "key participants" in three small group settings. After the interviews, the research team searched for specific ambiguity-oriented language (see the last sentence of the first paragraph on page 6 in the article) and broke the dialogue into research units. These units were then classified as either high ambiguity or low ambiguity by two independent coders, which is the independent variable in this study. If you remember the section on Cohen's kappa from Chapter 10, you will note that 0.86 is above the 0.70 designation described as necessary to be considered satisfactorily reliable for coders. The coders also determined whether the participant perceived the ambiguity as either beneficial or detrimental to the Comprehensive Community Health Model initiative's implementation, which is the dependent variable in this study. Ultimately, the coders created a 2 × 2 table (high ambiguity and low ambiguity) × (detrimental effects and beneficial effects). The actual 2 × 2 table can be seen on page 7 of the article.

RESULTS

The goal of this study was to see whether there was a difference in perception of the effects based on the level of ambiguity. Pearson's chi-square was reported as ($\chi^2 = 117.05$, 1 df, $p < 0.01$). Note that this format for presenting the chi-square information is slightly different than the one discussed in the APA write-ups. However, all of the same information is presented (N can be found in the table on page 7). So based on the results, people do perceive the effects of the implementation with regard to their perception of the ambiguity of the term "collaborative community health improvement."

Chi-squares Outside Academia

Chi-squares are fairly simple tests that actually have a number of benefits outside of traditional academic research. For example, what if you worked for an auto dealership and you wanted to know whether biological sex influenced the model of a car a customer buys? This is a clear case where you would have different categories (biological sex: female and male) and car model (every different auto manufacturer has a line of different car models). In this case, both variables would clearly be nominal, so the chi-square would be a great test to determine this outcome. These results could then be used to target customers. For example, if you learn that male customers are more likely to buy one model of car than women, then spending a lot of time trying to sell a female customer that other model of car may not be the best sales approach.

Another example of a chi-square outside of academia is determining whether different products sell better in different geographic locations. In fact, some companies are interested in product type, geographic location, and store location. Although we have added a third nominal variable here, the appropriate test would still be a chi-square. For example, maybe we want to see whether five different types of plants sell differently based on geographic location (north, south, east, west), based on whether those plants are in the front of the store or in a garden section. You can quickly see that we have a series of three nominal variables.

Overall, any time you want to test a business analytics problem that utilizes two or more sets of nominal variables, then the chi-square test will be a useful tool. The results one gains from these tests can really help an organization grow and thrive.

Conclusion

In this chapter, we have examined how to compute a chi-square statistic by hand, how to compute and interpret computer results of a chi-square statistic in both SPSS and Excel, and how to write up a chi-square tests using APA style. We have seen the chi-square statistic used in three different examples. In the next chapter we will discuss how to calculate t tests.

KEY TERMS

Calculated value	Cramer's phi (Φ)	Degrees of freedom
Chi-square (χ^2)	Critical value	Dunn–Sidak test

REFERENCES

Acock, A. C. (2010). *A gentle introduction to Stata* (3rd ed.). College Station, TX: Stata Press.

Brummans, B. H. J. M., & Miller, K. (2004). The effect of ambiguity on the implementation of a social change initiative. *Communication Research Reports, 21*, 1–10.

Levine, T. R., & Atkin, C. (2004). The accurate reporting of software-generated *p*-values: A cautionary research note. *Communication Research Reports, 21*, 324–327.

FURTHER READING

Abramson, J. H., & Abramson, Z. H. (2001). *Making sense of data: A self-instruction manual on the interpretation of epidemiological data* (3rd ed.). New York, NY: Oxford University Press.

Bruning, J. L., & Kintz, B. L. (1997). *Computational handbook of statistics* (4th ed.). New York, NY: Longman.

Gravetter, F. J., & Wallnau, L. B. (2000). *Statistics for the behavioral sciences* (5th ed.). Belmont, CA: Wadsworth/Thomson Learning.

Green, S. B., & Salkind, N. J. (2004). *Using SPSS for Windows and Macintosh: Analyzing and understanding data* (4th ed.). Upper Saddle River, NJ: Prentice Hall.

Greenwood, P. E., & Nikulin, M. S. (2004). *A guide to chi-square testing.* New York, NY: Wiley.

Hocking, J. E., Stacks, D. W., & McDermott, S. T. (2003). *Communication research* (3rd ed.). Boston, MA: Allyn & Bacon.

Hogan, T. P. (2010). *Bare-bones R: A brief introductory guide.* Los Angeles, CA: Sage.

Howell, D. C. (1997). *Statistical methods for psychology* (4th ed.). Belmont, CA: Duxbury Press.

Huff, D. (1954). *How to lie with statistics.* New York, NY: Norton.

Keller, D. K. (2006). *The Tao of statistics: A path to understanding (with no math).* Thousand Oaks, CA: Sage.

Muenchen, R. A. (2009). *R for SAS and SPSS users.* New York, NY: Springer.

Pyrczak, F. (1999). *Statistics with a sense of humor: A humorous workbook and guide to study skills* (2nd ed.). Los Angeles, CA: Pyrczak.

Reynolds, H. T. (1984). *Analysis of nominal data* (2nd ed.). Newbury Park, CA: Sage.

Salkind, N. J. (2004). *Statistics for people who (think they) hate statistics* (2nd ed.). Thousand Oaks, CA: Sage.

Salkind, N. J. (2011). *Excel statistics: A quick guide.* Los Angeles, CA: Sage.

Excel Institute. (2004). *Excel 9.1 Companion for Windows.* Cary, NC: Excel Press.

Schmuller, J. (2009). *Statistical analysis with Excel®: For dummies.* Hoboken, NJ: Wiley.

Singleton, R. A., Jr., & Straits, B. C. (1999). *Approach to social research* (3rd ed.). New York, NY: Oxford University Press.

Trochim, W. M. K. (2000). *The research methods knowledge base* (2nd ed.). Cincinnati, OH: Atomic Dog. Retrieved from http://www.socialresearchmethods.net/

Independent Samples *t* Tests

When we conducted a chi-square in the last chapter, both of the variables we analyzed had to be nominal or categorical variables (if you do not remember what this means, please reread Chapter 6 before continuing). An **independent samples *t* test** or Student's *t* test, by contrast, examines one nominal variable with two categories (two independent groups) and their scores on one dependent interval/ratio variable. The nominal variable in a *t* test is the independent variable and the interval/ratio variable is the dependent variable. A group is considered independent when one participant's place in one group does not influence anyone else's placement within that group or another group. In essence, the two groups are not related to each other. For example, one common nominal variable used in *t* tests is biological sex. With the nominal variable, biological sex, we have two groups: females and males. If the first participant in the sample is male, then the second participant in the sample could equally be either female or male because the first participant's biological sex has no impact on the second participant's biological sex. In addition to the two groups being independent from each other, every participant should have scores on two variables: the grouping/nominal variable (biological sex) and a test/dependent variable. In the case of an independent samples *t* test, the goal is to determine whether two groups' means differ on an interval/ratio variable of some kind. The groups function as the independent variable, and the interval/ratio variable is the dependent variable. For example, maybe we wanted to determine whether females and males (independent variable) differ in their levels of nonverbal sensitivity (dependent variable). Now that we have explained the basic purpose of an independent *t* test, we will examine an example of an independent samples *t* test.

Case Study Introduction

Imagine you are a teacher teaching an interpersonal communication seminar to two different classes with five students in each class ($n = 5$). In one class, you wear stylish clothing (Class A), and in the other class you wear clothes from the 1970s (Class B). You want to determine whether the style of clothing you wear affects the performance of your class on a test. You formulate a hypothesis that predicts that your wardrobe (stylish clothing vs. outdated clothing) influences the midterm examination grades of Class A and Class B.

Based on this description, you have one nominal variable (stylish clothing vs. outdated clothing) and one ratio variable (grades on a midterm). You might ask yourself why the grades on the midterm variable is considered a ratio variable. If a student answers none of the questions correctly on a test, then he or she could receive an absolute zero (assuming the professor does not give points for correctly spelling one's name). If you look on the chart at the end of Chapter 6 in this book, you will note that if you have one nominal variable and one interval/ratio variable, the correct statistical test to determine whether a difference exists is an independent *t* test. We will now examine a handful of important assumptions about the independent samples *t* test.

Independent Samples *t* Test Background Information

The independent samples *t* test allows a researcher to examine the differences on an interval or ratio variable between two nominal variables. The nominal variables always function as the independent variables in the *t* test. For example, maybe you wanted to determine the level of CA between females and males. The biological sex nominal variable (females and males) would be the independent variable and CA would be the dependent variable. If your nominal variable has more than two levels (e.g., political affiliation—Democrat, Republican, independent voter, not registered to vote), you cannot use an independent samples *t* test to ascertain differences; instead, the one-way analysis of variance, which will be discussed in the next chapter, should be used.

Now that we have discussed a couple of the basic aspects of the independent samples *t* test itself, we will look at the underlying assumptions of the independent samples *t* test:

1. The dependent variable must be an interval or ratio variable.
2. The independent variable must be a nominal variable.
3. The dependent variable (grade) should be normally distributed in both of the independent variable levels (stylish clothing vs. outdated clothing). Specifically, the distributions for both populations should not have a high skewness or kurtosis. In a real-world situation, it is recommended that each nominal category have at least 30 participants. (Because we are only performing an example in this chapter, we do not have 30 participants in each category to make the math easier to compute.)

$$t = \cfrac{(\overline{X}_1 - \overline{X}_2) - (\mu_1 - \mu_2)}{\sqrt{\left[\cfrac{\Sigma X^2_1 - \cfrac{(\Sigma X_1)^2}{n_1} + \Sigma X^2_2 - \cfrac{(\Sigma X_2)^2}{n_2}}{n_1 + n_2 - 2} \right] \left(\cfrac{1}{n_1} + \cfrac{1}{n_2} \right)}}$$

Figure 17.1 *t* test Formula

4. A sample should be drawn from populations with equal variances on the dependent variable (midterm grade). Variance in the *t* statistic formula is obtained by averaging the variance for both of the independent variables (stylish clothing vs. outdated clothing). Because the variance is obtained by averaging the variance of both independent variables, it makes sense that both values should be estimating the same population variance. If the independent variables are both estimating the same population variance, then you are said to have achieved the homogeneity of variance assumption (we will see this assumption again in the next chapter).

5. Finally, the participants contributing data should represent a random sample drawn from the population of interest (this is an assumption of most statistical tests).

These assumptions are extremely important because if one assumption is violated, the meaning of the *t* test is lost. Now that we have explained what a *t* test is and what the basic assumptions of the *t* test are, we can look at the basic *t* test formula given in Figure 17.1.

For some, this formula is scary looking. However, most of the formula is simply computing some basic descriptive statistics as we did in Chapter 15 and then plugging those answers into the formula as we go along.

How Beer Created the *t* Test

Ever heard of William Sealy Gosset? We are going to bet that you probably have not heard of him. Gosset is an important statistician and many of you have probably sampled the fruits of his labor without even knowing you have him to thank. Gosset graduated from New College, Oxford, with degrees in chemistry and mathematics. On graduation, he started working for Arthur Guinness & Son in Dublin, Ireland. Yep, that Guinness! You see, Gosset was attempting to help Guinness develop a statistical tool that could help Guinness achieve the best selection and yield of barley. Working with one of his contemporaries, Karl Pearson (of correlation fame), the two created the *t* test. You may be wondering why it is called the Student' *t* test and not the Gosset *t* test. Well, Guinness was afraid that their competitors would be able to use Gosset's mathematical formula to get the same advantage they had received, so they decided Gosset should publish the article under the pseudonym "Student."

Step-by-Step Approach to the Independent *t* Test

As we discussed earlier, the basic hypothesis being examined in this example is that there is a difference between Class A (fashionable dress) and Class B (outdated dress) and student performance on their midterm examinations. Figure 17.2 portrays the midterm test scores from all 12 student participants.

Step 1. The first step to solving the independent *t* test is to find the ΣX_1 (all five grades in Class A added together), $\overline{X}_1$ (the average for Class A), and the ΣX_1^2 (sum of squares for Class A). To find the ΣX_1, you must add all five scores for the midterm examination for Class A together ($90 + 85 + 88 + 98 + 90 = 451$). To find $\overline{X}_1$, take the sum you found for ΣX_1 (451) and divide it by *n*, which is the number of people in Class A ($451/5 = 90.2$). To get the ΣX_1^2 value (student grades in Class A) you start by first squaring each *X* value on the chart. For example, Natalie got a 90 on her test, so you take 90^2 or 90×90 and get 8,100. You then repeat this process for each student in Class A. Louise obtained an X^2 value of 7,225, Jimmy had a 7,744, Tika had a 9,604, and Kristen had an 8,100. You then add all of these X^2 values together to obtain the ΣX_1^2 ($8,100 + 7,225 + 7,744 + 9,604 + 8,100 = 40,773$). Once you have completed this process for Class A or X_1, you then repeat the process for Class B or X_2. Figure 17.3 contains the mathematical values for Class A (X_1) and Class B (X_2) necessary for computing the *t* test.

Step 2. As with any formula, you must start by doing things within parentheses and brackets first. The part we are going to solve for in Step 2 is shown in bold in Figure 17.4.

Both of these portions of the formula involve the ΣX_1 (451) and the ΣX_2 (364). The actual formula for this part is $(\Sigma X_1)^2/n_1$. Remember, the lowercase *n* stands for the number of students in each class, or the number 5 in this example. So the solution for this part of the formula would be this:

$$(\Sigma X_1)^2/n_1$$

$$(451)^2/5$$

$$(203,401)/5$$

$$40,680.2$$

So, $(\Sigma X_1)^2/n_1 = 40,680.20$.

We can now just repeat these steps for $(\Sigma X_2)^2/n_2$ to find the result:

$$(\Sigma X_2)^2/n_2$$

$$(364)^2/5$$

$$(132,496)/5$$

$$26,499.20$$

So, $(\Sigma X_2)^2/n_2 = 26,499.20$.

Summary of Data (Scores Out of 100)			
Class A (Fashionable Dress) Condition$_1$ (n = 5)		**Class B** (1970s Dress) Condition$_2$ (n = 5)	
Participant	X	Participant	X
1. Natalie	˙90	1. Dave	83
2. Louise	85	2. Tad	71
3. Jimmy	88	3. Penny	96
4. Tika	98	4. Kevin	52
5. Kirsten	90	5. Brenda	62

Figure 17.2 *t* Test Sample Data

| **Summary of Data (Scores Out of 100)** | | | | | |
| Class A
(Fashionable Dress)
Condition₁ (*n* = 5) | | | Class B
(1970s Dress)
Condition₂ (*n* = 5) | | |
Participant	*X*	*X²*	Participant	*X*	*X²*
1. Natalie	90	8100	1. Dave	83	6889
2. Louise	85	7225	2. Tad	71	5041
3. Jimmy	88	7744	3. Penny	96	9216
4. Tika	98	9604	4. Kevin	52	2704
5. Kirsten	90	8100	5. Brenda	62	3844
	$\Sigma X_1 = 451$	$\Sigma X_1^2 = 40773$		$\Sigma X_2 = 364$	$\Sigma X_2^2 = 27694$
	$\overline{X}_1 = 90.2$			$\overline{X}_2 = 72.8$	

Figure 17.3 Summary Data Table for *t* Test Example

$$t = \frac{(\overline{X}_1 - \overline{X}_2) - (\mu_1 - \mu_2)}{\sqrt{\left[\dfrac{\Sigma X_1^2 - \dfrac{(\Sigma X_1)^2}{n_1} + \Sigma X_2^2 - \dfrac{(\Sigma X_2)^2}{n_2}}{n_1 + n_2 - 2}\right]\left(\dfrac{1}{n_1} + \dfrac{1}{n_2}\right)}}$$

Figure 17.4 Step 2 *t* Test Computation

$$t = \frac{(\overline{X}_1 - \overline{X}_2) - (\mu_1 - \mu_2)}{\sqrt{\left[\dfrac{\boldsymbol{\Sigma X_1^2 - \dfrac{(\Sigma X_1)^2}{n_1} + \Sigma X_2^2 - \dfrac{(\Sigma X_2)^2}{n_2}}}{n_1 + n_2 - 2}\right]\left(\dfrac{1}{n_1} + \dfrac{1}{n_2}\right)}}$$

Figure 17.5 Step 3 *t* Test Computation

Step 3. At this point, we can do everything within the brackets on the top side of the numerator bar, which is shown in bold in Figure 17.5.

Now we must bring back our sum of square calculations for both Class A (X_1) and Class B (X_2). The sum of square calculation for Class A was $\Sigma X_1^2 = 40{,}773$, and the sum of square calculation for Class B was $\Sigma X_2^2 = 27{,}694$. In this part of the formula, we are subtracting the sum of square for X_1 from the portion of the formula for X_1 that was computed in Step 2 [$(\Sigma X_1)^2/n_1 = 40{,}680.20$]. In other words, we are subtracting 40,680.20 from 40,773:

$$\Sigma X_1^2 - [(\Sigma X_1)^2/n_1]$$

$$40{,}773 - 40{,}680.20 =$$

$$92.8$$

We then repeat this part of the formula for X_2. We are now going to subtract the sum of square for X_2 from the portion of the formula for X_2 that was computed in Step 2 [$(\Sigma X_2)^2/n_2 = 26{,}499.20$]. In other words, we are subtracting 26,499.20 from 27,694.

$$\Sigma X_2^2 - [(\Sigma X_2)^2/n_2]$$

$$27{,}694 - 26{,}499.20 =$$

$$1194.8$$

Step 4. Step 4 is threefold, but it is easy. First, we must add both of the numbers calculated in Step 3 together ($92.8 + 1194.8 = 1287.6$). Second, we must complete the formula immediately below what we just completed doing ($n_1 + n_2 - 2$). If you remember from above, $n_1 = 5$, which indicates that there are five students in Class A; and $n_2 = 5$, which indicates that there are five students in Class B. To complete the formula you do the mathematical computation ($5 + 5 - 2 = 8$). Finally, we must divide the first number calculated in this step (1,287.6) by the second number calculated in this step (8): $1{,}287.6/8 = 160.95$.

Step 5. In the fifth step of this equation, we must calculate everything in the big parentheses to the right of the part of the equation we just finished computing. This part of the equation reads $(1/n_1) + (1/n_2)$. As we already know, $n_1 = 5$ and $n_2 = 5$, so we just need to compute the formula:

$$(1/n_1) + (1/n_2)$$

$$(1/5) + (1/5)$$

$$(0.2) + (0.2)$$

$$0.4$$

So, $(1/n_1) + (1/n_2) = 0.4$.

Step 6. In this step, take the number calculated in the third part of Step 4 (160.95) and multiply it by the number calculated in Step 5 (0.4):

$$160.95 * 0.4 = 64.38$$

We now take this newly calculated number (64.38) and find its square root: $\sqrt{64.38} = 8.0237$. At this point, we have calculated everything on the bottom part of this formula.

Step 7. The seventh step will calculate the top portion of the formula, or the part that is in bold in Figure 17.6.

This part of the formula $\left(\overline{X}_1 - \overline{X}_2\right) - \left(\mu_1 - \mu_2\right)$ can be understood as the sample mean difference minus the population mean difference. As was previously explained, one of the assumptions of the basic *t* test is the homogeneity of variance, so the population mean difference should equal 0. In essence, all that must be computed in this part is $\left(\overline{X}_1 - \overline{X}_2\right)$. As stated in Figure 17.3, $\overline{X}_1 = 90.2$ and $\overline{X}_2 = 72.8$. At this point, we can complete this part of the formula:

$$\left(\overline{X}_1 - \overline{X}_2\right) - \left(\mu_2 - \mu_2\right)$$

$$\left(90.2 - 72.8\right) - \left(0\right)$$

$$17.4 - 0$$

$$17.4$$

$$t = \frac{\left(\overline{X}_1 - \overline{X}_2\right) - \left(\mu_1 - \mu_2\right)}{\sqrt{\left[\dfrac{\Sigma X_1^2 - \dfrac{\left(\Sigma X_1\right)^2}{n_1} + \Sigma X_2^2 - \dfrac{\left(\Sigma X_2\right)^2}{n_2}}{n_1 + n_2 - 2}\right] \left(\dfrac{1}{n_1}\quad\dfrac{1}{n_2}\right)}}$$

Figure 17.6 Step 7 *t* Test Computation

So, $\left(\overline{X}_1 - \overline{X}_2\right) - \left(\mu_1 - \mu_2\right) = 17.4$

Step 8. The final step in computing the *t* statistic is to simply divide the calculated value from Step 6 (8.0237) from the calculated value in Step 7 (17.4), or

$$17.4/8.0237 =$$

$$2.168575595 \text{ or } 2.169$$

This indicates that the calculated value that we obtained for *t* is 2.169. However, we still have a couple of steps to go before we can say that we are truly finished with this example.

Step 9. In this step we must calculate the degrees of freedom for the *t* computed in this example. The formula for the degrees of freedom for the *t* test is simple. In fact, we have already computed it as part of the formula of the *t* test in Step 4. The formula for the *t* test df is $(df = n_1 + n_2 - 2)$, or $(df = 5 + 5 - 2)$, or 8.

Step 10. Figure 17.7 contains the independent samples *t* test critical value table. Note that this critical value table is different from the table used to test for chi-square significance in the previous chapter. On the left-hand side is the column for the degrees of freedom. In our study, our degrees of freedom value, as calculated in Step 9, was 8, so we must compare the number we calculated for the *t* statistic in Step 8, 2.169, against the numbers in row 8 on this chart. If 2.169 (calculated value) is greater than the number listed in the columns (critical values), our *t* test is statistically significant at that *p* value level (shown at the top of each column). The first column represents $p < 0.10$, which is not statistically significant, as discussed in Chapter 14. The critical value in this column was 1.860, and our calculated *t* statistic was 2.169, which is greater than 1.860, so we would consider our *t* significant at the $p < 0.10$ level. However, 0.10 does not meet the 95%confidence interval discussed in the previous chapter, so we would not consider a *t* test statistically significant at this *p* value. The second column represents $p < 0.05$,

df	0.10	0.05	0.01	0.005	0.001
1	6.31	12.71	63.66	636.62	363.62
2	2.92	4.30	9.93	31.60	31.60
3	2.35	3.18	5.84	12.94	12.92
4	2.13	2.78	4.60	8.61	8.61
5	2.02	2.57	4.03	6.86	6.87
6	1.94	2.45	3.71	5.96	5.96
7	1.90	2.37	3.50	5.41	5.41
8	1.86	2.31	3.36	5.04	5.04
9	1.83	2.26	3.25	4.78	4.78
10	1.81	2.27	3.17	4.59	4.59
11	1.80	2.20	3.12	4.44	4.44
12	1.78	2.18	3.06	4.32	4.32
13	1.77	2.16	3.01	4.22	4.22
14	1.76	2.15	2.98	4.14	4.14
15	1.75	2.13	2.95	4.07	4.07
16	1.75	2.12	2.92	4.02	4.02
17	1.74	2.11	2.90	3.97	3.97
18	1.73	2.10	2.88	3.92	3.92
19	1.73	2.09	2.86	3.88	3.88
20	1.73	2.09	2.85	3.85	3.85

The entries in this table were computed by the authors.

Figure 17.7 *t* Test Critical Value Table (Two-Tailed Test)

which is statistically significant, as discussed in Chapter 14. The critical value in this column was 2.306, and our calculated *t* statistic was 2.169, which is not greater than 2.306, so our *t* test is not statistically significant at the $p < 0.05$ level. In essence, our *t* test is not statistically significant. We cannot be 95% confident that there is a difference between the two classes and their midterm examination scores, which means we must accept the null hypothesis that style of dress (fashionable and 1970s dress) did not affect the students' scores on the midterm examination.

Computer Printouts of the Independent *t* Test

Now that we have examined how independent *t* test can be calculated by hand, we will examine what output from two statistical computer programs, SPSS and Excel, looks like as well.

SPSS AND *t* TESTS

Using SPSS to compute an independent *t* test is fairly easy as long as you know how to follow instructions, so let's get started. First, open your SPSS software and then locate the file on the textbook's website in the SPSS folder called "*t* test" (Figure 17.8). When you open this file, you will see two variables listed, "class" and "score." Class is the variable name given to either Class A (fashionable dress) or Class B (1970s dress). The classes are only represented by the numbers 1 (Class A) and 2 (Class B). Remember, a statistics program can only understand numbers, so it is up to you as a researcher to remember how you classified the two groups when you are inputting the data. The "score" variable is the score that each participant received on the midterm examination.

To conduct the *t* test, go to the menu bar at the top of your screen and click "Analyze." When you click "Analyze," a drop-down menu will appear. Go to the fourth category on this

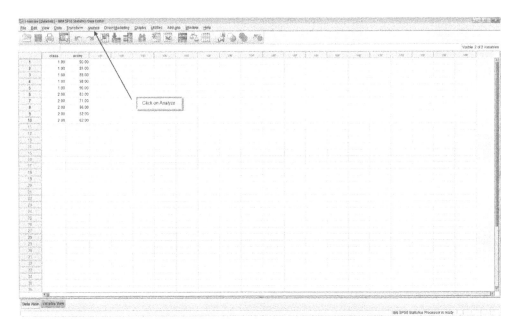

Figure 17.8 *t* Test Main Page

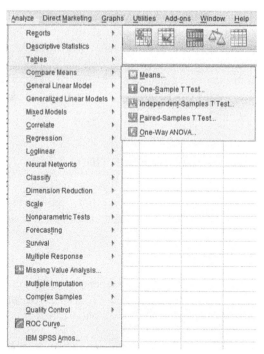

Figure 17.9 *t* Test Menu

menu, "Compare Means," scroll over the arrow, and another menu will appear to the right. The third option on the "Compare Means" menu is "Independent Samples T-Test"; click on it (Figure 17.9). At this point, the "Independent Samples T-Test" dialogue box will appear on your screen (Figure 17.10a). The screen has three major boxes on it. On the left-hand side is a box with your variables listed in it already. On the upper right is a box labeled "Test Variable(s)," and below that box is a small box labeled "Grouping Variable." Any dependent variables that you are attempting to analyze are placed in the "Test Variable(s)" box. Click on the dependent variable for this example "scores." When "scores" is highlighted blue, click the right arrow between the variable list box and the "Test Variable(s)" box (Figure 17.10b). After clicking the right arrow, "scores" should now appear in the "Test Variable(s)" box. Next, we must send our independent variable "class" to the "Grouping Variable" box as well. When conducting a *t* test, your independent variable will always be placed in the "Grouping Variable" box and your dependent variable(s) will always be placed in the "Test Variable(s)" box (Figure 17.10c).

You cannot click OK yet because you have not completely finished telling the computer what to do. Click on the word "class" in the "Grouping Variable" box if it is not already highlighted blue. In the "Grouping Variable" box, click the button labeled "Define Groups." When you click on "Define Groups," the "Define Groups" dialogue box will pop up (Figure 17.10d). In the "Define Groups" dialogue box you must tell the computer which two numbers in the variable "class" you are comparing. Remember, a *t* test can only be used if a nominal variable has two levels, so you must tell your computer what numbers you chose to represent those two levels. As mentioned above, we have chosen the numbers 1 and 2 to represent Class A (1) and Class B (2). We could have chosen 0 and 1 or 8 and 9—the numbers do not matter to the computer—what matters is that we clearly identify them to the computer. So, in the "Define Groups" dialogue box, you will note two places for you to enter information beside "Group 1" and "Group 2." Next to "Group 1," type the number "1" in the box, and next to "Group 2," type

a) Main Dialogue Box

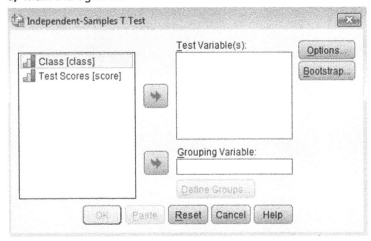

b) Dependent Variable to the "Test Variable(s):" Box

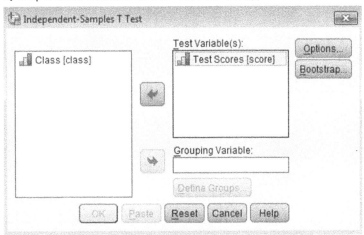

c) Independent Variable to the "Grouping Variable:" Box

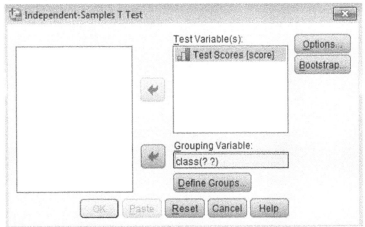

Figure 17.10 Independent Samples *t* Test Dialogue Box   *Continued*

Continued

d) Define Groups Dialogue Box

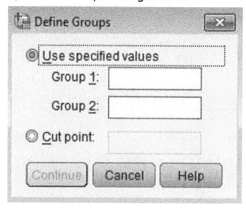

e) Defined Groups

the number "2" in the box (Figure 17.10e). Once you have clearly labeled the groups, you can then click on the "Continue" button. You will now be looking again at the "Independent Samples *T*-Test" dialogue box. At this point, you can click "OK." If for some reason you cannot click "OK," you have not entered your grouping variables correctly, so repeat the steps above and attempt to find out where you made your mistake. The results from SPSS will appear when you have clicked "OK" (Figure 17.11).

The first box that you will see in the results is simply a "Group Statistics" box. In this box you will see that the *N*, mean, standard deviation, and standard error means are listed for you for both Class A and Class B. The second box, or the "Independent Samples Test" box, is where the primary information about the *t* test itself is located. The first thing we must do when analyzing our computer printouts is to determine whether we have met the assumption discussed earlier called the "homogeneity of variance" assumption for *t* tests.

The second column in the "Independent Samples Test" box is labeled "Levene's Test for Equality of Variances." Levene's Test for Equality of Variances tests the homogeneity of variance assumption. If Levene's test is statistically significant, then the assumption has not been met. Remember, the assumption states that the variances would be equal, so when the two groups' variances are not equal, the assumption is not met. In the "Levene's Test for Equality of Variances" column, you will see two subcolumns, "F" and "Sig." If "Sig." is below 0.05,

T-Test

Group Statistics

	Class	N	Mean	Std. Deviation	Std. Error Mean
Test Scores	Class A	5	90.2000	4.8166	2.1541
	Class B	5	72.8000	17.2829	7.7292

Independent Samples Test

		Levene's Test for Equality of Variances		t-test for Equality of Means							
										95% Confidence Interval of the Difference	
		F	Sig.	t	df	Sig. (2-tailed)	Mean Difference	Std. Error Difference	Lower	Upper
Test Scores	Equal variances assumed	6.053	.039	2.169	8	.062	17.4000	8.0237	–1.1027	35.9027
	Equal variances not assumed			2.169	4.618	.087	17.4000	8.0237	–3.7501	38.5501

Figure 17.11 SPSS Results for *t* Test Example

then Levene's test for equality of variances is significant and the basic assumption of the *t* test has been violated, so equal variances cannot be assumed, which is the second row listed.

So, what does it mean when your *t* test indicates that equal variances cannot be assumed? It means that the *t* test we calculated by hand in the example must be tweaked since this assumption was violated. If you look at the "Independent Samples Test" box, you will see that there are *t* test results for both "equal variances assumed" and "equal variances cannot be assumed." If our Levene test for equal variances is statistically significant ($p < 0.05$), we must report the *t* test on the lower level. The biggest change that occurs is how we report our degrees of freedom. By lowering the degrees of freedom from 8 (like we calculated) to 4.618 (as seen for the "equal variances cannot be assumed"), we make it harder for a *t* test to be statistically significant to protect against possible type I errors. If you look at the significance levels for "equal variances assumed" ($p = 0.062$) and "equal variances cannot be assumed" ($p = 0.087$), you will see that the *p* value for equal variances being assumed is lower (greater chance of reaching statistical significance) than the *p* value for equal variances cannot be assumed (less of a chance of reaching statistical significance). You will see that the *t* value, the "Mean Difference," and the "Standard Error Difference" are all identical; the only values that are affected by the homogeneity of variance assumption are the 'df" and "Sig." values.

EXCEL AND *t* TESTS

To compare the means for independent samples in Excel, first open the "t-Test" file from the textbook's website. Once the file is opened, you will see data for the two dress groups. As we explained earlier, Excel uses the numeric representations of 1 and 2 for each of these groups (Class A and Class B). Click on the "Data" tab at the top of the spreadsheet, select "Data Analysis" from the right side of the screen, and choose the "*t*-Test: Two Sample Assuming

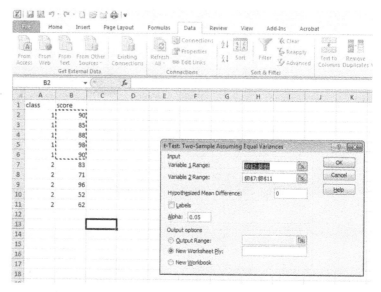

Figure 17.12 *t* Test: Two Sample Assuming Equal Variances

Equal Variances" option from the menu (Figure 17.12). To fill in the data ranges under the Input category, click the box labeled "Variable 1 Range" and highlight the values in cells B2 through B6 because this range corresponds with those in the first group. Next, click in the box titled "Variable 2 Range" and highlight the values in cells B7 through B11 because these scores correspond with those in the second group. Click the "Labels" box and the "New Worksheet Ply" box. A default of 0.05 is set for alpha, but this can be adjusted if desired. Click "OK" and the data output will appear in a new screen (Figure 17.13). In addition, the z-Test option is provided in the menu of options.

Please note that Excel does not provide you with the Levene test for equality of variances, so there is no way to ascertain whether this assumption of the *t* test is violated. You can repeat the test and run it where you assume that equal variances has been violated, but without Levene's test for equality of variances, it is hard to know whether the assumption has been violated.

Now that we have examined the *t* test itself, let's see how a researcher would write up this finding using APA style in a results section of an article.

APA WRITE-UP (SPSS)

An independent *t* test was conducted to determine whether an instructor's dress in a classroom (fashionable [$M = 90.20$, $SD = 4.82$] vs. out-of-date dress [$M = 72.80$, $SD = 7.73$]) affected the scores students received on their midterm examinations. Levene's test for equality of variances was significant ($F = 6.05$, $p < 0.04$), so equality of variances cannot be assumed, $t(4.62) = 2.17$, $p = 0.06$.

APA WRITE-UP (EXCEL)

A paired two sample for means *t* test was conducted to determine whether an instructor's dress in a classroom (fashionable [$M = 90.20$, $SD = 4.82$] vs. out-of-date dress [$M = 72.80$, $SD = 7.73$]) affected the scores students received on their midterm examinations. Overall, no significant difference was noted between the two groups, $t(8) = 2.31$, $p = 0.06$.

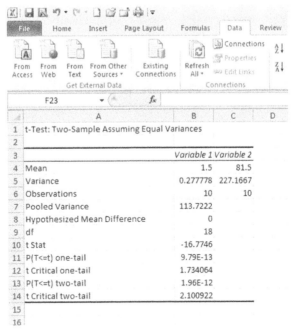

Figure 17.13 Computed *t* Test in Excel

DISCUSSION OF FINDINGS

So, now that we have completed the APA write-ups, you may be wondering what they actually tell us. To understand what the *t* test tell us, we must go back to the original purpose we had for conducting the *t* test. In our example, we had a schoolteacher who wanted to determine whether altering her dress between modern fashions in one class and outdated clothing from the 1970s in the other class would affect student learning. To test student learning, the teacher used the midterm examination as a benchmark. Based on the *t* test that we conducted, no difference was noted on the students' midterm examinations between the two classes. In a difference test, when we say that something is not significant or greater than 0.05, we are saying that a difference did not occur within our sample. In this case, the teacher's dress, whether fashionable or from the 1970s, did not change how students performed on the midterm examination.

Biological Sex and Communication Apprehension

In this example, we wanted to determine whether females and males differed in their reported CA levels. To test for a possible difference between females and males on the PRCA-24, we used the nominal variable biological sex and the interval variable communication apprehension. Figure 17.14 shows the findings from the SPSS results.

APA WRITE-UP (SPSS)

An independent *t* test was conducted to determine whether female ($M = 65.60$, $SD = 18.16$) and male ($M = 61.62$, $SD = 15.49$) reported levels of CA differed. Levene's test for equality of variances was significant ($F = 6.14$, $p < 0.05$), so equality of variances cannot be assumed: $t(615.46) = -2.96$, $p = 0.003$.

T-Test

Group Statistics

	Biological Sex	N	Mean	Std. Deviation	Std. Error Mean
Communication Apprehension Total	Male	314	61.6178	15.49195	.87426
	Female	317	65.5962	18.16314	1.02014

Independent Samples Test

		Levene's Test for Equality of Variances		*t*-test for Equality of Means						
		F	Sig.	t	df	Sig. (2-tailed)	Mean Difference	Std. Error Difference	95% Confidence Interval of the Difference Lower	Upper
Communication Apprehension Total	Equal variances assumed	4.850	.028	-2.959	629	.003	-3.97838	1.34452	-6.61868	-1.33808
	Equal variances not assumed			-2.961	615.457	.003	-3.97838	1.34351	-6.61680	-1.33996

Figure 17.14 SPSS Results of Sex and CA *t* Test

DISCUSSION

Let's examine how APA write-ups for *t* tests are conducted. First, note that when we described the two groups being compared, we also reported the group's means and standard deviations for the dependent variable (communication apprehension). We do this because we want to make the results easy to interpret. If the *t* test is significant, then the group with the higher mean has statistically significant higher levels on the dependent variable. In the case in front of us, females were shown to have higher levels of communication apprehension when compared to males. However, at this point, we still do not know how big this difference is, which is why we must calculate the effect size.

Calculating Effect Sizes

As mentioned in Chapters 6 and 14, one of the most important aspects related to difference research is the effect size, or the magnitude of the difference. Although statistics allows researchers to find small differences between two groups, the magnitude of this difference is not always known. In the example given earlier, females were shown to have significantly higher levels of CA when compared to males. As researchers, we must ask ourselves: Is a difference between 65.60 and 61.62 that big? Statistically, the relationship may be meaningful, but how big a difference are we talking about? For this reason, it is important to calculate an effect size any time one is calculating a difference using an independent t test. To test for an independent samples effect size, we use **Cohen's d** formula:

$$d = t \sqrt{\frac{N_1 + N_2}{N_1 N_2}}$$

t Test Effect Size Formula

You will note that all of the information we need to compute the effect size for the t test is located within the APA write-up itself. First, we need the computed t value, which was 2.961 in the study (for the purposes of this test, we do not need to worry about the negative sign). Second, we need the number of participants in the study ($N = 631$). Next, we must know how many people were in each group: $N_{1(female)} = 317$ and $N_{2(male)} = 314$. Once we have both of these pieces of information, it is simply a matter of completing the formula.

Step 1. The first step for computing d is to handle everything within the square-root function first. First, we will solve the information in the numerator ($N_1 + N_2$):

$$N_1 + N_2$$

$$317 + 314 = 631$$

Second, we want to solve the information within the denominator ($N_1 N_2$):

$$N_1 N_2$$

$$317 * 314 = 99,538$$

Third, we divide the result from Step 1 (122) by the result from Step 2 (3721):

$$(N_1 + N_2)/(N_1 N_2)$$

$$631/99,538 = 0.0327868852$$

Finally, we take the square root of the result we found in the third step (0.00633932875):

$$\sqrt{(N_1 + N_2)/(N_1 N_2)}$$

$$\sqrt{0.00633932875} = 0.0796196427$$

Step 2. The second step is to take the calculated t test value reported in the article (4.8) and multiply it by the number we found in the last part of Step 1:

$$(0.0796196427):$$

$$t\sqrt{(N_1 + N_2)/(N_1 N_2)}$$

$$2.961 \times 0.0796196427 = 0.235753762$$

or, Cohen's $d = 0.24$

To interpret t test effect sizes, use the following scale (Green & Salkind, 2004):

0.2—small effect size

0.5—medium effect size

0.8—large effect size

Based on this scale, the effect found (Cohen's $d = 0.24$) for the CA score differences between females ($M = 65.60$) and males ($M = 61.62$) is small.

Discussion of the Weber, Fornash, Corrigan, and Neupauer Article

To help you further understand the concept of the independent samples *t* test, we have included an article on the textbook's website that utilizes the statistical test. The 2004 article by Keith Weber, Bennie Fornash, Michael Corrigan, and Nicholas Neupauer entitled "The Effect of Interest on Recall: An Experiment" can be found in the folder titled "Articles." To view this article, you will must download a copy of the free Adobe Acrobat Reader (http://www.adobe.com/products/reader.html/) if you do not already have this program installed on your computer. We strongly encourage you to read the article first and then read our analysis of the article. The goal of this process is to make sure you understand how to read and interpret research results related to *t* tests.

ARTICLE PURPOSE

Have you ever had to sit through a lecture in which the professor used examples that were outdated and did not mean a lot to you? Apparently, these researchers had as well, and they wanted to determine whether these outdated examples affected student learning. The basic goal of this project was to determine whether presenting interest-based examples (examples that are meaningful to the student, are something the students know about so they can actually discuss the examples openly, and are examples that clearly make a difference in everyday life) create more interested students in the classroom and result in students who perform better on subsequent tests.

METHODOLOGY

In this study, the researchers divided participants into two groups and showed them a 10-minute video with a lecturer talking about public relations. In one video, the instructor (a male in his mid-30s) used examples that are not current but exist in most public relations textbooks (P. T. Barnum, Edward Bernays, and Ivy Ledbetter Lee). In the second video, the instructor (the same person as in the first video) used contemporary personalities such as Vince McMahon (wrestling promoter), Ray Lewis (professional football player), and Sean "Puffy" Combs (musician/entertainer/entrepreneur). The goal of this second video was to use examples that students would be familiar with and therefore, theoretically, cause them to be more interested in the course content as well.

After both groups watched the 10-minute videos, the groups were given a seven-item multiple-choice "quiz" to test their ability to understand the actual content from the videos. The groups also filled out a learner empowerment scale that measured the three concepts that represent interest-based examples (meaningfulness, competence, and impact).

The participants also filled out a nonverbal immediacy test to determine whether one group perceived the lecturer from the video as being more nonverbally immediate (and thus skewing the results from the examples). To test this notion, the researchers conducted an independent *t* test and did not find a significant difference between the textbook example and the modern example lecturer's nonverbal immediacy. This indicates that the lecturer did not alter his nonverbal communication significantly between the taping of one video and the next.

RESULTS

The first hypothesis in this study stated that "lectures utilizing interest-based examples should result in more interested participants" (p. 118). To examine this hypothesis, the researchers conducted an independent *t* test to determine whether students' interest in the videos (dependent variable) was different based on whether they watched the textbook-based example lecture versus the contemporary example lecture (independent variable). The researchers reported that the students who watched the video with the contemporary examples scored significantly higher on the interest scale than those students who watched the video with the traditional textbook examples. In other words, students are more interested in lectures that have examples they can relate to in a classroom. If you look at the way the authors of the article presented their results, you will note that they presented the *t* test as we previously discussed in this chapter and then presented the actual means for each group since the difference was significant. Although presenting the means is necessary, we strongly encourage you to always present both the mean and the standard deviation because they influence the meaningfulness of the findings. When presenting means in an article, it should look something like this ($M = \#$, $SD = \#$). Note that "M" and "SD" are both capitalized and italicized when presenting them in a research article.

The second hypothesis in this study predicted that "lectures utilizing interest-based examples should result in participants with higher scores on subsequent tests of cognitive recall" (p. 118). To examine this hypothesis, the researchers conducted an independent *t* test to determine whether students' scores on the seven-item quiz (dependent variable) were different based on whether they watched the textbook-based example lecture versus the contemporary example lecture (independent variable). The researchers reported that the students who watched the video with the contemporary examples scored significantly higher on the quiz than those students who watched the video with the traditional textbook examples. In other words, students will remember more and be able to recall it on a quiz when they listen to lectures that have examples they can relate to in a classroom.

The researchers then break the first hypothesis down and look at all three aspects of interest separately in three post hoc (after the fact) tests. In the post hoc analysis, the researchers conducted three more independent *t* tests examining the three factors of interest-based examples (competence, meaningfulness, and impact). The researchers report that they found differences between the two lecture groups on competence and meaningfulness, but not on impact. In other words, these results indicate that students in classrooms with modern examples feel that the examples are more meaningful to them and therefore are more competent to discuss these examples than students who listened to examples that came from traditional textbooks. However, the impact of both the contemporary and the textbook examples did not differ between the two groups.

Overall, this article is helpful because it emphasizes that college professors must stay on top of current events if they are going to be effective and affective teachers in the classroom. Sticking with examples that exist in the textbook and dismissing the notion that modern examples are needed will only do a disservice to the learning environment.

Paired *t* Tests

The majority of this chapter has been concerned with the independent samples *t* test or the Student *t* test. There is another type of *t* test that we think you should be aware of at this point. A **paired *t* test** is used to compare two interval/ratio level scores that are taken from the same group at two distinct time periods. Imagine you have run an experiment looking at individual's level of communication apprehension after interacting with a robot. To see whether interacting with a robot can decrease participant levels of CA with a robot, you take a baseline score of their Robot-CA (Time$_1$) and then take a second score after the interaction (Time$_2$). A paired *t* test can then be used to determine whether these two scores differ from one another. Because of the paired *t* test's ability to measure differences in this fashion, it is most commonly used in conjunction with experiments.

t Tests Outside Academia

As we discussed earlier in this chapter, the *t* test was created to help solve a practical problem that Guinness was facing. From the inception of the *t* test, it was designed to help solve a real organizational problem. Many organizations use *t* tests for a variety of different reasons. Any time an individual has two groups he or she wants to compare on an interval or ratio variable, then the *t* test is the most appropriate test to use. If you want to see whether female and male viewers have the same responses while watching a commercial, then you would probably want to use a *t* test. In fact, a lot of research that examines sex differences in the worlds of marketing and media rely heavily on the *t* test. In corporate training and development, a *t* test is often used to determine whether face-to-face and online training courses lead to similar levels of learning. You could also use a *t* test to examine a variety of business indicators against data from your organization's main rival. Whether you wanted to test issues like efficiency, productivity, or error rates against those of your competitor, a *t* test would be the tool you would want to use.

Conclusion

In this chapter, we have examined how to compute a *t* test by hand, how to compute and interpret computer results of a *t* test in both SPSS and Excel, and how to write up a *t* test using APA style. We have seen the *t* test used in four different examples and finally discussed how to compute a *t* test effect size.

KEY TERMS

Cohen's *d*
Paired *t* test
Independent samples *t* test

REFERENCES

Cohen, J. (1988). *Statistical power analysis for the behavioral sciences* (2nd ed.). Hillsdale, NJ: Erlbaum.

Weber, K., Fornash, B., Corrigan, M, & Neupauer, N. C. (2003). The effect of interest on recall: An experiment. *Communication Research Reports, 20,* 116–123.

FURTHER READING

Abramson, J. H., & Abramson, Z. H. (2001). *Making sense of data: A self-instruction manual on the interpretation of epidemiological data* (3rd ed.). New York, NY: Oxford University Press.

Bruning, J. L., & Kintz, B. L. (1997). *Computational handbook of statistics* (4th ed.). New York, NY: Longman.

Gravetter, F. J., & Wallnau, L. B. (2000). *Statistics for the behavioral sciences* (5th ed.). Belmont, CA: Wadsworth/Thomson Learning.

Green, S. B., & Salkind, N. J. (2004). *Using SPSS for Windows and Macintosh: Analyzing and understanding data* (4th ed.). Upper Saddle River, NJ: Prentice Hall.

Hocking, J. E., Stacks, D. W., & McDermott, S. T. (2003). *Communication research* (3rd ed.). Boston, MA: Allyn & Bacon.

Hogan, T. P. (2010). *Bare-bones R: A brief introductory guide*. Los Angeles, CA: Sage.

Howell, D. C. (1997). *Statistical methods for psychology* (4th ed.). Belmont, CA: Duxbury Press.

Huff, D. (1954). *How to lie with statistics*. New York, NY: Norton.

Keller, D. K. (2006). *The Tao of statistics: A path to understanding (with no math)*. Thousand Oaks, CA: Sage.

Muenchen, R. A. (2009). *R for SAS and SPSS users*. New York, NY: Springer.

Pyrczak, F. (1999). *Statistics with a sense of humor: A humorous workbook and guide to study skills* (2nd ed.). Los Angeles, CA: Pyrczak.

Salkind, N. J. (2004). *Statistics for people who (think they) hate statistics* (2nd ed.). Thousand Oaks, CA: Sage.

Salkind, N. J. (2011). *Excel statistics: A quick guide*. Los Angeles, CA: Sage.

Singleton, R. A., Jr., & Straits, B. C. (1999). *Approach to social research* (3rd ed.). New York, NY: Oxford University Press.

Tabachnick, B. G., & Fidell, L. S. (2001). *Using multivariate statistics* (4th ed.). Boston, MA: Allyn & Bacon.

Trochim, W. M. K. (2000). *The research methods knowledge base* (2nd ed.). Cincinnati, OH: Atomic Dog. Retrieved from http://www.socialresearchmethods.net/

CHAPTER 18

One-Way Analysis of Variance

1 Explain the purposes of a one-way analysis of variance (ANOVA).
2 Calculate a one-way ANOVA by hand.
3 Conduct a one-way ANOVA using both SPSS and Excel.
4 Interpret the printouts associated with a one-way ANOVA.
5 Examine a real-world one-way ANOVA analysis using the textbook's dataset.
6 Analyze the use of the one-way ANOVA in the article by Boiarsky, Long, and Thayer (1999).

When we conducted a *t* test in the previous chapter, one variable had to be nominal with no more than two independent groups and their scores on one dependent interval/ratio variable. A one-way analysis of variance (ANOVA), by contrast, has one nominal variable with two or more independent groups and their scores on one dependent interval/ratio variable. Once again, the nominal variable (with two or more groups) is the independent variable, and the interval/ratio variable is the dependent variable. A group is considered independent when one participant's place in one of the groups being tested does not influence anyone else's placement within that group or another group. In essence, the groups being tested are not related to each other. For example, one common nominal variable used in one-way ANOVA is political affiliation. With the nominal variable, political affiliation, as we have defined it in this text, there are four groups: Democrat, Republican, other political party affiliation, and not registered to vote. If the first participant in the sample is a Democrat, then the second participant in the sample could equally be a Democrat, Republican, other political party affiliation, registered to vote because the first participant's political affiliation has no impact on the second participant's political affiliation. In addition to the two or more groups being independent from each other, every participant should have scores on two variables: the grouping/nominal variable (political affiliation) and a test/dependent variable. In the case of a one-way ANOVA, the goal is to determine whether the two or more groups' means differ on an interval/ratio variable of some kind. The groups function as the independent variable, and the interval/ratio variable is the dependent variable. For example, maybe we wanted to determine whether people differ based on political affiliation (independent variable) in their levels of ethnocentrism (dependent variable).

The one-way analysis of variance is part of the family of statistical tests that belong to the **general linear model** (GLM) family. Although we wanted to mention here that the one-way ANOVA is a GLM test, we will discuss what the GLM is and how it functions when we talk about regressions in Chapter 20. Now that we have explained the basic purpose of a one-way ANOVA, we will examine an example of a one-way ANOVA.

Case Study Introduction

Have you ever noticed how some rooms just make you feel sleepy or physically drained? What if the color of the room caused this kind of reaction? In this example, a nonverbal communication researcher wants to find out whether the color of a room affects the speed with which a person can take a standard 10-item test. Using the same 10-item test, the researcher places 12 participants randomly into one of three rooms: white, yellow, and blue. When all was said and done, the researcher tested the time (in minutes) for the four participants in the white room, the four participants in the yellow room, and the four participants in the blue room.

In the previous chapter, we examined what was necessary to find a difference between a nominal variable with two levels (e.g., female and male) on an interval/ratio variable (communication apprehension). In this chapter, we will examine what is necessary to find a difference between a nominal variable with two or more levels (white, yellow, and blue) on an interval or ratio variable of some kind (time in minutes to complete the test). To perform this type of test, we calculate what is called a **one-way analysis of variance** (ANOVA).

One-Way ANOVA Background Information

The one-way ANOVA allows researchers to compare two or more groups on an interval variable using one test. If we attempted to do the example here using t tests, we would have to conduct three t tests with three unique null hypotheses:

H_0: $\mu_{white} = \mu_{yellow}$ ← mean time (in minutes) to take a test in the white room is equal to the mean time (in minutes) to take a test in the yellow room.

H_0: $\mu_{white} = \mu_{blue}$ ← mean time (in minutes) to take a test in the white room is equal to the mean time (in minutes) to take a test in the blue room.

H_0: $\mu_{yellow} = \mu_{blue}$ ← mean time (in minutes) to take a test in the yellow room is equal to the mean time (in minutes) to take a test in the blue room.

Although three groups and three t tests may not sound like a bad proposition, if we were comparing seven groups we would need 21 separate t tests. Not only would 21 tests be time-consuming, but, more important, it would also be inherently flawed because in each t test we accept a 5 percent chance of our conclusion being wrong (when we test for $p = 0.05$). So, in 21 tests we would *expect* (by probability) that one test would give us a false result. And, frankly, we do not like those odds at all. In a one-way ANOVA, the null hypothesis reads like this:

$$SS_{total} = \sum x^2 - \frac{G^2}{N} \qquad\qquad df_{total} = N - 1$$

$$SS_{between} = \frac{\sum T^2}{n} - \frac{G^2}{N} \qquad df_{between} = k - 1$$

$$SS_{within} = \sum SS_{\text{inside each treatment}} \qquad df_{within} = N - k$$

$$F = \frac{MS_{between}}{MS_{within}} \quad \text{Where each } MS = \frac{SS}{df}$$

Figure 18.1 One-Way ANOVA Formula

H_0: $\mu_{white} = \mu_{yellow} = \mu_{blue}$ ← mean time (in minutes) to take a test in the white room is equal to the mean time (in minutes) to take a test in the yellow room, which is equal to the mean time (in minutes) to take a test in the blue room.

Your hypothesis would then predict that at least one of the pairs (white and yellow, white and blue, and yellow and blue) is not equal, or

$$H_1: \mu_{white} \neq \mu_{yellow} \neq \mu_{blue}$$

Instead of doing 3 tests or 21 tests, the one-way ANOVA lets us perform one simple test to examine differences.

Now that we have discussed a couple of the basic aspects of the one-way ANOVA itself, we will look at the underlying assumptions of the one-way ANOVA:

1. The dependent variable must be an interval/ratio variable.
2. The independent variable must be a nominal variable.
3. The dependent variable (time to take the test in minutes) should be normally distributed in the independent variable levels (white room, yellow room, and blue room). Specifically, the distributions for all of the populations should not have a high skewness or kurtosis. In a real-world situation, it is recommended that each nominal category have at least 30 participants. (Because we are only performing an example in this chapter, we do not have 30 participants in each category to make the math easier to compute.)
4. The populations for all groupings in the independent variable (white room, yellow room, and blue room) should have equal variances. If the population in the largest group has no more than 1.5 times the number of participants than the number of participants in the smallest group, you will not violate the homogeneity assumption (Stevens, 1986).
5. Finally, the participants contributing data should represent a random sample drawn from the population of interest.

These assumptions are extremely important because if one assumption is violated, the meaning of the one-way ANOVA is lost. Now that we have explained what a one-way ANOVA is and what the basic assumptions of the one-way ANOVA are, we can look at the basic one-way ANOVA formula given in Figure 18.1.

Do not be scared by the formula; it is just as easy to calculate the one-way ANOVA as it was to calculate a chi-square or t test. Most of the one-way ANOVA formula is simply computing some basic descriptive statistics like we did in Chapter 15 and then plugging those answers into the formula as we go along.

Step-by-Step Approach to the One-Way ANOVA

As we discussed earlier, the basic hypothesis being examined in this example is that there is a difference in the time it takes participants to take a test in a white room versus a yellow room versus a blue room. Figure 18.2 portrays the raw data from all 12 participants in this study.

Step 1. The first step in computing a one-way ANOVA is to determine the X for each of the three groups. To find the X or T for each group, you add up each participant's score (in minutes). Figure 18.3 illustrates how this is accomplished.

Step 2. In the next two steps you will calculate the part of the formula represented in Figure 18.4.

The computed value you will attain in this step is called the **sum of squares between** (SSB). The SSB measures two different phenomena: (1) the differences between the groups that have been caused by the treatment effects (i.e., the difference in time it takes the participants to take the 10-item test caused by being in a white, yellow, or blue room) and (2) the differences between the treatments that are simply a result of chance. In this step we will calculate the first part of the SSB formula (T^2/n). To compute this formula, simply take the T values computed in Figure 18.4 and then square them and divide them by the number of participants in each column (4). So to compute the formula (T^2/n) for the white room group, you take the T value found in Step 1 (20) and square that value ($20 \times 20 = 400$). You then take 400 and divide it by n (the number of participants in the group or 4), or 400/4 = 100. So, for the white group, $T^2/n = 100$. You now compute this number for the other two groups as well:

$$T^2/n$$

$$((20)^2/4) + ((28)^2/4) + ((36)^2/4)$$

$$(400/4) + (784/4) + (1,296/4)$$

$$100 + 196 + 324$$

$$620$$

White	Yellow	Blue
5	5	8
6	6	10
5	10	10
4	7	8

Figure 18.2 Participant Scores from Chapter Example

White	Yellow	Blue
5	5	8
6	6	10
5	10	10
4	7	8
T = 5 + 6 + 5 + 4 = 20	5 + 6 + 10 + 7 = 28	8 + 10 + 10 + 8 = 36

Figure 18.3 Step One One-Way ANOVA

$$SS_{between} = \frac{\sum T^2}{n} - \frac{G^2}{N} \qquad df_{between} = k - 1$$

Figure 18.4 Sum of Squares Between Formula

So, $T^2/n = 620$.

Step 3. We now need to compute the part of the SSB formula that is represented by G^2/N. G is represented by the formula T, which is simply taking the T values found in Step 1 and adding them together to create a summed total. The T score for the white room group was 20; the T score for the yellow group was 28; and the T score for the blue group was 36. When you add these three numbers together $(20 + 28 + 36)$, you get a total of 84. Now that we have attained G, we must square that number $(84^2 = 7,056)$. The number we get for G^2 is then divided by the total number of participants in the study $(N = 12)$, or $7,056/12 = 588$.

Step 4. The next step of the one-way ANOVA will give us the actual value for the SSB. To compute the SSB, you must take the value created in Step 2 (620) and subtract it from the value created in Step 3 (588):

$$(T^2/n) - (G^2/N)$$

$$620 - 588 = 32$$

So, for our example, the SSB is equal to 32.

Step 5. In this step we will determine another important part of the one-way ANOVA puzzle called the **sum of squares within** (SSW). Figure 18.5 represents the formula portion for the SS_{within}.

Inside each condition or group tested in a one-way ANOVA we have participants who are treated exactly the same. In other words, the researcher treats all of the participants who take the test in the white room the same, so the researcher does nothing that could cause the individuals to have different scores within that room. When you look at the scores from Figure 18.2, you will see that people in the white room took the test at different speeds. Why did the four people in the white room take the test at different speeds? Well, the only answer that is plausible is that the people in the white room took the test at different speeds purely by chance. In other words, the SSW provides a measure of how much difference in the time it took to take the 10-item test used in this study is simply a result of chance.

To find the SSW, you have to compute a simple formula, which we have done before $SS_{inside\ each\ treatment}$. In other words, for each group of participants, we are going to determine the sum of squares for that group (white, yellow, and blue) and then add the three scores together to come up with the SSW.

To calculate the SSW, you must first find the mean for each group. In Figure 18.3, you take the T value computed for each group and then divide the T value by the number of participants in that group $(n = 4)$. For example, in the white group the T value is equal to 20 and there were 4 participants in the group, so to find the mean you simply divide 20 by 4 $(20/4 = 5)$. You then repeat this procedure for the other two groups: yellow $(28/4 = 7)$ and blue $(36/4 = 9)$.

Once you have the averages computed, you then subtract the individual scores for each participant in a group from the group average and then square that number (like we did in Chapter 15 when we first introduced the sum of squares concept). So, for the white group you take the first participant's score (5) and subtract that score from the mean score (5), or $5 - 5 = 0$. You then take this score (0) and square it. Of course, 0×0 is always going to equal 0. Let's follow the same procedure for the second participant in the white group. Take the second participant's score (6) and subtract that from the mean score (5), or $5 - 6 = -1$. You then take this score (-1) and square it. Of course, -1×-1 is always going to equal 1. Do not forget, when

$$SS_{within} = \Sigma SS_{inside\ each\ treatment} \qquad df_{within} = N - k$$

Figure 17.5 Sum of Squares Within Formula

	Group Average		Participant's Score				
White Room	5	–	5	=	0^2	=	0
	5	–	6	=	-1^2	=	1
	5	–	5	=	0^2	=	0
	5	–	4	=	1^2	=	1
					Sum		2

	Group Average		Participant's Score				
Yellow Room	7	–	5	=	2^2	=	4
	7	–	6	=	1^2	=	1
	7	–	10	=	-3^2	=	9
	7	–	7	=	0^2	=	0
					Sum		14

	Group Average		Participant's Score				
Blue Room	9	–	8	=	1^2	=	1
	9	–	10	=	-1^2	=	1
	9	–	10	=	-1^2	=	1
	9	–	8	=	1^2	=	1
					Sum		4

Figure 18.6 Computing the Sum of Squares Within

you multiply a negative number by a negative number, the two negatives cancel each other out. Let's now take the third participant's score (5) in the white group and subtract that from the mean score (5), or $5 - 5 = 0$. You then take this score (0) and square it. Of course, 0×0 is always going to equal 0. Last, we can take the fifth participant's score (4) in the white group and subtract it from the mean score (5), or $5 - 4 = 1$. You then take this score (1) and square it. Of course, 1×1 is always going to equal 1. You then add these four scores together: $0 + 1 + 0 + 1 = 2$, so the sum of squares for the white room is 2. You can now repeat these steps for both the yellow and the blue room groups. This process has been completed in Figure 18.6.

To compute the overall score for the SSW, you simply take the four scores calculated in Figure 18.5 and add them together ($2 + 14 + 4 = 20$). In our example, the SSW = 20.

Step 6. In this step, we will determine the sum of squares total (SS_{total}). To calculate the SS_{total}, you simply add the $SS_{between}$ from Step 4 (32) and the SS_{within} from Step 5 (20) together:

$$SS_{total} = SS_{between} + SS_{within}$$
$$32 + 20 = 52$$

So for this example, the $SS_{total} = 52$.

Step 7. At this point, we must compute the degrees of freedom for the one-way ANOVA. The one-way ANOVA has two different types of degrees of freedom (between and within). To calculate the between df, the formula is $K - 1$, or the number of groups (white, yellow, and blue) being examined in your study minus one ($3 - 1 = 2$). In this example, the between df = 2. To calculate the within df, the formula is $N - K$, or the total number of participants in a study (12 in our example) minus the number of groups (3 in our example) being examined in your study ($12 - 3 = 9$). In this example, the within df = 9.

Step 8. We can now calculate the two mean squares (MS) in this example. To calculate the **mean squares between** ($MS_{between}$), you divide the $SS_{between}$ calculated in Step 4 (32) by the between df calculated in Step 7 (2), or 32/2 = 16. So, in this example the $MS_{between}$ = 16. To calculate the **mean squares within** (MS_{within}), you divide the SS_{within} calculated in Step 5 (20) by the between df calculated in Step 7 (9), or 20/9 = 2.22. So, in this example the MS_{within} = 2.22.

Step 9. Once we have the $MS_{between}$ and the MS_{within}, we can calculate what is called the F ratio or **F test** value. To calculate the F ratio we simply divide the MS_{within} (2.22) from the $MS_{between}$ (16):

$$F = MS_{between}/MS_{within}$$
$$16/2.22 = 7.20$$

So, for our current example the F value = 7.20. The F value lets us know that the differences among the three groups (white room, yellow room, and blue room) and the time it took the participants to take a 10-item test is more than 7 percent bigger than we would expect to see randomly occurring. This could indicate that, yes, the participants did take the test at different speeds in the differently colored rooms (white, yellow, and blue). However, to truly determine whether a difference exists, we must determine whether the one-way ANOVA is statistically significant.

Step 10. Figure 18.7 contains the F value critical value table. You will notice that this critical value table is different than the other critical value tables we have already seen. On this chart, the df numbers run along the top and down the left-hand side of the table. The df numbers that run along the top of the chart (or the columns) represent the degrees of freedom numerator (**df between**), and the df numbers that are on the left-hand side of the chart (or the rows) represent the degrees of freedom denominator (**df within**). There are two separate

	1	2	3	4	5	6	7	8	9	10
					$\alpha = .05$					
1	161.00	200.00	216.00	225.00	230.00	234.00	237.00	239.00	241.00	242.00
2	18.51	19.00	19.16	19.25	19.30	19.33	19.36	19.37	19.38	19.39
3	10.13	9.55	9.28	9.12	9.01	8.94	8.88	8.84	8.81	8.78
4	7.71	6.94	6.59	6.39	6.26	6.16	6.09	6.04	6.00	5.96
5	6.61	5.79	5.41	5.19	5.05	4.95	4.88	4.82	4.78	4.74
6	5.99	5.14	4.76	4.53	4.39	4.28	4.21	4.15	4.10	4.06
7	5.59	4.74	4.35	4.12	3.97	3.87	3.79	3.73	3.68	3.63
8	5.32	4.46	4.07	3.84	3.69	3.58	3.50	3.44	3.39	3.34
9	5.12	4.26	3.86	3.63	3.48	3.37	3.29	3.23	3.18	3.13
10	4.96	4.10	3.71	3.48	3.33	3.22	3.14	3.07	3.02	2.97
11	4.84	3.98	3.59	3.36	3.20	3.09	3.01	2.95	2.90	2.86
12	4.75	3.88	3.49	3.26	3.11	3.00	2.92	2.85	2.80	2.76
13	4.67	3.80	3.41	3.18	3.02	2.92	2.84	2.77	2.72	2.67
14	4.60	3.74	3.34	3.11	2.96	2.85	2.77	2.70	2.65	2.60
15	4.54	3.68	3.29	3.06	2.90	2.79	2.70	2.64	2.59	2.55
16	4.49	3.63	3.24	3.01	2.85	2.74	2.66	2.59	2.54	2.49
17	4.45	3.59	3.20	2.96	2.81	2.70	2.62	2.55	2.50	2.45
18	4.41	3.55	3.16	2.93	2.77	2.66	2.58	2.51	2.46	2.41
19	4.38	3.52	3.13	2.90	2.74	2.63	2.55	2.48	2.43	2.38
20	4.35	3.49	3.10	2.87	2.71	2.60	2.52	2.45	2.40	2.35

Figure 18.7 Critical Values of the *F* Distribution

$\alpha = .01$

	1	2	3	4	5	6	7	8	9	10
1	4052.00	4999.00	5403.00	5625.00	5764 .00	5859.00	928.00	5981.00	6022.00	6056.00
2	98.49	99.01	99.17	99.25	99.30	99.33	99.34	99.36	99.38	99.40
3	34.12	30.81	29.46	28.71	28.24	27.91	27.67	27.49	27.34	27.23
4	21.20	18.00	16.69	15.98	15.52	15.21	14.98	14.80	14.66	14.54
5	16.26	13.27	12.06	11.39	10.97	10.67	10.45	10.27	10.15	10.05
6	13.74	10.92	9.78	9.15	8.75	8.47	8.26	8.10	7.98	7.87
7	12.25	9.55	8.45	7.85	7.46	7.19	7.00	6.84	6.71	6.62
8	11.26	8.65	7.59	7.01	6.63	6.37	6.19	6.03	5.91	5.82
9	10.56	8.02	6.99	6.42	6.06	5.80	5.62	5.47	5.35	5.26
10	10.04	7.56	6.55	5.99	5.64	5.39	5.21	5.06	4.95	4.85
11	9.65	7.20	6.22	5.67	5.32	5.07	4.88	4.74	4.63	4.54
12	9.33	6.93	5.95	5.41	5.06	4.82	4.65	4.50	4.39	4.30
13	9.07	6.70	5.74	5.20	4.86	4.62	4.44	4.30	4.19	4.10
14	8.86	6.51	5.56	5.03	4.69	4.46	4.28	4.14	4.03	3.94
15	8.68	6.36	5.42	4.89	4.56	4.32	4.14	4.00	3.89	3.80
16	8.53	6.23	5.29	4.77	4.44	4.20	4.03	3.89	3.78	3.69
17	8.40	6.11	5.18	4.67	4.34	4.10	3.93	3.79	3.68	3.59
18	8.28	6.01	5.09	4.58	4.25	4.01	3.85	3.71	3.60	3.51
19	8.18	5.93	5.01	4.50	4.17	3.94	3.77	3.63	3.52	3.43
20	8.10	5.85	4.94	4.43	4.10	3.87	3.71	3.56	3.45	3.37

The entries in this table were computed by the authors.

Source	df	SS	MS	F	p
Between	2	32	16	7.20	.05
Within	9	20	2.22		
Total	11	108			

Figure 18.8 ANOVA Summary Table

charts presented in Figure 18.7. The first chart examines the critical values at $p < 0.05$, and the second chart examines the critical values at $p < 0.01$. To analyze this chart, we need to remember the $df_{between}$ (2) and df_{within} (9) we calculated in Step 7. To determine our critical value to compare to our calculated value (7.20), we must go to the second column ($df_{between}$) and then go down to the ninth row (df_{within}). The critical value for F at $p < 0.05$ is 4.26. Since our calculated F value (7.20) is larger than the critical value of 4.26, we are statistically significant at the $p < 0.05$ level. To determine whether we are statistically significant at the $p < 0.01$ significance level (the second chart in Figure 18.7), we must go to the second column ($df_{between}$) and then go down to the ninth row (df_{within}) to find the critical value, which is 8.02. Because our calculated F value (7.20) is smaller than the critical value of 8.02, we are not statistically significant at the $p < 0.01$ level.

Step 11. The last step of the one-way ANOVA calculation is to create what is called an ANOVA summary table. Figure 18.8 is the ANOVA summary table for this example.

The ANOVA summary table arranges information that you have calculated in an easy-to-understand chart format. All of the basic information you need about the calculation of a one-way ANOVA can be found on this chart.

Computer Printouts of the One-Way ANOVA

Now that we have examined how a one-way ANOVA can be calculated by hand, we will examine what output from two statistical computer programs, SPSS and Excel, looks like.

SPSS AND ONE-WAY ANOVAS

Using SPSS to compute a one-way ANOVA is fairly easy as long as you follow the instructions, so let's get started. First, open your SPSS student version and then locate the file on the textbook's website in the SPSS folder called "One-Way ANOVA." When you open this file you will see two variables listed: "color" and "time." Color is the variable name given to the variable that contains the three room colors. Note, however, that the colors are only represented by the numbers 1 (white), 2 (yellow), and 3 (blue). Remember, a statistics program can only understand numbers, so it is up to you as a researcher to remember how you classified the two groups when you are inputting the data. The "time" variable is the amount of time in minutes it took each participant to complete the 10-item quiz.

To conduct the one-way ANOVA, go to the menu bar at the top of your screen and click on "Analyze" (Figure 18.9). When you click on "Analyze," a drop-down menu will appear. Go to the fifth category on this menu, "General Linear Model," and scroll over the arrow and another menu will appear to the right. The first option on the "General Linear Model" menu is "Univariate"; click on it (Figure 18.10). At this point, the "Univariate" dialogue box will appear on your screen (Figure 18.11a). On this screen you will see six boxes. The first box, on the left-hand side of the "Univariate" dialogue box, will contain your variables. To the right, on top is the "Dependent Variable" box, which is where dependent variables are placed (time). To place the variable "time" in this box, click and highlight in blue the variable time. When time is highlighted blue, click the right arrow button next to the "Dependent Variable" box (Figure 18.11b). Below that box is the "Fixed Factor(s)" box, which is where you place your

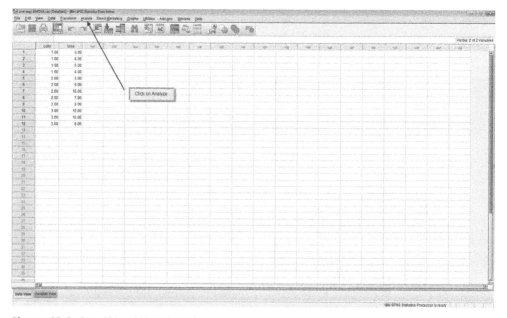

Figure 18.9 One-Way ANOVA Main

nominal independent variable (color). To place the variable "color" in this box, click and highlight in blue the variable color. When color is highlighted blue, click the right arrow button next to the "Fixed Factor(s)" box (Figure 18.11c).

To the right of those boxes, you will see six buttons: "Model," "Contrasts," "Plots," "Post Hoc," "Save," and "Options." Click on the button called "Post Hoc." The "Univariate: Post Hoc Multiple Comparisons for Observed Means" dialogue box will appear on your screen (Figure 18.11d). First, you must select the Factor(s) you want to compute a post hoc analysis

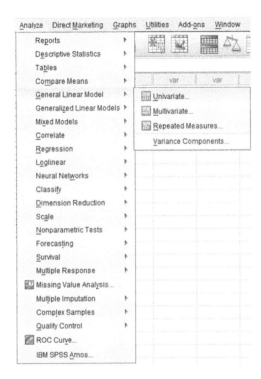

Figure 18.10 Univariate GLM Menu

a) Main Dialogue Box

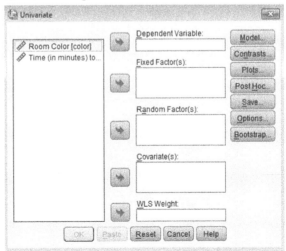

Figure 18.11 Univariate Dialogue Box

Continued

Continued

b) Move the Dependent Variable to the DV Box

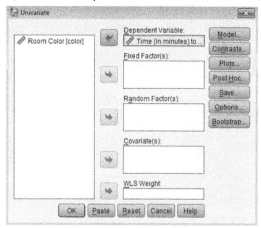

c) Move the Independent Variable to the "Fixed Factor(s)" Box

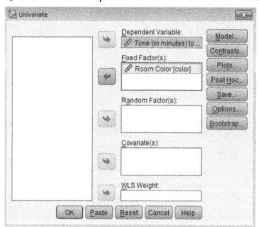

d) Univariate Post Hoc Dialogue Box

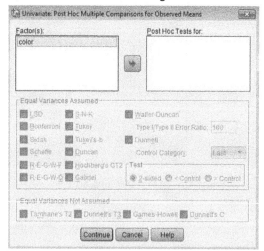

e) Shift Independent Variable to "Post Hoc Tests for:" Box

f) Select Desired Post Hoc Analyses

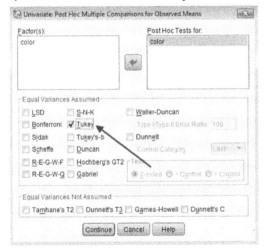

g) "Univariate: Options" Dialogue Box

Continued

Continued

h) Send Independent Variable (Color) to "Display Means for:" Box

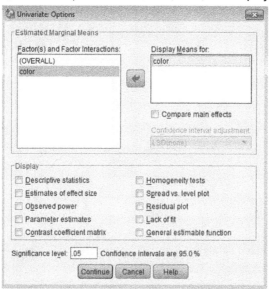

I) Select Desired Options

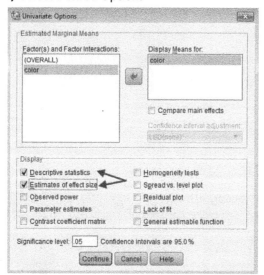

for by selecting the variable (color) and clicking the arrow between the "Factor(s)" box and the "Post Hoc Tests for" box. After you have sent your Factor variable over to the "Post Hoc Tests for" box, you will note that the various post hoc tests are now active (Figure 18.11e). In this box, there are two groupings for post hoc tests. One grouping is for "Equal Variances Assumed" and one is for "Equal Variances Not Assumed." We will go into more detail in a few minutes about post hoc tests, but for now, put a checkmark in the box next to the "Tukey" post hoc test under the "Equal Variances Assumed" list (it is the second one in the second column). Once "Tukey" is checked (Figure 18.11f), you can push the button at the bottom of the screen marked "Continue."

You should now have returned to the "Univariate" dialogue box. Now press the sixth button at the bottom of the dialogue box marked "Options." In the "Options" dialogue box, you will find two boxes on top and a variety of options at the bottom (Figure 18.11g). To have any options performed, you must select the variable (color) you want options for on the left in the "Factor(s) and Factor Interactions" box and send the variable over to the right box "Display Means for" by selecting the variable and pushing the arrow button between the two boxes. Once "color" is in the "Display Means for" box, we can then select a variety of options at the bottom of the page (Figure 18.11h). The bottom box is called the "Display" box and contains two items we must check at this point: "Descriptive Statistics" and "Estimates of Effect Size." Once you have selected "Descriptive Statistics" and "Estimates of Effect Size" (Figure 18.11i), click on the "Continue" button. Once you are back to the "Univariate" dialogue box, click the "OK" button to run the results. The results (excluding the post hoc) can be seen in Figure 18.12.

The results for the SPSS printouts are straightforward at this point. If you examine the three tables printed in Figure 18.12, you will see that the first table contains information about the independent variable, the second table contains simple descriptive statistics for the dependent variable, and the third table contains much of the same information as the ANOVA

Univariate Analysis of Variance

Between-Subjects Factors

		Value Label	N
Room	1.00	White	4
Color	2.00	Yellow	4
	3.00	Blue	4

Descriptive Statistics

Dependent Variable: Time (in minutes) to finish the test.

Room Color	Mean	Std. Deviation	N
White	5.0000	.8165	4
Yellow	7.0000	2.1602	4
Blue	9.0000	1.1547	4
Total	7.0000	2.1742	12

Test of Between-Subjects Effects

Dependent Variable: Time (in minutes) to finish the test.

Source	Type III Sum of Squares	df	Mean Square	F	Sig.	Eta Squares
Corrected Model	32.000[a]	2	16.000	7.200	.014	.615
Intercept	588.000	1	588.000	264.600	.000	.967
COLOR	32.000	2	16.000	7.200	.014	.615
Error	20.000	9	2.222			
Total	640.000	12				
Corrected Total	52.000	11				

[a.] R Squared = .615 (Adjusted R Squared = .530)

Figure 18.12 SPSS One-Way ANOVA Results

summary table we created in Step 11 earlier in this chapter. The third row, "COLOR," is the row that contains the information we calculated by hand earlier in this chapter. The major difference between the information contained in the SPSS ANOVA summary table and the one in Figure 18.8 is that the SPSS table gives you an exact calculation of the significance level ($p = 0.014$) and SPSS also calculates the effect size for the difference seen in the test ($\eta^2 = 0.615$). **Eta-square** (η^2) ranges from 0 to 1, with 0 indicating that there is no difference and 1 indicating that there is a difference between the groups but not a difference in scores within the groups. To interpret η^2, researchers rely on the following interpretation:

0.01—small effect size

0.06—medium effect size

0.14—large effect size

In this example, our effect size was 0.62, so we could say that there is a large proportion of the variance within the dependent variable (time it took to take the test) related to one of the groups (white, yellow, or blue). Based on this, we can conclude that a large portion of the time it took someone to fill out the survey was dependent on the color of room the participant was in. However, at this point, we cannot say which room had the most impact, so a multiple comparison test is needed.

One part of the one-way ANOVA that we did not calculate by hand is the **multiple comparison test**. At this point, all we know is that our one-way ANOVA test is significant (people take tests in different colored rooms at different speeds), but we do not know where those differences are. Maybe people in white rooms take tests slower than people in blue rooms but not slower than people in yellow rooms. Maybe people in yellow rooms take tests at similar speeds to people in white and blue rooms, but people in white rooms take tests faster than people in blue rooms. If you remember the null hypothesis we created at the beginning of this chapter, we wrote: "H_0: $\mu_{white} = \mu_{yellow} = \mu_{blue}$ ← mean time (in minutes) to take a test in the white room is equal to the mean time (in minutes) to take a test in the yellow room, which is equal to the mean time (in minutes) to take a test in the blue room." Your hypothesis would then predict that *at least one of the pairs* (white and yellow, white and blue, and yellow and blue) is not equal, or H_1: $\mu_{white} \neq \mu_{yellow} \neq \mu_{blue}$." Note that the boldfaced portion emphasizes that at least one pair will be different, but not all three different from each other. For this reason, when conducting a one-way ANOVA with an independent variable that has three or more levels (white, yellow, and blue), we must determine where the difference(s) actually exists. Because we cannot make these judgments based on a simple one-way ANOVA, we must conduct a post hoc (after-the-fact) multiple comparison test.

Multiple Comparison Tests

In the t test, we were able to compare the two groups directly to each other, which we can also do with a one-way ANOVA if, and only if, the nominal variable being used as the independent variable has two groups (such as females and males). If the nominal variable has more than two groups (like our example), the one-way ANOVA will determine whether at least one pair within a group is different from each other, but we will not know which pair is different until we perform a multiple comparison test. For example, if we are comparing three groups (white, yellow, and blue), a statistically significant one-way ANOVA will let us know whether these three groups differ in their means on a dependent variable. However, a one-way ANOVA will not say that people in the white room took more time to take the test than people in the blue room. To determine where the difference lies, a second test, the multiple comparison test, is conducted, which compares white and yellow, white and blue, and yellow and blue. The multiple comparison test then tells us where the specific difference actually lies.

If you remember from the SPSS steps above, when you entered into the "One-Way ANOVA: Post Hoc Multiple Comparisons" dialogue box, SPSS provides you with 18 different types of multiple comparison tests broken into two groups: "Equal Variances Assumed" and "Equal Variances Not Assumed." The four most common post hoc tests for a one-way ANOVA are **Fisher's Least Significant Difference (LSD)**, **Student Newman-Keuls (SNK)**, **Tukey's Honestly Significance Difference Test (Tukey)**, and **Scheffé (Scheffe)**. The order presented here (LSD, SNK, Tukey, and Scheffe) is a continuum from liberal to conservative post hoc tests. Liberal tests are called such because they make it easier to find significant differences between groups (white room, yellow room, and blue room). However, with a liberal test your chance of type I error also increases, so they should always be used with caution. Conservative tests make it harder to find significant differences between groups, and you have less of a chance of type I error. We will briefly explain the four post hoc tests. First, Fisher's LSD is the equivalent of running a series of paired t tests, but the alpha level is not controlled for, so the chance of compounded error is great. Second, SNK is a stepwise test for ordered means where the alpha level depends on the number of "steps apart" each of the means are from each other. This test is great when your data consist of ranges, but is not useful for pairwise comparisons. Furthermore, the SNK post hoc has more power, so you are more likely to find significant pairwise comparisons (Seaman, Levin, & Serlin, 1991). However, when you attempt to increase power, you run the risk of increasing your type I risk. Third, unlike the SNK, the Tukey HSD is able to test for pairwise comparisons while controlling your type I error and generating confidence intervals (Seaman et al., 1991). Finally, the Scheffé post hoc test assumes you wish to test all possible pairs and all possible combinations of means. For example, if you have three means, then there are six possible comparisons (white vs. blue, white vs. yellow, blue vs. yellow, white + blue vs. yellow, white + yellow vs. blue, and yellow + blue vs. white). The only real reason to use the Scheffé post hoc test is if you really need to examine all six possible combinations. For these reasons, we generally recommend using the Tukey HSD. The results for the post hoc analysis we selected earlier (Tukey HSD) can be seen in Figure 18.13.

In the "Multiple Comparisons" box in Figure 18.13, we see that the three colors are compared to each other. The first row compares people who took the test in the white room to people who took the test in the yellow and blue rooms. The second column in the "Multiple Comparisons" box is labeled "Mean Difference I-J," with "I" being the white room and "J" being both people in the yellow and people in the blue rooms. In essence, what this first row is testing is whether people in the white room took longer or less time to take the 10-item test than people in the yellow room and whether people in the white room took longer or less time to take the 10-item test than people in the blue room. The first room that the white room is compared to is the yellow room. If you look in the "Mean Difference" column, you will note that there is a mean difference between the two of –2.000. If a mean difference is negative, then the mean time spent taking the 10-item test in the group in the "I" column (in this case people in the white room) is less than the group it is being compared to in the "J" column (or yellow). However, people in the white room took less time to complete the test than people in the yellow room. The fourth column in the "Multiple Comparisons" SPSS printout box indicates that the significance is $p = 0.195$, which is not statistically significant. In other words, there is not a significant difference between the time it took people in the white and yellow rooms to complete the 10-item test.

At this point, we have used the first row on the "Multiple Comparisons" SPSS printout box to compare people in white rooms with people in yellow rooms. We now need to

Post Hoc Tests

Room Color

Multiple Comparisons

Dependent Variable: Time (in minutes) to finish the test.
Tukey HSD

(I) Room Color	(J) Room Color	Mean Difference (I-J)	Std. Error	Sig.	95% Confidence Interval	
					Lower Bound	Upper Bound
White	Yellow	-2.0000	1.0541	.195	-4.9431	.9431
	Blue	-4.0000*	1.0541	.011	-6.9431	-1.0569
Yellow	White	2.0000	1.0541	.195	-.9431	4.9431
	Blue	-2.0000	1.0541	.195	-4.9431	.9431
Blue	White	4.0000*	1.0541	.011	1.0569	6.9431
	Yellow	2.0000	1.0541	.195	-.9431	4.9431

Based on observed means.
 * The mean difference is significant at the .05 level.

Homogeneous Subsets

Time (in minutes) to finish the test.

Tukey HSD[a,b]

Room Color	N	Subset	
		1	2
White	4	5.0000	
Yellow	4	7.0000	7.0000
Blue	4		9.0000
Sig.		.195	.195

Means for groups in homogeneous subsets are displayed.
Based on Type III Sum of Squares
The error term is Mean Square(Error) = 2.222.
 [a] Uses Harmonic Mean Sample Size = 4.000.
 [b] Alpha = .05.

Figure 18.13 SPSS One-Way ANOVA Post Hoc Test

compare people in white rooms with people in blue rooms. On the first row, the second variable listed under the "J-Room Color" is blue. If you look in the "Mean Difference" column, you will see that there is a mean difference between white and blue of −4.000. Again this means that people in the white room took the test 4 minutes faster than the people in the blue room. You will note that next to the −4.000 beside blue in the "Mean Difference" column is an asterisk (*). SPSS automatically flags significant multiple comparisons if they are at the $p < 0.05$ level. In this case, the significance level listed in the fourth column of the "Multiple Comparisons" SPSS printout box was $p = 0.011$. At this point, we have found out that people in the white and yellow rooms did not complete the test at significantly different rates, but people in the white room did complete the test significantly faster than people in the blue room. At this point, there is only one other pairing that we have not examined; we have not examined whether people in yellow and blue rooms took the test at different speeds.

The second row in the "Multiple Comparisons" SPSS printout box now has yellow in the "(I) Room Color" column and white and blue in the "(J) Room Color" column. The first comparison that can be made compares yellow to white, but we did this comparison already so we are not concerned with it here. All of the comparisons are done twice in the printout, so be careful not to report both sets of multiple comparisons. Once you have reported the comparison between white and yellow, you do not need to report it a second time. In this case, we are only interested in the comparison between yellow and blue. Yet again, the mean difference between yellow and blue is –2.000, which indicates that people in the yellow room took the test on average 2 minutes faster than people in the blue room; however, this is not a significant difference, $p = 0.195$.

EXCEL AND ONE-WAY ANOVAS

To compute the one-way ANOVA in Excel, begin by locating the "One-Way ANOVA" spreadsheet on the textbook's website. After opening the file, you will see two columns of data. The "color" column represents the three room colors (1 = white, 2 = yellow, and 3 = blue). The column labeled "time" represents the number of minutes required to complete a 10-item quiz. First, you must separate out the time it took to take the test into three distinct columns. Excel needs the three groups separated into distinct columns (Figure 18.14). Next, click on the "Data" file tab at the top of the spreadsheet, select "Data Analysis" from the right side of the screen, and choose "Anova: Single Factor" from the drop-down menu (Figure 18.15). Highlight all the data included in cells D1 through F5. The data range will appear in the box labeled "Input Range." Be sure the "Columns," "Labels in First Row," and "New Worksheet Ply" options are all selected (Figure 18.15). Excel sets the Alpha default at 0.05, but this can be adjusted if you choose to do so. Click "OK" to proceed to the output worksheet (Figure 18.16).

APA WRITE-UP (WITHOUT CHART)

This research question wanted to determine whether there was a significant difference in the color of a room (white, yellow, and blue) and the length of time (in minutes) it took the participant to finish a 10-item test. A one-way ANOVA was calculated using the color of the room as the independent variable and length of time to finish the test (in minutes) as the dependent variable. A significant difference was noted: $F(2, 9) = 7.20$, $p < 0.001$, $\eta^2 = 0.62$. In a follow-up to this question, a Tukey HSD post hoc was conducted. The Tukey HSD post hoc indicated that there was a significant difference between people in the white room ($M = 5$, $SD = 0.82$) and people in the blue room ($M = 9$, $SD = 1.15$). However, the Tukey HSD post hoc test did not find a significant difference between people who took the test in the white room ($M = 5$, $SD = 0.82$) and people who took the test in the yellow room ($M = 7$, $SD = 2.16$), and the Tukey HSD also did not find a significant difference between people in the yellow room ($M = 7$, $SD = 2.16$) and people in the blue room ($M = 9$, $SD = 1.15$).

APA WRITE-UP (WITH CHART)

This research question wanted to determine whether there was a significant difference in the color of a room (white, yellow, and blue) and the length of time (in minutes) it took the participant to finish a 10-item test. A one-way ANOVA was calculated using the color of the room as the independent variable and length of time to finish the test (in minutes) as the dependent variable. A significant difference was noted: $F(2, 9) = 7.20$, $p < 0.05$, $\eta^2 = 0.62$. In a follow-up

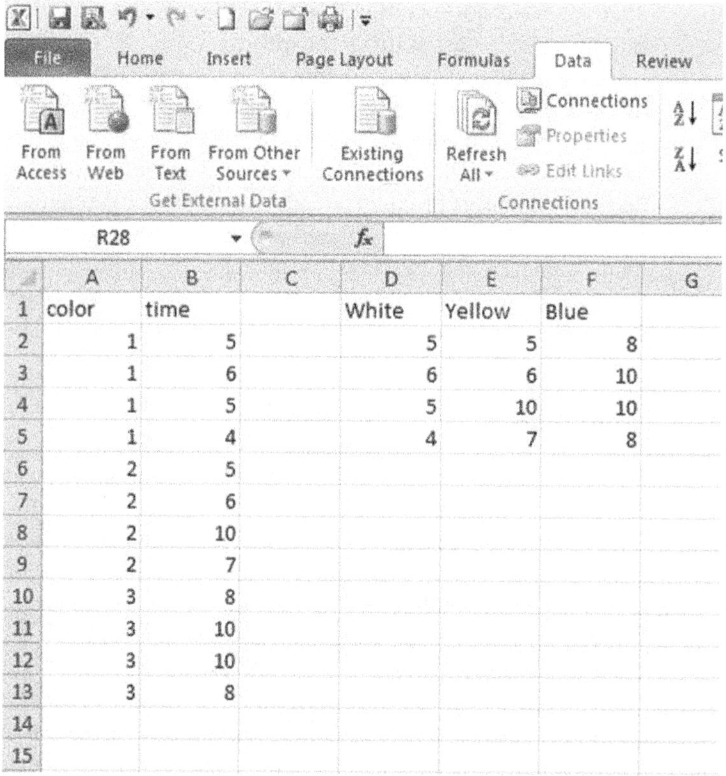

Figure 18.14 Select ANOVA: Single Factor

Figure 18.15 "ANOVA: Single Factor" Dialogue Box

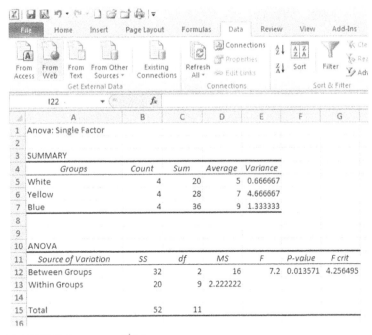

Figure 18.16 ANOVA Summary Table

to this question, a Tukey HSD post hoc was conducted. Figure 18.13 examines the exact differences that were noted.

DISCUSSION OF FINDINGS

After all of the work that we have done so far in this chapter, this is the point where we get to try to make some sense out of the results. To do this, let's go back to the initial question we asked. We wanted to determine whether the color of a room (white, yellow, or blue) caused people to take a 10-item test at different speeds. After calculating the one-way ANOVA, we found that the color of a room does cause people to take a 10-item test at different speeds. Based on this information, we performed a Tukey HSD post hoc analysis to see where that difference actually existed. Based on the Tukey HSD, we can say that people in white rooms and yellow rooms will take tests at roughly the same speed. We can also say that people in yellow rooms and blue rooms will take tests at roughly the same speed. However, we found out that people in white rooms finish tests faster than people in blue rooms. Now that we have completed a hypothetical example of a one-way ANOVA, we will examine results from an actual sample.

Political Affiliation and Humor Assessment

The purpose of this example was to see whether differences existed among political affiliations (Democrat, Republican, other, or not registered to vote) and an individual's humor assessment. Call this an "Are Democrats really funnier than Republicans?" question. To test for a possible difference among Democrats, Republicans, people belonging to other political parties, and people not registered to vote on the humor assessment inventory, we used the nominal variable politics (independent variable) and the interval variable humor assessment (dependent variable). Figure 18.17 represents the findings from the SPSS results.

APA WRITE-UP

This research question tests for a possible difference among Democrats, Republicans, people belonging to other political parties, and people not registered to vote on their reported levels of humor assessment. A one-way ANOVA was calculated using the four political party groupings as the independent variable and humor assessment as the dependent variable. The test was not significant: $F(3, 312) = 0.36$, $p = 078$.

DISCUSSION

For the test examining political affiliation and humor assessment, the p value was greater than 0.05, so the test was not statistically significant. It is important to note that once a test is reported as not statistically significant, we do not report either the eta-square or the post hoc analysis. We do not report the eta-square because eta-square is an effect size. When we say that the test is not statistically significant, we are saying that there is no effect, so reporting the effect size is meaningless. The same is also true for why we do not report post hoc analyses. We only run a post hoc analysis if the overall model is statistically significant. Once the one-way ANOVA model is shown to be not statistically significant, there is no reason to run a post hoc analysis.

Discussion of the Boiarsky et al. Article

To help you further understand the concept of the one-way ANVOA, we have included an article on the textbook's website that utilizes the one-way ANOVA in a unique way. The 1999 article by Greg Boiarsky, Marilee Long, and Greg Thayer entitled "Formal Features in

Univariate Analysis of Variance

Between-Subjects Factors

		Value Label	N
Political Affiliation	1.00	Democrat	217
	2.00	Republican	217
	3.00	Other	131
	4.00	Not Registered to Vote	63

Descriptive Statistics

Dependent Variable: Humor Assessment

Political Affiliation	Mean	Std. Deviation	N
Democrat	63.7373	9.63405	217
Republican	62.8940	9.84523	217
Other	63.4198	9.08418	131
Not Registered to Vote	62.7143	8.84532	63
Total	63.2771	9.50646	628

Figure 18.17 SPSS Results of Political Affiliation with Humor Assessment

Tests of Between-Subjects Effects

Dependent Variable: Humor Assessment

Source	Type III Sum of Squares	df	Mean Square	F	Sig.	Partial Eta Squared
Corrected Model	100.434[a]	3	33.478	.369	.775	.002
Intercept	1952449.491	1	1952449.491	21539.183	.000	.972
politics	100.434	3	33.478	.369	.775	.002
Error	56563.355	624	90.646			
Total	2571168.000	628				
Corrected Total	56663.790	627				

[a] R Squared = .002 (Adjusted R Squared = -.003)

Estimated Marginal Means

Political Affiliation

Dependent Variable: Humor Assessment

Political Affiliation	Mean	Std. Error	95% Confidence Interval	
			Lower Bound	Upper Bound
Democrat	63.737	.646	62.468	65.007
Republican	62.894	.646	61.625	64.163
Other	63.420	.832	61.786	65.053
Not Registered to Vote	62.714	1.200	60.359	65.070

Children's Science Television: Sound Effects, Visual Pace, and Topic Shifts" can be found in the folder titled "Articles." To view this article, you will need to download a copy of the Adobe Acrobat Reader (http://www.adobe.com/products/reader.html/) if you do not already have this program installed on your computer. We strongly encourage you to read the article first and then read our analysis of the article. The goal of this process is to ensure you understand how to read and interpret research results related to one-way ANOVAs.

ARTICLE PURPOSE

Children love television. Most of us have been raised on some form of child-centric television. Whether it was the *Muppets*, *Sesame Street*, *Mr. Rogers*, or *Captain Kangaroo*, we all enjoyed entertainment with a lesson. More recently, a new breed of children's television has surfaced known as children's science television. The purpose of this study was to determine whether four different children's television shows (*Beakman's World*, *Bill Nye the Science Guy*, *Magic School Bus*, and *Newton's Apple*) differed in their use of sound effects per minute, cuts per minute, fades/dissolves per minute, wipes per minute, and topic shifts per minute.

METHODOLOGY

In this study, the researchers analyzed a sampling the four children's science television shows during the 1995–1996 season. The shows were then coded to examine sound effects per minute, cuts per minute, fades/dissolves per minute, wipes per minute, and topic shifts per minute. To test for reliable program attribute coding, two independent researchers coded content pacing, sound effects, and visual pacing with Cohen's kappas ranging from 0.77 to 1.0. Although the 0.77 (content pacing's Cohen's kappas ranged from 0.77 to 0.87) is somewhat suspect (see Chapter 10 for information on intercoder reliability), all of the other coding was strong.

RESULTS

The researchers ran a series of five one-way ANOVAs using the four children's television shows (*Beakman's World*, *Bill Nye the Science Guy*, *Magic School Bus*, and *Newton's Apple*) as the independent variable and the program attributes (sound effects per minute, cuts per minute, fades/dissolves per minute, wipes per minute, and topic shifts per minute) as the dependent variables. All five of their one-way ANOVAs were significant. One problem with this article is seen in the reporting of the post hoc analyses. Although the authors do a good job explaining which television shows they perceive to have higher levels of specific program attributes, they do not explain what type of post hoc analysis was completed. Although this article was set up nicely overall, its discussion of the post hoc analyses used needed some help.

One-way ANOVAs Outside Academia

One-way ANOVAs are a common statistical tool for researches both inside and outside of academia. Maybe you are the head of a training and development department and you want to determine whether the time it takes to complete a task differs based on the type of training an employee has taken. For our purposes, you offer three different types of training: fully face-to-face, fully online, and a blended approach of both online and face-to-face training (one nominal variable with three levels). After people have completed their training, you could then examine the time it takes to complete a task (dependent variable).

Another example of using one-way ANOVAs outside of academia could be to test all of the major types of produce (apples, oranges, bananas, pears, other) and their sales rates. Through this one-way ANOVA, you could determine which form of produce is selling the best at your store if there is a statistical difference, or you could find out that your customers purchase produce in fairly equal amounts, when no statistical difference is found. One-way ANOVAs are often used when determining how different items measure up against one another when it comes to sales. When you have a limited amount of shelf space, know what your customers want can be beneficial.

A third example of using a one-way ANOVA outside of academia would be to determine whether different groups within an organization (lower-level works, upper-level workers, mid-level management, and upper-level management) differ in their perceptions of any number of **key performance indicators**, or quantifiable measures that help organizational decision makers evaluate organizational performance (e.g., meeting or exceeding strategic and organizational goals). For example, you could look for differences among these four groups on job satisfaction, employee motivation, productivity, etc.

Conclusion

In this chapter, we have examined how to compute a one-way ANOVA by hand, how to compute and interpret computer results of a one-way ANOVA in both SPSS and Excel, and how to write up a one-way ANOVA using APA style. We have seen the one-way ANOVA used in three different examples. Later in this book, we will discuss different types of ANOVAs (Chapter 21). For now, we are going to turn our attention to the next statistical test in this book, the correlation.

KEY TERMS

Degrees of freedom (df) between

Degrees of freedom (df) Within

Eta-square (η^2)

F test

Fisher's least significant difference (LSD)

General linear model

Key performance indicator

Mean squares between

Mean squares within

Multiple comparison tests

One-way analysis of variance

Scheffé

Student Newman–Keuls (SNK)

Sum of squares between

Sum of squares within

Tukey's honestly significant difference test (Tukey HSD)

REFERENCES

Boiarsky, G., Long, M., & Thayer, G. (1999). Formal features in children's science television: Sound effects, visual pace, and topic shifts. *Communication Research Reports, 16*, 185–192.

Seaman, M. A., Levin, J. R., & Serlin, R. C. (1991). New developments in pairwise multiple comparisons: Some powerful and practicable procedures. *Psychological Bulletin, 110*, 577–586.

FURTHER READING

Abramson, J. H., & Abramson, Z. H. (2001). *Making sense of data: A self-instruction manual on the interpretation of epidemiological data* (3rd ed.). New York, NY: Oxford University Press.

Bruning, J. L., & Kintz, B. L. (1997). *Computational handbook of statistics* (4th ed.). New York, NY: Longman.

Cortina, J. M., & Nouri, H. (1999). *Effect size for ANOVA designs.* Thousand Oaks, CA: Sage.

Fox, J., & Weisberg, S. (2011). *An R companion to applied regression* (2nd ed.). Los Angeles, CA: Sage.

Gravetter, F. J., & Wallnau, L. B. (2000). *Statistics for the behavioral sciences* (5th ed.). Belmont, CA: Wadsworth/Thomson Learning.

Green, S. B., & Salkind, N. J. (2004). *Using SPSS for Windows and Macintosh: Analyzing and understanding data* (4th ed.). Upper Saddle River, NJ: Prentice Hall.

Hocking, J. E., Stacks, D. W., & McDermott, S. T. (2003). *Communication research* (3rd ed.). Boston, MA: Allyn & Bacon.

Hogan, T. P. (2010). *Bare-bones R: A brief introductory guide.* Los Angeles, CA: Sage.

Howell, D. C. (1997). *Statistical methods for psychology* (4th ed.). Belmont, CA: Duxbury Press.

Iversen, G. R., & Norpoth, H. (2004). *Analysis of variance* (2nd ed.). Thousand Oaks, CA: Sage.

Keller, D. K. (2006). *The Tao of statistics: A path to understanding (with no math).* Thousand Oaks, CA: Sage.

Muenchen, R. A. (2009). *R for SAS and SPSS users.* New York, NY: Springer.

Salkind, N. J. (2004). *Statistics for people who (think they) hate statistics* (2nd ed.). Thousand Oaks, CA: Sage.

Salkind, N. J. (2011). *Excel statistics: A quick guide.* Los Angeles, CA: Sage.

Scheffé, H. (1959). *The analysis of variance.* New York, NY: Wiley.

Singleton, R. A., Jr., & Straits, B. C. (1999). *Approach to social research* (3rd ed.). New York, NY: Oxford University Press.

Stevens, J. (1986). *Applied multivariate statistics for the social sciences.* Hillsdale, NJ: Erlbaum.

Tabachnick, B. G., & Fidell, L. S. (2001). *Using multivariate statistics* (4th ed.). Boston, MA: Allyn & Bacon.

Trochim, W. M. K. (2000). *The research methods knowledge base* (2nd ed.). Cincinnati, OH: Atomic Dog. http://www.socialresearchmethods.net/

Turner, J. R., & Thayer, J. (2001). *Introduction to analysis of variance: Design, analysis, & interpretation.* Thousand Oaks, CA: Sage.

Weiss, D. J. (2005). *Analysis of variance and functional measurement: A practical guide.* New York, NY: Oxford University Press.

CHAPTER **19**

Correlation

CHAPTER OBJECTIVES

1   Describe the different types of relationships (positive, negative, curvilinear, and neutral).
2   Explain the purposes of a correlation.
3   Evaluate the idea that correlation does not equal causation.
4   Calculate a correlation by hand.
5   Conduct a correlation using both SPSS and Excel.
6   Interpret the printouts associated with a correlation.
7   Examine a real-world correlation analysis using the textbook's dataset.
8   Interpret large correlation tables.
9   Analyze the use of the correlations in the articles by Cheseboro (1999) and Punyanunt (2000).

In the previous chapter, we examined one-way ANOVA, which utilized one nominal variable (with two or more groups) and one interval/ratio variable. In fact, the first three tests examined (chi-square, *t* test, and one-way ANOVA) all utilized nominal variables to examine differences between groups. The correlation is not a difference test, so it does not utilize nominal variables at all. Instead, the Pearson product-moment correlation uses two interval/ratio variables.

The **Pearson product-moment correlation coefficient** (*r*) is a measure of the degree to which two quantitative variables (Likert/ratio) are linearly related in a sample (changes in one variable correspond to changes in another variable). To conduct a Pearson product-moment correlation, a researcher must obtain two scores (one for each variable) from each participant. If the correlation coefficient (*r*) is significant, there exists some type of relationship between the two variables. However, if the correlation coefficient (*r*) is not significant, then we cannot draw any conclusions about the nature of the relationship between the two variables. Let's look at a communication-related example in which the Pearson product-moment correlation could be used.

Correlation Background Information

The basic purpose of a correlation is to determine the relationship between two independent variables. In statistics, four types of relationships are theoretically possible. The purpose of a correlation is to measure whether as the score on one variable changes (goes up or down), the score on a second variable also changes (goes up or down). The four types of relationships are illustrated in Figure 19.1.

TYPES OF RELATIONSHIPS

The first type of relationship a researcher can find between two variables is called a positive relationship, or positive correlation. Figure 19.1a is an example of a positive correlation. In this example, you have two variables: humor assessment and popularity. This example is a positive relationship because as a person's use of interpersonal humor increases, so does her or his

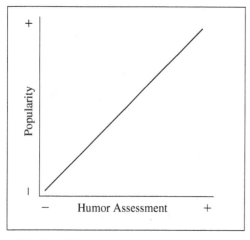

(a) Positive Relationship

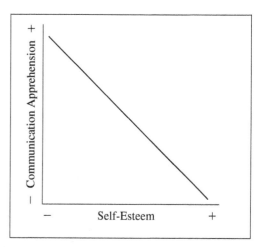

(b) Negative Relationship

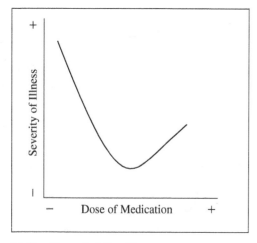

(c) Curvilinear Relationship

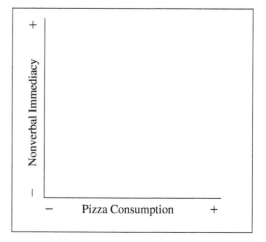

(d) No Relationship

Figure 19.1 Four Types of Relationships

popularity. This relationship indicates that the more humorous a person is, the more popular he or she will be, which is a positive relationship or correlation.

The second type of relationship, seen in Figure 19.1b, is a negative relationship. A negative relationship exists when the score on one variable goes up and the score on the other variable goes down. In the example in Figure 19.1b, we are examining the relationship between CA and self-esteem. As a person's level of CA goes up, her or his self-esteem goes down. The converse is also true; as a person's level of self-esteem goes up, her or his level of CA goes down.

The third example of a relationship, seen in Figure 19.1c, is called a **curvilinear relationship**. A curvilinear relationship is a relationship that is either positive or negative to a certain point and then starts to go in the other direction. In the example in Figure 19.1c, we have the severity of an illness and dose of medication. In an ideal world, the severity of an illness will go down as the dose of medication goes up. However, there does come a point when you can actually take too much medication for an illness (called an overdose) and the severity of your illness will go up. This is a good example of a curvilinear relationship.

Finally, as seen in Figure 19.1d, some variables are simply not related to each other at all, or a neutral relationship. In this example we are looking at an individual's pizza consumption and her or his nonverbal immediacy. These two variables simply do not make sense together in the first place, so clearly as one variable's score goes up or down, there should be no clear change in the score of the other variable.

CORRELATION NOT CAUSATION

Now that we have explained what the four basic types of relationships are, we must make one thing clear—correlation does not mean causation. In other words, being more humorous does not cause popularity, low self-esteem does not cause high levels of CA, and more medication does not cause the severity of the illness to change. You might be thinking "of course medication causes the severity of the illness to change," which might be true. However, the statistical tool called a correlation only examines whether two variables are linearly related to each other, *not* if one causes the change to occur in the other variable.

A published example of the "relationship versus **causation**" issue came from Eugene Volokh (2004), a professor in the UCLA School of Law, who conducted a study examining the relationship between ice cream consumption and the incidence of rape. In his study, Volokh (2004) used data from the international Dairy Foods Association's Dairy Facts (2000) publication to find out the monthly average of ice cream eaten (in millions of gallons). He then used data from the Federal Bureau of Investigation's Uniform Crime Reports (2000) to find out the number of rapes (percentage of 2,000 rapes) that occurred monthly as well. The two variables were strongly related to each other. An untrained person might say that this finding indicates that eating ice cream causes people to go out and rape others, but this is obviously a fairly idiotic statement. Instead, when one looks at the data more closely, there is a clear spike in the amount of ice cream consumed and the number of rapes that occur during the summer months. People eat more ice cream when it is hot, and people are outside more during the summer, which makes them more vulnerable to rape.

Another example of the problem of trying to create causation from correlation can be found in the study conducted by Janis Walworth (2001), who wanted to see whether there was a relationship between the number of Protestants living in a state and the incidence of tornados. Although there was no relationship between the number of Jews and Catholics living in a state and the number of tornados a state reports, this could not be said for Protestants. The relationship between the number of self-reported Protestants in a state and the number of tornados was strong ($r = 0.71$ for the statistically inclined). She further analyzed this phenomenon by examining the differences between reported categories of Protestantism (Lutheran,

Methodist, and Baptist) and the number of tornados. Lutherans apparently did not annoy God enough to spite them with a natural disaster because there was not a statistical relationship between the number of Lutherans living in a state and the number of tornados a state experiences. However, the numbers of both Methodists ($r = 0.52$) and Baptists ($r = 0.68$) positively related to the number of tornados a state has annually. Walworth concludes by saying, "this means that Texas could cut its average of 139 tornados per year in half by sending a few hundred thousand Baptists elsewhere (Alaska maybe?)" (p. 5), which has no tornados. Obviously, Walworth is joking in this article. However, we do see the interesting phenomenon that can occur if someone tries to create causal inferences from statistical relationships. One reason there may be a strong relationship between the number of Methodists and Baptists and the number of tornados is that more Methodists and Baptists live in the region of the United States known as tornado alley. Although there is a strong relationship, clearly having Methodists and Baptists in a state does not cause tornado activity.

Spurious Correlations

Need more evidence that correlation does not equal causation? Here are a number actual correlations that research scientists have discovered using the correlation:

- Pirate shortages and global temperature rates.
- The number of people who drowned in a year and the number of Nicholas Cage films.
- Per capita consumption of cheese and the number of people dying from tangled bed sheets.
- Per capita consumption of margarine and the death rate in Maine.
- Age of Miss America and the number of people dying from steam, hot vapors, and hot objects.
- Per capita consumption of chicken and U.S. crude oil imports.
- Quality of M. Night Shyamalan movies and newspaper purchasing rates.
- Number of Internet Explorer market share and murder rates.

Sources: http://stats.stackexchange.com/questions/36/examples-for-teaching-correlation-does-not-mean-causation http://www.tylervigen.com/
http://www.buzzfeed.com/kjh2110/the-10-most-bizarre-correlations/
ViGen, T. (2015). *Spurious correlations: Correlation does not equal causation*. New York, NY: Hachette.

CORRELATION ASSUMPTIONS

Now that we have examined some basic information about what a correlation is, we can turn our attention to the basic assumptions of the correlation:

1. Both the independent variable and the dependent variable should be interval (CA) or ratio (heart rate change).
2. A sample should be random.
3. Scores for both variables being compared must be obtained from each participant.
4. The relationship between the two scores should be linear (positive or negative) because the Pearson product-moment correlation (the test we will be conducting) does not test for curvilinear relationships.

$$r = \frac{N\Sigma xy - (\Sigma x)(\Sigma y)}{\sqrt{[N\Sigma x^2 - (\Sigma x)^2][N\Sigma y^2 - (\Sigma y)^2]}}$$

Figure 19.2 Pearson Product-Moment Correlation Formula

5. To avoid having an abnormal distribution, the Pearson product-moment correlation should have no fewer than 25 participants. (To make the math easy for this example, our example has fewer than 25 participants.)

These assumptions are extremely important, because if one assumption is violated, the meaning of the Pearson product-moment correlation is lost. Now that we have explained what a correlation is and what the basic assumptions of the correlation are, we can look at the basic correlation formula given in Figure 19.2.

In this formula we are solving for the mysterious "*r*" value. When you see an "*r*" reported in research, you can be guaranteed that you are seeing a Pearson product-moment correlation. Although the formula may look somewhat scary, it is just as easy as the other formulas previously computed in this book.

Case Study Introduction

Many people around the world suffer from CA. As we talked about in Chapter 6, CA can affect people in their interpersonal relationships, in health care, in organizations, and in intimate relationships. One area that CA clearly affects is one's ability to give speeches in a public setting. In this example, we have a researcher who is studying the relationship between a participant's score on the PRCA-24 and her or his change in heart rate while giving an impromptu speech—a speech without any time for preparation.

The researcher first has the participants fill out the PRCA-24. Then the participants are hooked up to a machine that monitors and records their heart rates. The participants are then asked to speak for 5 minutes about why they did or did not vote in the last election. The researcher records the participants' heart rate at the beginning of their speeches and throughout the speech, recording the highest heart rate achieved while speaking. After the fact, the researcher takes the highest heart rate and subtracts the baseline heart rate to obtain a figure called heart rate change. In essence, they are determining whether people who have higher scores on the PRCA-24 (interval variable) have faster heart rates (ratio variable because heart rate change could be equal to 0) while giving a speech than people who have lower levels of CA while giving a speech. Before we can calculate the correlation, some basic concepts related to correlations must be discussed.

Step-by-Step Approach to the Pearson Product-Moment Correlation

In our example, a researcher wants to determine whether an individual's level of CA (independent variable) relates positively or negatively to a participant's change in heart rate during an impromptu speaking situation. Figure 19.3 represents the raw data for this study. In this figure, PRCA scores are referred to as "*x*" scores and heart rate change as "*y*" scores.

Step 1. Before we can start completing any of the parts of the formula, we must do some simple descriptive statistics. First, we must find the sum of *x* multiplied by *y* (Σxy). To do this, we multiply everyone's *x* score (PRCA-24 score) by her or his *y* score (heart rate change). For

Participant	Communication Apprehension (X)	Change in Heart Rate (Y)
1	120	5.5
2	71	4.6
3	72	3.8
4	118	5
5	58	3.2
6	60	3.1
7	72	3.8
8	55	2
9	115	4.9
10	70	3.7
11	68	3.5
12	24	0
13	72	3.7
14	65	3.3
15	70	3.4
16	92	4
17	95	4.1
18	90	3.8
19	63	3.4
20	24	0

Figure 19.3 Raw Data for Correlation Example

example, the first participant's x score is 120 and her or his y score is 5.5. To obtain xy, we simply multiply 120 times 5.5, or $120 \times 5.5 = 660$. We have multiplied all of the xy scores in Figure 19.4 (as seen in the third column). Once you have computed all of the xy scores, you simply add them up to achieve the Σxy, which is equal to 5698.5.

Next, we must determine the sum of squares x and then the sum of squares y. As discussed in Chapter 7, to find the sum of squares x (Σx^2) you simply square each x value (individual's PRCA score) and then add those values. For example, to square the first participants score, you simply take her or his PRCA-24 score (120) and multiply it by itself ($120 \times 120 = 14,400$). After you have done this for all of the participants' x scores, you simply add the scores up to obtain the sum of squares x (Σx^2), which can be seen in the fourth column in Figure 19.4. Finally, you repeat the process for each participant's y scores (heart rate change) and then add these totals together to obtain the sum of squares y (Σy^2).

Figure 19.4 presents all of these totals for us. To complete the Pearson product-moment correlation formula, we must know the sum of X ($\Sigma x = 1,474$), the sum of X-squared ($\Sigma x^2 = 121,490$), the sum of Y ($\Sigma y = 68.8$), the sum of Y-squared ($\Sigma y^2 = 274.04$), the sum of $X \times Y$ ($\Sigma xy = 5698.5$), and the number of participants ($N = 20$). With these six numbers, we can now fill in every part of the correlation formula.

Step 2. The first part of the formula in Figure 19.2 we are going to complete is the part above the division line, $N\Sigma xy - (\Sigma x)(\Sigma y)$. At this point, we simply have to plug in the results from Step 1 into the formula and perform the calculation. Specifically, this formula asks us to multiply the number of participants ($N = 20$) by the sum of xy ($\Sigma xy = 5698.5$) and then subtract this total from the sum of x ($\Sigma x = 1,474$) multiplied by the sum of y ($\Sigma y = 68.8$).

$$(20 \times 5,698.5) - (1,474 \times 68.8)$$

$$(113,970) - (101,411.2)$$

$$12,558.8$$

So, the $N\Sigma xy - (\Sigma x)(\Sigma y) = 12,558.8$.

Participant	CA (x)	HR Change (y)	x*y	x*x	y*y
1	120	5.5	660	14400	30.25
2	71	4.6	326.6	5041	21.16
3	72	3.8	273.6	5184	14.44
4	118	5	590	13924	25
5	58	3.2	185.6	3364	10.24
6	60	3.1	186	3600	9.61
7	72	3.8	273.6	5184	14.44
8	55	2	10	3025	4
9	115	4.9	563.5	13225	24.01
10	70	3.7	259	4900	13.69
11	68	3.5	238	4624	12.25
12	24	0	0	576	0
13	72	3.7	266.4	5184	13.69
14	65	3.3	214.5	4225	10.89
15	70	3.4	238	4900	11.56
16	92	4	368	8464	16
17	95	4.1	389.5	9025	16.81
18	90	3.8	342	8100	14.44
19	63	3.4	214.2	3969	11.56
20	24	0	0	576	0
Sum =	1474	68.8	$5698.5 = \Sigma xy$	$121490 = \Sigma x^2$	$274.04 = \Sigma y^2$
Mean =	73.7	3.44	$284.925 = \Sigma xy$	$6074.5 = \Sigma x^2$	$13.702 = \Sigma y^2$

Figure 19.4 Descriptive Statistics for the Correlation Formula

Step 3. Next, we are now going to start computing the formula under the division line. To start with, we will work on the part of the formula under the division line that appears in the left bracket, $[N\Sigma x^2 - (\Sigma x)^2]$. Once again, this is simply a matter of plugging in the results we computed in Step 1. For this equation, we must multiply the number of participants ($N = 20$) by the sum of x-squared ($\Sigma x^2 = 121,490$) and then subtract this total from the sum of x ($\Sigma x = 1,474$) squared.

$$(20 \times 121,490) - (1,474)^2$$

$$(2,429,800) - (2,172,676)$$

$$257,124$$

$$\text{So, } [N\Sigma x^2 - (\Sigma x)^2] = 257,124.$$

Step 4. Next, we are now going to continue computing the formula under the division line by working on the part of the formula that appears in the right bracket, $[N\Sigma y^2 - (\Sigma y)^2]$. Once again, this is simply a matter of plugging in the results we computed in Step 1. For this equation, we must multiply the number of participants ($N = 20$) by the sum of y-squared ($\Sigma y^2 = 274.04$) and then subtract this total from the sum of y ($\Sigma y = 68.8$) squared.

$$(20 * 274.04) - (68.8)^2$$

$$(5,480.8) - (4,733.44)$$

$$747.36$$

$$\text{So, } [N\Sigma y^2 - (\Sigma y)^2] = 747.36$$

Step 5. In this step, we are going to do two basic computations. First we must multiply the answer from Step 3 (257,124) by the answer from Step 4 (747.36): 257,124 × 747.36 = 192,164,192.6. Once you have done that, you simply take the square root of that number, √192,164,192.6 = 13,862.32998.

Step 6. At this point, we have now calculated everything above the division line (Step 2 = 12,558.8) and everything below the division line (Step 5 = 13,862.32998). All we have to do now to obtain our *r* value is to divide 12,558.2 by 13,862.32998:

$$12,558.2/13,862.32998 = 0.905922743$$

So, for this example *r* = 0.91.

All Pearson product-moment correlation coefficients (*r*) exist on a scale from 0 to 1 or 0 to −1. The closer a correlation coefficient is to 1 or −1, the stronger the relationship is. To understand what *r* means, we must explore a concept called practical significance. Practical significance is not the same thing as statistical significance. Practical significance is an indicator of the strength of the relationship. The general agreed-on practical significance for an *r* value is that if it is under 0.30 (or −0.30) then it is a weak relationship (and somewhat questionable), if *r* is between 0.30 and 0.59 (or −0.30 to −0.59) then it is a moderate relationship (there is a clear relationship, but it is not strong), and if *r* is above 0.60 (or −0.60) it is a strong relationship (there is a clear, strong relationship between the two variables). In our example, we achieved an *r* value of 0.91, so there is a clear, strong, positive relationship between the two variables. However, practical significance does not mean anything unless it is statistically significant.

Step 7. In this step we are going to determine whether our *r* value (0.91) is statistically significant. Before we can determine this, we must calculate the degrees of freedom for the correlation. The formula for calculating the Pearson product-moment correlation degrees of freedom is *N* − 2, or the number of participants in a study (20) minus 2 (20 − 2 = 18). So for our example, the degree of freedom is 18.

On the left-hand side of Figure 19.5 runs the df for the Pearson product-moment correlation. Because our df calculated for this example was 18, we must go to the row with the number 18 listed as the df. In this row you will see the critical values listed for the calculated *r* value. As we have seen in previous chapters when examining a critical value table, if the *r* calculated is larger than the value in a column at a specific *p* value, then the *r* value is significant at that *p* value. For example, in the first column in row 18 is the critical value 0.3783. Because the calculated value for *r* (.91) is larger than the critical value (0.3783), then we can say the correlation is significant at *p* < 0.10. However, 0.10 does not meet the 95 percent confidence interval discussed in Chapter 14, so we would not consider a correlation statistically significant at this *p* value. However, if you look across the entire row of *p* values listed on the critical value chart (0.05, 0.01, and 0.001), the calculated *r* in this example (0.91) is larger than all three of the critical values (0.4438, 0.5614, and 0.6787, respectively). The lowest *p* value listed in the chart is 0.001, so we would have to declare 0.001 as the significance level since we do not have a more accurate significance level. However, it is probably significant at an even lower significance level, so we will examine how correlations are reported by SPSS and Excel.

Computer Printouts of the Pearson Product-Moment Correlation

Now that we have examined how the Pearson product-moment correlation can be calculated by hand, we will examine output from two statistical computer programs: SPSS and Excel.

| df | Level of Significance for a nondirectional two-tailed test | | | |
N – 2	0.10	0.05	0.01	0.001
1	0.9877	0.9969	0.9999	1.0000
2	0.9000	0.9500	0.9900	0.9990
3	0.8054	0.8783	0.9587	0.9912
4	0.7293	0.8114	0.9172	0.9741
5	0.6694	0.7545	0.8745	0.9507
6	0.6215	0.7067	0.8343	0.9249
7	0.5822	0.6664	0.7977	0.8982
8	0.5494	0.6319	0.7646	0.8721
9	0.5214	0.6021	0.7348	0.8471
10	0.4973	0.5760	0.7079	0.8233
11	0.4762	0.5529	0.6835	0.8010
12	0.4575	0.5324	0.6614	0.7800
13	0.4409	0.5139	0.6411	0.7603
14	0.4259	0.4973	0.6226	0.7420
15	0.4124	0.4821	0.6055	0.7246
16	0.4000	0.4683	0.5897	0.7084
17	0.3887	0.4555	0.5751	0.6932
18	0.3783	0.4438	0.5614	0.6787
19	0.3687	0.4329	0.5487	0.6652
20	0.3598	0.4227	0.5368	0.6524
25	0.3233	0.3809	0.4451	0.5974
30	0.2960	0.3494	0.4093	0.5541
35	0.2746	0.3246	0.3810	0.5189
40	0.2573	0.3044	0.3578	0.4896
45	0.2428	0.2875	0.3384	0.4648
50	0.2306	0.2732	0.3218	0.4433
60	0.2108	0.2500	0.2948	0.4078
70	0.1954	0.2319	0.2737	0.3799
80	0.1829	0.2172	0.2565	0.3568
90	0.1726	0.2050	0.2422	0.3375
100	0.1638	0.1946	0.2301	0.3211

The entries in this table were computed by the authors.

Figure 19.5 Critical Values Table for the Pearson Product-Moment Correlation

SPSS AND PEARSON PRODUCT-MOMENT CORRELATIONS

Using SPSS to compute a Pearson product-moment correlation is fairly easy as long as you follow instructions, so let's get started. First, open your SPSS software and locate the file on the textbook's website in the SPSS folder called "Correlation." When you open this file you will see two variables listed: "CA" and "hrchange." "CA" is the variable name for the participants' scores on the PRCA-24, and "HRChange" is the variable name for the participants' change in heart rates while giving the impromptu speech (Figure 19.6).

To conduct a Pearson product-moment correlation using SPSS, go to the menu bar at the top of your screen and click on "Analyze." When you click on "Analyze," a drop-down menu will appear. Go to the sixth category on this menu, "Correlate," and scroll over the arrow; another menu will appear to the right. Scroll over the first option in this list, "Bivariate," and click on it (Figure 19.7). The "Bivariate Correlations" dialogue box will appear (Figure 19.8a). There are two white boxes, one on the left-hand side of the screen (with your variables listed) and an empty one on the right-hand side of the screen labeled "Variables." Highlight both "ca" and "hrchange" and transfer them to the "Variables:" box (Figure 19.8b).

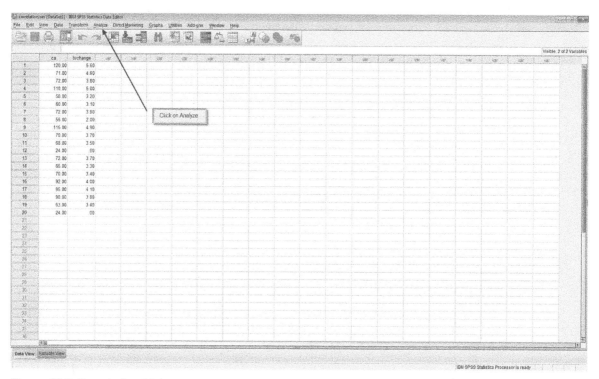

Figure 19.6 Correlation Main

You will also note that some correlation functions have been preselected. The SPSS "Bivariate Correlations" dialogue box allows you to perform three different types of correlations (Pearson's product-moment, Kendall's tau-b, and Spearman's rho). When you enter into the "Bivariate Correlations" dialogue box, "Pearson" is automatically checked because it is the most common form of correlation conducted by researchers. Below the three types of correlations, you will note that you can choose either a two-tailed significance test or a one-tailed significance test. If you remember from our discussion of significance in Chapter 14, you can use a one-tailed test if you have made a prediction about the direction of a correlation; however, it is recommended that you always use a two-tailed test since it is more conservative and less likely to cause type I errors. For this reason, SPSS automatically selects a two-tailed significance test unless told otherwise. Finally, you will see that SPSS has selected the "Flag Significant Correlations" box. When you look at the SPSS correlation printout, you will see an asterisk (*) next to any significant correlation.

To actually run the correlation using SPSS, simply highlight the variables you want to correlate. When the variables are highlighted in blue, hit the right arrow button and the variables will transfer to the "Variables" box. At this point, simply hit "OK." The results for the SPSS results can be seen in Figure 19.9.

When SPSS produces a correlation result, it correlates all of the variables listed as both the independent variable and the dependent variable. For this reason, in a correlation table each result will be presented twice. Furthermore, the computer program also correlates each variable with itself. If you correlate a thing with itself, then you will have a perfect correlation of 1.0. If you look at the answer listed in the first column and the first row (CA correlated with CA), you will note that they list 1.0 as the correlation coefficient. You will also note that in column 2/row 2 SPSS correlated HR Change with HR Change and reported a 1.0 correlation coefficient. For this reason, you will always end up with a diagonal line going through a

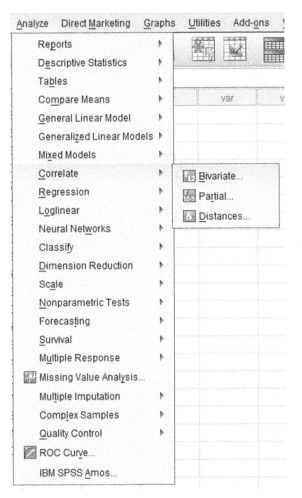

Figure 19.7 Correlate Bivariate Menu

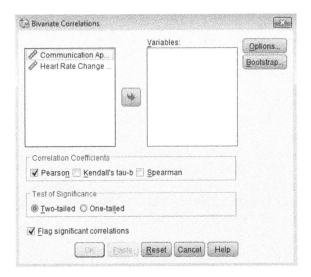

Figure 19.8a Correlation Dialogue Box

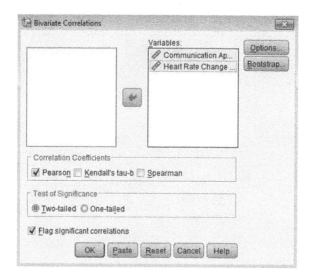

Figure 19.8b Correlation Dialogue Box

Correlations

Correlations

		Communication Apprehension	Heart Rate Change
Communication Apprehension	Pearson Correlation	1.000	**.906****
	Sig. (2-tailed)	.	.000
	N	20	20
Heart Rate Change	Pearson Correlation	.906**	1.000
	Sig. (2-tailed)	.000	.
	N	20	20

** Correlation is significant at the 0.01 level (2-tailed).

Figure 19.9 SPSS Results for CA and HR Change

correlation table where the program has correlated each variable with itself. On either side of that diagonal of 1.0 correlation coefficients will appear the exact same set of results. For this reason, it is recommended that you select one side of the line just to make sure you only report correlation results once.

In this example, you will see that the r value listed in the SPSS chart is identical to the one we computed by hand earlier in this chapter. You will also note that immediately under the r value is the significance (0.000) level, and immediately under that is the number of participants used in the correlation (20). The computer is able to obtain a much more exact p value than we could by looking at a critical value chart. In this case, the correlation was found to be significant at the $p < 0.0005$ level. The printout just says that the significance is 0.000; however, this means that the significance is lower than this level, so adding a 5 to the end of it is the most appropriate thing to do (Levine & Atkin, 2004). However, APA style informs us that we only report as the p value as low as $p < 0.001$.

EXCEL AND PEARSON PRODUCT-MOMENT CORRELATIONS

To calculate a correlation using Excel, open the file titled "correlation" in the Excel data file on the textbook's website. In this file, data for two variables will be listed—"CA" and "hrchange." "CA" represents the CA scores for each respondent, and "hrchange" reflects the change in heart rate when the respondent is asked to give an impromptu speech. The process for calculating the correlation is similar to other Excel statistical analyses. Click on the "Data" tab at the top of the spreadsheet, select "Data Analysis," and select "Correlation" from the menu. Click on "OK" and you will be prompted to enter the values in the "Input Range" box. Click on the box and highlight all of the data in cells A1 through B21—this includes the variable labels included in the first row of the spreadsheet. Check the options for "Labels in First Row" and "New Worksheet Ply" before clicking "OK" (Figure 19.10). The data output will appear in a new sheet (Figure 19.11). With the Excel file, you will have to look at the critical value table in Figure 19.5 to determine whether the test is statistically significant.

Again, we have bolded the significant correlation on the results to make it stand out more easily. Excel correlation tables can become somewhat confusing because they are not placed in a nice chart format like in SPSS. Although you may not notice this problem here, in a few minutes when we look at a larger example you will see it more clearly. Again, to make these tables easier to understand, we recommend finding the diagonal lines of 1.0 and marking a line through them with a highlighter to make it easier to view.

APA WRITE-UP

This research question tested for a relationship between an individual's level of communication apprehension and her or his increase in heart rate during an impromptu speaking situation, $r(20) = 0.91$, $p < 0.001$, which is considered a strong relationship.

DISCUSSION

After all of the work we have done so far in this chapter, this is the point where we get to try to make some sense out of our results. Let's go back to the initial research question we asked. The goal of this example was to see whether a person's level of CA related to a person's heart rate change while giving an impromptu speech. We found a strong, significant relationship between CA and HR change, which means that as a person's level of CA goes up, so did her or his heart

Figure 19.10 Excel Correlation Dialogue Box

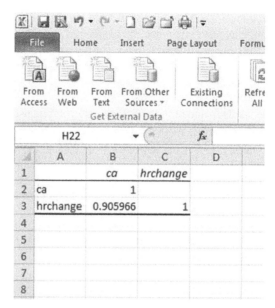

Figure 19.11 Excel Correlation Output

rate while giving a speech. Remember, this does not mean that an individual's CA caused the heart rate change, only that the two variables are positively related to each other. As another reminder, when dealing with numbers in APA style, we always round to the hundredth, or two numbers following the decimal. The only exception to this rule is the reporting of your p value.

Relationships among CA, WTC, and Beliefs about Public Speaking

The purpose of this example is to determine the relationships between an individual's CA, their WTC, and their belief that all students should be required to take public speaking in college (BELIEF). To analyze this question, we conducted three correlations: CA with WTC, CA with BELIEF, and WTC with BELIEF. Because we can calculate all of these correlations in one printout, Figure 19.12 shows the SPSS printout and Figure 19.13 the Excel printout.

In this example, you will note that both SPSS and Excel indicated that there were significant relationships between the three variables. To make it somewhat easier to see the results, we boldfaced the diagonal line of 1.0 correlation coefficients where the program correlates each variable with itself. You should only look at the results either to the right of the diagonal line or to the left of the diagonal line to make it easier to interpret your results. It does not matter if you look to the left or right of the diagonal line because the results are identical.

APA WRITE-UP

This research question was intended to examine the relationships between an individual's communication apprehension, willingness to communication, and the belief that all students should be required to take public speaking in college. To conduct this analysis, three Pearson product-moment correlations were conducted. Communication apprehension was found to be negatively related to an individual's willingness to communicate, $r(614) = -0.41$, $p < 0.001$, which is considered a moderate relationship. Communication apprehension was found to be negatively related to an individual's belief that all students should be required to take public

Correlations

Correlations

		Communication Apprehension Total	Willingness to Communicate Total	Everyone should be required to take public speaking in college
Communication Apprehension	Pearson Correlation Sig. (2-tailed) N	**1** **644**	.407** .000 614	**-.301** .000 615
Willingness to Communicate Total	Pearson Correlation Sig. (2-tailed) N	-.407** .000 614	**1** **622**	.141** .001 599
Everyone should be required to take public speaking in college	Pearson Correlation Sig. (2-tailed) N	**-.301** .000 615	.141** .001 599	**1** **623**

**. Correlation is significant at the 0.01 level (2-tailed).

Figure 19.12 SPSS Results for WTC, CA, and BELIEF

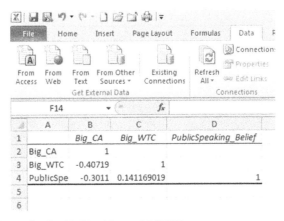

Figure 19.13 Excel Results for WTC, CA, and BELIEF

speaking in college, $r(615) = -0.30$, $p < 0.001$, which is considered a moderate relationship. Finally, willingness to communicate was found to positively relate to an individual's belief that all students should be required to take public speaking in college, $r(298) = 0.14$, $p = 0.001$, which is considered a minimal relationship.

A NOTE ABOUT R

Although PSPP will function in an identical way to SPSS with regards to running a correlation, R-commander does not produce the exact results that SPSS does. This is the one statistical test using R-commander where the results look drastically different. As such, we think it is important to add these results here and explain them for you. To run a correlation in R, you go to the "Statistics" drop-down menu, select "Summaries," and click on "Correlation matrix." Once you're in the Correlation matrix dialogue box, you simply click on the variables you want to correlate. Unlike SPSS, you must tell R that you want the program to calculate p values. If you look at Figure 19.14, you will see an arrow pointing toward the check box titled "Pairwise p-values for Pearson Spearman correlations." If this box is unchecked, the program

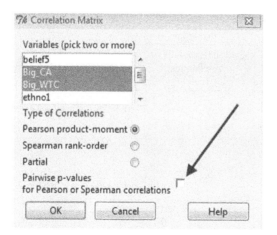

Figure 19.14 Correlation Matrix Dialogue Box in R

Big_CA	Big_CA	Big_WTC	PublicSpeaking_Belief
Big_CA	1.00	**-0.41**	-0.30
Big_WTC	-0.41	1.00	0.14
PublicSpeaking_Belief	-0.30	0.14	1.00

n= 592

P

	Big_CA	Big_WTC	PublicSpeaking_Belief
Big_CA		0e+00	0e+00
Big_WTC	0e+00		4e-04
PublicSpeaking_Belief	0e+00	4e-04	

Figure 19.15 R-Commander Results for WTC, CA, and BELIEF

will not report *p* values for the correlations. Once you have selected your variables and checked the pairwise *p* values box, you can simply click the "OK" button and the results seen in Figure 19.15 will appear.

The first set of numbers includes the *r* values and the second set of numbers includes the *p* values in scientific notation. The information is the same, but it is presented as two separate and distinct equations. You will also note that the correlation matrix function in R does not produce the *N*'s used for each correlation.

Reading Large Correlation Tables

Because correlations are probably the most common statistical tool used by social scientists, understanding how to read a correlation table is extremely important. For this reason, we have taken all of the variables from the real sample dataset on textbook's website (CA, ethnocentrism, humor assessment, nonverbal immediacy, assertiveness, responsiveness, WTC, belief that everyone should take public speaking in college, and attitude toward higher education) and run the correlations. To determine how many correlations you will actually must report, you can use the following formula: $[(N \times (N-1))/2]$, with *N* being the number of variables you want to correlate. In the sample dataset, we have nine unique variables, so the formula would be:

$$(9 \times (9 - 1))/2$$
$$(9 \times 8)/2$$
$$72/2$$
$$36$$

So, the correlation table will have 81 (36 correlations you must report on one side of the diagonal, 36 correlations that are replicated on the other side of the diagonal, and 9 correlations where the variable is correlated with itself), but only 36 of them are unique correlations. Figure 19.16 contains the SPSS results.

On the SPSS printout, to make it easier, we placed a big black line down the diagonal to point this out clearly. Also, we put a big black "X" through the left side of the diagonal, so we will only focus on those results found on the right side of the "X." Remember, the results on the left and right side of the diagonal of 1.0 are identical. To find the relationship between two variables, select a variable name from the top (columns) and one from the right side (rows). Where the column and row intersect, you will find the correlation information for the relationship between those two variables. For example, let's find the relationship between ethnocentrism and responsiveness. To do this, find the ethnocentrism row and then find the responsiveness column. The correlation you find at this intersect is $r(643) = -0.32$, $p < 0.001$. In other words, there is a moderate, but negative, relationship between ethnocentrism and responsiveness. Therefore, as a person's ethnocentrism goes up, her or his responsiveness goes down.

Discussion of the Chesebro Article

To help you understand how correlations appear in research, this section will examine two articles (both of which can be found on the textbook's website). The first article, by Joe Chesebro, "The Relationship between Listening Styles and Conversational Sensitivity," can be found in the folder titled "Articles." To view this article, you will need to download a copy of the Adobe Acrobat Reader (http://www.adobe.com/products/reader.html/) if you do not already have this program installed on your computer. We strongly encourage you to read the article first and then read our analysis of the article. The goal of this process is to ensure you understand how to read and interpret research results related to the Pearson product-moment correlation.

ARTICLE PURPOSE

Have you ever noticed that you can let a group of people watch a video and everyone will come away with something completely different? One reason this occurs is because of listening styles. In the Chesebro article, he talks about four listening styles (people, action, content, and time). People-oriented listeners listen for information-related feelings and emotions and areas of common interest. Action-oriented listeners like short and simple messages where people get to the point. Content-oriented listeners enjoy complex messages that they can evaluate and sink their teeth into. Finally, time-oriented listeners are more focused on their watches than on the messages. The purpose of this study was to see whether the four types of listener styles (people, action, content, and time) related to an individual's conversational sensitivity, or the degree to which an individual is attentive and responsive during a conversation.

METHODOLOGY

Chesebro had 239 participants in an introduction to communication course fill out scales. The set of scales the participants filled out measured listening styles and conversational sensitivity along with basic demographic information.

Correlations

		Communication Apprehension Total	Ethnocentrism	Humor Assessment	Nonverbal Immediacy	Assertiveness	Responsiveness	Willingness to Communicate Total	Everyone should be required to take public speaking in college.	Attitude about Higher Education
Communication Apprehension Total	Pearson Correlation	1	.157**	-.258**	-.331**	-.309**	-.072	-.407**	-.301**	-.094*
	Sig. (2-tailed)		.000	.000	.000	.000	.071	.000	.000	.020
	N	644	641	637	631	636	637	614	615	617
Ethnocentrism	Pearson Correlation	.157**	1	-.291**	-.360**	.091*	-.322**	-.124**	-.138**	-.190**
	Sig. (2-tailed)	.000		.000	.000	.021	.000	.002	.001	.000
	N	641	650	643	637	642	643	619	620	622
Humor Assessment	Pearson Correlation	-.258**	-.291**	1	.419**	.175**	.208**	.219**	.098*	.214**
	Sig. (2-tailed)	.000	.000		.000	.000	.000	.000	.015	.000
	N	637	643	646	639	641	642	617	617	619
Nonverbal Immediacy	Pearson Correlation	-.331**	-.360**	.419**	1	.117**	.386**	.334**	.125**	.281**
	Sig. (2-tailed)	.000	.000	.000		.003	.000	.000	.002	.000
	N	631	637	639	640	637	638	614	612	613
Assertiveness	Pearson Correlation	-.309**	.091*	.175**	.117**	1	.112**	.267**	.067	.145**
	Sig. (2-tailed)	.000	.021	.000	.003		.004	.000	.099	.000
	N	636	642	641	637	645	644	618	616	618
Responsiveness	Pearson Correlation	-.072	-.322**	.208**	.386**	.112**	1	.203**	.081*	.188**
	Sig. (2-tailed)	.071	.000	.000	.000	.004		.000	.045	.000
	N	637	643	642	638	644	646	619	617	619
Willingness to Communicate Total	Pearson Correlation	-.407**	-.124**	.219**	.334**	.267**	.203**	1	.141**	.156**
	Sig. (2-tailed)	.000	.002	.000	.000	.000	.000		.001	.000
	N	614	619	617	614	618	619	622	599	598
Everyone should be required to take public speaking in college.	Pearson Correlation	-.301**	-.138**	.098*	.125**	.067	.081*	.141**	1	.109**
	Sig. (2-tailed)	.000	.001	.015	.002	.099	.045	.001		.007
	N	615	620	617	612	616	617	599	623	617
Attitude about Higher Education	Pearson Correlation	-.094*	-.190**	.214**	.281**	.145**	.188**	.156**	.109**	1
	Sig. (2-tailed)	.020	.000	.000	.000	.000	.000	.000	.007	
	N	617	622	619	613	618	619	598	617	625

**. Correlation is significant at the 0.01 level (2-tailed).

*. Correlation is significant at the 0.05 level (2-tailed).

Figure 19.16 Reading Large SPSS Correlation Tables

RESULTS

If you look at the results on page 236 in Chesebro's article, they are straightforward. Chesebro used two different types of correlation (Pearson and partial correlations) in the article. A partial correlation is an advanced correlation tool. It (r_p) allows a researcher to determine actual relationships between variables that are highly interrelated. For example, the four listening styles are highly related constructs because they all involve listening and are measured using the same scale. To control for interference between the measurement of conversational sensitivity and one listening type (people), you can rule out the interference of the other variables (action, content, and time). Although this is by no means a complete description of what a partial correlation is, it should suffice to examine the results of this study.

The goal of this study was to examine the relationship between the independent variables (people, action, content, and time) and the dependent variable (conversational sensitivity). Looking at just the Pearson product-moment correlations, the people listening style is the only listening style that significantly relates to conversational sensitivity. Although two of the other listening styles did relate significantly when examining the partial correlations, the correlations were minimal and so probably not overwhelmingly meaningful.

Discussion of the Punyanunt Article

The 2000 article by Narissra Punyanunt entitled "The Effects of Humor on Perceptions of Compliance-Gaining in the College Classroom" can be found on the textbook's website in the folder titled "Articles." To view this article, you will need to download a copy of the Adobe Acrobat Reader (http://www.adobe.com/products/reader.html/) if you do not already have this program installed on your computer. We strongly encourage you to read the article first and then read our analysis of the article. The goal of this process is to ensure you understand how to read and interpret research results related to the Pearson product-moment correlation.

ARTICLE PURPOSE

The purpose of this article was to find the relationships between a teacher's use of humor, whether the teacher was effective at it, and how the teacher attempts to gain compliance and change behavior through communication in the college classroom. According to the article, a teacher in a college classroom can use 22 possible behavioral alteration techniques (BATs) to gain compliance and change behavior. The BATs are listed on page 34 of the Punyanunt article. The purpose of this article was to see whether there were relationships between students' perception of a teacher's use of humor in the classroom and the 22 BATs and to see whether a student's perception of a teacher's effectiveness at using humor in the classroom related to the 22 BATs.

METHODOLOGY

The 428 participants in this study were all students attending a large southwestern university. The participants were asked to fill out a modified version of the behavioral alteration techniques scale with one column asking participants to rate whether they thought their teacher used humor when using a specific behavioral alteration technique. This was measured using a 5-point Likert scale from 1 *never* to 5 *always*. The second column added to the BAT scale asked participants whether they thought their instructor was effective at using humor to deliver the specific behavioral alteration technique. This was measured using a 5-point Likert scale from 1 *very ineffective* to 5 *very effective*.

RESULTS

To examine the relationship among a teacher's use of humor, its effectiveness, and the use of a specific behavior alteration technique, Punyanunt correlated the BAT scores for each BAT with the use of humor and effectiveness use of humor questions. The results from these analyses can be seen in the charts on pages 34–35. These results demonstrated that teachers do use humor when trying to alter students' behavior in the classroom. For example, these results indicate that when using humor to guilt students into doing something, it may not be as effective as using humor to enhance a student's self-esteem.

Correlations Outside Academia

Of all the statistics, you probably hear about correlations more than any of the others because reports often "think" they understand correlations and what they mean. We use the quotation marks around the word "think" because often reporters fall into the correlation equals causation trap when reporting on data that are purely correlational. However, correlations can be important. For example, you may want to determine whether the number of new customers is positively related to sales rates. It is entirely possible that if you increase the number of people coming through your front door or website, you may see the same levels of purchases or even a dip in purchases. Ultimately, the question at hand here is do certain business practices actually lead to increased profits?

Do you want to know how an organization like Netflix makes recommendations for your next movie? Correlations. Basically, when you rate whether you liked a movie using their simple rating system of five stars, Netflix examines your ranking of that movie and looks for other people who ranked the same movie. So, let's say you ranked *Star Wars* *****. Netflix is going to find all of those people who also ranked *Star Wars* with five stars and then use correlations to see what other movies that whole giant group of *Star Wars* fans also ranks highly. Admittedly, the correlational models for this process can become extremely complex, but they are built on the basic backbone of a correlation.

In fact, much of what we have discussed in terms of "Big Data" is often based on correlational analyses. In an article published in the *New York Times* titled "How Companies Learn Your Secrets," Charles Duhigg (2012) discusses how organizations are using huge datasets to make some interesting and amazing predictions about people. This article has often been cheekily called the "Target Knows When You're Pregnant" article because Duhigg discusses how Target has created a data model (based on correlations) that can help them predict when women are pregnant based on purchasing different products. The article recalls the story of a father whose daughter started receiving pregnancy-related advertising at home before he knew she was even pregnant. He went so far as complaining to Target that they were sending his daughter these advertisements and Target was out of line. When he later found out that his daughter was indeed pregnant, he apologized to Target.

Conclusion

In this chapter, we have examined how to compute a Pearson product-moment correlation by hand, how to compute and interpret computer results of a Pearson product-moment correlation in both SPSS and Excel, and how to write up a Pearson product-moment correlation using APA style. We have also seen the Pearson product-moment correlation used in four different examples.

KEY TERMS

Causation
Correlation (*r*)

Curvilinear relationship
Negative relationship

Neutral relationship
Positive relationship

REFERENCES

Cheseboro, J. (1999). The relationship between listening styles and conversational sensitivity. *Communication Research Reports, 16*, 233–238.

Duhigg, C. (2012, February 16). How companies learn your secrets. *The New York Times Magazine*, p. MM30. Retrieved from http://www.nytimes.com/2012/02/19/magazine/shopping-habits .html?_r=3&pagewanted=1&hp/

Levine, T. R., & Atkin, C. (2004). The accurate reporting of software-generated *p*-values: A cautionary research note. *Communication Research Reports, 21*, 324–327.

Punyanunt, N. M. (2000). The effects of humor on perceptions of compliance-gaining in the college classroom. *Communication Research Reports, 176*, 30–38.

Volokh, E. (2004, July 13). *Ice cream production is closely correlated with the rate of forcible rape* [blog]. Message posted to http://volokh.com/archives/archive_2004_07_07.shtm/

Walworth, J. (2001, September/October). Does God punish gays? A statistical approach. *Gay & Lesbian Review Worldwide, 8* (5), 5.

FURTHER READING

Abramson, J. H., & Abramson, Z. H. (2001). *Making sense of data: A self-instruction manual on the interpretation of epidemiological data* (3rd ed.). New York, NY: Oxford University Press.

Bruning, J. L., & Kintz, B. L. (1997). *Computational handbook of statistics* (4th ed.). New York, NY: Longman.

Chen, P. Y., & Popovich, P. M. (2002). *Correlation: Parametric and nonparametric measures*. Thousand Oaks, CA: Sage.

Fox, J., & Weisberg, S. (2011). *An R companion to applied regression* (2nd ed.). Los Angeles, CA: Sage.

Gravetter, F. J., & Wallnau, L. B. (2000). *Statistics for the behavioral sciences* (5th ed.). Belmont, CA: Wadsworth/Thomson Learning.

Green, S. B., & Salkind, N. J. (2004). *Using SPSS for Windows and Macintosh: Analyzing and understanding data* (4th ed.). Upper Saddle River, NJ: Prentice Hall.

Hocking, J. E., Stacks, D. W., & McDermott, S. T. (2003). *Communication research* (3rd ed.). Boston, MA: Allyn & Bacon.

Hogan, T. P. (2010). *Bare-bones R: A brief introductory guide*. Los Angeles, CA: Sage.

Howell, D. C. (1997). *Statistical methods for psychology* (4th ed.). Belmont, CA: Duxbury Press.

Huff, D. (1954). *How to lie with statistics*. New York, NY: Norton.

Keller, D. K. (2006). *The Tao of statistics: A path to understanding (with no math)*. Thousand Oaks, CA: Sage.

Muenchen, R. A. (2009). *R for SAS and SPSS users*. New York, NY: Springer.

Pyrczak, F. (1999). *Statistics with a sense of humor: A humorous workbook and guide to study skills* (2nd ed.). Los Angeles, CA: Pyrczak.

Salkind, N. J. (2004). *Statistics for people who (think they) hate statistics* (2nd ed.). Thousand Oaks, CA: Sage.

Salkind, N. J. (2011). *Excel statistics: A quick guide*. Los Angeles, CA: Sage.

Singleton, R. A., Jr., & Straits, B. C. (1999). *Approach to social research* (3rd ed.). New York, NY: Oxford University Press.

Trochim, W. M. K. (2000). *The research methods knowledge base* (2nd ed.). Cincinnati, OH: Atomic Dog. http://www.socialresearchmethods.net/

Regression

Remember when you first learned how to graph a line in high school algebra? We all learned that the formula for graphing a line is $Y = mX + b$. For example, imagine that you have been asked to tutor students in public speaking during the next semester/quarter. Before you will tutor anyone, you get paid $20 to assess their skills, and then you charge $10 per hour of tutoring thereafter. One student, Fatwah, comes to you and wants you to tutor her for 5 hours. To determine how much you would get paid, you can plug it into the linear formula, with m equaling the charge per hour, X equaling the number of hours, and b equaling your $20 assessment fee, $Y = (10 \times 5) + 20$, or $70. If your next student, Bob, comes in and wants to be tutored for 8 hours, you can still use the same formula, $Y = (10 \times 8) + 20$, or $100. And the relationship between Fatwah's cost and Bob's cost would be a perfect relationship ($r = 1.0$). Furthermore, both scores would exist on a straight line if you graphed them because you are using the same formula to determine their overall cost. If Tika then comes to you and only wants to receive 2 hours of tutoring, you can once again use the formula to determine how

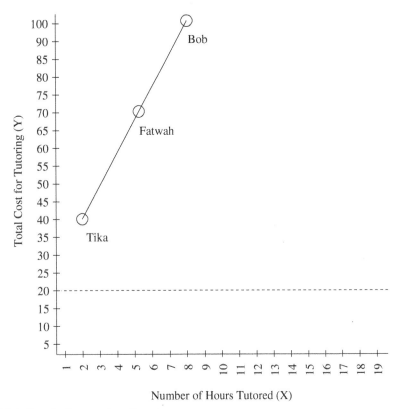

Figure 20.1 Simple Regression Graph

much she would be charged, $Y = (10 \times 2) + 20$, or \$40. Figure 20.1 shows these three situations on a graph. Remember, b values are points where the line intercepts the y axis. Note in this graph that the three points form a perfect line or have an r value of 1.0. Unfortunately, most relationships are not perfect ($r = 1.0$), so seeing perfect lines does not happen often in research. However, a simple linear regression can let us know how close to the perfect line the relationship between two variables is.

As mentioned in the chapter on one-way ANOVA, there is a series of statistical tests that all fall in the general category of general linear models (GLM), which includes regression. The easiest way to start understanding the GLM is through the discussion we had earlier regarding how two variables (time tutoring and amount paid) are linearly related to each other. Throughout this chapter we will be discussing the importance of linearity with reference to bivariate regression and multiple regression equations. Before we get into too much detail about linear equations, we will revisit the example from the previous chapter.

Case Study Introduction

In the previous chapter, we examined the relationship between an individual's score on the CAPRCA-24 and her or his change in heart rate while giving an impromptu speech in public. We found that there was a significant correlation between the two variables: $r(20) = 0.91$ and $p < 0.001$. This finding indicates that there is a strong, positive linear relationship between an individual's level of CA and her or his increase in heart rate (HR change) while giving an

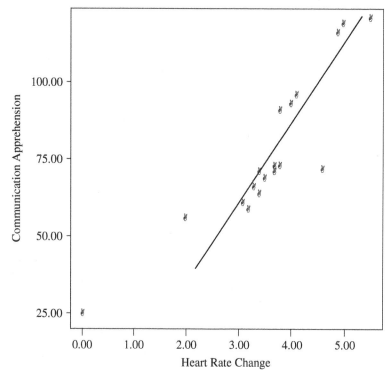

Figure 20.2 CA with HR Change Line

$$Y = m_{slope} X + b_{constant}$$

Figure 20.3 Regression Equation

$$m = \frac{\sum xy - (N * \mu x * \mu y)}{\sum X^2 - N\mu_{x2}}$$

$$b = \mu_y - m\mu_x$$

impromptu speech. This chapter is going to take the same example, but further develop the nature of the linear relationship between CA and HR change.

Let's compare the perfect line seen in Figure 20.1 to the line between CA and HR change from Chapter 18, which can be seen in Figure 20.2. The line drawn in on top of the scatter-plot (type of graph that illustrates where participants scores on the *x* axis value [HR change] and the *y* axis value [CA] intersect) runs through the means of both variables to demonstrate where the linear relationship exists. Note that most of the participants' scores for CA and HR change do not fall on the line perfectly. When this occurs, the predictive nature of the linear relationship is not perfect and we have some amount of error. Therefore, the formula for examining regressions must include an error term as seen in Figure 20.3.

Regression Background Information

Now that we have examined some basic information about what a **regression** is, we can turn our attention to the basic assumptions of the regression:

1. Both the independent variable(s) and the dependent variable should be interval (CA) or ratio (HR change).
2. Your sample should be random.
3. Scores for both variables being compared must be obtained from each participant.
4. The cases represent scores (on CA and HR change) that are independent of each other from one participant in your sample to the next participant. In other words, Jerry's level of CA cannot impact Heather's HR change.
5. The dependent variable (HR change) must be normally distributed in the population for each level of the independent variable. To ensure normal distributions, adequate sample sizes are necessary. Small samples may produce p values that are invalid.
6. The population variances of the dependent variable (HR change) are the same for all levels of the independent variable. If this assumption is violated, then the resulting p value for the overall F test is not trustworthy.

These assumptions are extremely important because if one assumption is violated, the meaning of the linear regression is lost.

Although a correlation does not require that you specifically determine independent and dependent variables, a regression requires that you know which variable is independent and which variable is dependent. In our example we are predicting that a person's CA (independent variable) can account for why a person's heart rate increases while giving an impromptu speech (dependent variable). You should also remember that independent variables and dependent variables often are not interchangeable. For example, it would not make sense to say that a person's change in heart rate while giving an impromptu speech causes her or his preexisting level of CA. With these two variables, there is clearly only one direction in which the linear equation can occur. Remember, correlations just test for relationships—regressions are creating predictive equation lines. It is the hope of the regression that if you are able to supply a person's CA score, then you can determine how much her or his heart rate will increase. If the correlation between two variables was 1.0, then the predictive nature of the line would be perfect. However, since our correlation between CA and HR change was 0.91, there is going to be some amount of error in our ability to predict a person's HR change from her or his CA score.

Step-by-Step Approach to a Linear Regression

In our example, a researcher wants to determine the nature of the **linear relationship** (R) between an individual's level of CA (independent variable) and her or his change in heart rate during an impromptu speaking situation. In essence, the goal is to find the "best fitting" straight line that was drawn in Figure 20.2 for the correlation data discussed in Chapter 18. This line is called a regression line. So what do we mean by "best fit?" For any set of data, it is possible to draw hundreds of lines that will pass through the data and appear meaningful. However, only one line is the best line to represent the relationship between the data and the actual relationship between the two variables, and this line is said to provide the "best fit" for the actual data points in a study. Before we can complete the linear aspect of the regression equation, we must retrieve some information from Chapter 18. We must know the sum of x ($\Sigma x = 1,474$), the sum of x-squared ($\Sigma x^2 = 121,490$), the sum of y ($\Sigma y = 68.8$), the sum of y-squared ($\Sigma y^2 = 274.04$), the sum of $X \times Y$ ($\Sigma xy = 5698.5$), and the number of participants ($N = 20$). If you forgot how these numbers were calculated, please refresh your memory by rereading the first part of Chapter 18.

Step 1. In this step we must find the mean of x (CA) and the mean of y (HR Change). To find the mean of x (μ_x), we simply take the sum of x (1,474) and divide it by N (20), or 1,474/20 = 73.7. Next we just repeat this process for the mean of y (μ_y), or 68.8/20 = 3.44.

Step 2. In this step we are going to compute the top portion of the formula for b, $\Sigma xy - (n \times \Sigma\mu_x \times \Sigma\mu_y)$. We already know the sum of $x \times y$ ($\Sigma xy = 5698.5$), the number of participants in the study ($N = 20$), the mean of x ($\mu_x = 73.7$), and the mean of y ($\mu_y = 3.44$). Since we have already calculated each of these numbers, all we have to do is complete the formula as follows:

$$\Sigma xy - (n \times \mu_x \times \mu_y)$$
$$5{,}698.5 - (20 \times 73.7 \times 3.44)$$
$$5{,}698.5 - 5{,}070.56$$
$$627.94$$

So, $\Sigma xy - (n \times \mu_x \times \mu_y) = 627.94$.

Step 3. Now we must calculate the part of the equation under the division bar, $\Sigma x^2 - N\mu_x^2$. Again, we have already calculated the sum of x-squared ($\Sigma x^2 = 121,490$), the number of people in the sample ($N = 20$), and the mean of x ($\mu_x = 73.7$). Since we have already calculated each of these numbers, all we have to do is complete the formula as follows:

$$\Sigma x^2 - N\mu_x^2$$
$$121{,}490 - (20 \times 73.7^2)$$
$$121{,}490 - (20 \times 5{,}431.69)$$
$$121{,}490 - 108{,}633.8$$
$$12{,}856.2$$

So, $\Sigma x^2 - N\mu_x^2 = 12,856.2$.

Step 4. In this step, we simply need to complete the equation by dividing the finding for Step 2 (627.94) by the finding in Step 3 (12,856.2), or 627.94/12,856.2 = 0.048433596. In other words, the slope of the linear relationship between CA and HR change is $m = 0.048433596$.

Step 5. Now that we have found m, we must switch gears and find the constant or b. To find b we simply have to fill in the following equation: $b = \mu_y - b\mu_x$. We already know the mean of y ($\mu_y = 3.44$), the slope of the line ($m = 0.048433596$), and the mean of x ($\mu_x = 73.7$), so we just need to fill in the formula:

$$\mu_y - b\mu_x$$
$$3.44 - (0.048433596 \times 73.7)$$
$$3.44 - (0.048433596 \times 73.7)$$
$$3.44 - 3.599755603$$
$$-0.159755603$$

So, $b = -0.159755603$.

Now we have all of the parts needed to complete the linear equation of $Y = mX + b$. So, the linear equation for the "best-fit" line between CA and HR change is

$$Y = mX + b$$

$$Y = 0.048433596X + - 0.159755603$$

At this point, we can turn our attention to the results from the computer to determine whether this "best-fit" line between CA and HR change is significant.

Computer Printouts of the Linear Regression

Now that we have examined how the linear regression line can be calculated by hand, we will examine the output from SPSS and Excel.

SPSS AND SIMPLE LINEAR REGRESSIONS

Using SPSS to compute a simple linear regression is easy, so let's get started. First, open your SPSS student version and then locate the file on the textbook's website in the SPSS folder called "Regression." When you open this file, you will see two variables listed, "ca" and "hrchange." "CA" is the variable name for individual's scores on the PRCA-24, and "HR Change" is the variable name for an individual's change in heart rate while giving the im-promptu speech (Figure 20.4). You could also use the file from the last chapter labeled "Cor-relation" since the data are identical.

To conduct a linear regression, go to the menu bar at the top of your screen and click on "Analyze." When you click on "Analyze," a drop-down menu will appear. Go to the seventh

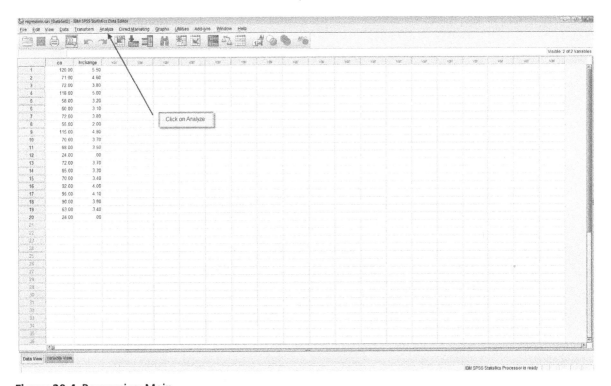

Figure 20.4 Regression Main

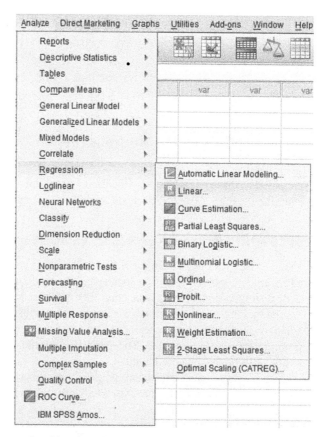

Figure 20.5 Regression Bivariate Menu

category on this menu, "Regression," scroll over the arrow, and another menu will appear to the right. Scroll over the first option in this list, "Linear," and click on it (Figure 20.5). The "Linear Regression" dialogue box will appear (Figure 20.6a). As we have previously noted, in this example a person's CA is the independent variable, so it should be placed in the second box down, labeled "Independent(s)." To do this, highlight the variable "ca" and then click the right arrow next to the box labeled "Independent(s)" (Figure 20.6b). Next, we must place the "hrchange" variable in the "Dependent" box by highlighting the variable "hrchange" and then click the right arrow next to the box labeled "Dependent" (Figure 20.6c). Once you have moved the variables, simply click "OK," and SPSS will produce the results that you see in Figure 20.7.

In the first box, SPSS tells you which variable(s) are the independent variables (in the "Variables Entered" box) and which variable was the dependent variable listed as "b" under the box itself. The second box of statistics is extremely important. The first column of results reports the "R" value for this linear regression. Since this is a bivariate linear regression (meaning we only looked at two variables—CA and HR change), the R value is the same computational value received for r in the last chapter, so $R = 0.91$. The second box indicates the **R-squared (R^2)** value. R^2 is an important concept to understand when talking about regressions. R^2 is a coefficient of determination, which means that R^2 determines what proportion of the variability in Y or your dependent variable (HR change) can be predicted by its relationship with X or your independent variable (CA). In our example, $R^2 = 0.821$, which indicates that 82%of the variance in an individual's heart rate changes while giving an impromptu speech

a) Highlight Dependent Variable

b) Send CA to "Independent(s):" Box

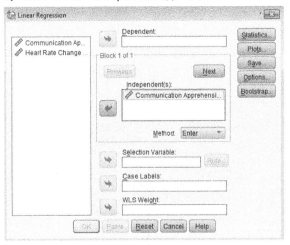

c) Send Heart Rate Change to "Dependent:" Box

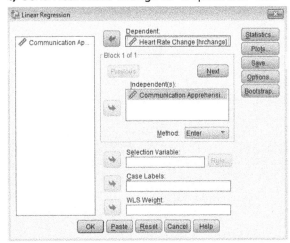

Figure 20.6 Regression Dialogue Box

Regression

Variables Entered/Removed[b]

Model	Variables Entered	Variables Removed	Method
1	Communication Apprehension[a]		Enter

[a] All requested variables entered.
[b] Dependent Variable: Heart Rate Change

Model Summary

Model	R	R Square	Adjusted R Square	Std. Error of the Estimate
1	.906[a]	.821	.811	.6100

[a] Predictors: (Constant), Communication Apprehension

ANOVA[b]

Model		Sum of Squares	df	Mean Square	F	Sig.
1	Regression	30.671	1	30.671	82.432	.000[a]
	Residual	6.697	18	.372		
	Total	37.368	19			

[a] Predictors: (Constant), Communication Apprehension
[b] Dependent Variable: Heart Rate Change

Coefficients[a]

Model		Unstandardized Coefficients		Standardized Coefficients	t	Sig.
		B	Std. Error	Beta		
1	(Constant)	-.160	.419		-.381	.708
	Communication Apprehension	4.884E-02	.005	.906	9.079	.000

[a] Dependent Variable: Heart Rate Change

Figure 20.7 SPSS Regression Results for CA and HR Change

can be predicted by an individual's level of CA. With that said, we should remember that to find out how much of the variance is not accounted for by our linear regression, we simply subtract R^2 from 1 ($1 - 0.821 = 0.179$). In other words, 17.9% of an individual's change in her or his heart rate while giving an impromptu speech cannot be predicted by the linear relationship with CA. In essence, not all of the increase in an individual's heart rate during an impromptu speech can be accounted for by her or his level CA. The next column, "Adjust R Square," is a mathematical adjustment to R^2 that attempts to more accurately reflect the goodness of fit in the overall linear regression. In essence, researchers may attempt to conduct a regression when they have enough participants to justify the number of independent variables they are using. When this happens, the adjusted R^2 is a more accurate portrayal of the variance accounted for. Datasets that use small samples and a large number of independent variables will see the greatest differences between R^2 and adjusted R^2. The last column, "Standard Error of Estimate," provides a measure of how accurately the regression equation predicts dependent variable values. The smaller your standard error of estimate is, the better you can predict that the independent variable(s) accounts for variance in the dependent variable. In this case, the standard distance between the actual data points seen in this example and the regression line is 0.61, which would indicate that the actual data points are fairly close to the regression line. The higher the standard error, the lower your R value will be.

The next table of results is also important because it is a traditional ANOVA summary table akin to the one we saw in Chapter 17 when we examined one-way ANOVAs. The reason we get an ANOVA summary table for a regression is because regressions, like one-way ANOVAs, are based on the GLM, so the F test allows us to determine whether our linear regression was statistically significant. If you need a refresher course in reading an ANOVA summary table, reread the discussion in Chapter 17 on how to create them.

The fourth box in the SPSS results, "Coefficients," is extremely important for regressions, but not necessarily for a simple linear bivariate regression like the example we used earlier. We will examine a more complicated regression model called a multiple linear regression later in this chapter and spend more time discussing this box at that point. However, we do want to point out that it contains the information you need for creating your line formula, $Y = mX + b$. The second column in this box is labeled "Unstandardized Coefficients," and in this column is the letter B. The first number listed under "B" is your constant (b) or y axis number (-0.160). The second number needed to create your linear equation is in the "Communication Apprehension" row (4.884E-02), which is scientific notation for 0.04884. When you put these two numbers together, you achieve the same linear formula that we calculated by hand earlier, $Y = 0.04X + -0.16$.

EXCEL AND THE SIMPLE LINEAR REGRESSION

To compute a regression in Excel, begin by opening the "Regression" data file on the textbook's website. In this spreadsheet, you will see two variables, "CA" and "hrchange". These are the same variables used in our calculation of correlations from the last chapter. Recall that "CA" represents an individual's scores on the PRCA-24, and "hrchange" reflects the change in an individual's heart rate while giving an impromptu speech. To begin, select the "Data" tab at the top of the spreadsheet, click on "Data Analysis" at the right side of the screen, and select "Regression" from the drop-down menu (Figure 20.8). Next, click on the "Input Y Range" box and highlight the data in cells A1 through A21. Select "Input X Range" and highlight the data in B1 through B21. Excel sets a default confidence interval of 95 percent for the regression statistic. Click on "New Worksheet Ply" and "Labels" before selecting "OK" (Figure 20.9). The output data will appear in a new sheet (Figure 20.10).

APA WRITE-UP

A bivariate linear regression was conducted to evaluate the prediction of heart rate change during an impromptu speech from an individual's level of communication apprehension (CA). The regression equation for predicting an individual's hear rate change is

$$\text{Change in heart rate} = (0.04 \times \text{CA}) + -0.16$$

The linear combination of CA and heart rate change was significant: $F(1, 18) = 82.43$, $p < 0.0001$. The sample multiple correlation coefficient (R) was 0.91, which indicates that approximately 82 percent of the variance in heart rate change in the sample can be accounted for by an individual's level of CA.

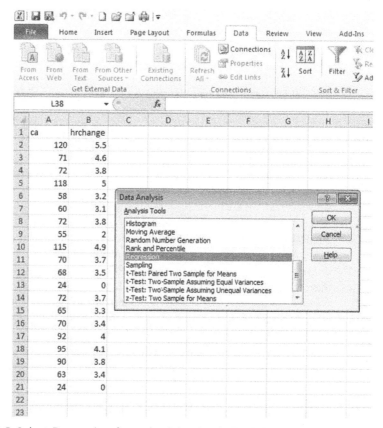

Figure 20.8 Select Regression from the Data Analysis Dialogue Box

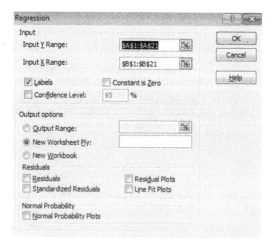

Figure 20.9 Regression Dialogue Box

DISCUSSION

We have now looked at this example for two complete chapters, so you are probably getting somewhat tired of trying to further your understanding of CA and the effect it has on heart rate change while a person delivers an impromptu speech. However, this simple example has

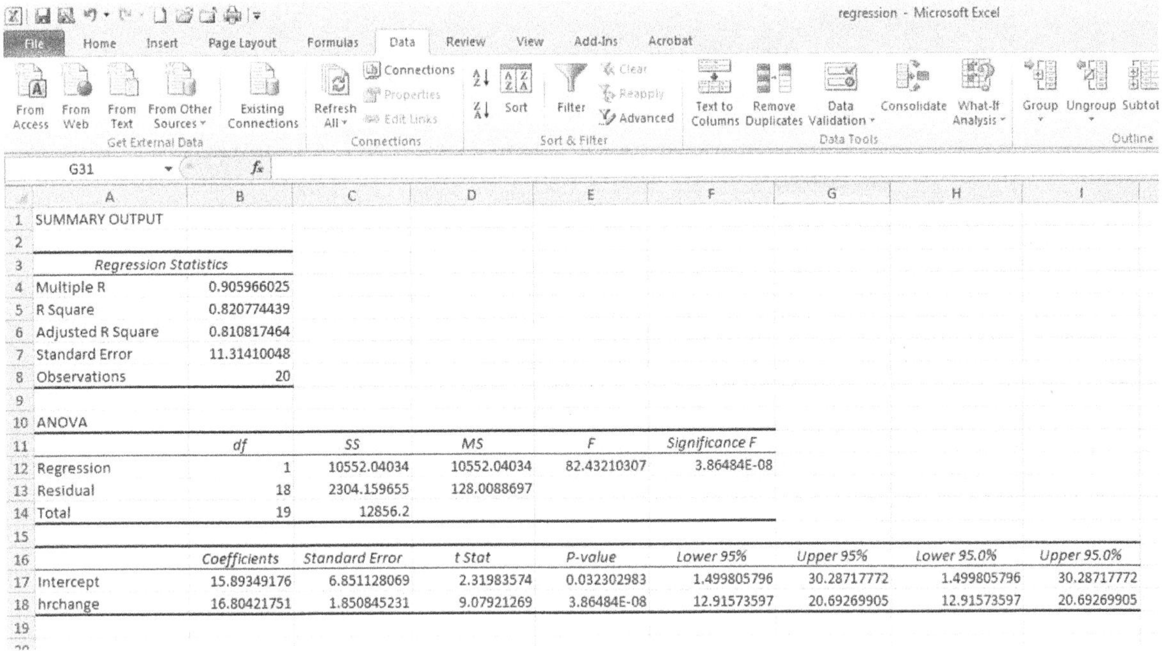

SUMMARY OUTPUT

Regression Statistics	
Multiple R	0.905966025
R Square	0.820774439
Adjusted R Square	0.810817464
Standard Error	11.31410048
Observations	20

ANOVA

	df	SS	MS	F	Significance F
Regression	1	10552.04034	10552.04034	82.43210307	3.86484E-08
Residual	18	2304.159655	128.0088697		
Total	19	12856.2			

	Coefficients	Standard Error	t Stat	P-value	Lower 95%	Upper 95%	Lower 95.0%	Upper 95.0%
Intercept	15.89349176	6.851128069	2.31983574	0.032302983	1.499805796	30.28717772	1.499805796	30.28717772
hrchange	16.80421751	1.850845231	9.07921269	3.86484E-08	12.91573597	20.69269905	12.91573597	20.69269905

Figure 20.10 Excel Regression Output

illustrated both how a Pearson product-moment correlation could be conducted and how a bivariate linear regression could be conducted. The regression finding indicates that there is a certain predictive nature between a person's level of CA and the change we could expect to see in her or his heart rate during an impromptu speech. Let's pretend that Pam has a CA score of 90. Using the equation generated by this example, we can actually predict how much Pam's heart rate will increase while giving an impromptu speech. We simply plug in Pam's CA score for *X*:

$$\text{Change in heart rate} = (0.04 \times \text{CA}) + -0.16$$

$$\text{Change in heart rate} = (0.04 \times 90) + -0.16$$

$$\text{Change in heart rate} = (3.6) + -0.16$$

$$\text{Change in heart rate} = 3.44$$

Given this finding, we would expect that Pam's heart rate would increase by 3.44 beats per minute during an impromptu speech. Admittedly, this is just an example and not based on actual research findings, but it does illustrate how regression equations can be used to make predictions.

Relationships between CA and Beliefs about Public Speaking

Here we present an example based on actual research collected from a college sample. In this research question, we want to see whether an individual's level of CA (independent variable) can predict an individual's belief that public speaking should be a required course for all

Regression

Variables Entered/Removed[a]

Model	Variables Entered	Variables Removed	Method
1	Communication Apprehension Total[b]	.	Enter

a. Dependent Variable: Everyone should be required to take public speaking in college.
b. All requested variables entered.

Model Summary

Model	R	R Square	Adjusted R Square	Std. Error of the Estimate
1	.301[a]	.091	.089	8.77707

a. Predictors: (Constant), Communication Apprehension Total

ANOVA[b]

Model		Sum of Squares	df	Mean Square	F	Sig.
1	Regression	4708.105	1	4708.105	61.115	.000[b]
	Residual	47223.693	613	77.037		
	Total	51931.798	614			

a. Dependent Variable: Everyone should be required to take public speaking in college.
b. Predictors: (Constant), Communication Apprehension Total

Coefficients[a]

Model		Unstandarized Coefficients		Standardized Coefficients		
		B	Std. Error	Beta	t	Sig.
1	(Constant)	33.746	1.370		24.636	.000
	Communication Apprehension Total	-.162	.021	-.301	-7.818	.000

a. Dependent Variable: Everyone should be required to take public speaking in college.

Figure 20.11 SPSS Results for Linear Regression of CA and Belief

college students. The findings for this linear regression can be seen in Figure 20.11 for the SPSS printout.

In this example, both SPSS and Excel results are basically identical in the linear regression equation, so let's look at the APA write-up.

APA WRITE-UP

A bivariate linear regression was conducted to evaluate the prediction of an individual's belief that all college students should be required to take public speaking from her or his level of

CA. The regression equation for predicting an individual's belief that all college students should be required to take public speaking is

$$\text{Belief about public speaking} = (-0.16 \times \text{CA}) + 33.75$$

The linear combination of CA and belief about public speaking was significant: $F(1, 613) = 61.12$, $p < 0.001$. The sample multiple correlation coefficient (R) was $-.30$, which indicates that approximately 9.1 percent of the variance in a person's belief that all college students should be required to take public speaking in the sample can be accounted for by an individual's level of CA.

Understanding Multiple Linear Regressions

Multiple linear regressions allow researchers to determine how a number of independent variables collectively account for the variance in a single dependent variable. For example, perhaps we wanted to go further than just CA and see how an individual's level of WTC, assertiveness, responsiveness, and CA accounted for the variance in her or his belief that all college students should take public speaking. Figure 20.12 is a pictorial representation of what we are asking in a multiple linear regression.

When we ran this research question in SPSS, we indicated that there were multiple independent variables (CA, WTC, assertiveness, and responsiveness) instead of just one, like we did in the previous two examples in this chapter, and one dependent variable (student belief about college). The results for what a multiple linear regression would look like can be seen in Figure 20.13 (SPSS).

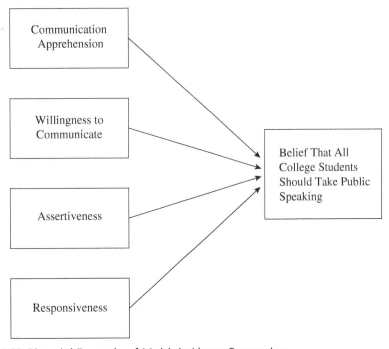

Figure 20.12 Pictorial Example of Multiple Linear Regression

Regression

Variables Entered/Removed[a]

Model	Variables Entered	Variables Removed	Method
1	Responsiveness, Assertiveness, Willingness to Communicate Total, Communication Apprehension Total[b]	–	Enter

[a.] Dependent Variable: Everyone should be required to take public speaking in college.
[b.] All requested variables entered.

Model Summary

Model	R	R Square	Adjusted R Square	Std. Error of the Estimate
1	.301[a]	.096	.090	8.83841

[a.] Predictors: (Constant), Responsiveness, Assertiveness, Willingness to Communicate Total, Communication Apprehension Total

ANOVA[b]

Model		Sum of Squares	df	Mean Square	F	Sig.
1	Regression	4849.869	4	1212.467	15.521	.000[b]
	Residual	45464.418	582	78.118		
	Total	50314.286	586			

[a.] Dependent Variable: Everyone should be required to take public speaking in college.
[b.] Predictors: (Constant), Responsiveness, Assertiveness, Willingness to Communicate Total, Communication Apprehension Total

Coefficients[a]

Model		Unstandarized Coefficients		Standardized Coefficients		
		B	Std. Error	Beta	t	Sig.
1	(Constant)	33.689	4.183		8.054	.000
	Communication Apprehension Total	-.165	.024	-.307	-6.904	.000
	Willingness to Communicate Total	.001	.001	.026	.578	.563
	Assertiveness	-.091	.063	-.061	-1.442	.150
	Responsiveness	.062	.062	.040	.999	.318

a. Dependent Variable: Everyone should be required to take public speaking in college.

Figure 20.13 SPSS Results for Multiple Linear Regression

Note that the output has not changed in how it is presented, but there is now more information presented in the "Coefficients" box in SPSS. For this reason we must discuss the results in the "Coefficients" box in SPSS. First, the column marked "B" in SPSS represents the same linear equation as seen in the bivariate linear regression in the previous two examples, but this one is more complex.

$$Y = -0.17X_{CA} + 0.00X_{WTC} + -0.09X_{ASSERTIVENESS} + -0.06X_{RESPONSIVENESS} + 33.69$$

It is still the same linear $Y = mX + b$, but now you have four mX statements—one for each independent variable you are examining. Ultimately, this is where the true power of the GLM comes into play for researchers. The next column is your standardized error for the "Unstandardized Coefficients" in SPSS.

This is followed by the "Standardized Coefficients" column in SPSS. The values represented in this column can be interpreted as correlation coefficients and are called beta weights. However, for a beta weight to be significant, the t value must be significant. For example, CA has a **beta (β) weight** of −0.307, a t value of −6.904, and a p value of 0.0005. In essence, this indicates that CA significantly accounts for a portion of the unique variance in a person's belief that public speaking should be required of all college students. However, if you look at responsiveness, the results indicate that it has a beta weight of −0.040, a t value of 0.999, and a p value of 0.318, which would indicate that responsiveness does not account for a portion of the unique variance in a person's belief that public speaking should be required for all college students. Beta weights are actually just standardized ways of examining the "Standardized Coefficients", which are actually unstandardized regression coefficients (B) or partial regression coefficients.

We have one note on running a multiple linear regression in Excel. Unfortunately, the regression function in Excel cannot have missing data. As such, the only way to run a multiple linear regression is to ensure that all data are accounted for and there are no missing data. Unfortunately, the dataset that came along with this textbook has missing data (and is quite large), so running multiple linear regressions in Excel with this dataset is highly problematic and leads to questions about the validity of the test.

APA WRITE-UP

A multiple regression was conducted to evaluate how well the independent variables (CA, WTC, assertiveness, and responsiveness) could predict the dependent variable (an individual's belief that all college students should be required to take public speaking). The linear combination of the independent variables was significantly related to an individual's belief that all college students should be required to take public speaking: $F(4, 582) = 15.52$, $p < 0.001$. The sample multiple correlation coefficient, R, was 0.31, which indicates that approximately 9.6 percent of the variance of an individual's belief that all college students should be required to take public speaking could be accounted for by the linear combination of CA, WTC, assertiveness, and responsiveness. However, only CA ($t = -6.904$, $p < 0.001$, $= β -0.31$) accounted for any of the unique variance in an individual's belief that all college students should be required to take public speaking.

DISCUSSION

So, what does this actually mean? A multiple regression allows us to see whether the linear combination of a variety of variables (CA, WTC, assertiveness, and responsiveness) can help

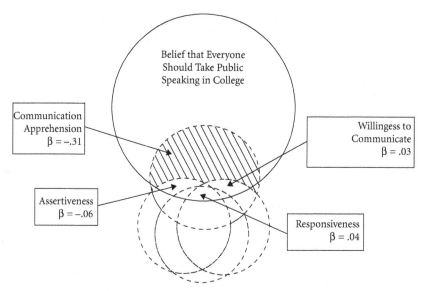

Figure 20.14 Multiple Linear Regression VennDiagram

predict a dependent variable (belief that all college students should be required to take public speaking). In this case, we found that only an individual's CA actually helps to predict her or his belief that all college students should be required to take public speaking. WTC, assertiveness, and responsiveness, by contrast, were not shown to add anything to one's ability to predict a person's belief that all college students should be required to take public speaking. As usual, the statistical process may be complex and unnerving at times, but the findings are generally straightforward.

To help us understand what is going on, let's look at this in terms of a Venn diagram. Figure 20.14 has an exaggerated replication of what we are seeing in this regression equation. In this Venn diagram, the larger, solid circle is representing the dependent variable (belief that everyone should take public speaking in college). The dashed circles are representing the independent variables used in this model (CA, WTC, assertiveness, and responsiveness). Although this is not exactly how this would really look if we plotted it with 100 percent accuracy, this diagram is useful for understanding what unique variance is. For our purposes, unique variance is represented by that part of CA that is shaded in the diagram. You will note that all four of the independent variables overlap with the dependent variable, but only CA is overlapping in a section of the dependent variable by itself. The other three variables, while overlapping with the dependent variable, do not overlap with the dependent variable in a unique fashion.

Discussion of the Wrench and Booth-Butterfield Article

Because regressions are commonly used in communication research, we are going to examine two studies that have utilized regressions in this chapter. The article by Jason Wrench and Melanie Booth-Butterfield (2003) entitled "Increasing Patient Satisfaction and Compliance: An Examination of Physician Humor Orientation, Compliance-Gaining Strategies, and Perceived Credibility" can be found on the textbook's website in the folder titled "Articles." To view this article, you will need to download a copy of the Adobe Acrobat Reader (http://www.

adobe.com/products/reader.html/) if you do not already have this program installed on your computer. We strongly encourage you to read the article first and then read our analysis. The goal of this process is to ensure you understand how to read and interpret research results related to the linear and multiple linear regressions.

ARTICLE PURPOSE

Have you ever noticed that some physicians have a good sense of humor when interacting with their patients and some simply do not? Well, this is what the authors of this study had noticed, and they wanted to determine how a physician's humor orientation (use of jokes and humorous story telling during interpersonal interactions) related to patient perceptions of credibility (competence, caring/goodwill and trustworthiness), patient satisfaction (affective, behavioral, and cognitive), use of compliance-gaining strategies (expectancies/consequences, relationship/ identification, and values/obligations), and actual patient compliance. (See the original article for a more detailed explanation of what each of these variables actually entails.)

METHODOLOGY

Participants in this study were college students ($N = 44$), professional educators in a Master's program ($N = 48$), people shopping at a mall ($N = 142$), and people online ($N = 26$). All participants were asked to fill out a variety of scales measuring the study variables using either a pen-and-paper test or an Internet-based survey.

RESULTS

The results from this study indicated that physician humor can help predict a patient's satisfaction (affective, behavioral, and cognitive) and a patient's perception of a physician's credibility (competence, trustworthiness, and caring/goodwill). In a multiple regression analysis using physician humor orientation, credibility, use of compliance-gaining strategies, and patient satisfaction as the independent variables and actual patient compliance as the dependent variable, 11 percent of the variance in compliance was accounted for by two compliance-gaining strategies (expectancies/consequences and values/obligations) and two forms of patient satisfaction (cognitive and behavioral).

Although humor was shown to be a strong predictor of satisfaction and patients' perceptions of physician credibility, it did not affect whether a patient would actually comply with a physician's treatment plan. We chose this article because the regression analyses are straightforward and are designed in a way that follows the reporting format that we have shown you in this chapter. You will also see that this article reported results for correlations and a one-way ANOVA as well, which is often the case in actual research. Most research does not rely on single statistical tests like the majority of the articles we have selected for inclusion on the textbook's website.

Discussion of the Rocca and Vogl-Bauer Article

The 1999 article by Kelly Rocca and Sally Vogl-Bauer entitled "Trait Verbal Aggression, Sports Fan Identification, and Perceptions of Appropriate Sports Fan Communication" can be found on the textbook's website in the folder titled "Articles." To view this article, you will need to download a copy of the Adobe Acrobat Reader (http://www.adobe.com/products/ reader.html/) if you do not already have this program installed on your computer. We strongly encourage you to read the article first and then read our analysis. The goal of this process is to ensure you understand how to read and interpret research results related to the linear and multiple linear regressions.

ARTICLE PURPOSE

Let's face it, sports fans are nuts!!! we are not talking about the average sports enthusiast (the person who enjoys a good game on a Sunday afternoon or Monday night). No, we are talking about the cheese head–wearing, body-painting, screaming, and yelling types that are often broadcast into our living rooms while we are watching any kind of athletic competition. Sometimes these sports fans can get out of control. Fans have been known to assault fans from other teams, destroy property, cause riots, and exhibit other antisocial forms of behavior. After noticing this phenomenon, Rocca and Vogl-Bauer wanted to determine what fans saw as appropriate forms of sports fan communication.

To examine appropriate fan behavior, Rocca and Vogl-Bauer created a new scale for measuring fan behavior. The scale consists of three subscales: verbal response (yelling at officials, taunting the opposing team, openly criticizing players and coaches, etc.), fan display (wearing clothing with team logos, wearing jewelry with team logos, buying a newspaper to read about the team, etc.), and violent response (destroying objects while watching a game, hitting someone during an intense game, being more violent than normal during a game, etc.). Ultimately, Rocca and Vogl-Bauer wanted to determine how fan display, verbal response, and physical response related to sports spectator identification (degree of connection a person feels with a specific sports team) and verbal aggression (personality construct where people use character attacks, competence attacks, insults, maledictions, teasing, profanity, and threats to attack the self-concept or self-esteem of another person).

METHODOLOGY

Participants in this study were undergraduates from either a large Eastern university ($N = 213$) or a medium-size Midwestern university ($N = 194$). The participants were asked to fill out three scales (verbal aggression, fan identification, a revised version of the sports identification behavior scale).

RESULTS

In this study there are only two basic research questions. The first research question examined the relationship between sports fans' verbal aggression and sports fans perceptions of appropriate communicative messages at a sporting event (behavioral identification, verbal response, and physical violence). The researchers examined how participants' perceptions of appropriateness of communicative behavior (behavioral identification, verbal harassment, and physical violence) could account for an individual's level of verbal aggression (dependent variable). The independent variables accounted for 12%of the variance in an individual's verbal aggression. Rocca and Vogl-Bauer found that fan display related negatively to verbal aggression ($\beta = -0.12$) and verbal response related positively to verbal aggression ($\beta = 0.28$), but violence did not significantly account for any of the unique variance in an individual's level of verbal aggression.

Next, Rocca and Vogl-Bauer examined how participants' perceptions of appropriateness of communicative behavior (behavioral identification, verbal harassment, and physical violence) could account for an individual's sport spectator identification (dependent variable). The independent variables accounted for 9 percent of the variance in an individual's sport spectator identification. Both verbal response ($\beta= 0.27$) and fan display ($\beta= 0.17$) related positively to sports spectator identification, but violence did not significantly account for any of the unique variance in an individual's level of sport spectator identification.

The regression equations used in this article are written up using APA style, which is slightly different from those used in the Wrench and Booth-Butterfield article discussed. This does not mean that one format is better than another, just that they are different. One of the things you will learn as you continue doing social scientific research is that there are a variety of ways to present the same information.

Regressions Outside Academia

By this point in life, you have probably come to know that everyone has a credit score, and this credit score determines the types of credit card, car, house, and other types of loans one can get. Furthermore, your credit rating also determines how much interest the credit lenders is going to throw on top of your loan as well. These credit ratings are based largely on regression models that help credit lenders determine whether an individual is a good investment or whether the individual will ultimately default on her or his loans. A wide range of different factors are examined. In fact, there are approximately 100 common variables used to determine your credit card score, but the major credit companies also stockpile huge amounts of other consumer information as well. In fact, one of the three large credit bureaus, Experian, says that they have 310 different variables in their dataset that can be utilized to make financial predictions (Experian, 2004). As you can imagine, this is a lot of data this company has at its disposal to create large regression models.

Besides determining your credit score, regressions are also beneficial in your daily life. In the business world, regressions are often used for a process called forecasting, or the use of historical data to make predictions about the future. Maybe an organization wants to predict how many products it must manufacture this year. Many different variables can impact customer purchases: economy, competitor sales, previous sales records, interest rates, etc. Any changes in these different variables could have huge impacts on the market's desire for your product. For example, during the economic crisis that hit the world starting in 2008, many organizations suddenly found the public's desire for their products dry up as it became more difficult for people to get loans with low interest rates. In parts of this country, giant home, condo, and apartment complex projects have halted for years because no one was making those types of large purchases. Being able to predict different possible scenarios that an organization may be facing is an important use of the regression.

As you can imagine, there are an endless supply of reasons to use multiple linear regressions in the modern business world. Want to find out what factors lead to employee burnout in your organization? Use a regression. Want to find out what website factors increase sales? Use a regression. Want to find out which recruitment mechanisms lead to the best job applicants? Use a regression. The possibilities are endless with multiple linear regressions.

Conclusion

In this chapter, we have used simple and complete ways of presenting information to educate you about all of the major facets of the tests we have studied in the past five chapters. This is not to say that we have taught you everything there is to know about any one test. In fact, there are graduate-level courses in ANOVAs and regressions alone, so the information presented here is to help you learn the basic terminology of statistics, see how simple statistics can be employed to answer real research questions, and provide you with enough information to allow you to read actual research in any field that employs social scientific statistical procedures. In the next chapter, we will explain a variety of more advanced statistical procedures.

KEY TERMS

Beta (β) weights
General linear model

Regression (*R*)
R-squared (*R*²)

REFERENCES

Rocca, K. A., & Vogl-Bauer, S. (1999). Trait verbal aggression, sports fan identification, and perceptions of appropriate sports fan communication. *Communication Research Reports, 16*, 239–248.

Wrench, J. S., & Booth-Butterfield, M. (2003). Increasing patient satisfaction and compliance: An examination of physician humor orientation, compliance-gaining strategies, and perceived credibility. *Communication Quarterly, 51*, 482–503.

FURTHER READING

Abramson, J. H., & Abramson, Z. H. (2001). *Making sense of data: A self-instruction manual on the interpretation of epidemiological data* (3rd ed.). New York, NY: Oxford University Press.

Achen, C. H. (1982). *Interpreting and using regression.* Newbury Park, CA: Sage.

Bruning, J. L., & Kintz, B. L. (1997). *Computational handbook of statistics* (4th ed.). New York, NY: Longman.

Chatterjee, S., Hadi, A. S., & Price, B. (2000). *Regression analysis by example* (3rd ed.). New York, NY: Wiley.

Experian. (2004). *Summarized credit statistics.* http://www.experian.com/assets/marketing-services/product-sheets/summarized-credit-stat.pdf/

Fox, J., & Weisberg, S. (2011). *An R companion to applied regression* (2nd ed.). Los Angeles, CA: Sage.

Gravetter, F. J., & Wallnau, L. B. (2000). *Statistics for the behavioral sciences* (5th ed.). Belmont, CA: Wadsworth/Thomson Learning.

Green, S. B., & Salkind, N. J. (2004). *Using SPSS for Windows and Macintosh: Analyzing and understanding data* (4th ed.). Upper Saddle River, NJ: Prentice Hall.

Hocking, J. E., Stacks, D. W., & McDermott, S. T. (2003). *Communication research* (3rd ed.). Boston, MA: Allyn & Bacon.

Hogan, T. P. (2010). *Bare-bones R: A brief introductory guide.* Los Angeles, CA: Sage.

Howell, D. C. (1997). *Statistical methods for psychology* (4th ed.). Belmont, CA: Duxbury Press.

Huff, D. (1954). *How to lie with statistics.* New York, NY: Norton.

Keith, T. Z. (2006). *Multiple regression and beyond.* Boston, MA: Allyn & Bacon.

Keller, D. K. (2006). *The Tao of statistics: A path to understanding (with no math).* Thousand Oaks, CA: Sage.

Muenchen, R. A. (2009). *R for SAS and SPSS users.* New York, NY: Springer.

Pyrczak, F. (1999). *Statistics with a sense of humor: A humorous workbook and guide to study skills* (2nd ed.). Los Angeles, CA: Pyrczak.

Salkind, N. J. (2004). *Statistics for people who (think they) hate statistics* (2nd ed.). Thousand Oaks, CA: Sage.

Salkind, N. J. (2011). *Excel statistics: A quick guide.* Los Angeles, CA: Sage.

Schroeder, L. D., Sjoquist, D. L., & Stephan, P. E. (1986). *Understanding regression analysis: An introductory guide.* Newbury Park, CA: Sage.

Seber, G. A. F., & Lee, A. J. (2003). *Linear regression analysis* (Rev. ed.). New York, NY: Wiley.

Singleton, R. A., Jr., & Straits, B. C. (1999). *Approach to social research* (3rd ed.). New York, NY: Oxford University Press.

Tabachnick, B. G., & Fidell, L. S. (2001). *Using multivariate statistics* (4th ed.). Boston, MA: Allyn & Bacon.

Trochim, W. M. K. (2000). *The research methods knowledge base* (2nd ed.). Cincinnati, OH: Atomic Dog. http://www.socialresearchmethods.net/

Advanced Statistical Procedures

1 Explain what a factorial ANOVA is and how it is presented in communication research.
2 Explain what an analysis of covariance (ANCOVA) is and how it is presented in communication research.
3 Explain what a multivariate analysis of variance (MANOVA) is and how it is presented in communication research.
4 Explain what a repeated measures ANOVA is and how it is presented in communication research.
5 Explain what a path analysis is and how it is presented in communication research.
6 Explain what a structural equation model is and how it is presented in communication research.
7 Explain what a factor analysis is and how it is presented in communication research.
8 Explain what a canonical correlation is and how it is presented in communication research.

In the previous five chapters, we have explained in great detail five common statistical procedures that communication researchers employ when doing social scientific empirical research. However, many research articles utilize a wide range of statistical tests, so this chapter is going to introduce you to four difference tests and four relationship tests that are currently found in communication journals. Most of these tests are useful because they allow researchers to be parsimonious. The **law of parsimony** states that scientists should look *for the simplest assumption in the formulation of a theory and the simplest test to interpret data*. Although we are not as concerned with the first part of this definition (theory), we are interested in the second part because of its depiction of how researchers should carry out data analysis. In essence, the law of parsimony states that researchers should find the simplest way to analyze their data. We have actually already conducted one statistical test in this book because of the law of parsimony, but we did not tell you so at the time. When someone conducts a one-way ANOVA that has an independent variable with three categories (A, B, and C), he or she could easily run one one-way ANOVA or three independent *t* tests (A and B; B and C; A and C). However, when we run three independent *t* tests, our error is compounded for each test, so the likelihood of type I error rises. Furthermore, conducting one one-way ANOVA is more frugal than running three *t* tests, so a one-way ANOVA is more parsimonious in this case. All of the advanced statistics could be conducted using the tests previously described in this text, but these tests are more parsimonious. Additionally, these advanced tests generally perform computations that the less parsimonious tests would not be able to compute, so we are able to ask more advanced questions about our data using a single test.

This chapter is not going to provide you with computer printouts or make you compute things by hand. If you would like to learn more about how to run these tests in SPSS, we encourage you to read Mertler and Vannatta (2005). If you want to see how many of these tests are calculated by hand, please read Bruning and Kintz (1997). Instead, this chapter will introduce you to a variety of advanced statistical procedures you may encounter while reading communication journals. Although there are literally hundreds of statistical tests that can be used, there are a handful of common statistical tests that you should at least be aware of at this point. To examine these tests, we are going to group them into two categories: difference tests and relationship tests. In the difference tests section, we will examine factorial ANOVAs, analysis of covariance (ANCOVA), multivariate analysis of variance (MANOVA), and repeated-measures ANOVA. In the relationship tests section, we will examine path analysis, structural equation modeling, factor analysis, and canonical correlations.

Difference Tests

FACTORIAL ANOVA

Example

Suppose that you wanted to find out whether there were differences between males and females and differences between political affiliations (Democrat, Republican, other, and not registered to vote) on college students' attitudes toward college. We could run two one-way ANOVAs to answer this question using both sex and political affiliations as two separate independent variables (remember in a one-way ANOVA the independent variable is always a nominal variable) looking for differences in the dependent variable (college students' attitudes toward college). (This example is actually based on the dataset found on the textbook's website.) Unfortunately, one thing we know about statistics is that the more statistical tests a researcher runs to answer the question, the greater the chance he or she will run into type I error. For this reason, running the two one-way ANOVAs is not considered parsimonious for this specific example. In statistics, we want the most frugal and simple (parsimonious) way to answer a single research question. For example, why run three linear regressions when one multiple linear regression will do the same thing? The same thing is true in this example as well. There is no need to run two separate one-way ANOVAs ("sex with attitude toward college" and "political affiliation with attitude toward college"). Instead, we simply run what is called a two-way or factorial ANOVA instead.

Explanation

When we originally talked about one-way ANOVAs, we mentioned that the independent variable is called a factor, so in a **factorial analysis of variance** you are simply dealing with more than one factor. In the example above, we have two levels in the first factor (male and female) and four levels in the second factor (Democrat, Republican, other, and not registered to vote). This design then would be considered a 2 × 4 factorial ANOVA. In a factorial ANOVA there are three types of difference tests. The first two differences calculated look for what are called **main effects** because they look for differences between each of the nominal independent variable's categories separately. For example, the difference computed in a factorial ANOVA looks at the first independent variable (female vs. male) and the dependent variable (attitude toward college). The second difference computed in a factorial ANOVA looks for differences among the categories in the second nominal independent variable (Democrat, Republican, other, and not registered to vote) and the dependent variable (attitude toward college). Again, the first differences look for main effects, whereas the third difference looks for an interaction effect between the two independent variables (sex and political affiliation) and the dependent variable (attitude toward college). The third difference test examined in a two-way ANOVA is called an **interaction effect** because it is looking for differences in the combination of the two factors (male Democrat, male Republican, male other, male not registered to vote, female Democrat, female Republican, female other, and female not registered to vote). In other words, the interaction test looks for differences between all of the following 8 groups (2 × 4 = 8): male Democrat, male Republican, male other, male not registered to vote, female Democrat, female Republican, female other, and female not registered to vote. So not only is a factorial ANOVA more parsimonious, but also it gives you a third type of difference test that cannot be done by simple one-way ANOVAs. You could even throw another factor into this study if you so desired, such as geographical location (north, south, east, or west), and get a 2 × 4 × 4. In this case you would end up with 32 comparisons being examined by the single interaction test and three main effect tests being reported by the factorial ANOVA test. Now that we have explained what a factorial ANOVA is, let's see how the APA write-up of a factorial ANOVA would appear in a journal.

APA Write-Up

A 2 × 4 ANOVA was conducted to evaluate the effects of biological sex (male and female) and political affiliation (Democrat, Republican, other, and not registered to vote) on college students' attitudes toward college. The means and standard deviations can be seen in Figure 21.1. The ANOVA indicated a significant main effect for sex with attitude toward college: $F(1, 304) = 4.45$, $p = 0.04$; did not indicate a significant main effect for political affiliation with attitude toward college: $F(3, 304) = 0.201$, $p = 0.90$; and did not indicate an interaction effect for sex by political affiliation with attitude toward college: $F(3, 304) = 0.144$, $p = 0.94$. The biological sex main effect indicated that females have more positive attitudes toward college than males.

Discussion

In this APA write-up, we see that there were three separate F tests reported in the one factorial ANOVA conducted to analyze this research question: two main effects tests and one interaction test. One of the main effect tests was significant, indicating that females reported having more positive attitudes toward college than males do. The other main effect test indicated that people in the four political affiliations (Democrat, Republic, other, and not registered to vote) did not differ in their attitudes toward college. Finally, we found that there were

Biological Sex	Political Affiliation	Mean	SD
Male	Democrat	35.86	6.19
	Republican	35.17	6.51
	Other	36.37	6.10
	Not Registered to Vote	34.46	6.02
	Total	35.52	6.29
Female	Democrat	37.78	5.19
	Republican	37.57	5.89
	Other	37.45	5.07
	Not Registered to Vote	37.50	7.48
	Total	37.65	5.54

Figure 21.1 Factorial ANOVA Means and SDs

no statistical differences between the eight combined groups (male Democrat, male Republican, male other, male not registered to vote, female Democrat, female Republican, female other, and female not registered to vote) and their attitudes toward college. In other words, female Republicans did not differ from males not registered to vote and so on. Overall, the factorial ANOVA allows researchers to answer more complex questions than could be accomplished using a simple one-way ANOVA.

ANALYSIS OF COVARIANCE

Example

Suppose you want to determine whether males and females differ in their level of communication apprehension. You have a group of college students fill out the Personal Report of Communication Apprehension–24. However, you realize that there is a strong negative relationship between an individual's communication apprehension and her or his willingness to communicate. For this reason, you want to see whether willingness to communicate is a confounding variable when determining whether females and males have different levels of communication apprehension. (This example is actually based on the dataset found on the textbook's website.)

Explanation

The **analysis of covariance (ANCOVA)** is an extension of the one-way ANOVA discussed in Chapter 18. You may be wondering how someone knows whether they should even look for a covariate in the first place. There are typically two reasons that a researcher may opt to use an ANCOVA. First, the researcher may want to exclude the effect of a given independent variable. For example, maybe you are conducting a study looking at sex differences and perceptions of political speeches. However, when you collect your data you find a significant difference between the ages of the females and males in your sample. To prevent age from becoming a factor while you are looking at the sex differences, you decide to use age as a covariate to exclude the effect that age may have on your participants' perceptions of the political speeches.

The second reason that a researcher may opt to use an ANCOVA is when there are two variables that are strongly related to each other. If someone is looking for a difference in a dependent variable, it is possible that the researcher will end up finding a difference in the variance accounted for by the dependent variable and another variable (the **covariate**). For this reason, the researcher may want to partial out the variance of the covariate, so he or she can only look for a difference in the variance not accounted for by the covariate. In our sample ANCOVA, we will test the second use of an ANCOVA. The purpose of our example ANCOVA is to allow a researcher to determine whether a difference lies between groups (female and male) on a dependent variable (communication apprehension) after the dependent variable has been mathematically adjusted for differences associated with one or more covariates (willingness to communicate). The basic test analyzed in an ANCOVA is similar to the one-way ANOVA in that both look for differences between groups. The ANCOVA, however, increases the power of the F test for a main effect or interaction by removing the predictable variance associated with the covariate (willingness to communicate) from the error term for the F test. In essence, a covariate (willingness to communicate) is a variable related to the dependent variable that can cause the participants' scores on the dependent variable (communication apprehension) to be skewed or altered, so the ANCOVA readjusts the dependent variable scores to prevent this skewing from occurring.

APA Write-Up

The purpose of this research question was to examine the possibility of a significant difference in communication apprehension based on biological sex (male and female) while controlling for an individual's willingness to communicate. A one-way analysis of covariance was conducted using biological sex (male and female) as the independent variable, communication apprehension as the dependent variable, and willingness to communicate as the covariate. A significant relationship was found between the dependent variable (communication apprehension) and the covariate (willingness to communicate): $F(1, 295) = 86.41$, $p < 0.001$, $\eta^2 = 0.23$. Furthermore, a significant difference was found between males ($M = 62.68$, $SD = 15.43$) and females ($M = 66.41$, $SD = 19.25$) on communication apprehension: $F(1, 295) = 8.78$, $p = 0.003$, $\eta^2 = 0.03$.

Discussion

These results indicate that there is a significant difference between males and females and their levels of communication apprehension. In Chapter 17, we ran the same test using an independent t test procedure and found no differences between males and females and communication apprehension. Because we used the same data off the textbook's website sample to ask this question, what caused the difference to appear now? The correction of communication apprehension that occurred by the covariate willingness to communicate is what ultimately caused this difference to occur. You will note that two separate F tests are reported in the ANCOVA. The first F test indicated that there was a significant relationship between the dependent variable (communication apprehension) and the covariate (willingness to communicate). The eta-squared ($\eta^2 = 0.23$) indicates that approximately 23 percent of the variance in communication apprehension can be accounted for by willingness to communicate. In an ANCOVA, you can think of eta-squared as being similar to R^2 in a regression.

The second F test examines the differences between males and females on communication apprehension. This test indicated that females do have slightly higher levels of communication apprehension than males in the sample. Note again that eta-squared is reported for this F test. Although males and females differ in their communication apprehension in this sample, biological sex only accounts for 2.9 percent of the variance, which is not much when you think about it.

MULTIVARIATE ANALYSIS OF VARIANCE

Example

A **multivariate analysis of variance** (**MANOVA**) allows a researcher to examine differences using one or more nominal independent variables with one or more dependent variables. Perhaps a researcher wants to see whether males and females differ in their levels of ethnocentrism, but wants to also see whether males and females differ in their levels of willingness to communicate with strangers. This could be answered using two one-way ANOVAs (sex with ethnocentrism and sex with willingness to communicate with strangers), but again, the more tests you use, the greater the chance you will end up with type I error. So to be parsimonious (simple and frugal), you would need to conduct a one-way MANOVA.

Explanation

A MANOVA, as discussed earlier, is considered a **multivariate test** because you have multiple dependent variables (ethnocentrism and willingness to communicate with strangers). A one-way ANOVA is considered a **univariate test** because you have one dependent variable. Often the dependent variables analyzed in a MANOVA are different measures of the same phenomenon. As in our example, we would think that people who have higher levels of ethnocentrism would be less willing to communicate with strangers, so these two variables could theoretically be related. However, the two do not need to be related, but should share a common conceptual meaning and some degree of linearity (remember all ANOVA tests are general linear model tests). In essence, the dependent variables in a MANOVA should go together in a way that makes sense, so you would not put both apples and oranges as dependent variables in the same MANOVA. Again, the purpose of this chapter is not to explain all of the mathematical aspects of the MANOVA procedure, but to introduce you to the basic concept. For this reason, we strongly urge you to read more information about the MANOVA elsewhere since it is the basis of a number of advanced statistical procedures.

APA Write-Up

The goal of this research question was to determine whether there was a difference between males and females on ethnocentrism and willingness to communicate with strangers. To analyze this question, a one-way MANOVA was calculated using biological sex (female and male) as the independent variable and the participant's scores for ethnocentrism and willingness to communicate with strangers as the dependent variables. Box's test (Box's $M = 3.58$) reveals that equal variances can be assumed: $F(3, 31993081) = 1.19, p > 0.05$; so Wilks's lambda ($\Lambda$) will be used as the test statistic. The Wilks's lambda criteria indicates significant group differences in biological sex for the overall model: Wilks's $\Lambda = 0.975, F(2, 302) = 3.94, p = 0.02$, multivariate $\eta^2 = 0.03$. Univariate ANOVA results were interpreted using alpha at 0.05. Results reveal that males ($M = 38.43, SD = 9.08$) and females ($M = 35.63, SD = 8.08$) significantly differ on ethnocentrism: $F(1, 303) = 7.91, p = 0.005$, partial $= \eta^2 = 0.03$. Results also revealed that males ($M = 47.86, SD = 24.86$) and females ($M = 48.86, SD = 26.67$) did not significantly differ on willingness to communicate with strangers: $F(1, 303) = 0.11, p = 0.74$.

Discussion

Let's start an analysis of these results by remembering the purpose of this research question. The goal was to use one independent variable (sex) to examine two dependent variables (ethnocentrism and willingness to communicate with strangers) using one test. The first result reported in the MANOVA is the test that measures for the equality of variances assumption. Like in other tests we have examined, the MANOVA has a basic assumption that the variances from the groups being examined are equal. Box's M test examines the equality of variances assumption and determines whether we can use Wilks's lambda (if Box's M is not significant—we accept the equality of variances assumption) or Pillai's trace (if Box's M is significant—we reject the equality of variances assumption). In this example, Box's M was not significant, so we were able to utilize Wilks's lambda. Wilks's lambda or Pillai's trace are two multivariate tests that examine statistical significance of the whole model (both independent variables and dependent variables).

The multivariate test is then followed by a series of univariate tests (F tests) for the independent variable (sex) with every dependent variable (ethnocentrism and willingness to communicate with strangers). The multivariate test essentially lets us know that a difference exists between the independent variable and dependent variables, but not where the difference actually is. In our example, the overall multivariate test was significant, so we needed to examine the univariate statistics (sex with ethnocentrism and sex with willingness to communicate with strangers). In our example, males had higher levels of ethnocentrism than females, but there was no difference between females and males in their willingness to communicate with strangers. However, once again, biological sex only accounted for a small amount of the variance in ethnocentrism (3%).

REPEATED-MEASURES ANOVA

Example

Suppose you are a public speaking teacher and you want to determine whether taking a public speaking course actually decreases a person's level of communication apprehension. One possible way to determine whether a person's level of communication apprehension decreases over the course of a public speaking class would be to test their CA level at the beginning of the course, test it again halfway through the course, and test it a third time at the end of the course. You could calculate three paired t tests to determine this research question ($Time_1$ to $Time_2$, $Time_2$ to $Time_3$, and $Time_1$ to $Time_3$), but again the more tests you run, the more error your findings will have. To avoid increasing your type I error, you can run a procedure called a repeated-measures ANOVA. (This example is hypothetical because the data on the textbook's website are not set up to answer a repeated-measures ANOVA question.)

Explanation

A **repeated-measures ANOVA** allows a researcher to determine whether differences occur in a variable over time. In the example above, we measured these differences occurring over time by having students fill out the Personal Report of Communication 24 at the beginning of the semester/quarter, in the middle of the semester/quarter, and at the end of the semester/quarter. By having the students fill out the survey all three times, we have a way of mapping what happens to communication apprehension levels throughout the course of a public speaking class. In essence, what we are testing is the null hypothesis that $Time_1 = Time_2 = Time_3$.

APA Write-Up

The goal of this research question was to determine whether a person's level of communication apprehension changes over the course of a public speaking class. A one-way within-subjects repeated measures ANOVA was conducted using three scores for communication apprehension taken at the beginning of the course ($M = 65.11$, $SD = 15.49$), the middle of the course ($M = 64.61$, $SD = 14.36$), and the end of the course ($M = 64.09$, $SD = 15.93$). This study found no significant differences between the measurements: Wilks's $\Lambda = 0.985$, $F(2, 125) = 0.96$, $p = 0.39$.

Discussion

In this APA write-up, we learned that there was not a significant difference among the beginning, middle, and end of the public speaking course and individual levels of communication apprehension. Although this test is considered a univariate test, it still relies on a multivariate test (Wilks's Λ) to determine the overall significance of the model. If the test had been significant, then we could have used paired t tests to determine where the actual difference existed (Time$_1$ to Time$_2$, Time$_1$ to Time$_3$, or Time$_2$ to Time$_3$).

It is also easy to make the repeated-measures ANOVA even more complicated by adding what is called a between-groups aspect to the test. For example, perhaps you wanted to see whether male and female levels of CA changed over the course of a public speaking course, which would give you one group within (everyone and CA) and one group between (males and females). Needless to say, more and more layers can be added to the repeated-measures ANOVA by adding multiple dependent variables, which would create a repeated-measures MANOVA.

Relationship Tests

PATH ANALYSIS

Example

Causal relationships are one of the areas that social scientific researchers are hesitant to discuss. One technique that has been developed to examine causal relationships is the path analysis. Perhaps you wanted to determine the causal relationships among communication apprehension, ethnocentrism, humor assessment, attitudes toward college, and people's belief that everyone should be required to take public speaking in college. You start doodling on a piece of paper and come up with a theoretical explanation for why people like college and others do not and why some people think everyone should take public speaking and others do not (Figure 21.2). You believe that people with higher levels of communication apprehension are less likely to like college and are less likely to believe that everyone in college should take public speaking (represented by the minus sign next to the lines). Furthermore, you believe that people who are more humorous will enjoy college more and believe that everyone in college should take public speaking (represented by the plus sign next to the lines). Finally, you believe that people who are ethnocentric are going to have more negative attitudes about college, but you do not think that there will be a relationship between an individual's level of ethnocentrism and her or his belief that everyone should take a public speaking class in college.

Explanation

In a **path analysis**, two different types of variables must be examined: endogenous and exogenous variables. **Endogenous variables** are explained by one or more of the other variables in the model (e.g., belief about public speaking and attitude about college). **Exogenous variables** are taken as a given, so the model does not try to explain them (CA, ethnocentrism, and HA). To calculate a path analysis, we calculate a series of multiple linear regressions using the exogenous variables as the independent variables (CA, ethnocentrism, and HA) and the endogenous variables as the dependent variables (belief about public speaking and attitude about college). From these regressions, you simply report the beta weights for each regression on the picture.

APA Write-Up

A path analysis was conducted to determine the causal effects among the variables communication apprehension, ethnocentrism, humor assessment, belief that everyone should take public speaking in college, and attitude about college. Before the analysis, an initial model was created (Figure 21.2). This model was not consistent with the empirical data. More specifically, two of the correlations exceeded a difference of 0.05, so the nonsignificant paths were removed from the model. Thus, a revised model was generated (Figure 21.3). Approximately 12% of the variance in a person's belief that a person should be required to take public speaking in college can be accounted for by the model, and approximately 17% f the variance in a person's attitude about college can be accounted for by the model.

Discussion

Overall, you can think of the path analysis as a pictorial way of presenting information about multiple regressions. The numbers shown to the left of the exogenous variables are Pearson product-moment correlations that were calculated among the exogenous variables. The numbers above the lines originating from an exogenous variable pointing toward an endogenous variable are beta weights calculated during multiple regressions and indicate whether there is a positive or negative relationship. What we can tell from these findings is that an individual's level of CA negatively relates to her or his belief that all college students should take public speaking. We also learned that there is a positive relationship between an individual's humor assessment and positive attitudes about college and that there is a negative relationship between an individual's ethnocentrism and positive attitudes about college. In other words, people who are more humorous feel more positively about college, whereas people who are more ethnocentric feel less positively about college.

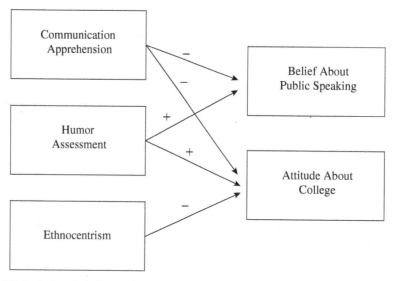

Figure 21.2 Path Analysis Example

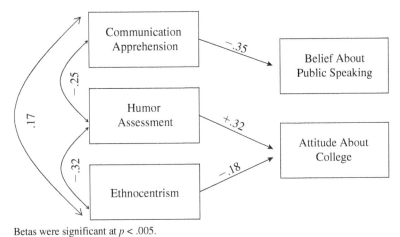

Betas were significant at $p < .005$.

Figure 21.3 Path Analysis Calculated

STRUCTURAL EQUATION MODELING

Example

As we have noted throughout this chapter and in previous chapters, the dataset that we collected for this textbook has indicated that there is a negative relationship between an individual's level of communication apprehension and her or his belief that all college students should be required to take public speaking. Suppose that you wanted to examine this relationship in light of the four subscales that allegedly make up communication apprehension. We could run a path analysis like we did in the previous section, but the problem with a path analysis is that it relies on the use of a number of linear and multivariate regressions, which simply is not parsimonious. For this reason, a newer statistical technique has been created called structural equation modeling. In this example, we want to see how well the four subscales of communication apprehension create this variable known as communication apprehension and how communication apprehension relates to a participant's belief that all students in college should be required to take public speaking. Figure 21.4 shows how this question would look pictorially. You will note that in this drawing we have a variety of circles and squares instead of just boxes. To further understand this research question, we will examine what a structural equation actually is.

Explanation

Structural equation modeling is similar in purpose to path analysis; however, the calculations are considerably more difficult but mathematically more meaningful. Ultimately, structural equation modeling is concerned with observed and latent variables. An observed variable can be an observation that a researcher directly collects (self-reports on a survey, scores on an achievement test, coded responses to interview questions, etc.). Latent variables are variables that are not directly measured, but we believe that our measurements help us understand this variable. For example, we believe that communication apprehension is a product of four subscales (group CA, meeting CA, interpersonal CA, and public CA). We do not measure a variable called "communication apprehension," but rather measure the four subscales together and then combine their results to create an overall score of communication apprehension. In essence, "communication apprehension" is the latent variable being measured by the four subscales (group CA, meeting CA, interpersonal CA, and public CA). As shown Figure 21.5,

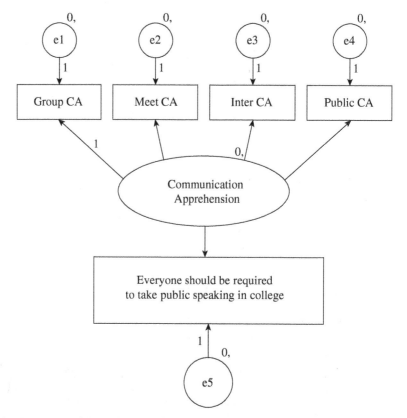

Figure 21.4 Structural Equation Model Hypothesis

we measured each of the four subscales in a rectangular box indicating that these variables are directly measured by the researcher. However, the variable listed as "communication apprehension" is an oval, indicating that CA is a latent variable.

In structural equation modeling like we saw in path analysis, there are two types of variables discussed: exogenous and endogenous. Exogenous latent variables are similar to independent variables because they can account for some of the variance in other variables in the model. Endogenous latent variables are similar to dependent variables because they are influenced by the exogenous variables. In our example, communication apprehension is an example of an exogenous variable because it attempts to account for some of the variance in an individual's belief that all college students should be required to take public speaking.

APA Write-Up

Using structural equation modeling, the relationships were examined between communication apprehension, a latent variable with four indicators (group CA, meeting CA, interpersonal CA, and public CA), and an individual's belief that public speaking be a required course in college. The hypothesized model is presented in Figure 21.4. Circles represent latent variables, and rectangles represent measured variables. Absence of a line connecting variables implies lack of a hypothesized relationship. Results indicated that the proposed structural model was problematic: $\chi^2(5, N = 325) = 24.20$, $p < 0.001$. However, because this model had more than 200 participants, other goodness-of-fit indices are necessary. All of the goodness-of-fit indices far exceeded the recommended levels: normed fit index (NFI) = 0.99, comparative fit index (CFI) = 0.99,

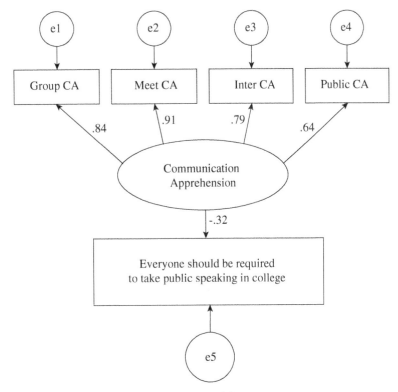

Figure 21.5 Calculated Structural Equation Model

relative fit index (RFI) = 0.98, incremental index of fit (IFI) = 0.99, and the Tucker–Lewis index (TLI) = 0.99. All of the indices of fit were over the 0.95 mark, which indicates that the model proposed is a superior fit. The final structural equation model can be seen in Figure 21.5.

Discussion

The goal of this research question was to see whether the four subscales of the PRCA-24 actually created a latent exogenous variable called communication apprehension and then to determine whether this latent exogenous variable was related to an individual's belief that everyone in college should be required to take public speaking. To examine these findings, we will first talk about the statistics involved and then examine the structural equation model in Figure 21.6. The first statistic that is reported is a chi-square test to determine whether the model is a good fit. When examining the chi-square test that is conducted for a structural equation model, there are two things that really should be examined: the chi-square statistic and the degrees of freedom. In an ideal test, the df is less than 5, and the closer the df is to the chi-square statistic, the stronger your model is said to be. However, the chi-square test of goodness-of-fit in the structural equation model is not always the best way to determine whether you have a strong model, especially if a study has more than 200 participants (Bollen & Long, 1993). If your study has more than 200 participants, your chi-square is almost always going to be significant, which is an indication of poor fit. For this reason, a number of other indices have been developed such as the ones reported in the results above: normed fit index (NFI), comparative fit index (CFI), relative fit index (RFI), incremental index of fit (IFI), and the Tucker–Lewis index (TLI). Without going into the mathematical reasoning for each of

1. I regularly communicate with others using humor.	.62
2. People usually laugh when I make a humorous remark.	.69
3. I am not funny or humorous.	-.66
4. I can be amusing or humorous without having to tell a joke.	.63
5. Being humorous is a natural communication orientation for me.	.70
6. I cannot relate an amusing idea well.	-.68
7. My friends would say that I am a humorous or funny person.	.68
8. People don't seem to pay close attention when I am being funny.	-.62
9. Even funny ideas and stories seem dull when I tell them.	-.67
10. I can easily relate funny or humorous ideas to the class.	.64
11. My friends would say that I am not a humorous person.	-.71
12. I cannot be funny, even when asked to do so.	-.68
13. I relate amusing stories, jokes, and funny things very well to others.	.64
14. Of all the people I know, I am one of the "least" amusing or funny persons.	-.65
15. I use humor to communicate in a variety of situations.	.68
16. On a regular basis, I do not communicate with others by being humorous or entertaining.	-.61

Figure 21.6 Factor Analysis Humor Assessment

these goodness-of-fit tests, each of these tests is designed to explain to us mathematically whether our model makes sense the way we designed it. All of these goodness-of-fit indices can range from 0 to 1 with scores above 0.95 generally being seen as acceptable (Byrne, 2010; Kelem, 2000). Overall, all of the goodness-fit-indices indicate that the model that we proposed in Figure 21.5 was a good model to explain the data.

Next to the goodness-of-fit indices, the most important part of the structural equation model is the standardized estimates seen in Figure 21.5. The standardized estimates can be seen as beta weights when determining the linearity of the relationship. In essence, all four subscales contribute to create the latent variable "communication apprehension" above 0.64, which indicates that the four subscales do actually measure the latent variable effectively. There is also a negative relationship between the latent exogenous variable "communication apprehension" and an individual's belief that all students should be required to take public speaking in college. Although this resembles the path analysis results from the previous section examining this question, the biggest difference between a path analysis and a structural equation model is that the structural equation model is more parsimonious and accounts for possible error that a series of multiple linear regressions cannot. Attached to every observed variable (the rectangles in the model), you will note that there is an error term (a small circle with the letter "e" followed by a number from 1 to 5). Again, to avoid going into the computational mathematics, understand that the error associated with observed variables (four CA subscales and belief about public speaking) accounts for measurement error. Measurement error can come from one of two places: random error and error uniqueness. Random error is simply random measurement error that occurs as a result of measuring things. Error uniqueness is a term that indicates that there was a form of error unique to a particular variable that is considered nonrandom measurement error.

FACTOR ANALYSIS

Example

Factor analysis is an extremely important technique to master if you want to understand how to create survey research measures like the PRCA-24, WTC, sociocommunicative orientation scale, or any of the other scales we have used in this textbook. One of the problems when creating a new scale is that you never know whether what you think you are measuring in your new scale is actually measuring what you say it should be measuring. Although the primary way we examine problems like this is through validity testing (see Chapter 8), another way we can attempt to understand whether a scale is measuring what we say it is measuring is through a factor analysis. In 2001, Richmond, Wrench, and Gorham created a new research scale to measure an individual's use of humor during interpersonal interactions. The scale itself consists of 16 Likert-type items using a 5-point scoring system from 1 *strongly disagree* to 5 *strongly agree*. How do we know that these 16 items actually measure anything? As discussed in Chapter 8, the HA has an alpha reliability of 0.91 ($M = 63.25$, $SD = 9.53$). So we know the scale is reliable, but do the 16 items in the HA actually measure just one thing? To determine whether a set of scale items (like the 16 items on the HA) is measuring one concept or multiple concepts, we conduct a factor analysis.

Explanation

A factor analysis is a technique that enables researchers to determine variation and covariation among research measures. For example, suppose we had two items being measured on a Likert scale ranging from 1 *strongly disagree* to 5 *strongly agree*. The first item in the scale reads, "People are innately good," and the second item reads, "Cats are the best animals." You give these two questions to a large sample and get the results back. Suppose you get an alpha reliability of 0.80, which is considered good. So your scale is reliable, but what is the scale measuring? Chances are your scale is not measuring one coherent concept, but rather two concepts that happen to be related to each other. The purpose of a factor analysis is to determine how many different concepts are being measured by a set of questions on a research scale. If you recall the discussion from Chapter 9 on creating surveys, we mentioned that a single research survey can only measure one thing. In the instance of the humor assessment, the purpose of the scale is to examine only an individual's use of humor during interpersonal interactions. The scale does not measure an individual's ability to use humor, an individual's sense of humor, or anything else. The scale has a single purpose, and all 16 scale items were written to reflect that conceptualization.

In the area of factor analysis, two basic types of factor analyses can be calculated. The first is called an exploratory factor analysis. Exploratory factor analysis occurs when a researcher has a set of scale items and wants to determine how many concepts the set of scale items is measuring. If you have 20 scale items, it is theoretically possible that each scale item is measuring a completely different concept and there is no unity between the set of scale items. However, it is also possible that all 20 items are only measuring a single variable. Most communication scales tend to measure between one and five distinct concepts. For example, of the scales used in this text book, only one scale measures two distinct variables. Know which scale it is? If you guessed the sociocommunicative orientation scale, then you were correct. The sociocommunicative orientation scale measures the degree to which an individual is assertive and the degree to which an individual is responsive. Each concept measured by a scale is called a factor. A factor analysis helps researchers group the individual scale items into coherent sets of concepts called factors. Sometimes you may think you have written 30 strong scale items to measure one single concept, cooperative communication, only to find out that your 30 items are actually measuring three different concepts—cooperative behavior, competitive behavior, and trust. Other times, the 30 items will hold strong and clearly measure one variable—cooperative communication.

The second type of factor analysis is called confirmatory factor analysis (CFA). Confirmatory factor analysis is when a researcher uses a factor analysis to make sure that a previously determined factor structure is consistent with present results. For example, in the last example looking at structural equation modeling, we used structural equation modeling to determine whether the four subscales of communication apprehension actually measure a variable called "communication apprehension." Although not an exact example of CFA, this is similar to what a CFA actually does, except in a true CFA we would have also tested whether each of the individual scale items clearly helps in creating the individual subscales (meeting CA, group CA, interpersonal CA, and public CA).

The last area of factor analysis that we must explain here is what we refer to as extraction methods and rotation. Extraction refers to the specific type of factor analysis that an individual is conducting. The most basic factor analysis extraction method is called a principal component factor analysis. Although we will not discuss the mathematical details of a principal component analysis, you should know that there are other forms of factor analysis, each of which is best used in different circumstances (unweighted least squares, generalized least squares, maximum likelihood, principal axis factor, etc.), and each factoring method contains differing mathematical reasoning and computations. For a good explanation of the different types of extraction methods and when to use one rather than another, we strongly encourage you to read Tabachnick and Fidell (2001) or Grimm and Yarnold (2000a, 2000b).

Another important concept in the world of factor analysis is factor rotation. When researchers calculate factor analyses, it is often difficult to ascertain a clear factor structure for the scale items involved. Trying to find factor structures is akin to looking at Impressionist art. Sometimes you have to step back from the art piece to see what is actually on the canvas, or maybe you will have to turn the canvass sideways to see what the artist intended her or his viewing audience to see. Examining factor structures often involves a certain amount of scrutiny and manipulation. Imagine that we have all of the data points on a graph. If we look at the graph straight on we may not see much, but if we turn the page slightly, a clear linear structure may appear on the paper. When we rotate the data points along either the x or the y axis, we have rotated the factor structure. This is a simplistic view of what happens in a factor analysis rotation, but it gives you a basic idea of what happens when a researcher must rotate a factor to determine the actual structure of the factor analysis.

APA Write-Up

The humor assessment instrument (HA) was developed to measure an individual's predisposition to use humor as a communicative tool during interpersonal situations. The HA is a 16-item, self-report measure that uses a 5-point Likert format ranging from 1 *strongly disagree* to 5 *strongly agree*.

The dimensionality of the 16 items for the HA was analyzed using an unrotated principal component factor analysis. Four criteria were used to determine the number of factors to rotate: sampling adequacy, the a priori hypothesis that the measure was unidimensional, the scree plot, and the interpretability of the factor solution. To examine sampling adequacy, Kaiser's measure of sampling adequacy (MSA) was used. The MSA obtained was 0.92, which is considered "marvelous" for conducting a factor analysis (Kaiser, 1974). The scree plot indicated that our initial hypothesis of unidimensionality was correct. The principal component analysis revealed a strong primary factor. The factor loadings can be seen in Figure 21.6.

Discussion

First, let's remember the basic research question involved in calculating the factor analysis. Our goal was to determine whether the 16 scale items created by Richmond et al. (2001) measure an individual's use of humor in interpersonal interactions using one factor. To analyze the above results, we will start by discussing some of the main features mentioned in the results section. First, the results mention that the researchers utilized an unrotated principal component analysis. In this example, there was no need to rotate the principal component analysis because the factor structure was clear without a rotation.

Second, Kaiser's MSA was used to determine whether the sample was adequate for performing a factor analysis. The Kaiser's MSA is a tool to determine whether your sample is sufficient (robust) enough to perform the factor analysis on the number of items in a scale. The way to interpret Kaiser's MSA is to use the system Kaiser (1974) created for determining whether the dataset is appropriate for the factor analysis: 0.9 and above is marvelous, 0.8–0.9 is meritory, 0.7–0.8 is middling, 0.6–0.7 is mediocre, 0.5–0.6 is miserable, and 0.5 and lower is unacceptable. As a general rule, Kaiser's MSA must be at least 0.6 or above, but most journals expect a Kaiser's MSA of 0.8 or above, with preference given to scores above 0.9.

The third part of the factor analysis results indicates that a scree plot was used to determine whether the model was unidimensional (contained only one factor). A scree plot is a plot of eigenvalues. Without going into detail, an eigenvalue describes the variance of the set of data points in a multivariate space that has one axis for each variable (Tabachnick & Fidell, 2001). You probably just hit your head on the table and think that sentence makes absolutely no sense whatsoever. Do not fear, we are here to help. In any dataset, the maximum number of the eigenvalues is equal to the number of scale items being factor analyzed. For example, in the HA there are 16 scale items, so the combined eigenvalue for the scale is 16. The question becomes, can we minimize the eigenvalue sum (16) so that only one eigenvalue is above the number 1? For example, in our survey, the first component had an eigenvalue of 6.966, which accounted for 43.54% of the variance. In other words, one factor accounts for 43.54% of the variance in the HA scale. Ideally, for each eigenvalue above 1.0 in a factor analysis, you will extract one factor. In the example above, there were actually three factors that had eigenvalues above 1.0 (component 2, 1.30: and component 3, 1.12). However, researchers have shown that relying on the eigenvalues alone for extracting factors can be misleading. For this reason, it is also encouraged that you examine a scree plot when extracting factors (Figure 21.7).

In Figure 21.7, the scree plot is actually the plot of the eigenvalues themselves. The word "scree" is actually a geological term referring to the debris that collects toward the bottom of a rocky slope. If you look at Figure 21.7, the figure is kind of reminiscent of a rocky slope. The scree plot has a clear downward trajectory that then levels off and flattens out to the right. The first data point is placed at 6.966 and the second point is plotted at 1.30. To determine how many factors to extract using a scree plot, it is best to use the concept of looking at the elbow. On a scree plot there will always be at least one eigenvalue above 1.0. In our example, the first eigenvalue 6.966 is considerably larger than the rest of the eigenvalues. In fact, if you look at the scree plot, it is hard to clearly delineate the 15 eigenvalues from each other as far as how they are plotted. This leveling off of a scree plot is called the elbow of the plot. Any eigenvalues separated from the elbow are considered actual factors, and those eigenvalues in the elbow or in the tail of the scree plot are considered residuals of that primary factor. Figure 21.8 shows the scree plot associated with the factor analysis of the sociocommunicative orientation scale. Remember, the sociocommunicative orientation measures two factors—assertiveness and responsiveness.

You will note that in Figure 21.9 that there are two clear eigenvalue plots—one at 6.17 and one at 3.36—and then you see a big dip and the creation of the elbow of the scree plot.

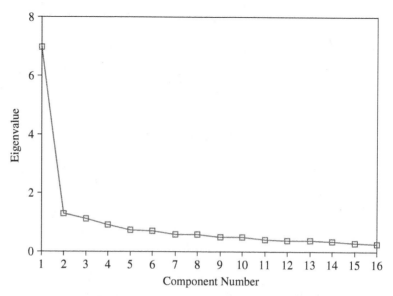

Figure 21.7 Scree Plot for Humor Assessment

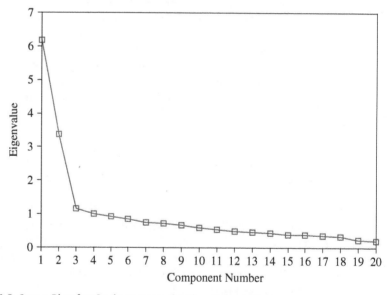

Figure 21.8 Scree Plot for Sociocommunicative Orientation

This is an example of what it looks like when a factor analysis has two clear factors that must be extracted from the data.

Once we have determined how many factors must be extracted from the data, we can examine how the values actually load. In our example we only extracted one actual factor, which can be seen in Figure 21.7. When examining the factor loadings (number in the right column in Figure 21.7), you will note that all of the loadings are 0.61 and higher. Even if a number has a minus in front of it, it is considered a high loading on the factor analysis. If you look carefully, you will see that all of those items that have negative factor loadings are items that are reverse coded on the scale. A factor analysis has the ability to factor a set of variables even if items have not been reverse coded because the factor analysis is attempting to determine whether people answer a set of scale items in a coherent fashion or whether participants respond one way to a certain type of questions and another way to a different type of question. As a rule of thumb, items should load on a single factor at 0.50 or higher and not load another factor at 0.30 or higher. Often, when more than one factor is extracted from a factor analysis, an item will load equally high for two different factors. In essence, this means that the scale item is actually not measuring either factor but is an index of both factors, and since a scale can only measure one thing, that scale item must be removed from the scale if it is to be statistically valid.

CANONICAL CORRELATIONS

Example

In the variable communication apprehension, there are four subscales that can be examined: group CA, meeting CA, interpersonal CA, and public CA. There are four subscales in willingness to communicate as well: group WTC, meeting WTC, interpersonal WTC, and public WTC. Suppose that you wanted to determine the nature of the relationship between the four subscales of communication apprehension with the four subscales of willingness to communicate. You could run a lot of correlations, or you could conduct one canonical correlation.

Explanation

A **canonical correlation** is a statistical tool that allows a researcher to investigate the relationships among two or more variable sets. In our example, we have two different variable sets: communication apprehension (group, meeting, interpersonal, and public) and willingness to communicate (group, meeting, interpersonal, and public). Variables in a canonical correlation must be either interval or ratio level variables. All of the variables used in our example are interval variables, so the canonical correlation is a good statistical tool to determine the interrelationships among the variables. Ultimately, a canonical analysis is the best test to use when examining statistical relationships between multiple interval/ratio independent variables with multiple interval/ratio dependent variables.

APA Write-Up

The goal of this research question was to examine the relationships among the four communication apprehension subscales (group, meeting, interpersonal, and public) and the four willingness to communicate subscales (group, meeting, interpersonal, and public). A canonical correlation was calculated using the four communication apprehension subscales as the predictors of the four willingness to communicate subscales. Using Wilks's Λ, the overall model was significant—Wilks's $\Lambda = 0.68$, $F(16, 889.66) = 7.54$, $p < 0.001$—which indicates that the two variable sets are significantly associated by the canonical correlation. Only the first two canonical correlations were found to be significant in this study: canonical correlation 1, Wilks's $\Lambda = 0.68$, $F(16, 889.66) = 7.54$, $p < 0.001$; and canonical correlation 2, Wilks's $\Lambda = 0.91$, $F(9, 710.80) = 3.10$, $p = 0.001$. Canonical correlations 3 and 4 were not significant: canonical correlation 3, Wilks's $\Lambda = 0.99$, $F(4, 586) = 0.94$, $p = 0.44$; and canonical correlation 4, Wilks's $\Lambda = 0.99$, $F(1, 294) = 0.07$, $p = 0.80$. The first variate accounted for approximately 26% of the variance in the dependent variable (canonical correlation [rc] = 0.51), and the second variate accounted for approximately 7.84% of the variance in the dependent variable (rc = 0.28). The exact canonical loadings for each variable can be seen in Figure 21.9.

Variable	Variate One	Variate Two
Group Communication Apprehension	−.81	.16
Meeting Communication Apprehension	−.94	−.13
Interpersonal Communication Apprehension	−.88	.41
Public Communication Apprehension	−.74	−.46
Group Willingness to Communicate	.81	−.41
Meeting Willingness to Communicate	.89	−.17
Interpersonal Willingness to Communicate	.61	−.67
Public Willingness to Communicate	.94	.08

Figure 21.9 Canonical Variate Loadings

Discussion

When examining a canonical analysis, it is always important to remember what is actually being correlated. In this example, we were examining the relationships between the four communication apprehension subscales (group, meeting, interpersonal, and public) and the four willingness to communicate subscales (group, meeting, interpersonal, and public). The first statistic that is reported is the significance test for the whole model. Because our independent variable (communication apprehension) had four variables (group, meeting, interpersonal, and public), we end up with four canonical correlations to be calculated. The results indicated that only the first two canonical correlations were significant. This does not mean that only the relationships between group CA and meeting CA are significant. Instead, in a canonical correlation, the model allows for the possibility that each independent variable may function uniquely and thus need its own variate. To understand what the two significant canonical correlations mean, you must look at how all of the variables (both independent and dependent) load on the significant canonical variates (see Figure 21.9). We interpret each significant canonical variate separately in a fashion similar to interpreting a factor analysis. The stronger a variable loads on an individual variate (the closer that variable is to 1), then the more commonality that variable has with that specific variate. When looking at Figure 21.9, you will see that the communication apprehension variables load negatively on the first variate and the willingness to communicate variables load positively on the first variate. This should be expected since CA and WTC are negatively related constructs. However, the story does not end there. When you look at the second variate, a new story is developing. The cutoff point for meaningfulness of a loaded variable on a variate is 0.30 (Tabachnick & Fidell, 2001), so in our example in Figure 21.9, group CA, meeting CA, meeting WTC, and public WTC did not load on the second variate at all. Most of the variables are loaded moderately on the variate (interpersonal CA, public CA, and group WTC). Interpersonal WTC is actually loaded negatively higher on the second variate than on the first variate. It should also be noted that interpersonal CA loads positively on the second variate.

So, what does all of this mean about the relationship between the CA subscale variables and WTC subscale variables? A lot. First, we learn that CA and WTC are clearly negatively related. However, the exact nature of that relationship does depend on the subscales themselves because they do not simply negatively relate. The second variate indicates that although interpersonal WTC, public CA, and group WTC may be low, it is still possible for someone to have a higher level of interpersonal CA. In other words, there are some people who do not exhibit high levels of public speaking CA, but may still experience high levels of interpersonal CA.

Conclusion

In this chapter we have introduced you to a variety of advanced statistical techniques, shown you how their results may appear in a research article, and discussed seven research questions (that could be answered using the dataset on the textbook's website) as well as one hypothetical research question. We have looked at four difference tests (factorial ANOVA, ANCOVA, MANOVA, and repeated-measures ANOVA) and four relationship tests (path analysis, structural equation modeling, factor analysis, and canonical correlation). This chapter concludes our investigation of actual statistical techniques that communication researchers employ to answer social scientific research questions. The next chapter will examine what to do with your research study when you are done with the paper/project.

KEY TERMS

Analysis of covariance (ANCOVA)
Canonical correlation
Covariate
Endogenous variable
Exogenous variable
Factor analysis

Factorial ANOVA
Interaction effect
Law of parsimony
Main effect
Multivariate analysis of variance (MANOVA)

Multivariate test
Path analysis
Repeated-measures ANOVA
Structural equation model
Univariate test

REFERENCES

Bollen, K. A., & Long, S. J. (1993). *Testing structural equation models*. Newbury Park, CA: Sage.

Byrne, B. M. (2010). *Structural equation modeling with AMOS: Basic concepts, applications and programming* (2nd ed.). New York, NY: Routledge.

Grimm, L. G., & Yarnold, P. R. (Eds.). (2000a). *Reading and understanding multivariate statistics*. Washington, DC: American Psychological Association.

Grimm, L. G., & Yarnold, P. R. (Eds.). (2000b). *Reading and understanding more multivariate statistics*. Washington, DC: American Psychological Association.

Kaiser, H. F. (1974). An index of factorial simplicity. *Psychometrika, 39*, 401–415.

Mertler, C. A., & Vannatta, R. A. (2005). *Advanced and multivariate statistical methods* (3rd ed.). Glendale, CA: Pyrczak.

Richmond, V. P., Wrench, J. S., Gorham, J. (2001). *Communication, affect, and learning in the classroom*. Acton, MA: Tapestry Press.

Tabachnick, B. G., & Fidell, L. S. (2001). *Using multivariate statistics* (4th ed.). Boston, MA: Allyn & Bacon.

FURTHER READING

Asher, H. B. (1983). *Causal modeling* (2nd ed.). Newbury Park, CA: Sage.

Bruning, J. L., & Kintz, B. L. (1997). *Computational handbook of statistics* (4th ed.). New York, NY: Longman.

Fox, J., & Weisberg, S. (2011). *An R companion to applied regression* (2nd ed.). Los Angeles, CA: Sage.

CHAPTER 22

Presenting Research

CHAPTER OBJECTIVES

1 Write a discussion section in response to the rest of the paper.

2 Explain the five goals of a discussion section.

3 Write an abstract.

4 Explain the purposes of conference presentations.

5 Differentiate among the three types of conference presentations (paper, poster, and panel).

6 Explain the process one goes through for submitting a paper to a conference.

7 Describe process one goes through for submitting a paper to an academic journal.

8 Explain the three responses an author may receive from a journal editor (accept for publication, revise and resubmit, and reject).

This book has taken you on a journey to demonstrate how communication researchers conduct quantitative research. In the first three chapters, we introduced you to the basic underlying assumptions in scientific communication research and how to conduct yourself ethically as a researcher. Chapters 4 and 5 then discussed how to go about searching for existing literature and then incorporate this literature into a *literature review*. This literature review then enabled you to create a series of arguments that formed hypotheses and research questions in your *rationale section*. Chapter 6 then explained what variables are and how communication researchers utilize variables. Chapters 8 and 9 discussed how we measure variables in communication, whereas Chapter 7 explained how mathematics can be used to describe collected variable data. Chapter 10 introduced us to conducting survey research, Chapter 11 introduced content analysis, and Chapter 12 introduced experimental research. Chapter 13 then explained the different types of samples that researchers could utilize while conducting research. Chapters 6 through 13 provided you with the nuts and bolts of conduct quantitative research, which is the information one generally provides in her or his *method section*.

Chapter 14 then introduced you to the theoretical premises behind hypothesis testing before actually showing you a variety of statistical tests, covered in Chapters 15 through 20. In those chapters, we provided you with numerous examples of how to write up research results using APA style. The results section of a research paper consists of conducting the most parsimonious tests to answer the hypotheses and research questions you formulated in your rationale section at the end of the literature review. In other words, for every hypothesis or research question you posed in your rationale section, you should have a corresponding section in your *results section*. But we do not stop the research process just because we have written our results.

By this point in your research project, you have completed your data analysis and are probably ready to exhale a huge sigh of relief. But what good are results for a study if the author fails to explain what the information means for the reader? In this chapter, we will describe the process of writing the discussion section of a research paper, presenting at conferences, and publishing your research.

Too often, students or authors spend countless hours completing a research project only to have it sit in a file folder. Our purpose in conducting research is to share our knowledge and expand our understanding of phenomena in our discipline. In this chapter we will describe the steps involved in preparing your work for conference presentations and publication. After all, it would be a shame to keep your research findings on a shelf.

However, before we can talk about disseminating our research, there are two final parts of the research project we must examine: the discussion section and the abstract.

Writing a Discussion Section

The six previous chapters have been dedicated to the data analysis phase of the research project. Each chapter has provided you with information on how to present the findings of your analyses in the results section using APA format guidelines. But do you recall our instructions to provide "just the facts" in the results section and resist the temptation to engage in any interpretation of the data? There was a reason for that—each research project concludes with a discussion section, and this section provides the author with the opportunity to provide an interpretation of the findings.

Students often report that they find the discussion section to be the most interesting part of a journal article. After all, this is where the author's own voice is heard. The discussion section allows the researcher to create links between the study and previous work, discuss any roadblocks that were encountered during the research process, and provide suggestions as to how other scholars can build upon this new information. In essence, the discussion section is like the last chapter in a good book. It provides a conclusion to the research project.

Depending on the type of research methodology employed, the format of the discussion section could vary. Qualitative studies sometimes combine results and discussion sections together because it is difficult to present findings without simultaneously interpreting them for the reader. The focus of this chapter will be on writing the discussion section for quantitative studies. As a general rule, there are typically five goals for this section:

1. Provide the reader with a summary of the major results or findings of the study.
2. Provide an interpretation or the meaning of these findings.
3. Discuss the relationship between the findings and previous research.
4. Acknowledge any limitations of the study.
5. Discuss the implications of the findings and suggest future research directions.

PROVIDING A SUMMARY OF MAJOR FINDINGS

Discussion sections begin with one or two paragraphs summarizing the major findings of the study. In essence, the introductory paragraph serves as an abstract for the discussion section. If the results section is strong, the reader already has the statistical information and knows whether the research questions and hypotheses were supported, so this is not the place to re-iterate statistics. Instead, a clear and succinct summary of the results should be presented. Figure 22.1 shows the introductory paragraph from the discussion section of Wrench and Booth-Butterfield's (2003) study on patient compliance. Note how the authors succinctly summarize the major findings of the study and transition into an interpretation of these results.

They begin the discussion by stating the primary goal for the study. This information creates the foundation for the remainder of the section by reminding the reader of the overall purpose for the project. Next, a concise summary of the overall findings is presented. This statement is especially important in studies where extensive data analyses are conducted. It enables the reader, who may not have a strong grasp of statistical analyses, the opportunity to understand the overall results. Wrench and Booth-Butterfield conclude the paragraph with a preview of the information to be discussed in the section. Previews such as these allow the author to subtly remind the reader what research questions and hypotheses were proposed in the study.

PROVIDING AN INTERPRETATION OF FINDINGS

At this point in the research process, you have spent countless hours formulating, examining, and analyzing questions and data. Now is the time to present your interpretation of the study. The discussion section of the research report provides you with the opportunity to allow your voice to be heard. A second goal of the discussion section is to explain the meaning of the results and share insight into why the findings are relevant or important. Typically, the author will devote a paragraph of discussion for each research question or hypothesis proposed in the study. A good way to start each paragraph is by paraphrasing the question or hypothesis being discussed. Follow this with a concise statement that clearly states the direction of the relationship between the independent and dependent variables. Subsequent sentences focus on the author's interpretation of why the findings are important. The use of language in interpreting

> The primary goal of this study was to determine how physicians' humor orientation, credibility, and use of compliance-gaining strategies relate to patient satisfaction and compliance. The findings revealed significant relationships suggesting that better physician communication skills were associated with improved patient perceptions of physician credibility and patient satisfaction. The following paragraphs focus on the relationship that a physician's humor orientation has on patient satisfaction and physician credibility, the relationship between patient satisfaction and physician credibility, the relationship of compliance-gaining strategies with physician–patient interactions, and the post–hoc analysis of the data sources used.

Figure 22.1 Introducing the Discussion Section

the results is particularly important in this section. Resist the temptation to use definitive language to describe your results. Rather than stating that "results proved" something, consider evaluating results by applying language such as "results suggest" or "indicate."

Review the Wrench and Booth-Butterfield (2003) article and note how each paragraph provides a succinct overview of the research question or hypothesis that was examined. No statistical information was included in the summaries. Rather, they summarize the statistical results using descriptive terms such as "positive relationship," "negative relationship," and "statistically significant." Declarative statements are avoided. Instead, the language used to interpret their findings includes phrases such as "the results appear to show" and "suggest" to avoid making claims that may later need to be defended.

DISCUSSING THE RELATIONSHIP BETWEEN FINDINGS AND PREVIOUS STUDIES

Remember the review of literature that was completed at the beginning of the research project? Although you may have thought the only purpose of the review was to provide information for formulating the research question or hypothesis, there is one more opportunity to incorporate the information in your paper. One of the primary goals of research is to build a body of knowledge. Because the review of literature serves as the foundation for a research project, it is important to show how the current study builds on the existing knowledge. A third goal of the discussion section is to discuss the relationship between the study's findings and previous studies. How do your findings compare with those of related studies? Discussing the relationship between the current study and previous studies creates a context for the results. If the current study was the result of an idea for future research proposed by a previous study, now is the opportunity to acknowledge this information. Some common phrases used to make connections between studies include "supports the findings of Smith (1998)" or "contribute to the differences found in the current study and those reported by Smith (1998)." The last goal of the discussion section is to demonstrate how your results support and build on theory. As we mentioned in Chapter 4, one of the reasons many researchers conduct research is to test and extend existing theories. The discussion section is where a researcher is able to shed light on the theory he or she is examining based on the results in her or his study. Did the researcher's results support the assumptions of the theory, or did the results negate the assumptions of the theory? Ultimately, clearly demonstrating how one's results impact our understanding of theory is extremely important because your discussion will influence how other people understand the theory.

Wrench and Booth-Butterfield (2003) incorporate previous research findings to provide a rationale for their results. Several references are made throughout the discussion section to previous results to demonstrate that a pattern of similar findings exists across studies. This serves to strengthen the conclusions proposed by the authors. Note that references to previous studies are separate from the discussion of the findings. Rather, they are woven throughout the discussion to provide the reader with a "big picture" of the major findings and how they relate to earlier work.

ACKNOWLEDGING LIMITATIONS

Every research study is affected by **limitations**. It is better for the author to identify and address the limitations of the study in the discussion section than to have a reader or reviewer point them out later. You are not claiming that the study was poorly designed by pointing out these flaws; rather, you are sharing the insight gained by looking at the big picture. Later in this chapter we will provide recommendations for submitting research for presentation or publication. An author who points out the weaknesses in her or his study will enhance his or her credibility as a researcher. In addition to highlighting limitations, the discussion section provides the author with an opportunity to propose methods for overcoming these flaws in future studies. Examples of limitations often addressed in this section include inappropriateness in the design, population, methods, or instrumentation.

Although the Wrench and Booth-Butterfield (2003) study provides valuable insight into understanding the relationship between physicians' use of humor and patient satisfaction, the study has limitations. The authors highlight these limitations through the use of the subheading "limitations" and devote two paragraphs to address the limitations with measurement instruments and sampling methods. Note that they incorporate examples of previous research by other scholars to provide support for their recommendations.

DISCUSSING IMPLICATIONS AND FUTURE DIRECTIONS

The discussion section should conclude with a summary of the theoretical or practical **research implications** of the study and recommendations for **future directions** in research. If the study supports existing theory, it is appropriate to point out the contributions it makes in this section. Perhaps your results offer practical implications for the reader. Use this opportunity to discuss the benefits of the information. In their article, Wrench and Booth-Butterfield (2003) conclude by emphasizing the benefits of the study for enhancing interactions between patients and physicians and potentially decreasing the number of malpractice claims that are filed as a result of dissatisfaction.

Although the research project is designed to answer questions, the end result may actually result in questions that are unanswered. Some of these questions may evolve because of the findings of your study. The concluding paragraphs of the discussion section provide the author with an opportunity to suggest directions for future research. Reflecting on the current study, ideas are proposed for the next step in research that examines similar variables. Some of these may evolve out of the limitations of the existing study. Others may be the result of comparing results with similar studies. The future directions provide other researchers with ideas to launch their own research projects.

Once the discussion section is finished, your research task may seem to be complete. But not so fast—after all, has the study contributed to the body of literature on a subject if it remains on your computer or in a file folder? Given the time and energy dedicated to the project, it is important to share the data with others. Several outlets for research exist. These include presenting your research at professional conferences or conventions and submitting your study for publication in an academic journal.

Writing the Abstract

Once you have concluded your discussion section, it is time to write your study's abstract. As we discussed in Chapter 5, the APA's Style Manual (2010) says that an abstract should be accurate, self-contained, and concise/specific. To be accurate, an abstract should correctly reflect what occurs in the paper itself. To be self-contained, an abstract should not need any specialized information for the reader to understand what the abstract is communicating. Finally, a good abstract should be concise and specific. You should not attempt to retell your entire study, but you should give as much information to a potential reader that he or she understands what you did in your study by discussing any relevant results and conclusions. However, many research projects can have 10–20 results or major conclusions, so it is usually best to limit your number of conclusions in the abstract to the five most important findings, because in APA style your abstract is limited to 120 words.

Now that we have taken you through the world of creating, conducting, and writing quantitative research projects, it is time to talk about how to disseminate your findings to other researchers by both presenting at conferences and publishing.

Presenting at Conferences

Each professional discipline has its own associations that are designed to promote the research and scholarly activities of its members. In the communication discipline, there are associations at the state, regional, national, and international levels. Depending on your area of specialization, there may even be additional opportunities to network and share research. For example, if you completed a study examining humor in organizations, you could present your research at business conferences, psychology conferences, or humor conferences instead of communication conferences. Figure 22.2 lists the communication associations that host conventions or conferences where research is presented. The majority of these associations host annual conventions that feature research presentations by students and faculty. Some convention feature special preconferences, which focus on undergraduate and graduate research. All of the regional communication associations (Central [http://www.csca-net.org/], Eastern [http://www.ecasite.org], Southern [http://www.ssca.net/], and Western [http://www.west-comm.org/]) have undergraduate conferences that coincide with those organization's annual convention. Furthermore, there are a number of colleges and universities that sponsor communication conferences targeted for undergraduate research . The best place to find information on these conferences is in either the National Communication Association's (NCA) monthly newsletter *Spectra* or by joining the NCA listserv Communication, Research, and Theory Network (CRTNET, http://www.natcom.org/crtnet/). Deadlines for conference submissions vary, and it is best to consult the organization's website for submission information.

As a student, there are many reasons why a communication conference should be of interest to you. Conferences provide students with an opportunity to meet and hear from scholars in the field, to learn about new methodologies and applications in research, and to present their own research. Networking and research presentation opportunities are the primary focus of these events. Faculty and alumni from various institutions catch up and share research and teaching ideas. Many schools recruit future graduate students at these events. After all, if an undergraduate student has an interest in presenting research and getting involved in professional associations, this is a good indicator of her or his potential as a graduate student. Before we continue, it is important to remember that conferences are professional events, so you should always dress appropriately. In other words, if you are presenting, you should be in formal business attire, and if you are just attending but not presenting, you can go with business casual.

Divisions and Interest Groups

An important benefit provided by conferences is the opportunity provided to network with colleagues with similar interests. Perhaps the best way to meet other scholars with similar interests is to attend presentations sponsored by specific interest groups or divisions. Most associations provide their members with the opportunity to affiliate with several **academic divisions/interest groups** that represent various communication contexts. The National

INTERNATIONAL
International Communication Association
World Communication Association

NATIONAL
American Communication Association
National Communication Association

REGIONAL
Central States Communication Association
Eastern Communication Association
Southern States Communication Association
Western Communication Association

STATE
Arizona Communication Association
Arkansas Speech Communication Association
California Speech Communication Association
Carolinas Communication Association
Florida Communication Association
Georgia Communication Association
Illinois Speech & Theatre Association
Iowa Communication Association
Kansas Speech Communication Association
Kentucky Communication Association
Louisiana Communication Association
Maryland Communication Association
Michigan Association of Speech Communication
Minnesota, Communication and Theatre
    Association
Mississippi Speech Communication Association
Missouri, Speech and Theatre Association of
Nebraska Speech Communication and Theatre
    Association
New Jersey Communication Association
New York State Communication Association
North Dakota Speech and Theatre Association
North West Communication Association
Ohio Communication Association
Oklahoma Speech Theatre Communication
    Association
Oregon Speech Communication Association

Pennsylvania, Speech Communication
    Association of
Rocky Mountain Communication Association
South Dakota, Speech Communication
    Association
Tennessee Speech Communication Association
Texas Speech Communication Association
Virginia Association of Communication Arts
    and Sciences
Wisconsin Communication Association

SAMPLE OF SPECIALIZED OR RELATED
    ASSOCIATIONS
Academy of Management
American Association of Public Opinion Research
American College of Physicians
American Public Health Association
American Society for the History of Rhetoric
Association for Business Communication
Association for Women in Communications
Association for Education in Journalism and
    Mass Communication
Broadcast Education Association
Gerontological Society of America
International Association for Conflict Management
International Association for Humor Studies
International Association for Intercultural
    Communication Studies
International Association for Media and
    Communication Research
International Association for Relationship
    Research
International Listening Association
International Public Relations Association
Kenneth Burke Society
Media Ecology Association
National Council on Family Relations
Public Relations Society of America
Religious Communication Association
Rhetoric Society of America
Society for Personality and Social Psychology
Society for Risk Analysis

Figure 22.2 Professional Communication Associations

Communication Association currently has around 50 divisions and sections representing a variety of interests (the 2012 list of NCA divisions can be seen in Figure 22.3). Each of these groups schedules programs of research presentations at an annual convention, so whatever your interests are, there is an outlet for presentation.

SUBMITTING RESEARCH FOR CONFERENCE REVIEW

Once you have decided to submit your research paper to a professional conference, you should consult the call for programs on the organization's website. The call for programs document provides important information on submitting your paper or proposal for review. Typically the deadlines for convention submissions are 6–9 months prior to the actual event. A sample of the **call for papers** for submissions to the Organizational Communication Division of ECA

Activism and Social Justice Division
African American Communication and Culture Division
American Studies Division
Applied Communication Division
Argumentation and Forensics Division
Asian/Pacific American Communication Studies Division
Basic Course Division
Communication and Aging Division
Communication and the Future Division
Communication and Law Division
Communication and Sport Division
Communication Apprehension and Competence Division
Communication Assessment Division
Communication as Social Construction Division
Communication Ethics Division
Communication and Social Cognition Division
Critical and Cultural Studies Division
Environmental Communication Division
Ethnography Division
Experiential Learning in Communication Division
Family Communication Division
Feminist and Women Studies Division
Freedom of Expression Division
Game Studies Division
Gay, Lesbian, Bisexual, Transgender, and Queer Communication Studies Division
Group Communication Division
Health Communication Division
Human Communication and Technology Division
Instructional Development Division
International and Intercultural Communication Division
Interpersonal Communication Division
Language and Social Interaction Division
Latino/ Latina Communication Studies Division
Mass Communication Division
Nonverbal Communication Division
Organizational Communication Division
Peace and Conflict Communication Division
Performance Studies Division
Philosophy of Communication Division
Political Communication Division
Public Address Division
Public Dialogue and Deliberation Division
Public Relations Division
Rhetorical and Communication Theory Division
Spiritual Communication Division
Theatre, Film, and New Multi-Media Division
Training and Development Division
Visual Communication Division
This list was accurate as of January 2012.

Figure 22.3 National Communication Association—2011 Divisions and Sections

(Figure 22.4) illustrates many of the guidelines provided for submissions. We should note that the regional associations (as of 2012) still accept submissions via e-mail, but the national and international associations now have a website where all submissions are conducted. As always, please check the individual association's website for more information on how they accept submitted manuscripts.

EASTERN COMMUNICATION ASSOCIATION

ORGANIZATIONAL COMMUNICATION DIVISION

Copies of Papers: 1 [in electronic form only; NO hard copies]
Deadline: October 15, 20xx
Specify student papers: yes
Maximum length: 25 pages, excluding title page, abstract, references, tables, and figures

The Organizational Communication Division invites competitive papers and panel proposals on the theory, research, and teaching of organizational communication. The Division embraces all theoretical and methodological approaches to research. The submission of papers and panels pursuing the convention theme, "Insert Theme Here," is strongly encouraged.

Completed Paper Submissions should be emailed with the following:

1. TWO attached Microsoft Word (.doc or .rtf) files:

   - File 1) title page with the paper title and the author name (s)* and contact information (affiliation, mailing address, telephone number, email address) and a statement of professional responsibility (see below).
   - (File 2) text of the paper starting with a one-page abstract. All author identifiers should be removed from the text (excluding previous scholarly works cited in the paper and listed in the reference section). The word "Debut" should be marked on papers by authors who have not presented previously at a regional or national convention.
   - Statement of professional responsibility on the abstract page (see below).

2. The email subject line should include the abbreviation "ECA" and the title of the paper. The email text should include any requests for presentation aids such as overhead projector, TV/DVD player, etc. (see below).

Panel Proposal Submissions should be emailed and include the following:

1. ONE Microsoft Word (.doc or .rtf) file containing:

   - A thematic title for the program
   - Names of the chair and respondents, if any. Please do not have chairs act as respondents.
   - Names, mailing addresses, telephone numbers, email addresses, and institutional affiliations of all participants
   - Titles and abstracts for each paper or presentation
   - A program copy (NO MORE than a 75-word description) as it should appear in the final program
   - A detailed rationale for the program/panel
   - A statement of professional responsibility (see below)

2. The email subject line should include the abbreviation "ECA" and the title of the panel. The email text should include any requests for presentation aids such as overhead projector, TV/DVD player, etc. (see below).

Papers and panels not meeting these submission guidelines will not be distributed for review.

Figure 22.4 Sample Call for Convention Papers

Continued

Statement of Professional Responsibility

ALL submissions must include (on either the abstract or the second page of the panel proposal) a statement of professional responsibility that reads:

"In submitting the attached paper/panel, I/we recognize this submission is a professional responsibility. I/We agree to present this paper/panel if it is accepted and programmed. I/We further recognize that all who attend or present at ECA's annual meeting must register and pay required fees."

ECA Technology Policy

ECA has a Technology Policy (available in full text at http://www.ecasite.org/pdf/technologypolicy042007.pdf). Please note in particular the section that reads, "ECA will not approve requests for the following technology: personal computers, laser printers, satellite links, teleconference equipment, LCD panels and projectors, video data projects, and digital versatile/video disc equipment."

Questions & Additional Information

Please contact the Organizational Communication program planner, **Chair of the Organizational Communication Division**, at chair@genericuniversity.edu if you have any questions. Additional information about the convention, including short courses and other programming, is available on the ECA website, http://www.ecasite.org/.

The call will specify whether the paper should be submitted in electronic format or mailed to the coordinator. Be sure to note what file format is preferred for submissions. Instructions provide guidelines as to page length limitations and deadlines for submission. Specific information on formatting of submissions is included, and often items such as a title page, abstract, key terms, and audiovisual needs are detailed. Some divisions schedule special panels or present awards to the top papers authored by students. To be considered for these, you should include the phrase "student authored" or "student paper" on the title page.

All conference submissions are submitted to blind peer review to ensure that the papers are given an equal opportunity for programming. The blind review process requires all authors to remove any identifying information from the text of the paper to ensure that no preferential treatment will be shown in the evaluation. Most of the information that would need to be changed is located in the methods section of the research paper, and changes are often relatively simple. For example, if you initially reported in the paper that participants were students enrolled in classes at Ohio University, the name of the institution could be concealed by changing the description to students enrolled in classes at a large Midwestern university.

TYPES OF CONFERENCE PRESENTATIONS

Paper Presentations

Presentations take one of three forms at a professional conference: paper presentations, poster presentations, or panel discussions. **Paper presentations** involve an oral report about the research project, typically followed by a response from a scholar who has conducted research in the area. If time permits, the audience may choose to ask authors questions about their projects. Depending on the topic, an average of three to six papers may be scheduled to be presented during the same session. This typically means that an author can expect to have between 10 and 15 minutes to talk about the research project. That is not a lot of time, so if your paper is selected for presentation, you will need to give careful consideration to what you will highlight in your presentation and rehearse to ensure that your presentation meets the time constraints.

If you have only 10–15 minutes, how do you condense a 25- to 30-page paper to that short period of time? Here is what we recommend. First, start your presentation by introducing your title and giving a short background about how the project was initiated. Did you see a hole in a theory? Did you notice that a communication variable had not been explored in a new context? Whatever the reasoning you have for your study, explain why you initiated the project in the first place. Explaining why you conducted your study should take no more than 1 minute.

Second, introduce the minimal research background necessary for your audience to understand your research variables. If you are dealing with a widely known concept like communication apprehension, you may need to provide a quick definition and a review of one or two studies that set up how you are looking at communication apprehension in your study. Presenting your study's variables should take no more than 2–5 minutes.

Third, explain the methods you used in your study. Start by giving a brief overview of how you collected your sample and any important demographics (sex, age, ethnicity, etc.). Next, explain the procedure that you used in your study as briefly as possible. If you conducted a complicated experiment, you may need to allow yourself a little more time to explain your experimental procedures. Then discuss the instrumentation used in your study. At this point, it is not really necessary to go into detail about alpha reliabilities, means, and standard deviations—just refer your audience to the paper for the specific statistical information. Presenting your methods should take only 1–3 minutes.

Fourth, systematically deliver your results. We recommend (1) telling your audience what a specific hypothesis or research question was, (2) explaining how you tested the hypothesis or research question, (3) presenting the general result for the hypothesis or research question, and (4) providing your audience a brief analysis of what your findings mean. This four-step process should be repeated for each of your major hypotheses and research questions. If, however, your study has many hypotheses and research questions or is overly complex, you may need to break your results into chunks of information that can be easily digested orally by your audience. While presenting your results, you do not want to get yourself hung up on long strings of numbers that confuse your audience. For example, if you are reporting a regression, just say that the regression was significant, what R^2 was, and whether any beta weights accounted for unique variance. Do not attempt to read all of the numbers in the F test, because saying that the regression was statistically significant will cover this in an oral presentation. You can also provide a basic interpretation of what each result means as you are discussing each finding. This section may take 2–5 minutes depending on your time limit, so keep it moving steadily.

Fifth, explain your limitations briefly (30 seconds max) and any major future directions you believe this line of research should take in the future. Finally, explain why this research is important and where you see this line of research heading in the future. This last part should be a quick summation of why the overall project was important and how it helps us understand human communication better.

After all of the presentations are complete, you may or may not have a respondent for your paper. A respondent is an academic who is trained in your area of research who will provide feedback on your manuscript's writing, analysis, and conclusions. The respondent will discuss each person's paper separately, so it is possible that it will feel like you are getting picked on during this process. The respondent is not trying to hurt your feelings or make you feel inferior; he or she really wants to offer you advice on how to make your paper stronger. While listening to the respondent, it is important not to become argumentative even if you think the respondent is wrong. Instead, listen and take notes about what the respondent is saying and then later decide whether you agree or disagree. If you start arguing with the respondent, either out loud or inside your head, you may end up missing some useful advice.

After the respondent is finished, the people who are attending the panel session are allowed to ask questions as time allows. As researchers, you should be ready for almost any type of question related to your study. People may ask you about why you used specific scales or why you chose your specific statistical analysis. If you are presented with a question that you are not completely sure you can answer, we recommend that you simply say that you are not sure, but you would be glad to find the answer for the questioner if he or she would provide you with an e-mail address at the conclusion of the session.

In the event that you are asked to present your paper at a conference or convention, we have some helpful hints for you:

1. DO NOT read us your paper. Okay, we are communication scholars who have taken public speaking. However, many people who present will actually read their manuscript in a fairly monotone fashion. Instead, we recommend making an outline of notes that you can use to deliver your presentation in an extemporaneous fashion—just as you learned to do in public speaking.

2. Make sure you know how much time you will have to present, and then make sure that your presentation can be made in the allotted time frame. Please realize that some speakers will alter their speaking rate once they are in front of an audience. If you know that you are someone who tends to slow down or talk too much in front of an audience, then you must plan your presentation accordingly.

3. When discussing your literature review, give only the absolutely necessary highlights. People are more interested in your new research than they are in what is already out there. However, if your research involves any complex terms that may not be familiar to a general communication audience, then you should provide definitions so people will understand the research.

4. Do not rely on having technology for your presentation. Increasingly, people want to use PowerPoint or other presentation software systems during a paper presentation. Unfortunately, the cost of such technology is often prohibitive for conferences and conventions. Even if you want to bring in your own laptop and projector, you should check with a conference or convention organizer to make sure that this is okay. Many conferences and conventions are held in locations that have strict rules about the use of technology (e.g., conference centers, hotels, etc.). Some conference and convention locations will allow individuals to bring in outside technology with no extra charge to the conference or convention. Conversely, some conference and convention locations will actually charge the conference or convention an electricity use fee for any technology used.

5. Always have a backup plan if you intend to use some kind of technology during your presentation. There is an old presenter's rule that states that if your technology can break down while presenting, it will. For this reason, you should always have a backup plan. One easy backup plan is to have a handout you can give your audience members. If the technology you wanted to use does not lend itself to a handout, you should think about how you can present without the technology in case something does go wrong. It is always better to have thought out a worst case scenario before it happens than to come up with a plan during the crisis.

6. Decide whether to stand or not to stand. One of the hardest questions some presenters have to make is whether they should stand or sit during their presentations. There is no standard rule for this issue. On some panels, everyone stands while presenting, whereas on other panels no one stands while presenting. From a basic public speaking perspective, standing is generally going to lead to a stronger connection with one's audience, so as a rule, we recommend standing. However, ultimately you should do what is most comfortable for you as a presenter.

Poster Presentations

A **poster presentation** is a great opportunity for individuals just getting their feet wet presenting at academic conferences and conventions. According to Nicol and Pexman (2003a, 2003b), the goal of a poster "is to summarize findings in a clear, interesting way to facilitate comprehension. Ultimately, the aim is for visitors to the poster to understand what the study was about and what the results were. The more visually appealing, well organized, and informative the poster is, the more likely people are to understand the study and findings" (p. 159). During a typical poster presentation, an author or group of authors will stand next to their poster and individuals will walk around reading the posters and talking to the author(s) about the study. One of the nice things about poster sessions is that they tend to be fairly low key and full of energy. You may even want to consider making a handout that summarizes your study to individuals who talk to you about your study. You could also have a stack of copies of your actual paper to hand out to individuals as they talk to you during the poster session. For undergraduate and graduate students, all of the regional communication associations have competitive poster competitions during their conventions. Presenting your original research at a communication conference is a good resume builder whether you plan on entering graduate school or the corporate sector, and poster sessions provide a fairly nonthreatening way to do this even for individuals who have high public speaking anxiety.

At this point, you may be asking yourself, "What does a poster actually look like that is presented at a communication conference?" To give you a general idea of how posters are typically formatted, we have created a simple graphic to help you understand (Figure 22.5). First, every conference or convention has different requirements for the sizes of the poster, so

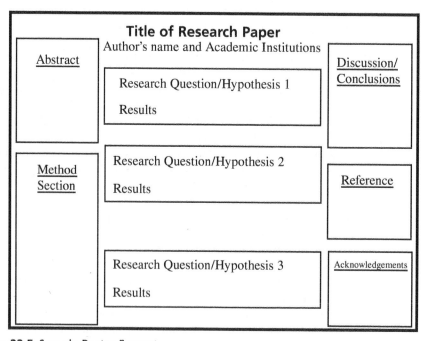

Figure 22.5 Sample Poster Format

ensure you find out how large your poster can be before you get to the conference. Furthermore, you will want to know whether your poster should be freestanding (such as on a table), displayable on an easel, or tacked to a cork board. The most common size poster is probably the 36" × 48" poster, and because this is the most common size of foam board, it is often used for trifold posters. Foam board is probably the number one choice for easel displays, whereas trifold posters are great for tabletop displays and easels. The reason we suggest both the foam board and trifold posters is because they tend to have a thickness to them that allows them to stand up on their own on an easel. If you try to use regular poster board, you will have a lot of problems keeping the poster in place.

Once you know the basic size of the poster, it is time to determine what information must be put on the poster board. First , your poster cannot be a simple retelling of your study. we have all seen lazy poster presenters who literally tack up their entire paper on the poster with no changes at all. As communication scholars, we have all taken public speaking and should know a little about the importance of visual aids, and that is exactly what a poster should be—a visual aid. Remember that the purpose of a poster session is to interact with other people discussing your research study as they walk by your poster. The more interesting the poster is, the more likely people are going to stop and talk to you about your research.

You will note in Figure 22.5 that there are a number of different parts commonly seen on a poster. The first part is the name of your study centered at the top of the poster, along with the author(s) names and college/university affiliations. After the paper title and your names, everything else is more creative. We provided you a simple format you can follow in Figure 22.5, but this is by no means the only format you could use for your poster. For example, if you have a large number of research questions and hypotheses, you may not end up including the references or acknowledgment sections on your poster. If you have too many research questions and hypotheses, you may end up only putting the three or four most important findings on your poster.

The first box you will see on the poster is the abstract box. We think it is a good idea to include your abstract on your poster because it gives a general overview of your paper. People may not stop and ask you questions, but they are more likely to walk by and quickly read your abstract. Furthermore, abstracts are often great conversation starters with people reading your poster.

The second box we have included on our sample poster in Figure 22.5 is the method box. Whether you conducted a qualitative, quantitative, or rhetorical/crucial study, people are going to want to know a little about your methodology. Obviously, you cannot provide all of the intricate details of the method you used in your study, but you can provide enough information to quickly explain what it is that you did.

The third, fourth, and fifth boxes are designed for the real heart of your study or your research questions and/or hypotheses. Some individuals like to clump all of their research questions and/or hypotheses into one box and then their results in another box, but we think this ultimately ends up confusing people examining your poster. For this reason, we recommend listing a research question or hypothesis, followed by what you found. Ultimately, this will help you demonstrate exactly what it is that you found in your study in a quick and efficient manner.

The sixth box is for your overall conclusions from your study. We often call this the "so what" box, or the "why should we really care about these findings?" box. If you have multiple important conclusions that can be made as a result of your study, we strongly recommend bulleting them to make them easier to read.

The seventh and eighth boxes contain information that may or may not be overly relevant. The seventh box contains a list of important references or works cited. Obviously, you cannot include all of the references or works cited listed in your manuscript. However, if there are a handful that are important, list them on your poster. The eighth box is one that is technically only necessary if your project was funded by someone. Many research projects receive grant funding for the project, and one common requirement of grants is that any presentation made about the study funded by the grant must acknowledge the source of funds.

In this section we have examined the different parts of Figure 22.5 in an effort to help you understand how to create a top-notch research poster. Before we move on to the next section, we want to stress a number of key elements in making a stellar poster:

1. Black and white is boring, so make sure you add color. But do not go overboard and start bedazzling your poster—there comes a point when there is too much flash.

2. Twelve-point Times New Roman or Courier New font may look great on the page, but cannot be read at a distance. When making your poster, stand at least 5 feet away from all words and see whether you can easily read them. If you cannot read your poster, no one else will bother trying.

3. A poster is a not a research paper, so there is no need to double space text that appears on the poster.

4. A poster is not an instant message or text message, so avoid Internet lingo on your poster (unless relevant). And make sure you use both upper- and lowercase letters.

5. Too much text on a poster can be boring, so using lists and bullets of information will be greatly appreciated by your readers. Furthermore, graphs, charts, and pictures are pretty and can help get information across much faster.

6. Make sure you use headings for each section of your poster. People get lost easily, so headings help them follow what you are saying.

7. A poster is a visual aid that should aid you in having a discussion with someone about your research project. The goal of your poster is to help you, not hinder you.

Scholar-to-Scholar Posters

Scholar-to-scholar presentations are similar to poster sessions. Although some scholar-to-scholar presenters will still utilize a traditional poster, others have gone beyond the traditional poster to include audio and video presentations. The purpose of the scholar-to-scholar sessions is to provide poster presenters with an opportunity to discuss their poster with top-notch scholars in the field of communication. In essence, a scholar-to-scholar presentation functions like a poster session, but top scholars whose research relates to the research being presented during the scholar-to-scholar sessions are invited to interact with the individuals presenting. scholar-to-scholar presentations provide a great way for you get feedback about your research study from some of the top minds in the field of communication.

Panel Discussions

Panel discussions are composed of three or more individuals who discuss a common topic in an informal format. Rather than each presenter delivering a formal presentation, they may be asked to offer their insight or opinions while a facilitator guides the discussion. Audience members are often encouraged to participate during panel sessions by asking questions or offering comments.

Although we wish we could say that all presentations are created equally, they really are not perceived this way in academia. Typically speaking, people who are presenting original research on a competitive panel generally are perceived as more prestigious than people presenting posters or sitting on panel discussions. In fact, some universities will not even count posters or panels as research presentations. We say this not to devalue posters and panels, but to warn you that you must know how your academic institution places value on these different presentational formats, especially if you decide to make a career in academia. Now that you understand the opportunities offered by professional associations for young scholars, we hope that you will consider submitting your research projects for review. After all, the format of a convention paper is nearly identical to the format discussed for research papers in this text.

Publication

One of the best ways to ensure that your research study contributes to the body of knowledge in the field is to submit it for publication to an academic journal. Articles submitted to academic journals are scholarly in nature. "Scholarly" indicates that facts and information included in the study are documented by citing the author and date of publication for relevant research. It is important to note that although authors of convention papers often receive feedback in 2–3 months, the journal review process is considerably longer. It may take anywhere from 1 to 5 years before an article submitted for review actually ends up in print. To better understand the time required for publishing journal articles, let's take a closer look at the review process.

JOURNAL REVIEW PROCESS

All articles submitted to academic journals are peer reviewed. The **peer review** process for academic journals is similar to that used by professional conventions with one notable exception. Feedback provided in a journal article review is much more comprehensive than the comments provided by a convention review panel. Whereas convention reviewers may simply rank papers they think should be presented, the process is much more rigorous when reviewing articles for publication. Journal review board members are often asked to provide one of four recommendations to the editor: (1) publish as is; (2) publish pending revisions; (3) revise and resubmit before a decision is made; or (4) reject the study. If the article is rejected, some editors and reviewers may offer suggestions for alternative outlets for the study to be considered for publication. Whether a study is accepted or rejected, authors typically receive extensive feedback from a panel of two or three anonymous reviewers. Let's take a look at the two processes involved in journal publication more closely: the submission process and the review process.

Submission Process

Once you have decided to submit your research for review, the next question is often, "Which journal is most appropriate for this study?" There are several options to choose from in determining which outlet is best for your research. Many of the associations listed in Figure 22.2 publish one or more academic journals, and the focus of each journal is unique in terms of the types of methodologies, communication contexts, and length of articles published. To determine which outlet is best suited for your research, review the call for manuscripts for more detailed guidelines. Samples of call for manuscripts are provided in Figure 22.6 for two prominent communication journals: *Communication Education* (*CE*) and *Communication Research Reports* (*CRR*).

Each of these samples provides scholars with information on the types of articles that are typically published with regard to methodology and contextual focus. In addition, format guidelines are provided as well as information about page length and how to submit articles. One obvious difference in the calls for *CE* and *CRR* is their page length requirements: *CRR* has a limit of 12 pages, whereas *CE* accepts manuscripts up to 30 pages in length. Another distinction can be found in the research contexts included in the journal: *CE* encourages manuscripts focusing on classroom communication phenomenon, whereas *CRR* welcomes manuscripts on a wide variety of topics focusing on human communication. Three basic factors will help guide your decision as to which journal is right for your research: (1) focus on communication context, (2) research methodologies, and (3) page length. To see a list of possible publication outlets that publish communication scholarship, review the chart of communication-related journals in Figure 4.6 from Chapter 4.

---

a) Communication Education (an NCA Journal)

Communication Education invites original, social science research on communication in instructional contexts. These should be methodologically rigorous studies that advance practice and theory in instruction generally, and in communication education specifically. I encourage submissions from well-designed, systematic and programmatic research, theoretically-grounded projects, rigorous literature reviews and meta-analyses. Importantly, these studies must be data-based and have a substantive impact on educational processes.

Sound studies that examine constructs that are important to teaching/learning processes will be emphasized; e.g., teacher/student interaction, verbal/non-verbal interaction in the teaching-learning context, classroom management, information processing, mediated or technology education, educational communication constructs, development and assessment, and learning outcomes will be considered.

One goal is high credibility and visibility of *Communication Education* as a premiere source of the highest level knowledge and information on communication in educational contexts. Therefore, comprehensive, major literature reviews, either empirical or narrative, will be featured. Such reviews should be thorough, detailed, and unbiased, and provide extensive background as well as the latest research on major instructional concepts.

Both new and experienced scholars are encouraged to submit their works, and will receive feedback that is both expedient and helpful. Correspondingly, all authors must submit articles that meet the highest standards of writing, grammar, and mechanics (emphasizing brevity). Authors who need editorial assistance can find support in online proofreading services, such as www.proofreadnow.com .

Given the distinctive missions of each of the NCA journals, book reviews are should be submitted to the more appropriate NCA journal, *The Review of Communication*, and articles focusing on teaching practices should be submitted to *Communication Teacher*.

Manuscript Submission

Communication Education has moved to an entirely electronic system for submissions and reviews. To facilitate rapid accessibility and review, manuscripts should be submitted online at Communication Education's ScholarOne site .

New users should first create an account. Once a user is logged onto the site, submissions must be made via the Author Center. Please submit papers formatted in MS Word in a

---

Figure 22.6 Call for Manuscripts for Communication Education and Communication Research Reports

Continued

PC-compatible version. To ensure a blind review process, any identifying information is entered during the online submission process where prompted, along with any other relevant information concerning the basis of the study (e.g., a dissertation, grant or paid consulting) and other background (e.g., prior presentations of results, grant support). Please keep all identifying information separate from the attached manuscript.

Manuscripts should be no longer than 25 double-spaced pages (not including tables and references), and must conform to the conventions of the 6th edition of the *Publication Manual of the American Psychological Association*. Manuscripts that do not conform to these guidelines will not be reviewed.

Manuscripts submitted to *Communication Education* must not be under consideration in other outlets, or have appeared in any other published form. Upon notification of acceptance, authors must assign copyright to the National Communication Association and provide copyright clearance for any copyrighted material used.

b) *Communication Research Reports* (an ECA Journal)

Communication Research Reports publishes brief empirical articles (approximately 10 double-spaced pages or less excluding tables and references) on a variety of topics of human communication. Empirical studies in the general contexts of interpersonal, organizational, communication traits, intercultural, nonverbal, small group, health, persuasion, mass, political, relational, computer mediated, life-span, and instructional communication are appropriate for submission. Consistent with the mission of the journal, the main portion of submitted manuscripts should focus on the method, results, and interpretation of the results. However, manuscripts must contain a concise theoretical rationale and relevant literature review.

Particular manuscripts may be designated as a Brief Report. At the discretion of the Editor, manuscripts that are designated as such will have gone through the complete review process (as full length manuscripts), provide value for the readership, yet not warrant a full-length article. Brief reports will be no longer than 3 to 5 pages (excluding tables and references) with the focus highlighting a specific finding and implications for the discipline. All sections traditionally included in a manuscript will be required, but must be brief and to the point. All extraneous information must be eliminated. Manuscripts that are submitted as a Brief Report will not be reviewed. The Brief Report designation is a function of editorial decision. Also at the discretion of the Editor will be one manuscript per issue designated as a Spotlight on Method/Analysis piece. These articles will be solicited by the Editor and will be 5–8 pages in length (excluding tables and references) highlighting topics that will range from novel methodological approaches and/or statistical techniques to common misconceptions/issues of contemporary controversy related to method/analysis. Each issue of CRR will contain one such manuscript that will be solicited and/or determined by the Editor.

Review Policy. Manuscripts will be blind-reviewed by at least two experts in the relevant subject matter. These evaluations will constitute the basis for the Editor's decision. *Communication Research Reports* is committed to completing the review process as efficiently and quickly as possible. Manuscripts that do not conform to submission guidelines will not be reviewed. No manuscript submitted for review can be previously published or be under consideration by any other journal at the time of submission.

Continued

Submission of Full-Length Manuscripts. *Communication Research Reports* will accept all manuscript submissions electronically via the ScholarOne Manuscripts website located at http://mc.manuscriptcentral.com/crr. For technical support regarding the ScholarOne Manuscripts system, you may contact them at http://scholarone.com/services/support. For all other inquiries, please contact Communication Research Reports at editor@genericuniversity.edu. Submitted manuscripts must be the original work of the author(s) and have all identifiers removed from the document. Authors should submit their files per the submission protocol found on ScholarOne. Manuscripts should be prepared using MS WORD and must conform to the 6th edition of the Publication Manual of the American Psychological Association. All general inquiries about the journal, it policies, or procedures should be directed to Theodore A. Avtgis, Editor.

Proofs. One set of page proofs will be sent to the designated corresponding author. Proofs should be checked and returned promptly as directed.

Complimentary Policy/Reprints. Each corresponding author will receive 50 complimentary reprints of their article upon registration with Rightslink, our authorized reprint provider. Authors will need to create a unique account and register with Rightslink for this free service. Complimentary reprints are not available past publication. Each corresponding author will also receive one complimentary copy of the issue in which their article appears.

Once you have determined which journal is appropriate for your research, be sure to adhere to all instructions for manuscript preparation detailed in the call. In particular, pay close attention to guidelines for page length, limits on the number of words to be included in the abstract, and preferred style format (APA or MLA). Be sure to carefully edit the manuscript to avoid any embarrassing mistakes. When you submit your paper, it is often a good idea to draft a short cover letter to the editor pointing out the unique contributions of your paper and how it "fits" with the journal content. Some editors may request that you add a statement confirming that the article has not been published elsewhere and is not being submitted simultaneously for review by another journal.

Review Process

As discussed earlier, the journal review process is lengthy and sometimes frustrating. Once you have reached this point in the process, be prepared to wait. Journal editors will often review the list of references included in your article to identify potential reviewers. Throughout the process, the author(s) and reviewer(s) remain anonymous. However, authors often include information in the manuscript that provides the reviewer with clues as to their identity. To maintain your anonymity, refrain from including too many references to your own work, and be sure to remove any and all identifying information from the manuscript. Citing references from the journal to which you are submitting your article is another way of demonstrating to the reviewers and editor how your research fits with what the journal is already publishing.

Prepare yourself for the feedback you will receive. After all, reviewers often feel obligated to find some issues with your study. Rarely do papers get accepted on the initial submission. Many papers undergo two to three revisions before they are ready for publication. Editors will send typed comments from the reviewers along with their anonymous recommendation for

Communication and Critical/Cultural Studies	11%
Communication Education	4.4%
Communication Monographs	12%
Communication Teacher	25%
Critical Studies in Media Communication	6.0%
Journal of Applied Communication Research	12.6%
The Quarterly Journal of Speech	0.13%
Review of Communication	42%
Text and Performance Quarterly	20%

Acceptance rates are calculated on the three-year editorial term of the previous editor.
SOURCE: https://www.natcom.org/uploadedFiles/More_Scholarly_Resources/List%20of%20Communication%20Journals2.xls
All represent 2012 numbers

Figure 22.7 NCA Journal Acceptance Rates

acceptance, revision, or rejection. If the recommendation from reviewers is to revise and re-submit your article, take heed and be sure to address the concerns identified in their reviews. Once you have made the recommended changes, it is a good idea to draft a letter to the reviewers letting them know that you have made the changes requested in their review. Address each recommendation made by the reviewer and explain how you responded to it in the revised manuscript. Doing so will communicate to the reviewers and the editor that you are committed to addressing their concerns and value their feedback.

Let's face it, not every manuscript that is submitted to a journal gets accepted. In fact, most communication journals average an acceptance rate of between 10 and 20 percent. That means that 80–90 percent of the articles are rejected. A summary of the acceptance rates for journals published by NCA (Figure 22.7) should provide you with additional insight into journal acceptance rates.

If you decide to submit your research for publication, chances are that you will experience rejections along the way. Although rejection is frustrating, you can adopt a positive view of the process if you utilize the feedback provided by the reviewers to help you revise the paper for submission to a different journal. Ask a colleague or professor to read the paper and share the feedback provided by reviewers to get their suggestions. Although nobody likes being rejected, it is important to remember that it is part of the publication process. Trust us—the satisfaction you will experience on receiving your first acceptance letter will make this entire process worth the effort.

Research Outside the Walls of Academia

Discussions of research abound in the twenty-first century. We are constantly bombarded with information related to quantitative information, so making the information easy to navigate for those who do not have a background in quantitative research methods is extremely important. For our purposes, we want to discuss two specific aspects of research reporting: writing for business and writing for the general public.

WRITING FOR BUSINESS

In Chapter 5 we discussed O'Shea's (1986) nine steps to writing a business research report: (1) executive summary, (2) project background, (3) objectives/scope, (4) methods, (5) analysis, (6) findings/conclusions, (7) recommendations, (8) benefits, and (9) implantation guide. Whether you are presenting your research in a written fashion or asked to orally present the information, this nine-step process is good for all basic presentation needs outside academia.

O'Shea (1986) also offers seven keys to writing a readable report that we think should be reiterated here as well:

1. Write short reports. Most people in the business world do not have the time to read long documents, so research reports should be written as shortly and directly as possible.

2. Arrange material for emphasis. You do not want to get your biggest finding or your number one recommendation lost because it is buried somewhere in the middle of the report. This is one reason why you should really lay out information in a matter that draws attention to material you want emphasized.

3. Avoid long, complex paragraphs and sentences. As academics ourselves, we know that a gorgeous, flowing, long-winded sentence can be a lot of fun to write. But in the world outside of academia, people want things to the point.

4. Avoid jargon. Writing about statistics and avoiding jargon can be difficult. As such, if you must use technical ideas and information, you must ensure that you provide a simple explanation for the jargon. If possible, avoid the jargon.

5. Use active voice and direct, descriptive words rather than euphemisms. Again, you want your reader to actively engage with your writing. If you are writing in a straightforward manner, people are more likely to read and remember what you have written.

6. Use pictures and graphs. People like pictures and graphics. We recommend also thinking about strategic use of color as well. However, you do not want to go overboard. We have seen some reports in which every other page is a picture or graph, which can become tedious. Remember, if you try to call attention to everything, you will end up calling attention to nothing. For this reason, use pictures and graphs to emphasize pieces of information you want your readers to remember and understand.

7. Use numbers selectively. Obviously, when you are discussing statistics you are going to have to use some numbers. However, you do not need to include every number. For example, one of our coauthors was working on a consulting project that involved correlations. Instead of presenting the correlation coefficients for each relationship in a correlation matrix, he placed a + sign for positive relationships, a − sign for negative relationships, and NR in spaces where no relationship was found. This more visual approach made it easier to understand for readers who were not schooled in quantitative research methods.

RESEARCH AND THE GENERAL PUBLIC

When writing up research that will be disseminated to the general public, it is important to remember that most people in the general public are functionally numerically illiterate. As such, any description of statistical analysis and data should be kept short and clear. Admittedly, it is often difficult for researchers to adjust to this type of writing because we get so used to writing for our colleagues who understand the different research methods, statistical tests, and results. According to the United Nations Economic Commission for Europe (2009), a statistical story is one that "doesn't just recite data in words. It tells a story about the data. Readers tend to recall ideas more easily than they do data. A statistical story conveys a message that tells readers what happened, who did it, when and where it happened, and hopefully, why and how it happened" (p. 1). A good statistical story is one where the data can help inform people about various issues that affect them and their environment. The presentation should focus on how the information from a research study can be used by readers while preventing the story from getting bogged down by the researcher's methods and statistics. A good statistical story should accurately represent the research, but the goal of this type of writing is journalist and designed for a general audience with little to no research background.

Writing Statistical Stories

According to United Nations Economic Commission for Europe (2009), the goal of a successful statistical story contains three primary components: (1) has a successful headline that grips the attention of readers; (2) provides the "story behind the numbers in an easily understood, interesting and entertaining fashion" (p. 1); and demonstrates to both the general public and journalists how statistical information can impact how news stories are told. As you can quickly see, statistical storytelling could also be called statistical journalism. Unfortunately, most journalists do not take courses in school related to understanding and handling statistical information. As such, they often rely on others to explain the significance of statistical information. One common tool that many researchers use is the simple press release. Press releases related to statistical information can help frame how the numbers and the findings get discussed by those in the media. In fact, it is not uncommon that press releases quickly turn into entire stories with little to no editing by news outlets looking for good content.

Historically, the field of communication has done a poor job of communicating the importance of our research to the general public. We have a number of notable public scholars who appear on daytime talk shows, but many of the findings published in our academic journals are read only by those in our own field or closely related fields. In 2005 the National Communication Association stepped in and created the field's first online magazine devoted to making communication research accessible for those in the general public (http://www.communicationcurrents.com/). *Communication Currents* is designed to take complicated research and discuss it in a manner that people in the general public can understand. Many of the articles found in *Communication Currents* are good examples of statistical stories. Other articles approach communication from either a qualitative/interpretive or a rhetorical/critical epistemological perspective.

So, how does one write a good statistical story? Figure 22.8 shows the difference between academic and journalistic writing. Academic writing starts off with a broad focus as you investigate your literature review. Over time, your focus narrows as you go into your rationale section leading to your hypotheses and or research questions. Ultimately, academic writing gets to its narrowest point during the results and discussion section, where you make sense of what you found. Journalistic writing, on the other hand, is the opposite of academic writing with regard to structure. In journalistic writing, you start your writing by focusing on the famous who, what, when, where, and why of the story. You want to get to the important parts of the story first before you lose your readers' attentions. From there, journalistic writing goes

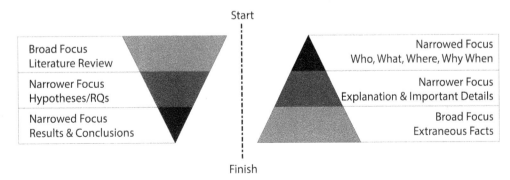

Figure 22.8 Academic versus Journalistic Writing Process

into the supporting information in the forms of explanations and important details needed to understand the full scope and context of the introduction. In journalistic writing, the broad part is generally extraneous information that is left to the end of the article. In fact, most of this extraneous information will eventually get cut by an editor in need of page space.

Although there is a fundamental difference in how academics and journalists approach the writing process, the goal is still to ensure that their readers understand the material that is presented. To help with journalistic writing, United Nations Economic Commission for Europe (2009) recommends that when writing about statistical information, writers should use the following:

- Language that people understand;
- Short sentences, short paragraphs;
- One main idea per paragraph;
- Subheadings to guide the reader's eye;
- Simple language: "Get," not "acquire." "About," not "approximately." "Same," not "identical";
- Bulleted lists for easy scanning;
- A good editor. Go beyond Spell-Check; ask a colleague to read your article;
- Active voice. "We found that . . ." Not: "It was found that . . .";
- Numbers in a consistent fashion: For example, choose 20 or twenty, and stick with your choice;
- Rounded numbers (both long decimals and big numbers);
- Embedded quotes (these are sentences that generally explain "how" or "why" and which journalists like to use verbatim in their news stories in quotes);
- URLs, or electronic links to provide your reader with a full report containing further information.
  Avoid:
- "Elevator statistics": This went up, this went down, this went up;
- Jargon and technical terms;
- Acronyms;
- All capital letters and all italics: Mixed upper and lower case is easier to read;
- "Table reading", that is, describing every cell of a complex table in your text. (p. 6)

Although the United Nations Economic Commission for Europe's ideas on writing seem simplistic, their approach to statistical science writing is actually appropriate to ensure the general public will understand.

Infographics

In recent years, substantial statistical information has started to crop up in books, magazines, and online visually. An information graphic (**infographic**) is a visual representation of data, information, or knowledge condensed into a combination of images and text designed to help viewers quickly grasp complex material quickly and clearly. Although the Internet did not create infographics, the Internet has definitely popularized the art form in recent years.

Thankfully, you do not have to be a great artist to create compelling infographics. There are a number of websites where you can purchase stock infographics and then reformat them for your own needs (e.g., http://www.vectorstock.org/, https://www.dollarphotoclub.com/). There are also a few places online where you can get free infographic templates that can be used: http://piktochart.com/, http://www.freepik.com/, etc.). You will need some experience working with a graphics editing software program to use these templates. Two common proprietary software packages used for making infographics come from Adobe called Photoshop and Illustrator (https://creative.adobe.com/), but you can find free software that is just as effective Gimp (http://www.gimp.org/) and Inkscape (https://inkscape.org/en/).

Figure 22.9 is an example of an infographic designed based on content found in the dataset collected for this book. Although this data are not necessarily the most conducive for overly creative infographics, the basic gist of the data is easily understood.

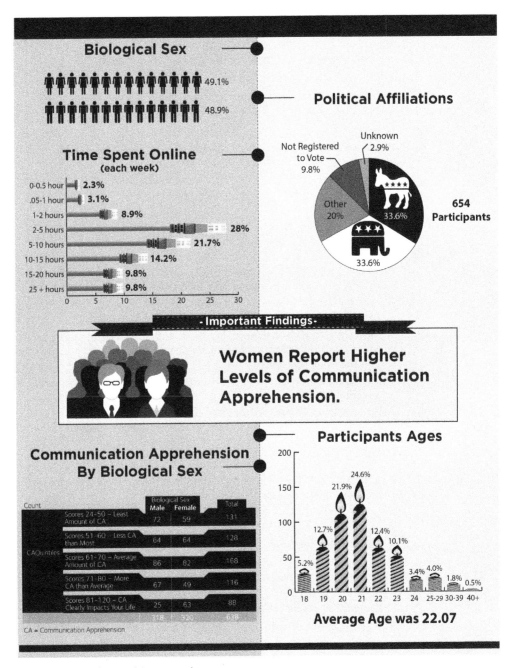

Figure 22.9 Infographic Example

Conclusion

Throughout this text, we have described the process involved in writing and conducting scholarly research. As you have noticed, this process takes time, and it would be a shame not to share the results of your hard work with others. In this chapter, we have provided information to assist you in writing up the discussion section of your paper. Various elements and suggestions for language use are provided to interpret results for the reader. We chose to conclude this text with an explanation of the options available and a description of the processes involved in submitting your research for conference presentation or journal publication. As you begin your journey as a communication scholar, we encourage you to share your work with others—after all, you are the future scholars of our field!

KEY TERMS

Abstract	Future directions	Poster presentation
Academic divisions/interest groups	Limitations	Research implications
	Panel discussion	Scholar-to-scholar
Call for papers	Paper presentation	Presentations
Discussion	Peer review	

REFERENCES

American Psychological Association. (2010). *Publication manual of the American Psychological Association* (6th ed.). Washington, DC: American Psychological Association.

O'Shea, T. J. (1986). Presentation of results. In S. W. Barcus & J. W. Wilkinson (Eds.), *Management consulting services* (pp. 235–252). New York, NY: McGraw–Hill.

Wrench, J. S., & Booth-Butterfield, M. (2003). Increasing patient satisfaction and compliance: An examination of physician humor orientation, compliance-gaining strategies, and perceived credibility. *Communication Quarterly, 51*, 482–503.

United Nations Economic Commission for Europe. (2009). *Making data meaningful: Part 1—A guide to writing stories about numbers.* [online] Retrieved from http://www.unece.org/fileadmin/DAM/stats/documents/writing/MDM_Part1_English.pdf/

FURTHER READING

Alexander, A., & Potter, W. J. (Eds.). (2001). *How to publish your communication research: An insider's guide.* Thousand Oaks, CA: Sage.

Kitchin, R., & Fuller, D. (2005). *Academics guide to publishing.* Thousand Oaks, CA: Sage.

Knapp, M. L., & Daly, J. A. (2004). *A guide to publishing in scholarly communication journals.* Mahwah, NJ: Erlbaum.

McInerney, D. M. (2002). *Publishing your psychology research: A guide to writing for journals in psychology and related fields.* Thousand Oaks, CA: Sage.

Nicol, A. A. M., & Pexman, P. M. (2003a). *Displaying your findings: A practical guide for creating figures, posters, and presentations.* Washington, DC: American Psychological Association.

Nicol, A. A. M., & Pexman, P. M. (2003b). *Presenting your findings: A practical guide for creating tables.* Washington, DC: American Psychological Association.

GLOSSARY

Abstract: Accurate, self-contained, concise description of a research study.

Abstract Variables: Variables that change or differ over time or across situations or contexts.

Academic Division/Interest Group: Group of people who study a specific area of communication (e.g., organizational, instructional, intercultural, mass mediated).

Accelerated Longitudinal Design: Form of survey design in which a research creates mini age cohorts and studies them over a short period of time to ascertain how changes would occur across age groups over a longer period of time.

Acquiescence: When an individual fakes responses to cooperate with the investigator and give the researcher what he or she wants.

Alternate Forms Reliability: Reliability test in which two measures of the same phenomenon are used to measure the same group at two different times.

Alternative Hypothesis (H_1): Prediction that there is a relationship or a difference that has not occurred by chance or random error.

American Psychological Association (APA) Style: Components or features of a research manuscript that dictate how the manuscript should be presented beyond the scope of actual content as dictated by the American Psychological Association's style manual.

Analysis of Covariance (ANCOVA): Statistical test that allows a researcher to determine whether a difference lies between groups on a dependent variable after the dependent variable has been mathematically adjusted for differences associated with one or more covariates.

Analytical Survey: Type of survey that explains people's attitudes and behaviors by identifying likely causal influences.

Anonymity: When a researcher does not know who participated in a study or which results belong to which participants in a study.

Antecedent: (1) The "if" statement within a logical proof. (2) What happened earlier in time.

Antecedent Variable: Variable that occurs prior to the experiment that could impact the way an independent variable or dependent variable functions.

Apparatus: Any appliance or device used in the conducting of a study.

Appeal to Authority: When people explain a phenomenon by believing that an authority has made it occur.

Appeal to General Empirical Rules: Explaining phenomena through proven scientific facts.

Argument: Set of propositions in which one follows logically as a conclusion from the others.

Assertiveness: Capacity to make requests, actively disagree, express positive or negative personal rights and feelings, initiate, maintain, or disengage from conversations, and stand up for oneself without attacking another.

Attitude: Predisposition to respond to people, ideas, or objects in an evaluative way.

Attributes: Specific values of a variable.

Attrition: Number of participants who left a study since it began.

Audience-Specific Behavior: Behavior exhibited in front of one audience that does not occur in front of other audiences.

Author Search: Database search for author's name in the author field.

Authorship Credit: Ethical principal that states that all researchers involved in a project should receive acknowledgment for their work on a research project.

Axiom: Generally accepted principle or rule.

Backtracking: The process a researcher uses when he or she examines the references of one article in an effort to help her- or himself find other articles and books that may be relevant.

Baseline: Initial score on some variable of interest.

Belief: Perception of reality about whether something is true or false.

Belmont Report: The 1979 report by the National Commission for the Protection of Human Subjects of Biomedical and Behavioral Research that established three basic guidelines for working with human participants: consent, beneficence, and justice.

Beta (β) Weights (regression coefficients): Value in a multiple linear regression that helps explain the degree to which a dependent variable takes varying values and can be interpreted as correlations.

Big Data: Data that is simply too large to store on a single computer and are beyond the scope of traditional statistical research software.

Bimodal: When two values larger than the other values in a dataset occur at equal frequency within the dataset.

Boolean Logic: Form of symbolic logic created by George Boole that is the basis for electronic search engine technology.

Calculated Value: End result after completion of a mathematical formula related to a specific statistical test.

Call for Papers: Posting requesting scholars to send in manuscripts for possible consideration for a conference/convention or for journal publication.

Canonical Correlation: A statistical tool that allows a researcher to investigate the relationships among two or more variable sets.

Categorical/Topical Order: Organizing a literature review by main topics or issues and emphasizing the relationship of the issues to the main problem.

Causation: Ability to determine that an act or agency truly produces an effect.

Cause and Effect: Literature review organizational pattern used to explain what causes a specific situation and what the effect of that situation is.

Central Limits Theorem: Theoretical idea that the mean of the scores obtained from the probability sample will be equal to the mean of the scores obtained from the population.

Certificate of Confidentiality: Certification granted by the Secretary of Health and Human Services that enables a researcher engaged in biomedical, behavioral, clinical, or other research to protect the privacy of research participants even if the participants are engaged in illicit or illegal behavior.

Channel: Method used to send a message (verbal, nonverbal, or mediated).

Chi (χ)-Square: Statistical test that evaluates whether the proportions of individuals who fall into categories of two or more nominal variables are equal to hypothesized values.

Chronological Order: Organizing a literature review by historical progression in terms of time.

Citation: When an author gives credit to another individual's thoughts.

Cluster Sample: Sample created by identifying naturally occurring clusters of people with a target variable in a target population, randomly selected to participate in a research project.

Codebook: Book researcher creates to explain the operationalization in a clear and succinct way.

Coder: Person actively involved in the coding process.

Coding: Process a researcher goes through to group one's variable of interest in a consistent way.

Coding Form: Form that contains all of the information in the codebook in a simple check-off sheet to make it easier for coders to code information quickly.

Cognitive Knowledge: Degree to which someone has actually learned a specific concept or skill.

Cohen's d: Effect size test utilized in an independent samples **t** test.

Cohen's Kappa (κ): Statistic used to calculate intercoder reliability for two coders where none of the data are missing.

Common Rule, the: Title 45, Code of Federal Regulations, Part 46 (45 CFR 46), which established a set of guidelines for the rights, welfare, and protection of research participants.

Communication: Process whereby one person stimulates meaning in the mind of another person (or persons) through verbal and nonverbal messages.

Communication Apprehension: Fear or anxiety associated with either real or anticipated communication with another person or persons.

Communication Trait: Hypothetical construct that accounts for certain kinds of communication behaviors.

Communications: Array of mass-mediated technologies people utilize to send messages.

Compare-and-Contrast Order: Organizing a literature review to show how research studies are similar to and different from each other.

Conceptual Equivalence: Issue involved in translating surveys from one language to another concerned with whether the basic concept a researcher is attempting to study in one culture even exists within another culture.

Conceptualization: Development and clarification of concepts or your germinal idea.

Concrete Variables: Variables that are stable or consistent.

Concurrent Validity: Form of validity concerned with whether scores taken at the same time are related to each other.

Confederate: Individual who, without the participants' knowledge, is actually part of the experiment being conducted.

Confidence Interval: The degree to which a researcher is certain he or she will accept a true null hypothesis.

Confidence Level: Level of confidence that the results found within a study are generalizable to the population and not a result of chance.

Confidentiality: The treatment of information an individual has disclosed in a relationship of trust with the expectation that it will not, without permission, be divulged to others in ways inconsistent with the understanding of the original disclosure.

Conflict of interest: When financial or other personal considerations prevent a researcher from abiding by or can give the appearance of compromising scientific and ethical principles.

Confounding Variables: Variables that obscure the effects of your independent variable.

Consequent: The "then" statement within a logical proof.

Construct Validity: Degree to which the survey measures an intended nonobservable trait, which is used to explain observable behavior.

Constructive Replication: When a researcher duplicates a previous study but uses entirely new instrumentation, experimental procedures, and sample and data analysis techniques.

Content Analysis: Summarizing, quantitative analysis of messages.

Control: Process by which an individual both prevents personal biases from interfering with the research study and ensures there are no other explanations for what is seen in the study.

Control Group: Group that the researcher measures without attempting to manipulate in any way.

Convenience Sample: When participants are selected nonrandomly based on availability.

Correlation (r): Statistical test that determines whether two variables are positively, negatively, or not related to each other.

Covariate: A variable that is a possible predictive or explanatory variable that is observed rather than manipulated but can have an effect on the dependent variable.

Cramér's Phi (F): Effect size test utilized in a chi-square.

Criterion Validity: Form of validity concerned with how accurately a new measure can predict a well-accepted criterion or previously validated concept.

Critical Value: (1) Value of the random variable at the boundary for accepting or reject the null hypothesis. (2) Value that a calculated value must be greater than to achieve statistical significance at a calculated confidence level.

Cronbach's Alpha (α): Scale reliability test that determines how well a set of items measures a unidimensional hypothetical construct.

Cross-Sectional Survey Design: Type of survey design in which a researcher receives information from a group of participants at a given point in time.

Culture Shock: State of disorientation and anxiety that affects an individual who is exposed to a new culture or co-culture.

Curvilinear Relationship: Relationship between two variables plotted along a curve instead of a straight line.

Data: Collected measures of independent and dependent variables that can be used for statistical calculations.

Data Analytics: Set of tools used to make predictions about the future based on information from the past.

Data Falsification: Any time you manipulate or alter the data to achieve the results wanted by a researcher.

Data Mining: The process of examining data for new, useful information.

Data Science: The emerging field that attempts to extract knowledge from data through advanced mathematical analyses, computers, and databases.

Data Sharing: Ethical principle by which researchers share their data with other researchers to help further science.

Debriefing: Period following an experiment when a researcher corrects any deception, reaffirms the value of the experiment, and determines whether the answers were changed based on what the participant assumed was occurring.

Decoding: Process a receiver goes through to assign meaning to a source's message.

Degrees of Freedom: Number of participant scores in a sample that can or are free to vary.

Deidentify Data: Making sure the data cannot be linked back to the participants themselves.

Dependent Variable: Measured variable in a study whose changes are determined by changes in one or more independent variables.

Descriptive Analytics: Data analytics associated with describing the data

Descriptive Statistics: Statistical tests used to describe the shape of a dataset.

Descriptive Survey: Type of survey designed to find out how common a phenomenon is within a given group of people.

df Between: In a one-way ANOVA, number of participant scores in a sample that can or are free to vary between multiple groups.

df Within: In a one-way ANOVA, number of participant scores in a sample that can or are free to vary within a single group.

Difference: The degree to which one person or a group of people are dissimilar from another person or group of people.

Differences in Kind: Differences that occur when two or more groups do different things associated with their groups.

Differences of Degree: When scores from two or more groups significantly differ from each other.

Diminished Autonomy: When possible participants do not have the ability to intellectually discern for themselves whether participation in a research endeavor is okay.

Directional Research Question: When a researcher asks whether there is either a positive or a negative relationship or a specific significant difference between two or more variables.

Discussion Section: Section of a research manuscript that appears after the results section to provide an interpretation of the findings, acknowledge limitations, and propose future research.

Dunn-Sidak Test: Statistical test that readjusts the probability level to correct for possible compounded error resulting from multiple pairwise comparisons to help prevent type I error.

Duplicate Data Publication: Publishing the same set of data in two different research publications.

Effect Size: Strength of a relationship or the magnitude of difference occurring between two variables or the degree to which a null hypothesis is false.

Electronic Database: Computerized system for searching and retrieving information.

Empirical Generalization: Attempt to describe a phenomenon based on what we know about it at this time.

Empiricism: Belief that science is only acceptable insofar as the phenomenon in question can be "sensed" by average people.

Encoding: Process of creating messages we believe represent the meaning to be communicated and are likely to stimulate similar meaning in the mind of a receiver.

Endogenous Variable: Variable in a path analysis or structural equation model that is explained by one or more of the other variables in the model.

Ends: Outcomes that one desires to achieve.

Epistemology: Way of knowing.

Ethical Behavior: When a researcher uses positive means to achieve a positive end.

Ethics: Study of means and ends.

Ethnocentrism: View of one's culture as the center of the universe.

Evoke Empathy: Showing that a phenomenon had good, just, or moral reasons.

Exempt Review: Level of review performed by an IRB where a protocol is determined to be exempt from the guidelines established in 45 CFR 46.

Exogenous Variable: Variable in a path analysis or structural equation model that is taken as a given, measured variable.

Expedited Review: Level of review performed by an IRB where a protocol involves no more than minimal risk, does not include intentional deception, does not utilize vulnerable populations, and includes appropriate consent procedures.

Experiment: When a researcher purposefully manipulates one or more variables (independent variables) in the hope of seeing how this manipulation effects change or lack of change of other variables of interest (dependent variables).

Experimental Group(s): Group(s) that a researcher attempts to manipulate in some clear way.

Experimenter Effects: Effects caused unknowingly by the experimenter on the participants.

Explanation: Attempt to satisfy one's curiosity about an observable event.

Eta-Square (η^2): Effect size test utilized in a one-way analysis of variance.

Extraneous Variables: Variables not being measured in your study but affecting your results (see intervening and confounding variables).

F Test: Any statistical test that determines whether two population variances are equal.

Face (Content) Validity: Form of validity where a researcher determines whether the measure determines the appropriate construct by examining the specific questions.

Factor Analysis: A statistical device that enables researchers to determine whether the responses on a set of scale items actually measure a single construct or multiple constructs.

Factorial Analysis of Variance: Statistical test in which a researcher has multiple nominal independent variables and one interval/ratio dependent variable.

Factorial Experimental Design: Experimental design that utilizes two or more independent variables.

Faking Responses: Any circumstance in which a respondent to our instrument deliberately attempts to alter the results in some specific way.

Fisher's Least Significant Difference (LSD): Post hoc test that is the equivalent of running a series of paired *t* tests, but for which the alpha level is not controlled, so the chance of compounded error is great.

Frequency Distribution: Record of the number of occurrences for each value in the dataset.

Full-Board Review: Level of review performed by an IRB where a protocol involves more than minimal risk, uses intentional deception, or uses vulnerable populations.

Future Directions: Subsection of the discussion section in which an author discusses where he or she thinks the research should continue.

General Linear Model (GLM): Linear model ($Y = mX + b$) where each object can have multiple measurements. The GLM underlies many different statistical tests, including one-way analysis of variance and regression.

General-to-Specific Order: Organizing a literature review to examine broad-based research first and then focus on specific studies that relate to the topic.

Generalizability: Notion that the results found from studying a sample can be assumed to be true of the entire population.

Germinal Idea: Spark that causes an individual to realize that something new can be researched or measured.

Hasty Generalization: Generalizing about something when not enough evidence is available to do so.

Hawthorne Effect: Effect caused when study participants know they are being observed.

Historical Flaw: Threat to a study's external validity that occurs because a historical event has caused a sample to change in a way that is not measurable.

Humor Assessment: Mental measure created by Wrench and Richmond (2004) to measure an individual's use of humor in interpersonal interactions.

Hypothesis: Tentative statement about the relationship between independent and dependent variables.

Hypothesis Testing: Process a researcher goes through using inferential statistics to determine whether we reject or accept the null hypothesis.

Illustration: Generalizable stories that can be applied to a variety of different contexts.

Immediacy: The degree of perceived physical or psychological distance between people in a relationship.

Independent Samples *t*-Test: Statistical test that evaluates whether there is a difference between two groups on a dependent variable.

Independent Variable: (1) Variable whose numeric value determines the value of other variables. (2) Part of the research experiment that is manipulated or changed.

Inferential Statistics: Statistical tests that allow researchers to make inferences about some unknown aspect of a population from a sample.

Information Graphic (Infographic): A visual representation of data, information, or knowledge condensed into a combination of images and text designed to help viewers quickly grasp complex information quickly and clearly.

Informed Consent: A person's voluntary agreement, based on adequate knowledge and understanding of relevant information, to participate in research.

Institutional Review Board: Panel of people at institutions that receive federal funds established by Title 45, Code of Federal Regulations, Part 46 (45 CFR 46), which reviews all research proposals for possible risks to research participants and to ensure that all research participants are informed of their rights as research participants.

Instrumental Replication: When a researcher duplicates a previous study by measuring the dependent variable in the same way as the first study, but changes the independent variable to see whether a different operationalization of the experimental procedures will give the same results.

Instrumentation: Section of a literature review where a researcher explains which research measures were used to measure the specific study variables.

Interaction Effect: Statistical difference test in a factorial ANOVA where differences on a dependent variable are examined by analyzing the combinations of the independent variables.

Intercoder Reliability: Test to determine whether multiple coders are coding pieces of data in a stable, consistent fashion (most commonly reported as Cohen's kappa or Krippendorff's alpha).

Internet of things: The process of connecting a wide variety of our lives together through the Internet.

Interval Variable: Variable in which the values of the categories are classified in a logical order that represents equal distances between levels within each category.

Intervening Variable: Variable that intervenes between the independent variable and the dependent variable.

Interview Schedule: List of survey questions an interviewer asks an interviewee when conducting an oral survey.

Introduction: The first portion of a paper that contains an attention-getter, a link to the topic, the significance of the topic, an espousal of the credibility of the writer, a thesis statement, and a preview of the main points of the paper.

Isomorphism: Identity or similarity of form.

Item Nonresponse: Form of nonresponse that occurs when an individual participant fails to answer individual or groups of questions on a survey.

Justice: The third ethical standard taken from the Belmont Report that explains that those individuals who take the risks of research should also receive the benefits from that research.

Key Performance Indicator (KPI): Quantifiable measures that help organizational decision makers evaluate organizational performance (e.g., meeting or exceeding strategic and organizational goals).

Known-to-Unknown Order: Organizing a literature review to examine current literature about the problem and then identify at the end what still is not known.

Kurtosis: The degree of peakedness of a distribution of scores.

Label the Phenomenon: Giving the phenomenon a name.

Language: A system of symbols or codes that represent certain ideas or meanings.

Latent/Hypothetical Variable: Variable that a researcher cannot directly observe, but can be inferred from other variables that are observable and measured directly.

Law of Parsimony: Law of science that states that scientists should look for the simplest assumption in the formulation of a theory and the simplest test to interpret data.

Likert Scale: Scale in which participants are presented with a declarative statement and then asked to respond to the statements with a range of possible choices: strongly disagree, disagree, neither agree or disagree, agree, or strongly agree.

Limitations: Subsection in a manuscript's discussion section that highlights the weaknesses of the study, including inappropriateness in the design, population, methods, or instrumentation.

Linear Relationship: Any equation where increasing or decreasing one variable will produce a corresponding change in a secondary variable.

Literal Replication: When a researcher duplicates a previous study keeping the instrumentation, experimental procedures, and sample as similar as possible.

Literature Reviews: Selection of available documents (published and unpublished) on a given topic that contain information, opinions, data, and evidence written from a particular point of view that aid in a reader's understanding of pertinent literature prior to examining the results and discussion in a research study.

Longitudinal Survey Design: Type of survey design in which a researcher gathers information from a group of participants multiple times over a period of time.

Lurker Variable: Variable that explains both the independent variable and the dependent variable.

Machiavellian Ethic: When a researcher uses bad means to achieve a good end.

Machine Learning: Branch of science involving the creation of algorithms that enable a computer to learn and make decisions when exposed to new data.

Main Effects: Statistical difference test in a factorial ANOVA where differences on a dependent variable are examined for each independent variable separately.

Major Premise: Premise of a syllogism that contains the major term (which is the predicate of the conclusion).

Manipulation Check: Procedure by which a researcher inserts a quantitative measurement into a study to determine whether different conditions perceive the independent variable differently.

Manipulation of an Independent Variable: Process a researcher goes through to purposefully alter or change an independent variable to see whether this alteration in the independent variable has an effect on the dependent variable during an experiment.

Maturation: Threat to validity that occurs because it is possible that a portion of the estimated change is not as a result of independent variable manipulations, but as a result of the passage of time between the first measure of a dependent variable to follow-up measures of the dependent variable.

Mean: Sum of all of the scores in a sample divided by the number of scores in the sample.

Mean Squares Between: In a one-way ANOVA, the value calculated by dividing the between sum of squares by the between degrees of freedom.

Mean Squares Within: In a one-way ANOVA, the value calculated by dividing the within sum of squares by the within degrees of freedom.

Means: Tools or behaviors that one employs to achieve a desired outcome.

Measurement: Process of systematic observation and assignment of numbers to objects or events according to rules.

Measures of Central Tendency: Statistics that help describe the center of a distribution of data (e.g., mean, median, and mode).

Median: Middle value in a list of data.

Mediated Channel: Any channel that uses some kind of mediating device to help transmit information.

Mental Measure: Any tool used for the measurement of mental functions like attitudes, beliefs, cognitive knowledge, perceived knowledge, and personality/behavioral traits.

Message: Information the source is stimulating in the mind of the receiver.

Method Section: Section of a research manuscript that discusses participants, apparatuses, procedures, and instrumentation.

Minor Premise: Premise of a syllogism that contains the minor term (the subject of the conclusion).

Mode: Number(s) that occur most frequently within a dataset.

Modified Direct Translation: Form of translation where a translator performs a simple direct translation, after which the translation is given to a panel of experts to decide whether the survey translation is appropriate.

Mono-operation Bias: Validity flaw related to the single use of an independent variable, cause, program, or treatment in a study.

Multiple Comparison Test: A statistical test conducted after a significant difference is noted to ascertain where the significant differences exist statistically among three or more groups (commonly called post-hoc tests).

Multivariate Analysis of Variance: Difference test that can utilize one or more nominal, independent variables and two or more related interval/ratio dependent variables.

Multivariate Tests: Statistical tests with two or more related dependent variables.

Negative Relationship: When a decrease in one variable corresponds to an increase in the other variable or vice versa.

Network Sample: Participants are asked to refer researchers to other people who could serve as participants.

Neutral Relationship: When the change of one variable does not correspond with a change in another variable.

Nominal Variable: Qualitative variable in which categories are mutually exclusive, equivalent, and exhaustive where the categories are not numerically oriented.

Nondirectional Research Question: When a researcher asks whether there is a relationship between two or more variables or a significant difference occurs between two or more variables.

Nonparametric: Statistical tests that are associated with categories and ordering; these are tests observed at the nominal/ordinal levels.

Nonprobability Sampling: Samples that are not randomly selected.

Nonproportionate Quota Samples: Quota sampling technique by which a researcher recruits volunteers until the determined number of participants has been recruited.

Nonresponse: When a sampled unit does not respond to the request to be surveyed (unit nonresponse) or to particular survey questions (item nonresponse).

Nonresponse Bias: Systematic distortion of a statistic as a result of unit and item nonresponse.

Nonverbal Immediacy: The perceived physical and/or psychological closeness a receiver feels exists between her- or himself and a source that occurs as a result of nonverbal behavior.

Nonverbal Messages: Any communicated messages other than verbal messages.

Normative Equivalence: Issue involved in translating surveys from one language to another language concerned with whether norms or social conventions will influence participants' responses during a survey.

Null Hypothesis (H_0): Hypothesis that predicts that groups will not vary on a dependent variable or that there is not a relationship between two variables.

Objective: The desire to create knowledge by examining facts through the scientific method without distorting one's findings through personal feelings, prejudices, and interpretations.

Observations: The part of the part of the scientific method where a researcher attempts to test the hypotheses created.

One-Tailed Hypothesis: Hypothesis that predicts the specific nature of the relationship or difference.

One-Way Analysis of Variance: Statistical test that evaluates whether there is a difference between two or more groups on a dependent variable.

Operationalization: Detailed description of the research operations or procedures necessary to assign units of analysis to the categories of a variable to represent conceptual properties.

Operational Replication: When a researcher duplicates a previous study keeping the experimental procedures and sample as similar as possible, but changes the instrumentation.

Ordinal Variable: Qualitative variable in which categories are mutually exclusive, equivalent, or exhaustive where the categories represent clear numerical gradients, which allows for the rank ordering of the categories.

Outlier: A data point that is far away from the other data points.

Paper Presentation: Oral report about the research project typically followed by a response from a scholar who has conducted research in the area.

Pancultural: When something is the same across all cultures.

Panel Design: Type of longitudinal survey design used to examine participants who agree to be surveyed periodically over a given period of time.

Panel Discussion: Form of conference presentation by which three or more individuals discuss a common topic in an informal format.

Paired *t* Test: Statistical test used to compare two interval/ratio level scores that are taken from the same group at two distinct time periods.

Parallel Blind Technique: Form of translation by which two translators perform a simple direct translation on the same survey and then compare their translations.

Parameter: A value of a population.

Parametric: Statistical tests assume that the level of measurement that was employed in obtaining the data was at the interval/ratio level.

Paraphrasing: Including another author's ideas in your own words; involves summarizing or highlighting one or two important points.

Parenthetical Citation: Citation used within the text body of a manuscript that enables a reader to know where the information is being taken from—also referred to as internal citations.

Participant Section: Section of a literature review (under the method section) where a researcher describes her or his participants and any important demographic characteristics.

Path Analysis: Extension of general linear model used to test the fit two or more causal models.

Pearson Product Moment Correlation: Statistical test created by Karl Pearson to examine the linear relationship between two variables (most common form of correlation).

Peer Review: Process whereby an individual's scholarly work is critiqued by people who also conduct research in a specific area to make sure the new scholarly work is of a quality worthy of publication.

Perceived Knowledge: Degree to which someone believes that he or she has learned a specific concept or skill.

Personality: Total psychological makeup of an individual, which is a reflection of her or his experiences, motivations, attitudes, beliefs, values, and behaviors, derived from the interaction of these elements with the environment external to the individual.

Physical Sciences: Study of the objective aspects of nature.

Pilot Study: Small-scale study a researcher conducts to test the effectiveness of a survey or research procedures.

Plagiarism: Any time a writer does not properly cite or give credit to the source where he or she is getting information.

Population: An entire set of objects, observations, or scores that have some characteristic in common.

Positive Relationship: When an increase in one variable corresponds to an increase in another variable or a decrease in a variable corresponds to a decrease in another variable.

Poster Presentation: Visual report about the research project where people mingle and ask questions about research projects that interest them.

Post Hoc Hypothesis Revision: The revision of hypotheses once an individual receives her or his results.

Power: Degree to which a researcher is certain he or she can reject a false null hypothesis.

Predictive (Prospective) Validity: Form of validity concerned with whether a person's score on a new measure can be used to predict future scores on another measure.

Prescriptive Analytics: Data analytics designed to determine possible courses of action and what the ramifications would be of these different courses of action.

Preview: Point in the introduction when a writer lists the specific sections that he or she is planning to cover in the main body of the literature review.

Primary Source: An original document that examines a phenomenon (e.g., poems, diaries, court records, and interviews to research results generated by experiments, surveys, ethnographies).

Principle of Beneficence: Researchers must ensure that during the research process they maximize possible benefits and minimize possible harms to the research participants themselves.

Privacy: The individual control over the extent, timing, and circumstances of sharing oneself (physically, behaviorally, or intellectually) with others.

Probability: Relative frequency with which a phenomenon is likely to occur.

Probability Level: One minus the percentile confidence level.

Probability Sampling: Randomly selecting participants from a population of interest so all potential participants have an equal chance of being selected for the sample.

Probability Theory: The score that occurs most frequently in the sample will also be the score that should occur most frequently in the population.

Probability Value (*p* value): Probability of obtaining a result at least as extreme as that calculated, which assumes that the null hypothesis is true (result occurred by chance).

Problem–Cause–Solution Order: Organizing a literature review so that it moves from the problem to the solution.

Procedures: The sequence of actions or instructions a researcher follows while conducting a study.

Proportionate Quota Samples: Quota sampling technique by which a researcher ensures that the number of volunteers recruited for the study is proportionate or equal to the number of group members in the population.

Proposition: A statement that either confirms something or denies something.

Protected Health Information (PHI): Any individually identifiable health information (e.g., demographic data and biological specimens) transmitted or maintained by a covered entity.

Psychological Order: Literature review organizational pattern in which a researcher attempts to demonstrate a logical sequencing of events, or how "a" leads to "b" and "b" leads to "c."

Purposive Sample: Participants are nonrandomly picked to be in a study because of a specific characteristic the researcher is investigating.

Quasi-Experimental Design: Looks like an experimental design but likes randomization.

Questionnaire: A form containing a series of questions and mental measures given to a group of people in an attempt to gain statistical information about the group as part of a survey.

Quota Sample: Participants are separated into strata and then nonrandomly selected for participation in the study.

Quotation: Exact use of another author's words in your writing.

Random Assignment: Procedures experimenters use for placing participants into a research condition that ensures that every participant in the sample has an equal chance of being in a research condition.

Random Probe Translation: Form of translation by which a translator performs a simple direct translation and then the researcher pilot tests the translation with a group of bilingual participants to determine whether the researcher's own understanding of the mental measure and that of the participants is the same.

Range: Distance between the largest value and the smallest value in the dataset.

Ratio Variable: Variable in which the values of the categories are classified in a logical order that represents equal distances between levels within each category with the presence of an absolute zero point.

Rationale: Section of a research manuscript that explains the fundamental reasons for the hypotheses and research questions posed in the study.

R-Squared (R^2): Indicates what proportion of the variability in a dependent variable can be predicted by its relationship with an independent variable(s).

Receiver: Person who interprets a message (decoder).

Reference page: The page in an APA formatted document where all of the sources that have been internally cited within the manuscript are referenced.

Regression: Statistical test that examines whether an independent variable can linearly account for any of the variance in a dependent variable.

Regression to the Mean: The tendency for extreme scorers on one measurement to move (regress) closer to the mean on a later measurement causing a change that would normally not happen in the population.

Reinforcer Variables: Variables that enhance the effect of the independent variable on the dependent variable.

Relationship: Correspondence between two variables.

Reliability: Whether a measure produces stable, consistent values.

Repeated-Measures ANOVA: Statistical test that allows a researcher to determine whether differences in the same interval/ratio variable occur over three or more measurements of the variable.

Replication: Conducting more research on a specific topic to determine whether original results occurred by error or remain consistent.

Research: Investigation or experimentation aimed at the discovery and interpretation of facts, revision of accepted theories or laws, and/or practical application of new or revised theories or laws.

Research Implications: Subsection in discussion section in which an author indicates what her or his findings mean for the larger community of scholars' understanding of the topic.

Research Participant: A living individual about whom a researcher obtains either: (1) data through intervention or interaction with the individual; or (2) identifiable private information.

Research Question: Explicit question researchers ask about variables of interest.

Response Rate: Percentage of surveys returned compared to the percentage of surveys distributed.

Response Set: Any tendency that causes a person to give different responses to test items than he or he would if the item were presented in a different form.

Responsiveness: Capacity to be sensitive to the communication of others, to be a good listener, to make others comfortable in communicating, and to recognize the needs and desires of others.

Results Section: Section of a research manuscript in which a researcher presents her or his empirical findings.

Retrospective Validity: Form of validity by which a research attempts to relate a previously taken measure of a phenomenon with a newly designed measure of a phenomenon.

Rhetorical Question: Type of question that asks a listener to think about the question without audibly responding to it.

Sample: People or units that a researcher includes in the study.

Sampling: Selecting people or units for inclusion in a research study.

Sampling Bias: Systematic differences between the population and the sample that result from failing to draw representative cases.

Sampling Error: Degree to which a sample differs with respect to a specific variable from a population.

Sampling Frame: All members of the population accessible to the researcher.

Scalogram: Type of research scale that consists of a set of unidimensional items designed to measure an attitude or opinion where agreement with one item implies agreement with the preceding, less extreme items.

Scheffé: Post hoc test that assumes you wish to test all possible pairs and all possible combinations of means.

Scholar-to-Scholar Presentations: Form of poster presenters by which the researcher has an opportunity to discuss her or his poster with top-notch scholars in the field of communication who specialize in a specific content area.

Science: The study of natural phenomena through quantitative observation, theoretical explanation, and experimentation.

Scientific Method: Empirical process by which a researcher attempts to understand a phenomenon using existing theories to make predictions, empirically observe the phenomenon based on the predictions, and use the observations to make empirical generalizations that then help to refine the original theory.

Secondary Source: Restatements or analyses of primary sources.

Selection Threat: Threat to the validity of an experiment caused by whether the participants who have been selected to participate in an experiment have some characteristic that could slant the findings of the study.

Semantic Differential/Bipolar Scale: Type of research scale that asks respondents to rate their opinion on a linear scale that exists between two endpoints that have opposite meanings (e.g., Good/Bad, Dirty/Clean, Slow/Fast, Weak/Strong, Light/Heavy, Moral/Immoral).

Semantic Equivalence: Issue involved in translating surveys from one language to another concerned with whether scale items are translatable semantically from one language to the next.

Significance Testing: The process to determine whether chance causes a difference or relationship between two or more variables.

Simple Direct Translation: Form of survey translation by which a researcher recruits a bilingual individual who takes the original survey and then translates this survey from the primary language to the secondary language.

Simple Random Sample: Sample created through some means of randomly deciding who in a target population will be asked to participate.

Situational (State) Behavior: Behavior that varies from one situation to another within the same context.

Skewness: Positive or negative direction an asymmetrical set of data points takes.

Specific-to-General Order: Organizing a literature review to try to make sense out of specific research studies so that conclusions can be drawn.

Split-Half Reliability: Scale reliability test in which all of the items are randomly divided into two groups and then a correlation is calculated between the two sets of scores.

Sociocommunicative Orientation: An individual's trait assertive and responsive communicative behavior.

Sociocommunicative Style: An individual's assertive and responsive communicative behavior as perceived by another individual.

Social Desirability Bias: When a participant changes how he or she scores on a measure to be perceived in a "better light" than her or his actual scores would reveal.

Social Sciences: A group of fields that set out to study how humans live and interact.

Socially Desirable Responding: When an individual fakes responses to indicate beliefs that he or she thinks society accepts.

Source: Person who sends the message (encoder).

Standard Deviation: (1) Measure of the distribution of a set of data points around the mean. (2) Square root of the sum of squares divided by the number of data points minus one.

Statistic: The calculated numerical value that represents a sample or population.

Stratified Random Sample: Sample created by dividing a population into specific strata (group based on a characteristic important to the study) and then randomly selecting participants from each strata for inclusion.

Structural Equation Model: Powerful multivariate analysis that enables a variety of specialized versions of other statistical tests including regression models, causal modeling, confirmatory factor analysis, second-order factor analysis, covariance structure models, and correlation structure models.

Student Newman–Keuls (SNK): Post hoc stepwise test for ordered means in which the alpha level depends upon the number of "steps apart" each of the means are from each other.

Subject Search: Database search for key terms that the author has submitted to the subject field to describe the article or book.

Subjective Ethic: When a researcher uses good means, but achieves a bad end result.

Subscale: A subdivision of a research measure.

Sum of Squares: Sum of all squared values for a set of data points minus the sum of data points squared divided by the number of data points.

Sum of Squares Between: Variation between groups in a study calculated by comparing the mean of each group with the mean of the overall sample.

Sum of Squares Within: Variation within groups in a study calculated by summing the squared deviations between scores on a dependent variable for each group and then summing the group values.

Suppressor Variables: Variables that suppress or reduce the effect of the independent variable on the dependent variable.

Survey: A social scientific method for gathering quantifiable information about a specific group of people by asking the group members questions about their individual attitudes, values, beliefs, behaviors, knowledge, and perceptions.

Syllogism: Form of logical argumentation where the logic deductively flows from a major premise to a minor premise to a conclusion.

Systematic Sample: Sample created by determining the sample size needed from a target population and then picking every nth person from the population for selection.

Test–Retest Reliability: The same measure is administered to the same group on two separate occasions and the relationship between both measurements is calculated.

Testing Flaw: Threat to a study's validity that occurs because the measurement of a dependent variable at Time 1 affects the measurement of a dependent variable at Time 2.

Theory: Proposed explanation for how a set of natural phenomena will occur, capable of making predictions about the phenomena for the future, and capable of being falsified through empirical observation.

Theory of Natural Selection: The process in nature by which only the organisms best adapted to their environment tend to survive and transmit their genetic characteristics in increasing numbers to succeeding generations, whereas those less adapted tend to be eliminated.

Theoretical Population: All of the members of a specific population, both accessible and not accessible to the researcher.

Thesis: Short declarative sentence that explains to a listener the purpose of a paper.

Threshold Effects: When changes in a specific dependent variable are only seen after an independent variable reaches a certain level.

Time Order: Idea that researchers can establish an exact order to when things occur—T_1 occurred and then T_2 occurred—through experimental procedures.

Title Search: Database search of the title field for words included in the title of an article or book.

Trait Behavior: Behavior assumed to be consistent across contexts and specific situations within particular constructs.

Translation/Backtranslation: Form of translation by which a translator performs a simple direct translation, after which another bilingual individual translates the work back to the first language.

Trend Design: Type of longitudinal survey design used to examine different samples of people at different points in time.

Truncation Symbols: Symbols used to ensure that your search looks for every possible version of a word.

Tukey's Honest Significant Difference Test (Tukey): Post hoc test for pairwise comparisons while controlling for type I error and generating confidence intervals.

Two-Tailed Hypothesis: Hypothesis that predicts a significant relationship or difference, but does not indicate the specific nature of the relationship.

Type I (α) Error: When a researcher rejects a null hypothesis based on a sample when the null should be accepted.

Type II (β) Error: When a researcher accepts a null hypothesis based on a sample when the null hypothesis should be rejected.

Unethical Behavior: When a researcher uses bad means to achieve a bad end.

Unit of Analysis: Major phenomenon being analyzed within a study.

Unit Nonresponse: Form of nonresponse when a researcher has a failure to obtain any survey measurements on a sample unit.

Univariate Test: Statistical test with one dependent variable.

Validity: Degree to which the measuring instrument measures what it is intended to measure.

Values: Numerical aspect directly associated with a specific attribute of a variable.

Variable: Any entity that can take on different values.

Variance: (1) Degree of variability around a mean. (2) Sum of squares divided by the number of data points minus one.

Verbal Immediacy: Use of language to foster an individual's perception of psychological and physical closeness.

Verbal Messages: Use of language to communicate a message.

Volunteer Sample: Participants who choose to be in a study; typically based on some form of reward.

Willingness to Communicate: A person's general level of desire to initiate communication with others.

INDEX

Page numbers followed by *f* indicate a figure on the designated page

abstract variables, 128
abstracts
    APA style formatting, 83*f,* 91, 92*f,*
        98–99, 519
    article example, 99*f*
    creating, 91
    in databases, 71*f,* 71*f*–72*f,* 76–77
    key word searches in, 73
    length/word limitation in, 532
    on poster, 526*f*
    reading/studying of, by students, 38
    reviewing, 65
    writing, 518–19
academic divisions/interest groups, 519–20, 520*f*
accelerated longitudinal survey design, 224–25
achievement tests, 170
acquiescence, 213
Adobe Acrobat Reader, 80
adolescent alcohol consumption project
        study, 32
Adrian, Allyson, 185
African American men, untreated disease
        study, 29–30
algebra, 472–73
algorithms, 290–91, 292, 296, 304
alpha reliability. *See* Cronbach's Alpha
        Reliability test
alternate forms reliability, 192
alternative hypothesis, 329–31, 332, 344
Amazon, Glacier cold data program, 299
Amazon Echo, 290
Amazon Web Services, 298–99, 300*f*
ambiguous pronoun references, 181
American Psychological Association (APA),
        9, 50, 51
American Psychological Association (APA)
        style
    abstract page, 91, 92*f,* 99*f*
    ANCOVA write-up in, 498

canonical correlations write-up in, 511–12
chi-square test post-hoc write-up in, 401
chi-square test write-up in, 395, 403, 404
citing sources with, 81–84, 83*f,* 85, 86*f*–87*f*
content analysis write-up, 256–58
cover page, 90*f*
cover (title) page, 89–91, 90*f*
factor analysis write-up in, 508
factorial ANOVA write-up in, 496
first page, 91–93, 93*f*
information referenced by, 82*f*
internal citations, 89*f*
linear regression write-up in, 481, 484–85
MANOVA write-up in, 499
mean notation, 112, 159
multiple linear regressions write-up in, 487
one-way ANOVA write-up for, 443, 445
paper formatting, 89–93
paraphrasing, 88–89
parenthetical citations, 85, 87*f,* 88, 89*f*
for Pearson product-moment correlation
        coefficient, 463–64
quotations, 88, 89
reference page, 84, 85*f,* 94–95, 94*f*
reference samples, 85*f,* 86*f*
repeated-measures ANOVA write-up in,
        500–501
scale write-up in, 159–60, 161*f*–162*f,*
        200–201, 201*f*
source record card, 81*f*
structural equation modeling write-up in,
        504–5
style checklist, 83*f*
title page, 89–91, 90*f*
for *t*-tests, 418, 419, 421
types of information being referenced,
        84–85
write-up for range, 159, 161*f,* 199
write-up for SPSS, 199

analysis of covariance (ANCOVA)
    APA style write-up of, 498
    dependent variables in, 497–98
    example of, 497
    explanation of, 497–98
    independent variables in, 497, 498
analytical surveys, 217
ANCOVA. *See* analysis of covariance
Annals of Improbable Research, 36
anonymity, 38
anonymous sex study, 31
antecedent, 19
antecedent variables, 135
anthropology, 1
apparatus subsection, of method section, 112
appealing to authority, 18
appealing to general empirical rules, 18
apprehension, 4
argument, 19–20
Aristotle, 2, 20
Arnold, W. E., 171
artificial intelligence, 290–91
assertiveness, 153–54, 177
*Assessing Organizational Communication:
    Strategic Communication Audits* (Downs
    and Adrian), 185
Associated Press, 295–96
associations, communication-related,
    519, 520*f*
Atkin, Charles, 343
atomic bomb, 35
AT&T facial database, 292
attention-getter, in introduction, 99–102
    acknowledged facts in, 100–101
    claims/statistics in, 100
    illustrations, stories in, 101
    link to topic from, 101–2
    quoting/acknowledging sources in, 101
    rhetorical question in, 100
attitudes. *See also* Generalized Attitude
    Measure
    defined, 157
    measurement of, 158*f,* 162*f,* 173, 175
attitudinal research scales, 170–71. *See also*
    Bogardus Social Distance Scale
attractiveness, 250–51, 252*f,* 254
attributes of variables, 130
attrition, 275
audience-specific behavior, 145
author search, in databases, 73
authorities, in gaining knowledge, 15
authorship credit, 50
axioms, of uncertainty reduction
    theory, 59–60

Babbie, E., 15
backtracking, 65
backtranslation/translation, 237, 238
Bacon, Francis, 16, 17
Banks, W. C., 31–32
Barbato, C. A., 129
Bardhan, N., 318
Barnum, P. T., 422
baseline score, 274
Beatty, Michael, 130, 131, 144
behavioral alteration techniques (BAT),
    469, 470
BELIEF, 464–66, 465*f*–466*f*
beliefs
    defined, 157
    measurement of, 157, 158*f,* 162*f,* 175, 204*f*
    mental measures and, 170
    personality and, 143
    relation to public speaking, 464–66
    research scales classification of, 175
    source credibility measure of, 182*f*
    surveys of, 217
Bell Curve, 336*f,* 337, 338*f*
Bell Telephone Company, 6
Belmont Report, 45, 53
    effect on research ethics, 35–36
    on informed consent, 35
    on justice, 36
    origins/creation of, 31, 33
    on principle of beneficence, 35–36
Bem, Sandra, 107, 153
Bem Sex-Role Inventory (BSRI), 153
beneficence principle, 35–36
Berger, C., 59–60
Berlo, David, 3
beta (β) weights, 487
Big Brother TV show, 59
Big Data, 122, 287–306
    the cloud and, 299–300
    algorithms in, 290–91, 292, 296, 304
    anomalies in, 301–2
    communication and, 302–3
    correlation analyses of, 470
    data analytics and, 288, 291–92, 295,
        304, 305
    data mining, 239*f,* 243*f,* 294, 301
    data science and, 291, 291*f*
    data variety in, 294–95
    data velocity in, 294
    data volume in, 292–94, 293*f*
    defined, 288, 290
    differentiation of, 290–92
    ethics, 303–6
    free sources of, 300*f*

identity concerns, 304–5
information ownership concerns, 305
machine learning and, 290–91
monitoring, 301
online reputation concerns, 305–6
privacy issues, 303–4
value of, 297
variability of, 296
veracity of, 295–96
visualization of, 296–97
bimodal datasets, 353, 362–63
Binet, Alfred, 170
Binet-Simon scale, 170
biological sex, 21, 24, 112, 113*f*, 122
    ANOVA evaluation of effects of, 496
    BSRI, U.S. data, 153
    CA based on, 498
    chi-square test on, 378, 379, 380, 389, 395,
        401, 402*f*, 404
    as concrete variable, 128
    factorial ANOVA means and SDs, 497*f*
    frequency distributions for, 356, 357*f*
    as nominal variable, 142
    political affiliation and, 495–97, 497*f*
    as reported in method section, 159
    t-test and, 406–7, 419, 420*f*
    variable attributes of, 130
    variable values of, 130
    WTC and, 497–98
birth order, 128
bivariate correlations, 459–60, 461*f*
bivariate linear regression, 116*f*, 478, 481, 483,
    484–85, 487
"black hat" activities, 291
Bogardus, Emory S., 170
Bogardus Social Distance Scale, 170–71
Boiarsky, Greg, 105, 178, 446–48
Book of Optics (Ibn al-Haytham), 17
Boolean logic, 73, 74*f*
Booth-Butterfield, Melanie, 58, 63, 103, 105,
    112, 114, 116, 174, 178, 488–89, 517, 518
Booth-Butterfield, Steven, 58, 174, 178
Borisoff, Deborah, 8
Box's test, 499
Brady, R., 267
brainstorming map, 63–64, 63*f*
Bruess, C. J., 319
Brummans, Boris, 101, 105, 403
Bruner, Gordon, 185
Bruning, J. L., 495
Buckingham, A., 226
Bureau of Applied Social Research, 3
Burgoon, Judee, 155
Buros, Oscar K., 184

Burros, Marian, 301
Bush, George W., 18
Bushmen, 18
business research reports, 533–34

CA. *See* communication apprehension
Calabrese, R., 59–60
calculated value, 336
    for chi-square test, 381*f*, 382, 387–89
call for papers, 520–21
Calo, R., 305
canonical correlations
    APA write-up for, 511
    dependent variables in, 511
    explanation/example of, 511
    variate loadings, 512*f*
card catalogues, 70
categorical/topical organizational pattern, 108
Cattell, James McKeen, 169–70, 216–17
causal relationships, 108, 262, 263, 284, 501
causation, 453–54, 470
cause-and-effect organizational pattern, 107
CD-ROMs, 298
Centers for Disease Control and Prevention, 218
central limits theorem, 312
Certificate of Confidentiality, 39
Chan, K., 319
channel
    defined, 6
    mediated, 7
charts
    frequency distributions and, 360, 361*f*–363*f*,
        362–63
Chesebro, James, 8, 100–101, 102, 105, 330,
    467, 469
The Chicago Manual of Style, 58
chimpanzees study, 32
chi-square ($\chi 2$) test of independence, 377–404
    APA style write-up for, 395, 403, 404
    assumptions for, 379
    background information, 379–80
    for biological sex, 378, 379, 380, 389, 395,
        401, 402*f*, 404
    Brummans and Miller article on, 403
    calculated value for, 381*f*, 382, 387–89
    case study introduction of, 378
    computer printouts of, 383–99
    Cramér's phi and, 388–89, 389*f*, 395, 401
    critical values for, 382
    degrees of freedom for, 382, 383*f*, 387
    as difference test, 395
    Excel and, 389, 390*f*–392*f*, 392, 393*f*–394*f*
    expected frequency formula, 380–81, 381*f*
    formula for, 379*f*

chi-square (*Continued*)
multiple comparison procedure for, 396, 397*f*
multiple definitions of, 377–78
outside academia, 404
post-hoc APA style write-up, 401
probability values of, 383*f*
purpose of, 378
SPSS and, 383–85, 389, 396, 401, 402*f*
in statistical analysis, 136
step-by-step approach to, 380–82, 380*f*–381*f*
t-test comparison, 406
on university classification, 383–85, 383*f*–384*f*, 386*f*–388*f*, 387–89, 390*f*–395*f*, 392, 395, 397*f*–399*f*
Chory, R. M., 64
chronological order organizational pattern, 106
citations, APA style, 81–84, 83*f*, 85, 86*f*–87*f*
Clement VIII (Pope), 34
Clever Hans: The Horse of Mr. Von Osten (Pfungst), 22–23
closed-ended questions, 233
cloud storage, 80, 289
cloud/cloud computing
Big Data and, 297–300
data and, 298–99
description, 298
scalability, redundancy, speed, and, 299
types of delivery services, 299–300
cluster samples, 311, 315
Code of Federal Regulations (CFR), 37, 45, 46
codebook, 251, 252*f*, 253–54, 256–57
coder fatigue, 257
coders/coding, 251, 252*f*, 253–58, 254*f*–255*f*
coding form, 251, 252*f*, 253, 254, 256, 257
coefficients, 478, 480*f*, 481, 484*f*, 486*f. See also* Pearson product-moment correlation coefficient
cognitive knowledge, 175–76
cognitive learning, 105
Cohen, J. E., 304
Cohen's *d* formula, 421–22
Cohen's kappa (κ), 256, 257*f*, 258, 403, 448
color reactions case study, 427–45
Combs, Sean "Puffy," 422
Common Rule, 37
communication
categories of, 4*f*, 13
defined/goal of, 5–6
mediated, 7
nature of, 5–7
SMCR model, 6
Communication, Research, and Theory Network (CRTNET) listserv, 519

Communication and Mass Media Complete database (CMMC), 58, 72
communication apprehension (CA)
biological sex and, 498
Boolean search for articles on, 73, 74*f*, 76
construct in PRCA-24, 211
contextually-based, 148
defined, 146
dependent variable in, 104, 269
descriptive statistics for, 371*f*
intercultural, 221
linear regression and, 473–78, 479*f*–480*f*, 481
literature reviews and, 104–5, 106, 107, 109
null hypothesis in, 330
path analysis example for, 502*f*
PRCA-24 use in assessment, 146, 147*f*, 160
relation to public speaking, 464–66, 483–85, 484*f*
rhetorical question on, 100
structural equation modeling and, 503–4, 505*f*
subscales of, 503–4, 504*f*–505*f*
trait behavior and, 174
t-tests and, 407, 419, 420*f*, 424
types of, 146, 148
WTC, BELIEF correlations to, 464–66, 465*f*–466*f*
Communication Institute for Online Scholarship (CIOS), 76–77
communication satisfaction study, 134–35
communication trait, 145
communication-related associations, 519
comparative fit index (CFI), 504–5
compare and contrast organizational pattern, 107
Compliance-Gaining Questionnaire, 113*f*
Comprehensive Community Health Models Initiative, 403
computer printouts
of chi-square test, 383–99
of Cronbach's alpha reliability test, 193–94
of linear regression, 477–78, 477*f*–480*f*, 480–83, 482*f*–483*f*
of one-way ANOVA, 434–40, 434*f*–439*f*
of Pearson product-moment correlation coefficient, 458–64
of *t*-tests, 413–14, 413*f*–419*f*, 416–19
computerized databases. *See* electronic databases
conceptualization, 91, 177
for content analysis, 249–50
conclusion (concluding section), 119, 119*f*
concurrent validity, 209
confederates, 264, 267, 268, 273

conference presentations
    academic divisions/interest groups for,
        519–20, 520*f*
    associations for, 519, 520*f*
    call for papers for, 520–21
    panel discussions, 523, 528–29
    paper presentations, 515, 523–26
    poster presentations, 526–28, 526*f*
    research submission for review, 520–21,
        521*f*–523*f*
    scholar-to-scholar presentations, 528
    types of, 523–29
    of unethical research, 49
confidence intervals, 320, 321*f,* 333–34
confidence levels, 333
confidentiality, 38–39, 43
confirmatory factor analysis (CFA), 508
conflict management, 129
conflicts of interest, 50
confounding variables, 271, 278, 497
consequent, 19
conservative post hoc tests, 441
construct validity, 209–10
constructive replication, 277
constructs, 211
Consumer Privacy Bill of Rights, 305
content analysis
    APA style write-up for, 256–58
    coding in, 251, 252*f,* 253–58, 254*f*–257*f*
    conceptualization for, 249–50
    contexts for, 248–49
    defined, 247–48
    operationalization for, 250–51
    sampling decisions, 253
    steps for conducting, 249–58
    theory and rationale for, 249
    training and pilot reliability, 253–56
    unit of analysis in, 250
content pacing, 105
content validity, 208
control, 22
control group, 267
convenience samples, 311, 317
conversational sensitivity, 105
Converse, J. M., 220
Conway, Drew, 291
Copeland, Peter, 144
correlations *(r),* 451–71. *See also* Pearson
        product-moment correlation coefficient
    assumptions of, 454–55
    background information, 453–55
    between BELIEF, CA, WTC, 464–66,
        465*f*–466*f*
    Big Data analyses, 470

    bivariate, 459–60, 461*f*
    canonical, 511–12, 512*f*
    causation compared to, 453–54
    Chesebro article on, 467, 469
    independent variables in, 452, 454, 455,
        460, 469
    outside academia, 470
    Protestantism tornado study, 452–53
    Punyanunt article on, 469–70
    reading large tables of, 466–67, 468*f*
    spurious, 454
Corrigan, M. W., 101, 134, 221, 267, 327,
        422–23
covariate, 497–98
cover letter, 160, 235, 241, 532
Cramér's phi (Φ), 388–89, 389*f,* 395, 401
credibility
    evaluation of, 79, 85
    influence on persuasion, 3
    introduction's espousal of, 102
    literature reviews and, 105
    theories on, 27
criterion validity, 208
critical values, 336–37, 343
    for chi-square test, 382
    for one-way ANOVA, 432*f,* 433
    for Pearson product-moment correlation
        coefficient, 459*f*
    for *t*-tests, 412–13, 412*t*
Cronbach's Alpha Reliability test,
        192–200, 212
    case processing summary, 197*f*
    computer printouts of, 193–94
    Excel and, 193, 199–200, 199*f*–201*f*
    item statistics, 198*f*
    item-total statistics, 198*f*
    measurement issues, 212
    reliability statistics, 197*f*
    scale statistics, 198*f*
    SPSS and, 193–95, 196*f,* 197–98
Cross-Out Test, 170
cross-section survey design, 223
Crudup, Billy, 32
cultural studies, 1
curvilinear relationships, 452*f,* 453, 454

DaaS (data as a service), 299
Dairy Foods Association's Dairy Facts, 453
Darley, John, 31
Darwin, Charles, 2, 169
data. *See also* Big Data
    accuracy of, 48
    analysis of, 16, 17, 130, 225
    antecedent variables and, 135

558　INDEX

data (*Continued*)
  bimodal, 353, 362–63
  coding, 253, 254, 257–58
  coding initial, 254
  collection of, 129, 252*f*
  defined, 288, 349
  deidentification of, 49, 303–4
  duplicate publication of, 49
  ethics and, 31, 37, 38
  falsification, 48
  human-generated, 289
  interpretation of, 17
  interval level, 141, 171, 173
  Laney's report on, 292–95
  machine-generated, 289–90
  measurement of, 192–93
  metadata, 289, 294, 300*f*
  nominal data, 135–36
  ordinal data, 136, 221
  processing, 225
  sharing, 48–49
  stealing, 50
Data Analysis ToolPak, 360
data analytics
  Big Data, 304, 305
  defined, 291–92
  descriptive, 292
  predictive, 288, 291
  prescriptive, 292
  real-time, 288
data as a service (DaaS), 299
data hackers, 291
data mining, 239*f*, 243*f*, 294, 301
data science, 291, 291*f*
data variety, 294–95
data velocity, 294
data volume, 292–94, 293*f*
databases. *See* electronic databases
Data.gov, 300*f*
dataset variability, 371, 372*f*–375*f*
Davis, K., 305
Dawson, R. J. M., 294
De Gail, M. A., 267
debriefing, 273–74
deception
  after-effects of, 64
  debriefing and, 273
  ethics of, 44, 271
  expedited review and, 47
  interpersonal, 59
  legitimate research reason for, 272, 324
decoding, 6
definition, 155
degrees of freedom

for chi-square test, 382, 383*f*, 387
for one-way ANOVA, 431–32
degrees of freedom (df) between, 428*f*, 432–33, 433*f*
degrees of freedom (df) within, 428*f*, 432–33, 433*f*
deidentifying data, 49, 303–4
Dell Computers, 26–27
demographic characteristics, 112
dependent variables, 111, 134–35
  in ANCOVA, 497–98
  in canonical correlations, 511
  in design of research project, 241
  in factorial ANOVA, 495, 496
  in MANOVA, 499–500
  measurement of, 269–70, 273, 277, 278–83
  in one-way ANOVA, 426–28, 434, 436*f*, 439*f*, 440, 442*f*, 443, 445
  in regressions, 475, 479*f*–480*f*, 481, 484*f*, 485, 486*f*, 487–88, 489
  in *t*-tests, 406–8, 414, 415*f*, 420, 423
Descartes, René, 16, 17
descriptive data analytics, 292
descriptive statistics, 197, 347–75
  for CA, 371*f*
  in data analysis, 136
  defined, 349
  Excel calculations, 372*f*–373*f*
  inferential statistics comparison, 349–50
  in Item Statistics box, 198
  measures of central tendency for, 350–65
  nominal level questions, 220
  SPSS calculating in, 373*f*–374*f*
  sum of squares in, 366
descriptive surveys, 217
Designing a Research Project Worksheet, 238–42
  completed worksheet, 243*f*–244*f*
  dependent variables, 241–42
  hypotheses/research questions, 242
  independent variables, 241
  participants section, 241
  principal researcher(s), 242
  question section, 238, 239–40*f*
  setting section, 240–41
  statistical tests choice, 242
  study design section, 240
  tentative study title, 242
desktop computers, 289
differences
  defined, 131–32
  between people/groups of people, 131–32
  reasons for emergence of, 128–29

statistical differences, 133
in variables, 134
differences in kind, 132–33
differences of degree, 133, 133*f*
Dillman, D. A., 231, 232, 233, 322
diminished autonomy, 32
directional research questions, 329
Directory of Open Access Journals (DOAJ), 76
discussion section, 116–19, 117*f*
example, 117*f*
future directions subsection, 119, 121, 518
interpretation of findings in, 516–17, 516*f*
introduction, 516*f*
limitations subsection, 118, 517–18
present *vs.* past findings, 517
research implications, 518
results subsection, 116–17
review of, 81
skimming, 65
summary of major findings in, 516
writing, 515
"disguiser" plagiarism, 51
dispersion, measures of, 365
DOAJ. *See* Directory of Open Access Journals
Docear software, 80–81
double negatives/positives, 181
double questions, 180
Downs, Cal, 185
Dropbox, 298, 299
Duhigg, Charles, 470
Dunn–Sidak test, 400, 400*f*
DVD-ROMs, 298

Eastern Communication Association, 522*f*–523*f*
Eastin, M. S., 267
EBSCOhost, 58, 72
ecological fallacy, 24–35, 129
Educational Testing Services (ETS), 170, 184
educational theory, 7
"The Effect of Ambiguity on the Implementation of Social Change Initiative" (Brummans and Miller), 403
"The Effect of Interest on Recall: An Experiment" (Weber, Fornash, Corrigan, Neupauer), 422–23
effect size
hypothesis testing and, 339–41, 340*f*
t tests calculating, 420–22
"The Effects of Humor on Perceptions of Compliance-Gaining in the Classroom" (Punyanunt), 469–70
electronic databases, 58, 67, 70, 71*f*–72*f*, 72–74, 76–77

Eltinge, J. L., 231
e-mail, 7, 59, 77, 80
e-mail sampling recruitment, 322, 323*f*
emotionally loaded items, 180, 204
empirical generalizations, 23–25
empirical research, 12–27
empirical rules, appealing to, 18
empiricism, 19, 22
encoding, 6
Encyclopedia Britannica, 70
encyclopedias, subject-specific, 62*f,* 65, 66*f,* 67, 70
endogenous variables, 501–2
epistemology, 13–14
ERIC (Education Resource Information Center) database, 72
error
sampling, 312, 314, 315, 316, 333–35
standard error of estimate, 481
type I, 341*f,* 344, 400, 401, 417, 441, 460, 495
type II, 335, 339, 341*f,* 344
understanding, 341–42, 341*f*
eta square (η^2), 439*f,* 440, 446, 447*f*
ethical behavior, 33–34, 34*f*
ethical matrix, 34*f*
Ethical Principles and Guidelines for the Protection of Human Subjects of Research. *See* Belmont Report
ethics, 29–53
of Big Data, 303–6
of deception, 271
defining, 33–35
examples of studies, 29–31
gaining knowledge and, 16
Machiavellian, 34
non-academic issues, 53
research-related issues, 48–53
subjective, 34
ethics, issues for research
authorship credit, 50
conflicts of interest, 50
data accuracy, 48
data sharing, 48–49
duplicate data publication, 49
participant identity disclosures, 49–50
plagiarism, 51–53
post hoc hypothesis revision, 49
recruitment for samples, 323–24
ethnocentrism
correlation testing of variables of, 225
defined, 148–49
in large SPSS correlation table, 468f
one-way ANOVA for, 427, 499
one-way MANOVA for, 499–500

ethnocentrism (*Continued*)
  path analysis example for, 501–2, 502*f*, 502*f*–503*f*
  reliability for book dataset variables, 202*f*
  responsiveness' relation to, 467
  SPSS dataset statistics for, 374*f*
  Wrench, Corrigan, McCroskey, Punyanunt-Carter study of, 221–22
  WTC and, 499, 500
Ethnocentrism Scale, 149*f*, 161*f*, 203*f*
European Union Open Data Portal, 300*f*
evaluating information, 80–81
evoking empathy, 18
ex post facto design, 283
examples, giving, 18
Excel
  Big Data and, 293
  caveats regarding use of, 359
  chi-square test and, 389, 390*f*–392*f*, 392, 393*f*–394*f*
  Cronbach's alpha reliability test and, 193, 199–200, 199*f*–201*f*
  "Data" menu in, 360*f*
  descriptive statistics calculated in, 372*f*–373*f*
  "Find and Select" in, 359
  frequency distributions and, 354, 359–60, 359*f*–360*f*
  linear regression and, 481–83, 482*f*–483*f*
  multiple linear regressions in, 487
  one-way ANOVA and, 443
  Pearson product-moment correlation coefficient and, 458, 462–63, 464*f*–465*f*
  "PivotTable"/"Pivot Chart" options, 360*f*
  replacing #NULL! in, 359
  statistic's difficulty with, 354
  t-tests and, 417–18, 419*f*
exception fallacy, 25
executive summary, 120
exempt review, from IRBs, 46–47, 47*f*
exogenous variables, 501–2, 504, 505, 506
expected frequency formula, 256*f*, 380–81, 381*f*
expedited review, for IRBs, 47–48
experimental design
  aspects of, 263–72
  debriefing in, 273–74
  dependent variable manipulation and, 269–70, 272, 273, 274, 277, 278–83
  factorial, 268, 268*f*
  independent variable manipulation and, 266–70, 268*f*, 273, 278, 278–83
  pre-, 277–78
  problems with, 279
  quasi-, 279–81

  random assignment and, 264–66, 264*f*–266*f*, 272
  true, 281–83
experimental group, 262–63, 267, 278, 280
experimenter effects, 270
experiments
  conducting, 272–74
  controlling, 270–72
  defined, 262
  obtaining consent for, 272
  rationale for, 262–63
  threats to validity of, 274–77
explanations, 18
explanatory surveys, 217
exploratory factor analysis, 507–8
extraction methods, in factor analysis, 508
extraneous variables, 271

F test, 432, 433*f*, 475, 481, 498, 524
face validity, 208
Facebook
  daily data analysis, 287
  recruitment ads on, 322
  reputation concerns, 306
  "thumbs-up" symbol, 289
  user manipulation study, 33
face-to-face interviewing (FtF), 227–28, 322
factor analysis
  APA style write-up for, 508
  confirmatory, 508
  defined, 182–83, 210
  example of, 507
  explanation of, 507–8
  exploratory, 507–8
  extraction method in, 508
  for humor assessment, 506*f*, 509–11, 510*f*
  Kaiser's MSA and, 508, 509
  rotation in, 508
  scree plot for, 510*f*
  types of, 507–8
factor loading, 506*f*, 508
factorial ANOVA. *See also* one-way analysis of variance
  APA style write-up of, 496
  dependent/independent variables in, 495, 496
  example of, 495
  explanation of, 496
  means and SDs of, 497*f*
factorial experiment design, 268, 268*f*
factorial validity, 209–10
Factual, 299
Fahrenheit system, 168
faking responses, 213

fallacy
  ecological, 24–35
  exception, 25
false premises, 180–81
falsification of theories, 19
Family Educational Rights and Privacy Act, 38
Fediuk, T. A., 267
Ferdowsi, Arash, 298
Fidell, L. S., 508
field experiments, 284
Fink, A., 220
first page, 76, 89, 91–93, 93*f*
Fisher, R. A., 330
Fisher's Least Significant Difference Test
    (LSD), 441
flight attendants-humor hypothesis, 21–22
floppy disks, 293
focus groups, 26, 37
Food and Drug Administration (FDA), 37
"forgotten footnoter/referencer" plagiarism, 52
"Formal Features in Children's Science
    Television" (Boiarsky, Long, Thayer),
    446–47
format choices for research, 58
Fornash, Bennie, 101, 134, 267, 327, 422–23
Fowler, F. J., 234
frequency distributions
  for biological sex, 356, 357*f*
  charts and, 360, 361*f*–363*f*, 362–63
  creating, 354
  Excel and, 354, 359–60, 359*f*–360*f*
  histograms and, 360, 362–63, 362*f*, 363*f*–364*f*
  for political affiliation, 159–60, 353, 358*f*
  SPSS and, 354, 355*f*, 356, 357*f*–358*f*
  for Time Spent Online, 358*f*
  for University Classification, 358*f*
Frymier, A. B., 101, 207, 211
Fulcher, Glenn, 199, 199*f*, 200
full-board review, of IRBs, 48
future directions subsection, 119, 121, 518

Galilee, Galileo, 17, 24
Galton, Francis, 169
"gaps" in research, 59
Garramone, G. M., 32
Gates, Arthur, 170
general linear models (GLM), 427, 435*f*, 473.
    See also linear regressions; one-way
    analysis of variance
general to specific organizational pattern,
    108–9
generalizability
  content analysis and, 247
  experimental designs and, 284

replication and, 276–77
restrictions across constructs, 211
sampling process and, 310–11
in surveys, 219, 234
generalizations
  empirical, 23–25
  exception fallacy and, 25
  hasty, 24
Generalized Attitude Measure, 173, 175
  consistent scoring example, 191*f*
  description, 157, 162*f*, 192–93, 199
  of "Higher Education," 190*f*
  inconsistent scoring example, 190*f*
  reliability of, 192–200, 194*f*–200*f*, 204*f*
  sample questionnaire questions, 224*f*
Generalized Belief Scale, 157, 158*f*, 162*f*, 204*f*
germinal idea, 177, 178, 249–50
"ghostwriter" plagiarism, 51
Glacier cold data program, 299
Global Positioning System (GPS), 289, 294
Gnip, 299, 303
The Gods Must Be Crazy (film), 18
Goodall, Jane, 32
Goodboy, A., 64
Google Books Library Project, 296, 297*f*
Google Docs, 299
Google Scholar, 75–76
Gorham, Joan, 77, 507
Gosset, William Sealy, 408
Graham, E. E., 129
Gray, John, 24
Grimm, L. G., 508
group communication apprehension (CA),
    503–4, 504*f*, 512*f*
Groves, R. M., 231
Grunig, L. A., 318
Guéguen, N., 267
Guttman, L., 3, 212
Guttman scale, 140

HA. *See* humor assessment
hacking, 291
Hairston, M., 64
Hamer, Dean, 144
handbooks, 62*f*, 65, 66*f*, 67, 69–70
Haney, C., 31–32
hasty generalizations, 24
Hawthorne effect, 270–71, 274
Health Insurance Portability and
    Accountability Act (HIPAA), 38, 304
HealthData.gov, 300*f*
Heise, D. R., 173
Hereditary Genius (Galton), 169
Hildebrand, D. K., 221

Hippocrates, 2, 170
histograms
    frequency distributions and, 360, 362–63, 362*f*, 363*f*–364*f*
    SPSS and, 362–63, 362*f*–363*f*
historical flaws, 274
Hollander, E. P., 143–44
Homonegativity Short Form, 137, 138*f*
Houston, Drew, 298
Hovland, Carl, 3
"How Companies Learn Your Secrets" (Duhigg), 470
"How to Make Our Ideas Clear" (Peirce), 16
Hoyt reliability, 191
human sexuality research, 228
human-generated data, 289
humanism, 2
Hume, David, 17
humor, of physicians, 99*f*, 103*f*, 115*f*, 116*f*, 117*f*
humor assessment (HA), 150*f*, *161*f, 161*f*
    description, 508
    factor analysis for, 506*f*, 509–11, 510*f*
    one-way ANOVA for, 445–46, 446*f*–447*f*
    path analysis example for, 502*f*
    reliability of, 203*f*
    scree plot for, 510*f*
    as variable, 106, 150–51, 150*f*
Humor Orientation scale, 113*f*, 115*f*, 161*f*, 174, 176, 203*f*
Humphreys, Laud, 31
Hunt, Everett Lee, 2–3
Hussein, Saddam, 18
hypothesis testing, 326–45
    case study, 331–32
    effect sizes and, 339–41, 340*f*
    error understanding for, 341–42, 341*f*
    power testing in, 338–39
    significance testing in, 334–38, 336*f*–338*f*
hypothesis/hypotheses, 17
    alternative, 329–31, 332, 344
    defined, 19
    in design of research project, 242
    flight attendants-humor, 21–22
    good hypotheses elements, 326–28
    "if"/"then" statements in, 327
    null, 329, 330–32, 334–35, 338–39, 341*f*, 342–44
    observations in, 21
    one-tailed, 328, 339
    post hoc revision of, 49
    in preview of introduction, 103
    in the rationale section, 515, 535
    research question comparison, 111
    for structural equation modeling, 503–4, 504*f*

in theories, 19–21
    two-tailed, 328, 338*f*, 339
hypothetical questions, 181
hypothetical variable, 171

IaaS (infrastructure as a service), 299
IBM Statistical Package for the Social Sciences (SPSS), version 20.0, 9
Ibn al-Haytham, 17
ideology, 13
Ig Nobels, 36
illustrations, 101
immediacy, 151–52. *See also* nonverbal immediacy
"Increasing Patient Satisfaction and Compliance" (Wrench, M. Booth-Butterfield), 488–89
incremental index of fit (IFI), 505
Independent Samples Test, 416–17, 417*f*, 420*f*
independent samples *t*-tests. *See t*-tests
independent variables, 134–35
    in ANCOVA, 497, 498
    canonical correlations and, 511
    in correlations, 452, 454, 455, 460, 469
    in design of research project, 241
    exogenous latent variables comparison, 504
    in factorial ANOVA, 495–96
    manipulation of, 266–70, 268*f*, 273, 278, 278–83
    in MANOVA, 499–500
    in one-way ANOVA, 426–27, 428, 435, 436*f*–438*f*, 439–40, 443, 495
    in regressions, 475, 478, 479*f*, 480–81, 483–84, 485, 487
    in *t*-tests, 406–7, 414, 415*f*, 423
inferential statistics
    defined, 349
    descriptive statistics comparison, 349–50
    hypothesis testing and, 331
    sum of squares in, 366
Infochimp, 299
infographics, 536–37, 537*f*
information sources
    locating, 67, 68*f*–69*f*, 69–70, 71*f*–72*f*, 72–80
    primary, 64–65, 80
    secondary, 64–65, 80
    types, 65, 66*f*, 67
informed consent
    Belmont Report on, 35
    defined, 35
    IRB forms for, 39–40, 41*f*–42, 43–45
    in research projects, 241
    student consent forms and, 32

infrastructure as a service (Iaas), 299

Instagram, 289

Institute for Communications Research
(University of Illinois), 3

institutional review boards (IRBs), 37–48

  basics of, 37–39

  communication researchers and, 39

  ethical dilemmas of, 37–38

  exempt categories, 47*f*

  exempt review from, 46–47, 47*f*

  expedited review, 47–48

  full-board review, 48

  functions, advanced, 46

  functions, basic, 45–46

  informed consent forms and, 39–40, 41*f*–42,
    43–45

  origins of, 37

  processes, 45–48

  recruitment strategy approval, 323–24

instrumentation subsection, 114–15, 115*f,* 160.
  See also measurement

interaction effects, 496

intercoder reliability, 254–58, 257*f*

intercultural communication apprehension, 221

*International Encyclopedia of
Communication,* 70

Internet. *See also* time spent on Internet; World
Wide Web

  blogger/blogging on, 26

  electronic databases, 58, 67, 70, 71*f*–72*f,*
    72–74, 76–77

  evaluating sources on, 78–79

  evolution of, 7, 59

  research benefits of, 12, 75

  survey administration, 38, 185, 229–30

  Wikipedia problem, 53, 79–80

Internet of things, 290

interpersonal communication apprehension
(CA), 503–4, 504*f,* 512*f*

interpersonal willingness to communicate
(WTC), 512*f*

interpretive research, 13

interval level questions, 231–32

interval measurement, 137, 168. *See also* Likert
scales; scalogram scale; semantic
differential/bipolar scale

interval variables

  audience-specific behavior, 145

  communication apprehension (*See*
communication apprehension)

  communication traits, 145–46, 145*f*

  defined, 137

  ethnocentrism (*See* ethnocentrism)

  Likert scale measure of, 137, 138*f*

nonverbal immediacy (*See* nonverbal
immediacy)

  personality, 143–44

  scalogram measure of, 138, 140, 140*f*

  semantic differential/bipolar scale measure
    of, 137

  situational behavior, 145

  sociocommunicative orientation (*See*
sociocommunicative orientation)

  Staple scale measure of, 138

  trait behavior, 144–45

  willingness to communicate (*See* willingness
to communicate)

intervening variables, 135

interview schedule, 217, 220, 226

interviewing

  encouraging responses in, 232–33

  face-to-face (FtF), 227–28, 322

  telephone, 228–29

introduction (to research paper)

  acknowledged facts in, 100–101

  attention getter in, 99–101

  claims/statistics in, 100

  credibility espoused in, 102

  illustration/story in, 101

  link to topic in, 101–2

  preview in, 102–3

  quotations acknowledged in, 101

  rhetorical question in, 100

  significance of topic, 102

  sources acknowledged in, 101

  thesis in, 102

iPad, 289

iPhone, 289

IRBs. *See* institutional review boards

isomorphism, 166–67

item nonresponse, 232–33

Jaffe, D., 31–32

John Paul II (Pope), 24

Johnson, Aaron, 102, 161*f,* 173, 210

journal review process, 529–30, 530*f*–532*f,*
  532–33

journals, communication-related, 68*f*–69*f*

Jowett, G. S., 3

justice, Belmont Report on, 36

Kaiser's measure of sampling adequacy
(Kaiser's MSA), 508, 509

Kellogg Foundation, 403

Kelly, Frederick, 170, 175

Kelvin scale, 168, 169

Kennamer, J. D., 32

key performance indicators, 448

key term identification, 61, 63–64, 63*f*
Khan, A., 51
King, J. H., 304
Kinsey, Alfred, 228
Kintz, B. L., 495
Klein, P., 13, 14
knowledge
    cognitive, 175–76
    measurement of, 175–77
    perceived, 176
    ways of gaining, 13–16
known to unknown organizational
        pattern, 109
Krippendorff's alpha, 258
Kuhn, Tim, 129
Kumblaeus, 248
kurtosis, 365, 365*f,* 371*f*

labeling of phenomena, 18
Lachlan, K., 267
Laing, J. D., 221
Laio, Alessandro, 292
Laney, Doug, 292–95
language, defined, 6
laptop computers, 289
Latané, Bibb, 31
latent variable, 171, 173
law of parsimony, 484–95
Lazarsfeld, P., 3
leading items, 204
learner empowerment, 105
Lesser, V., 232
Levene's Test for Equality of Variances,
        416–18, 417*f,* 419, 420*f*
Levine, T. R., 343
Lewis, Ray, 422
liberal post hoc tests, 441
librarians, working with, 77–78
Likert, R., 3
Likert, Rensis, 3, 171
Likert scales, 114.
    anchors, 171, 172*f*
    closed-ended questions in, 233
    constructing questions for, 179–81
    history of, 171
    interval variables measured by, 137
Lime Survey, 231
limitations subsection, 117–18, 118*f,* 517–18
linear regressions. *See also* multiple linear
        regressions
    APA style write-up for, 481, 484–85
    background information, 474–75
    bivariate, 116*f,* 478, 481, 483, 484–85, 487
    case study introduction to, 473–74

computer printouts of, 477–78, 477*f*–480*f,*
        480–83, 482*f*–483*f*
    Excel and, 481–83, 482*f*–483*f*
    Rocca and Vogl-Bauer article on, 489–91
    SPSS, 477–78, 477*f*–480*f,* 480–81, 484*f*
    step-by-step approach to, 475–77
    Wrench and M. Booth-Butterfield article on,
        488–89
linear relationship, 116*f,* 473–74, 475–76, 480
link to topic, 101–2
literal replication, 277
literature review, 104–9, 514
    categorical/topical organizational pattern
        in, 108
    cause-and-effect organizational pattern
        in, 107
    chronological order in, 106
    compare-and-contrast method in, 107
    concluding section, 119, 119*f*
    discussion section, 116–19, 117*f*
    first draft preparation, 121–24
    general to specific organizational pattern
        in, 108–9
    known to unknown organizational pattern
        in, 109
    method section, 111–15, 115*f*
    pitfalls in writing, 124
    previous research cited in, 106
    problem-cause-solution format in, 108
    psychological organizational pattern in, 108
    rationale section of, 109, 111, 111*f*
    reasons for, 104–5
    results section, 115–16, 116*f*
    segment (example), 110*f*
    specific to general organizational
        pattern in, 109
Little, R. J. A., 231
loaded items, 204
Long, Marilee, 105, 178, 446–48
longitudinal survey design, 223
LSD. *See* Fisher's Least Significant Difference
        Test
lurker variables, 272

Machiavelli, Niccolò, 34
Machiavellian ethic, 34, 34*f*
machine learning, 290–91
machine-generated data, 289–90
Mahmood, A., 51
Mahmood, S. T., 51
mailed administration, of surveys, 229
main effects, 496–98
major premise, 20–21
Malik, A. B., 51

manipulation check, 272–73
MANOVA. *See* multivariate analysis of variance
Masling, Joseph, 272
Mason, R., 232
mass administration, of surveys, 229
mass-mediated messages, 248–49
maturation, 274
McCroskey, James, 6, 102, 105, 107, 137, 144, 148, 153, 155, 160, 161*f*, 171, 173, 177, 182, 200, 210, 221. *See also* Ethnocentrism Scale; Personal Report of Communication Apprehension-24
McMahon, Vince, 422
McNutt, L. A., 43
mean
    APA style notation for, 112, 159
    calculating, 350–51, 350*f*–351*f*
    central limits theorem and, 312
    defined, 184, 350
    in descriptive statistics for CA, 371*f*
    in descriptive statistics in SPSS, 373*f*
    Excel calculation, 372*f*
    of population, 350*f*
    of PRCA-24, 350–51, 353*f*
    regression to, 275, 275*f*, 279
    in reliabilities for book's dataset variables, 202*f*
    in Risk Knowledge Index, 176*f*
    skewness and, 365*f*
    in SPSS Cronbach's alpha reliability, 198*f*
    in SPSS output of exam scores, 362, 362*f*
    standard error of (SE_M), 333
    in VAS (example), 114
mean squares (MS), 432, 433*f*
mean squares between, 432, 433*f*
mean squares within, 432, 433*f*
measure of sampling adequacy. *See* Kaiser's measure of sampling adequacy
measurement, 165–86. *See also* reliability; research scales; validity
    of attitudes, 175
    of beliefs, 175
    for communication, 173–77
    conceptualization and, 177
    constructing questions, 179–81
    defined, 165–66
    factors for avoiding confusion, 181–83
    for gaining knowledge, 16
    germinal idea and, 177, 178, 249–50
    history of, 169–73
    interval, 137, 168
    of knowledge, 175–77
    levels of, 137, 167–69

nominal, 167
numbers/"things" and, 166–67
operationalization and, 178
ordinal, 167–68
outside academia, 185
outside the walls of academia, 214
of personality traits/states, 174–75
problems with, 212–14
question construction for, 179–81
ratio scale for, 169
reliability improvements for, 202, 204
results section example, 115*f*
statistical analysis and, 184–85
of variables, 128
measures of central tendency, 350–65. *See also* kurtosis; mean; median; mode; skewness
measures of variability, 365–71. *See also* range; standard deviation; sum of squares; variance
median
    calculating, 351–52
    defined, 351
    in descriptive statistics for CA, 371*f*
    in descriptive statistics in SPSS, 373*f*
    of PRCA-24, 353*f*
    skewness and, 363–64, 365*f*
    in SPSS output of exam scores, 362, 362*f*
mediated channel, 7
mediated communications, 7
mediated messages, 248–49
mediating variables, 271
meeting communication apprehension (CA), 503–4, 504*f*, 512*f*
meeting willingness to communicate (WTC), 512*f*
Menager-Beeley, R., 53
mental measures. *See* research scales
Mental Measures Yearbook (Buros), 184
mental replication, 277
Mertler, C. A., 495
message, 6–7
metadata, 289, 294, 300*f*
method section (of research paper), 111–15, 514
    apparatus subsection, 112
    defined, 111–12
    example, 113*f*
    instrumentation subsection, 114–15, 115*f*, 160
    participant subsection, 112, 159–60
    procedure subsection, 112, 114, 160
metric system, 166
Microsoft Excel. *See* Excel
Microsoft OneDrive, 299

Milgram, Stanley, 32
Milgram Study, 32, 34
Miller, Katherine, 101, 105, 403
Millhouse, B., 266
Million Song Database, 300*f*
Milloy, S., 301
minor premise, 20–21
"misinformer" plagiarism, 52
mode
    calculating, 353–54, 353*f*
    defined, 136, 353
    in descriptive statistics for CA, 371*f*
    for political affiliation, 353
    of PRCA-24, 353*f*
    skewness and, 363–64, 365*f*
    in SPSS output of exam scores,
        362, 362*f*
Modern Language Association (MLA), 58
modified direct translation of surveys, 237
mono-operation bias, 210–11
Moore, Gordon E., 293
Moore's Law, 293
Morse code, 7
Moser, P. K., 13
multiple comparison tests
    chi-square test and, 396, 397*f*
    for one-way ANOVA, 440–43
multiple linear regressions
    APA style write-up for, 487
    Excel and, 487
    pictorial example of, 485*f*
    Rocca and Vogl-Bauer article on, 489–91
    SPSS results for, 485, 486*f*, 487
    understanding, 485, 486*f*, 487–88
    Venn diagram of, 488*f*
    Wrench and M. Booth-Butterfield article on,
        488–89
multiple time series design, 280
multiple-choice test, 175
multivariate analysis of variance (MANOVA),
    499–500
multivariate test, 499, 500, 501

Narayanan, Arvind, 304
Nass, Clifford, 26
Nathan, Rebekah (Cathy Small), 32
National Commission for the Protection of
    Human Subjects of Biomedical and
    Behavioral Research, 31, 35
National Communication Association (NCA),
    231–32, 519–20, 521*f*
National Institutes of Health (NIH), 37
National Research Act (1974), 31
natural selection theory (Darwin), 2

NCA. *See* National Communication
    Association
negative relationships, 131, 132*f*, 452*f*, 453,
    454, 455
Netflix, 299, 304
Netherlands Institute of Public Opinion, 138
Nettler, Gwynn, 18
network sampling, 319
Neuendorf, K. A., 247–48
Neuliep, J. W., 148, 161*f*, 203*f*. *See also*
    Ethnocentrism Scale
Neupauer, Nicholas, 101, 134, 267, 327, 422–23
neutral relationships, 131, 132*f*, 453
Newton, Isaac, 1, 2, 17
Nicol, A. A. M., 526
No Child Left Behind Act, 38
nominal level data, 135–36
nominal measurement, 167
nominal variables
    biological sex as, 142, 244*f*, 378, 401
    categorization rules, 135–36
    chi-square test evaluation, 379, 382
    data gathering rules, 221
    frequency table, 358*f*
    political affiliation as, 142
    school classification variable as, 378
    soft drink preference as, 378
    t test examination of, 406
    testing for differences, 225
nondirectional research questions, 329
nonmediated messages, 249
nonparametric statistical testing, 184–85
nonprobability samples, 311, 316–17, 319
nonproportionate quota samples, 318
nonresponse
    bias, 234
    effects of, 234
    item, 232–33
    unit, 231–32
nonverbal immediacy, 105, 151–53, 159
    relationships of, 342–43, 452*f*
    SPSS dataset information on, 374*f*
    survey research and, 222
    t-test of, 422
    Zhang's examination of, 236
Nonverbal Immediacy Scale, 161*f*, 210
Nonverbal Immediacy Scale-Self-Report
    (NIS-S), 151, 152*f*, 175
    reliability of, 202*f*–203*f*, 210
    validity of, 210
nonverbal messages, 6–7
normative equivalence, 236–37
normed fit index (NFI), 504, 505
Note Pad datasets, 354

null hypothesis
    in the case study, 332
    Confidence Interval and, 342
    effect sizes and, 339
    error understanding and, 341*f*, 342
    in one-way ANOVA, 42–428, 440
    power and, 343
    power testing and, 338–39
    probability determination and, 331
    reasons for testing, 330
    significance testing and, 334–35
    type I/II error and, 344

objective/objectivity, 22
observations, 17, 21–23
O'Donnell, V., 3
Office of Human Research Protections
    (OHRP), 47
OK Cupid mismatching people study, 33
one-group pretest posttest, 278
one-shot case study, 277–78
one-tailed hypothesis, 328, 339
one-way analysis of variance (one-way
    ANOVA), 141*f*, 426–49. *See also* factorial
    ANOVA; multivariate analysis of
    variance; repeated-measures ANOVA
    APA style write-up for, 443, 445
    background information for, 427–28
    Boiarsky, Long, Thayer article on, 446–48
    case study introduction to, 427
    computer printouts for, 434–40, 434*f*–439*f*
    critical values for, 432*f*, 433
    degrees of freedom for, 431–32
    dependent variables in, 426–28, 434, 436*f*,
        439*f*, 440, 442*f*, 443, 445
    Excel and, 443
    F test value for, 432, 433*f*
    formula for, 428*f*
    for humor assessment, 445–46, 446*f*–447*f*
    independent variables in, 426–28, 435,
        436*f*–438*f*, 439–40, 443, 495
    law of parsimony and, 495
    mean squares for, 432, 433*f*
    multiple comparison tests for, 440–43
    null hypothesis in, 42–428, 440
    outside academia, 448
    for political affiliation, 426–27, 445–46,
        446*f*, 447*f*
    post hoc tests for, 438–39, 441–43, 445–46
    regression and, 473, 480*f*, 481, 484*f*, 486*f*,
        489, 491
    SPSS and, 434–35, 439–43, 439*f*, 442*f*, 446*f*
    SSB and, 429–30, 429*f*
    SSW and, 430, 430*f*–431*f*

    step-by-step approach to, 429–33, 429*f*,
        431*f*–433*f*
    summary table for, 433*f*, 438–39, 440, 445*f*
    t-tests compared to, 407
online databases. *See* electronic databases
open-access communication sources, 77
open-ended questions
    advantages of, 222–23
    analytic tools for, 223
    in face-to-face interviewing, 227
    in self-administered surveys, 233
    in telephone interviewing, 228
    in translating scales, 238
Opera Solutions, 299
operational replication, 277
operationalization
    for content analysis, 250–51
    developing, 178
    of variables, 104
opinions
    ignorance and, 2
    public, 3
    value of, 16, 26
Oracle, 299
ordinal level questions, 221
ordinal measurement, 167–68
ordinal variables, 136–37
    in book's dataset, 143
    categorization rules, 136–37
    relationship testing of, 141
    time spent online as, 143, 162*f*
    university clarification as, 143
ordinary ways of knowing, 14–16
organizational ambiguity, 105
organizational effects, 105
organizational patterns
    categorical/topical, 108
    cause-and-effect, 107
    chronological, 106
    compare and contrast, 107
    general to specific, 108–9
    known to unknown, 109
    problem-cause-solution, 108
    psychological order, 108
    specific to general, 109
organized writers, 90–91
organizing information, 80–81
Origin of Species (Darwin), 2, 169
Osgood, C. E., 3, 171
O'Shea, T. J., 120, 533–34
outliers, 362

PaaS (platform as a service), 299
paired *t*-tests, 423–24

panculturalism, 148

Pandora, 289

panel discussions, 523, 528–29

panel survey design, 224

paper formatting, APA style, 89–93
  abstract page, 91, 92*f*
  cover (title) page, 89–91, 90*f*
  first page, 91–93, 93*f*
  introduction, 99–103
  title page, 89–91, 90*f*

paper presentations, 515, 523–26

parallel blind technique, 238

parameters, 184, 328, 347–48

parametric statistical testing, 184–85, 328

paraphrasing, 88–89

parenthetical (internal) citations, 85, 87*f*,
  88, 89*f*

parsimony, law of, 484–95

participant identity disclosures, 49–50

participant subsection, of method section, 112,
  159–60

path analysis
  APA style write-up for, 502
  calculation, 503*f*
  example of, 501, 502*f*
  explanation of, 501–2
  structural equation model comparison,
    504, 506

Patient Satisfaction Scale, 113*f*

Patterson, D., 305

Paulos, L., 53

Pearson, Karl, 319, 408

Pearson product-moment correlation
  coefficient
  APA style write-up for, 463–64
  case study introduction for, 455
  computer printouts of, 458–64
  critical values for, 459*f*
  curvilinear relationships, 452*f*, 453, 454
  defined, 451
  descriptive statistics for formula, 457*f*
  Excel and, 458, 462–63, 464*f*–465*f*
  formula for, 455*f*
  negative relationships, 452*f*, 453, 454, 455
  neutral relationships, 453
  positive relationships, 452–53, 452*f*, 458
  PRCA-24 and, 455–56, 459
  relationships for, 452–53
  SPSS and, 459–60, 460*f*–462*f*, 462
  step-by-step approach to, 455–58, 456*f*–457*f*

Pearson Spearman correlations, 465–66

Peirce, Charles Sanders, 16, 17

Perceived Credibility Scale, 113*f*

perceived knowledge, 176

perception, 4

"perfect crime" plagiarism, 52–53

periodical indexes, 70

Perse, E. M., 129

Personal Report of Communication
  Apprehension-24 (PRCA-24)
  analysis of covariance and, 497
  CA construct in PRCA-24, 211
  criterion validity and, 208
  description, 160, 161*f*, 174–75, 203*f*
  descriptive statistics and, 347–48
  latent variables and, 171
  mean scores of, 350–51
  median of, 353*f*
  mode of, 353*f*
  Pearson product-moment correlation and,
    455–56, 459
  range in, 147*f*
  reliability of, 203*f*
  repeated-measures ANOVA and, 500
  statistics on, 347–50
  subconstructs of, 211
  use in measuring CA, 146, 147*f*, 160

Personal Report of Public Speaking Anxiety
  (PRPSA), 137

personality, 143–46

personality theory, 2

personality traits/states, 174–75

petabyte hard drives, 293

Peters, J. M., 301

Pew Research Center, 300*f*

Pexman, P. M., 526

Pfungst, Oskar, 23

phenomena, 18, 22

Philosophiae Naturalis Principia Mathematica
  (Newton), 2

"photocopier" plagiarism, 51

physical sciences, 1, 2, 262

physician's humor orientation, 99*f*, 103*f*, 115*f*,
  116*f*, 117*f*

pilot testing, of surveys, 225–26

plagiarism
  defined, 51
  secondary sources and, 64–65
  sources-cited types, 52–53
  sources-not-cited types, 51–52

platform as a service (PaaS), 299

Plato, 2

political affiliation
  ANOVA evaluation of effects of, 496
  biological sex and, 495–97, 497*f*
  factorial ANOVA example, 495–97, 497*f*
  frequency distributions for, 159–60,
    353, 358*f*

as nominal variable, 135–36, 142
one-way ANOVA for, 426–27, 445–46, 446*f*, 447*f*
Poole, Marshall Scott, 129
Popper, Karl, 17
populations
defined, 219, 253, 310
generalizability and, 219
parameter value of, 184–85
sampling process and, 310–12
in surveys, 226–30
theoretical, 311
variable levels in, 135
positive relationships, 130–31, 131*f*, 452–53, 452*f*, 458
positivism/postpositivism communication, 13
post hoc hypothesis revision, 49
postdictive validity, 209
poster presentations, 526–28, 526*f*
"potluck writer" plagiarism, 51
power testing, 338–39
predictions
of the future, 19
narrowing/fine-tuning of, 14
in theories, 19–21
predictive data analytics, 288, 291
predictive validity, 208–9
pre-experimental design
one-group pretest posttest, 278
one-shot case study, 277–78
static group comparisons, 278–79
premises, 20–21
prescriptive data analytics, 292
Presser, S., 220
Pressy, L. W., 170
Pressy, S. L., 170
pretest-posttest design, 279, 281
preview, in paper introduction, 102–3
Prichard, S., 171
primary sources of information, 64–65, 80, 103*f*, 106, 122
prison simulation study, 31–32
privacy, 38
probability, 331, 344
probability level, 335, 336, 339, 343*f*, 344, 383*f*
probability sampling, 311, 312, 314–16, 324
probability theory, 312
probability value, 335, 343*f*, 344, 383*f*
problem-cause-solution organizational pattern, 108
procedure subsection, of method section, 112, 114, 160
proportionate quota samples, 318
proposition, defined, 19

prospective validity, 208–9
protected health information (PHI), 38
Protestantism tornado correlation study, 452–53
PRPSA. *See* Personal Report of Public Speaking Anxiety
PSPP statistical software, 9, 193, 354, 371, 393
psychological organizational pattern, 108
psychopharmacology, 19
public communication apprehension (CA), 503–4, 504*f*, 512*f*
Public Health Act, 39
public speaking
anxiety from, 128, 130–31, 131*f*–132*f*, 137
beliefs about taking, in college, 157, 158*f*, 159, 162*f*, 204*f*, 330, 349, 378–79, 378*f*, 464–66
chi-test case study and, 378–80, 382, 389
Likert scale measurement, 190
relationships between CA and beliefs about, 483–85, 484*f*
Winans'/Hunt's research, 2–3
WTC for, 155, 156*f*
public willingness to communicate (WTC), 512*f*
publication
NCA journal acceptance rates, 533*f*
peer review for, 529
review process for, 532–33
submission process for, 529–30, 530*f*–532*f*
Publication Manual of the American Psychological Association (APA), 51, 98
Punyanunt, Narissra M., 105, 221, 348, 469–70
purposive samples, 317–18

qualitative research, 8, 13, 14, 26
journals containing, 69*f*
mode in, 354
open-ended questions in, 227
purposive sampling in, 318
results/discussion combined in, 515
statistical stories about, 535
types of data examined in, 50, 217
variables in, 135, 136
quasi-experimental design
multiple time series, 280
pretest-posttest, 279
switching replications, 280–81
time series, 279
question clarification, 60–61, 62*f*–63*f*
questionnaires.
consent forms and, 43, 44, 160
defined, 217
in dyad research, 129
as indirect research method, 22
sample questions, 224*f*
on workplace aggression tolerance, 129

questions
    closed-ended, 233
    construction guidelines, 179–81
    directional, 329
    double, 180
    factor analysis of responses, 182–83
    on Humor Orientation Scale, 174
    hypothetical, 181
    interval level, 221–22
    for Likert-scales, 179–81
    measurement-related, 167, 169
    nominal level, 220–21
    nondirectional, 329
    open-ended, 222–23, 227–28, 233, 238
    ordinal level, 221
    on PRCA-24, 174
    ratio level, 222
    rhetorical, 100
    on scalogram scale, 175
    for surveys/questionnaires, 220–23
    "yes" or "no," 170
quota samples, 318–19
quotations
    APA style of, 88, 89
    in introduction, 101

R statistical software, 9, 193, 354, 371, 393,
        465–66, 466f
random assignment, 264–66, 264f–266f,
        272, 313
random probe translation of surveys, 238
random samples
    confidence intervals in, 333–34
    Excel providing, 314
    population variances, 333
    simple, 311, 312–15, 313f
    stratified, 311, 314–15, 318–19
    in t-tests, 408
randomized switching replications
        design, 282
range
    APA write-up style, 159, 161f, 199
    calculating, 365–66
    confidence intervals and, 320, 333
    defined, 365
    in descriptive statistics for CA, 371f
    in Likert scale, 227
    in PRCA-24, 147f, 160, 161f
    in PRPSA, 137
    in Risk Knowledge Index, 177
    in sampling error, 316
    in SPSS frequency distribution, 365f
    in willingness to communication, 156f

rank-order measurement. See ordinal
        measurement
ratio level questions, 222
ratio variables, 141, 141f, 142, 159, 371, 451
rationale section, 109–11
    defined, 110, 112
    example, 111f
    hypotheses in, 515, 535
    research questions in, 328–29, 331, 514
reading literature, to gain knowledge, 16
real-time data analytics, 288
recall issues, 181
receiver, defined, 6
redundancy of backup copies, 299
reference page, APA style, 84, 85f, 94–95, 94f
regression (R), 472–92. See also multiple linear
        regressions
    assumptions of, 474–75
    bivariate linear, 116f, 478, 481, 483,
        484–85, 487
    dependent variables in, 475, 479f–480f,
        481, 484f
    equation for, 474f
    independent variables in, 475, 478, 479f,
        479f–480f, 480–81, 483–84, 484f, 485,
        486f, 487–88, 489
    one-way ANOVA and, 473, 480f, 481, 484f,
        486f, 489, 491
    outside academia, 491
    simple graph of, 473f
regression to the mean, 274–75, 275f, 280
reinforcer variable, 271
relational databases, 294–95, 295f
"The Relationship between Listening Styles
        and Conversational Sensitivity"
        (Chesebro), 467, 469
relationship tests
    canonical correlations, 511–12
    factor analysis, 507–10, 510f
    path analysis, 501–2, 502f–503f
    structural equation modeling, 503–4,
        504f–505f
relationships
    causal, 108, 262, 263, 284, 501
    as CRR top concept, 4
    curvilinear, 452f, 453, 454
    dependent variables and, 241–42
    interpersonal, 36, 161f, 174, 203f
    interval measurement and, 168
    negative, 131, 132f, 452f, 453, 454, 455
    neutral, 131, 132f, 453
    ordinal measurement and, 167–68
    positive, 130–31, 131f, 452–53, 452f, 458

power and, 338–39
as research concept, 130
survey design and, 223
relative fit index (RFI), 505
reliability
alternate forms, 192
analysis dialogue box, 195*f*–196*f*
analysis menu, 194*f*
APA style write-up for, 203*f*–204*f*
article alpha reliabilities, 205*f*–206*f*
for book's dataset, 202*f*
coding/intercoder, 254–58, 257*f*
Cronbach's alpha, 192–200, 194*f*–200*f*
defined, 188–89
of Ethnocentrism Scale, 203*f*
of Generalized Attitude Measure, 192–200,
194*f*–200*f*, 204*f*
of Generalized Belief Scale, 204*f*
of Humor Assessment, 203*f*
intercoder, 254
of measurement improvements, 202, 204
of Nonverbal Immediacy Scale, 203*f*
outside of academia, 201–2
pilot, 253
of PRCA-24, 203*f*
research outside academia, 214
scalar, 189–91
of Sociocommunicative Orientation Scale,
161*f*, 203*f*
split-half, 192
test-retest, 191–92
of Verbal Aggression Scale, 114
of Willingness to Communicate instrument,
203*f*–204*f*
religious fundamentalism, 221
religious identity and credibility
study, 267
repeated-measures ANOVA, 500–501
replication, 275, 277
research, defined, 12–13
research implications, 518
research participants
analysis of responses of, 182–83
APA style write-up for, 112, 159–60
Belmont Report on, 35–36
Common Rule on rights for, 37
identity disclosures, 49–50
informed consent and, 42*f*, 44
NIH on, 37
researcher preferences for, 40
responsibilities of IRBs, 45
strategies for getting, 230, 322
Research Planning Worksheet, 62*f*–63*f*

research questions
defined, 328–29
directional, 329
in discussion section, 116–17
epistemology and, 13–14
hypothesis comparison, 111
identifying key terms for, 61, 62*f*, 63, 63*f*
in literature review, 105
nondirectional, 329
participant's rights and, 42*f*
questionnaires and, 225
in rationale section, 104, 249
in research project worksheet, 240*f*, 244*f*
in results section, 115
topic stated as, 60–61
unit of analysis in, 250
variable identification and, 134, 135
writing, 128, 220
research scales (mental measures). *See also*
Likert scales; semantic differential/bipolar
scale
APA write-up, 159–60, 161*f*–162*f*,
200–201, 201*f*
attitudes, beliefs, and, 174–75
conceptualization and, 177, 178
creation problems, 177
germinal ideas for, 178
history of, 170
operationalizing, 178
personality traits/states, and, 174–75
question construction for, 179–81
reliability of, 189–91, 190*f*–191*f*
resources for finding, 183–84
subscales, 182–83
"resourceful citer" plagiarism, 52
resources for research, 58
response rate
defined, 231–32
improving, 234–35
item nonresponse and, 232–33
nonresponse bias and, 234
unit nonresponse and, 231–32
responsiveness, 154, 177
results discussion subsection, 115–16, 116*f*, 515
retrospective validity, 209
rhetorical communication, 13, 14
rhetorical question, 106
Richards, N. M., 304
Richmond, V. P., 4
Richmond, Virginia Peck, 77, 102, 105, 107,
137, 153, 155, 173, 174, 177, 210, 507.
Riddle, D. L., 317
Risk Knowledge Index, 176, 176*f*, 177

Rocca, Kelly A., 105, 114, 129, 223, 329, 489–91
Rodriguez, Alex, 292
Rosenthal, H., 221
R-squared (R^2) value, 478–79
Ruszkiewicz, J. J., 64
Rutherford, Ernest, 2

SaaS (software as a service), 299
samples
    anonymity, confidentiality, and, 40–41, 221
    choosing, 114, 184–85, 219, 228
    cluster, 311, 315
    common sense recruitment, 320–23, 323*f*
    for content analysis, 253
    convenience, 311, 317
    defined, 347–48
    design selection, 311–12
    ethical recruitment, 323–24
    generalizability and, 219
    network, 319
    nonprobability, 311, 316–17, 319
    overrepresentations, 36
    probability, 311, 312, 314–16, 324
    purposive, 317–18
    quota, 318–19
    random (*See* random samples)
    reference, for APA style, 85*f*, 86*f*
    response rate of, 230–33
    size determination, 226, 319–20, 321*f*
    systematic, 311, 315–16
    volunteer, 311, 317, 318, 319
sampling
    in content analysis, 253
    defined, 310
    error, 312, 314, 315, 316, 333–35
    network, 319
    process, 310–11
sampling bias, 312, 317
sampling error, 312, 314, 315, 316, 333–35
sampling frame, 311
SAT. *See* Stanford Achievement Test
Saunders, P., 226
scalability of data storage, 299
scalogram (Guttman) scale, 138, 140, 140*f*, 212
Scheffé (Scheffe) test, 441
scholar-to-scholar presentations, 528
school classification. *See* University Classification
Schramm, Wilbur, 3
science, 2, 15–17, 19, 22, 26
scientific method, 16–25, 17*f*
    basic steps, 17
    defined, 16

empirical generalizations in, 23–25
    hypotheses in, 17
    observations in, 17, 21–23
    predictions/hypotheses in, 19–20
    theories in, 17, 18–19
scientific ways of knowing, 14–16
search engines, 65, 75, 75*f*, 76, 77
secondary sources of information, 64–65, 80, 103*f*, 106
selection threat, 275
self-addressed stamped envelope (SASE), 229, 234
self-administered surveys, 229–31
    advantages/disadvantages of, 230–31
    Internet administration, 229–30
    mailed administration, 229
    mass administration, 229
    open-ended questions in, 233
"self-stealer" plagiarism, 51
semantic differential/bipolar scale
    belief statement measurement, 162*f*, 204*f*
    closed-ended questions in, 233
    commonality of, 168
    description, 137, 171, 173
    history of, 171, 173
    interval variables measured by, 137
    interval/ordinal level questions and, 221
    online survey programs and, 231
    Work Motivation example, 139*f*
semantic equivalence, 235
sex. *See* biological sex
Sextus Empiricus, 19
Shannon, Claude, 6
Shannon and Weaver communication model, 6
shared communication networks, 60
Sharp, D., 266
Sherblom, J. C., 4
Shmatikov, Vitaly, 304
shyness, 73, 74*f*, 155–57
significance testing, 334–38, 336*f*–338*f*
    calculated value in, 335
    critical value in, 336–38
    defined, 334
    setting the probability level, 335
Simon, Theodore, 170
simple direct translation of surveys, 237
simple random samples, 311, 312–15, 313*f*
situational behavior, 145
Skalski, P., 267
skewness, 363–64, 364*f*–365*f*, 371, 371*f*
SlideShare, 306
Small, Cathy (aka Rebekah Nathan), 32
SMCR (source-message-channel-receiver) model, 6

Smith, Heather, 102, 173, 517
SNK test. *See* Student Newman-Keuls test
snowball recruitment technique, 322
social desirability bias, 212
social networking, 31, 33, 230, 298, 302–3, 306
social sciences
    databases, 71t
    description, 1–2
    historical background, 2–3, 169
    hypothesis as the backbone in, 189, 326
    physical sciences comparison, 2
    processes used in, 21
    reliability testing in, 189, 193
    use of research experiments, 252
social threats to validity, 211–12
socially desirable responding to surveys, 218
social-scientific communication, 13
sociocommunicative orientation
    assertiveness measured in, 153–54, 177
    attributes of, 130
    categorical/topical pattern and, 108
    compare and contrast discussion about, 107
    example, 154*f*
    Likert scale measure of, 161*f*
    responsiveness measured in, 154, 177
    scree plot for, 510*f*
    as self-report scale, 154–55
    study examination of, 108
    as variable, 105, 107, 130
    variable attributes of, 130
Sociocommunicative Orientation Scale,
        153–54, 154*f*, 161*f*, 203*f*
Socrates, 175
software. *See also* Excel; Statistical Package
        for Social Sciences
    PSPP, 9, 193, 354, 371, 393
    R, 9, 193, 354, 371, 393, 465–66, 466*f*
software as a service (SaaS), 299
Solomon Four-Group design, 283
Songs of Zion, 248
Source Credibility Measure, 182, 182*f*, 183
sources
    APA style for citing, 57, 80–85, 88
    evaluating, 78–80, 123
    knowledge of receivers, 6
    locating, 64–65, 67, 70–78
    plagiarism and, 51, 52
    primary, 64–65, 80, 103*f*, 106, 122
    secondary, 64–65, 80, 103*f*, 106
    types of, 13, 15, 57, 58, 60, 65, 66*f*, 67
sources for research topics, 57, 58–59
sources-cited types of plagiarism, 52–53
sources-not-cited types of plagiarism, 51–52
specific to general organizational pattern, 109

Spectra newsletter (NCA), 519
split-half reliability, 192
sports fan communication, 129, 489–91
Spotify, 289
SPSS. *See* Statistical Package for Social
        Sciences
spurious correlations, 454
SSB. *See* sum of squares between
SSW. *See* sum of squares within
staged burglary study, 31
standard deviation
    in Bell Curve, 336*f*, 337
    in descriptive statistics for CA, 371*f*
    in descriptive statistics in SPSS, 373*f*
    equation of, 368*f*
    notation style, 112, 114
    percentiles and, 368*f*
    skewness and, 365*f*
    SPSS calculating, 368–69, 369*f*–370*f*
standard error of estimate, 481
standard error of the mean (SE_M), 333
Stanford Achievement Test (SAT), 170
Stanford Prison Experiment (film), 32
Stapel, Diederik, 33
Staple, Jan, 138
Staple scale, 138, 139*f*
state behavior, 174
State Communication Apprehension Measure
        (SCAM), 209
static group comparisons, 278
statistical analysis
    chi-square test of independence in, 136
    measurement and, 184–85
    null hypothesis and, 343
    quantifying ordinal level data for, 136
    reason for choosing, 525
    time-test reliability and, 191–92
    variable values in, 130
    view of interval/ratio characteristics, 141
Statistical Package for Social Sciences (SPSS)
    APA write-up for, 199
    chi-square test and, 383–85, 389, 396,
        401, 402*f*
    Cronbach's Alpha Reliability test and,
        193–95, 196*f*, 197–98
    dataset recoded image, 194*f*, 197–98
    descriptive statistics calculated in,
        373*f*–374*f*
    frequencies dialogue box, 368, 369*f*
    frequency distributions and, 354, 355*f*, 356,
        357*f*–358*f*
    histograms and, 362–63, 362*f*–363*f*
    linear regression and, 477–78, 477*f*–480*f*,
        480–81, 484*f*

Statistical Package for Social Sciences (SPSS) (*Continued*)
multiple linear regressions results with, 485, 486*f*, 487
one-way ANOVA and, 434–35, 439–43, 439*f*, 442*f*, 446*f*
Pearson product-moment correlation coefficient and, 459–60, 460*f*–462*f*, 462
skewness and, 364–65, 365*f*
standard deviation calculation with, 368–69, 369*f*–370*f*
t-tests and, 413–14, 413*f*–417*f*, 416–17
statistical power, 338–39
statistical stories, 535–36, 535*f*
statistical testing
alternate forms reliability and, 192
in analyzing variables, 141, 141*f*
calculated value in, 336
conducting, 335
Cronbach alpha reliability test and, 192–93
factor analysis and, 182
nonparametric, 184–85
ordinal level questions and, 221
outside of academia, 120
parametric, 184–85, 328
ratio variables and, 141
in research project design, 240*f*, 242, 244*f*
semantic differential/bipolar scale in, 137
split-half reliability and, 192
test-retest reliability, 191–92
statistics
benefits of, 348–49
for chi-square test, 381–82, 381*f*
defined, 348
descriptive *vs.* inferential, 349–50
inferential, 331, 349–50, 366
on PRCA-24, 347–50
step-by-step approach
to chi-square test, 380–82, 380*f*–381*f*
to linear regression, 475–77
to one-way ANOVA, 429–33, 429*f*, 431*f*–433*f*
to Pearson product-moment correlation coefficient, 455–58, 456*f*–457*f*
to t-tests, 408–13, 409*f*–412*f*
stereotyping, 25, 129, 153–54, 157, 207
Stern, L., 53
Stewart, R. A., 267
stories, 101
stratified random samples, 311, 314–15, 318–19
structural equation modeling
APA style write-up for, 504–5
calculated, 505*f*

example, 503
hypothesis for, 503–4, 504*f*
student life study, 30
Student Newman-Keuls test (SNK), 441
Student' *t*-test, 408
Stumpf, Carl, 23
style checklist, APA style, 83*f*
subject search, in databases, 73
subjective ethic, 34, 34*f*
subscales, 182–83
Suci, G. J., 171
sum of squares, 366–67, 368, 431
in ANOVA, 480*f*, 484*f*, 486*f*
calculating, 366*f*–367*f*
defined, 366
in regression, 486*f*
type III, 439*f*, 442*f*, 447*f*
x and *y*, 456
sum of squares between (SSB), 429–30, 429*f*
sum of squares within (SSW), 430, 430*f*–431*f*
sum of *x*, 475
sum of *X x Y*, 475, 476
sum of *x*-squared, 475, 476
sum of *y*, 475, 476
sum of *y*-squared, 475
suppressor variable, 271
survey companies, 231
surveys. *See also* questionnaires
accelerated longitudinal design, 224–25
analytical, 217
of cognitive knowledge of students, 175–76
conducting, 219–26
confidentiality and, 38–39, 43
consent forms and, 40–41, 160
cross-section design, 223
as cultural mainstay, 216–17
data needs determined for, 217–18
data processing and analysis, 225
defined, 217
descriptive, 217
design for, 223–25
differences of degree and, 133
disseminating, 227–31
expedited review and, 47
explanatory, 217
Fink's five steps, 220
generalizability in, 219
hesitancy of participants, 219
instructions for, 223
Internet administration, 38, 185, 229–30
interval level questions, 221–22
interview schedule, 217, 220, 226
IRBs and, 37, 38
longitudinal design, 223

mailed administration of, 229
mass administration of, 229
nominal level questions, 220–21
online, 38, 185
open-ended questions, 222–23
operationalization and, 178
ordinal level questions, 221
outside of academia, 242, 244–45
panel design, 224
pilot testing, 225–26
prevalence in communication research, 183
as primary sources, 64
problem areas, 231–35
questions for, 217
ratio level questions, 222
research ethics and, 30
response rate issues, 231–35
scale creation and, 179
self-administered, 229–31
socially desirable responding to, 218
translating into other languages, 235–38
trend design, 223–24
validity and, 211
when to use, 217–19
Sweeney, Lynn, 221
switching replications design, 280–81
syllogism, 20
synonymous term identification, 61, 63–64, 63*f*
systematic samples, 315–16

Tabachnick, B. G., 508
Tamborini, R., 267
Tannenbaum, P. H., 171
telephone interviewing, 228–29
televangelist case study, 331–32, 334–36, 336*f*
television, 7
Terman, Lewis, 170
terms, defining, 18
testing flaw, 274–75
test-retest reliability, 191–92
Teven, Jason, 182
text messaging, 7
Thayer, Greg, 105, 178, 446–48
theoretical populations, 311
theory(ies)
    defined/components, 18–19, 25, 125
    determining value of, 25–26
    opinion *vs.*, 26
Thomas, C., 58, 105
Thomas, William Isaac, 3
Thomas-Maddox, Candice E., 401
Thompson, B., 161*f*, 366
Thorndike, E. L., 170
threshold effects, 270

time order, 261–63, 264, 269, 284
time series design, 279
time spent on Internet
    frequency distributions for, 358*f*
    hypothesis testing and, 327
    mean difference and, 441
    ordinal variables and, 143
title page, 83*f*, 84, 89–91, 522
title search, 73
Titles World Cloud *(CRR)*, 5*f*
Today's Speech, 171, 173
"too-perfect paraphraser" plagiarism, 52
topic choice
    brainstorming map, 63–64, 63*f*
    identification of, 57–60
    key/synonymous term identification, 61,
        63–64, 63*f*
    link to, in introduction, 101–2
    locating information sources, 67, 68*f*–69*f*,
        69–70, 71*f*–72*f*, 72–80
    organizing/evaluating information, 80–81
    question clarification, 60–61
    Research Planning Worksheet, 62*f*
    significance of (in introduction), 102
    types of information sources, 65, 66*f*, 67
traditions, in gaining knowledge, 15
trait behavior, 144, 174
"Trait Verbal Aggression, Sports Fan
        Identification, and Perceptions of
        Appropriate Sports Fan Communication"
        (Rocca and Vogl-Bauer), 489–91
translation of surveys
    conceptual equivalence issue, 235–36
    modified direct, 237
    normative equivalence issue, 236–37
    parallel blind technique, 238
    random probe, 238
    semantic equivalence issue, 235
    simple direct, 237
    translation/backtranslation method,
        237, 238
translation/backtranslation, 237, 238
Traugott, M. W., 232
trend survey design, 223–24
true experimental design
    pretest-posttest, 281
    randomized switching replications, 282–83
    Solomon Four-Group, 282–283
    two-group posttest-only, 281–82
true-or-false test, 170, 175
truncation symbols, 73–74
t-tests, 406–24
    APA style write-ups for, 418, 419, 421
    background information, 407–8

t-tests (*Continued*)
  beer's creation of, 408
  biological sex in, 406–7, 419, 420*f*
  CA in, 407, 419, 420*f,* 424
  case study introduction to, 407
  chi-square test comparison, 406
  computer printouts of, 413–14, 413*f*–419*f,*
    416–19
  critical values for, 412–13, 412*t*
  defined, 141
  dependent variables in, 406–8, 414, 415*f,*
    420, 423
  effect size calculation for, 420–22
  Excel and, 417–18, 419*f*
  formula for, 408*f*
  independent variables in, 406–7, 414,
    415*f,* 423
  law of parsimony and, 495
  of nonverbal immediacy, 422
  one-way ANOVA compared to, 407
  outside academia, 424
  paired, 423–24
  SPSS and, 413–14, 413*f*–417*f,* 416–17
  step-by-step approach to, 408–13, 409*f*–412*f*
  Student' *t*-test, 408
  variances and, 407–8, 411, 416–18,
    417*f*–418*f,* 419, 420*f*
  Weber, Fornash, Corrigan, Neupauer article
    on, 422–23
Tucker-Lewis index (TLI), 505
Tukey's Honestly Significance Difference Test
    (Tukey), 441
Tuskegee Syphilis Study, 31, 36, 37, 53
tweeting, 289, 294
Twitter, 289, 294, 306
two-group posttest-only design, 281–82
two-tailed hypothesis, 328, 338*f,* 339
type I errors (alpha (α) errors), 341*f,* 344, 400,
    401, 417, 441, 460, 495
type II errors (beta (β) errors), 335, 339,
    341*f,* 344

uncertainty reduction theory (URT), 59–60
unethical behavior, 24, 34–35, 34*f,* 48–49, 50
unit nonresponse, 231–32
unit of analysis, 128, 129, 178, 250
United Nations Economic Commission for
    Europe, 534–36
univariate test, 499, 500, 501
University Classification
  chi-square test on, 383–85, 383*f*–384*f,*
    386*f*–388*f,* 387–89, 390*f*–395*f,* 392, 395,
    397*f*–399*f*
  frequency distributions for, 358*f*

updating research, 59, 79
upselling, 26–27
U.S. Department of Health and Human
    Services, 37, 39, 47
U.S. Office of War Information, 3
U.S. Public Health Service, 31
USB flash drives, 298

Valencic, Kristin, 144
validity
  concurrent, 209
  construct or factorial, 209–10
  criterion, 208
  defined, 206
  face/content, 208
  importance of, 207–8
  of PRCA-24, 208
  prospective of predictive, 208–9
  research outside academia, 214
  retrospective or postdictive, 209
  threats to, 210–12, 274–77
  of verbal aggression scales, 114
value of Big Data, 297
values of variables, 130
van Rijmenam, M., 295–98
Vannatta, R. A., 495
variability
  of Big Data, 296
  dataset, 371, 372*f*–375*f*
  measures of, 365–71
variables. *See also* dependent variables;
    independent variables; interval variables;
    nominal variables; ordinal variables
  abstract, 128
  affective, 101
  antecedent, 135
  attributes of, 130
  concrete, 128
  confounding, 271, 278, 497
  defined, 128
  differences in, 134
  endogenous, 501–2
  exogenous, 501–2, 504, 505, 506
  extraneous, 271
  hypothetical, 171
  intervening, 135
  latent, 171, 173
  levels of, 135–41
  literature reviews and, 104–9, 110*f,* 111
  lurker, 272
  mediating, 271
  operationalization of, 104
  of personality, 57
  ratio, 141, 141*f,* 142, 159, 371, 451

reinforcer, 271
relationships as, 13–131, 131*f*
researcher control of, 21
statistical tests, 141*f*
suppressor variable, 271
types of, 134–37
values of, 130
Yale group study of, 3
variance, 367–68, 367*f. See also* analysis of
    covariance; measures of variability;
    multivariate analysis of variance; one-way
    analysis of variance
  central limits theorem and, 312
  Cognitive Satisfaction measure, 116*f*
  Cramér's phi and, 388–89
  defined/equation, 367, 367*f*
  Excel/SPSS calculation, 368
  Humor Orientation measure, 116*f*
  multiple linear regressions and, 485,
    487–88
  population, 408, 475
  standard deviation and, 367–68
  t-tests and, 407–8, 411, 416–18, 417*f*–418*f*,
    419, 420*f*
Vaughan, T. R., 31
Venn diagram, for multiple linear
    regressions, 488*f*
veracity of Big Data, 295–96
verbal aggression, 105, 129, 133
Verbal Aggression Scale (VAS), 114
verbal immediacy, 151–52
verbal messages, 6
video games, 248, 269–70
Vimeo, 306
visualization of Big Data, 296–97
Vogl-Bauer, Sally, 105, 114, 129, 223, 329,
    489–91
Volokh, Eugene, 453
volume, 292–94, 293*f*
volunteer samples, 311, 317, 318, 319
Von Osten, Wilhelm, 22–23

Wales, Jimmy, 80
Walworth, Janis, 453
Wanzer, M. B., 101, 207, 211
Weaver, Warren, 6. *See also* Shannon and
    Weaver communication model

Weber, Keith, 101, 105, 134, 267, 327, 328,
    422–23
West Virginia University (WVU), 7–8
Wheeless, L. R., 6
Wichita Jury Study, 31
Wickersham, J. A., 4
WikiData, 300*f*
Wikipedia, 53, 79–80
Wilk's lambda criteria, 499
willingness to communicate (WTC), 155–57
  biological sex and, 497–98
  book dataset variables and, 202*f*
  CA, BELIEF correlations to, 464–66,
    465*f*–466*f*
  CA's relation to, 155, 157
  defined, 155
  gender, ethnocentrism, and, 499, 500
  relation to public speaking, 464–66
  shyness mistaken for, 155–57
  subscales of, 512*f*
Willingness to Communicate instrument, 156*f*,
    203*f*–204*f*
Winans, James A., 2–3
Woodworth, Robert, 170
Woodworth Personal Data Sheet, 170
Work Motivation Scale, 139*f*
Workplace Aggression Tolerance Questionnaire
    (WATQ), 129
workplace verbal aggression, 129
World War I, 3, 170
World War II, 3, 31, 32
World Wide Web (WWW), 65, 66*f*, 67, 75–77,
    113*f. See also* Internet
Wrench, Jason S., 61, 63, 77, 85*f*, 103, 105, 112,
    114, 116, 137, 174, 177, 221, 266, 273, 401,
    488–89, 507, 517, 518
WTC. *See* willingness to communicate

Yarnold, P. R., 508
Yelp's Academic Dataset, 300*f*
Yen, Corina, 26

Zhang, Q., 236
Zimbardo, P. G., 31–32
Znaniecki, Florian, 3
Zoomerang, 231
Zuckerberg, Mark, 304–5